Capturing the Moment
Single Session Therapy and Walk-In Services

Edited by

Michael F. Hoyt, PhD
&
Moshe Talmon, PhD

Crown House Publishing Limited
www.crownhouse.co.uk
www.crownhousepublishing.com

Published by

Crown House Publishing Ltd
Crown Buildings
Bancyfelin, Carmarthen, Wales SA33 5ND, UK
www.crownhouse.co.uk

and

Crown House Publishing Company, LLC
6 Trowbridge Drive, Suite 5, Bethel, CT 06801-2858, USA
www.crownhousepublishing.com

British Library Cataloging-in-Publication Data
A catalog entry for this book is available
from the British Library.

ISBN
978-1845908935 (print)
978-1845909369 (mobi)
978-1845909376 (epub)

LCCN: 2014947499

Shalom

("Hello, Peace, Goodbye")

Contents

Contributors

The Editors

Michael F. Hoyt, Ph.D. (Yale, 1976) is a psychologist based in Mill Valley, California. For more than three decades he was a staff member at the Kaiser Permanente Medical Center in San Rafael and Hayward, California. He is a recipient of the APF Cummings Psyche Prize for lifetime contributions to the role of psychologists in organized healthcare. He has been honored as a Continuing Education Distinguished Speaker by both the American Psychological Association and the International Association of Marriage and Family Counselors and as a Contributor of Note by the Milton H. Erickson Foundation. He has authored and edited numerous books, including *Brief Therapy and Managed Care; Some Stories Are Better than Others; The Present is a Gift; Brief Psychotherapies: Principles and Practices; The Handbook of Constructive Therapies; Interviews with Brief Therapy Experts*; and *Therapist Stories of Inspiration, Passion, and Renewal: What's Love Got to Do with It?*

Moshe Talmon, Ph.D. (University of Pennsylvania, 1982) is a senior lecturer at Tel-Aviv University and at the Academic College of Tel Aviv-Yaffo, Israel; and is the founder and Director of the International Center for SST. He provides training and supervision worldwide. He is the author of the bestselling *Single-Session Therapy: Maximizing the Effect of the First (and Often Only) Therapeutic Encounter* (which has been translated into many languages); as well as the follow-up book (intended for clients who avoid therapy), *Single Session Solutions: A Guide to Practical, Effective, and Affordable Therapy*; and (in Hebrew) *Worthwhile for Every Soul: The Brief Way to an Effective Psychotherapy*.

The Authors

Steve Andreas, M.A.
NLP Comprehensive
Private Practice
Boulder, Colorado

Rubin Battino, M.S. (Mental Health Counseling), Ph.D. (Chemistry)
Licensed Professional Clinical Counselor
Private Practice
Yellow Springs, Ohio

Bernard L. Bloom, Ph.D.
Professor Emeritus of Psychology
University of Colorado
Boulder, Colorado

Monte Bobele, Ph.D.
Professor of Psychology
Our Lady of the Lake University
San Antonio, Texas

Patricia A. Boyhan, M. Counseling
Registered Psychologist and Family Therapist
Australian Psychological Society and Australian
    Association of Family Therapists
Melbourne, Victoria, Australia

Dawson Church, Ph.D.
President of the National Institute for Integrative Healthcare
Private Practice
Fulton, California

Douglas Flemons, Ph.D., L.M.F.T.
Professor of Family Therapy
Nova Southeastern University
Ft. Lauderdale, Florida

Evan George, M.A., M.Science
Cofounder of BRIEF (formerly known as
the Brief Therapy Practice)
Private Practice
London, England

Shelley K. Green, Ph.D., L.M.F.T.
Professor of Family Therapy
Nova Southeastern University
Ft. Lauderdale, Florida

James P. Gustafson, M.D.
Professor of Psychiatry
University of Wisconsin Medical School
Madison, Wisconsin

Chris Iveson, B.Science
Cofounder of BRIEF (formerly known as
the Brief Therapy Practice)
Private Practice
London, England

Bradford Keeney, Ph.D.
Clinical Psychologist
Private Practice
New Orleans, Louisiana

Hillary Keeney, Ph.D.
Clinical Psychologist
Private Practice
New Orleans, Louisiana

Bruce Maclaurin, M.S.W., Ph.D.
Assistant Professor at the Faculty of Social Work
University of Calgary
Senior Researcher at Wood's Homes
Calgary, Alberta, Canada

Susan H. McDaniel, Ph.D.
Professor of Psychiatry and Family Medicine
University of Rochester School of Medicine and Dentistry
 Rochester, New York
Board of Directors of the American Psychological Association
 Washington, DC

Nancy McElheran, R.N., M.N., R.M.F.T.
Clinical Nurse Specialist, Approved Supervisor with AAMFT,
 and Clinical Associate with the Faculty of Nursing at the
 University of Calgary
Independent Practice
Calgary, Alberta, Canada

John K. Miller, Ph.D.
Director of the Sino-American Family Therapy Institute and Professor
 in the Family Therapy Program
Nova Southeastern University
Member of the Board of AAMFT
Ft. Lauderdale, Florida

Debora Mondellini, M.A.
Professor in the Masters in Counseling Psychology Program
Alliant International University
Mexico City, Mexico

Jennifer Newman, B.H.Science
Data Analyst in the Research Department at Wood's Homes
Calgary, Alberta, Canada

Jason J. Platt, Ph.D.
Director of the Masters in Counseling Psychology Program
Alliant International University
Approved Supervisor with AAMFT
Mexico City, Mexico

Harvey Ratner, B.A.
Cofounder of BRIEF (formerly known as the Brief Therapy Practice)
Private Practice
London, England

Michele Ritterman, Ph.D.
Clinical Psychologist
Private Practice
Berkeley, California

Robert Rosenbaum, Ph.D.
Psychotherapist, Neuropsychologist, and Teacher of Qigong
    (Wild Goose) Meditation.
Private Practice
Arnold, California

Tziporah Rosenberg, Ph.D., L.M.F.T.
Assistant Professor of Psychiatry and Family Medicine
University of Rochester School of Medicine and its
    Institute for the Family.
Approved Supervisor with AAMFT
Rochester, New York

Ernest L. Rossi, Ph.D.
Clinical Psychologist
Private Practice
Los Osos, California

Kathryn L. Rossi, Ph.D.
Clinical Psychologist
Private Practice
Los Osos, California

Pam Rycroft, M.S.
Psychologist and Family Therapist
The Bouverie Centre at La Trobe University
Melbourne, Victoria, Australia

Arnold Slive, Ph.D.
Clinical Psychologist and Approved Supervisor with AAMFT
Private Practice
    Austin, Texas
Lecturer at Our Lady of the Lake University
    San Antonio, Texas

Dean Soenen, M.B.A.
Director with Wood's Homes Eastside Family Centre
    and Street Services
Calgary, Alberta, Canada

Janet Stewart, M.Ed., R. Psych.
Registered Psychologist
Wood's Homes Eastside Family Centre
Calgary, Alberta, Canada

Shane Weir, B.A., B.S.W., M.F.T.
Manager of the Community Services Team
The Bouverie Centre at La Trobe University
Melbourne, Victoria, Australia

Jeff Young, Ph.D.
Director of The Bouverie Centre at La Trobe University
Past-President of the Victorian Association of Family Therapists and
    Past-President of the Board of *The Australian and New Zealand
    Journal of Family Therapy*
Melbourne, Victoria, Australia

Foreword

Bernard L. Bloom

In 1956, when I accepted the position as Chief Psychologist and Director of Research at the Territorial Hospital (later Hawaii State Hospital), I had the happy occasion to meet and subsequently befriend Stanley Porteus, Not many of you will remember him—an Australian by birth and a clinical psychologist by training who led an unusual professional life for many years by working in New Jersey during the warm weather and moving to Hawaii each year to work during the mainland cold weather. When I met him, he had retired in Hawaii with his family. He welcomed me into the psychologist community there and generously helped me settle in.

Stanley had developed a presumably culture-free psychological test instrument for assessing intelligence, the Porteus Mazes, now deeply buried in the history of psychology. Frankly, I knew of him but thought he had been dead for years. I was astonished that he was still alive, although elderly, and very much alive at that. One day he laughingly mentioned to me that at a recent annual meeting of the American Psychological Association, someone stopped him and said, "Didn't you used to be Stanley Porteus?" Ever since he told me that story I have been waiting for someone to stop me and ask, "Didn't you used to be Bernie Bloom?" Perhaps my early involvement with very brief psychotherapy will do the trick.

That involvement began nearly 40 years ago in the late 1970s when I received a phone call from Simon Budman at the Harvard Community Health Plan. He had heard that I was studying single session psychotherapy and invited me to participate in a conference to be held the following year. I don't remember how he had learned of my interest in brief psychotherapy, but I acknowledged that it had seemed to me that brief psychotherapy should play a significant role as a clinical component of the newly-developing field of community mental health and I was happy to accept his invitation. The conference was quite splendid, resulting in a collection of papers on brief psychotherapy entitled *Forms of Brief Therapy* (edited by S.H. Budman, 1981, Guilford Press). Included in that volume was my first paper, "Focused Single Session Therapy: Initial Development and Evaluation."

For some reason, I was attracted to the numerous parenthetical references to single session psychotherapy in the literature: "brief psychotherapy (often as brief as a single session) has been found..." I was drawn to search for and review what literature there was on single session psychotherapy and to learn more about it. Interestingly, there wasn't a great deal of literature and much of it was written by classically-trained psychoanalysts who realized that, while their long-term therapy was helpful to those who could afford it, it could not play a significant role in a population-oriented program. If there was to be any hope for the concepts that supported the field of community mental health there had to be attention paid to brief clinical interventions.

At the same time, insurance providers saw brief psychotherapy as a way of reducing their costs. (Believe it or not, there was a time in the early reimbursement of the costs of psychotherapy when some insurance companies reimbursed for the complete costs of a psychoanalysis!) It didn't take long before insurance companies used emerging brief psychotherapy outcome data as the justification for limiting reimbursement just to the brief forms of treatment. The rush to brief psychotherapy was on.

Since then, I have witnessed the birth and explosive growth of brief psychotherapy as a field all its own, with single session psychotherapy as a legitimate sub-specialty. With the publication of this outstanding volume, the justification for the growing interest in very brief psychotherapy continues. Readers will learn many ways in which "less can be more," with the benefits of single session therapy going far beyond cost containment and waiting-list management.

'Nuff said!

Acknowledgments

The growing awareness of the benefits of single session therapy and walk-in services is the result of excellent clinical and research work conducted by many outstanding people, a number of whom contributed chapters to this volume. *THANK YOU! TODA! CHEERS! GOOD ON YA, MATES! !MUCHAS GRACIAS!* and *XIE XIE!* to the authors who generously shared their experience and wisdom. Our additional heartfelt *MAHALO!* to Bernie Bloom for his fine Foreword.

Along the long way of training, practice, and research we also have been fortunate to enjoy the inspiration, the originality, and the warm support of many teachers. They all had passed away prior to the inception of this book, but all were significant influences on us and are always remembered with deep appreciation: Jerome Frank, Steve de Shazer, Insoo Kim Berg, Jay Haley, John Weakland, Carl Whitaker, Bob and Mary Goulding, Milton Erickson, Alan Gurman, and Mordecai Kaffman. Their spirit and outstanding work in our field is forever present and can be felt throughout the pages of this volume.

We did very well choosing Crown House Publishing as the home for this volume. We thank Mark Tracten for his able and caring support of this project from its initiation. We also extend our appreciation to editor Rachel Ursitti and to all the people whose labor (design, printing, sales, delivery, and others) have made this project possible.

Thanks to Kaiser Permanente and to the Academic College of Tel Aviv-Yaffo, Israel, for their support. In the mid-1980s we and our colleague Robert Rosenbaum were recipients of Kaiser's first Stanley Garfield Memorial Award for Clinical Innovation for research in the area of mental health and psychiatry. Kaiser was more than a place of employment for us. The outstanding staff of the Department of Psychiatry at Kaiser-Hayward, with the special leadership of Norman Weinstein, was an excellent multidisciplinary hotbed for our clinical and research work. Michael Hoyt is honored to be a recipient (2007) of the APF Cummings Psyche Prize. A special thanks to Nick Cummings for being one of the very first to identify, research, and teach the value of single session encounters in an HMO medical setting. Also, special gratitude goes to Salvador Minuchin for his mentorship of Moshe.

Thanks also to the Bouverie Centre at La Trobe University, Melbourne, Australia, for its friendship and for sponsoring and hosting the *Capture the Moment: First International Symposium on Single Session Therapy and Walk-In Services* (March 21–23, 2012) which was the springboard for the production of this volume.

Kudos to the Kaiser-San Rafael Medical Library, the Mill Valley Public Library, Rachel Wu and Chandra Lakin at the Milton H. Erickson Foundation, and Penny Wong at the Bouverie Centre for their excellent assistance.

Great thanks to our clients and patients, who have taught us the most about resilience and change.

As friends, colleagues, and co-editors, we have mutually enjoyed the stimulating opportunity of working together to bring this volume to fruition. Well done, mate!

And to our families, parents, spouses, and children—your love, support, and grace are blessings with us always.

Michael F. Hoyt, Mill Valley, California
Moshe Talmon, Herzeliya, Israel

"Brevity is the soul of wit."
—WILLIAM SHAKESPEARE (*Hamlet,*
ACT II, SCENE 2)

Questioner: What time is it?
Yogi Berra: "Do you mean NOW?"

"....the fierce urgency of now...."
—DR. MARTIN LUTHER KING, JR., "I
HAVE A DREAM," 28 AUGUST 1963

"Each new hour holds new chances
For a new beginning.
[....]
The horizon leans forward,
Offering you space
To place new steps of change."
—MAYA ANGELOU, "ON THE PULSE
OF MORNING," 20 JANUARY 1993

"I think the development of psychiatric skill consists in very consider-
able measure of doing a lot with very little—making a rather precise
move which has a high probability of achieving what you're attempting
to achieve, with a minimum of time and words."
—HARRY STACK SULLIVAN (*The*
Psychiatric Interview, 1954, p. 224)

"Moshe, if you want to get somewhere fast, go slowly."
—MILTON H. ERICKSON, M.D., 1978,
PHOENIX, AZ

"We once assumed that long-term therapy was the base from which
all therapy was to be judged. Now it appears that therapy of a single
interview could become the standard for estimating how long and how
successful therapy should be."
—JAY HALEY (FLYLEAF, M. TALMON,
1993, *Single Session Solutions*)

Chapter One

Editors' Introduction: Single Session Therapy and Walk-In Services

Michael F. Hoyt and Moshe Talmon

Could one therapy session be enough for some people? Collaborating with our esteemed colleague, Robert Rosenbaum, in the 1980s we began a series of studies to explore the possibility of a single therapy session being adequate and appropriate for some client/patients. We became curious when we noticed that, in the clinic where we were then working, about one-third of patients did not come back after their initial intake appointment. At first, we thought these must all be dissatisfied customers and therapeutic failures. Reviewing the existing literature, however, we found studies reporting both the negative effects of so-called "drop-outs" as well as numerous anecdotes describing one session successes from many of the "who's who" names in the psychotherapy field, including Freud's single session treatment of Katarina and his cure of Gustav Mahler's impotency during a long walk (see Kuehn, 1965; Rosenbaum, et al., 1990).[1] We also read the reports of David Malan, et al. (1968, 1975) from the Tavistock Clinic in London, in which a series of patients who made significant improvements after a single diagnostic interview were studied; as well as Bernard Bloom's fine 1981 paper, "Focused Single Session Therapy: Initial Development and Evaluation," in

---

1. See Appendix A for a listing of recent single session therapy case reports plus a summary of the research literature.

which he cited numerous one session clinical reports and several preliminary research investigations, and concluded:

> There is no question but that mental health professionals tend to view early and unilateral termination by clients as a sign of therapeutic failure and client dissatisfaction. Thus, it may be reassuring to know that empirical studies of client satisfaction and length of treatment (with particular reference to single session therapy), consistently fail to support this view. (p. 171)

Bloom (1981, 1992a) also offered some valuable suggestions for possible SSTs:

1. Identify a focal problem.
2. Do not underestimate clients' strengths.
3. Be prudently active.
4. Explore, then present interpretations tentatively.
5. Encourage the expression of affect.
6. Use the interview to start a problem-solving process.
7. Keep track of time.
8. Do not be overambitious.
9. Keep factual questions to a minimum.
10. Do not be overly concerned about the precipitating event.
11. Avoid detours.
12. Do not overestimate a client's self-awareness (i.e., don't ignore what may seem obvious).
13. Help mobilize social supports.
14. Educate when patients appear to lack information.
15. Build in a follow-up plan.

We then reviewed the charts and called 200 patients who had been seen for only one intake visit in our Psychiatry Department—and were pleasantly surprised by how many of them reported improvement and satisfaction. Encouraged by these retrospective findings, we approached our employer at the time (Kaiser Permanente) and received a grant to do a prospective study of potential single session therapy. In our middle- and working-class HMO clinic, we saw a series of 58 consecutive outpatients, ages 8 to 80, having a wide variety of diagnoses and presenting problems. With some of the cases, we called them in advance of their appointment and asked them, *a la* de Shazer's (1988) Skeleton Key Question, to notice what was going on in their lives that they would want to have continue to happen. At the beginning of each in-office session (which included consent forms and videotaping when clients gave their approval), we essentially said: "The purpose of our meeting today is to work together to find a solution to the problem that has brought you here. We may be able to do it in one visit, but if not, we can schedule more sessions. Are you interested in that?" The therapy was thus not necessarily single session, but the seed for such an option was planted. We elected not to employ a single protocol or methodology. Each of the three therapists (and their respective clients) used whatever skills, theories, and techniques they might bring to bear. At the end of the initial therapy session, we asked clients if they wanted to make another appointment or if the one session had been helpful and adequate for now. Regardless of the clients' choice, we followed up by telephone with all clients (SST and on-going therapy) anywhere from three months to two years after the last session.

We found that 34 of 58 (58.6%) elected to complete their therapy in the one visit. When we followed up with them by telephone, we found that most reported significant improvements in both their original "presenting complaint" (88%) as well as in related ("ripple") areas of functioning (65%). SST clients were as satisfied and as improved as the on-going clients, despite the fact that we were much better trained in on-going and relatively long-term therapy than we were in conducting SST.

We first described these findings at the large Brief Therapy Conference, sponsored by the Milton H. Erickson Foundation and held in San Francisco in December 1988, then at the 1989 annual convention of the American Psychological Association (held in New Orleans that year); and then in two full-length books, *Single Session Therapy: Maximizing the Effect of the First (and Often Only) Therapeutic Encounter* and *Single Session Solutions: A Guide to Practical, Effective, and Affordable Therapy* (Talmon, 1990, 1993) and in a series of papers (e.g., Hoyt, et al., 1992; Hoyt, 1994a, 2000; Rosenbaum, et al., 1990/1995; Rosenbaum, 1993, 1994). We also developed a training videotape (Talmon, Hoyt, Rosenbaum, and Short, 1990) that was based on transcripts from SST sessions that were recorded with clients' full permission.

Based on our findings, we described some possible indications and contraindications, sketched some sample cases, and offered a series of general principles:

1. Expect change.
2. View each encounter as a whole, complete in itself.
3. Do not rush or try to be brilliant.
4. Emphasize abilities and strengths rather than pathology.
5. Life, not therapy, is the great teacher.
6. More is not necessarily better. Often less is more. In any case, better is indeed better.
7. Big problems do not always require big solutions. Clients with serious problems are often not as psychologically minded as their therapists and such clients are usually seeking pragmatic help rather than wanting to explore the nooks and crannies of psychosocial and psychosexual development. "Avoid the poor," advised Haley (1969) tongue-in-cheek, "because they will insist upon results and cannot be distracted with insightful conversations" (p. 76).
8. The essence of therapy is more about helping clients to help themselves than about the therapist's need to be needed.
9. Most clients (as well as healthcare organizations) have limited resources (time and money) and these should be preserved and respected.
10. Terminate in a way that allows the client to realize useful implications. "In terminating the session, the... therapist may help a client remember to remember, forget to remember, remember to forget, or forget to remember... The degree of closure appropriate to a termination covers a wide range and is influenced by the extent to which the therapy was seeking resolution of some issue or attempting to open up new possibilities" (Rosenbaum, et al., 1990, pp. 184–185).

These led to some clinical guidelines:

1. "Seed" change through induction and preparation.
2. Develop an alliance by co-creating, with the client, obtainable treatment goals.
3. Allow enough time for the session to be a complete process or intervention.

4. Look for ways to meet the clients in their worldview while, at the same time, offering a new perspective or hope about the possibility of seeing and acting differently.
5. Go slowly and look for the clients' strengths and resources.
6. Focus on "pivot chords," ambiguous or conflictual situations that can be reframed in therapeutic ways.
7. Practice solutions experientially, using the session to help clients rehearse solutions, thus inspiring hope, readiness for change, and forward movement.
8. Consider taking a time-out, break, or pause during the session to think, consult, focus, prepare, and punctuate.
9. Allow time for last-minute issues, to help clients have the sense that the session has been complete and satisfactory.
10. Give feedback, emphasizing the client's understanding and competency to make changes.
11. Leave the door open, follow up, and let the client decide if the session has been sufficiently helpful or if another session (or more) is needed.

Nevertheless, we emphasized that there is no single method or goal for attempting SST other than being with patients and using the skills that patient and therapist bring to the endeavor. As Hoyt (2009) has noted:

> Treatments may be as varied as the patients (and therapists) and what they come to accomplish. Single session therapies, like all forms of psychotherapy, can occur either by default (usually when the patient stops unilaterally) or by design (when patient and therapist mutually agree that additional sessions are not then indicated). The choice of a single session (or more, or less) should, whenever possible and appropriate, be left to the patient. "Let's see what we can get done today" is much more "user friendly" and likely to succeed than the resistance-stimulating "We're only going to meet one time." Most effective SST is thus *not* time-limited therapy—it is open-ended, the therapist may mention the possibility of one session perhaps being enough, and the patient may elect to stop after one visit. (p. 63)

Our results were generally well received, and we were gratified when Jay Haley wrote (see Talmon, 1993, flyleaf): "We once assumed that long-term therapy was the base from which all therapy was to be judged. Now it appears that therapy of a single interview could become the standard for estimating how long and how successful therapy should be." The results also stirred controversy (see Cummings, 2000), since they challenged the notion that effective therapy needs to be a prolonged, expensive (read: lucrative) process. Some readers misinterpreted us to be saying that people should only get one session, or that one session was best for everyone, or that one session was all that was needed and more were inappropriate. (They didn't seem to attend to the word *may* when we said about potential SSTs that "the first session may be the last.") Still, many people—especially patients and professionals in healthcare organizations, community clinics, emergency room and primary-care physician offices, as well as hospital inpatient medical departments and insurance agencies—embraced the ideas and requested our training.

We saw ourselves as part of a larger movement (e.g., Haley, 1973; Fisch, Weakland, & Segal, 1982; de Shazer, 1985, 1988; O'Hanlon & Weiner-Davis, 1989; Ray & Keeney, 1994; White & Epston, 1990; also see Hoyt, 1994b, 1996, 1998, 2009; Hubble, Duncan, & Miller, 1999; Wampold, 2001) toward focusing more on people's strengths and resources rather than on their weaknesses and problems—some of this spirit originated in the innovative work of Milton Erickson, which highlighted using clients' positive strengths for problem-solving action (see Erickson, 1980; Haley, 1973, 1994, 2010). In 1993, Talmon wrote: "These concepts represent an alternative to the traditional model in psychiatry and psychotherapy: psychohealth replacing psychopathology, solutions replacing problems, and partnership replacing patronization, domination, and hierarchy" (p. 73). Privileging clients' ways of knowing, and their competencies to help them achieve outcomes they defined as successful, heralded a paradigm shift (see Hoyt, 2011). We were upsetting the psychiatric-industrial complex, asking: *Who's in charge here? Whose therapy is it? Who really holds the keys and the power? And how will therapists make enough money if their clients only come one time?*

We began to receive more and more calls to teach and do trainings on single session therapy (and brief therapy) from all around the world. We also continued to see our own clients, often for "one session at a time." Some felt one session was sufficient, others elected to meet with us intermittently, while others elected to be seen for regular, ongoing therapy.

Multiple Branches and Roots

Other colleagues were doing related work in other vineyards. Recognition was given to the idea that one could have a single session deliberately, that is, the client and therapist have the advance understanding that they will only meet once—e.g., when clients come to a clinic expecting a complete-unto-itself, self-contained one-visit experience (Slive, et al., 1995—see Chapters 5 and 6 this volume) or when they volunteer to be a therapy demonstration subject at a workshop (Barber, 1990) or for a training videotape (e.g., Carlson & Kjos, 2000). A deliberate single session could also occur when a patient seeing another clinician meets with a different therapist as an understood one-time ("second opinion") consultation, sometimes in a "trouble-shooting" or supervision clinic (see Chapters 23 and 24 this volume; also see Gustafson, 1995, 2005, and Chapter 19 this volume); or when family members are brought in for a single meeting in the course of a patient's longer therapy (sometimes in inpatient and residential settings, as well as in outpatient offices) or in the course of a patient's medical treatment (see Chapter 18 this volume).

Walk-in SST has also been found very useful in humanitarian-emergency situations, where limited resources and somewhat chaotic conditions make return visits unlikely. The one meeting is it. In his excellent report on single session disaster mental health counseling in the wake of Hurricane Katrina, for example, John Miller (2011) recommends:

- Therapy begins at the first moment of meeting, often focused by the first question: "What is the single most important concern that you have right now?"
- Seeking client resources, often with questions such as: "What things have you tried?" and "What inner strengths would it be useful for us to know about?"
- Helping clients prioritize problems and goals, as guided by the question: "What will be the smallest change to show you that things are heading in the right direction?"
- Focusing on pragmatism versus any specific model of intervention, evaluation of results being based on whether the session was able to meet the client's stated goal, not on whether the problem was entirely resolved. Helping clients to adjust to and deal with the range of needs and emotions that emerge from the trauma is primary.

- Fostering a relationship with the service rather than an individual therapist by informing clients at the end of the session that they could return as needed and desired, and that another worker would be available and would welcome talking with them.

In addition to echoing these general suggestions and guidelines, Paul and van Ommeren (2013) also provide a valuable primer on the potential application of walk-in SSTs in acute emergency settings (they cite Hurricane Katrina, Haiti, and providing services in the midst of Colombia's internal armed conflict as examples). Their advice, which can apply to a range of SSTs, not just ones occurring in disaster situations, includes:

- Use various evidence-based approaches and techniques that fit your training, skill level, experience, and the client's presenting needs.
- Ensure the approaches and techniques fit within the culture or context.
- Keep the client focused on what is happening in the moment.
- Recognize that a single session is good for some people, but not always enough for many.
- Allow couples, individuals and small groups to participate in a session together.
- Help clients create a relationship with the service rather than the individual professional.
- Consider how providing single session services can help strengthen the existing mental healthcare delivery system.
- Provide the service in an accessible location where those who need help can access it at the time of need (community halls, schools, information centers, etc.).
- Ensure cooperation between single session service provides and professionals within the broader mental healthcare and psychosocial support system.

In an early review, Rockwell and Pinkerton (1982, p. 39) wrote: "The therapist must be alert to the possibility [of SST occurring], must assess quickly when s/he has a [potential SST] case in hand, set the process in motion, and determine a satisfactory stopping point." Eric Berne (originator of Transactional Analysis; quoted by Goulding

& Goulding, 1979, p. 4) said that he approached every group therapy session with the thought, "How can I cure everyone in this room *today?*" Mary and Bob Goulding (1979), recognizing that the power is ultimately in the patient and wanting to develop Berne's concept of *contractual therapy* to respect clients' stated treatment goals, would start their Redecision Therapy sessions by asking, "What are you willing to change today?" Jay Haley asked, "*If* I told you we're only going to meet one time, what would you want to talk about?" (see Hoyt, 2002). K.K. Lewin (1970, pp. 49–69) observed: "If a patient is seen even for a single interview, it should be a therapeutic experience. Sometimes it is not enough to offer the patient a mirror in which to see himself; often he must be encouraged to open his eyes and be shown where to look.... [T]he interview becomes an awakening, an intense stimulation of mind and spirit, and hopefully a corrective emotional experience." D.W. Winnicott's (1971) *Therapeutic Consultations in Child Psychiatry* featured one session interviews. Stephen Appelbaum (1975) articulated Parkinson's Law in Psychotherapy: work expands or contracts to fit the time allotted. Wells and Phelps (1990, p. 16) noted the economic pressures for briefer, more efficient treatment and predicted "The Survival of the Shortest." Bernard Bloom (1992a, 2001; see his Foreword this volume) updated his review of focused single session therapy and published (1992b) *Planned Short-Term Psychotherapy: A Clinical Handbook.*

Brief strategic approaches were developed in Palo Alto (Watzlawick, et al., 1974; Fisch, et al., 1982), Milwaukee (de Shazer, 1982, 1985) and Milan (Boscolo, et al., 1987). Bill O'Hanlon and Michele Weiner-Davis (1989) authored *In Search of Solutions* and wrote (pp. 77–78): "We have observed enough 'one-session cures' to be utterly convinced that they are neither flukes, miracles, nor magic. Rather, something powerfully therapeutic occurs in the interaction between therapist and client during these sessions." Budman, Hoyt, and Friedman (1992) edited *The First Session in Brief Therapy.* Nick Cummings (Cummings & Sayama, 1995) wrote about brief (including one session) focused intermittent treatment episodes throughout the life cycle. Pollin (1995, p. 128) discussed seeing "one-time-only patients" in medical crisis counseling. Irvin Yalom (Yalom & Leszcz, 2005, p. 488) noted that the composition of inpatient psychiatric groups changes rapidly: "I believe that the inpatient group therapist must consider the life of the group to be only a single session." Long ago, William James (1902) studied life-changing moments; almost a century later, Miller and C'de Baca (2001) wrote *Quantum*

Change: When Epiphanies and Sudden Insights Transform Ordinary Lives. Jim Gustafson (2005) published *Very Brief Psychotherapy*, and Rubin Battino (2006) published *Expectation: The Very Brief Therapy Book*—the latter two authors' chapters follow herein.

In the mid-1960s, the Haight-Ashbury Free Clinic was established in San Francisco (Smith, 1971), and then a few years later, the Walk-In Counseling Center was opened in Minneapolis, Minnesota (Schoener, 2011). Kupers (1981) called for a different way to treat patients in public mental health clinics to help reduce the high "no-show" rate. In Calgary, Alberta, Canada, the Wood's Homes Eastside Family Centre began in 1990 to provide walk-in single session community-based mental health services (Clements, et al., 2011; Slive, et al., 1995, Slive, et al., 2008; see also Chapters 5, 6, and 10 this volume). The walk-in movement in Canada has proliferated (see Clouthier, et al., 1996; Bhanot-Malhotra, Livingstone, & Stalker, 2010) and continues to grow. In Toronto, Ontario, Canada, Karen Young and her colleagues at the Reach Out Centre for Kids (ROCK) began to provide innovative and effective walk-in services based on narrative therapy practices (Young, 2011a, 2011b; Young, et al., 2008). In the early 1990s, Monte Bobele made a fortuitous site visit to Calgary, saw the innovative walk-in single session work being done, brought the idea back to Our Lady of the Lake University in San Antonio, Texas, and began to establish training and service provision programs there.

Fast forwarding to 2011, our colleagues Arnie Slive and Monte Bobele (who have contributed two fine chapters to this volume) edited a book entitled, *When One Hour is All You Have: Effective Therapy for Walk-In Clients*, in which they highlighted the practice of having clinics in which a client could walk in for therapy with the expectation that it would be a one-visit encounter (what our Aussie and British colleagues might call a "one-off"). As Slive, et al. (2009, p. 6) wrote in an earlier article:

> Developed...as a result of community demands for greater accessibility to mental health services, walk-in therapy enables clients to meet with a mental health professional at their moment of choosing. There is no red tape, no triage, no intake process, no waiting list, and no wait. There is no formal assessment, no formal diagnostic process, just one hour of therapy focused on clients' stated wants. As well as meeting client needs, walk-in therapy is highly rewarding to professionals due to the simple fact

that the clients' ability to access the service at their chosen moments of need without having to jump over multiple hurdles means that a large percentage are highly motivated. Also, with walk-in therapy there are no missed appointments or cancellations, thereby increasing efficiency.

Meanwhile, in Australia, the walk-in option was implemented in various community clinics, and in a study of more than 100,000 cases more than 40% elected to complete therapy with a single session—even when more sessions were available (Weir, et al., 2008—see Chapters 7–9, this volume). In March 2012, the "Capture the Moment: Inaugural International Symposium on Single Session Therapies and Walk-In Services" was held near Melbourne, Australia. (We borrowed the title of this book from the conference; see Young & Rycroft, 1997. A symposium with the title "Single Session Therapy—Capturing the Moment" was also held at the annual convention of the American Psychological Association in Honolulu, July 2013—see Hoyt, Talmon, Young, Slive & Bobele, 2013.) The Australian conference, organized and graciously hosted by the Bouverie Centre at La Trobe University, brought together our original SST team (Talmon, Rosenbaum and Hoyt) as well as other leaders, practitioners, and students from several countries and continents. Adaptations of some of the papers that were presented there, as well as others describing SST possibilities, are included in this book.

Terminology

The terms *client* or *patient* will be used back and forth throughout this volume, following the preference of particular authors. Each term may carry certain implications about the nature of the therapeutic relationship and the various reasons for professional contact. *Client* may emphasize the egalitarian and minimize the implication of pathology, whereas *patient* may connote both a medical model (sickness and doctor-patient hierarchy) as well as the idea of the problem having to do with the alleviation of suffering. What one calls the participants and the process (*therapy*? *counseling*? *treatment*? *intervention*? *consultation*? *facilitation*? *work*? *practice*? *meeting*? *encounter*? *conversation*? *coaching*?) helps to establish a meaning context (topics, roles, power relations, ideas about how change occurs), and thus, influences their work together (see Hoyt, 1995, 2009).

We have also generally used the term *single session therapy* (and the acronym *SST*) rather than using another valid term such as *single session work* (see Boyhan, 2006; and Gibbons & Plath, 2012), *single session intervention* (Campbell, 1999; Miller, 2011), or *single session consultation* (Boyhan, 1996; Fry, 2012), partly for continuity with the literature and partly because the present volume focuses on clinical applications (sometimes conducted in a medical setting). (McKenzie, 2013, has also described *single session peer work*, with the acronym *SSPW*.) Again, the terms may have somewhat different connotations about the nature of the problem, the participants, and the process.

Young and Rycroft (2012) point out another conundrum:

> The term 'Single Session Therapy' is a great misnomer, given that almost universally, it would seem, about half the clients who are seen within this approach go on to engage in further therapy work…It is not, as some critics (and researchers) assume, the same as only offering one session of therapy. So why call it Single Session Therapy?[…]We have stuck with it, partly out of loyalty to Moshe Talmon's original (1990) book title (though he tells us that this was his publisher's, rather than his own preferred title![2]) and partly because we have failed to find a term that encompasses what we are trying to offer in this work: the possibility that clients can be helped in one single encounter, as well as the possibility that it may well be useful for client families to engage in further work, and that this decision is best made not by the therapist alone, but in consultation with our clients…It has become clear, too, that for many therapists, counselors, support workers, social workers in general hospital settings, outreach workers and others, they only get one 'go' at being helpful with clients, and the idea of making the most of any encounter fits really well for them. (pp. 3–4)

The term *walk-in* refers to the idea that the client/patient simply walks in—or arrives—without prescheduled appointment, when he or she is ready. ("The readiness is all" said Shakespeare, *Hamlet*, Act V, Scene 2.) "Walk-in" therapy clients usually have the expectation of a complete, one-time experience—as well as the awareness

---

2. See Chapter 2, p. 30.

that they may return again sometime in the future if they so desire. As Slive and Bobele (2011, p. 38) note: "Walk-in counseling does not necessarily mean a single session....However, with a walk-in mindset, therapists are always thinking that the current session is potentially the final one. We organize our session with that thought in mind and strive to be maximally effective in every session." Although we traditionally think of therapy (including walk-ins) occurring face-to-face in a bricks-and-mortar building, with modern technology a "walk-in" (contact when ready) session could actually be a "call-in" (using the telephone) or "click-in" (Internet therapy). Call-in radio shows and newspaper advice columns generally are educational/informational and not intended to be true clinical SSTs.

Writing about their child and youth mental health services in Ontario, Canada, Duval, et al. (2012, pp. 4–5) note: "Brief service delivery systems that provide immediate access at the front door of our systems include walk-in clinics, intake as first session, extended intake and focused consultation." Other "single session" contacts are also possible, of course, such as one-time encounters during hospital consultation-liaison or in an emergency room when on-call. These encounters are usually forms of *crisis intervention*, emergency psychological care aimed at assisting individuals to restore equilibrium to their biopsychosocial functioning and to minimize the potential for psychological trauma. Such crises usually are temporary, no longer than a month. Crisis intervention is often ultra brief, but SST is not necessarily aimed to be a crisis intervention unless this is what the client needs at the moment.

Even the word *psychotherapy* can be questioned. Thus, in describing the Mental Research Institute (MRI) strategic interactional approach, Paul Watzlawick deliberately omitted the prefix *psycho* before the word *therapy*. He explained (in Nardone & Watzlawick, 2005, p. 3): "[M]odern family therapy...no longer asks, 'Why is the identified patient behaving in this bizarre, irrational fashion?' but rather, 'In what sort of human system does this behavior make sense and is perhaps the only possible behavior?' and 'What sort of solutions has this system so far attempted?'...Let me merely point out at this juncture therapy has little, if anything, to do with concepts beginning with prefix *psycho-*, such as psychology, psychopathology, and psychotherapy. For it is no longer just the individual, monadic psyche that concerns us here, but the superindividual structures arising out of the interaction between individuals" (p. 12). As Haley (2010, p. 303) explained: "What came with systems theory...was the theory that metaphors should be horizontal and go round and round. The sequences in a self corrective system were the problem to change." Steve de Shazer (1991a, p. 50) succinctly stated, "Between, not inside."

When a therapist and patient endeavor to get from Point A (the problem that led to therapy) to Point B (the resolution that ends therapy) via a direct, parsimonious, and efficient route, we say that they are engaging in *brief therapy* (Hoyt, 2009, p. 2); "as few sessions as possible, not even one more than is necessary" is how de Shazer (1991b, p. ix–x) put it. Synonymous with brief therapy is the phrase *planned short-term therapy*, meaning literally a "deliberately concise remedy/restoration/improvement." As Bloom (1992b, p. 3) has written, "The word *planned* is important; these works describe short-term treatment that is intended to accomplish a set of therapeutic objectives within a sharply limited time frame." *Focused single-session therapy* (Bloom, 1981, 1992a) and *focused brief therapy* (Cummings & Sayama, 1995) are related terms. For Hymmen, et al. (2012, p. 2), "SST refers to a planned single session intervention—not to the situation where a client is offered more sessions but chooses to attend just one. The single session may be previously scheduled or provided in a 'walk-in counseling clinic.'" The terms *by design* or *by default* (Budman & Gurman, 1988) address the distinction of whether there was a respective intention to be brief, or whether the therapy simply fizzled and ended or the client became a "no show" for the scheduled next appointment. Not all "no shows" indicate failure or dissatisfaction, of course, as found by our phone calls to *de facto* SST clients in our preliminary Kaiser study (Talmon, 1990)—although some do. It would be better to clarify clients' intentions at the end of the session rather than to have them schedule something they will fail to do—a poor ending to the therapy, and a waste of resources. Not assuming more sessions will be needed is a basic attitude shift in preparing oneself to being open to seeing what can get done in a single session. Because we were open to the *possibility* of one session being enough but did not insist on a single session, cases that required more than one visit were not thought of as "failures in SST" but simply as cases needing more time. The basic idea was "making the most of each session," no more than needed. If more were needed, SST with some clients would help make the additional time available for others.

The appellation *time-limited therapy* emphasizes the temporal boundaries of the treatment. (Would the reader consider a single marathon session, such as the 10-hour treatment reported by Berenbaum [1969], to be a prolonged brief therapy or a brief prolonged therapy?) Planned (deliberate) SST could be the extreme (asymptote) for time-limited therapy, as when clients walk-in and expect to meet only one time; but SST could also be seen as planned very brief *time-unlimited therapy*, as when clients are told, "We have found that a large number of our patients can benefit from a single visit here. Of course, if you need more therapy, we can provide it. But I want to let you know that I am willing to work with you hard today to help resolve your problem quickly, perhaps even in this single visit, as long as you are ready to start doing whatever is necessary" (Hoyt, Rosenbaum & Talmon, 1990, pp. 37–38). As Rosenbaum (2008, p. 8) has written: "Psychotherapy is not long or short; to view it this way sets up a false dichotomy. Psychotherapy depends instead on 'good moments' where something profound shifts for a client. All the rest is preparation and consolidation." Maybe in one session!

Capturing the Moment: The Book in Hand

Let us now turn to a preview of some ways an effective one-session therapy can be provided. The authors of the following chapters draw on various brief therapy approaches involving a wide range of creative methods from differing theoretical orientations. Some describe formats and approaches related to our original Kaiser study, which was somewhat influenced by de Shazer and Berg's (1985, 1988) work on solution-focused brief therapy (as well as other approaches including redecision therapy, brief psychodynamic therapy, hypnotherapy, and family therapy—see Chapter 2 this volume); others depict additional methods that can be useful within a single session therapy context. SST often involves a walk-in service delivery system as well as specific clinical procedures; hence, some of the chapters also describe important organizational and administrative issues. It is a pleasure to note the international scope of SST and walk-in services: the reports contained herein come from the United States, Canada, Israel, Australia, England, Mexico, and China. More information about the respective authors is available in the "Contributors" section that precedes this introduction.

In Chapter 2, "When Less is More: Lessons from 25 Years of Attempting to Maximize the Effects of Each (and Often Only) Therapeutic Encounter," Talmon notes that there are multiple approaches to successful SST (not "one size fits all"), and that SST is not for every client—or therapist. He further observes that the essence of successful SST involves the therapist and the client/patient collaboratively bringing their various gifts and skills to bear in the present.

In Chapter 3, "The Time of Your Life," Bob Rosenbaum notes that therapy does not take place in clock time, but in *being time*. Psychological time has a reality of its own, with its own separate rhythms and durations. When viewed as taking place in being time, therapy is neither short nor long (Rosenbaum, 2008). Twenty years ago, Bob wrote (in Hoyt et al., 1992, p. 81): "My desire is not to see everyone for one session; my desire is to see everyone for one full moment, as long as that takes." Drawing on his awareness as a therapist, a neuropsychologist, and as a student and teacher of Buddhist principles (Rosenbaum, 1999, 2013) and Dayan (Wild Goose) Qigong, here he explores and expands some of the implications of that idea, and more.

In Chapter 4, "Psychology and My Gallbladder: An Insider's Account of a Single Session Therapy," Hoyt describes his subjective experience of being an SST patient when preparing to undergo a surgical procedure. He presents a narrative of events along with interspersed comments about internal processes and reflections, emphasizing that single session therapy may be an unfolding event with many components and contributors adding to its success.

In Chapter 5, "Walk-In Single Session Therapy: Accessible Mental Health Services," Arnie Slive and Monte Bobele focus on the concept of *walking in* as a form of service delivery. They note that walk-ins address the issue of accessibility of mental health services, that "one" is the modal length of therapy, and that there has been a general proliferation of walk-in services. They present a case example, answer some frequently asked questions, and draw upon their extensive experience to provide valuable suggestions for starting a walk-in service.

In Chapter 6, "One Session at a Time: When You Have a Whole Hour," Bobele and Slive continue their discussion, now focusing directly on clinical matters, elaborating the single session mindset, describing a clinical model, and providing another detailed case example.

In Chapter 7, "Implementing Single Session Therapy: Practical Wisdoms from Down Under," Jeff Young, Pam Rycroft, and Shane Weir report on the development and implementation of single session work in community mental health in Australia. Their experience with 100,000 cases, more than 40,000 of whom finished in one visit, has implications for the wide use of SST as well as for the study of the implementation of large-scale program change.

In Chapter 8, "SST in Australia: Learning from Teaching," Pam Rycroft and Jeff Young describe the evolution of their training program at the Bouverie Centre, including the use of innovative exercises, ever-expanding applications, and outreach to the broader professional community. Their focus on developing strong clinical skills refreshingly trumps discussions about short versus long, individual versus family, and strengths versus pathology.

In Chapter 9, "Innovative Uses for Single Session Therapy: Two Case Studies," Patricia Boyhan describes how, while completing a postgraduate placement at the Bouverie Centre in Melbourne, she learned that SST was helpful for far more than just waiting list management; she discovered that it could be an excellent strategy to encourage reluctant participants to attend counseling (especially where there was often resistance to seeking assistance for psychological difficulties due to shame and denial). She presents two cases: the first involves a 12-year-old girl who was refusing to attend counseling with her parents, although they were concerned about her high-risk behavior; and the second involves a highly complex cross-cultural situation.

In Chapter 10, "Walk-In Single Session Therapy at the Eastside Family Centre," Nancy McElheran, Bruce Maclaurin, Dean Soenen, Janet Stewart, and Jennifer Newman describe the walk-in single session therapy service of the Eastside Family Centre (EFC) of Wood's Homes, a child and adolescent mental health treatment center in Calgary, Alberta, Canada. In the 25 years since the EFC opened its doors, 2,500 walk-in sessions a year on average have taken place, with presenting concerns including family conflict, mental health issues, parent-child problems, addictions, and risk/safety issues. Variations of the EFC walk-in single session counseling approach have been introduced in other centers across Canada and the U.S. Theoretical foundations and useful interventions, management of risk and safety issues, the central role of the multidisciplinary treatment team, and recent data on specific symptoms presentations are described and three case examples presented.

In Chapter 11, "Single Session Therapy in China," John Miller notes that the practice of therapy has recently undergone rapid development in China, and studies indicate that, when made available, the majority of people there prefer approaches that are short-term, problem-focused, solution-oriented and directive rather than more open-ended and long-term. With this in mind, he discusses a brief, single session, consultation-based service he developed in China as part of a U.S. Fulbright-funded clinical and research project. Clinical examples illustrate ways of adapting single session therapy to the Chinese context; he also cautions against accepting any single story about a culture or individual and highlights the importance of cross-cultural collaboration being a two-way exchange.

In Chapter 12, "Single Session Walk-In Therapy for Street Robbery Victims in Mexico City," Jason Platt and Debora Mondellini describe the innovative program they have been developing in response to the disproportionately high number of street crimes that result, for some people, in a loss of a sense of safety, relational conflicts, and a serious disruption of daily activities. Adapting the single session approach for the national culture of Mexico, they use case examples to highlight the benefits that a single session may provide a person in making meaning of the event in a way that is beneficial to them.

In Chapter 13, "Opening the Heart and Mind with Single Session Psychotherapy and Therapeutic Hypnosis: A Final Meeting with Milton H. Erickson, M.D.—Part I," Kathryn and Ernest Rossi present the edited transcript of a videotape made in 1980 by Marion Moore, M.D., and Milton Erickson, M.D., utilizing therapeutic hypnosis for the professional training of their post-doctoral student, Ernest Rossi, Ph.D. Erickson was a master of brief and single session therapy nonpareil, and the videotape (made just a few months before his death) illustrates some of his novel activity-dependent approaches for facilitating naturalistic and utilization methods to optimize a subject's consciousness, emotional development, and psychological growth.

In Chapter 14, "Opening the Heart and Mind with Single Session Psychotherapy and Therapeutic Hypnosis: Utilizing the General Waking Trance, Empathy and Novelty in Life Transitions—Part II," Rossi and Rossi continue their presentation. The original words and commentaries made in 1980 are now supplemented with a 33-year follow-up by Rossi from the new psychosocial genomic perspective of the 4-stage creative process and the microdynamics of therapeutic hypnosis and mind-body healing that he has developed over the intervening years and which he connects to this single session.

In Chapter 15, "SST with NLP: Rapid Transformations Using Content-Free Instructions," Steve Andreas describes how he uses Neurolinguistic Programming (NLP) to help clients. He sees addressing how the mind builds its sense of reality as the key to change. He describes two different content-free processes in which instructions are given to help clients alter *how* they create and hold their experience (imagery, feeling, meaning), then presents the complete transcripts of single session examples of each, one involving the rapid resolution of a specific phobia and the other involving the altering of the internal negative self-talk that underlies many clients' problems with anxiety and low self-esteem.

In Chapter 16, "Clinical EFT (Emotional Freedom Techniques) as Single Session Therapy: Cases, Research, Indications, and Cautions," Dawson Church gives a thumbnail overview of one of the new "energy" therapies (see Church, 2009; Craig, 2011) that combines elements of exposure and cognitive therapies with the manual stimulation of acupuncture points. He provides numerous case examples in which EFT yielded one-session success, and also cautions that EFT may not work so quickly with other problems and that therapists and clients should have optimistic but not unrealistic expectations.

In Chapter 17, "Love is All Around: A Solution-Focused Single Session Therapy," Chris Iveson, Evan George, and Harvey Ratner, of BRIEF, the premier European brief therapy training and service provision agency based in London, report that while they do not set out necessarily to provide one-session treatments, one meeting is the modal (most common) attendance for clients—happening in their experience about 50% of the time. Central to solution-focused practice is the notion that each session, including the first, is to be treated as if it might be the last. The authors discuss their shift to enhancing effectiveness by focusing almost exclusively on descriptions of the expressed best wishes of the client. A transcribed case example is provided.

In Chapter 18, "Single Session Medical Family Therapy and the Patient-Centered Medical Home," Tziporah Rosenberg and Susan McDaniel describe how they apply a biopsychosocial model to assist patients and families at the University of Rochester who are challenged by medical problems. They combine two core paradigms, medical family therapy and integrated care, and present several single session cases illustrating their work in a variety of situations.

In Chapter 19, "Collisions of the Social Body and the Individual Body in An Hour's One-Time Consultation," James Gustafson takes us inside his weekly case conference at the Brief Psychotherapy Clinic at the University of Wisconsin-Madison. A "Linnaeus of tormented tales as well as a cartographer of routes to territories less twisted" (Hoyt, 2000, p. 69), Gustafson works succinctly by taking in the whole from a third position. He has elsewhere (e.g.., Gustafson, 1986, 1992) portrayed the main stories of persons on fields of power as involving subservience, bureaucratic delay, and overpowering. Here, in a context similar to the one D.W. Winnicott (1971) used for his one-session consultations in *Therapeutic Consultations in Child Psychiatry*, he illustrates with a dream interpretation intervention how, with one brief step—the right step—he helps a patient break out of a painful, reiterating trap.

In Chapter 20, "One-Session Therapy: Fast New Stance Using the Slo-Mo Three-Minute Trance," Michele Ritterman describes how she helps clients slow down time to identify what is disturbing them and then helps them to develop a new way of thinking and reacting. After she reports how she first learned this method by observing Milton Erickson, she guides the reader to have a "Slo-Mo" experience, and then provides six single session clinical examples to illustrate her "Trance and Stance" method.

In Chapter 21, "Expectation: The Essence of Very Brief Therapy," Rubin Battino identifies the key expectation of both the therapist and the client as the belief that helping the client get what s/he wants can be done in one (or two) sessions. He sees the origins of this approach in the work of the de Shazer-Berg group at the Brief Family Therapy Center in Milwaukee. After briefly reviewing their research and other work on expectancy, he then goes on to describe a variety of approaches designed to work in one session, as well as two case studies, as well as his preferred method of "chatting," and the use of hypnosis. He notes that there is much evidence regarding expectation as a psychotherapeutic placebo effect, which, in practice, can be achieved by acting "as if" something is real and true.

In Chapter 22, "Quickies: Single Session Sex Therapy," Douglas Flemons and Shelley Green note that although they don't restrict their practice to stand-alone appointments, as brief therapists they are committed to working as efficiently as possible, facilitating resolution of client conundrums in ways that underscore clients' resources, expertise, and capacity for transformation. They approach each appointment with clients as a singular opportunity for initiating a significant shift in orientation or experience. Because they specialize in applying brief therapy ideas and methods to individuals and couples with sexual concerns, other clinicians will sometimes refer them clients for one-session sex therapy consultations. A case example is described.

In Chapter 23, "Horse Sense: Equine-Assisted Single Session Consultations," Shelley Green describes how her clinical work utilizing horses in single session consultations with couples is very much influenced by brief therapy and relational principles. She describes a 90-minute, single session consultation with a couple who were participating in ongoing, intensive therapy with other clinicians. The work is conducted on the ground—nobody is riding the two or more horses that join the couple, the therapist, and an equine specialist in an outdoor ring—and the therapy is fundamentally experiential, requiring extemporaneous utilization by the therapist and inviting metaphorically meaningful discoveries by the clients.

In Chapter 24, "Deconstructing Therapy: Case Study of a Single Session Crisis Intervention," Hillary and Bradford Keeney emphasize improving and using distinctions and frames that are resourceful, illustrating how single session work can be guided by the overarching structure of a three-act dramatic play. The beginning act with its communications concerning problems and crises is bridged to a middle act that enables more choices of understanding and action that, in turn, enables further movement forward to a resource-focused final act. Problem discourse is minimized and resourceful themes are highlighted, moving the session from an impoverished context to one that provides more opportunity for positive action. Therapy itself becomes rendered a less resourceful contextual frame in favor of the family shifting to their needing some life coaching that mobilizes the parents to take more responsibility for their leadership. Implications of how a single session focus and a consideration of decontexualizing therapy—for therapeutic reasons—are discussed.

In Chapter 25, "Moments are Forever: SST and Walk-In Services Now and in the Future," we highlight some of the themes and lessons to be gleaned and discuss future implications.

Two appendices complete the volume. The first, "What the Research Literature Says: An Annotated Bibliography," is a citation-rich compendium of studies of SST and walk-in services; some suggestions for further research are also included. The second, "The Temporal Structure of Brief Therapy: Some Questions Often Associated with Different Phases of Sessions and Treatments," presents a schema for organizing key issues and helpful questions that may be especially pertinent at different times (pre-, early, middle, late, and follow-through) during the course of a SST.

Readers can work their way through the book from front to back, or turn immediately to certain chapters that may hold special interest. Whatever your approach, eventually don't miss any—they're all excellent!

References

Appelbaum, S.A. (1975) Parkinson's Law in psychotherapy. *International Journal of Psychoanalytic Psychotherapy*, 4, 426–436.

Barber, J. (1990) Miracle cures? Therapeutic consequences of clinical demonstrations. In J.K. Zeig, & S.G. Gilligan (Eds.), *Brief therapy: Myths, methods, and metaphors* (pp. 437–442). New York: Brunner/Mazel.

Battino, R. (2006) *Expectation: The very brief therapy book.* Norwalk, CT: Crown House Publishing.

Berenbaum, H. (1969) Massed time-limit psychotherapy. *Psychotherapy: Theory, Research, and Practice*, 6, 54–56.

Bhanot-Malhotra, S., Livingstone, S., & Stalker, C.A. (2010) *An inventory of walk-in counseling clinics in Ontario.* Unpublished report. Available at http://www.wlu.ca/documents/46045/Walk_in_Inventory-_June_6_final.pdf.

Bloom, B.L. (1981) Focused single-session therapy: Initial development and evaluation. In S.H. Budman (Ed.), *Forms of brief therapy* (pp. 167–216). New York: Guilford Press.

Bloom, B.L. (1992a) Bloom's focused single-session therapy. In *Planned short-term psychotherapy: A clinical handbook* (2nd ed.; pp. 97–121). Boston: Allyn & Bacon.

Bloom, B.L. (1992b) *Planned short-term psychotherapy: A clinical handbook* (2nd ed.). Boston: Allyn & Bacon

Bloom, B.L. (2001) Focused single-session psychotherapy: A review of the clinical and research literature. *Brief Treatment and Crisis Intervention*, 1, 75–86.

Boscolo, L., Cecchin, G., Hoffman, L., & Penn, P. (1987) *Milan systemic family therapy: Conversations in theory and practice.* New York: Norton.

Boyhan, P.A. (1996) Clients' perceptions of single session consultations as an option to waiting for family therapy. *Australian and New Zealand Journal of Family Therapy*, 17(2), 85–96.

Boyhan, P.A. (2006) Single session work (SSW): Implementation resource parcel. *Journal of Family Studies*, 12(2), 286–290.

Budman, S.H., & Gurman, A.S. (1988) *Theory and practice of brief therapy.* New York: Guilford Press.

Budman, S.H., Hoyt, M.F., & Friedman, S. (Eds.) (1992) *The first session in brief therapy.* New York: Guilford Press.

Carlson, J., & Kjos, D. (Hosts) (2000) *Brief therapy inside out.* Videotape series. Phoenix, AZ: Zeig, Tucker, & Theisen.

Church, D. (2009) *The genie in your genes: Epigenetic medicine and the new biology of intention.* Santa Rosa, CA: Energy Psychology Press.

Clements, R., McElheran, N., Hackney, L., & Park, H. (2011) The Eastside Family Centre: 20 years of single-session walk-in therapy: Where we have been and where we are going. In A. Slive & M. Bobele (Eds.), *When one hour is all you have: Effective therapy for walk-in clients* (pp. 109–127). Phoenix, AZ: Zeig, Tucker & Theisen.

Clouthier, K., Fennema, D., Johnston, J., Veenendaal, K., & Viksne, U. (1996) Expanding the influence of a single-session consultation program. *Journal of Systemic Therapies*, 15(4), 1–11.

Craig, G. (2011) *The EFT manual* (2nd ed.). Santa Rosa, CA: Energy Psychology Press.

Cummings, N.A. (2000) The single-session misunderstanding. In *The collected papers of Nicholas A. Cummings, Vol. 1: The value of psychological treatment* (p. 77). Phoenix, AZ: Zeig, Tucker & Theisen.

Cummings, N.A., & Sayama, M. (1995) *Focused psychotherapy: A casebook of brief, intermittent psychotherapy throughout the life cycle.* New York: Brunner/Mazel.

de Shazer, S. (1982) *Patterns of brief family therapy.* New York: Guilford Press.

de Shazer, S. (1985) *Keys to solution in brief therapy.* New York: Norton.

de Shazer, S. (1988) *Clues: Investigating solutions in brief therapy.* New York: Norton.

de Shazer, S. (1991a) *Putting difference to work.* New York: Norton.

de Shazer, S. (1991b) Foreword. In Y.M. Dolan, *Resolving sexual abuse* (pp. ix–x). New York: Norton.

Duval, J., Young, K., & Kays-Burden, A. (2012, November) *No more, no less: Brief mental health services for children and youth.* Policy paper, Ontario Centre of Excellence for Child and Youth Mental Health. Available from www.excellenceforchildandyouth.ca.

Erickson, M.H. (1980) *Collected papers* (Vols. 1–4; E.L. Rossi, Ed.). New York: Irvington.

Fisch, R., Weakland, J.H., & Segal, L. (1982) *The tactics of change: Doing therapy briefly.* San Francisco: Jossey-Bass.

Fry, D. (2012) Implementing single session family consultation: A reflective team approach. *Australian and New Zealand Journal of Family Therapy*, 33(1), 54–69.

Gibbons, J., & Plath, D. (2012) Single session social work in hospitals. *Australian and New Zealand Journal of Family Therapy*, 33(1), 39–53.

Goulding, M.M., & Goulding, R.L. (1979) *Changing lives through redecision therapy.* New York: Grove Press.

Gustafson, J. P. (1986). *The complex secret of brief psychotherapy.* New York: Norton.

Gustafson, J. P. (1992). *Self-delight in a harsh world: The main stories of individual, marital and family psychotherapy.* New York: Norton.

Gustafson, J. P. (1995). *Brief versus long psychotherapy: When, why, and how.* Northvale, NJ: Jason Aronson.

Gustafson, J.P. (2005). *Very brief psychotherapy.* New York: Routledge.

Haley, J. (1969). The art of being a failure as a therapist. In *The power tactics of Jesus Christ and other essays* (pp. 69–78). New York: Avon.

Haley, J. (1973). *Uncommon therapy: The psychiatric techniques of Milton H. Erickson, M.D.* New York: Norton.

Haley, J. (1994). Typically Erickson. In *Jay Haley on Milton H. Erickson* (pp. 176–199). New York: Brunner/Mazel.

Haley, J. (2010). The brief, brief therapy of Milton H. Erickson. In M. Richeport-Haley & J. Carlson (Eds.), *Jay Haley revisited* (pp. 284–306). New York: Routledge.

Hoyt, M.F. (1994a). Single session solutions. In M.F. Hoyt (Ed.), *Constructive therapies* (Vol. 1, pp. 140–159). New York: Guilford Press.

Hoyt, M. F. (Ed.) (1994b). *Constructive therapies* (Vol. 1). New York: Guilford Press.

Hoyt, M. F. (1995). *Brief therapy and managed care.* San Francisco: Jossey-Bass.

Hoyt, M. F. (Ed.) (1996). *Constructive therapies* (Vol. 2). New York: Guilford Press.

Hoyt, M. F. (Ed.) (1998). *The handbook of constructive therapies.* San Francisco: Jossey-Bass.

Hoyt, M. F. (2000). A single-session therapy retold: Evolving and restoried understandings. In *Some stories are better than others* (pp. 169–188). Philadelphia: Brunner/Mazel.

Hoyt, M. F. (2002). Video review of *Learning and teaching therapy with Jay Haley: A videotape series. American Journal of Family Therapy,* 30(1), 105–112.

Hoyt, M. F. (2009). *Brief psychotherapies: Principles and practices.* Phoenix, AZ: Zeig, Tucker & Theisen.

Hoyt, M. F. (2011). Foreword. In A. Slive & M. Bobele (Eds.), *When one hour is all you have: Effective therapy for walk-in clients* (pp.ix–xv). Phoenix, AZ: Zeig, Tucker & Theisen.

Hoyt, M.F., Rosenbaum, R., & Talmon, M. (1990) Effective single-session therapy: Step-by-step guidelines. In M. Talmon, *Single-session therapy: Maximizing the effect of the first (and often only) therapeutic encounter* (pp. 34–56). San Francisco: Jossey-Bass.

Hoyt, M.F., Rosenbaum, R., & Talmon, M. (1992) Planned single-session psychotherapy. In S.H. Budman, M.F. Hoyt, & S. Friedman (Eds.), *The first session in brief therapy* (pp. 59–86). New York: Guilford Press.

Hoyt, M.F. (Chair), Talmon, M., Young, J., Slive, A., & Bobele, M. (2013) *Single-Session Therapy—Capturing the Moment.* Symposium held at the annual convention of the American Psychological Association, July 31, Honolulu, HI.

Hubble, M.A., Duncan, B.L., & Miller, S.D. (Eds.) (1999). *The heart and soul of change: What works in therapy.* Washington, DC: APA Books.

Hymmen, P., Stalker, C., & Cait, C . A. (2012). The case for single-session therapy: Does the empirical evidence support the increased prevalence of this service delivery model? *Journal of Mental Health,* Early OnLine, 1–12.

James, W. (1902) *The varieties of religious experience.* Cambridge, MA: Harvard University Press.

Kuehn, J. L. (1965) Encounter at Leyden: Gustav Mahler consults Sigmund Freud. *Psychoanalytic Review,* 52, 345–364.

Kupers, T. A. (1981) *Public therapy: The practice of psychotherapy in the public mental health clinic.* New York: Free Press/Macmillan.

Lewin, K. K. (1970) *Brief psychotherapy: Brief encounters.* St. Louis, MO: Warren H. Green.

Malan, D. H., Bacal, H. A., Heath, E. S., & Balfour, F. H. G. (1968). A study of psychodynamic changes in untreated neurotic patients: Improvements that are questionable on dynamic criteria. *British Journal of Psychiatry,* 114, 525–551.

Malan, D.H., Heath, E., Bascal, H., & Balfour, H. (1975). Psychodynamic changes in untreated neurotic patients, II. Apparently genuine improvements. *Archives of General Psychiatry, 32*, 110–126.

McKenzie, P. (2013) Single session peer work: A framework for peer support. In C. Chapman, K. Kellehear, M. Everett, et al., *Recovering citizenship: Cairns Conference Proceedings 2012* (pp. 161–165). Mental Health Services Conference of Australia and New Zealand, Cairns, Queensland, Australia; August 21–24.

Miller, J.K. (2011) Single-session intervention in the wake of Hurricane Katrina: Strategies for disaster mental health counseling. In A. Slive & M. Bobele (Eds.), *When one session is all you have: Effective therapy for walk-in clients* (pp. 185–202). Phoenix, AZ: Zeig, Tucker & Theisen.

Miller, W.R., & C'de Baca, J. (2001) *Quantum change: When epiphanies and sudden insights transform ordinary lives.* New York: Guilford Press.

Nardone, G., & Watzlawick, P. (2005) *Brief strategic therapy: Philosophy, techniques, and research.* New York: Jason Aronson.

O'Hanlon, W.H., & Weiner-Davis, M. (1989) *In search of solutions: A new direction in psychotherapy.* New York: Norton.

Paul, K.E., & van Ommeren, M. (2013) A primer on single session therapy and its potential application in humanitarian situations. *Intervention, 11*(1), 8–23.

Pollin, I. (1995) *Medical crisis counseling: Short-term therapy for long-term illness.* New York: Norton.

Ray, W.A., & Keeney, B. (1994) *Resource focused therapy.* London: Karnac Books.

Rockwell, W.J.K., & Pinkerton, R.S. (1982) Single-session psychotherapy. *American Journal of Psychotherapy, 36*, 32–40.

Rosenbaum, R. (1993) Heavy ideals: Strategic single-session hypnotherapy. In R.A. Wells & V.J. Giannetti (Eds.), *Casebook of the brief psychotherapies* (pp. 109–128). New York: Plenum Press.

Rosenbaum, R. (1994) Single-session therapies: Intrinsic integration? *Journal of Psychotherapy Integration, 4*(3), 229–252.

Rosenbaum, R. (1999) *Zen and the heart of psychotherapy.* Philadelphia: Brunner/Mazel.

Rosenbaum, R. (2008) Psychotherapy is not short or long. *Monitor on Psychology, 39*(7), 4, 8.

Rosenbaum, R. (2013) *Walking the way: 81 Zen encounters with the Tao Te Ching.* Somerville, MA: Wisdom Publications.

Rosenbaum, R., Hoyt, M.F., & Talmon, M. (1990) The challenge of single-session therapies: Creating pivotal moments. In R.A. Wells & V.J. Giannetti (Eds.), *Handbook of the brief psychotherapies* (pp. 165–189). New York: Plenum Press.

Schnoener, G.R. (2011) Walk-In Counseling Center: Minneapolis, Minnesota. In A. Slive & M. Bobele (Eds.), *When one hour is all you have: Effective therapy for walk-in clients* (pp. 95–108). Phoenix, AZ: Zeig, Tucker, & Theisen.

Slive, A., & Bobele, M. (Eds.) (2011) *When one hour is all you have: Effective therapy for walk-in clients.* Phoenix, AZ: Zeig, Tucker & Theisen.

Slive, A., MacLaurin, B., Oakander, M., & Amundson, J. (1995) Walk-in single sessions: A new paradigm in clinical service delivery. *Journal of Systemic Therapies*, 14, 3–11.

Slive, A., McElheran, N., & Lawson, A. (2009) How brief does it get? Walk-in single session therapy. *Journal of Systemic Therapies*, 27, 5–22.

Smith, D.E. (1971) *Love needs care: A history of San Francisco's Haight-Ashbury Free Medical Clinic and its pioneer role in treating drug abuse problems*. Boston: Little, Brown.

Talmon, M. (1990) *Single session therapy: Maximizing the effect of the first (and often only) therapeutic encounter*. San Francisco: Jossey-Bass.

Talmon, M. (1993) *Single session solutions: A guide to practical, effective, and affordable therapy*. Reading, MA: Addison-Wesley.

Talmon, M., Hoyt, M.F., Rosenbaum, R., & Short, L. (1990) *Single session therapy*. Professional training videotape. Kansas City, MI: Golden Triad Films.

Wampold, B.E. (2001) *The great psychotherapy debate: Models, methods and findings*. Mahnah, NJ: Lawrence Erlbaum Associates.

Watzalawick, P., Weakland, J.H., & Fisch, R. (1974) *Change: Principles of problem formation and problem resolution*. New York: Norton.

Weir, S., Wills, M., Young, J., & Perlesz, A. (2008) *The implementation of single session work in community health*. Brunswick, Victoria, Australia: The Bouverie Centre, La Trobe University.

Wells, R.A., & Phelps, P.A. (1990) The brief psychotherapies: A selective overview. In R.A. Wells & V.J. Giannetti (Eds.), *Handbook of the brief psychotherapies* (pp. 3–26). New York: Plenum.

White, M., & Epston, D. (1990) *Narrative means to therapeutic ends*. New York: Norton.

Winnicott, D.W. (1971) *Therapeutic consultations in child psychiatry*. New York: Basic Books.

Yalom, I., & Leszcz, M. (2005) *The theory and practice of group psychotherapy* (5th ed.). New York: Basic Books.

Young, J., & Rycroft, P. (1997) Single-session therapy: Capturing the moment. *Psychotherapy in Australia*, 4(1), 18–23.

Young, J., & Rycroft, P. (2012) Single session therapy: What's in a name? *Australian and New Zealand Journal of Family Therapy*, 33(1), 3–5.

Young, K. (2011a) When all the time you have is NOW: Re-visiting practices and narrative therapy in a walk-in clinic. In J. Duvall & L. Beres (Eds.), *Innovations in narrative therapy: Connecting practice, training, and research* (pp. 147–166). New York: Norton.

Young, K. (2011b) Narrative practices at a walk-in therapy clinic. In A. Slive & M. Bobele (Eds.), *When one hour is all you have: Effective therapy for walk-in clients* (pp. 149–166). Phoenix, AZ: Zeig, Tucker, & Theisen.

Young, K., Dick, M., Herring, K., & Lee, J. (2008) From waiting lists to walk-in: Stories from a walk-in therapy clinic. *Journal of Systemic Therapies*, 27(4), 23–39.

Chapter Two

When Less is More: Maximizing the Effect of the First (and Often Only) Therapeutic Encounter

Moshe Talmon

In life, like in science, the most significant findings are often discovered by accident. I stumbled upon the single session therapy (SST) phenomenon while working at the Kaiser Permanente Medical Group in Northern California during the 1980s. I had joined that organization after researching, practicing, and teaching psychotherapy for 8 years. At that point in time, I felt quite competent and experienced as a psychotherapist and hoped to keep doing what worked quite well for me. Since much of my experience up to then was with children and families, I was assigned to the Child and Family Team. Although I had quite extensive training, I was never trained as a brief therapist, nor aimed to be one. In my former position as a clinical director of a child and family clinic (serving

A version of this chapter was presented as a keynote address at the *Capture the Moment: The Inaugural Symposium on Single-Session Therapies and Walk-In Services* held on Phillip Island, Victoria, Australia, in March 2012. Portions were also presented as part of the symposium, *Capturing the Moment: Single-Session Therapy and Walk-In Services*, held at the annual convention of the American Psychological Association, Honolulu, HI, July 31, 2013. An abbreviated version was first published in the *Australian and New Zealand Journal of Family Therapy*, 2012, 33(1), 6–14. Used with permission.

the kibbutz population in Israel) and in my part-time private practice (in an affluent neighborhood of Tel Aviv), I had practically no experience with "drop-outs." By and large, all my clients showed up on time, paid on time, and gladly engaged in long-term, open-ended therapy once or twice a week. I enjoyed working with the sensitive, reflective, verbal, psychologically-minded therapy believers. I, myself, had just finished 8½ years of studying for three degrees in psychology, a predoctoral internship, a postdoctoral residency, and a long-term in-depth analysis myself. I was ready for a good return on my long-term investment in psychology and psychotherapy, with no ground and zero motivation for conducting a brief or time-limited therapy in a practice which was on a fee-for-time basis.

I was trained to believe that just the initial phase of therapy takes about 8 sessions (including assessment, testing and diagnosis, joining and working through inevitable resistances, etc.). I assumed that the problems of my patients were hard and complex and deeply rooted in their past. They all deserved in-depth and long-term therapy. This was my basis.

Since the Child and Family Team I had just joined at Kaiser had a very long-term waiting list, I volunteered to see two new cases each working day until my caseload would be full. It never got filled! I continued to have two new slots every week for the next six years. I soon collected a significant number of unplanned dropouts ("no shows"). I was quite upset about it. For one, it had never happened to me before. Second, I hated to do the extensive paperwork required when opening and closing cases. Third, at the time California was a "lawsuit happy society," particularly toward big organizations like Kaiser—the largest HMO around. Last but not least, I was assuming all dropouts were failures on my part. Once I noticed the Psychiatry Department statistics (going back ten years before I joined), I learned that unplanned SST was the most common length of therapy among all thirty providers in our Department. I began to follow-up with my own unplanned SST clients, who often surprised me with the positive outcome of their single sessions. Our Kaiser SST study was thus exploratory by nature. We studied 58 cases in which we attempted to conduct a planned single session, while leaving the door open for each client/family to continue with the same therapist for on-going longer therapy or to renew therapy later. Fifty-eight percent of our cases used only a single session.

The Kaiser SST Project

The three main findings of our further studies, conducted by Hoyt, Rosenbaum, and myself during the years 1986–1990 at the Kaiser Permanente Medical Group in Hayward, California, were as follows:

1. Single session was the most common length of psychotherapy, regardless of therapist orientation, patient's diagnosis, or treatment plan;
2. The first session in psychotherapy is potentially the most therapeutic and often has the greatest influence on the outcome of therapy, regardless of the total number of sessions eventually used;
3. Single session therapy (SST) is the most cost-effective mode of therapy. Furthermore, patients who use SST tend to be at least as satisfied and show as much improvement (including long-term and ripple-effect changes) when compared to patients who opted for longer-term therapy (Rosenbaum, Hoyt & Talmon, 1990; Hoyt, Rosenbaum & Talmon, 1992; Talmon, 1990, 1993, 1996).

These findings held both in cases of planned and unplanned SSTs (Bloom, 1981, 2001; Talmon, 1990), and the positive outcome and satisfaction levels were found to be stable on follow-ups ranging from a few weeks to several years.

Contextually and historically, it is easy to understand the need for abbreviated therapy as the treatment of choice in settings such as community mental health centers (CMHCs) and health maintenance organizations (HMOs) as well as other public or large-scale organizations such as managed healthcare (MHC), employee assistance programs (EAPs), and the national health services (NHSs) that exist in countries such as Canada, England, Australia, and others. Such organizations are often dealing with limited staff and budget, lengthy waiting lists, and other concerns regarding the somewhat complex and problematic relationship between cost and effectiveness in psychotherapy as well as other healthcare services. It was remarkable that although Hoyt, Rosenbaum, and I were employed by a large HMO at the time of our study, there was no pressure on us to shorten the therapy in our department: the majority of our colleagues were trained in and mostly experienced in long-term therapy. As part of the Child and Family Team, I was quite proud of having used my own systemic approach to change the I.P. (identified patient) name on the medical chart so as to allow families to get more than the 20 yearly sessions allowed by their HMO insurance. Even when our SST research yielded the clear evidence of one session being so helpful to many patients, Kaiser (who employed us and had funded our research) did not want to be associated with our findings. In preparing me for a television interview, the head of public relations at Kaiser explained: "We prefer the image of being the IBM of healthcare and not the McDonald's."

Yet a broader historical perspective shows that many of the therapists who have launched, practiced, and studied SST and brief therapy have done so in private and small settings. Reports on the significance of SST started with Freud in Vienna (Breuer & Freud, 1893–1895; Kuehn, 1965) and continued in later years with Malan (Malan, et al., 1968, 1975) at the Tavistock Clinic in London; MRI (Watzlawick, Weakland, & Fisch, 1974; Fisch, Weakland & Segal, 1982) in Palo Alto, California; the Milan group (Boscolo, Cecchin, Hoffman, & Penn, 1987) in Italy; and de Shazer (1982, 1985) and his group in Milwaukee, to name some of those reviewed in my books *Single Session Therapy* (1990) and *Single Session Solutions* (1993)—also see Appendix A this volume.

Still, based on our training and years of clinical experience that we had at the time, we found it difficult to believe that what we had simply considered the initial intake for ongoing therapy could also be so effective in treating complex, longstanding problems. We originally anticipated some benefit for the so-called "worried well" and potentially for those suffering, in *DSM* terms, from "adjustment disorders." We approached each case as an open-ended choice regarding the eventual length of therapy. We found, to our surprise, that among the successful SST cases were much more severe conditions, including personality disorders, obesity, family violence, and other clinical problems, none of which we had considered likely candidates for SST.

Different therapists will interpret our findings differently.[1] The way I see it, SST (planned or unplanned) is far from a rare, magi-

---

1. I first titled my book *Once Upon a Therapy* to hint at the possibility of being seen only once but mostly to indicate my realization that therapy is different than what I assumed, expected, or had been told in my training and that it is mostly what happens when we (as therapists) make all kinds of plans and tell legends. My outstanding editor, Gracia Alkema, insisted that *Single Session Therapy* is clearer and more "catchy," and we compromised by adding the excellent but somewhat long subtitle: *Maximizing the Therapeutic Effect of the First (and Often Only) Session.*

cal event that can only be performed by a few master therapists or a few outstanding clients. It is a very common, very useful way of conducting therapy, and employs many different approaches and methods to address a wide range of presenting problems. Indeed, effective utilization of SST can benefit many patients and can also shorten waiting lists. Furthermore, it can free up more time and resources for clients who may benefit from longer therapy.

Expanding Our Understanding

When we started our SST project, Rosenbaum had trained in brief psychodynamic therapy and was then fascinated with non-directive hypnosis *a la* Milton Erickson. Hoyt had done an internship with Carl Whitaker, trained in brief psychodynamic therapy, and was then taken by the work of Mary and Bob Goulding (1979), which combined Transactional Analysis (TA) and Gestalt into what they called Redecision Therapy, a very directive form of treatment. I was primarily a systemic therapist working with the Child and Family Team while Hoyt and Rosenbaum worked with the Adult team. When we started the project I was quite intrigued by the simple elegance of solution-focused therapy developed by de Shazer, Berg, et al. (de Shazer, 1985, 1988) in Milwaukee. I met them shortly before our project started and they were a main force in spreading the word about our initial findings long before we published anything.

As the project developed, Hoyt, Rosenbaum, and I were also somewhat influenced by postmodern, constructivist philosophy (Gergen, 1985; also see Hoyt & Ziegler, 2004). In that context, SST is viewed as a constructive minimalist approach. The constructive therapist realizes that he or she always works with a selective partial knowledge and a subjective narrative; and therefore, he or she does not attempt to give the "right" diagnosis or the "correct" intervention. The therapist's main goal is to search for the least restrictive, least intrusive, and most cost-effective intervention with the basic assumption that therapy's main goal is to help people help themselves—or at least that the therapist should "do no harm," to echo the Hippocratic Oath. Hoyt has since edited three outstanding volumes on constructive therapies (Hoyt, 1994, 1996, 1998) and has broadened his competence-based approaches (2000, 2004, 2009), while Rosenbaum has deepened his studies of Zen Buddhism. Rosenbaum's application of the Japanese Zen Buddhist teacher Dogen's idea of *Uji* ("Time-

Present/Being Time") to the field of psychotherapy and behavioral medicine (Rosenbaum, 1992, 1999, 2013—also see Chapter 3 this volume) is a remarkable extension of SST. It is also an example of how an up-to-date neuropsychologist can merge old and new wisdom.

Today, if I still adhere to any ideology in my ongoing practice of SST, it is probably the ecological belief in maximizing the therapeutic effect of each session. As noted by Goleman (2009), we still have a long way to go in developing our ecological intelligence in order to be less wasteful of our important resources such as food, land, water, time, and money.

Nevertheless, looking back on my own SST work and that of others, I conclude that SST does not necessarily require a strong theoretical or ideological stance from every therapist. As I view it, it is more a reflection of certain attitudes:

- It is about respecting each client's choices, culture, and belief system.
- It is about being experienced enough (or, if you prefer: flexible enough) to leave aside therapy by the book, by the protocol, or by the theory.
- It is about being present and seeing each and every session as a whole.
- It is about allowing yourself again and again to know that you don't know everything, so that you can be surprised and learn something new from every new client and every first session.

When I was a student of Salvador Minuchin, I was sure that he, as my mentor, knew exactly what, how, and when to make each move in therapy. In the last year of my four years at the University of Pennsylvania and the Philadelphia Child Guidance Clinic, I had the rare opportunity to live in Pat and Sal Minuchin's house, and I often drove with Sal to the clinic and back. On our final drive home, right after another outstanding demonstration he had given at the clinic, he told me that in 90% of his family sessions, he was "walking in total darkness." It was a very valuable last lesson, given by a master to his devoted student.

SST: Psychotic Optimism?

Some people define SST and other ultra-brief therapies as a "psychotically optimistic" way of conducting therapy. Trusting human potential, internal and external resources, as well as the ever-surprising capabilities of the mental immune system to recover and heal is indeed relentlessly optimistic. I agree and yet I tend to see SST more as a very realistic, practical, no bullshit, and down-to-earth form of therapy.

An anecdote may be enlightening at this point. As I was concluding the first draft of *Single Session Therapy*, I met for breakfast with the (now late) John Weakland near his office at the Mental Research Institute in Palo Alto, California. My publisher wanted him to read and comment on the book. Paraphrasing the title of Jim Gustafson's (1986) important book, *The Complex Secret of Brief Psychotherapy*, I asked Weakland:

> "What is, in your opinion, the simple secret of brief therapy?"
>
> He answered, "The simple secret of brief therapy is that life is one damn thing after another."
>
> "In that case," I continued, "what would you say is the simple secret of long-term therapy?"
>
> To which John replied, "The idea that you can make it not so."

I was quite intrigued. John often made me think in a new way. His answer suggested that long-term therapists might be more optimistic than short-term ones. From what I know of John's wisdom, he would suggest to us that we should enter each session simply by walking in and staying curious. As for the necessary level of optimism needed in SST, he would advise us to keep hoping for the best while always being ready for the worst.

Although others define SST as a form of abbreviated psychotherapy (e.g., Pekarik, 1996), I don't necessarily consider myself a brief therapist, nor have I tried to train others to be briefer therapists than they already are. As of today, I cherish my long-term clients as much as my short-term ones. Having conducted SST for more than 25 years in public and private settings, I now have many more SST than long-term clients. My goal did not change: to make the most of every therapeutic session, whether I am seeing a client only once or over a long period of time. I try not to lose sight of that goal with my long-term clients, although with the luxury of time and stable and dependable income, I suspect that I occasionally do.

SST: A "One-Size-Fits-All"?

My partners and I have always made it very clear in all of our writings and teaching that SST is not right for every client—or for every therapist. We have always resisted the idea of developing "one size fits all" solutions or any attempt to create a universal formula or protocol. I have occasionally been approached by big insurance companies and healthcare institutions requesting such a formula or protocol. As much as I personally might like to have claimed fame and fortune by doing so, the concept went too much against the essence of SST, as I have experienced it, and I had to decline such offers. Although, I was pleased when Jay Haley in his endorsement on the cover of my 1993 book wrote:

> "We once assumed that long-term therapy was the base from which all therapy was to be judged. Now it appears that therapy of a single interview could become the standard for estimating how long and how successful therapy should be."

I was also worried—alas, rightly so—that some managed-care companies would begin to expect and demand a single session therapy for all of their customers. Nick Cummings (2000, p. 77) made the same observation:

> "When Moshe Talmon came to Kaiser....he took this idea of 'single session' psychotherapy and later expanded it into his book on this subject....Indeed, sometimes there are single-session treatments that can be the right thing for some patients, but this should not be interpreted too broadly. It is for those who choose a single session that the benefits can be significant."[2]

I still view our work more as an open-ended form of therapy than as time-limited therapy. To me, SST is not a rigid or structured therapeutic model, but a highly flexible, integrative, and creative one.

---

2. In his foreword to the earlier book, *Single Session Therapy,* Jerome Frank (1990, p. xiii) similarly wrote: "Readers should not overlook the author's explicit recognition that, while perhaps as many as four-fifths of psychiatric outpatients receiving single session therapy respond favorably, the remaining one-fifth, as well as most inpatients, require considerably more treatment."

I tend to view the "DNA" of good SST as very similar to that of any effective psychotherapy:

- Establishing a positive therapeutic relationship, often helped by the therapist's caring, empathy, acceptance, affirmation, and encouragement;
- Mutually identifying a "pivot-chord" (Rosenbaum, Hoyt, & Talmon, 1990) that offers a better understanding of the patient's problem while also identifying the potential for a solution or giving hope for change. If you practice psychotherapy long enough, you see how often problems are part of solutions, how weaknesses are part of strengths, and how "ups" are part of "downs." If "both sides of the coin" are embraced, respected, and understood by both client and therapist, therapeutic moments of a creative pivot-chord emerge that embody the problem and the solution together. (A good example of this phenomenon is provided by Rosenbaum's [1993] case of "I've always had the weight of the ideal child.")
- Mobilizing so-called "client and extra-therapeutic factors" such as the client's underlying strengths, supportive elements in the environment, and chance events of spontaneous healing. Clearly, helping clients to define what they might do after the first session or between sessions is an important part of good therapy.

Some General Guidelines

In retrospect, I don't know if we should have published a more unified set of guidelines, or even a protocol, for SST. This approach might have allowed more research, better structured training and a wider usage of SST as was done in the state of Victoria, Australia (Young, et al., 2006—see Chapters 7–9 this volume). Leading researchers in the field of psychotherapy have sometimes attempted to offer unified, trans-theoretical schemes and protocols. Most notable are Prochaska's (1999) six stages of change, best suited to the field of behavioral medicine and addictive behaviors; and more recently, David Barlow's (Barlow, et al., 2010) unified protocol for the transdiagnostic treatment of emotional disorders.

We have not taken this path. In our writings and training tapes, we have mostly advocated many more ways to do it right, using various theories, techniques, and therapeutic settings where SST can be employed. Nevertheless, if we were to offer a few general guidelines specifically for SST, they might include:

Always be present, in all three meanings of the word: presence, gift, and present tense.

a. Show your human presence in the here-and-now of each session and with each client. Be prudently active in your listening, attunement, and response to each client. When appropriate, allow the client and yourself to be fully present, including nonverbal expressions such as tears, hugs, or holding hands when they support opening up and help form a positive human alliance.

b. Exchange gifts with your clients. The so-called "transference" and "countertransference" of the therapeutic relationship often takes place immediately, in the first minutes of the first session. By fully attending to and willingly embracing the client's gift to you—their opening up by bringing to the session their verbal story and physical presence—you may receive an immediate gift. Carl Jung once said, "When two people meet anything can happen." Irvin Yalom (2002) calls it "the gift of therapy." Open your client's gift, unwrap it slowly and never forget to thank and appreciate them for the very special gift they have brought with them. Don't let them leave before giving in response your gift to them: your appreciation of their strengths; your offer of a reliable sense of hope and perspective; and, at times, a ritual or suggestion for a small step in the right direction. Any or all may serve as a valuable gift you can give back to your client.

c. Utilize the power of the here and now. When I treat a session as potentially my first as well as last meeting with a client, I am not as governed by the limits imposed by the fifty-minute hour of "clock time," nor am I as bound to focus either on the pain and grief of the past (taking a history, getting to the root of the problem, identifying the disorders, uncovering the conflicts, etc.) or the worries, fears, and concerns about the future (the client's fears of failure, rejection, commitment as well as the therapist's need to come up with a treatment plan and a prognosis). Clearly, human brains as well as initial therapeutic sessions tend to operate in all three tenses. In SST, one focuses more on the present tense, keeping in mind that talking about the past as well as expectations or fears of the future, are also mainly a representation of the present (Gilbert, 2005). The Melbourne group nicely summarized this concept: "We believe the delicate dilemma for a single session clinician is not who is appropriate for a single session and who is not, but rather how do I maintain the possibility that one session may be enough and feel free to initiate further sessions should they be necessary" (Young & Rycroft, 1997, p. 20).

When possible: Keep it simple, focused, and brief.
Most of my failures in SST are due to my trying too much and offering too much in the first session. Patients bring us very complex stories with far more than one problem or disorder. As an experienced therapist, I understand these problems with multi-layered and multi-focal views. It is vital to avoid trying to appear overly smart, sophisticated, or right in your replies. Don't try to know everything in order to be helpful. You may feel you are being active in your talking and persuasiveness, but don't try to rush the process or accomplish too much. Take it slowly, and play it as it lies.

Very complex and longstanding problems can often be helped with very simple solutions. In a study comparing three methods of treating alcoholics in Great Britain (Baer, Marlatt, Kivlahan, et al., 1992), the members of the single-day treatment group were bluntly told at the end of the day-long assessment process: "You have a problem. It's called drinking. There is only one good solution to this problem and that is to stop drinking now. Many people are worried about you and may want to help you stop drinking, but there is only one person who can do it and that is you!"

Stay humble.
Not all problems have good solutions. Not all conflicts have good resolutions. Not all disorders can be cured. Yes, I remain a strength-based, solution-focused, and optimistic therapist, but SST is at times also about surrendering to our limits. Some therapists choose to offer more and more therapy when they encounter such cases. I prefer to humbly acknowledge my own limitations and those of psychotherapy as well as our limitations as humans. At such

times, I might find myself telling clients something like: "I wish solving problems were like baking a cake. Then, I could give you a good recipe and you could go home, follow my instructions, put it in the oven and shortly after that enjoy the cake."

When possible: Use a win-win approach.

As Jeff Young and Pam Rycroft (1997, p. 22) have said: "Rather than promoting one session cures, single session therapy aims to develop an openness and an attitude in both therapists and clients, that each session may be the last. In doing so, it optimizes clients' readiness to change and creates a structure for respectful, focused and responsive therapy."

I have never tried to convince clients that all they need is one session, nor do I try to convince them that they need to see me for at least twice a week for years to come. I see each session as a whole, complete in itself. This approach enables me to allow room for the full potential of that session, and to allow the client and the outcome to dictate what may come next. Clients are the real heroes (Duncan & Miller, 2000) of any successful therapy. It is our clients who should be the main source of guidance for us, letting us know when to stop and when to continue with our sessions.

References

Baer, J.S., Marlatt, G.A., Kivlahan, D.R., Fromme, E., Larimer, M.E., & Williams, E. (1992) An experimental test of three methods of alcohol risk reduction with young adults. *Journal of Consulting and Clinical Psychology, 60*, 974–979.

Barlow, D.H., Ellard, K.K., Fairholme, C.P., Farchione, T.J., Boisseau, C.L., Allen, L.B., & Ehrenreich-May, J.T. (2010) *Unified protocol for the transdiagnostic treatment of emotional disorders: Workbook*. New York: Oxford University Press.

Bloom, B.L. (1981) Focused single-session therapy: Initial development and evaluation. In S.H. Budman (Ed.), *Forms of brief therapy* (pp. 167–216). New York: Guilford Press.

Bloom, B.L. (2001) Focused single-session psychotherapy: A review of the clinical and research literature. *Brief Treatment and Crisis Intervention, 1*, 75–86.

Boscolo, L., Cecchin, G., Hoffman, L., & Penn, P. (1987) *Milan systemic family therapy*. New York: Basic Books.

Breuer, J., & Freud, S. (1893–1895) Studies in hysteria. In *Standard edition of the complete psychological works of Sigmund Freud* (Vol. 2, pp. 1–319). London: Hogarth Press, 1955.

Cummings, N.A. (2000) The single-session misunderstanding. In *The collected papers of Nicholas A. Cummings. Vol. 1: The value of psychological treatment* (p. 77). Phoenix, AZ: Zeig, Tucker & Theisen.

de Shazer, S. (1982) *Patterns of brief family therapy.* New York: Guilford Press.

de Shazer, S. (1985) *Keys to solution in brief therapy.* New York: Norton.

de Shazer, S. (1988) *Clues: Investigating solutions in brief therapy.* New York: Norton.

Duncan, B.L., & Miller, S.D. (2000) *The heroic client: Doing client-directed, outcome-oriented therapy.* San Francisco: Jossey-Bass.

Fisch, R., Weakland, J.H., & Segal, L. (1982) *The tactics of change: Doing therapy briefly.* San Francisco: Jossey-Bass.

Frank, J.D. (1990) Foreword. In M. Talmon, *Single session therapy: Maximizing the effect of the first (and often only) therapeutic encounter* (pp. xi–xiii). San Francisco: Jossey-Bass.

Gergen, K.J. (1985) The social constructionist movement in modern psychology. *American Psychologist,* 40, 266–275.

Gilbert, D. (2005) *Stumbling on happiness.* New York: Knopf.

Goleman, D. (2009) *Ecological intelligence.* London: Penguin Books.

Goulding, M.M., & Goulding, R.L. (1979) *Changing lives through redecision therapy.* New York: Grove Press.

Gustafson, J.P. (1986) *The complex secret of brief psychotherapy.* New York: Norton.

Hoyt, M.F. (Ed.) (1994) *Constructive therapies.* New York: Guilford Press.

Hoyt, M.F. (1995) *Brief therapy and managed care: Readings for contemporary practice.* San Francisco: Jossey-Bass.

Hoyt, M.F. (Ed.) (1996) *Constructive therapies* (Vol. 2). New York: Guilford Press.

Hoyt, M.F. (Ed.) (1998) *The handbook of constructive therapies.* San Francisco: Jossey-Bass.

Hoyt, M.F. (2000) *Some stories are better than others: Doing what works in brief therapy and managed care.* Philadelphia: Brunner/Mazel.

Hoyt, M.F. (2004) *The present is a gift: Mo' better stories from the world of brief therapy.* New York: iUniverse.

Hoyt, M.F. (2009) *Brief psychotherapies: Principles and practices.* Phoenix, AZ: Zeig, Tucker & Theisen.

Hoyt, M.F., Rosenbaum, R., & Talmon, M. (1992) Planned single-session therapy. In S.H. Budman, M.F. Hoyt, & S. Friedman (Eds.), *The first session in brief therapy* (pp. 59–86). New York: Guilford Press.

Hoyt, M.F., & Ziegler, P. (2004) The pros and cons of postmodernism in psychotherapy: Stepping back from the abyss. In M.F. Hoyt, *The present is a gift* (pp. 132–181). New York: iUniverse.

Kuehn, J.L. (1965) Encounter at Leyden: Gustav Mahler consults Sigmund Freud. *Psychoanalytic Review,* 52, 345–364.

Malan, D.H., Bacal, H.A., Heath, E.S., & Balfour, F.H.G. (1968) A study of psychodynamic changes in untreated neurotic patients: Improvements that are questionable on dynamic criteria. *British Journal of Psychiatry,* 114, 525–551.

Malan, D.H., Heath, E.S., Bacal, H.A., & Balfour, H.G. (1975) Psychodynamic changes in untreated neurotic patients. II. Apparently genuine improvements. *Archives of General Psychiatry,* 32, 110–126.

Pekarik, G. (1996) *Psychotherapy abbreviation: A practical guide.* New York: Haworth Press.

Prochaska, J.O. (1999) How do people change, and how can we change to help many more people? In M.A. Hubble, B.L. Duncan, & S.D. Miller (Eds.), *The heart and soul of change: What works in therapy* (pp. 227–255). Washington, DC: APA Books.

Rosenbaum, R. (1992) *Single-session therapy: The time being.* Paper presented at the annual meeting of the American Psychological Association, Washington, DC.

Rosenbaum, R. (1993) Heavy ideals: Strategic single-session hypnotherapy. In R.A. Wells & V.J. Giannetti (Eds.), *Casebook of the brief psychotherapies* (pp. 109–129). New York: Plenum Press.

Rosenbaum, R. (1999) *Zen and the heart of psychotherapy.* New York: Brunner/ Mazel.

Rosenbaum, R. (2013) *Walking the way: 81 Zen encounters with the Tao Te Ching.* Somerville, MA: Wisdom Publications.

Rosenbaum, R., Hoyt, M.F., & Talmon, M. (1990) The challenge of single-session therapies: Creating pivotal moments. In R.A. Wells & V. J. Giannetti (Eds.), *Handbook of the brief psychotherapies* (pp. 165–189). New York: Plenum Press.

Talmon, M. (1990) *Single session therapy: Maximizing the effect of the first (and often only) therapeutic encounter.* San Francisco: Jossey-Bass.

Talmon, M. (1993) *Single-session solutions: A guide to practical, effective, and affordable therapy.* New York: Addison-Wesley.

Talmon, M. (1996) (in Hebrew) *Worthwhile for every soul: The brief way to an effective psychotherapy.* Tel Aviv, Israel: Chamed Books.

Watzlawick, P., Weakland, J.H., & Fisch, R. (1974) *Change: Principles of problem formation and problem resolution.* New York: Norton.

Yalom, I.D. (2002) *The gift of therapy.* New York: HarperCollins.

Young, J., & Rycroft, P. (1997) Single-session therapy: Capturing the moment. *Psychotherapy in Australia,* 4(1), 18–23.

Young, J., Weir, S., Rycroft, P., & Whittle, T. (2006) *Single session work (SSW) implementation resource parcel.* The Bouverie Centre, La Trobe University, Melbourne, Australia.

Chapter Three

The Time of Your Life

Robert Rosenbaum

You are the time of your life. Consequently, psychotherapy is neither long nor short, unless we make it so.

*

I was originally trained psychoanalytically, and thought therapy required years. Then I worked in community mental health clinics and started learning brief psychodynamic psychotherapies; one model used 40 sessions, another worked with 20 sessions. Subsequently, I learned two models of time-limited dynamic psychotherapy where the number was fixed at 12 sessions to activate existential themes of loss and separation.

When I started working at Kaiser Permanente, it seemed many clients got better even in six or eight sessions. Learning hypnosis and strategic therapies seemed to often be effective in even fewer sessions. Finally, Moshe Talmon came to me and invited me to join him and Michael Hoyt in a new project: investigating single session therapies. I agreed, but inwardly protested: "Come on, single sessions? Not possible!"

The next weekend, while hiking in the Sierra Nevada, I looked at the mountains and mused: "People might get a little better in a few sessions of therapy, but there's no way fundamental change can take place quickly. People are like these mountains; their psy-

A version of this chapter was presented as a keynote address at the *Capture the Moment: The Inaugural Symposium on Single Session Therapies and Walk-In Services* held on Phillip Island, Victoria, Australia, in March 2012.

chological structures have to change slowly just as the mountains change, by the gradual erosion of wind and rain."

At that moment I rounded a corner of the trail and found the path blocked. It had been overrun by a massive avalanche that winter. The entire face of the mountain had been transformed in a few seconds.

I looked up at the sky and said, "OK, OK, I get the message..."

Figure 1. Avalanche

But I didn't really get the message. I still thought change takes time. I hadn't yet realized change *is* time, and that pivotal moments transcend both time and timelessness in the eternal here and now.

*

Everyone knows subjective time varies according to the quality of an experience. Pleasures seem all too short; pains seem all too long. We think these time spans are somehow less "real" than the time measured by clocks. Why? Our body-mind and mechanical timepieces are different measurement instruments, but neither has a monopoly on the truth. The "feel" of an experience, though, is more intimate and, ultimately, matters more to us than the tick-tock of gears linked to an expanding spring or a swinging pendulum. Modern clocks synchronize with the decay of a cesium atom in the computer servers of the National Institute of Standards and Technology, but the decay of the cells of our body provides the most inexorable measure of our life-and-death.

*

Time "keeping" is simply a matter of counting cycles or units of time. A clock is what does the counting. We have many different body clocks, each counting a different cycle. While we live, our cells are constantly dying and being replenished. Each cell in our body has a mitotic "clock" that keeps track of cell divisions and when cells will stop dividing.

How old are you? You replace all your skin cells roughly every two weeks and all your red blood cells every four months or so, but the cells in your liver take somewhere over a year (roughly 300 to 500 days) to regenerate the entire organ. Your entire skeleton is replaced every 10 years; the average age of most of your muscles (but not the heart) is roughly 15 years. So, when someone asks you how old you are, the answer depends: the age of your liver cells may be of paramount importance if the person is asking you to join them in another glass of wine, but irrelevant if it is movie ticket-taker checking if you qualify for a senior discount. Chronological years may not be the most relevant measure of how you spend your time. Perhaps you are young enough to play a game of chess with your children but too old to accompany them to the climbing gym.

*

The very question "How old are you?" is prejudiced; it assumes time has a fixed metric, but the metric varies from culture to culture. Traditional Chinese measure a person's age starting with conception; in that view, you may be one year "older" than you think you are. Some cultures don't start measuring a person's age until they survive childhood and become adults in a welcoming ritual; other cultures dispense entirely with keeping track of birthdays.

Within our own culture, our age may obscure the existential reality of our lifespan. Norman Fischer points out that when you are sixty, it may seem three-quarters of your life expectancy has elapsed as measured by years, but since older people perceive time as slipping by two or three times faster than young people (two months until Christmas seems like eons to a first grader but like an eye blink to a septuagenarian); at "sixty" you may have only 10% of your life left when you measure by experiential time.

*

A corollary for psychotherapists: a child is not a half-grown woman; a wise crone is not a decayed adult woman. Each is complete in herself.

*

A thirty-eight year old woman came to therapy concerned she might be vulnerable to a relapse of anorexia and bulimia, which she had struggled with while a teenager learning ballet. She had stopped dancing after marrying and having two young children. Now they were both attending school, and she had begun ballet lessons again to provide herself an enjoyable exercise. But she found herself looking at the lithe teens and slender twenty-somethings in the class and started feeling larger and older. She said: "How can I be willowy like them when I am a grown woman in a grown woman's body?"

I said to her, "Yes, you've grown up and matured. What does it feel like to be a grown woman in a grown woman's body?"

A look of pleased surprise resulted in a change of posture, facial expression and emotional tone. "I am a grown woman!" she said. "And I'm happy! I don't need to worry about being an anguished teenage anorexic."

She had a successful outcome with a single session of psychotherapy.

*

Life is not merely linear. It is also composed of cycles—and it is cycles that clocks count. Our body temperature, blood pressure, GI tract activity, muscle coordination, mental efficiency, cortisol levels and melatonin secretion all vary according to a 24-hour cycle. More remarkably, this is true even on the cellular level. Every single cell has periods of rest and activity tied to a roughly 24-hour cycle, and

Figure 2. Circadian Cycle

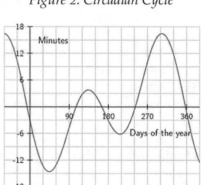

this is observable even if you take the cells out of the body and place them in a petri dish.

It is a bit misleading, though, to say that circadian rhythms function on a 24-hour cycle, because days are not 24 hours long. Days are not 24 hours long because the earth wobbles on its axis; it is eccentric in its orbit around the sun and oblique in its ecliptic. The length of the day can be as much as 16 minutes longer or 14 minutes shorter than 24 hours. The equation of time (see Fig. 2 above) is the difference, over the course of a year, between time as read from a sundial and a clock measuring the 1,440 minutes a day "should" take.

Hours, minutes, days—convenient conventions, but don't mistake them for invariable constants. The 24 hours of our circadian cycles are variable rather than constant: our biological periods reset themselves to the earth's rotation. Research has found variation of about +16 minutes in the duration of our circadian rhythms, which is in close accord with the amount of variation in the length of the days over the course of a year.

*

The alternation of light and dark is an important signal to the body for maintaining and re-setting the pulse of our circadian rhythms. Psychotherapy is one process by which we adjust the balance of our existential light and darkness: our sorrows and joys, our bright clarity of purpose throwing long shadows over our souls.

Perhaps this is why our emotional lives affect our sleep and our guts along with many other body functions—and why alterations in these body functions affect our psychological states as well as our body clocks.

*

Our perception of time varies widely because the brain has several different ways of marking time. The cerebellum helps coordinate the timing of motor movements; the lateral intraparietal lobe seems to monitor elapsed time intervals of moderate duration. The suprachiasmatic nucleus regulates circadian rhythms in response to light and dark registered by the optic nerve but also functions independently, regulated by gene activity, GABA (gamma-aminobutyric acid) and vasoactive intestinal polypeptides; there are connections with the pineal gland and melatonin secretion.

The brain also has an interval timer: when an event impinges on our neural circuits, cells within the basal ganglia fire in unison and a signal is sent from the substantia nigra to the striatum, creating a "time stamp" for the pattern's onset. At the end of the pattern, another signal is sent from the striatum to the thalamus to the cortex. This allows us to mark spans of time ranging from seconds to hours. It is possible to train the brain's interval timer, but its accuracy when compared to mechanical clocks is quite variable, diverging by anywhere from 5% to 60% from clock time.

People vary in the accuracy of their ability to judge time intervals, and this appears to be at least partially influenced by genetics. But no matter your skill in estimating clock time, it is subject to large changes depending on the state of your biochemistry. Time perception is influenced by the availability of the neurotransmitter dopamine; marijuana lowers dopamine availability and "slows" time, while stimulants increase dopamine availability and time seems to speed up. Thus, from a neuropsychological standpoint, time is not a "what" but multiple "hows." We keep track and coordinate the movement of our life and its surroundings.

*

We use clocks to coordinate our schedules. But if you synchronize clocks, they will not stay that way for long. Physics informs us it is impossible for even two clocks to stay synchronized; they will run faster and slower because of slightly different characteristics in their physical makeup and environments, plus the effects of acceleration and gravity.

Many people are familiar with the findings of relativity theory, that the faster we go the slower our clocks run so that one twin leaving earth on a spaceship traveling at close to the speed of light will, on his return, find himself younger than the twin who stayed at home. Einstein's special theory of relativity showed absolute simultaneity does not exist; observers detecting an event will assign a different time to it depending on how fast each is going. According to general relativity theory, clock time can only apply to small patches of the universe

But modern physics questions the very existence of time. Some versions of string theory do not need to include time as a variable. When Einstein's equations for gravity are re-written in the same form as equations for electromagnetism to develop a unified quantum theory, time completely vanishes from the resulting Wheeler-Dewitt equation.

Many physicists suggest our assumption that time flows from past to future may be more feeling than fact. They point out that

Newton's laws work just as well going backward or forward in time, and although we cannot go back in time, this doesn't imply time flows in one direction; nature abounds in irreversible processes (e.g., the tendency toward entropy as described by the second law of thermodynamics).

The fact that time's arrow "points" toward the future doesn't mean the arrow is itself moving toward the future any more than a compass needle pointing north means the compass is traveling north; the arrow indicates an asymmetry, not a movement. If time "flows," it means one thing is moving relative to another thing: if time is itself moving, we would have to specify what it is moving relative to.

Some physicists suggest each moment has its own existence. Rudolf Rucker, in *Geometry, Relativity, and the Fourth Dimension*, spells out the implications of this: "Every instant of your life exists always. Time does not pass. *We are in fact at each instant of our lives* [my italics]. Every moment of past and future history exists permanently in the framework of four-dimensional space-time."

*

We usually think we live embedded in time as if it were a flowing stream. This was expressed well by Marcus Aurelius, who wrote: "Time is a sort of river of passing events, and strong is its current; no sooner is a thing brought to sight than it is swept by and another takes its place, and this too will be swept away."

But there is another way of approaching time. Thornton Wilder refutes Marcus Aurelius, saying: "It is only in appearance that time is a river. It is rather a vast landscape and it is the eye of the beholder that moves."

Jorge Luis Borges: "Time is the substance from which I am made. Time is a river which carries me along, but I am the river; it is a tiger that devours me, but I am the tiger; it is a fire that consumes me, but I am the fire."

*

Craig Callender, writing in a special issue of *Scientific American* devoted to the physics of the time, suggests that "The apparent flow of time is a product of our surreptitiously putting into the river a witness of its course; we then forget to put ourselves and our connections to the world into the picture. In this picture, physical time emerges by virtue of our thinking ourselves as separate from everything else."

We are not separate from everything else. We are connected. If we weren't connected, psychotherapy could not exist.

*

We cannot "keep" time because there is nothing to hold on to. The Diamond Sutra, a core text in early Buddhism, states something we know, but rarely pay attention to: the past is gone, the future is not here yet, and the present cannot be grasped.

What time, then, do you exist in? How could therapy "take" time?

*

Therapy, like life, does not "take" time because time is not a dimension we exist "in." We are time, and time is us.

As Eihei Dogen, the founder of Soto Zen in 13th century Japan, puts it: "Time itself is being, and all being is time."

*

In Dogen's fascicle *Uji* (*The Time Being*) he says: "Time is not separate from you, and as you are present, time does not go away. Do not think that time merely flies away....If time merely flies away, you would be separated from time. People only see time's coming and going, and do not thoroughly understand that the time-being abides in each moment."

We are often advised: "be in the moment." But a moment is not a very brief instant of time.

Zen teacher Shunryu Suzuki used to say that in a single finger-snap there are millions of instants of time. When you meditate, you become quite aware of this.

A lot can happen in less than a second. Psychology research shows chronological resolution of perception is quite variable but can be measured in milliseconds (visually the fusion threshold is around 40 milliseconds, aurally about two milliseconds). Neural impulses can travel as fast as 350 feet per second, although when you are reading and thinking they go only about a quarter as fast.

*

Moments, are best viewed not as short intervals on a time line but rather as meeting points: attention meets thought, action meets object, self meets other. This moment is defined by you reading what I have written.

*

Points are defined in geometry, as in life, by intersections. In geometry, a point has no dimensions, neither length nor width nor depth. Extending the analogy, we can say a point in time is, in a way, timeless.

Moments are pivot points, each an opportunity to turn this way or that, openings in which experience unfolds. Psychotherapy is an intersection of self and other, points of time where therapist and client jointly create pivotal moments. In single session therapy, we often find problems being maintained by ineffective attempts at a solution; conversely, we often can discover pivot chords where—like a musical chord that simultaneously implies two keys and facilitates modulation from one to the other—a problem can suggest the seeds of its own resolution. These pivot chords are most likely to arise when client and therapist feel fully "present." At that moment an opening blossoms here-and-now.

Each moment is forever. This rather esoteric saying actually conforms to our subjective experience of time. It is only when we stop and look back that, surprised, we say: "Look how much time has gone by." When we are fully absorbed in an activity, moment by moment, we don't notice the passage of time.

Good moments in therapy are fully absorbing. They resonate back to before and create openings to ever after.

*

Mind and moment are inseparable. As Dogen says: "The mind arises in this moment; a moment arises in this mind....This is the understanding that the self is time."

*

Dogen alerts us to a crucial issue for therapists doing therapy moment by moment. He points out that "Since there is nothing but just this moment, the time-being is all the time there is. Each moment is all being, is the entire world."

This is not an abstraction but a liberating gateway to our life. To say "the time-being is all the time there is" doesn't mean we must "seize the moment" (which is impossible, since time cannot be grasped), nor that we should indulge ourselves because time is fleeting. "There is nothing but just this moment" means: this is your life. It's right here, right now.

*

Step off the treadmill of time and you can turn self and world inside out and all around simply by opening yourself up to the realization: this moment is you.

As Dogen puts it, "In essence, all things in the entire worlds are linked with one another as moments. Because all moments are the time-being, they are your time-being."

This is why single session therapy is possible.

*

Implications for therapy are innumerable. Hypnotherapists use time distortion, age regression and progression; strategic therapists may schedule a symptom or alter its rhythm or speed; psychodynamic therapists may use time-limited therapy to activate issues of separation and loss.

Clinicians have explored how time perception varies with depression, anxiety, and other emotional states. The rhythm of therapy sessions, their duration and frequency, may alter its effects. Some suggested readings are appended.

*

Every therapy session demarcates a beginning and an end in the continuous flow of experience. We break it into small pieces to make it manageable, but rely on that which can never be broken.

Appreciating time as ungraspable and the self as time, we find time is not our enemy but our ally on the path of liberation.

In this view of time, anything is possible any moment. This is the attitude for doing single session psychotherapy.

*

Nothing is ever finished, but everything is always complete.

*

To quote the Xinxin Ming ("Faith in Mind,") a poem attributed to the third Chinese Zen ancestor, Jianzhi Sengcan (Jap. Kanshi Sosan):

"Words!
The Way is beyond words,
for in it
there is no yesterday, today, or tomorrow."

Sources of Quotations and Suggested Further Reading

Citations are ineluctably tied to the past; we need to honor the past but need to make it present. I, therefore, purposely wrote this chapter without putting citations in standard academic style (i.e., with an accompanying date) in the hopes of encouraging the reader to enter a different mind-set that might foster a new sense of the time being.

The works below contain the sources for the specific quotations I used; in each case I named the author. I've also included authors below I did not quote directly, but whose works on time and psychotherapy have influenced my thinking, and I recommend each of the works cited below to readers interested in taking the time to delve further.

Aurelius, M. (c.178/1956). *Meditations* (Book IV, Section 43; Trans. G. Long). Chicago: Henry Regnery Company. (p. 41)

Borges, J.L. (1946/1962). A new refutation of time. In *Labyrinths: Selected stories and other writings*. New York: New Directions (p. 205).

Boscolo, L. & Bertrando, P. (1993). *The times of time: A new perspective in systemic therapy and consultation*. New York: Norton.

Callender, C. (2012). Is time an illusion? *Scientific American, A Matter of Time*, 21(1), pp. 14–21. (originally appeared in *Scientific American*, June 2010, pp. 40–47)

Cooper, L. & Erickson, M. (1959/1982). *Time distortion in hypnosis: An experimental and clinical investigation*. (2nd ed.). Boca Raton, FL: OTC *Publishing Corp.*

Dogen, E. (1240/2010). Uji, The Time Being. In K. Tanahashi, (Ed.), Treasury *of the true dharma eye: Zen master Dogen's Shobo Genzo* (Trans. D. Welch & K. Tanahashi; pp. 104–111). Boston: Shambala.

Edgette, J. H., & Edgette, J. S. (1995). Toying with time. In *The handbook of hypnotic phenomena in psychotherapy* (pp. 89–142). New York: Brunner/Mazel.

Falk, D. (2008). *In search of time: The science of a curious dimension*. New York: Thomas Dunne Books/St. Martin's Press.

Fischer, N. (2013). *Training in compassion: Zen teachings on the practice of Lojong*. Boston: Shambala. (Reference is on p. 6, loc 330 of the Kindle e-book.)

Hawking, S. (1988). *A brief history of time*. New York: Bantam.

Hoyt, M.F. (1995). On time in brief therapy. In *Brief therapy and managed care* (pp. 69–104). San Francisco: Jossey-Bass.

Lakoff, G. & Johnson, M. (1999). Time. In *Philosophy in the flesh: The embodied mind and its challenge to Western thought* (pp. 137–169). New York: Basic Books.

Mann. J. (1980). *Time-limited psychotherapy*. Cambridge, MA: Harvard University Press.

Melges, F. (1982). *Time and the inner future: A temporal approach to psychiatric disorders*. New York: Wiley.

Ritterman, M. (1995, January/February). Stopping the clock. *Family Therapy Networker*, pp. 163–169.

Rosenbaum, R. (2013). *Walking the way: 81 Zen encounters with the Tao Te Ching*. Boston, MA: Wisdom Publications.

Rosenbaum, R. (1999). Zen and the heart of psychotherapy. Philadelphia, PA: Brunner/Mazel.

Rosenbaum, R., & Dyckman, J. (1996). "No self? No problem!" In M.F Hoyt (Ed.), *Constructive psychotherapies* (Vol. 2, pp. 238–274). New York: Guilford Press.

Rosenbaum, R., Hoyt, M.F., & Talmon, M. (1990). The challenge of single-session psychotherapies: Creating pivotal moments (pp. 65–189). In R.A. Wells & V.J. Giannetti (Eds.), *Handbook of the brief psychotherapies*. (pp. 165–192). New York: Plenum.

Rucker, R. (1977). *Geometry, relativity, and the fourth dimension*. Mineola, NY: Courier Dover Publications.

Smolin, L. (2013). *Time reborn: From the crisis in physics to the future of the universe*. New York: Houghton Mifflin Harcourt.

Talmon, M. (1990). *Single session therapy: Maximizing the effect of the first (and often only) therapeutic encounter*. San Francisco: Jossey-Bass.

Wallisch, P. (2008, February). An odd sense of timing. *Scientific American Mind*, pp. 37–43.

Young, J. (1994). The loss of time in chronic systems: An intervention model for working with longer term conditions. *Australia and New Zealand Journal of Family Therapy, 15*(2), pp. 73–80.

Chapter Four

Psychology and My Gallbladder: An Insider's Account of a Single Session Therapy

Michael F. Hoyt

I have lived on the lip of insanity, wanting to know reasons, knocking on a door. It opens. I've been knocking from the inside!
—JELALUDDIN RUMI (1207–1273, QUOTED IN BARKS & GREEN, 1997, PP. 36–37)

I am one of those blessed people who, at the age of 59, could say "I have never really been sick." My body has always been my friend. I had pitched no-hitters in Little League, won a junior golf tournament,

The information contained herein describes the subjective experience of the author and is not intended to replace professional medical and/or psychological advice. Special thanks to Carol A. Erickson, John Frykman, Murray Korngold, Jennifer Lillard, and (the late) Jeffry Ordover for their help. A version of this chapter was first presented at the University of Rochester Medical Center, Department of Psychiatry, on March 31, 2009; another version was presented as a keynote address at the *Capture the Moment: The Inaugural International Symposium on Single-Session Therapies and Walk-In Services* held on Phillip Island, Victoria, Australia, in March 2012; and a version was presented as part of the First Online Conference on Ericksonian Approaches to Psychotherapy (sponsored by the M.H. Erickson Institute of Tasmania, Australia). A modified version was first published in the *Journal of Clinical Psychology: In Session*, 2011, 67(8), 766–775; used by agreement. Figure 1© M.F. Hoyt, 2013. Used by agreement.

played competitive basketball, ran marathons, and hiked and back-packed a lot. I still get up in the morning and do push-ups and sit-ups and stretches. I have taken antibiotics a few times, busted my nose and sprained an ankle playing sports, have had the flu and thrown up, but I had never been in the hospital nor had surgery. I never had a tooth pulled, never even had an I.V. It thus came as quite a shock when the doctor said, "You have a large stone, almost 4.5 centimeters, in your gallbladder. The wall of the gallbladder is very inflamed. It has to come out. It would be better to wait until it's not so inflamed, but you need to have a cholecystectomy, soon." *(When I retold this conversation to friends, it became: "The doctor told me, 'You don't really have any choice.' 'What do you mean, no choice?' I responded indignantly. 'Well, if you get an attack while you're backpacking, maybe your buddies can take it out with a can opener; or if you're on vacation some-where, you can hope that the village doctor knows what to do—but if it were me, I'd want to have it on my schedule and my terms in a clean operating room here at the hospital.' And I told him, 'Hey, if you ever get tired of medi-cine, you've got a career in sales waiting for you!'" Fear + wit = bravado.)*

History

A year earlier I had some pain in my hip. An X-ray showed nothing structurally wrong with my hip, but a then 3 centimeter gallstone had been detected incidentally. At that time, my internist said, in essence, "If it's not bothering you, ignore it." (The hip prob-lem went away quickly with some physical therapy exercises.) I got a second opinion about the gallbladder from a consulting sur-geon, who recommended preemptive removal; I thanked her and promptly went into denial. *(When I looked up gallbladder surgery on the Internet, the words 'pain,' 'complications,' and 'possible post-surgical greasy diarrhea' leapt out of the computer and slapped me in the eye.)* I had a few minor episodes of 'mild indigestion,' but nothing I could not ignore, until the night, many months later, when I had really bad pain that went on for eight hours. Writhing, gasping, whimper-ing—in the middle of the night my wife said, "Maybe we should go to the Emergency Room." I didn't want to: "If I go to the E.R., they'll want to operate on me." She replied, "Well, maybe they should." I stubbornly *(perhaps foolishly)* made it through the long, sleepless night at home—but wrung-out in the morning, I saw the internist again, and got the on-call surgeon's insistent recommendation.

I called the office of the surgeon I had seen initially. *(There are other good surgeons on the staff, but I had done my due diligence and she was the one I wanted.)* The crisis had temporarily subsided. We scheduled a date. Between her calendar and mine, it was over a month off, although I was cautioned to come in immediately if I had another acute bout.

I am rational *(kind of)* and knew surgery was needed. Nonetheless, a few days later I awoke in the middle of the night having a panic attack. And then another. And another. During the day I was okay (most of the time), but my nightmares began to unreel: *I was being wheeled into surgery when it was announced that my surgeon was suddenly not available and another doctor would replace her. I would get angry and sit up and pull out the I.V. and get off the table, cursing and fleeing.*

I became extra careful about my diet (minimal fats, no dairy, no red meat). I began taking vitamins daily and started doing lots of pushups, sit-ups, and other exercises. I was having no gallbladder symptoms. I went off to Wisconsin to teach a workshop that had been scheduled almost a year earlier. One afternoon, I was playing golf with some fellows. It turned out that one of them was an internist. "Know much about gallbladders?" I asked, casually.

"Of course."

I told him my situation and asked his advice: what would he recommend to make things go better?

"I don't know if you smoke, but I wouldn't smoke anything for the next month."

"Sure, no problem—but why not?"

"To reduce having a cough after surgery. You're going to have some stitches in your abdomen. If you take vitamins, that's okay—but stop Vitamin E a week before surgery because it can increase bleeding. I also recommend that you give up all alcohol, and get yourself into the best physical shape you can. It will help your recovery."

"Okay. Anything else?"

"I sure hope you have a laparoscopy. If they can do it with a laparoscope, it's *much* better. Otherwise, you could be in the hospital for a week or two with a big, deep incision and lots of pain and morphine, and a long recovery."

"Ohhhh."

I had been on my way to my best golf round of the year, but I then hit my next three shots off to the side and into a lateral water hazard.

A couple of weeks later, I was in New York. I had stopped over on my way to the APA Convention in Boston to see my friend, Jeff, who was in the hospital. It turned out that he was too ill for a visit, but I stayed over with another buddy. The next day I went to the Museum of Modern Art. There was a big Salvador Dali show. On the top floor, there was also a temporary exhibit with lots of video screens. When I looked, I discovered that on one screen there was a continuous one-minute loop of a surgeon pulling some gizzard from someone's abdomen and cutting it off, over and over. I stood there, transfixed. Yikes! I wandered around the MoMA, but kept coming back to watch again and again.

Preparing for Surgery: The Single Session Begins

As it happens, every three weeks or so, I have a long lunch meeting with some friends. We are all experienced psychotherapists, and we discuss cases, professional gossip, movies, personal stuff, and so forth. We were at Murray's house when I announced: "I need your help. I'm freaking out." I explained my medical situation and my fearful reactions. In the course of our discussion, Murray, who was then 88 years old, said, "Do you know why I'm 88?" "No," I replied, not yet getting his message. "Because I've had surgery, several times—it's your friend." He told a story about his first surgery, when he was in his 20's. When he finished, Carol asked me to respond with my first, uncensored thoughts to a series of questions:
"How tall are you?" ("6 foot 3 and ¾ inches.")
"What sex are you?" ("Male.")
"Which hand do you write with?" ("Left.")
"How old is the person who is scared?" ("6.")
It just popped out: "6." "No wonder you're scared—you're reacting from your 6-year-old self." We discussed ways to cope better. Rather than simply telling me to stop acting like I was 6, I was advised to fasten the seatbelt on the passenger side when I was driving and have reassuring discussions with the (imaginary) 6-year-old who was riding with me. She also suggested that I write out a list of statements I wanted the surgeon to make (and not make) while I was in surgery and ask the surgeon to be sure to say them. "That's brilliant," said Murray, "it puts him in a meta position—you'll still have some control even while you're out." Just then our other friend, John, arrived. He caught up quickly, then reminded us that he had, years earlier, been a consultant with a surgical group in which they found that what the surgeons said while the patient was "out" had significant

implications for healing, amount of pain, days in hospital, etc. While I was taking all this in, Carol offered to meet with me a couple of days before the surgery, to talk and do some hypnotherapy. My scheduled surgery was impending, and there was an implicit understanding that the one session would be helpful. I accepted her invitation.

Carol very kindly stopped by my house to drop off some professional hypnosis tapes she had made, to help me practice my going-into-trance skills. I listened to one of the tapes a couple of times—at first I was rushed and impatient, but then slowed myself down and tuned in. She also asked me to write out an imagery scene that I found comforting and that she could use when we did our hypnotherapy work. I did so, and mailed the scene to her. Here's what I wrote:

Secret Beach.

My #1 place I like to go, in reality and in my head, is Secret Beach on the north side of Kauai. I am at the cottage and looking out toward the ocean, then I walk across the large lawn until I get to the top of the cliff. Looking down at the ocean, watching it, blue washing up against the white sand shore. I climb down the cliffside, back and forth, then one ladder of stairs, then the other, then down the last of the hillside until I land on the beach. I kick off my sandals and leave them under the big tree with the rope, then walk out on to the warm—almost hot, keep walking—sand. It's a longish walk in the powdery sand, a 100 yards or more, but not too far. The shore slants down near the water. The sand gets damp. I love walking in, slowly, the water over my feet, then around my ankles, then up to my knees and thighs—then I pause, and gasp a bit as it hits my tummy—cool, yet tropic warm. I like the beach because it is so gradual and easy—I can slowly walk out until the water is up to my chest and over my shoulders. I duck under a rolling wave, then swim a bit. It's like a big bathtub. I go back and forth, paralleling the shore, knowing I can put my feet down if I want to—sometimes swimming out a bit further, but coming back to the safe warm enclosure. Turning and looking back toward the cliff, I see the trees and then looking along to the right, the place where the wall juts out a bit and around the corner the small waterfall trickles down the rocks. I walk out and go over. The waterfall is freshwater—it runs on my head, rinsing the salt from my face. I tip my head back and take a drink, then turn and look back toward the ocean.

(In retrospect, this was another way I was practicing going into trance and accessing internal resources—even before our session.)

At my pre-op appointment, the surgeon was very nice and professional. She answered my questions, then asked me a few medical questions and examined me. She had me lie back on the examination table and pull up my shirt. She pressed around in my belly and asked a few more things. She explained the situation and my options. I asked her to touch the exact places where incisions would be made. She lightly touched four small spots—one in the bottom of my belly button, another a few inches above, two others over to the side: "That's if we're able to do this laparoscopically." She explained that would be the first choice, but if there were problems they would need to "go in" with a regular incision. "Where would that be?" I asked. She traced a line *(a long line)* on my right side, under my rib cage. *(Remember the famous photo of President Lyndon Johnson in 1965 pulling up his shirt to show his ugly gallbladder incision?)*

When we were finishing, she asked if I had any more questions. I hesitated, then noticed the poster on the wall behind her. It was titled "Attitude Matters" and extolled some of the advantages of a positive outlook when dealing with cancer. I smiled. "This is your regular examining room, right?" She nodded. "Seeing that poster makes me think you'll understand the importance of what I'm going to ask. I would really like it if you would carefully and consciously say certain things while I'm out and you're operating—and not say other things."

"Like what?"

I pulled a slip of yellow paper out of the file I had brought. "Here."

On it was written:

SAY:
"Doing very well."
"Everything looks good."
"Will heal nicely."

DON'T SAY:
"That's going to be painful."
"That's a lot of blood."
"Oops!"

She laughed at the last entry, then smiled: "No problem—I'll be sure to say the right ones." She told me that she'd see me just before the surgery, and that she would call me at home a couple of days after. As we finished up, we shook hands. I held hers and did not let go, but gently turned it over, palm up. "What are you looking at?" she asked. "Are you going to stick that in me?" I asked with pseudo-jocularity *(or should I say, 'pseudo-jock-hilarity'?)*. "Well, carefully—if I have to—but we have long instruments so I may not need to." *(Her quick reply made me feel confident that she was on top of it and in charge.)*

I also met with the anesthesiologist. She explained the anesthesia procedure and answered my questions. She looked at the back of my hand (where an I.V. would be placed) and said "Oh, you have beautiful veins" and then looked into my mouth (where a breathing tube would be inserted after I was unconscious) and said, "Oh, you have a beautiful throat." *(I suddenly realized that many years ago a dentist had told me what a nice mouth—big and spacious—I had to work in; ever since I proudly open wide whenever I sit in a dentist's chair.)* I smiled and said, "You have beautiful diction."

When Saturday came, I drove over to where Carol lives; she has her office in her home. I had been there before, for luncheons, but this time we went down the hall and into her therapy room. It was full of stuff, everywhere—books, pictures, knick-knacks, plants, stuffed toy animals, curios, more stuff, more books, everywhere. She introduced me to a couple of her stuffed animals *(a little weird, but done playfully and signaling to me that we were going into imaginal space)* then asked me to look around and find the mate of one of them. I naturally looked into her box full of various animals; I pulled a few out but didn't find the mate. I looked around a bit: "I give. Where is it?" She looked around a bit—"not in the box." I looked around some more. Carol looked up at a picture on the wall above the toy box. I followed her gaze: there was a picture of a beautiful black panther with green eyes. She told me its name and introduced us. *(As I thought about the 'outside the box' message of seeing more the more one looked, I relaxed. I let my guard down and decided to 'go with it.')* We talked about lots of things, eventually getting around to my situation. I explained:

"I'm basically scared."

"Of what?"

I made a dumb frown: "Of pain, and surgery, and getting nauseated. I don't want them to find a tumor the size of a cantaloupe. I don't want a scar on my belly. And trouble with my digestion. I'm not really scared of dying—I think I'll wake up—but the rest of it is a fucking disaster and a mess."

Carol smiled kindly. "Can you see it?"

"What?"

She leaned forward a bit. "Now?"

"No—what?"

She moved her chair over, very close to me.

"Now?"

"No—what?"

She pointed to her neck. If I leaned forward and squinted, I could just sort of make out a thin white line that blended into a natural crease in her skin.

"Not much of a scar, huh?" I recalled that she had told me earlier about having had, years prior, a major operation to remove a growth that had threatened her vocal cords. (*I got the message: it was inconsequential and that scars fade.*)

She smiled. "I can see we've got some work to do. So, what do you want to have happen?"

"I don't want to have any pain, not one iota."

"Well, we can't be sure of that. How about: 'I'd like to have the maximum comfort and the least discomfort available in the situation'?"

"Sounds good."

We talked for a few more minutes, including about my meeting to prepare the surgeon. She then suggested that we do some more formal trancework, and asked if I had been listening to the tapes she had dropped off. I told her that I had, a couple of times. She suggested that I get comfortable, whatever way would be easiest for me to go into trance.

"Let me show you what I mean. You may want to jot down some notes." She gave me a pen and piece of paper. She got comfortable, then closed her eyes and began to speak. Here is what I wrote:

> Wise Unconscious—
>
> Assist me to do this in the wisest way...to use my resources...doing my part...take care of me...help me walk in calm, comfortable...how do I want to do this? Put them at *their* ease...they're taking good care of me...help my body...resting, relaxed...Wise Unconscious, help me to dissociate—do things, forget other things...maximum comfort available in the circumstances...get back quickly to feeling good...Thank you, Wise Unconscious—I don't

know how you do it...Say aloud so that all parts—unconscious, body, and conscious—hear it.

Carol smiled. "OK?"

I nodded, then took off my glasses and closed my eyes. I listened to her voice and also to my thoughts, back and forth. I began to get a bit spacy, then sleepy, then found myself drifting. It seemed that I heard her voice, somewhere in the background. My breathing slowed. Various thoughts flitted through my mind. I heard Carol: "Calm. Competent. Comfortable. Cooperative." I saw the beach. I felt drowsy. I relaxed, then opened my eyes a crack. "As you see that you're safe you can feel comfortable and let yourself go a bit further—you can always put your feet down when you want." I went a bit deeper. "Healing...taking good care of me..." I seemed to be floating, inside my head. I'm not sure for how long (*20–30 minutes?*). "Calm. Comfortable. Competent. Cooperative." After awhile, I began to "come back." I was aware that I was in the room, Carol sitting across from me. I slowly opened my eyes.

Carol smiled benignly. We just sat there. After a bit, she asked: "Have you ever had shoes with green shoelaces, or red shoelaces?" I was still entranced, and the question seemed natural (not a decontextualized *non sequitur*). I paused, then thought. My eyes rolled up to the side as I searched my memory. "No, not green ones." I looked around in my head some more. I suddenly saw them, in the bottom of my closet, in the back. "Yeah. I did used to have some with red laces. I gave them to one of my son's friends." I sat there, amused by the recall of the distant memory.

"Isn't that interesting," she said in her soft drawl, "all the things that you can recall if you just look in the right place...It's very interesting...Your mind is full of things you could think about—interesting things—the plants in your garden, and friends, and things you've read and things you want to write, pictures and memories and ideas, all sorts of interesting things you'll find if you look."

(*It felt like little computer files were popping open in my head.*) "Yeah! There are lots of things I can think about. There are all the plants, the tops of the leaves *and* the underside of the leaves. Wow! And movies. And sex. And conversations. There are lots of things I can focus on."

We sat for a few more minutes. I asked her some questions about the experience. She said that it seemed my trance state fluctuated from 4 to 7. I confirmed that impression, and said I had noticed that when I had briefly opened my eyes she had utilized my coming up as a way to facilitate going a bit deeper. We talked about "calibration," adjusting responses to the particular client. I also commented on hearing, several times: "Calm. Cooperative. Comfortable. Competent." and that the alliteration had been pleasantly predictable.

I quipped: "Hey, you're good at this!"

Carol nodded: "You are, too!" (*Appreciating the compliment while returning power to me.*)

The meeting was almost over. Carol leaned forward and said, in the nicest way: "You know, you're going to have to deal with this like a man." (*It was said as a friendly encouragement to use my resources. Suddenly, I recalled a time, some years earlier, when in a somewhat different situation I had told a friend that I felt anxious and out of control like I was on a runaway horse.*) I told Carol about the time, and how my friend had helpfully said: "Hey, man, grab the reins!"

After we finished our meeting, I drove over and joined my wife and some friends at a picnic. I was calm and relaxed. After the picnic, we had time before meeting some other friends for dinner. I had my golf clubs in the car and we stopped at a driving range near the restaurant. My wife bought a soda and sat in the bar working on her laptop computer while I hit a big bucket of balls. Then we went to dinner.

Sunday passed. I gardened and wrote a short letter to my son. I called my friend Jeff. He was still very ill and in the hospital, but I needed to speak with him. When I told the person who answered to tell him that *I* was having surgery the next day, she put him on. We spoke for a bit. He was positive and reassuring. Himself a physician, he asked some medical questions, then told me I'd be okay and wished me well. I slept okay that night (all things considered) and got up early. No liquids or food after midnight. I read the newspaper, did some push-ups and sit-ups, shaved and showered, spritzed on some favorite cologne (*its sweet tuberose scent aimed me at Hawaii and Secret Beach*) and announced, "Let's go—bring it on."

My wife drove us to the hospital. I knew I was on autopilot, in a trance. We parked. As we were walking toward the building with the admitting office, I suddenly thought of my mother and how she had conducted herself when she first went into the care facility where she spent the last two years of her life. (*My thought was not morbid, not about her dying. Rather, it was remembering watching her going around to each person, each nurse, each clerk or orderly or house-keeper, shaking people's hand and saying, "Hi. I'm Ruth Hoyt. Let's be friends. What's your name? Do you have any children?" As I remembered seeing her, I heard the words: 'CALM, COOPERATIVE, COMPETENT, COMFORTABLE.' I understood how they could work for me.)*

I was pleasant and cooperative with the admitting clerks *(although they seemed a little slow and distracted for my taste)*. My wife and I went to the waiting area. After awhile, my name was called. We were guided into a changing room. I put on a hospital gown and some paper booties. We sat around for a few minutes, waiting. I noticed on the bulletin board, amidst various articles and announcements, a cheap plaster plaque with some cherubs and a motto: "Angels Gather Here." *(It was probably given by a grateful patient or well-intended nurse and meant to be reassuring, but I didn't like it—to me, the angels seemed funereal. I thought it was creepy and considered throwing it in the trashcan, but decided that it didn't matter and it would be better to stay focused on my positive resources and not act out my anxiety.)* We hung out for a bit, then a door opened. A nurse smiled. "We're ready." My wife and I hugged and said our *'Love you*'s and *See you later*'s, then I was led into the pre-op room.

I met two nurses. They had me climb onto a gurney. I looked around at the high-tech equipment. It looked a little like we were on the command deck of the Spaceship Enterprise. I told them this was my very first time. "Don't worry—we'll take very good care of you." As we chatted, they started an I.V. into the back of my hand (it pricked for a moment, but didn't really hurt). They gave me some fast-acting relaxant that soon had me grinning. One woman then produced an electric clipper from a drawer and shaved me "to within an inch of your life" *(as she put it—I'd say two inches)*. My surgeon popped in, to say hello and make sure everything was going right. I said 'Hi' and noticed that she had my yellow slip of paper taped to the front of the chart she was carrying.

"Everything OK?" she asked.

"Sure."

After a while (and a little more medication) they put a green surgical "party hat" on my head and rolled me down the hallway. We went into a very bright room. Big round lights. White walls. Everyone with pale green gowns and surgical masks. I looked around.

"Hi, everyone!" I said brashly as I transferred from the gurney to the table. "I'm Michael. We're all in this together. I hope you've got your 'A' game!"

They gathered around. Someone tapped me on the shoulder, then began to place a see-through mask over my face. I looked back to see who it was...

Surgery

My eyes slowly opened and I became aware that I was staring at a curtain beside my gurney in the recovery room. *(Three hours later.)* I slowly looked around, coming to. Just then, a nurse's face came into my field of vision—she leaned in close and asked, "Hi—how are you?"

"Uhh. I just came to—give me a moment."

I looked around, and my wife's head popped in from behind the curtain.

"Hi, honey! You're alive!"

She came over and gave me a little peck on the cheek. The nurse then asked, "Let me ask you: How would you rate your pain?" I didn't feel like being bothered. A voice in the back of my head whispered: "COOPERATIVE."

"Did I have the laparoscope or the open incision?"

The nurse replied: "Oh, the laparoscope."

I smiled. "I'm OK—and I'd rather not think about pain right now. Could you ask me again in a bit?"

She smiled, and disappeared. A few minutes later, when she returned, I rated my pain "a 2 or a 3." She suggested that I start some medication, to stay ahead of any developing pain, and held out a pill and a little glass of water.

"What's that?"

"It's a pain pill. The doctor wants you to take it."

"What kind is it, and how many milligrams?" I asked, pointedly. *(I could sense my brother, who I had watched be a patient for many years, always checking any pills before taking them. He may have seemed cautious and a bit paranoid, but he far outlived his expected lifespan.)* My wife began to step forward, probably a bit embarrassed by my sudden abruptness with the kind post-op nurse.

"It's a regular post-operative pain pill, dear." *(I heard "COOPERATIVE" and "CALM.")*

"I'm sorry. I didn't mean to bark. It's just that I'm a little nervous—kind of having a big day here, you know? And I'd like to know exactly what I'm taking. So, what is it?"

The nurse told me the name and milligrams. I held out my hand and popped it in my mouth, then took a big sip of water. "Thanks."

Back at Home

I stayed in the recovery area for a while, then went home. Once home, I took pain meds for two days. When I went into the bathroom to pee, I would pull up my pajama shirt and look at the four little band-aids stuck to my abdomen. The second day I tried to write an e-mail to a friend, saw that it was garbled and had many typos, but hit the 'Send' button anyway. I wrote another: "Okay, but screwed up on pain meds. Call me." An hour later, I got a call. I stopped the medication after two days. I was experiencing no real pain, I feared constipation, and wanted to stop being so dopey. I had some cramps and knew something had happened, but nothing sharp or horrible. The next day, my surgeon called to check up on me; I called Carol to say hi; Murray came to visit; then John and his wife. I walked around the house and yard a bit. I went upstairs to groom the geraniums on the deck. Coming back in, I looked into the bathroom mirror and caught my eye. Suddenly, I burst into tears! *(Crying at the happy ending—the danger had passed and it was safe to experience my feelings; see Weiss, 1952.)*

Two weeks went by. I read and daydreamed and dozed a lot. I saw the surgeon for a follow-up appointment, then finally went back to work. At first I tired easily, but began to get my strength back. I told people about my experience. One patient, who fears medical procedures, seemed to benefit from the details; another wondered why I was going on and on.

I began to get eager to resume some exercise, both to flex my muscles and to establish that I was completely 'back.' The surgeon had cautioned no strenuous exercise for a full month, to allow healing, and then to ease back in. I waited the 30 days, then went to the local driving range. I was rusty and had lost distance. I hit one okay, then a couple off to the side.

A fellow was standing there and started kibitzing with me.

"How you doing?" he asked.

"Great! Are you kidding? Man, a month ago I was in surgery. *EVERY* one I hit is great!"

Lessons Learned and Offered

I have a much greater appreciation for what surgical patients go through. My operation was relatively easy. My heart goes out to people having their chests cracked, their hips and knees replaced, their breasts removed, and so on. It is more than daunting to recall the many surgeries my older brother went through because of his Crohn's Disease. I tip my hat to his courage.

Psychotherapy (including hypnotherapy) can be invaluable in helping people prepare and cope, mentally and physically. Reducing anxiety (*let's call it what it really is: FEAR*) is important in its own right, and may also enhance the body's healing.[1] Effective therapy involves developing an alliance, having achievable goals, and evoking relevant resources (Hoyt, 2000a, p. 3). Language matters. Consistent with Shakespeare's line, "Our remedies often in ourselves do lie" (from *All's Well that Ends Well*—Act I, Scene 1, line 216), smart therapists strategically amplify and utilize patients' existing healthful resources and responses. Memories of my brother and mother were evoked as allies, a useful "re-membering" (White, 1997). Some stories are better than others (Hoyt, 2000a), some ways of looking are more encouraging and empowering than others— they tap into our strengths and competencies.

I expect that an "analytic" therapist would have invited me to think about the origins or meanings of my panic attacks in terms of feelings about my brother's medical history. This would not have been a "Wow—I never thought of that!" unconscious revelation, of course; but the choice does not have to be an either/or. We can acknowledge painful material while focusing on strengths. For example, in a single session clinical demonstration (transcribed in Cummings & Cummings, 2000, pp. 193–208) in which I was the therapist working with someone anxious about his young daughter having major surgery, we explored what impact his own little baby sister's death many years before might be having. When he affirmed that there was a connection, I asked, "How do you remind yourself that your sister is not your daughter, that what happened with your sister doesn't mean anything in terms of the outcome for your daughter?" Guiding him toward rationality—

---

1. "Words of comfort" is the humane answer to the question, "What treatment in an emergency is administered by ear?" that is asked by the chief surgeon in Abraham Verghese's (2009, pp. 520–521) bestselling medical novel, *Cutting for Stone*.

not just warded-off anxiety—helped him to control his potential emotional spillover.

When alliance/goals/resources overlap (see Figure 1), we're creating a *context of competence* in which effective brief (time-sensitive) therapy can take place. This way of thinking was not a fresh "lesson learned"; I had previously put this Venn diagram on the board many times when teaching workshops. Expectations can be helpfully self-fulfilling (Appelbaum, 1975; Battino, 2006—see Chapter 21 this volume) and my "brief" and "competence-based" orientation helped me to be open to the possibility of one-session help.

Figure 1. Context of Competence

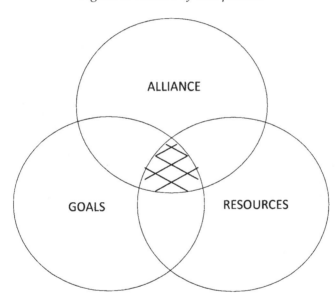

We are "on time in brief therapy" (Hoyt, 1990—also see Rosenbaum, Chapter 3). Effective therapy sometimes only requires a single session, especially if a "good moment" (Rosenbaum, 2008) can be evoked in which something profound shifts for the patient. "My desire is not to see everyone for one session; my desire is to see everyone for one full moment, as long as that takes" (Rosenbaum, in Hoyt et al., 1992, p. 80). Because the therapy is not prolonged and the locus of control is experienced inside the client (rather than depending on the therapist), termination (letting go) may be relatively simple (see Hoyt, 2000b).

Carol and I shared an intimate (therapeutic) moment. It was not merely a "professional consultation." Consistent with the brief therapy idea of focused intermittent treatment throughout the life cycle (Cummings & Sayama, 1995), it was not intended to "restructure my personality," but it was "personal therapy": I was there as a person, and it affected me personally. I was anxious and I let myself be vulnerable; I was a "patient" seeking help for my mind-body. Brevity (including "single session") does not necessarily mean superficial; the right haiku can be much more soul stirring and "deep" than a long, plodding novel. ("Deep" is another metaphor, "rooted" in the body—Lakoff & Johnson, 1999.) As Haley (2012, p. 303) has noted, "Part of the prejudice against brief therapy was caused by the metaphors developed in long-term therapy ideology. It was said, for example, that long-term therapy was 'deep' and the past was 'buried.' Brief therapy was said to be 'shallow'...Who would want a therapy that was shallow and dealt with only the surface and couldn't deal with buried complexes." Although the area of therapeutic focus was circumscribed, SSTs often do more than just stabilize or resolve a "presenting problem": they can lead to enduring changes that may "ripple" to other areas of personality and interpersonal functioning.

Interestingly, more than a year after the episode recounted here, I underwent a routine but less-than-charming medical procedure (colonoscopy).[2] Going into the procedure, I started to get very nervous, then heard in my mind the words "Calm...Competent...Cooperative...Comfortable." I heard the words in *my* voice—not Carol's—and became calm and comfortable. I expect that I will be able to access this resource again if and when medical challenges arise in the future.

When choosing a psychotherapist, pick a good match. I chose my friend Carol, who is a licensed clinical social worker, as my therapist in this episode because I knew and trusted her as a person, because she made herself available at a time of need, and because I knew that she was smart and that her approach would be compatible with my desired ways of working and being—trying to get to the heart of the matter, closely attending to what the client wants now that would be helpful, and emphasizing client competency and empowerment rather than weakness and pathology. Carol's theoretical orientation is Ericksonian. Indeed, her last name

---

2. Anyone hesitating to have this important cancer screening procedure should read the article by Oz (2011).

is "Erickson" and she is the oldest daughter of Milton H. Erickson, the legendary pioneer of many strategic and hypnotic techniques (see M. Erickson, 1980; Haley, 1973; Short, Erickson & Klein, 2005). Mind you, Carol is her own person, with her own personality and methods. Nevertheless, her overarching orientation, focusing on and working with clients' strengths and resources, is very much in the spirit of Dr. Erickson's competency-seeking ideas about *utilization* (see C.A. Erickson, 2013) and also fits nicely with evidence (see Duncan & Miller, 2000; Lambert, 2005; Sprenkle, Davis, & Lebow, 2009; Wampold, 2001) that it is the client's (not therapist's) contributions that most influence good outcomes. Carol and I both know ourselves and each other fairly well; we are informed and good communicators, and felt we could proceed with likely benefit and without undue present or future clinical, ethical, or social risk (see Heaton & Black, 2010; Younggren & Gottlieb, 2004).

People craft their healing from a variety of internal and external resources (Bohart & Tallman, 1999; Dreier, 2008; Rosenbaum, 1994). I actually sought help in a variety of ways. My friends, my wife, my surgeon, the nurses, and my hypnotherapist all provided support and encouragement. Effective single session therapy helps people organize and catalyze, integrate and motivate, so that they can better access their own resources. When attempting to help someone via brief intervention, it is particularly important to appreciate and help them utilize their own strengths. No therapy is often the treatment of choice (Frances & Clarkin, 1981)—people do it on their own. When we are involved as therapists, we should try to help the client as much as possible to use his/her/their own abilities. To my mind, our primary therapeutic effort and expertise should be directed toward encouraging, eliciting, evoking, exploring, and elaborating whatever the client brings that can be helpful to get them to where they want to go.

"When the doctor is the patient" can be difficult: our professional knowledge can be helpful, but we therapists can sometimes let "knowing" interfere with participating in the vulnerable client role (see Kaslow, 1984). Fortunately, in my situation the doctor and hypnotherapist built confidence with their manner and skillfulness; seeing my yellow paper on the surgeon's chart and receiving her promised follow-up call were reassuring. Negotiating a realistic goal ("maximum comfort, minimal discomfort available in the situation") was much more helpful than indulging a fantasy ("not one iota of pain") that would have left me panicked as soon as it began to crumble. My therapist worked *with* my experience (frightened 6-year-old) rather than simply trying to abolish it (see Flemons, 2002). The alliterative mnemonic ("Calm. Comfortable. Cooperative. Competent.") was comforting and easy to recall (McDowell, 2008, pp. 84–92; Rosen, 1982; Zeig, 1990). Reminding me of and pointing me toward some of my many resources, as well as gently challenging me to use them ("deal with this like a man"), was very helpful. Indeed, writing this report, stepping back and putting my experience into words, has served to help me feel a greater sense of competence, control, coherence, and completion—as I hope it may invite others to do who are facing similar challenges. I have tried to be true to Geller's (2005, p. 96) call "to set for ourselves the task of finding narrative formats that would enable therapists to explore the nonrational and irrational sources of their handling of the ambiguities and unscripted aspects of therapy."

Readers whose ears perked up at the mention of golf may especially find some useful lessons in my paper, "A Golfer's Guide to Brief Therapy (with Footnotes for Baseball Fans)" (Hoyt, 2000c), in which, following the layout of a golf course, I describe 18 brief therapy concepts (along with "Making the Turn," "Back in the Clubhouse," and some supporting footnotes drawn from baseball anecdotes). As golfers and ballplayers know, many a useful principle has been revealed on various fields of dreams.

Finally, let us remember: It *is* thin ice on which we all skate. In his magnificent novel, *Ransom*, David Malouf (2009, p. 184) recreates the famous scene from the *Iliad* in which King Priam goes to Achilles to claim back the body of his dead son, Hector: "'Achilles,' he says, his voice steady now, 'you know, as I do, what we men are. We are mortals, not gods. We die. Death is in our nature. Without that fee paid in advance, the world does not come to us. That is the hard bargain life makes with us—with all of us, every one—and the condition we share.'" Verily: life is a single session. Capture the moment and count your blessings.

References

Appelbaum, S.A. (1975) Parkinson's Law in psychotherapy. *International Journal of Psychoanalytic Psychotherapy*, 4, 426–436.

Barks, C., & Green, M. (1997) *The illuminated Rumi*. New York: Broadway Books.

Battino, R. (2006) *Expectation: The very brief therapy book*. Norwalk, CT: Crown House.

Bohart, A.C., & Tallman, K. (1999) *How clients make therapy work: The process of active self-healing*. Washington, DC: APA Books.

Cummings, N.A., & Cummings, J.L. (2000) A sampling of current masters: Michael F. Hoyt, Ph.D.: John—The present is a gift. In *The essence of psychotherapy: Reinventing the art in the new era of data* (pp. 193–208). San Diego, CA: Academic Press.

Cummings, N.A., & Sayama, M. (1995) *Focused psychotherapy: A casebook of brief, intermittent psychotherapy throughout the life cycle*. New York: Brunner/Mazel.

Dreier, O. (2008) *Psychotherapy in everyday life*. New York: Cambridge University Press.

Duncan, B.L., & Miller, S.D. (2000) *The heroic client: Doing client-directed outcome-oriented therapy*. San Francisco: Jossey-Bass.

Erickson, C.A. (2013) It warms my heart. In M.F. Hoyt (Ed.), *Therapist stories of inspiration, passion, and renewal: What's love got to do with It?* (pp. 67–74). New York: Routledge.

Erickson, M.H. (1980) *Collected papers* (Vols. 1–4). (E.L. Rossi, Ed.). New York: Irvington.

Flemons, D. (2002) *Of one mind: The logic of hypnosis, the practice of therapy*. New York: Norton.

Francis, A., & Clarkin, J.F. (1981) No treatment as the prescription of choice. *Archives of General Psychiatry*, 38, 542–545.

Geller, J.D. (2005) My experiences as a patient in five psychoanalytic psychotherapies. In J.D. Geller, J.C. Norcross, & Orlinsky, D.E. (Eds.), *The psychotherapist's own psychotherapy: and clinician perspectives* (pp. 81–97). New York: Oxford University Press.

Haley, J. (1973) *Uncommon therapy: The psychiatric techniques of Milton H. Erickson, M.D.* York: Norton.

Haley, J. (2012) The brief, brief therapy of Milton H. Erickson. In M. Richeport-Haley & J. Carlson (Eds.), *Jay Haley revisited* (pp. 284–306). New York: Routledge.

Heaton, K.J., & Black, L.L. (2010) I knew you when: A case study of managing preexisting nonamorous relationships in counseling. *The Family Journal: Counseling and Therapy for Couples and Families*, 17(2), 134–138.

Hoyt, M.F. (1990) On time in brief therapy. In R.A. Wells & V.J. Giannetti (Eds.), *Handbook of the brief psychotherapies* (pp. 115–143). New York: Plenum.

Hoyt, M.F. (2000a) *Some stories are better than others: Doing what works in brief therapy and managed care*. Philadelphia: Brunner/Mazel.

Hoyt, M.F. (2000b) The last session in brief therapy: Why and how to say "when." In *Some stories are better than others* (pp. 237–261). Philadelphia: Brunner/Mazel.

Hoyt, M.F. (2000c) A golfer's guide to brief therapy (with footnotes for baseball fans). In *Some stories are better than others* (pp. 5–15). Philadelphia: Brunner/Mazel.

Hoyt, M.F. (2009) *Brief psychotherapies: Principles and practices*. Phoenix, AZ: Zeig, Tucker & Theisen.

Hoyt, M.F., Rosenbaum, R., & Talmon, M. (1992) Planned single-session psychotherapy. In S.H. Budman, M.F. Hoyt, & S. Friedman (Eds.), *The first session in brief therapy* (pp. 59–86). New York: Guilford Press.

Kaslow, F.W. (Ed.) (1984) *Psychotherapy with psychotherapists*. New York: Haworth Press.

Lakoff, G., & Johnson, M. (1999) *Philosophy in the flesh: The embodied mind and its challenge to Western thought*. New York: Basic Books.

Lambert, M.J. (Ed.) (2005) Enhancing psychotherapy outcome through feedback. *Journal of Clinical Psychology/In Session*, 61, 141–217. [whole issue]

Malouf, D.S. (2009) *Ransom*. New York: Pantheon.

McDowell, R. (2008) *Poetry as spiritual practice*. New York: Free Press.

Oz, M. (2011) What I learned from my cancer scare. *Time*, 177, 24, 50–55.

Rosen, S. (1982) *My voice will go with you: The teaching tales of Milton H. Erickson*. New York: Norton.

Rosenbaum, R. (1994) Single-session therapies: Intrinsic integration? *Journal of Psychotherapy Integration*, 6, 107–118.

Rosenbaum, R. (2008) Psychotherapy is not short or long. *Monitor on Psychology*, 39(7), 4, 8.

Short, D., Erickson, B.A., & Klein, R.E. (2005) *Hope and resiliency: Understanding the psychotherapeutic strategies of Milton H. Erickson, M.D.* Norwalk, CT: Crown House.

Sprenkle, D.H., & Davis, S.D., & Lebow, J.L. (2009) *Common factors in couple and family therapy: The overlooked foundation for effective practice*. New York: Guilford Press.

Verghese, A. (2009) *Cutting for stone: A novel*. New York: Random House/Vintage.

Wampold, B.E. (2001) *The great psychotherapy debate: Models, methods, and findings*. Mahwah, NJ: Lawrence Erlbaum Associates.

Weiss, J. (1952) Crying at the happy ending. *Psychoanalytic Review*, 39, 338.

White, M. (1997) *Narratives of therapists' lives*. Adelaide, S.A., Australia: Dulwich Centre Publications.

Younggren, J.N., & Gottlieb, M.C. (2004) Managing risk when contemplating multiple relationships. *Professional Psychology: Research and Practice*, 35(3), 255–260.

Zeig, J.K. (1990) Seeding. In J.K. Zeig & S.G. Gilligan (Eds.), *Brief therapy: Myths, methods, and metaphors* (pp. 221–246). New York: Brunner/Mazel.

Chapter Five

Walk-In Single Session Therapy: Accessible Mental Health Services

Arnold Slive and Monte Bobele

Candace and her 11-year-old son, Taj, arrived at the Austin Child Guidance Center's walk-in counseling service. On the brief intake form, Candace responded to the question, "What is the single most important concern you would like to discuss today?" with "My son's behavior since the accident." The therapist, Arnie, greeted them in the waiting room and immediately noticed the two dark marks under Taj's eyes, which are sometimes indicative of head trauma.

After they were seated in the session room, Arnie explained how the walk-in service works, explained the limits of confidentiality, and obtained the appropriate consent signatures. He began by asking, "What are you hoping for from today's session?" Candace answered that she didn't know how to deal with Taj's recent behavior and wondered if he might need counseling. Candace then described their current situation. She was a single mother who, with her four

A version of this chapter was presented as a keynote address at the *Capture the Moment: The Inaugural Symposium on Single-Session Therapies and Walk-In Services* held on Phillip Island, Victoria, Australia, in March 2012. Portions were also presented as part of the symposium, *Capturing the Moment: Single-Session Therapy and Walk-In Services*, held at the annual convention of the American Psychological Association, Honolulu, HI, July 31, 2013.

children, had for the last eight months lived together in one room at a homeless shelter. She has three sons, 12, 11 and 8 years old, and an 8-month-old daughter. They had been living in the shelter since the daughter was two weeks old. Most days after school, Taj and his older brother, Jason, rode a city bus to spend time at a nearby public library. The staff members at the library knew the boys. Candace frequently called the library to check up on them or to ask that they be sent home for dinner.

In a voice that sometimes trembled, Candace then described an event that had occurred nine days earlier. Taj came home from school that day and took the bus to join Jason who was already at the library. He got off of the bus across the street from the library, crossed in front of the bus into the street, and was hit by a truck. The driver of the truck sped away. Taj was knocked unconscious and was transported by ambulance to the nearby children's hospital. The hospital called Candace telling her that Taj was in the hospital. She rushed to join Taj at the hospital where he remained for two more days. For the first 24 hours, he was in and out of consciousness, but he improved considerably the next day. No permanent neurological damage was found. The only thing Taj remembered about the accident was a brief glimpse of a "white truck." He very quickly returned to his regular activities, such as attending school without any difficulties. Taj remained silent as his mother continued to fill in the therapist.

Next, Candace explained why they walked in for a session that day. Since the accident, Taj had been leaving the homeless shelter unannounced, and without Candace's permission, to go to the library. Sometimes she did not know that he had gone. Other times she saw him leaving, but he refused his mother's requests that he stay home. He either would not or could not answer his mother's questions about why he was doing this. She took him to the family doctor who suggested counseling.

Taj sat quietly while his mother told this story. When Arnie asked him if he had any comments about what his mother had said, he said, "No." When asked if he was in agreement with the details, he said, "Yes." Arnie then complimented Taj on getting back so quickly into his regular life after such a scary event. Taj said, "But, I'm still scared." When asked what he meant, he explained that he now looks much more carefully when he crosses a street. Arnie said, "It's good that you were able to learn something valuable from such an awful experience." Taj nodded his head as if to say "Yes."

Arnie decided against asking Taj the same "why" question that his mother had been asking about his recent trips to the library. Instead, he asked Taj what he was doing at the library in the week or so after the accident. He answered that he had not been going into the library; instead, he stood outside on the sidewalk in front of the library.
Arnie: What do you do when you stand on the sidewalk?
Taj: I look for the white truck.
Arnie (surprised): Oh! Well what would you do if you saw it?
Taj: I'd call 911.
Arnie: I get it! You're being a detective.
For the first time Taj smiled broadly as he vigorously nodded his head in agreement.
Candace had not heard this explanation for Taj's behavior before. She appeared relieved. Taj's behavior now made sense to her. This explanation seemed to relieve her fears that something was wrong with her son.
With Arnie's encouragement, Candace told Taj that she was prepared to support Taj's "detective work." Taj and his mother then negotiated an agreement about his trips to the library. If he agreed to ask permission, his mother would say "Yes," most of the time. But he also agreed not to go if his mother did not give permission. When offered the option of making an appointment for ongoing counseling or returning for another walk-in session at any point in the future, Candace indicated that she and Taj could now manage the situation. She said they would walk in again "if we need to."

Walking In for Services: An Everyday Occurrence

We live in a fast-paced culture. Schedules are tight, meetings and appointments get squeezed into ever narrowing time-frames. In this environment, there are times when it isn't possible to plan ahead and make appointments. The business world has adapted to this shift by offering services that are immediately accessible without a pre-arranged appointment. Hence, we have fast food, drive-in banks, walk-in hair stylists, "no appointment necessary" income tax services, and even walk-in wedding chapels. In Calgary, Canada, walk-in medical clinics boomed during the 1980's and became one of the models for walk-in counseling services. Medical patients have the option of walking in to see a doctor without an appointment. If they return, they may or may not be treated by the same doctor, though the next doctor will access the records from previous visits. Many dental and veterinary practices also encourage walk-ins. Church confessionals are usually available on a walk-in basis. "Walk-ins Welcome" signs are a common fixture in our lives. They are common because they fit our on-demand lifestyles. With the presence of these services all around us, it makes sense for mental health professionals to adopt the walk-in idea.

This chapter examines walk-in counseling as a type of brief and single session therapy, outlines its rationale, and answers some frequently asked questions; it concludes with some suggestions for starting a walk-in service. The following chapter then highlights clinical aspects of our walk-in single session approach.

It's a Type of Single Session Therapy

Walk-in therapy and single session therapy are two related forms of brief therapy. Brief therapy approaches have developed extensively over the last several decades. These models challenge the idea that enduring change must come through lengthy and laborious mental health interventions. There is consistent evidence of the effectiveness of brief interventions in the literature. The development of brief therapy models has been influenced by schools of thought ranging from psychodynamic to systemic to behavior therapy (Hoyt, 2009). All are based on the idea that important changes can occur in relatively few sessions.

Walk-in therapy is both similar to and different from single session therapy (Talmon, 1990; Hoyt, 1994). Both treat each session as a complete therapy, in and of itself. In both approaches, clients present a concern and therapists help the clients construct goals. Both therapies aim for clients to leave with a sense of hopefulness, knowing that they have been heard, and a feeling of having gained an increased awareness of their strengths and resources. In some circumstances, clients may have also begun to develop a plan on how to address their issues.

An obvious difference between the two is that walk-in therapy requires no appointment—clients just arrive for a session. Unlike conventional "by appointment" services, there is little pre-screening of clients, and there is a wide range of presenting concerns and family constellations (individuals, couples, families). It is up to the clients to decide who needs to attend a session. Another difference is that there is usually no pre- or post-session contact with the client. In most walk-in settings, clients are invited to return as often as they wish, at their convenience, although they may not see the same therapists. Walk-in services are designed to reduce red tape and to minimize medicalized procedures like *DSM* diagnoses, formal testing, and time consuming paperwork. It is one hour with as much of that time as possible devoted to the therapeutic conversation.

The Where and How of Walk-in Counseling Services

The availability of walk-in counseling has begun to flourish in North America (Duvall, Young, & Kays-Burden, 2012; Slive & Bobele, 2011) as well as elsewhere (e.g., Boyhan, 1996; Price, 1994). It has been offered at an agency in Minneapolis since 1969 (Schoener, 2011). Most others have started since the founding of the Eastside Family Centre in Calgary, Canada in 1990 (Slive, et al., 1995). We have been directly involved with the development of these resources in Calgary as well as in Austin and San Antonio, Texas. It is available in agencies that serve the general population, in private practices, as well as in organizations that specialize in serving children (Young, et al., 2008). The model has been deployed to survivors of Hurricane Katrina (Miller, 2011) and in other humanitarian crisis situations (Paul & van Ommeren, 2013). Walking-in for a Valentine's Day "relationship tune up" has been a regular offering in at least one university counseling center. A clinic in México City has offered walk-in relationship tune-ups for couples and help for robbery victims (see Chapter 12 this volume). Walk-in counseling is more established in Canada than anywhere else in the world. At present, there are more than 20 such services in the Province of Ontario alone (Duvall, Young, K., & Kays-Burden, A., 2012).

Some clinics offer "no appointment" services exclusively. In others, this is but one aspect of an agency's entire spectrum of services. It may be available anywhere from one half-day per week to full time (5 or 6 days per week). In some instances, it has become an agency's intake mechanism. Some walk-in services are embedded in medical networks such as hospital-based and outpatient medical and mental health systems. Most operate as part of non-profit organizations. Some charge no fee for the walk-in session, others charge a fee using a sliding fee scale and still others accept third-party health insurance. Some private practices set aside time for walk-in sessions for new or existing clients. Even though some of these services primarily function as intake interviews, the application that we describe in this chapter is one that functions as a single complete session of counseling.

The Case for Walk-in Counseling

There is increasing research evidence that supports the efficacy of walk-in/single session therapy (Duvall et al., 2012; Harper-Jaques & Foucault, 2013; Miller, 2008; Miller & Slive, 2004). For the purpose of the discussion to follow, we summarize the following salient points:

- High percentages of clients report improvement in their presenting concerns, even months after a single walk-in session. The rates of these positive outcomes are comparable to those found in multi-session therapy.
- Walk-in clients report high rates of satisfaction with their walk-in sessions.
- Many clients report that a single walk-in session is sufficient and that no further sessions are needed.

Beyond the research about the frequent brevity of therapy, we suggest that there are a number of other reasons for considering the development of a walk-in option. In order for clients to receive treatment, many traditional counseling agencies require several steps be taken first. Typically, the prospective client phones to make an appointment. This call leads to intake procedures that may involve the completion of forms and, perhaps after waiting, a meeting with an intake coordinator. There may be another delay before the first session with a therapist. Some practitioners may consider that first session (or sessions) an assessment. Only after the assessment does the actual therapy begin. The time from the initial phone call to the beginning of therapy will vary depending on the length of the agency's waiting list. Clients might have to wait from a few days to many months. Young and Rycroft (2012) described how these barriers to treatment encouraged them to begin to experiment with a single session model over eighteen years ago.

In contrast, not even a phone call is required for someone to walk in. The only steps are to show up, fill out a brief form, and wait for the session to start. There is no screening—anyone who shows up is seen. The "first" session is not an assessment—it is a therapy session. If clients want more sessions, they can show up again in the same way as often as they would like. According to Barrett, et al. (2008), 50% of prospective clients who make an initial phone call to a public mental agency choose not to follow through with the initial intake meeting. Perhaps the wait time is discouraging. If they could simply walk in, how many more of those callers would become actual clients?

Agencies could shorten lengthy waiting lists and increase cost effectiveness by offering a "no appointment" alternative for help. Clinics may set aside specific hours of the week and inform callers requesting counseling services about the convenience of walking in as a way to avoid waiting for an appointment. In fact, establishing walk-in hours might eliminate the need for a separate intake process altogether. A significant percentage of those clients (Miller & Slive, 2004) will be satisfied with their single walk-in session and not require further ongoing counseling by appointment. Agencies may serve more clients more quickly with the same number of staff. The bottleneck at the point of entry will have eased or been erased. A Canadian pilot study (Horton, et al., 2012) assessed the economic effects of providing walk-in/single sessions and found that clients were diverted from using more costly services and returned to work sooner. They stated that these benefits exceeded the cost of the service delivery.

Most clients want therapy to be as brief as possible. At Our Lady of the Lake University's Community Counseling Service (CCS) in San Antonio, many clients decide before they arrive that they have come for only one session and expect that the session will help them (Correia, 2013; Scamardo, Bobele, & Biever, 2004). Often, traditionally trained therapists, not clients, think that therapy should continue beyond the first session. We have found that when additional appointments are suggested at the end of the session, some clients seem surprised and disappointed. We think this provides a choice for us as mental health professionals. We can try to fit our clients into the traditional, unsupported belief that change takes a long time, perhaps many sessions over months or even years, or we can adjust our thinking to fit the many clients who want only one or a few sessions. We have found that offering walk-in/single sessions addresses our clients' needs.

A "no appointment necessary" option also means that we see clients when it is most convenient, most practical (e.g., does not conflict with work or school schedules) or most meaningful (a key moment to deal with a life problem) for them. Some of our clients drop-in because they were driving by and saw the CCS's "No Appointment Necessary" sign. Some come because a critical episode has occurred with a longstanding issue (e.g., an employer threatens to fire a client when he once again arrives late for work). Some are in the midst of dealing with an urgent crisis. When clients arrive at their moment of choosing, they are more likely to be highly motivated. We have found that helping clients at these opportune moments promotes good outcomes and is rewarding for therapists.

In spite of remarkable increases in the numbers of mental health services and providers, underserved populations still face obstacles to treatment: clients may not know how to initiate the process; social and cultural factors stigmatize mental illness; cultural beliefs about healing may not include psychotherapy as a solution; the appointment-making process can be intimidating; long waiting lists delay appointments; there are issues with transportation; work schedules interfere with clinic schedules; and child care may be expensive and unreliable. It is no wonder that many are discouraged about mental health services. Our "no appointment" option in San Antonio is available to a large number of Latino/a clients, and it seems to be a good cultural fit. Clients can come at times that suit their schedules, they do not have to wait, and they do not need to commit to long-term counseling. Perhaps the American tradition of living with well-planned schedules is giving way to a preference for more on-demand, drive-through, fast-food lifestyles among younger generations and some cultural groups.

Providing walk-in/single sessions can be rewarding for therapists because:

- Most of the clients are ready to have therapeutic conversations that will lead to change.
- There aren't any "no shows."
- Sessions are about 50-minutes, leaving time for therapists to complete a brief session note.
- Once the session and session note are completed there is usually no more work to be done—no follow-up phone calls, no missed appointments to deal with, no discharge and closing paperwork.
- Only the administrative task of collecting from third-party payers may remain. It is simple and straightforward. Usually both the therapists and clients feel a sense of accomplishment.

- Our students, who often felt demoralized when a client came for "only" one session, have learned to celebrate their single session "successes." Now, when a client wants to return for another session, we sometimes joke that we must have failed to be helpful in the previous session!

Experience with this model of treatment delivery can benefit professionals and professionals in training. Many use a team format where therapists work together supporting and learning from one another. In some settings, the walk-in/single sessions are provided in whole or in part by mental health professionals who have volunteered their talents. Less experienced professionals gain valuable experience with a wide range of clients in a short period of time. Adding a walk-in option to a community's array of mental health and social service resources can provide a safety net for those in immediate crisis. Many are first time mental health customers. They are not looking for "therapy"—rather, they are searching for a resource that will effectively and promptly address their needs. For some of them, one session will be sufficient. Others might return for additional walk-in sessions. Still others will be referred to community resources that are a better fit for their particular issues. Their single session becomes a starting point for further services. Hospital emergency services in Calgary, for example, send clients to walk-in clinics for counseling after they have been assessed to be at low risk for self-harm. Conversely, high-risk clients may be sent to an emergency room for evaluation or may be connected with child protection services. A client whose therapist is on vacation may make use of walk-in sessions as a "booster" for their ongoing treatment or to deal with an immediate crisis (Mallozzi, 2009).

Frequently Asked Questions

Don't some clients have problems that are too severe or too chronic for a single session walk-in service?

In addition to the mistaken notion that "more is always better," Hoyt (2009) and Duval et al. (2012) list various attitudes and beliefs—such as that SST is only helpful with simple problems and with psychologically unsophisticated clients, and that "real therapy" takes thorough prior assessment and a long time—that may impede effective (including single session) therapy.

However, walk-in clients choose us, we don't choose them. There is no pre-screening or assessment. The worst that can happen is that the client has a one-hour counseling session and is ultimately redirected to a more appropriate resource. But we also adhere to the principle that any client can benefit from a single session of therapy. For example, we do not treat "schizophrenia;" although we can assist people with serious mental health diagnoses to address their life problems. One of our clients who had been diagnosed with schizophrenia was concerned that his landlord was going to evict him because he was talking to himself in the halls of his apartment building. In addition to advising the client to consult with his psychiatrist about his medication, we role-played how to have a reassuring conversation with the landlord. Another client with a longstanding history of depression used her walk-in session to explore ideas that would help her get out of bed early enough to get to work on time. Clients are never only their "diagnosis." They have many "normal" issues that can be addressed and helped via a single session of a walk-in therapy.

Aren't there some clients who want something that you cannot give them?

Yes, that happens. We invite our clients to tell us as soon as possible what they want from the session so that we can learn quickly if the client wants something we cannot provide. For example, occasionally clients want a formal psychological assessment or a forensic opinion. Another client might ask for medication. In each of those instances, we inform the client that we do not offer that and provide information about where to get it. Sometimes, after being so informed, the client still wants their hour of counseling and we negotiate an achievable goal for that session. We prefer to promise less and deliver more.

What about clients who want to return again and again?

Actually, we routinely invite our clients to return if additional difficulties arise. It is common that about 30% to 40% of walk-in clients have had previous sessions (Clements et al., 2011). Sometimes they have returned after a few days or weeks and sometimes after several years. We are pleased when a client returns for another session. We think that means we have done a good job. We want our clients to be satisfied enough that they will come back as needed, like taking another dose of aspirin. In some important ways, though, walk-in/single sessions are different from ongoing counseling. Resembling walk-in medical clinics, clients who return to our clinic may, or may not, see the same therapist. Unlike traditional therapeutic relationships, we want our clients to develop relationships with the agency, more so than with a particular therapist. As a practical matter, the same therapist is not likely to be available when a client returns. A very small percentage of clients use our walk-in service for ongoing psychotherapy, even though they may see a number of different therapists over an extended period of time. Sometimes we can accommodate them, especially if repeat visits are not disruptive to the clinic. In other instances, we may encourage them to connect with another agency when it is more appropriate for their needs.

How do you respond to at-risk clients?

Walk-in clients, more frequently than most typical outpatient clients, are dealing with immediate crises. So it is not surprising that some of them will present with risk issues such as child abuse, elder abuse, domestic violence, threats of violence to others, and thoughts of suicide or self-harm. In these crises, we work collaboratively with the client and his or her significant others to assess the risks as well as the strengths and resources that can be incorporated in the development of a safety plan. When we are required to report to child protection authorities or the legal system, we do so. In those instances, we make every effort to make the process as collaborative as possible with the client and significant others. In some high-risk situations, the usual 50-minute expectations may fall by the wayside. The session lasts as long as is necessary. Nevertheless, we focus more on how we can help the client/family in the here and now and less on "covering our behinds" by pretending we can foresee or avoid all future risks.

What about follow-ups?

As mentioned earlier, each session is a self contained unit—a whole therapy. There is no routine follow-up appointment or phone call. We conceptualize our sessions as a consultation in which the therapist is the consultant and the client is the consultee. In a consulting relationship, the therapist's job is to provide ideas, feedback or suggestions, and the client's job to decide what do with the therapist's input. In other words, the client is the decision maker. The client decides when to come, what to address, what to do with whatever ideas may have emerged from the conversation, and when, if at all, to return. Therefore, follow-up contact usually occurs when the client arranges it either by walking in again or by making an appointment for ongoing counseling. The exception is that follow-up phone calls may be made when certain risk issues are involved. For example, we might call to follow-up about a suicide prevention safety plan that had been developed during the session. Other than in these restricted situations, follow-up contacts are limited to research purposes.

At recent workshops that we have conducted, participants have raised some additional interesting observations about follow-up contact after therapy has ended (even if it is a single session of therapy). One person noted that this could create boundary confusion since post-session contact could imply to the client that the therapist thinks therapy is continuing even when the client does not. This led to a discussion about the infrequency with which questions are raised about whether to routinely initiate follow-up contact when therapy ends after 3 sessions, or 10 sessions, or six months. It is not clear why not. Does a single session of therapy somehow make follow-up more necessary? Is follow-up contact more the therapist's need to know or stay in contact; does it interfere with the client who endeavors to address life struggles without therapy?

Can't you be overwhelmed with more clients than you can handle?

"You'll be overwhelmed" was a comment we sometimes heard in the months preceding the opening of the Eastside Family Centre in Calgary (Slive, et al., 1995). Because our desire was to address the issue of accessibility, we took this warning as a sign that we were on the right track—we really were about to make ourselves more available to our community. Of course, we did not know how many people would come. When we first opened our doors, after an initial promotional effort in the community, response was low. Gradually, though, more and more clients began to take advantage of the Eastside's convenience. We have found this slow start to be typical of the beginning of new walk-in services. We've also found that occasionally more people arrive than can be handled on a given "shift." When that occurs, we do some triaging. The supervisor/shift coordinator, perhaps along with the reception/intake person, reviews waiting clients' intake forms to ensure that anyone who might be at risk gets a session. Infrequently we need to tell those who can't be seen that they will be "put at the head of the line" when they return.

Isn't this a superficial, Band-Aid™ approach?

We've been asked this question so many times that we decided to do some research on the topic of "bandages." According to archaeologists, bandages have been around at least since the time the pyramids were being built in Egypt. They have been widely used ever since. The reasons for the millennia-long application of this relatively low-tech invention are simple: bandages promote healing and prevent the spread of infection. We've come to think of our walk-in single sessions as a form of band-aid. Sometimes first aid is all that is necessary. At times it is an important starting point for additional treatment, and at other times one may require a band-aid following a major surgery. So when we are asked if we are offering a Band-Aid™ approach we say, "Yes! Thank you for the compliment."

Is this primarily for low-income and minority groups?

Walking in is neither better nor worse than other forms of counseling. Rather, it adds to the choices available to a community. Some folks choose a no-appointment option for a haircut rather than make an appointment. They do this because it fits their schedule or lifestyle. Similarly, a client chooses "no appointment" counseling because it is a good fit for that client at that point in time. Earlier, we noted that our agency tends to serve a high number of low-income clients partly because it is located in a low-income area of the city. Also, walking in is a logical choice for those who have difficulty planning ahead or who are in immediate crises (circumstances that many low-income people face on a daily basis). A significant proportion of our clients are from minority cultural and ethnic groups. Walking in is culturally syntonic for many in our community who are very familiar with walk-in medical clinics, emergency rooms, beauty salons, and church confessionals. However, we caution the reader not to assume that single, walk-in sessions are exclusively for low-income and minority clients. Often times our clients are Caucasian and some are well-off financially. Since everyone is familiar with walking in for a variety of services, choosing a walk-in counseling option can be a good fit for them as well.

You Say You Want to Start a Walk-In Service?

On many occasions, we have been asked about how to start a walk-in counseling service. We would like to share some ideas with readers who may be considering that. This is not meant as a list of "how to's." Rather, these are thoughts to consider as you begin to plan.

Making the case to community members and professional colleagues

We find that community members who are not mental health-providers usually immediately understand the idea of walking in. After all, this is an option that many businesses offer. It is something we are all used to. In the months leading up to the opening of our clinic in Calgary (Slive, 1995), we had numerous meetings with a wide variety of community members: educators, political representatives, grassroots community leaders, clergy, police, and funders. Almost without exception, they told us that ours was a great idea. That's because they wanted mental health services to be more accessible. They helped us to understand that the word *accessible* drew immediate positive attention to the concept.

When making a case to mental health professionals, on the other hand, it is best to emphasize that research has found one session to be the mode and the increasing evidence for the efficacy of walk-in single sessions (see Appendix A this volume). In addition to the efficacy research on walk-in sessions, here are the four chief benefits of walk-in services that will resonate for mental health professionals and administrators:

More clients can be served with the same agency resources

Agencies eliminate or shorten wait lists

Clients access counseling with no red tape and no wait

Clients are motivated when they first decide to seek help

Fitting the service into existing mental health continuums of resources

It is helpful to carefully consider the resources already available in the community and how this new idea will fit in and meet the existing needs of a particular community. For example, will it be stand-alone or part of a larger organization? What will be its connection to local schools and to primary care physicians and pediatricians? Will it operate under the umbrella of an existing continuum, as one part of a medical/psychiatric complex, for example? What about community counseling agencies? Can it form partnerships with those agencies by providing an immediate resource for clients on an agency's wait list or for clients of therapists who are on vacation? How might it link to area emergency rooms for those in need of urgent assistance? Can the emergency room make use of the availability of walk-in counseling for immediate follow-up assistance for those who do not require hospital admission?

If walk-in counseling is new to an existing agency, how will it interface with the other agency components? What about the agency's waiting list? Is the goal to use the walk-in/single sessions as a means to reduce the wait list? Perhaps it will eliminate the wait list entirely as the Austin Child Guidance Center did when it started its walk-in service. Now when someone calls ACGC for an initial counseling appointment, an appointment may be scheduled if a therapist has an opening within the following two weeks. If no appointment is available at the time of call, the person is asked to call again. However, they are also invited to walk-in as an alternative or until an appointment becomes available. Eventually, some of those who walk-in for one or two sessions decide that is sufficient and no longer need an appointment.

Single sessions also occur in private offices. Some private practitioners raise concerns about the prospect of having too many single sessions. After all, we all want to make a good living and longer-term clients are a foundation of many private practices. However, single sessions in a private practice can be an important addition.

When one of us (A.S.) operated a full-time practice, he had many single sessions. There was mutual satisfaction whenever a first session ended on a positive note and with a decision by the client not to return. Satisfied customers are the best marketing tool, and they might have recommended him to other prospective clients. Some private practitioners have even established walk-in hours. For example, they might schedule times during the week when new clients can walk-in, former clients can return, or current clients can arrive for emergency sessions. Should no clients arrive during those hours, the practitioner can do paperwork, return phone calls, or perhaps enjoy a latte.

Staffing a walk-in service

One staffing option is for existing therapists to do one or more shifts in the walk-in service. This has the advantage of spreading the awareness of the service to other parts of the agency and increasing the skill level of clinicians with single session, brief therapy work. Another option is to recruit volunteer therapists for the walk-in service. Schoener (2011) and Slive et al. (1995) have described the successful use of volunteers. The volunteers can be licensed mental-health professionals, professionals in the process of licensing, or graduate students doing walk-in counseling as part of their training. The attraction of this option to volunteers is the excellent experience that comes from working with highly motivated clients and the opportunity to contribute to their community. The attraction to the agency is that an already low-cost service component becomes even more cost efficient.

Deciding on hours of operation

There is wide variety in the hours of the week that agencies offer walk-in counseling. Some clinics operate only one half-day per week. Still others are open for walk-ins full-time. For example, in Calgary, Alberta, Canada, the Eastside Family Centre currently operates from 11a.m. to 8 p.m. Monday to Friday as well as daytime hours on Saturdays (Clements et al., 2011). There is another walk-in facility in Calgary that is open on Sundays (Harper-Jaques & Leahey, 2011). As a result, Calgary has walk-in availability throughout the week. We recommend offering hours of operation that are spread out during the week so that prospective clients do not have to wait too long after deciding they want to receive help. For example, if an agency decides to have 10 hours per week of walk-in sessions, it's better to distribute those hours over two or three days instead of all on one day. Time of day is also a factor. The Calgary experience, after more than 23 years, is that early morning hours and late evening hours are underutilized. Hence, they operate from 11a.m. to 8 p.m.. In deciding on hours of operation, the key word is accessibility.

Giving it a name

You may have noticed that we tend to use the term *counseling* rather than *therapy* in naming walk-in services. When A.S. was involved in starting the Eastside Family Centre in Calgary in 1990, a community task force was formed to advise on its start-up; the majority of its members were not mental health professionals. They suggested that we use the term "walk-in counseling" because "counseling" sounds less intimidating than "therapy" to potential users (clients/patients). In this chapter, though, we use terms like *counseling, therapy, consultation,* and *treatment* interchangeably. We teach in a counseling psychology doctoral program accredited by the American Psychological Association. The faculty and doctoral students are affiliated with APA's Society of Counseling Psychology. Most of our masters' students become Licensed Professional Counselors. We refer to our graduate students as either counselors- or therapists-in-training, and we describe what they do as counseling, therapy, psychotherapy, or treatment. We think all of these terms fit. However, when naming a service we encourage you to think from the perspective of the people you plan to serve. What will be most meaningful and least intimidating to them? We think the term *walk-in counseling* works rather well.

Generating referrals: Promotion and advertising

As we have said, clients may not walk-in in large numbers at first. It takes time to raise awareness about something new, unusual, and innovative—so don't get discouraged if the flow of clients is slow at first. The best promotion is through providing a quality product.

You will know you are making progress when an increasing number of referrals come from former clients.

Walk-in services that are one piece of a large network of resources (for example, a large healthcare system) have an easier time, because there is a large existing referral network. Here are a few additional ideas for promoting the service:

a. Schools distribute to families
b. Presentations at conferences or workshops
c. Newspaper or magazine article about a new innovative service
d. Public service announcements on radio stations
e. Advertise at transportation sites such as bus stops
f. Advertise in newspapers
g. On-line resources such as Angie's List, *Psychology Today*, or Google Ads.

Supporting the new service

This form of service delivery is an innovation. As such, it requires special kinds of attention to start well and to become an established part of a community's or an agency's resources (Young, Weir & Rycroft, 2012). It is a new offering for an agency, and most mental health professionals are not trained to provide walk-in/single sessions. We have found that therapists who practice from a variety of clinical models can provide effective walk-in therapy, although it is crucial that all therapists embrace the idea that a single session can make a meaningful difference for clients. Institutional supports are critical. There needs to be "buy-in" at the highest levels of the organization as well as from the immediate supervisors of the therapists who will be providing the walk-in sessions. We can anticipate that without buy-in, there will be insurmountable hurdles to overcome. Some therapists will be challenged to learn how to conduct single sessions. They will need support and encouragement. Also, as mentioned earlier, sometimes a walk-in service starts slowly as the community gets used to this new concept. There needs to be a message that the organization is standing behind this new idea and is committed to making it a success. In 1990, when we rented space for our new walk-in service in Calgary, the Board of the parent organization, Wood's Homes, insisted that we take out a five-year lease (as opposed to one year) as a way of giving a message to both the community and the staff that we were in this for the long term.

One way that the organization can support a new innovation is to develop supportive agency policies. Examples could be the re-writing of therapists' job descriptions that include walk-in counseling as one job responsibility. Another is to include observation of walk-in sessions as part of the orientation of new therapists. We think it is ideal to have one or more in-house "clinical champions" for the walk-in work—these would be therapists with a passion for the concept who are respected by other therapists who are learning to do the work. They are also colleagues who can be turned to for advice and encouragement by those who are just starting to pro-vide single session therapy. The "champions" may or may not be in formal leadership positions.

Training opportunities for staff and volunteers

Offering a formal training workshop is often a good way to start. A one- or two-day workshop that concentrates on theory and tech-nique will generate enthusiasm and confidence for newcomers to this form of service delivery. A few months later, a follow-up workshop can be held after therapists have had actual experience with single session work. That second workshop can be tailored to the initial clinical and organizational challenges that have been en-countered. We have also found it to be useful to invite one or more agency therapists to visit an already established walk-in counseling provider to observe the day-to-day implementation.

Working as a team

The Eastside Family Centre in Calgary, the Community Coun-seling Service in San Antonio, and other clinics that offer walk-in services frequently use therapy teams. There are many ways to organize a team, but, in essence, two or more therapists work together at the same time of day providing walk-in sessions and use each other as consultants. A team approach reduces stress for therapists because they know they can rely on their colleagues for support. Furthermore, it is stimulating for therapists to learn from one another, and it is a way for an agency to improve quality. The successful implementation of a walk-in service does not require a team approach. However, even in agencies where clinicians conduct their sessions alone, it is helpful for them to be able to consult with colleagues about their work.

Conclusion

Walk-in counseling is one way of addressing roadblocks to mental health care. It is an option that gives clients the opportunity to have a therapeutic conversation at a moment that is meaningful to them. Clients aren't forced to do a lot of planning. Walking in is familiar and it decreases frustrations with "the system." For therapists, working with highly motivated clients is rewarding. For mental health administrators, walk-in services are cost efficient. The very existence of walk-in single sessions conveys a message to the public and to service providers that psychotherapy does not have to be a lengthy process over months or years. Help can be available now!

References

Barrett, M. S., Chua, W., Crits-Christoph, P., Gibbons, M., & Thompson, D. (2008). Early withdrawal from mental health treatment: Implications for psychotherapy practice. *Psychotherapy: Theory, Research, Practice, Training, 45*, 247–267.

Bobele, M., Lopez, S., Scamardo, M., & Solorzano, B. (2008). Single-session walk-in therapy with Mexican-American clients. *Journal of Systemic Therapies, 27*(4), 75–89.

Boyhan, Patricia A. (1996). Client's perceptions of single session consultations as an option to waiting for family therapy. *Australian and New Zealand Journal of Family Therapy, 17*(2), 85–96.

Clements, R., McElheran, N., Hackney, L. & Park, H. (2011). The Eastside Family Centre: 20 years of single-session, walk-in therapy. Where we have been and where we are going. In A. Slive & M. Bobele (Eds.), *When one hour is all you have: Effective therapy for walk-in clients* (pp. 109–127) Phoenix, AZ: Zeig, Tucker, & Theisen.

Correia, T.D. (2013). *Once was enough: A phenomenological inquiry into clients' experiences with single session therapy.* (3536011 PsyD), Our Lady of the Lake University, Ann Arbor.

Duvall, J., Young, K., & Kays-Burden, A. (2012). *No more, no less: Brief mental health services for children and youth.* Ontario, Canada, Ontario Centre of Excellence for Child and Youth Mental Health.

Green, K., Correia, T., Bobele, M. & Slive, A. (2011). The research case for walk-in single sessions. In A. Slive & M. Bobele (Eds.), *When one hour is all you have: Effective therapy for walk-in clients* (pp. 23–36) Phoenix, AZ: Zeig, Tucker, & Theisen.

Hampson, R., O'Hanlon, Franklin, A., Pentony, M., Fridgant, L., & Heins, T. (1999). The place of single session consultations: Five years' experience in Canberra. *Australian and New Zealand Journal of Family Therapy, 20*(4), 195–200.

Harper-Jaques, S. & Foucault, D. (2013). Clinical outcomes & client satisfaction of a mental health walk-in single-session therapy service. (submitted for publication)

Harper-Jaques, S. & Leahey, M. (2011). From imagination to reality: mental health walk-in at South Calgary Health Centre. In A. Slive & M. Bobele (Eds.), *When one hour is all you have: Effective therapy for walk-in clients* (pp. 167–183). Phoenix, AZ: Zeig, Tucker, & Theisen.

Horton, S., Stalker, C., Cait, S. & Josling, L. (2012). Sustaining walk-in counseling services: An economic assessment from a pilot study. *Healthcare Quarterly, 15*(3), 44–49.

Hoyt, M.F. (1994). Single session solutions. In M.F. Hoyt (Ed.), *Constructive therapies* (pp. 140–159). New York: Guilford Press.

Hoyt, M.F. (2009). *Brief psychotherapies: Principles and practices.* Phoenix, AZ: Zeig, Tucker, & Theisen.

Mallozzi, V. (2009). Answers to life's worries, in 3 minute bursts. *The New York Times.* August. 30, Retrieved from http://www.nytimes.com/2009/08/31/nyregion/31therapy.html?_r=0 .

Miller, J. (2011). Single-session intervention in the wake of Hurricane Katrina: Strategies for disaster mental health counseling. In A. Slive & M. Bobele (Eds.), *When one hour is all you have: Effective therapy for walk-in clients* (pp.185–202). Phoenix, AZ: Zeig, Tucker, & Theisen.

Miller, J. (2008). Walk-in single session therapy: A study of client satisfaction. *Journal of Systemic Therapies 27*, 78–94.

Miller, J. & Slive, A. (2004). Breaking down the barriers to clinical service delivery: Walk-in family therapy. *Journal of Marital and Family Therapy, 30*, 95–105.

Paul, K., & van Ommeren, M. (2013). A primer on single session therapy and its potential application in humanitarian situations. *Intervention, 11* (1) 8–23.

Price, C. (1994). Open days: Making family therapy accessible in working class suburbs. *Australian and New Zealand Journal of Family Therapy, 15*(4), 191–196.

Scamardo, M., Bobele, M., & Biever, J.L. (2004). A new perspective on client dropouts. *Journal of Systemic Therapies, 23*(2), 27–38.

Schoener, G. R. (2011). Walk-in Counseling Center: Minneapolis, Minnesota. In A. Slive & M. Bobele (Eds.), *When one hour is all you have: Effective therapy for walk-in clients* (pp. 95–108). Phoenix, AZ: Zeig, Tucker, & Theisen.

Slive, A., & Bobele, M (2011). *When one hour is all you have: Effective therapy for walk-in clients.* Phoenix, AZ: Zeig, Tucker, & Theisen.

Slive, A., MacLaurin, B., Oakander, M., & Amundson, J. (1995). Walk-in single sessions: A new paradigm in clinical service delivery. *Journal of Systemic Therapies, 14*, 3–11.

Talmon, M. (1990). *Single-session therapy: Maximizing the effect of the first (and often only) therapeutic encounter.* San Francisco: Jossey-Bass.

Young, J., & Rycroft, P. (2012). Single session therapy: What's in a name? *The Australia and New Zealand Journal of Family Therapy, 33*, 3–5.

Young, J., Weir, S. & Rycroft, P. (2012). Implementing single session therapy. *The Australia and New Zealand Journal of Family Therapy, 33*, 84–97.

Young, K, Dick, M., Herring, K. & Lee, J. (2008). From waiting lists to walk-in: Stories from a walk-in therapy clinic. *Journal of Systemic Therapies, 4*, 23–39.

Chapter Six

One Session at a Time: When You Have a Whole Hour

Monte Bobele and Arnold Slive

Imagine that a new client calls to make an appointment.[1] You handle the call in your usual manner, perhaps inquiring about basic demographic information, maybe even a bit of a problem description. Then, the day before the client has been scheduled, he calls back to say that he is moving to a distant city the day after the appointment and that the scheduled time will be his only opportunity to talk with you. Nonetheless, he is still anxious to meet with you. How will you handle this one session differently than an ordinary first session? Although this scenario may be dramatic, it is not unusual. At least, the "I'll never see this client again" part is not uncommon. One is not only the loneliest number; indeed, it is the most frequent number of psychotherapy visits. We have found viewing each session as potentially the last opportunity we might have to be helpful has changed our practices in significant ways.

A version of this chapter was presented as a keynote address at the *Capture the Moment: The Inaugural Symposium on Single-Session Therapies and Walk-In Services* held on Phillip Island, Victoria, Australia, in March 2012. Portions were also presented as part of the symposium, *Capturing the Moment: Single-Session Therapies and Walk-In Services,* held at the annual convention of the American Psychological Association, Honolulu, HI, July 31, 2013.

1. We are indebted to our colleagues Jeff Young, Pam Rycroft, and Shane Weir for this exercise—see Chapters 7–8 this volume.

When You Have a Whole Hour

DR. MOLLY GRISWOLD: Roy, Roy... why are you here?
ROY 'TIN CUP' MCAVOY: Therapy.
DR. GRISWOLD: You've come for therapy? Okay, look, Roy, you know, you really need to make an appointment. Because, I have a client in a half an hour.
ROY 'TIN CUP' MCAVOY: That's enough time. Thirty minutes? Hell, I'm not THAT fucked up![2]

We originally titled our book "*When One Hour is All You Have*" (Slive & Bobele, 2011). Recently, a workshop participant pointed out that thinking about "an hour being ALL we have" was inconsistent with our message. She pointed out that we should have titled the book "*When You Have a WHOLE Hour.*" And she was right! We missed the opportunity to stress that an hour was frequently more than enough time to help clients achieve some small progress toward their goals. We often learn from our students. Recently, a couple arrived at our clinic 45 minutes late. As our team was discussing how to handle the late-comers, various options arose: go ahead and see them and postpone starting the next case, reschedule them and send them home, ask them to wait and work them in if we had a later cancellation or no-show, and so on. Finally, a sharp student pointed out, "We have 15 minutes. Let's see what we can get done." She had grasped the fundamental notion that a therapy session should be distinguished by what was accomplished, not by how much time had elapsed. The team proceeded to use the 15 minutes available to them to set a goal with the clients and help them with the issue that brought them in that day. The clients left feeling helped and with a plan for their next steps. Many clients are less concerned about the length of the therapy session and more interested in results.

Single Session Therapy

We have described walk-in services in Chapter 5 in this book and elsewhere (Slive & Bobele, 2011). Here we illustrate how we use a single session framework in our walk-in clinic. The single ses-

---

2. From the 1996 film *Tin Cup*, starring Kevin Costner and Rene Russo. Thanks to Michael Hoyt for this wonderful example of clients' perspectives on therapy.

sion work that we do is somewhat different from that originally described by the Kaiser Permanente team (Hoyt, Rosenbaum, & Talmon, 1992; Talmon, 1990). The original work of Talmon and his colleagues at Kaiser, and more recently by the Bouverie group in Australia (Young, Weir, & Rycroft, 2012; see Chapters 7 and 8 this volume) could actually be considered as three session, not single session, therapy. According to their model, therapy consists of a pre-session phone call where screening and minimal interventions are offered. When the client actually arrives for their therapy (the single session), they often begin with a check on the results of the telephone intervention/homework. The session is typically well more than an hour in length. Finally, clients are contacted again by telephone for a follow-up session. This model has been well established in Australia where Young and his colleagues have developed a sophisticated training program that incorporates pre-session phone calls, a therapy session, and a follow-up phone call.

Our walk-in setting by definition makes pre-session screening calls rarely possible. Occasionally we do have information beforehand about a walk-in client if they have called ahead to get information about our services, but more often than not, we know nothing until they arrive for their appointment and complete a very brief intake form. Our sessions are typically one hour in length and, except in some risk situations, we do not call clients routinely for follow-up as an extension of the clinic visit. We think these differences are non-trivial. Single session work is frequently depicted as more cost-effective than some conventional treatment models. We would note, however, that the staff time invested in pre-session and post-session phone calls is not without cost. In the United States, we usually only charge for services delivered in an office. Third party payers do not commonly reimburse providers for non-face-to-face services.

The Single Session Mindset

Many researchers have found single sessions are common and surprisingly effective in a variety of clinical settings (Bloom, 2001; Başoğlu, Şalcioğlu, & Livanou, 2007; Miller, 2008; Ollendick, et al., 2009; Perkins, 2006; Perkins & Scarlett, 2008; Talmon, 1990; see Appendix A this volume). They have also found that most clients, even those with long-standing issues, can be helped in only one session. These findings have encouraged our belief that any session could be the last session. We do not conduct any session as if there will be another session. In other words, we do *one session at a time*. We prefer to think of walk-in therapy as a solitary pearl. Pearls begin as a solution to an oyster's problem. The formation of a pearl has a beginning, a middle, and a point where it is complete. If a jeweler anticipates making a long string of pearls, then each one is understood as related to, connected to, the one before and the one to come. Therapy is a lot like this process. If therapists view each session as connected to the one before and a precursor to the ones to come, then no session truly stands on its own. Instead, it is always contextualized by what came before and the anticipation of what is coming after.

We encourage therapists to always consider the session as the creation of a solitary pearl. Of course another session may have occurred before the current one, and other sessions may follow, but the current session is complete and stands on its own. The extra-therapeutic factors that we take seriously tell us that clients have informal "therapeutic" encounters such as conversations with clergy, advice from friends, even the occasional self-help book. These factors are at work before, during, and after every session we have with clients. A single therapeutic encounter is never an isolated event in a client's life.

For therapists to capitalize on this phenomenon, what they need are alternate ways to think about psychotherapy—a different mindset. We have come to believe that this single session mindset is essential to be effective as a walk-in therapist. It may be more important than any particular model of psychotherapy practice. Therefore, a crucial element for conducting successful single therapy is the therapists' own beliefs about the effectiveness of brief therapy. Therapists' expectations are communicated overtly and covertly to their clients about how rapid and how much change can be expected (Hunsley, Aubry, Verstervelt, & Vito, 1999; Scamardo, Bobele, & Biever, 2004; Hoyt, 2009). We have also developed a motto that we repeat like a mantra to our trainees: *Every case has the potential to be a single session case!*

Our single session mindset consists of a number of ideas:

We think clients know what works best for them.

Clients are far less interested in psychotherapy than are therapists, and prefer brief therapeutic encounters.

Not only do most clients frequently choose to attend only one session of therapy, they overwhelmingly express satisfaction with that session (Miller, 2008; Harper-Jaques & Foucault, 2013).

A common finding is that clients make dramatic improvements at the beginning of a therapy experience and show less session to session improvement as the number of therapy sessions increases (Bloom, 2001; Howard, Kopta, Krause, & Orlinsky, 1986; Seligman, 1995). The dose-response and the phase models researchers also have described these substantial improvements in the early stages of psychotherapy followed by ever-decreasing improvements as psychotherapy continues (Baldwin, Berkeljon, Atkins, Olsen, & Nielsen, 2009; Feaster, Newman, & Rice, 2003; Hansen & Lambert, 2003; Harnett, O'Donovan, & Lambert, 2010; Lambert & Forman, 2002; Wolgast, et al., 2003).

We have observed that rapid change is not only possible, but also common in human experience. There is no established direct correlation between the duration of the complaint or the severity of the complaint and the duration of the treatment (O'Hanlon & Weiner-Davis, 1989).

Making the Most of Single Sessions

Therapists and their clients are not rushed in our one-session-at-a-time consultations. To help therapists pay close attention to the nuances of the client's communication, we encourage them to slow down, sit back in the chair and breathe. As we have said, one hour is plenty of time. In fact, we know a therapist at a walk-in service in British Columbia, Canada, who regularly conducts 30-minute sessions (Philip Perry, personal communication, March 24, 2006)!

Our minimal goals in walk-in/single session therapy are that clients leave with a sense of emotional relief and increased hope. For one client, a positive outcome may be as straightforward as knowing that someone has listened supportively to his or her story. Another may leave with a new way of thinking about a problem— the beginning of a new story. This new way of thinking about a problem may, in another instance, involve deciding that the original situation was not problematic after all. Some clients might walk away with a specific task; a new way of approaching a troubling issue. Or, a client may leave with ideas about where to get further help. Many leave with a new appreciation of mental health services and may be more likely to return for another visit in the future because they were helped. The following ideas have contributed to the achievement these outcomes.

Fisch (1994) argued that the narrower the scope of the therapeutic conversation, the briefer, more potentially efficient the therapy. We begin by concentrating on the problem as it occurs in the present. We do not explore the past, theories of underlying causes, or the function of the problem. We have borrowed from solution-focused and narrative therapists (Berg & Miller, 1992; Freedman & Coombs, 1996; Lipchik, 2002; White, 1986; White & Epston, 1990) who all assert that "the problem is the problem" as the client presents it. We collaborate with each client to establish specific behavioral goals that efficiently directs the therapy and structures the session to work toward those goals.

Although our work is beholden to the strength-based approaches mentioned above, meta-analyses of four decades of psychotherapy outcome research have concluded that the effectiveness of therapies in general is not due to the uniqueness of the various models of therapy, but instead to the common ways the approaches empower factors associated with positive client outcomes (Baardseth, et al., 2012; Duncan, Miller, Wampold & Hubble, 2010; Duncan, Miller & Sparks, 2004). These researchers have concluded that much of the outcome variance in therapeutic change is attributable to a strong therapeutic relationship that effectively capitalizes on existing client strengths and resources. We apply the common factors research by attending to clients' motivations, attending to the clients' goals, linking hope with expectations for improvement, and soliciting continuous feedback from clients about how our methods fit with their own ideas about what is helpful.

We begin each session assuming that it will comprise the whole therapy, as if the present session is not only the first, but also the last opportunity we will have to help the client. This idea was well articulated by Ray and Keeney (1993) when they advised that all sessions should aim to be a whole therapy by focusing on a beginning, middle, and end. That is not to say that a client might not come back for another session, but each subsequent session is treated as a new therapeutic episode. This sentiment was echoed by Haley: "Maybe you don't have a case really, except for the first interview. That would be nice I think. Every therapist should shoot for one session" (Haley & Richeport-Haley, 2003, p. 33).

We prefer to think of walk-in/single session therapy as a consultation process where the therapist offers ideas (many of which may have come from the client), and the client decides whether to accept them, reject them, or put them on hold. A consultation stance helps therapists to resist the temptation to take responsibility for client change. We believe that clients are their own greatest resource. Clients are in the best position to evaluate the ideas generated during the session. Our job is to create a context that enables clients to discover those resources and teach us how to be their guide.

Organization of the Single Session

The format of our single sessions follows the guidelines originally described by Hoyt, Rosenbaum, and Talmon (1990), which were loosely adapted from solution-focused brief therapy (de Shazer, 1985, 1988; also see Appendix B this volume). We have found it helpful to develop an agenda with suggested timelines for our sessions.

Pre-Session

Usually, our walk-in clients have completed a brief intake form that provides us with some general demographic information, a brief description of the presenting problem and goals. In the 5 to 10 minute presession we chose therapists to work with the case (based on therapist learning goals and their needs for experience with certain kinds of clients) and make preliminary plans for the session based on the information on the intake form. These plans might include:

Key questions such as: What does the client want today? Why is this a concern now? Who else is involved in the problem?

How to include all family members that are present in the conversation.

How to address possible risk issues based on intake form information.

Addressing strengths that are hinted at in the intake form.

Asking about pre-session change.

Session: The Conversation

The first part of the session lasts for about 30 to 45 minutes.

Joining. Therapists must establish a collaborative, therapeutic relationship with clients as early as possible. We want to remove obstacles to forming a therapeutic alliance. Moving administrative tasks to a later point in the session facilitates this. Joining first enables us to learn about our clients' jobs, families, education, and other facets of their lives that help us connect with them and help demonstrate to them we are interested in them as people.

Consent and Outcome Rating Scale (ORS). When therapists and clients are at ease and feel comfortable with one another, we provide clients with standard consent information and ask them to complete an ORS (Miller & Duncan, 2000). We are able to explain these procedures more clearly to clients when we calibrate our vocabulary as a result of the earlier joining. We have often found that knowing something about them helps us customize our presentations of the clinic policies and procedures more clearly.

Orientation to the Walk-In Session. We then describe how a walk-in session works: "Some clients find one session to be sufficient for now, some would like to walk in again, and some would like to schedule an appointment." Sometimes we use the analogy of medical clinics that offer walk-in options. We explain that this will be discussed again at the end of the session. We introduce them to the team approach with an explanation, such as, "In our experience we have found that we have found that six heads are better than two in helping our clients." We also inform clients that we may take a break part way through to consult with the team that is observing via closed-circuit TV. Clients rarely object to the use of the team. In fact, many readily overcome any initial worries about it. If clients object to this process, they are referred to alternative services in the community. Occasionally, clients meet the rest of the team.

Problem/Goal Definition. We collaborate with clients to establish small goals.

Clients often have a story to tell, and having someone listen to that story is sometimes essential. Nevertheless, we frequently begin a session with an inquiry into "What would you want to accomplish today?" (The word "today" is key since it orients clients to the idea that one session could be enough.) Other questions could include:

"Why did you decide to walk in today?"

"What's been helpful in the past?"

"What would tell you when you are leaving that this has been a good use of your time?"

Just before the break we might ask:

"What's been helpful so far?"

"Is there anything that we didn't think to ask so far that would be useful for us to know?"

Consultation Break

During the intersession break (typically, 5–10 minutes), the therapists review strengths and assets identified during the session. When a team is available, having several observers capturing clients' strengths facilitates this process. The break is an opportunity for the therapist to develop a plan to help the clients use the identified strengths and assets in the solution of their presenting problem. Sometimes a homework task is formulated.

The Closing

The last portion of the session (typically 10–15 minutes) with the client usually begins with some reflections from the therapist about what assets and strengths have been observed. We often find that clients are expecting the session to end with a diagnosis or some other recitation of their shortcomings. Typically, we might say:

"We have been impressed with how you have been struggling with this problem for some time now" or

"Many parents would not have spent as much time trying to get their child the help they needed" or

"Given the unsuccessful attempts you have made to get help in
the past, we are impressed with your refusal to give up on
trying to improve your situation."

In some situations, the discussion of assets and resources may
conclude the session. However, we may also ask about what remains to be done. We do not ask, "Is this a good time to meet again
next week?" or similar questions that imply future appointments
are necessary. The previous chapter on conducting walk-in sessions
describes how we approach additional appointments. But, having
an idea about what our clients want helps us polish the homework
task we may offer.

Homework/Task

Not all clients leave with a homework task. For some, the main
objective was a chance to tell their story and be heard. In those instances, the session may conclude with the reflections of strengths
and assets. In other situations, the session may conclude with a discussion of a new way of thinking about a problem. For example, the
distress over a job loss could be reframed as an opportunity to take
advantage of a period of free time or to explore new opportunities.
In the majority of sessions, though, there is the addition of a homework task or an idea that maintains the change begun by the therapy session. We have recently experimented with asking clients to
use the break to design their own homework assignment or task that
will assist them in taking the next step toward achieving their goal.
Other times, we asked clients to observe and record any improvements in their situation so that they can provide that information to
their next therapist. Sometimes there may be a rather elaborate task
designed to address the current dilemma. Other times, the task may
be as simple as an idea for client self-care. In the case that follows,
we said to the clients, "The team had an idea about something that
you might experiment with, whether you come back or not."

Team Debriefing

After the client leaves, the team briefly (5–10 minutes) reviews
the session by identifying what went well and what areas could

have been handled differently, writes the notes, and gets ready for the next session.

An Example of a Single Session

Manny and Vera had called earlier in the day to make an appointment for marital counseling; but, when told about the walk-in option, they elected to come to the clinic right away. They arrived during a time when we were co-supervising a team of six graduate student therapists at the Community Counseling Service (CCS), a training clinic operated by Our Lady of the Lake University in San Antonio, Texas. The structure of CCS and our team based, live-supervision model has been described elsewhere (Bobele, Lopez, Scamardo & Solórzano, 2008). Typically, the teams schedule one appointment per hour and are also available for walk-ins. In the CCS, two therapists conduct the session with one or more team members observing. The therapists take a break to consult with their team part way through the session.[3] In this instance, we decided to see the couple as a demonstration for the students, with the students acting as our observing team. The session was recorded and is presented here, with minor editing and with the clients' permission.

ARNIE: So maybe we could start, and just explain a little about how we work, to see if you have any questions. You've come for what we call our walk-in service. You can come as you have today; you didn't need an appointment. If you want to at some point in the future, you could come back in the same way. Some people find that one session works for them. You know, they get what they want from it and leave, and that's that. Some people decide they want to walk in again. Some people decide they'd like to make an appointment and see somebody here. When we get to the end, we can talk about that. So what are you hoping for today in coming here?

MANNY: Well, we've been together for a little over a year. And we've had, you know, problems in our relation-

---

3. It should be noted that while our training setting allows for a team of therapists, neither a team nor co-therapists are necessary to do walk-in work.

ship, and we want to try to—I don't know if fix them, but to find out a reason why they're happening, try to find a solution. And I personally think I have a lot of problems psychologically. So I would like try to find a reason why, or at least try to understand why I have the behavior that I've been having throughout my adult life.

MONTE: And how did you guys come to the decision to come today to talk about those things?

VERA: Well, it was my idea. I had already talked to him (Manny) about this several months ago. But we never did anything. But he's threatened to take his own life at least five times in the last two weeks.

We think it is important to find out early in the session what clients expect from the session. In a sense, we have borrowed from the world of business where customers are always right, and the successful business gives them what they want. Early in the session, we learned that Manny had no plans to harm himself. He reassured us that his threats to kill himself had been signals of his desperation and hopelessness. Three weeks earlier, Manny and Vera separated when Manny failed to comply with their landlord's demand for rent, which resulted in the family's eviction from their apartment.

ARNIE: So what are you hoping for from today's session?

We want to ask questions that put the presenting concern into context. We do this by asking about why the couple had chosen to come today. Which one of them was more interested in coming? Who else was involved in the development or maintenance of the problem? Who in their lives would be most affected when they make positive changes?

MONTE: And how did you guys come to the decision to come today to talk about those things?

VERA: Well, it was my idea. I had already talked to him about this months ago. But, we never did anything. But he's threatened to take his own life at least five times in the last two weeks. So I talked to him, and I told him, you know, everything has a solution. And I told him that I would call the police. And then he—

he said it at least five times. And then the last time I
talked to him, I told him that we should try to see a
counselor. And I guess—we're here.

MONTE: And so what happened that you decided to come
today?

VERA: Because he called. Well, I called and left a message.
And then he called, and they told him that today was
the best day to go. I mean, to—for walk-ins.

ARNIE: You called here, and they told you about the option of just coming today.

VERA: Yeah.

MANNY: Right.

ARNIE: So you decided, you know, okay, if we can come
today, we'll come today.

VERA: Yeah. And he needs help. And I'm sure I need help,
too. And we need to see if our relationship can be
fixed and can be better.

*According to the common factors research (Duncan, et al., 2010),
extra-therapeutic factors in clients' lives, such as their own resources, are the most powerful contributors to therapeutic change.
We listened carefully for the couple's descriptions of these resources.
In the following segment, Manny offers us an idea about his im-
pressive personal resources.*

MANNY: I'm not dumb. I consider myself to be an intelligent person. I know how to do things. I know how to
fix things. I know a lot more than the average person
does. Yet, I'm unable to find gainful employment or
one that lasts or one where I can be successful. I asked
her (Vera) earlier, "How many jobs do you think I've
had since I've been working?" And she just took a
guess. Twenty. I've had about 20 jobs in the last 12
years. And it's not because I'm not good at them. It's
just I get tired of them. I get bored.

And a little later:

MANNY: I haven't gone to a job interview where I haven't
gotten the job.

We invite clients to guide us toward the most helpful under-standings of their situation and possible solutions to their dilem-mas. We also think it is important to gain an understanding of a client's theory of change (Duncan, et al., 1998; Duncan, et al., 2004). We do this by asking them what they want from the therapy process, their beliefs about the problem ("theory of the problem"), and their ideas about how to reach their goals ("theory of change"). In this case, we have learned from Manny that he is self taught. He is confident that he can learn on his own "when he sets his mind to it." So we think he can teach himself to make the necessary changes.

MANNY: Well, there's a lot of things that I can do. I learned to speak English on my own without going to school to learn to speak English. I lived in Mexico until I was 17. Everything recent that I know about computers, fixing computers, I learned on my own. Fixing cars. I do signs. I learned to do that on my own. Basically, I do graphic design. And I learned to do that on my own, never going to school to learn that. So a lot of those things I just know because I like to read. I like to learn stuff, and I'm quick at learning something.

We strongly adhere to the notion that only clients can solve their problems, and all clients have resources that can be directed toward problem solving. The job of the therapist is to direct the conversa-tion in such a way that resources that could be used for problem solving are discovered.

We strive to define small, obtainable goals during the session. Single session goals may be thought of as the first steps on the way to meeting larger goals. So, when Manny said that his goal was to be more hope-ful, we began to narrow that down to behavioral specifications.

MONTE: So, if you were to begin to feel a little bit more hope-ful, Manny, what might Vera see that would be a sign to her that you were more hopeful? What would she see?
MANNY: What would she need to see in order to believe that? That I can be held accountable for my actions, first of all, that—
MONTE: What would be a little sign that you were being more accountable?

MANNY: Talk to the people that I had hurt that were involved in this mess. Her parents.

MONTE: Oh, her parents. That you would talk with them? And what would you say that would give her some hope that—

MANNY: I don't know what would give her hope, but I know that they didn't have to do everything they did, that I had to help her when she had to move her stuff, that they didn't have to do that.

ARNIE: I think you may be saying if you apologized to these people—

MANNY: Right.

So, we helped Manny identify a specific behavior, apologizing, that would be a step toward achieving his goal of becoming hopeful and accountable. Vera caught on quickly and offered a big goal that needed paring down.

VERA: Well, to me, a big change would be if he stops looking at himself as the victim, because he does this a lot.

MONTE: So, that would be a big change?

VERA: That would be a huge change, if he stops that behavior for a considerable amount of time so that I can see that he really wants to change.

MONTE: What does he do now that gives you the idea that he's thinking of himself as a victim?

VERA: Well, he says, "Oh, nothing's going well for me. You know, all the doors have closed to me. I'm just a worthless person," or, you know, stuff like that.

ARNIE: So, when he becomes really hopeless and—

VERA: Yeah. Instead of saying, "Well, you know what? I did everything wrong, but I'm going to try and fix it."

ARNIE: So—okay. "So I've screwed up, but this is what I can do about it?"

VERA: Yeah. Instead of saying, "Oh, you know, I feel sorry for myself, because—"

MANNY: I've never said I felt sorry for myself.

VERA: Okay, not in those words, but you—

MONTE: But, that's what you hear?

VERA: Yes.

MONTE: Okay. If he were to start turning the corner there, he might say something like that to you? He might say, "Well, I didn't get that job, but maybe I'll be able to get another job," or something like that. That would be a small sign to you that he was moving away from feeling like a victim?

VERA: Yeah. Well, first of all, accept the fact that he was wrong and all this. But he has been saying this, and then he blames it on me. And then he goes back and forth, you know.

MONTE: Okay.

VERA: So—and he says that, first of all. If he really—the last thing I told him before we actually decided to talk and come here was, "You know what? I—you just stop saying all these things. I mean, you need to show me, not just say it, because that's kind of getting old, so—"

Here we tried to get an idea of what Vera is hoping to see Manny do when he abandoned his victim stance.

ARNIE: And showing you. What would that look like?

VERA: Showing me that he's really willing to change. Like he's not feeling sorry for himself, and he really wants to try and change and make things better, you know.

ARNIE: And how would you know? What might he do that would tell you he's taken a step in that direction of showing you?

VERA: First of all, act responsible. And if he needs to apologize to some people, he needs to do that. And—

MONTE: So, that would be one thing—being responsible and apologizing. What would be something else?

VERA: Well, he's trying to find a job, which I think is a positive thing.

MONTE: So if he was looking for a job, that would be a bit more responsible.

At this juncture, we took a short break, explaining to the couple that we wanted to consult with our team. After about 10 minutes, we returned.

The end of every session begins with feedback from the therapists and might then be followed with a homework task. Frequently we refer to the feedback as "commendations" to remind ourselves that the feedback should be aimed at underscoring the resources and strengths that we have noted during the session. Whether or not clients have previous experience with therapy, they frequently are apprehensive about how we might judge them. They steel themselves in preparation for criticism and diagnostic language. We have found that beginning the last part of the session with commendations puts them at ease, increases hope and expectations, and mobilizes their resources for change.

After a short consultation break with our team, we returned to the therapy room and began with commendations:

MONTE: The team observed that, as a couple, the two of you seem to have a lot of strengths that you can build on. You obviously love one another a lot, or you wouldn't be here. The crisis that you went through in getting evicted from your home and all of the emotional upset that you went through could have really been devastating. And I'm not saying that you weren't both deeply hurt by it. But you're wanting to overcome that and somehow put this relationship back together. So it's clear that the two of you care about one another a lot. You respect one another, and that's really clear, you may be hurt and have been hurt over the last several months. But it's clear that you have a lot of respect for one another, that you listen to what one another is saying. You might not like what you hear sometimes, but it's clear that you listen to one another. I'm guessing that she thinks you're likely to be a pretty good dad, or she wouldn't have moved in with you and brought you into her family with her daughter.

VERA: Oh, he's great with her. He's a good dad to her, and she adores him. Yeah.

ARNIE: I was going to say, I bet she really digs him.

VERA: They have a great relationship. Yeah.

ARNIE: And, Manny, we also know that when you set your mind to get good at something, that you do it. You gave us a number of examples of things that you really have decided you were going to learn, and you just did it. And actually, one of the things I sort of was saying to the team, and they suggested that I say to you, is that you set your mind to learn English, and not only have you learned English really well, and you sound more like a Texan than I do. [*Arnie was born in Chicago and spent many years living in Calgary, Canada, and, to his regret, has not yet acquired a Texan's accent.*]

MANNY: Most of the time I worked on the phone. And you learn to do that [*mimic accents*], and people accept that better, because they feel like they're with somebody that they can relate to.

MONTE: Wow! [*to Vera*] So he's pretty sensitive about picking up kind of cues like that from people over the phone and stuff. That's something that we didn't know about him, too.

Whether or not clients express an interest in returning for another session, we try to devise a homework assignment that will keep the therapy session alive after we are done. Frequently before the consultation break, we will ask clients what has been helpful about the session thus far. Their answers often offer clues about a useful homework assignment. A second useful question we ask before the break elicits what the client is thinking about future appointments and when they might happen. In any case, we tailor the homework to fit with their expectations.

ARNIE: [*to Manny*] So, you're a talented guy. When we left, right before the break, we asked if the two of you together could think about how you were going to use those talents to get really, really good at being partners in a relationship, even better as parents to Vera's daughter. You both talked about Manny being more responsible in his work life. Manny, you've impressed all of us as somebody who, if you decided that you were going to figure out how to do that, it would be hard and it would take time, but you would do it. You would do it, because you've done it before. The best sign that you're going to do something in the future is if you've done it before. There'd be struggles with it. It would be—it would feel like slow going at times. But you'd figure it out. And in that process—you're a self-learner. You went to school and you said you know, the formal education—like college. You know, and it didn't quite fit for you. And you—but you know how to teach yourself.

And, in considering the next step and future appointments:

ARNIE: You could use us as your learning consultant. You could, walk in like you did today, or you could set up an appointment to come back, if that made the most sense to you to do it that way. But—so we could be your consultants in that process. You know the best learning path, the best learning methodology that you would figure that out, because you've done it before. So we're very confident about that. You can think about do you want to leave it that you'll come back the same way you have today, by walking in, or do you want to set up a time? So we'll talk about that.

So we have left the next step up to them.

ARNIE: And, we also had a specific idea, a suggestion for you to experiment with.
MONTE: Right, whether you come back or not. One of the things, Vera, that the team heard loud and clear from you was that you wanted to see some more signs of responsibility from Manny. And it seemed to us that one that you've already seen at least one that we know of. And that is coming here with you today and taking responsibility for the relationship. Is that the kind of thing that you were looking for in terms of responsibility?
VERA: Yes.
MONTE: And you mentioned that maybe another big sign would be if he was to apologize to your family for the things that was responsible for recently. Is that your parents and your daughter that you're thinking about?
VERA: Yes.
MONTE: Okay. So you know that he's capable of doing those things. He's already done one. And you wouldn't even be asking him to apologize if you didn't think he was capable of doing it. So you have some confidence that he could do that.
VERA: Yeah.

MONTE: Okay. The team had an idea about something that you might experiment with, whether you come back or not. Manny, as Dr. Slive said, you're a self-learner. Could you give some thought to maybe one or two little things that you could do that would be small signs of responsibility? Maybe not even as big as apologizing to her parents, but some small things you would do that she would see as a sign of your taking more responsibility for yourself and for the relationship. *[Manny nods and begins to speak.]* But don't tell me, and don't tell her. These would be things that you might surprise her with. And don't even tell her if you did it. You know, it would be useful for us—if you come back—if you were to tell us what you did, and maybe even tell us what her reaction was to it.

ARNIE: *[to Vera]* So, you don't tell him that you noticed it.

VERA: Okay.

ARNIE: And, Manny, a lot of times, we have a way of just responding to something. So your job is to kind of watch for something, some sign that she's noticed what you did.

MONTE: And we couldn't tell Manny what to do, because that would be like taking a class in college where we'd be telling you what to do. But you're smart enough to figure out on your own what works.

ARNIE: He figures things out himself. He wouldn't pay attention to what we said anyway, you know.

MONTE: And if we gave him an idea, it would be a bad one anyway, so—

MANNY: Probably so.

Early in the session, both Manny and Vera said they wanted to understand why Manny had been behaving as he had. Even though we believe that "why" questions are often unanswerable, we thought it important to address this client want.

ARNIE: Now, there's one other thing. You're curious about understanding what's been going on with you. Why is it that you've been doing some of the things that you've been doing? And what we find is that many times when people start to do some things differently, and especially in your case because you're a smart guy and you teach yourself, that as you start to do new things, some ideas will start percolating for you, that will start to help you to understand yourself in a different way. So those ideas about 'Who am I? What's going on with me?' will be answered when you try these new things out.

MONTE: He gave us an example early on when he said that he had kind of given up on being the kind of guy that would be involved in a relationship and have a family. He tried that; it didn't work out. He decided that that just wasn't going to be part of his life. Then he met Vera. And all of a sudden, he began to have a different understanding of himself because of his relationship with Vera. And you learned something new and different about yourself when you met her. That's what we're talking about. As you begin now to make other changes in your life, you'll develop new understandings that you didn't have before.

ARNIE: Yeah, discoveries.

MONTE: Discoveries. You'll discover new things. Does that make sense?

MANNY: Yes. Absolutely. If I get out of my everyday pattern, I guess, and try to do the things that I wouldn't have done before.

Manny tells us that we have answered the basic question that he began the session with.

Manny and Vera agreed that they would need to come back at some point in the future, but not right away. They both agreed that the session had been helpful to them. They had talked about a number of issues that needed airing. They had a plan for what they could do in the short-term to begin repairing their relationship. We reminded that they could return as walk-in clients, either together or separately, or they could call and schedule an appointment in the conventional manner. As frequently happens, Manny walked in several months later for a consultation about some of his concerns about Vera. The couple had reunited since their first walk-in session, and continued to have some relationship concerns. Threats of harm appeared to have disappeared as an issue for them. A different therapy team saw Manny for the second session, and it, too, was conducted as a self-contained, single session.

Conclusion

In this chapter we have described how we conduct walk-in/single session psychotherapy in our context. Walk-in services require some modification of the original single session model, but the essence of Hoyt, Talmon, and Rosenbaum's work is still evident in our clinic. We have not insisted that clients be limited to a single session of therapy, but we have been guided by the idea that every session has the potential to be a single session. Every session may be the last opportunity that a therapist has to assist a client.

The case we presented was not unusual. If anything, it was typical of most of the cases we see in our walk-in clinic. By our focus on this couple's immediate concerns and our offer of suggestions consistent with the clients' own ideas about change, they left with increased optimism and hope as well as a new idea to try out. They chose, at that time, not to schedule a return session. This case illustrated the single session mindset and some ideas for conducting effective walk-in sessions. Because we do not assume that the clients will return, we treat each session as a whole therapy. If they should return, the therapy will be another self-contained whole. We do one session at a time. After all, we have a whole hour.

References

Baldwin, S. A., Berkeljon, A., Atkins, D. C., Olsen, J. A., & Nielsen, S. L. (2009). Rates of change in naturalistic psychotherapy: Contrasting dose-effect and good-enough level models of change. *Journal of Consulting & Clinical Psychology*, 77, 203–211. doi: 10.1037/a0015235.

Baardseth, T.P., Goldberg, S.B., Pace, B.T., Wislocki, A.P., Frost, N.D., Siddiqui, J.R. Wampold, B.E. (2013). Cognitive-behavioral therapy versus other therapies: Redux. *Clinical Psychology Review*, 33(3), 395–405. doi: http://dx.doi.org/10.1016/j.cpr.2013.01.004.

Başoğlu, Metin, Şalcioğlu, Ebru, & Livanou, Maria. (2007). A randomized controlled study of single-session behavioural treatment of earthquake-related post-traumatic stress disorder using an earthquake simulator. *Psychological Medicine: A Journal of Research in Psychiatry and the Allied Sciences*, 37(2), 203–213. doi: 10.1017/S0033291706009123

Berg, I.K., & Miller, S.D. (1992). *Working with the problem drinker: A solution-focused approach*. New York: Norton.

Bloom, B.L. (2001). Focused single-session psychotherapy: A review of the clinical and research literature. *Brief Treatment and Crisis Intervention*, 1, 75–86.

Bobele, M., Lopez, S., Scamardo, M., & Solórzano, B. (2008). Single-session walk-in therapy with Mexican-American clients. *Journal of Systemic Therapies, 27*, 75–89.

de Shazer, S. (1985) *Keys to solution in brief therapy*. New York: Norton.

de Shazer, S. (1988) Clues: Investigating solutions in brief therapy. New York: Norton.

Duncan, B.L., Hubble, M.A., Miller, S.D., & Coleman, S.T. (1998). Escaping the lost world of impossibility: Honoring clients' language, motivation, and theories of change. In M.F. Hoyt (Ed.), *The handbook of constructive therapies* (pp. 293–313). San Francisco: Jossey-Bass.

Duncan, B.L., Miller, S.D., & Sparks, J. (2004). *The heroic client: A revolutionary way to improve effectiveness through client-directed, outcome informed therapy*. San Francisco: Jossey-Bass.

Duncan, B., Miller, S., Wampold, B., & Hubble, M. (Eds.). (2010). *The heart and soul of change: Delivering what works in therapy*. Washington, DC: American Psychological Association.

Feaster, D. J., Newman, F. L., & Rice, C. (2003). Longitudinal analysis when the experimenter does not determine when treatment ends: What is dose, response? *Clinical Psychology & Psychotherapy, 10*, 352–360. doi: 10.1002/cpp.382.

Fisch, R. (1994). Basic elements in the brief therapies. In M.F. Hoyt (Ed.), *Constructive therapies* (Vol. 1, pp. 126–139). New York: Guilford Press.

Freedman, J., & Coombs, G. (1996). *Narrative therapy: The social construction of preferred realities*. New York: Norton .

Haley, J., & Richeport-Haley, M. (2003). *The art of strategic therapy*. New York: Bruner-Routledge.

Hansen, N. B., & Lambert, M. J. (2003). An evaluation of the dose-response relationship in naturalistic treatment settings using survival analysis. *Mental Health Services Research, 5*(1), 1–12. doi: 10.1023/a:1021751307358.

Harnett, P., O'Donovan, A., & Lambert, M. J. (2010). The dose response relationship in psychotherapy: Implications for social policy. *Clinical Psychologist, 14*, 39–44. doi: 10.1080/13284207.2010.500309.

Harper-Jaques, S., & Foucault, D. (2013). Clinical outcomes and client satisfaction of a mental health walk-in single session therapy service. (submitted for publication)

Howard, K. I., Kopta, S. M., Krause, M. S., & Orlinsky, D. E. (1986). The dose-effect relationship in psychotherapy. *American Psychologist, 41*, 159–164.

Hoyt, M. F., Rosenbaum, R., & Talmon, M. (1990). Effective single-session therapy: Step-by-step guidelines. In M. Talmon, *Single session therapy: Maximizing the effect of the first (and often only) therapeutic encounter* (pp. 34–56). San Francisco: Jossey-Bass.

Hoyt, M. F., Rosenbaum, R., & Talmon, M. (1992). Planned single session therapy. In S. H. Budman, M. Hoyt & S. Friedman (Eds.), *The first session in brief therapy* (pp. 59–86). New York: Guilford Press.

Hoyt, M. F. (2009). *Brief therapies: Principles and practices*. Phoenix, AZ: Zeig, Tucker, & Theisen.

Hunsley, J., Aubry, T.D., Verstervelt, C.M., & Vito, D. (1999). Comparing therapist and client perspectives on reasons for psychotherapy termination. *Psychotherapy: Theory, Research, Practice, Training*, 36(4), 380–388.

Lambert, M., & Forman, E. (2002). The psychotherapy dose-response effect and its implications for treatment delivery services. *Clinical Psychology: Science and Practice*, 9, 330.

Lipchik, E. (2002). Beyond technique in solution-focused therapy. New York: Guilford.

Miller, S.D., & Duncan, B.L. (2000). Outcome and session rating scales administration and scoring manual. Chicago, IL: Institute for the Study of Therapeutic Change.

Miller, J. (2008). Walk-in single session therapy: A study of client satisfaction. *Journal of Systemic Therapies* 27, 78–94.

O'Hanlon, W.H., & Weiner-Davis, M. (1989). *In search of solutions: A new direction in psychotherapy*. New York: Norton.

Ollendick, Thomas H., Öst, Lars-Göran, Reuterskiöld, Lena, Costa, Natalie, Cederlund, Rio, Sirbu, Cristian,...Jarrett, Matthew A. (2009). One-session treatment of specific phobias in youth: A randomized clinical trial in the United States and Sweden. *Journal of Consulting and Clinical Psychology*, 77(3), 504–516. doi: 10.1037/a0015158

Perkins, R. (2006). "The effectiveness of one session of therapy using a single-session therapy approach for children and adolescents with mental health problems." *Psychology & Psychotherapy*, 79(Pt 2): 215–227.

Perkins, R. and G. Scarlett (2008). "The effectiveness of single session therapy in child and adolescent mental health. Part 2: An 18-month follow-up study." *Psychology & Psychotherapy: Theory, Research & Practice*, 81(2): 143–156.

Ray, W., & Keeney, B. (1993). *Resource focused therapy*. London: Karnac.

Scamardo, M., Bobele, M., & Biever, J.L. (2004). A new perspective on client dropouts. *Journal of Systemic Therapies*, 23(2), 27–38.

Seligman, M. E. P. (1995). The effectiveness of psychotherapy: The Consumer Reports study. *American Psychologist*, 50, 965–974. doi: 10.1037/0003-066x.50.12.965.

Slive, A. (2008). (Ed.) Special section: Walk-in single session therapy. *Journal of Systemic Therapies*, 27, 1–89.

Slive, A., & Bobele, M. (Eds.). (2011). *When one hour is all you have: Effective therapy for walk-in clients*. Phoenix, AZ: Zeig, Tucker & Theisen.

Slive, A., MacLaurin, B., Oakander, M., & Amundson, J. (1995). Walk-in single sessions: A new paradigm in clinical service delivery. *Journal of Systemic Therapies*, 14(1), 3–11.

Talmon, M. (1990). Single-session therapy: Maximizing the effect of the first (and often only) therapeutic encounter. San Francisco: Jossey-Bass.

White, M. (1986). Negative explanation, restraint and double description: A template for family therapy. *Family Process*, 25, 169–184.

White, M., & Epston, D. (1990). *Narrative means to therapeutic ends*. New York: Norton .

Wolgast, B. M., Lambert, M. J., & Puschner, B. (2003). The dose-response relationship at a college counseling center: Implications for setting session limits. *Journal of College Student Psychotherapy, 18*(2), 15–29. doi: 10.1300/Jo35v18no2.

Young, J., Weir, S., & Rycroft, P. (2012). Implementing single session therapy. *Australian & New Zealand Journal of Family Therapy, 33*(1), 84–97. doi: 10.1017/aft.2012.8.

Chapter Seven

Implementing Single Session Therapy: Practical Wisdoms from Down Under

Jeff Young, Pam Rycroft, and Shane Weir

Until recently, the therapeutic world has been focused on the development of new evidence-based approaches with little regard to their implementation into regular service delivery. As a result, an abundance of new and proven practices never make it into widespread clinical practice or into service delivery, thus wasting valuable healthcare dollars and depriving the community of the latest clinical developments in the human service sectors (Proctor, et al., 2009). The goal of this chapter is to raise some of the conceptual ideas and practical wisdoms regarding how to translate new theories into practice, based on the collective experiences of The Bouverie Centre: Victoria's Family Institute, La Trobe University in Australia. Since 1996, The Bouverie Centre staff have trained thousands of individual practitioners in Single Session Therapy (SST), helped hundreds of organizations implement SST into their services and project managed three large scale state-wide implementation

A version of this chapter was presented as a keynote address at the *Capture the Moment: The Inaugural Symposium on Single-Session Therapies and Walk-In Services* held on Phillip Island, Victoria, Australia, in March 2012. Portions were also presented as part of the symposium, *Capturing the Moment: Single-Session Therapy and Walk-In Services,* held at the annual convention of the American Psychological Association, Honolulu, HI, July 31, 2013.

strategies, two using SST concepts to introduce family work into individual-focused organizations. These experiences, together with several research projects evaluating this work (including the implementation of SST into our own organization), have had a profound impact on us as family therapists, trainers, and wider service system consultants and implementers. Our hope is to generate interest and discussion in the art of implementation, also called implementation science, translation research, dissemination, uptake, adoption and diffusion of innovation—rather than pretend we have anything definitive to share. Although our focus is on the implementation of SST and the more generic termed Single Session Work (SSW), as well as our family-focused Single Session Family Consultation (SSFC) approach, the ideas raised and the discussions provoked may have relevance to practitioners, managers, service CEOs or to external trainers interested in any practice change project.

Definition and Description of SST, SSW and SSFC

Like many approaches in the counselling realm that do not possess a universally accepted definition, SST is open to different interpretations, particularly due to its radical name. To avoid misunderstanding, we begin this chapter with our definition and description of SST and its derivatives, SSW and SSFC. It has been surprisingly difficult to articulate a clear definition that accounts for all of the essential components of SST, SSW and SSFC, including their differences as well as the organizational processes that are needed to support them. The implementation literature makes the distinction between elements of an innovation that can be adapted to suit local conditions and those elements that cannot be changed without losing the integrity of the innovation. The following definition is an attempt to cover all of the elements we see as essential for an SST approach whilst allowing flexibility for local adaptions, a key part of effective implementation. We argue for an attitudinal definition of SST/SSW/SSFC rather than a precise and practice definition and this is essentially everything that results from genuinely accepting the following three research findings (Talmon 1990; Young & Rycroft, 1997; Young, et al., 2012):

1. A large proportion of clients only attend one occasion of care, irrespective of diagnosis, severity or practitioner expectation;

2. The majority of clients who elect not to return after the first session do so because they are satisfied rather than dissatisfied with the service they have received; and

3. It is essentially impossible or impractical for practitioners to predict which clients will attend only one session and which clients will elect to attend more than one session.

At a practitioner level, these three findings lead workers to approach the first session as if it may also be the last. This attitude encourages practitioners to make it apparent that the first session may be the only contact, which creates a context for both practitioner and client to try and make most of the first (and subsequent) session(s). In most situations this translates to responding to what clients (and practitioners) see as a priority to address in the session at hand. It also means neither assuming that a client will come back for further sessions, nor blocking a client from returning for more work. This work entails either explicitly following up with clients after the first session to determine if they want to seek further support or simply finishing the session by ensuring return visits are easy and possible. In our service, and many that we have assisted, further treatment decisions are made by clients during a follow-up phone call rather than at the end of the first session. However, the method of communication is dependent on the clientele and local service contexts. For example, some clients may not have mobile phones!

At a service level, accepting the three research findings above means providing an environment where attending only one session is seen as common practice whilst ensuring there are no impediments to clients accessing further service. It also requires the creation of an accessible service delivery system that will allow clients and workers to achieve the most from the first session. Therapeutic goals should be defined collaboratively by client and worker, but largely by the client (if possible) rather than stipulating cumbersome universal assessment procedures. Assessments are done as needed to address the most pressing problem(s). By promoting creative structures and processes, clients and practitioners will be helped in jointly making the most of all, but particularly the first session, as it may be the only meeting many clients attend. A pre-session questionnaire is mailed out to client(s), inviting them to articulate the most pressing concerns, their strengths that may help address these concerns, and what success would look like, as well as any questions they would like addressed during the session (see www.bouverie.org for SST resources including the questionnaire our center routinely mails out to clients). For a more detailed description of the SST process we employ at our center see O'Neill and Rottem (2012).

We, the authors, use *SST* and *SSW* as interchangeable terms, depending on the context of the work. We introduced the title SSW when translating SST ideas into work contexts where practitioners do not describe the work they do as therapy or counselling. These practitioners do not identify themselves as therapists, despite often providing counselling and therapeutic-type services as part of their role. We find, for example, that these practitioners, including maternal and child-health workers, hospital social workers and youth workers, find SSW a particularly helpful framework because their clients often do not attend regular, multiple or predictable appointments or they act as *occasional counsellors* in between providing other services, such as case management or practical support. We encourage participants in our SST workshops and implementation projects to use descriptors that make sense to them, to their clients and to their context. As a result, many of our SST-trained practitioners use terms such as *initial consult, get-togethers,* and *purposeful extended consultation* to describe their SST approach.

SSFC simply refers to using SST/SSW with more than one person: families, partners, social networks, etc. SSFC emerged as a simple and implementable way to help practitioners in individually focused healthcare organizations (such as Mental Health Services, Alcohol and Other Drug [AOD] Services and Gambling Services) engage the relational supports of their individual clients. The practical application of *making the most of each session* invites a consultative, needs-driven and non-pathologizing approach. We have found SSFC to be a relatively easy way to teach basic family work meeting skills to non-family therapists and to introduce client and family led contextual practice. In Mental Health organizations and Alcohol and Drug services for example, SSFC can be used to bring family members together, including the client, to identify what they would find most helpful, how they want to be involved in their family member's care and how the client wants them to be involved. Often it addresses how family members can better support their relative who is experiencing a mental health or substance use problem. SSFCs can be the setting for sharing information, providing education (both general education about the service and basic psychoeducation), solving day-to-day problems, making decisions, establishing a communication strategy, negotiating differences, etc. (see Young, Weir, O'Hanlon, *FIP Guidelines*, in press). The SSFC has the advantage that it can be used flexibly as a stand-alone encounter or as the start of ongoing work, which may be continuous or intermittent and which can provide a "pathway" to more specialized family treatments or therapeutic approaches.

Increasingly, we see SST and its derivatives as service delivery models rather than clinical or therapeutic models. The introduction of SST, SSW or SSFC requires practitioners to shape their established ways of working, but not to surrender their favorite therapeutic approach entirely, thus making implementation more palatable to a wider range of practitioners. For example, at a large inner-city community health service a CBT-trained psychologist, a family therapist and a social worker with a degree in Gestalt therapy were able to discuss their SST cases together from each of their therapeutic perspectives which led to greater team cohesion and very healthy morale.

Implementing SST

The implementation strategies and practical hints provided in this chapter are written to help practitioners recruit colleagues, managers, and CEOs in the change process; to provide ideas for CEOs and managers to inform their organizational implementation plans; and as a guide to help external trainers and implementers be more effective at engaging services in the change process. These practical ideas should be augmented by an awareness of the implementation literature, if for no other reason than to appreciate that significant thought, planning, strategy, and resources are usually required to achieve any significant organizational or practice change. We provide a brief introduction to the literature in the following section.

Implementing Evidence-Based Practices in General: A Brief Reflection

Implementation of new ideas is not easy! Boren and Balas (1999) estimate that new evidence-based interventions languish for between 15–20 years before they are incorporated into practice, and then only a small proportion of innovations ever find their way into core service delivery (Grimshaw & Eccles, 2004; Fixsen, et al., 2005). Apart from the cost, the community misses out on the health benefits of the latest treatments and healthcare innovations that have proven efficacy, leading Proctor, et al. (2009, p. 24) to argue that "one of the most critical issues in mental health services is the gap between what is known about effective treatment and what is provided to consumers in routine care."

As a result of recent efforts to bridge this gap between discovery of effective and innovative healthcare practices and translation of these practices into everyday service provision, interest in implementation science is growing. For example, The American National Institute of Health (NIH) established an annual conference on the Science of Dissemination and Implementation and an associated journal in 2006. In Australia, a similar trend is beginning as evidenced by the implementation focus of major funding bodies such as the National Institute of Clinical Studies. The literature strongly argues that successful implementation of new ideas is usually hard won, requiring long term systemic (Proctor, et al., 2009), multi-level approaches (Greenhalgh, et al., 2004; Damschroder, et al., 2009), guided by coherent frameworks (Rogers, 2003; Fixsen, et al., 2005; Damschroder, et al., 2009; Meyers, et al., 2012) and a strong understanding of the internal and external world (Damschroder, et al., 2009) surrounding the implementation site. Key meta-analyses of the implementation research have been published, most notably by Greenhalgh, et al. (2004), Fixsen, et al., (2005), Damschroder, et al. (2009), and Meyers, et al. (2012), which provide comprehensive frameworks for those brave enough to embark on a service-wide implementation journey.

Policy makers, funders, service managers and practitioners are all beginning to consider implementation more seriously and much earlier in the process of their work. At Bouverie, we now clearly see our old "train and hope" model as inadequate to generate consistent or sustainable practice change and considerations of implementation influence the design of our workforce development projects from the start. We recommend that readers wanting to introduce SST/SSW/SSFC into an organization consult the implementation frameworks (especially Rogers, 2003; Damschroder, et al., 2009; Meyers, et al., 2012) available in the literature and read Young, Weir and Rycroft (2012) for greater detail about the research that informed the practice-change wisdoms specifically associated with SST/SSW/SSFC presented in this chapter.

Practical Strategies for Implementing SST

We believe that strategies of implementation should reflect the values underlying the innovation being implemented. Whilst we no longer experience the hostility we faced in our early SST training (see Chapter 8 this volume), we try to hold onto these early memories to remind ourselves how practitioners in our field have a strong commitment and passion for their work and do not like changes that they suspect may reduce services to their clients or affect the quality, enjoyment, or established rhythms of their work. We understand that practice change is an emotional enterprise as much as a practical one and that sufficient support is required, backed up by a clear and logical rationale to make sense of the need for change.

Underlying our approach to implementation is an appreciation that most practitioners, managers and CEOs are driven by wanting the best experience, satisfaction and outcomes for their clients, although they typically focus on different elements of achieving this outcome and their approach sometimes inadvertently does not lead to ideal client outcomes.

A rationale for change: What's the problem and how can SST address this problem?

A useful starting point to engage practitioners, managers, CEOs or funders around SST or its derivatives is to discover, articulate, or make overt a problem that prevents clients (or at least some clients) getting the best possible service; a problem SST/SSW/SSFC can help address. People tend not to change if their current approach seems to be working well. Striving for long-term engagement has face validity, feels respectful and fits with traditional counsellor training; hence, it can be seen as the "right thing to do" especially in the absence of practitioners seeking feedback from clients who do not fit this standard approach. Articulating a problem is often a key part of creating a rationale for the need for change. Ideally, the problem should be articulated by the practitioners, managers or CEOs themselves, but understandably the need to change may be forced on services from external factors, such as policy directives or the identification of poor service outcomes by interested stakeholders. We commonly point out to services that SST approaches can minimize the risk that clients continue to face through abuse or other risks whilst on long waiting lists. We point out that SST approaches provide a better service to clients who only ever attend one or two sessions and can help satisfy external policy expectations for accessible services responsive to individual client need including providing services to engage hard-to-reach clients. Pertinent to our center's role, it also assists with the policy directives to improve services to families or to comply with family sensitive policies, introduced in Australia in the past two decades.

SST may solve the problem but it needs to fit with practitioner values and the philosophy of the host organization

Whilst general guidelines and frameworks help guide our implementation work, it is important to understand the unique culture of each implementation site and the underlying values of the different workforces involved and make an explicit link between SST and these cultures and values. Generally the stronger the link that can be made between the new practice and practitioner values and the philosophy underlying the organization, the easier implementation will be (Rogers, 1995). For example, we have had greater success implementing SST in services which embrace a social model of health and celebrate client empowerment (see Young, et al., 2012) and less success with services who value the expertise of the professional staff to determine the direction of client care. A colleague who has been an advocate of SST and SSFC in a services system that values practitioner expertise told us he was asked, *How do you know that one session can be helpful?* He responded that clients report this in significant numbers to which the questioner retorted, *Clients don't necessary know what is good for them!*

Link SST to existing organizational processes, procedures, policy and strategic directions

Although usually a challenge in the early stages, embedding SST into existing organizational processes and procedures will usually lead to improved implementation success in the long term and sustainability of the new practice. Organizations have limited capacity for change and hence if SST can be seen as part of the overall strategic direction of the organization the implementation is likely to enjoy greater momentum. "Surf others' waves," as a colleague of ours puts it, by which he means, surf the energy and interest generated by other compatible initiatives of the organization. This will vary depending on the particular service demands and funding environment influencing each sector. Over the past 10 years, The Bouverie Centre has assisted organizations to apply SST/SSW/SSFC in a diverse range of service sectors for a variety of reasons. Some low-cost community-based counselling services have implemented SST as a result of the overwhelming consumer demand on the services. Others, such as Child and Youth Mental Health Services and Community Health Services, have used SSFC as a means to effectively triage clients and provide an effective first response to support the client's pathway through the service system. Adult mental health and alcohol and drug services have used SSFC to meet the policy requirements of government to include families and careers in their treatment strategy. Family service organizations have utilized SST and SSFC as an approach to engage vulnerable families who have had long-term involvement with family and child welfare services. Perhaps the most interesting uses of the approach have been sponsored by the Victorian Responsible Gambling Foundation (VRGF). The VRGF have supported SST and SSFC for two reasons. Firstly, as a useful approach for Gambler's Help counsellors to provide timely support to individual clients and families. Secondly, they have also brokered Bouverie to provide SST and SSFC training and implementation support to bring Gambler's Help counsellors, mental health, alcohol and other drug services and family service practitioners together through the use of SSFC, which has application across all service sectors. The use of SSFC as a vehicle to promote cross-sector collaboration helped the VRGF respond to research that indicates people with problematic gambling behavior often have other co-occurring conditions but are more likely to present with these other conditions leaving the problematic gambling undetected and untreated.

Get champions, managers and leaders on side

The need to get "buy-in" from the implementation site is well understood. What is less understood is the need to engage multiple levels of an organization. It is important to accept that practitioners, managers and leaders may be affected by different change cultures within an organization. For example, CEOs may be interested in cutting-edge innovations that reflect the policy context whilst practitioners may be more client-focused. Each host agency will also have a specific culture which will need to be understood. For example, some organizations value exciting innovations; some prefer high-status programs, others research projects, others pilot programs, others partnerships and some just do not want to be left behind.

We have learned the hard way to engage middle managers as well as practitioners and CEOs. Practitioners understand the personal or professional benefit of training and new ideas. CEOs are typically excited by new initiatives that make their organization look better, but middle managers are often the ones who have to make these new ideas actually work, usually without any additional resources. Just as middle managers are sometimes forgotten, intake workers are often not included in training or the change process, possibly because their role is seen as low status or not clinical. However, the inclusion of intake workers was a key element in a highly successful state-wide implementation project we conducted which led to the introduction of SST as a formal service delivery model in 49% of the 89 community health services which participated in the project (Young, et al., 2012).

External implementers particularly are advised to engage champions, rather than getting them off-side. Typical ways of getting potential champions off-side include coming in as the experts without acknowledging the contribution of existing staff, or engaging high-status staff at the expense of champions who have been doing work similar to the innovation. An effective way of getting champions on-side is to include them in implementation teams or (in smaller organizations) putting a champion in charge of the implementation process.

Create an implementation team, an implementation process and plan

Most practitioners love opportunities for reflective practice and working alongside colleagues on exciting new projects. Creating a new implementation team or charging an existing service development team with the responsibility for embedding SST into core practice is endorsed by 68% of the 25 implementation frameworks that Meyers, et al. (2012) reviewed. As external implementers, we have found that a locally established implementation team has the advantage of knowing how decisions are made and how to get things done in the particular organization. If the membership is thoughtfully selected the implementation can be driven by this team supported by external facilitators. It is hard to be "prophets in your own land" and hence external trainers and consultants can make it easier for local teams to be taken seriously. In large-scale implementation projects across a number of services or across different service types, implementation teams can be put in touch with other teams via newsletters or web-based communities of practice (Wenger & Snyder, 2000) and possibly brought together occasionally for best practice symposia so that each individual participant and team can see they are part of a bigger change program. For example, one of our SSFC implementation projects involved 32 organizations and 400 practitioners from the mental health and alcohol and other drugs sectors. Participating organizations were asked to nominate at least two champion practitioners to be involved in monthly, two-hour supervision sessions or Participant Enquiry Groups (PEGs). Participants were allocated by region and the sessions were facilitated by a Bouverie staff member. Discussion focused on the clinical application and implementation of family inclusive work and opportunities were provided to explore the challenges and barriers staff were encountering. PEG facilitators fostered an atmosphere of mutual learning and respect, and provided support and motivation to develop the new SSFC practices. Implementation leadership groups were also convened for middle managers every 4 to 6 months during the life of the project.

A good task for the implementation team is to agree on an SST implementation plan and a clear process for making SST work in practice. A process essentially has to put in place the practical tasks needed for starting the new practice, support processes and procedures, as well as allowing feedback on what is working and what needs adapting. We used an action research format to re-introduce SST to our own service several years ago (O'Neill & Rottem, 2012), in which clinical staff met once a month using the Observe-Reflect-Plan-Act-Observe participatory action research process (e.g., Kemmis and McTaggart, 2005). We facilitate a similar process in the implementation groups we establish in our larger projects. Adaptation of the SST/SSW/SSFC approaches is encouraged as an important ingredient of a successful local implementation. We believe that as long as the three research findings outlined in the attitudinal definition described earlier in this chapter are observed, agencies do not have to worry too much about the fidelity of the innovation.

It probably goes without saying but the success of any process or plan, no matter how good, is reliant on a functional organization with effective management. For example, in one of our evaluation studies, staff were busting to start conducting SST but management was unresponsive although rhetorically supportive of the idea, and this reflected a historical pattern of disorganization and repeated leadership changes.

Provide good short-term training AND long-term support

We have changed our previous strategy of comprehensive training and minimal follow-up support. We now provide sufficient but minimal training followed by ongoing implementation support. We have found that if workshop participants do not put new ideas and approaches into practice almost immediately, they often lose their nerve and confidence and resort to their usual and comfortable practice. If ongoing support is not provided, practitioners often take recourse to familiar approaches as soon as they face dilemmas, complexities, or anxieties. Our approach, called the Beacon Systemic Implementation Strategy, provides basic training and then booster sessions when our participants come up against such difficulties. For example, after meeting with families after the basic two-day SSFC training, workers are often challenged by managing conflict between family members and the expression of strong emotions; hence, we provide one-day booster workshops to provide extra skills and techniques to address these concerns. Because the topics have been identified by the participants themselves, they have basic experiences on which to build and are highly motivated to engage in the boosters, the material being real and relevant.

We also provide facilitation and technical support to the implementation teams. Support may be provided face-to-face, via telephone, or online. The essential consideration is to ensure implementation teams and practitioners get what they need. Paradoxically, implementing SST is not a single session!

Provide resources to support implementation—time, technical support, processes

Resource allocation should reflect the size and importance of the implementation process. Significant organizational change cannot be expected if accompanied by minimal dedicated staff time or supports. Whilst this is a no-brainer, many organizations (especially small agencies) can fall into the trap of expecting new projects to be done over and above existing commitments. The importance of technical support, which may include expert advice, supervision or coaching, is endorsed by 80% of the 25 implementation frameworks Meyers, et al. (2012) reviewed. We have developed a range of resources to assist services to implement SST/SSW/SSFC into their organizations (available from Bouverie.org.au) including training DVDs and implementation flow charts for clinicians, intake workers, and managers.

Evaluation, numbers and feedback systems

We have found that one of the most powerful incentives for practitioners to change their default practice is client feedback. We personally still have trouble believing that many clients with a range of difficulties, including some of the most serious and complex problems, could be satisfied with one or two *single sessions* as outlined in the literature. However, when it is confirmed by our follow-up phone calls and evaluations conducted in our implementation sites, we are convinced all over again. This is how we were initially convinced about the value of SST: not from what we read in the literature, but from listening to our clients' feedback. Even in our own service, which has strong advocates for SST approaches, some practitioners were only reassured during our re-implementation process by the support of the approach we received from families attending our center. An interesting finding from our own evaluation research was that whilst some practitioners were concerned that SST may lead clients to feel they were encouraged not to return for further sessions, clients indicated that this was not a concern for them (O'Neill and Rottem, 2012). It seems our clients are often more robust and improve quicker than we therapists expect. A trend in our evaluation, supported by a number of more robust research projects in the literature designed to specifically test this finding, is that practitioners repeatedly predict that clients will require more sessions than clients predict they will need (Pekarik, 1991).

We have learnt in our larger state-wide implementation projects to get services to record the actual number of SST sessions they actually conduct, because some agencies talk up their success and others down play it. Having a tangible and objective measure also acts as a feedback mechanism for the implementation process. In our large state-wide project involving AOD agencies implementing SSFC, we wanted a measure of the work implemented over the life of the project (3 years) that would capture the diversity of implementation approaches. We also wanted a measure that could be displayed publicly for all the participants. Due to the disparity in the size of teams and the number of clients accessing service types we devised a pictorial representation we called the *Implementation Tree Questionnaire*. The questionnaire was purposefully designed to be a creative and interventive measuring tool that would stimulate staff reflection on their agency's implementation activity, identify gaps and guide further development, monitor progress of the implementation and provide engaging visual feedback.

The image of a tree was used as a metaphor for the growth of family work. Questions related to root development were designed to capture those organizational activities that assist family inclusive practice to become embedded within agency culture, activities that may not be seen and yet are important for SST to take *root* in the organization, such as policies and procedures. Additionally, questions related to canopy growth would illustrate activities of direct practice. AOD teams were encouraged to complete the questionnaires as a whole staff group (workers and managers together), to reflect, review and plan further implementation activity on a 6-monthly basis. Managers and workers reported that the *Implementation Tree Questionnaire* had a positive effect on influencing the uptake and sustainability of family inclusive practice.

Plan for sustainability from the start

Although embedding SST service delivery in the core processes, procedures and systems of an organization helps, our experience is that even successful SST services tend to last only about 5 years unless services continue to support the development of the approach. Many services, including our own, that reported positive experi-

ences of conducting SST stopped when key staff left the organization, intake procedures changed or waiting-list pressures relaxed.
Research and evaluation to inform continual service improvement,
clinical practice discussions to expand clinical skills and the interest
of clinicians, opportunities to write papers, teach others or to apply
SST ideas to new areas or client groups are examples of developments that we have found help sustain SST practice.

We are currently exploring the use of SSFC as a tool for helping
practitioners talk to colleagues across disciplines and across service systems. For example, there is a significant body of research
evidence indicating the value of working with families in Mental
Health Services, Alcohol and Drug Services, Gambling and other
services, and yet families are often equally neglected in these fields
(Copello, et al., 2006; Cohen, et al., 2008). The SSFC approach is an
ideal service delivery framework of practice that allows practitioners across different service systems to respond to complex clients
with co-occurring conditions. The utilitarian nature of SST/SSW/
SSFC means that it appeals to workers with quite different roles
and preferred models of practice. SSFC is proving a useful tool for
us to help the Australian Government achieve its goals of reducing
siloed service delivery.

Further Practical Tips for Implementing SST

We would like to share some specific practical tips that will not
be found in the general implementation literature, but have proven
very useful in our efforts to implement SST approaches, both externally and internally.

Use agencies' existing client contact data

A very effective way of preparing to conduct a SST workshop or
implementation project is to obtain the existing client contact data
of the host organization and to use this data as a rationale for providing a good service to all clients, whether they attend for one
or 20 occasions of care. Often this data will surprise practitioners
because of what Cohen and Cohen (1984) called the *clinician's illusion* where a large amount of a clinician's time is spent working
with a few long-term clients, and a relatively smaller amount of

time working briefly with a lot of clients, thus rendering invisible the high number of clients who attend few sessions (Young, Weir & Rycroft, 2012). Contact data, an example of which is shown in Figure 1, results in a similar shaped graph in most services (although the actually figures change), and hence is a powerful meme or image, allowing implementers to emphasis SST as an effective way to provide a good service to people no matter how often they attend rather than as an economic rationalist intervention aimed at reducing services to the bare minimum.

Figure 1. Client contact data collated for Community Health Counseling Services across the state of Victoria, Australia

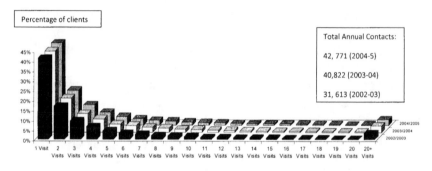

The contact data shown in Figure 1 was used to justify introducing SST to Community Health Services (CHS) across Victoria, Australia but nearly led to a very different response, and thus serves as a cautionary tale. One of the authors (J.Y.) and a colleague (Colin Riess, the former director of The Bouverie Centre) were asked to provide expert consultation to a review of the counselling practices within CHS. Community health centers were set up across Australia in the 1970s to provide a mix of direct services, community development and health promotion, based on a social model of health. Initially conceptualized as closely connected to local communities, these services have been influenced by the different policies of governments over time, but retain a philosophy of being accessible and responsive to all members of the community, especially those who experience disadvantage.

The purpose of the review was to increase the quality of all of the counselling services delivered by the CHS. In line with this goal, an organizational consultant presented what he saw as a worrying statistic that 50%[1] of the annual 35,000 counselling clients attended only 1–2 sessions across the state. He invited the expert panel to provide ideas on how to increase the number of sessions and by implication, the quality of counselling services provided. The Bouverie consultants indicated that it would be futile to attempt to increase the number of sessions because they were consistent with contact data research across the world in almost every service type. Instead, we suggested that training community health counselling staff in SST would possibly improve the experience of clients (and practitioners) in these 1–2 sessions, in line with the core goal of providing a quality service to all potential clients. The final report of the review made recommendations which led to a state-wide and ultimately very effective implementation of SST across community health counselling services.

Present the positives and negatives of introducing SST to everyone involved

Rogers (2003), an early adopter of implementation science, points out that implementation is easier with innovations that provide a good cost/benefit ratio for effort. Hence, pointing out how everyone is likely to benefit from SST approaches is as important as is making room for discussing concerns and potential costs, such as less ongoing working relationships with clients and disruptions to familiar and comfortable ways of working. Cost/benefits will vary for different contexts but some of the key positives we point out include:

- The opportunity for SSFC practitioners to work in co-therapy given the resource friendly nature of SST approaches.
- The likely increase in throughput for managers concerned about waiting lists.
- Opportunities for having open days (Price, 1994) where staff conduct SST at the same time and then discuss the work or celebrate over lunch or drinks.
- Opportunities to create more accessible services.
- The advantage of a service delivery model that allows practitioners to remain loyal to different therapeutic models and

---

1.   The actual figures were higher (60% of clients attended once or twice) as indicated in Figure 1, which we discovered later in this project.

yet all work within a common framework and the potential benefits for team cohesion than can result.

- A service which invites clients to take an active role in their own treatment.
- The opportunity for practitioners and services to carry out their own 'practice-based evidence' and learn from their clients what works best for their clients.

Timing

Finally, even the most well thought out implementation plan will struggle if the timing is not right for the host organization. Restructuring or relocation plans, competing projects, financial difficulties and incompatible policies that need to be implemented can all make it hard or impossible to introduce new practices.

Conclusion

Although the introduction of any new approach into routine practice is usually, as Greenhalgh, et al. (2004, p. 610) point out, "a nonlinear process characterized by multiple shocks, setbacks, and unanticipated events," we have found the implementation of SST approaches to be *relatively* easy compared to other innovations because it appeals to managers and CEOs, to clients and eventually to practitioners, once understood and seen to fit within their underlying practice values.

We have found it a pleasure to help organizations to implement an approach that leads to accessible services for a greater range of clients. Furthermore, the underlying principles of SST continue to inspire respectful and effective approaches to engaging groups historically marginalized by traditional counselling approaches, such as walk-in services described by Slive and Bobele in Chapters 5–6 in this volume (also see Slive and Bobele, 2011), which have shown promise, for example, in making the value of counselling accessible to disadvantaged Hispanic communities.

Clinically, SST has challenged our views about client change and the role of therapy and of the therapist in that change; training colleagues in SST approaches has broadened our views about how SST ideas can be applied and helping small organizations and large state-wide services implement SST/SSW/SSFC has extended our appreciation of how the underlying principles of SST can contribute to making health and welfare services accessible, cost-effective and respectful.

References

Boren, S. A. and Balas, E. A. (1999). Evidence-based quality measurement. *Journal of Ambulatory Care Management*, 22(3), 17–23.

Cohen, P. and Cohen, J. (1984). The clinician's illusion. *Archives of General Psychiatry*, Dec; 41(12), 1178–1182.

Cohen, A. N., Glynn, S. M., Murray-Swank, A.B., Barrio, C., Fisher, E.P., McCutcheon, S.J., Perlick, D.A., Rotondi, A.J., Sayers, S.L., Sherman, M.D., & Dixon, S.B. (2008). The family forum: Directions for the implementation of family psychoeducation for severe mental illness. *Psychiatric Services*, 59(1), 40–48.

Copello, A.G., Templeton, L., and Velleman, R. (2006). Family interventions for drug and alcohol misuse: Is there a best practice? *Current Opinions in Psychiatry*, 19(3), 271–276.

Damschroder, L.J., Aron, D. C., Keith, R.E., Kirsh, S. R., Alexander, J.A., & Lowery, J.C. (2009). Fostering implementation of health services research findings into practice: A consolidated framework for advancing implementation science. *Open Access: http://www.implementationscience.com/content/4/1/50.*

Fixsen, D. L., Naoom, S. F., Blase, K. A., Friedman, R. M., & Wallace, F. (2005). *Implementation research: A synthesis of the literature.* Tampa, FL: University of South Florida, Louis de la Parte Mental Health Research Institute, The National Implementation Research Network.

Greenhalgh, T., Robert, G., Macfarlane, F., Bate, P., & Kyriakidou, O. (2004). Diffusion of innovations in service organizations: Systematic review and recommendations. *The Milbank Quarterly*, 82(4), 581–629.

Grimshaw, J.M., & Eccles, M. P. (2004). Is evidence-based implementation of evidence-based care possible? *Medical Journal of Australia*, 180, S50–S51.

Kemmis, S., & McTaggart, R. (2005). Participatory action research: Communicative action and the public sphere. In N. Denzin (Ed.), *The SAGE handbook of qualitative research* (3rd ed., pp. 559–603). Thousand Oaks, CA: SAGE Publications.

Meyers, D. C., Durlak, J. A., & Wandersman, A. (2012). The quality implementation framework: A synthesis of critical steps in the implementation process. *American Journal of Community Psychology*, 50, 462–480.

O'Neill, I., & Rottem, N. (2012). Reflections and learning from an agency-wide implementation of single session work in family therapy. *Australian and New Zealand Journal of Family Therapy*, 33(1), 70–83.

Pekarik, G. (1991) Relationship of expected and actual treatment duration for adult and child clients. *Journal of Clinical Child Psychology*, 20(2), 121–125.

Price, C. (1994). Open days: Making family therapy accessible in working class suburbs. *Australian and New Zealand Journal of Family Therapy,* 15(4), 191–196.

Proctor, E. K., Landsverk, J., Aarons, G., Chambers, D., Glisson, C., & Mittman, B. (2009). Implementation research in mental health services: An emerging science with conceptual, methodological, and training challenges. *Administration and Policy in Mental Health,* 36, 24–34, DOI 10.1007/s10488-0197-4.

Rogers, E. M. (1995). *Diffusion of innovations.* New York: Free Press.

Rogers, E. M. (2003). *Diffusion of innovations* (5th ed.). New York: Free Press

Slive, A., & Bobele, M. (Eds.) (2011). *When one hour is all you have: Effective therapy for walk-in clients.* Phoenix, AZ: Zeig, Tucker, & Theisen.

Talmon, M. (1990). *Single-session therapy: Maximizing the effect of the first (and often only) therapeutic encounter.* San Francisco: Jossey-Bass.

Wenger, E., & Snyder, W. (2000). Communities of practice: the organizational frontier. *Harvard Business Review,* January–February, 139–145.

Young, J., & Rycroft, P. (1997). Single session therapy: Capturing the moment. *Psychotherapy in Australia,* 4(1), 18–23.

Young, J., Weir, S., and Rycroft, P. (2012). Implementing single session therapy. *Australian and New Zealand Journal of Family Therapy,* 33(1), 84–97.

Young, J., Weir, S., & O'Hanlon, B. (in press). *Family inclusive practice clinical guidelines.* Produced for the Department of Health, Mental Health, Drugs and Regions Division by The Bouverie Centre, Victoria, Australia.

Chapter Eight

Single Session Therapy in Australia: Learning from Teaching

Pamela Rycroft and Jeff Young

"In learning you will teach, and in teaching you will learn."
—PHIL COLLINS

The Bouverie Centre, originally the Bouverie Street Clinic, was established in 1956 as a child guidance clinic. It developed into the only publicly-funded clinical family therapy service in Australia during the 1970s, when Geoff Goding, its founder, travelled to the United States. It was there that he heard Salvador Minuchin, Walter Kempler and others spreading the excitement of those relatively early days of family therapy theory and practice. Very quickly after that, Bouverie became known for its training in family therapy. Over time the training diversified and spread to different audiences, so that now The Bouverie Centre has formal family therapy streams (including introductory workshops, graduate certificates, masters and doctorate level programs). The center also provides a continuing education calendar full of short courses in many areas, from working with various mental health issues to compassion fatigue and No Bullshit Therapy (NBT), and a range of training

Portions of this chapter were presented at the *Capture the Moment: The Inaugural Symposium on Single Session Therapies and Walk-In Services* held on Phillip Island, Victoria, Australia, in March 2012.

programs delivered on-site to various organizations. Throughout this time, it is fair to say that these courses have developed, by and large, directly out of our clinical practice. In particular, we have been stretched to respond to what our clients are asking of us and have improved our own thinking beyond our particular and initial practice habits. This growth led to the creation of specialist clinical teams who took up the particular challenges in these areas of work, always with a focus on families and systemic practice. As our thinking progressed, so did our clinical practice. As our clinical practice progressed, so did our thinking. Consequently, the change transformed our service into the integrated clinical/academic/research center it is today (see www.bouverie.org.au).

In the early 1990s, many robust discussions were had around the question of how to rationalise scarce clinical resources in a responsive, equitable way, without resorting to the common practice of allocating the same (apparently random) number of sessions to each family. Then, in 1994, we heard about staff at the Dalmar Child and Family Centre in New South Wales providing single sessions to clients sitting on their waiting lists, with surprisingly positive outcomes (Price, 1994). A student on a university counselling placement was looking for a research project and this led to Pat Boyhan's research on a single session approach in our clinical service (see Chapter 9 this volume). She introduced us, among other things, to Moshe Talmon's seminal text, *Single Session Therapy: Maximizing the Effect of the First (and Often Only) Therapeutic Encounter* (1990).

Following our own clinical research (Boyhan, 1996) and the establishment of this approach in our general family therapy service (which led to a significant reduction in our waiting list), our colleagues became interested in what we were doing and asked if we would run some training.

Responses to this early dissemination of the SST approach ranged from strong scepticism and suspicion that this was yet another economic rationalist strategy to get health professionals to provide more with less (which was a message being reflected in general political terms at the time) to a quiet excitement about a very different way of responding to an often overwhelming demand. There was a lot of concern at this time about contraindications and exactly which client presentations were appropriate for SST. Our training messages reflected our own journey with this work, as we began to realise that (apart from major risk issues requiring a more pro-active response), there were very few of our client families who were not suitable to be seen within a single session framework, so long as we weren't trying (as we did initially) to predict who would do well with just one session.

During these early years, we had a visit from Ralph Hampson, a member of the original team from the Child and Adolescent Mental Health Service (CAMHS) in Canberra, our national capital, which was the second organisation to introduce SST in Australia (see Hampson, et al., 1999). He talked of SST as having increased morale to the point that it had been the single greatest inspiration in refreshing his interest in clinical work. He went on, though, to mention that this approach tended to be invested in particular colleagues, who had since left, taking the driver for SST with them (Hampson, personal communication, 1995). Hence our later interest in sustainable implementation (see Chapter 7 this volume.)

Our Earliest Training

It was in February, 1996—just less than two years after first trialling it—when our newly formed Single Session Team decided to deliver a day-long training in this approach. A large conference room was filled with social workers, family therapists and generalist counsellors. The history and philosophy of SST were outlined, and our own research findings presented, as well as the growing statistics about the number of families who were reporting that they were doing well after a single therapeutic encounter. The most common question asked in our early workshops was about indicators and contraindications, namely, "How do you know whether SST is appropriate for a client or not?" After initially struggling to answer this question (because we like others found it impossible to predict), we eventually found the answer: "Make sure you don't have to ask this question! Embed SST into your service system so that clients can have further sessions when they need them, whether immediately or at a later time." This question also led to reflections on the research that showed no relationship between diagnosis, severity or complexity and the number of sessions.

Our early workshops included a segment which was headed "Single Session Clinical Practice Versus Ongoing Clinical Work," aiming to investigate the difference between SST and longer-term therapeutic practice. Experiential exercises, verbatim role-plays, and video excerpts were used to demonstrate clinical aspects of single session work. The second half of the day was dedicated to workshopping, in small groups, ideas about implementing SST in the workplace. This was followed up by a panel of folk who had begun to introduce SST in their own work contexts, and who could address some of the issues the small groups came up with. At the end of the day, there was a whole group review of ideas generated, unanswered questions, and uncovered topics. Lastly, the concept of developing a network of professionals interested in SST approaches was canvassed, and a meeting time planned.

Some Useful Exercises

Some of the exercises we developed for this first training proved to be so useful in engaging participants' own reflections that they have stayed with us and remain a part of our current training. One of these involves a guided imagery, in which participants are invited to close their eyes and imagine a first meeting with a client who was fairly typical to their service. They are taken through a series of questions, such as:

What are you thinking and feeling as you are about to meet this person/these people for the first time?

How do you greet your client, build rapport, and explain what is about to happen?

What are your favorite ways of beginning a session, and establishing your job with this client?

As the session continues, how are you feeling about how it's going, what is the ambience of the session?

How do you want to work towards finishing the session?

What are you thinking and feeling at the end of the session and how do you finish the session and book in the next session?

They are asked to set this image aside, and then to imagine the same client coming along to a first session, while making it clear that this is the only session possible, given a sudden move interstate. Participants are taken through a similar guided imagery, involving the same questions, and then asked to compare the two. More recently, we have added specific questions to raise the dilemmas we know many new to SST experience, such as: *What do you focus on, given the many options?* and: *How do you manage the large amount of information you have, given you have little time?* Most often, they will reflect that in the second guided imagery, they are more focused, get down to business sooner, are more energized, are keener to hear what the client needs now, want to ensure that the session stays on track and feel keen to follow up in some way (even if it is to ensure a referral to another professional interstate). This is a great lead into what we see as the philosophy and some of the core principles of SST practice: to work with the client's agenda; to be as helpful as possible in the moment; to keep a clear focus and check in with the client through the session; and to arrange a follow-up, keeping the door open for further contact. The exercise essentially invites our workshop participants to conduct their own virtual SST and offers an insight into how a SST framework would transform their existing approach. It is also a great way to have clinicians 'check in with themselves' in relation to their feelings about offering a single session. There are two major responses: one group reports feeling more pressured to achieve a positive outcome, while others feel liberated by the idea that they could do their best to be helpful knowing that after that, it was up to the client. For example, this exercise alone led to greater lightness and sense of relief recently for a group used to conducting an initial session expecting it to be the first of fifty sessions! It provides an opportunity for each participant to experience how an SST approach would influence their own therapeutic model and counselling style and provides the foundation for vibrant discussions about the nature of collaboration with clients, the locus and level of responsibility for change (clients vis-a-vis practitioners), our often unspoken models and assumptions, and our "default" practice habits.

Another exercise, which came about as a response to beliefs that "real" change can only occur over time, involves having participants reflect firstly on what their own theoretical model teaches them about change, and then to reflect on change in their own personal lives, and finally to compare the two. This highlights beautifully the fact that change can happen in many different ways and in pivotal moments as well as over time. It also identifies that a number of participants discovered a 'disconnect' between their professional theories and their personal experience of change. One participant, for example, had expressed a passionate alliance to the idea that real, deep change can only happen slowly and gradually, requiring long-term work. On doing this exercise, he was taken back to a time when a particular film had changed the course of his life from that time on. Rather than get into debates about the possibility that change can happen in a single encounter, we began to encourage people to seek their own practice-based evidence, and (just as Moshe Talmon had done originally) ASK THEIR CLIENTS about their models of change! In regard to participant's professional theories of change, we found that SST follow-ups with clients proved to be the single greatest factor in challenging therapists' fixed ideas about change.

Our early SST training not only challenged participants' views about change but also challenged practitioners about professional ways of conducting a session. We found that many therapists when introduced to the SST framework found it impolite and therefore difficult to interrupt or be more direct with clients. We argued that if there is limited time, clients usually appreciate focusing on the areas that they bring to the table and are almost reassured if the professional respectfully keeps the conversation on track, re-orientating the discussion if needed. An exercise we developed to help participants explore being more active as practitioners and also experience being actively directed to stay on track involved getting people to role play being a radio interviewer. Keeping strictly to time (3 minutes), we would invite participants to interview a fellow group member as if the interview was conducted on radio with a live audience. With the warning that dead time (silence) is the enemy of radio, interviewers were given instructions to conduct an interesting interview for the listening (general public) audience, whilst maintaining co-operation of the interviewee. Topics ranged from the interviewee's theory of change, their areas of resilience, approach to therapy or special talents. The radio interview exercise is a fun way to experience some of the elements of SST and how it may differ from long-term work. Participants experienced interrupting, being interrupted, and staying on track whilst maintaining the relationship. They discovered the amount of information and engagement that can be elicited in a short amount of time.

The Network Meetings

The first network meeting was held three months after that initial training day. Individuals and agency groups were invited to attend, whether their interest was clinical, research, or implementation. These network meetings continued to be held every few months over the seven years, hosted by the Bouverie Single Session Team. During their lifetime they provided a very stimulating forum in which to think together about different elements of the SST approach. Various people from different therapeutic contexts presented on topics such as:

- *The Research on SST*
  which highlighted the fact that our own research findings echoed the international findings reflecting that for about fifty percent of clients attending a planned SST service, one therapeutic encounter was sufficient

- *Feedback from Clients*
  which included letters from clients, more formal evaluations, and a recorded interview with a family after attending an SST. Almost universally, professionals were delighted, surprised, and came to appreciate how useful it is to get feedback directly from clients about particular sessions and about the SST process.

- *SST and Assessment*
  In response to one of the significant dilemmas for clinicians working in services that expect formal comprehensive assessments as the first step of providing services, this presentation identified the SST approach to assessment is in response to the client's needs, not a broad generic assessment of which only a small portion is relevant to the client's presenting problem.

- *Make Time Your Friend*
  Rather than be pressured by the perceived lack of time when using a SST approach another way is to make time your friend by making overt the time limits and using this constraint to help shape the conversation, usually making it focussed, targeted and responsive to the client's (or worker's) key priorities.

- *Adolescents and SST*
  There was acknowledgment from workers in the youth field that their work is by nature opportunistic. Rather than working hard to engage adolescents to come back, working

in the moment without assuming ongoing work was liberating and often (paradoxically) led to greater engagement

- *SST in a Gambling Service*
  Again, gambling service professionals felt that an SST framework was a natural fit with existing patterns of client contacts and helped them to validate the potential in every single encounter. It also provided a way to engage partners in treatment, given they were not expected to make a major commitment to therapy.

- *Grief and SST*
  Given that grief is a natural process which takes place over time, it was assumed initially not to lend itself to an SST approach. However, a case was presented in which two sessions had helped a young family in acute grief confront the relational impact of losing a central family member and to bridge some distance between surviving members.

- *SST with a Holocaust Survivor and His Family*
  Some of our families agreed for us to film their sessions in order to help professionals learn from them. One such family came along with a Holocaust trauma history and twenty years of nightmares. It was a privilege to be able to deconstruct the single session, hear about the follow-up and to be challenged in our common assumptions that serious, long-term problems require serious, long-term work.

- *Essential Elements of SST*
  With feedback from our clients, we began to formulate our own ideas about what is essential to this way of working: we decided that, for us, a pre-session questionnaire, a phone follow-up, and an open-door policy were essential elements. In terms of the session itself, we encouraged therapists to work from their own preferred models and strengths, while suggesting a broad framework for the session which allowed time to reflect in front of the client before reaching session closure.

At the same time, the word had spread and various health and welfare agencies were asking us to deliver training to their staff on site. We became cautious about this, being very conscious that some managers were picking up on the Single Session Therapy title, making assumptions that this referred to an approach offering just one session to all clients. Interestingly, in our own clinical work, we were also struggling at times to leave behind the idea that good single session work meant that our clients were totally happy after one session. We used the "no-fail" statistics—showing that approximately half of our SST clients would go on to do further work and half would not—to remind devotees of SST that ongoing work was a key part of SST and to remind people convinced that longer term work was essential that a large proportion of their clients exit after one session. Like our SST colleagues, we were keen to describe SST as neither a brief therapy nor a long-term therapy, but as a therapy that reflected the natural contact clients have with a counsellor. Once reconciled to this, we found it liberating in our own clinical program, because it freed us to use our limited resources more creatively. Thus our training informed our own clinical work and vice versa, in a very helpful way. A workshop participant helped us to reframe the SST approach as offering more, not less, to clients, provided that all other options remained available to them following the initial single session.

Ongoing Interest

What became clear to us over time was that interest in SST training persisted, even while our own clinical commitment to this approach waxed and waned. This kept us honest: we needed to keep refreshing our own thinking in relation to SST. Further, clinicians were coming along to learn about it from a different starting point: no longer needing to be persuaded by statistics and research that SST is an ethical approach to the reality that most clients attend services once or twice—now they were asking more questions about *how to do* good Single Session Therapy. We began to hear from practitioners who worked in various contexts wherein they often had only one or at most two chances to do effective work with clients. This provided an avenue for our center into settings we traditionally hadn't been strongly connected with, including rural outreach, hospital ward social work, homeless shelters, working with adolescents and with people in palliative care and other diverse settings. Workers in these services wanted to find out how to optimise the brief clinical opportunity available to them. In response, we began to think harder about the skills involved in offering a single session approach.

The Community Health Project

One of the most valuable boosts to the development of our training came out of a review of Victoria's state-wide Community Health Counselling statistics, (Department of Human Services, Victoria, 2002). The author of this review, John Pead, after noting that more than 50% of all clients across a 3-year period attended once or twice only, recommended training in SST to take best advantage of this phenomenon. This led to all (300+) Community Health counsellors at that time (2004/5) receiving subsidised 2-day training in single session approaches. It also led to the development of training resources: workbooks and increased videoing of our work, as well as more emphasis on role-plays, both by facilitators and participants. In order to be inclusive of practitioners who did not identify as therapists, but who could benefit from this approach, we changed the title from Single Session Therapy to Single Session Work (SSW). We also began to focus on implementation issues, being clear that SSW was a service provision process, not a model of counselling or therapy (see Chapter 7 this volume). With the Community Health project also came the development of a more professionally produced "Implementation Parcel" (Young, Weir, Rycroft & Whittle, 2006), which included a booklet, DVD example of a single session, and various resources (see review by Boyhan, 2006) that could be adapted for those interested in implementing SSW across their service.

The training grew in content at this time, from one day to two days, in order to include ideas and exercises on implementation. Further, we were receiving feedback from participants that they no longer needed or wanted to be "persuaded" by the research on the efficacy of SST—they wanted to know more about *what needs to happen to make a single session approach as effective as possible and how to implement it into their organization*. A broad template for a single session was developed, as were (particularly for the Community Health context) step-by-step guidelines for intake and follow-up calls. The training structure changed to follow the SSW process, so that, after a brief introduction and history of SST, participants were taken through an intake process (principles, demonstration, and role-play), with the role-play "client" in each small group filling out a mock pre-session questionnaire to be used later in the role-play of the face-to-face session. Similarly with the session itself and the follow-up call, so that everyone heard about the process in detail, watched a demonstration, and had a go at it themselves.

Apart from the demonstration DVD, which had involved an enactment of SST with an individual '"client," we also showed tapes of real clinical sessions with families who had given permission. These were always popular; however, their use became more limited as our audiences began to include professionals from diverse settings, many of whom did not identify as therapists. We spent more time workshopping ways in which participants could engage colleagues and managers in a process of implementation.

Our Current Training

We continue to train a variety of professionals, from alcohol and other drug (AOD) services, gambling services, mental health, university counselling and a range of non-government agencies across the state, and now also across state lines.

By and large, the major change most recently in our training is a deconstruction of some of the clinical skills that we believe are involved in providing a high-quality single session. Ideas from this work have been incorporated into other training contexts (e.g., in assisting clinicians to develop frameworks for involving families in work which is primarily individual), and this has honed the need for a skills-based approach to training, while giving a consistent message that clinicians need to work from their existing strengths. So, apart from the more standard 2-day training in SST on offer to health and welfare professionals, we have developed training on Single Session Family Consultations for the many clinicians who are being asked to include family members in their work, but who don't identify as family therapists. Single session work as a "container" is enormously helpful in this context.

The skills focus means that we encourage conversations and experiential exercises around particular aspects of this work, building on attitudes and a skill set so that it is experienced as more accessible. We include skills such as:

- Negotiating a joint session with an individual client
- Creating a shared agenda, and establishing the clients' priorities
- 'Checking in' with clients
- Interrupting respectfully
- Staying on track

- Using time efficiently
- Providing honest, clear and helpful reflections
- Ending well, and
- Following up with clients

These skills are taught through facilitator demonstration, use of DVD examples (*Focus on Families*, 2006; *From Individual to Families—Single Session Family Consultations*, 2012) and participant role-play. Rather than role-playing an entire SSW session, it has proved to be less daunting and more efficient to "chunk" a few skills and have small groups practise these together, giving each other clear feedback about one thing they really liked, and one thing that could have happened differently. The experience of "sitting in the shoes of" particular family members, apart from conducting the role-play session, provides great learning. This structure also allows for greater participation across the large group. One exercise we have added more recently—"Real SSW"—invites participants to interview each other in pairs for 15 minutes each using the clinical principles we have introduced them to:

- Viewing each contact as complete in itself
- Working with a greater sense of urgency to clarify what needs to be achieved in this contact
- Prioritizing what to work on during the session
- Checking in with the client to ensure that the session is on track
- Sharing any thoughts and ideas with the 'client' (particularly with reference to the client's own agenda)

In this case, however, they are asked to talk with each other about actual life issues, rather than role-playing. It seems that this exercise, possibly more than any other, surprises and delights them when they realise how helpful such a brief, focused experience can be.

We tend to be training three major groups these days:

- Individual therapists/counsellors from a range of contexts
- Mental health/Alcohol and Other Drugs/Gambling service workers, who tend to identify as case managers, and
- Whole teams (university counselling services; palliative care teams; child and adolescent mental health teams; ABI (Acquired Brain Injury) and disability workers, hospital in the home workers)

The experience of training an entire Community Health counselling workforce taught us a number of things (see Chapter 7 this volume) including that there is a distinct advantage, in terms of sustainability, when team leaders and managers are included in both training and implementation. The nomination of "champions" or "lead clinicians" who receive ongoing support has also been a great development. One such champion from an outlying area of Melbourne was keen enough to prepare and co-train with one of the authors, with a view to training others in her broader service.

The Inaugural International Symposium on SST and Walk-In Services

In March, 2012 the first SST "conference" was held in Melbourne. This brought together a number of key authors and researchers in the field, including the original Kaiser Permanente SST team: Moshe Talmon, Michael Hoyt and Robert Rosenbaum. It also brought to us practice ideas and stunning outcome data from Walk-In services, with presentations from Arnie Slive and his colleagues, Monte Bobele, Nancy McElheran, Lee Hackney and Margie Oakander (see Chapters 5, 6, 10 this volume). Further, there were many presentations from more local practitioners, who had adapted SST to their practice in varied and creative ways. The symposium generated some very positive outcomes, including the envisioning of an international network of SST practitioners supported via a website hosted by The Bouverie Centre (see www. Bouverie.org.au), with the potential to include written material, resources, and DVDs.

Summary and Reflections

The Bouverie Centre has offered training in SST/SSW for 18 years. It has never ceased to be a popular training option, for individual practitioners, teams and whole organisations. This has led us to continue refreshing the training, and alongside this, our own practice. At a time recently when we realised that we had put a lot of resource into our external training while neglecting our own staff, clinicians at The Bouverie Centre were engaged in an SST action learning group. As distinct from seeing single session work as a separate "arm" of our clinical work, it was integrated into our regular clinical practice such that all new families are expected to be seen within a SST framework, with two therapists, one of whom follows up and continues with the family, while the second therapist becomes "consultant" to the first, and conducts a review of the work at session six, should the family continue to that point. This project created a rich forum for discussions between trainers and clinicians and highlighted a number of concerns held by staff in relation to SST work (O'Neill & Rottem, 2012). Interestingly, some staff members continue to see SST as something extra demanded of them, or of their trainees, and tend to "default" to their more usual clinical practice habits. Rather than seeing this as a problem, in some ways it is helpful in reminding us of the very human issues in implementation. For example, how does an organisation which values difference and individual choices implement an "across the board" approach to clinical practice?

Our early training experience included reviews of the research literature and reported data on how many clients attended only once. Initially, we ourselves had found it difficult to believe that useful therapeutic work could occur in single encounters. Once we had the benefit of learning from our own clients that it could, we may well have come across (and some participant feedback suggested this) as SSW zealots. As time went on, we positioned ourselves a little differently, suggesting that participants start from their own contact data and carry out their own clinical research rather than taking our word for it. In this way, the review of community services counselling contact data provided an immense springboard from which to assist counsellors in capitalizing on the client contact available to them.

The major changes across time in our training could be summed up in the following:

- The development of various trainings tailored to various groups (from two-hour introductions to the philosophy and practice of SST to a two-day workshop with follow-up consultations
- The inclusion of implementation ideas (inviting organizations to consider how and where an SST approach may fit within their service)
- Greater clarity about the value of the clinical practice principles inherent in SST, regardless of whether organizations take on SST as a whole service approach

- An ever-widening group of examples of applications of these ideas (As *a framework for providing "constructive minimalist" intervention* to those clients who can take advantage of this; as a non-blaming way to *provide a service to clients who attend only irregularly;* a*s a way to engage clients* who wouldn't otherwise attend; as a *second opinion* or *live consultation* within the context of ongoing work; as *an extension of an intake process* when normal intake has not sufficiently established that the client is appropriate for the service; as *a framework for setting a contract* and/or *including workers from other systems.*)
- Focusing on encouraging organizations to consider SST as a vehicle for staff development and team-building. We provide examples from groups we have worked with, where SST has given professional groups reason to co-work, to share ideas about what works best for their clients, to dedicate time to reflecting together and to learn together from clients' feedback at follow-up.
- The development of skills-based training for professionals who don't identify as therapists, or who engage in "incidental counselling."
- The development of various resources: a workbook, an implementation package, and various DVD examples (www. bouverie.org.au).
- The integration of SST values into the training itself: we work to assess what participants most want from the training, check in with them across the training, and follow them up afterwards, offering an "open door" to individuals and organizations who may need support in implementing SST.

When we began conducting single session training, SOME colleagues were outraged by the title and what they thought SST stood for: actively focusing on reducing the number of contacts; saving money by ignoring the importance of the therapeutic relationship; a conspiracy of economic rationalists and anti-therapy bureaucrats. By the end of our training, a significant portion of participants would come around to seeing SST as a respectful approach that allows therapists to be using their expertise at the same time as providing a service that actively invites clients' expertise on their own lives. We often get to hear the irony that, when we work as if the first session may also be the last, and "roll up our sleeves" to be as helpful as possible in each contact, clients engage well and often return for further single sessions.

A gratifying question often asked these days within the training groups goes something like: "…but isn't this just good practice?" We agree.

References

Boyhan, P. (1996). Clients' perceptions of single session consultations as an option waiting for family therapy. *Australian and New Zealand Journal of Family Therapy*, 17(2), 85–96.

Boyhan, P. (2006). DVD and User's guide; SSW Implementation Booklet; Compact Disc with electronic versions of all necessary SSW paperwork; and Detailed Flow Charts *Journal of Family Studies*, 12(2), 286–290.

Department of Human Services, Victoria. (2002). *Review of counselling services in community health: discussion paper.* Primary and Community Health Branch, Rural and Regional Health and Aged Services Division, Melbourne.

Focus on families: Interviews with Bouverie's family therapists. (2006, DVD). The Bouverie Centre, La Trobe University, Brunswick, Victoria, Australia.

From individual to families: Single session family consultations. (2012, DVD). Produced in partnership by The Bouverie Centre and NADA.

Hampson, R., O'Hanlon, J., Franklin, A., Pentony, M., Fridgant, L. & Heins, T. (1999). The place of single session family consultations: five years' experience in Canberra. *Australian and New Zealand Journal of Family Therapy*, 20(4), 195–200.

O'Neill, I. & Rottem, N. (2012). Reflections and learning from an agency-wide implementation of single session work in family therapy. *Australian and New Zealand Journal of Family Therapy*, 33(1), 70–83.

Price, C. (1994). Open days: making family therapy accessible in working class suburbs. *Australian and New Zealand Journal of Family Therapy*, 15(4), 191–196.

Talmon, M. (1990). *Single session therapy: Maximizing the effect of the first (and often only) therapeutic encounter.* San Francisco: Jossey-Bass.

Young, J., Weir, S., & Rycroft, P. (2012). Implementing single session therapy. *Australian and New Zealand Journal of Family Therapy*, 33(1), 80–96.

Young, J., Weir, S., Rycroft, P., & Whittle, T. (2006). *Single session work (SSW) implementation resource parcel.* The Bouverie Centre, La Trobe University, Melbourne, Australia.

Chapter Nine

Innovative Uses for Single Session Therapy: Two Case Studies

Patricia A. Boyhan

In the 1990s, I was completing a post-graduate placement at Bouverie Centre (then known as Bouverie Family Therapy Centre) in Melbourne, Australia. There was a conservative government in power, and economic policies were impacting funding for both government and not-for-profit organizations. This contributed to long waiting lists in agencies and mental health facilities, and Bouverie Centre was anxious to develop waiting-list management strategies.

Bouverie staff members had attended a family therapy conference the previous year, when Dalmar Child and Family Therapy Services from Penrith, New South Wales, presented results from their pilot project which used single session therapy (SST) as a waiting-list management tool (Price, 1994). Dalmar had been experiencing government cutbacks, associated with inadequate resources in

I would like to acknowledge the professional support and encouragement I received from Rosalie Hearne when I originally joined CatholicCare. Her own enthusiasm for innovative practice and cross-cultural counselling, and her encouragement of me, enabled the implementation of SST as an option for clients who otherwise would have waited on long waiting lists. It also opened the learning opportunity for new and innovative ways to use SST, as shown in the presentation of the two cases that follow.

I am also grateful to St. Luke's Innovative Resources, Bendigo, for granting permission for the "Strength Cards for Kids" to be reproduced in this chapter (the an economically disadvantaged area, resulting in waiting lists of six months or longer for families seeking therapy in Sydney's outer western suburbs.

I flew to New South Wales and trained with the Dalmar therapists. After I returned to Melbourne, the SST Team was established at Bouverie and of the first 50 families who were the subjects for my research project, 36 families agreed to have their data used. Client families who were deemed suitable for a single session consultation (that is those who were not legal/protective referrals, nor those who would normally be referred directly to Bouverie's specialist teams, e.g., Sexual Abuse, Acquired Brain Injury, Serious Mental Illness, and HIV/AIDS) were offered the option of a one-off consultation, as an alternative to waiting for approximately three months. Despite the inclusion/exclusion criteria adopted by Bouverie, a range of problems of varying complexity (which had not been disclosed at telephone intake) was presented at consultations. These included sibling incest, grief and loss due to death, domestic violence, alcohol and drug misuse and other serious issues. By far the major problem area was related to conflict in the parent/child context, both for adult and dependent children. In the study, 'conflict' varied from relatively minor issues, such as one case of childhood sleeping disorder, through to more serious issues, such as a mother threatening to "throw out" her 10-year-old son (Boyhan, 1996).

At the same time as the Bouverie study was being conducted, therapists at a Child and Adolescent Mental Health Facility in Canberra, with waiting lists of up to 5 months, were trialling SST to assist with high unmet demand for service (Hampson, et al., 1999). Results of this study, as well as those of Price (1994) and Boyhan (1996) were compared and indicated a high level of client satisfaction with the services (Boyhan, 1996) and as a result, SST was adopted as a viable alternative to allowing clients to languish unattended on long waiting lists.

---

original cards appear in color). The cards have been a valuable resource across my professional career, as have many more of their products. Additional thanks to Maggie Loffler and Dr. Lawrie Moloney for assistance with editing, and to Cesca Gerner for invaluable IT support.

Finally, I am indebted to my clients for trusting me to share their stories. I continue to learn from them and am constantly inspired by their resilience in the face of adversity.

Portions of this chapter were presented as part of the symposium, *Capture the Moment: The Inaugural Symposium on Single-Session Therapies and Walk-In Services*, held on Phillip Island, Victoria, Australia, in March 2012.

After graduating, I was appointed to a position in a family and relationship counselling agency (CatholicCare, then known as Centacare Catholic Family Services) where, in order to deal with waiting lists, I continued to use SST in my own practice and also to train other staff members. As I became more experienced, however, I discovered SST was a valuable strategy to encourage reluctant participants to attend counselling (especially adolescents) and was also far more acceptable to clients in our cross-cultural work, where due to stigma, shame and denial around mental health problems, there was often resistance to seeking assistance for psychological difficulties.

This chapter will focus on two case studies in which SST was found to be a successful innovative intervention. The first involved a 12-year-old girl whose parents were concerned about her risk-taking behavior, but who was refusing to attend counselling with them. The second was a highly complex cross-cultural case in which serendipity provided an opportunity for the therapists "to capture the moment" and "to let the client lead the way" (Talmon, 2001). In both cases, names and other identifying features have been changed to protect privacy.

Case 1: Reluctant Adolescent

Josephine and Tom recontacted CatholicCare, with concerns about their 12-year-old daughter (Lucy). They were former clients having attended two years previously with their son Josh (then 16 years of age) who, at that time, was using illicit drugs. Josh had been referred to a drug and alcohol specialist youth service, and Josephine, Tom, Josh, and Lucy were seen for family therapy at CatholicCare. The outcome had been successful and Josh had returned to school and re-engaged with his former friendship group, who were not drug users. The therapist who worked with the family had subsequently left the agency and when Josephine and Tom recontacted, I was asked to see them.

The story Josephine and Tom told at the intake session was very worrying. Although Josh was continuing to do well, Lucy had become defiant and oppositional. She appeared to be achieving and well-connected at school, but at home "she was a nightmare." She was staying out at night, climbing out of her bedroom window and going to nightclubs with an older group of friends. Her parents believed she was at serious risk of becoming involved in drugs ("like her brother"), and also were fearful of her being attacked or taken advantage of by older men. They said although she was only 12 she looked much older when she was "dressed up." They had contacted the school counsellor, but after attending a couple of times, Lucy refused to continue. She was also adamant she was not returning to CatholicCare. Lucy believed she was fine—her parents needed to stop being over-protective and let her enjoy life.

Josephine, Tom and I discussed appropriate boundaries for a 12 year old; what their responsibilities and rights were as her parents; whether there had been a trigger for the change in Lucy's behavior; what they had tried already; what had worked/what had not. We also explored their parenting styles and some family-of-origin issues in an endeavor to identify what had shaped their attitudes to parenting and family life. Josephine had been born in India and had been sent to boarding school as a young child. She was anxious to ensure her children had a happier childhood than she had experienced; however, she acknowledged she set high standards as she wanted them to succeed academically. She also had an expectation that both children would do a few chores in the house. Tom, who was several years older than Josephine, said he also had a pretty tough time growing up but was probably a "bit more laid back" in his parenting attitudes. Despite this, he tried to be supportive and did not argue about parenting issues in front of the children. Both parents said they encouraged Josh and Lucy to bring friends home and their house was a bit of a "drop-in center" for young people in the area.

All this sounded relatively positive from my perspective, and I was curious and puzzled about what was happening in the "system." I agreed with Josephine and Tom that it would be helpful to get Lucy along to counselling and I saw an opportunity for SST. After explaining the fundamentals of SST, I obtained permission from Josephine and Tom to write to Lucy inviting her to come in for a single session of therapy, and to send her a questionnaire (see Table 1). I also took the opportunity to do some 'seeding' with the parents. I explained my primary aim would be for Lucy to be given the opportunity to tell her story from her 'map of the world'. I asked them not to be reactive, not to assume they were being judged or that they had to defend their position to Lucy, or to me.

My reason for working this way is that I believe it is important for children and young people to be given a voice in the counselling room, without too much focus on 'the truth'. A genuine acknowledgement of 'their experience and reality' often provides the trigger for an openness to explore other possibilities—and other

Table 1: One-Off Consultation Questionnaire for Reluctant Participants

Welcome to CatholicCare. Thank you for agreeing to attend a single session of therapy.

To assist us to maximize the effectiveness of the consultation, would you please take the time to fill out the following information and bring to the session with you.

Family name _____

Name of person filling out the form _____

What are the main problems which you bring to counselling?

1. Greatest problem

   _____

2. Second greatest problem

   _____

What other problems are you coping with now?

_____

Are there any issues you DO NOT want to discuss in counselling?

_____

How do you think counselling could help you deal with the problem(s)?

_____

If counselling was successful, what would you and your family be doing differently?

_____

Since speaking with the counsellor, what have you noticed happening to you and your family that you would like to keep happening in the future?

_____

'truths'. I reassured Josephine and Tom I would not allow Lucy to be abusive or disruptive, but I was hoping that, as the significant adults in Lucy's life for that short period, we could tolerate a bit of acting out. Tom and Josephine appeared to understand and accept these concepts and I prepared and sent a letter to Lucy.

A week or so later I heard from Lucy. She agreed to come in for the single session, but stipulated it would only be with her father. She did not want her mother to attend. She said she had discussed this with her parents and they had agreed. I gave her an appointment within the next few days.

When Tom and Lucy arrived I went to greet them and was somewhat thrown off guard by the sight of Lucy. She was extremely tall, physically developed, and looked about 19 years of age. I immediately understood her parents' anxiety about her vulnerability in the risky situations to which she was exposing herself. However, once we entered the counselling room and she started talking, I realised her looks were deceiving. She was clearly functioning within a developmental range of a 12 year old, with very little emotional congruity and with a strong sense of entitlement and self-focus. Despite this, I found her likeable and engaging and I was looking forward to getting to know her more in the next 90 minutes or so.

I used the questionnaire to focus on what Lucy was prepared to discuss and then she launched into a diatribe about what old-fashioned parents she had, how they would not allow her to have fun and enjoy life, even though she was achieving good results at school. She said she was the "ONLY" person in her friendship group whose parents had such out-dated ideas and she was not prepared to let them "ruin her life." She talked about the problems her brother had been through and said she had learnt from his mistakes. She was not going to use drugs and she was quite capable of keeping herself safe when she went out. She said she was staying with friends when she stayed out beyond her curfew, because she didn't want to go home and be hassled by her mother and father. After I took time to acknowledge her map of the world, I encouraged her to talk about what she enjoyed in her life, even though she thought her parents were over-protective. She was able to acknowledge some good things, especially the fact that her parents were welcoming to her friends. She said some of her friends thought her parents were "awesome, but they didn't have to live with them." I attempted to explore with her what might be reasonable expectations of parents with a 12 year old, and what might be reasonable for a 12 year old to accept in terms of boundaries and limitations. However, this intervention did not go well and she reverted to her belligerent stance. At this stage I was feeling fairly powerless and inwardly empathized with her parents' struggle.

Tom had been well-controlled in the session—he had obviously taken notice of the 'seeding' I had done when we discussed SST in the earlier session with Josephine. He had not attempted to defend his position, and had reflected back to his daughter he understood her need to establish her independence. He had, however, left most of 'the work' to me. Then he suddenly became proactive. He told Lucy he was going to share a family secret which he had held for many years. Her mother knew the secret, but he had not shared it with Josh or Lucy before. He had been married when he was very young and had a daughter. He had been through a very nasty divorce and his former wife would not allow him to have contact with his daughter. This caused him enormous grief as he longed to see her and to be part of her life. He told Lucy, because he had already lost one daughter, she was incredibly precious to him and he lived in fear of losing her also. He MUST do everything in his power to protect and keep her safe. By this time both Lucy and Tom were in tears, and I was using all my skills to contain my own emotional response.

I felt privileged to have witnessed a significant event. For Tom and Lucy to have reached such depth in a single session was truly remarkable, but I was struggling to know where to take it from there. Being mindful of my agreement with Lucy that she had only committed to one session I did not want to overstep her boundaries by suggesting further counselling. After Tom and Lucy had regained composure I asked them what they thought would be helpful for the future. I commended them both for what they had achieved that day and ran through the single session options, i.e., go away and try any interventions suggested with a follow-up phone call in about 4 weeks or book another SST. Lucy said she needed time to think about the implications of having a sister, but she would like to come back to counselling with both her parents. We booked another appointment.

Over the next few days I continued to reflect on the session. I was confident SST had provided an opportunity to engage with Lucy which would not otherwise have been available. Nonetheless, I was curious about why Tom had not disclosed the family secret in other settings. After all, the family had attended counselling for an extended period two years earlier when Josh was using drugs. Why didn't he disclose then? What was different for him this time? I remembered Moshe Talmon's workshop (Talmon, 2001) when he said, "Success in psychotherapy is dependent on timing. Readiness allows for change to occur." I decided to ring Tom to check it out with him.

During our telephone conversation Tom told me there was something quite significant for him in the SST. He said he realised this might be the last chance he had to speak with Lucy about the existence of her sister with the support of a professional in the room. Therefore, Tom had taken the risk and was very pleased with the outcome. After the SST, he and Josephine had a family meeting and also told Josh about his half-sister.

The family came for a few more sessions and reached some agreements about boundaries for Lucy. Although she remained feisty, she was no longer defiant and oppositional. At the final session, I reinforced the SST 'open door' policy ensuring the family knew they could contact me for a telephone catch-up, or to book another appointment at any time in the future

Reflection

SST had proven to be an effective way to engage a very reluctant adolescent, but had also been a catalyst that provided an opportunity for Tom to finally talk about his grief and to share the loss with his family. Being mindful that the change process begins before the session occurs and continues well after, I hoped for ongoing growth in family relationships as each person realized the importance of connection and support between all members, regardless of the family hierarchy. I was also hopeful Lucy had learnt her parents could be vulnerable, too, and that the compassion she expressed towards her father in the SST would be part of her enduring relationship with them. When providing SST training, I am frequently challenged about 'the lack of depth' able to be achieved in one session. This case example (and many more I could discuss) reinforces the power of capturing the moment when clients are at 'the height of readiness for change' and shows that 'depth' does not always depend on length or frequency of the counselling process.

Case 2: Cross-Cultural Counselling

CatholicCare has long been considered a leader in the field of cross-cultural counselling in Melbourne, Victoria. This started in the 1990s following a wave of refugees from Vietnam, and has continued through to today when we provide support via our Refugee & Settlement and Asylum Seeker Programs to people from Africa, Afghanistan, Burma, and other war-torn countries. We have always worked with cultural guides from a range of different ethnic backgrounds and these are an excellent resource for advice and training.

An ongoing challenge to therapists is the reluctance of some cultures to attend 'therapy', which is negatively associated with mental health disorders and not accepted by some communities. In fact, for many people having a relative with a mental health disorder is a source of stigma and shame. SST has been used successfully to engage with some of these clients.

In the early 2000s our services included a Vietnamese Family Support Group, with Vietnamese practitioners working alongside non-Vietnamese therapists, to try to provide for the needs of a large Vietnamese community which had come to Australia post the Vietnam War. The following case sets out the story of one family with multiple issues, and also provides some insight into the challenges faced by workers attempting to deal with complex family relationships/family law/migration law/cultural presentations, and how SST was helpful in the process. The case laid a foundation for the work we have continued to the present day.

Due to the complexity of the case I have provided a genogram below and the reader is invited to use it as a guide.

I was contacted by one of our Vietnamese Family Support Workers who was working with a recently-arrived Vietnamese man. She told me this story. Tran and Bing lived in Vietnam with their two children, but life was difficult following the Vietnamese/American war. Tran decided to come to Australia to establish a better life and then send

Figure 1. Cross-Cultural Genogram

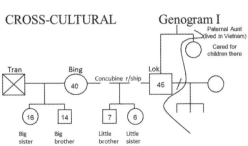

for his family. After he left Vietnam, Bing lived as a concubine with another family, which was quite culturally acceptable, and was the only option she saw for herself, as she needed assistance to care for her children. She and her lover/patron (Lok) had two more children. When Tran arranged for Bing to come to Australia she brought her two older children and left the two younger ones in the care of their paternal aunt, who had been a significant person in their lives. Lok continued to provide for his children and to see them regularly. Bing was heartbroken at the loss of her two younger children and always hoped she could find a way to be reunited with them.

Tran and Bing were extremely successful in establishing a business in Australia and became well connected in the Vietnamese community. The two older children thrived and achieved academically. Unfortunately, after several years Tran died. Bing immediately started to plan reunification of her family. She wrote to Lok and asked him to leave his wife and family and bring their children to Australia. She offered to pay airfares and said she would live with him in a de facto relationship and apply to sponsor him once he came to Australia. Lok thought this would be a wonderful opportunity for him and the two children and after much soul-searching he agreed to leave his family in Vietnam.

On the day he arrived in Australia, Lok said that Bing and the two older children met him at the airport and took the two younger children, and that Bing told Lok she was not prepared to see him again, and he would not have contact with the children. Lok was devastated—he had 'abandoned' his family in Vietnam and now found himself alone in Australia with no source of support. He was referred to CatholicCare and a worker was appointed as his Case Manager.

The Vietnamese Family Support Team arranged for temporary accommodation and linked Lok into a sympathetic family. They consulted with a migration law specialist, as Lok did not want to return to Vietnam and his legal status was precarious. His case manager also met with Bing to discuss the possibility of Lok having some contact with his children. Within the Team there was significant concern for the children, given that their father had been a constant figure in their young lives and they had suddenly been separated from him, when they had been whisked away by their mother and siblings at the airport. How well were they coping? Bing was adamant she would not allow Lok access to the children. She said there had been domestic violence in their relationship when she was his concubine, she had no feelings for him, her two older children were hostile towards him and none of them wanted him to be part of their lives. She reassured the worker the younger children had settled into their new home and were enjoying being with their siblings and family friends.

It was at this stage the case manager and the clinical practice director (Rosalie Hearne) approached me for a consultation. Rosalie also had experience in SST and together we developed a plan. Bing would be asked to come in for a single session of therapy, with no obligation to engage in future sessions. She would be invited to bring a support person. Lok would also attend with his case manager. The aim would be to provide Lok with the opportunity to see his children in a supervised space and for Bing and Lok to discuss options. Bing reluctantly agreed to attend, but only for one session.

On the day of the SST we had fortunately booked a large room as we had the following attendees:

1. Bing (English and Vietnamese speaking)
2. Big Sister (English and Vietnamese speaking)
3. Big Brother (English and Vietnamese speaking)
4. Little Sister (Vietnamese speaking)
5. Little Brother (Vietnamese speaking)
6. Bing's support person and her infant in a pram (English and Vietnamese speaking)
7. Lok (Vietnamese speaking)
8. Lok's case manager (English and Vietnamese speaking)
9. An independent translator (multi-lingual)
10. Therapist Rosalie (English speaking)
11. Therapist Pat (English speaking).

After we had settled Bing, the children and her support person in the room, Lok and his case manager joined us. Little Sister immediately ran to her mother, buried her face in her mother's lap and appeared to be frightened. Rosalie and I had previously developed a trusting synergy as co-counsellors and we immediately recognized we were both concerned we may have set up a situation where the children could be exposed to trauma. To put some space between the two younger children and their father she asked them, via the interpreter, if they would like to go into her office, which was off to the side of the counselling room. From there they were able to see their mother and older siblings, but their father was out of their sight. The children agreed and Rosalie guided them through. As she was leaving her office she noticed a box of Strength Cards for Kids (St. Luke's Strength Cards for Kids, 1996), which are brightly colored cards, each depicting a cartoon of an animal and nominating a 'strength'. Rosalie thought the children might like to play with them, so she scattered them on the floor. (*It is important to point out here that we had been told by our Vietnamese colleagues these cards were not a culturally appropriate resource to use with Vietnamese communities as it is considered disrespectful to depict people as animals. However, Rosalie presumed they would stay in her office and not be seen by the adult members of the group.*)

Rosalie returned to the counselling room and we commenced the engagement process. Bing presented as an extremely powerful woman, with strong opinions and a clear vision of what she wanted for her family. She spoke about her successful business and the stable home she could provide for the four children, as well as the opportunities available to them, both socially and academically. Big Sister was also strong and eager to support her mother. She spoke disdainfully about Lok and referred to his physical abuse of her mother when they were living with him and his family in Vietnam. Lok appeared to be demoralized, disconnected, and somewhat bewildered. He was obviously still recovering from the shock of how things had changed so dramatically for him. Despite this, he was able to speak decisively about the fact that he loved his children, he had sacrificed a great deal to come to Australia, and he wanted to have ongoing contact with the children.

There were significant difficulties with the mixture of English/ Non-English speaking participants, and Rosalie and I were challenged with the process of working with an interpreter, and trying to ensure all conversations were understood and acknowledged. Additionally, despite the best efforts of all professionals involved, Bing would not negotiate and Lok was helpless in the face of the strength of the liaison between Big Sister and Bing. We appeared to have hit an impasse.

THEN change occurred. The younger children returned to the group, and started showing the Strength Cards to their mother and older siblings. Despite the advice we had received from our Vietnamese colleagues, the whole group became engaged with the cards. Rosalie and I again exchanged glances. We believed serendipity had intervened and provided us with an opportunity, but we remained cautious. Moshe Talmon's (2001 workshop) voice was in my head: "Take advantage of the moment"; "The strength is with the client—let the client lead"; "Follow the client—let the client teach you"; "Therapist should not be right, rather be useful"; and "…. an important part of the therapeutic process is the humble knowledge that we do not know everything and what we do know might or might not be useful for the individual client" (Talmon, 1990, p. 122). So, with a nod of our heads we decided to take a chance and use the opportunity that had arisen. Neither of us dared to look at the Vietnamese case manager! We collected all the cards and spread them on the floor in the middle of the group. Everyone was invited to choose a card and we would then have a discussion. We were aware there would be differences in how family members used the cards, depending on their understanding of English. Bing, Big Sister and Big Brother's choices would be influenced by both the picture and the strength caption, while Lok and the 2 younger children would only use the pictures to guide their choices.

Lok's choice:

Figure 2. I forgive people when they make mistakes.

Lok could not read the strength caption, but when asked why he chose his card, he replied through the interpreter "Families should stay together". Rosalie said she noticed one fish was swimming in a different direction to the others, and as Lok's eyes filled with tears, he merely responded "Yes!"

Big Brother's choice:

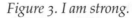

Figure 3. I am strong.

Big Brother was asked to give feedback and he said he needed to be strong as he was "the man" in the family and needed to help his mother, especially now that his younger brother and sister had come to live with them.

Little Brother's choice:

Figure 4. I am an interesting person.

Little Brother could not read the strength caption, but when asked why he chose his card he said "I want to be like my brother." Big Sister's choice:

Figure 5. I stick up for myself.

Big Sister's choice was self-explanatory, but she had no hesitation in telling everyone in the room why she chose her card and gave a clear message she was determined and forthright.

Little Sister's choice:

Figure 6. I have good manners.

Little Sister was not able to read the strength caption, but she was eager to talk about the picture. She stayed close to her mother and through the interpreter said she was the little kangaroo in the mother's pouch. The kangaroo holding down the fence was Dad and he was going to let the wire go and hurt her and her mother. Both Rosalie and I were shocked as we had both anticipated the kangaroo holding down the fence would be Big Sister, attempting to help her mother. Lok was also visibly disturbed by Little Sister's story and he spoke quickly to his case manager, who interpreted back to the group that he had never hurt Little Sister and he had no intention of harming anyone now. He asked Little Sister why she was frightened of him, but she refused to answer and clung to her mother.

Bing's choice:

Figure 7. I help others.

Bing said her job was to help her children and she would make sure they had everything they needed to be protected and safe. Having her family together was very important for them all, and she was determined to provide a good life for them in Australia.

At this stage Lok interrupted and said that in his culture "children belonged with their mother—mothers looked after the children". For the good of his children he would withdraw from their lives and allow them to connect with their new family. He would not cause any more problems for the family, but he wanted the children to understand he loved them and he would miss them for the rest of his life.

Again, there was a sudden shift in the room. Bing softened and thanked Lok for accepting how important it was for the younger children to be with their family. She acknowledged he and his sister had cared for the children well in Vietnam after she left them behind, and she would always be grateful for that. She then said she would allow Lok to see the children, as long as the visits were supervised. She asked her support person (a personal friend) if Lok could visit the children at her home. The support person agreed. Arrangements were made, and after thanking everyone for their participation, acknowledging the achievements they had all accomplished, and reinforcing our 'open door' policy, Rosalie and I ended the session.

Reflections

SST had provided an opportunity to engage a reluctant participant (Bing) who had been refusing to attend counselling with Lok. The SST option appeared to be less challenging to her, as she was not being asked to commit to anything other than a 'one-off'. It also provided an opportunity for the whole family to come together, with appropriate support people. The older siblings would not have come to counselling, nor would the younger children's voices have been heard, if the significant adults in their lives had not agreed to SST.

The session itself was challenging, with a mix of participants with different language proficiencies (English speaking, Vietnamese speaking, and multi-lingual). It took time and patience for conversations to be interpreted, and spontaneity could have been lost without a skilled and experienced Interpreter.

There was a significant power imbalance between Lok and Bing, which was a complete reversal to their previous relationship. To be helpful in the SST, Rosalie and I needed to remain neutral and non-judgmental, although we were challenged by, and empathized with, each of the participants:

- What was it like for Lok to 'abandon' his family in Vietnam and come to Australia trusting in the commitment made by Bing that she would live with him and support his application for residency, only to find on arrival it had all been a lie? What were his options now? Could he go back to Vietnam and reconnect with his family? What about the shame and loss of 'face'? How could he survive in Australia? What hope did he have of being granted residency? BUT, what about his alleged violence towards Bing, which had been witnessed by Big Brother and Big Sister?

- What was it like for Bing to have lived as a concubine and been abused by Lok, then to have been forced to leave her 2 younger children in Vietnam? Did she see the promise she made to Lok as the only pathway to bringing her children to Australia? How could she enter into a de facto relationship with a man she did not love and had been abusive to her? BUT, what about the commitment she made to Lok, how could she now abandon him and separate him from his children?

- What was it like for the two younger children to be met at the airport by their mother and older siblings, with whom they did not have a relationship; to be suddenly separated from their father and taken to a strange home in a strange country? Their mother said they had coped well, BUT would they need professional support to make the necessary adjustments?

- What was it like for Big Sister and Big Brother? They had both witnessed the abuse of their mother and they were now eager to support her in her quest to reunite the family. Why should they have any loyalty to the man who had been the abuser? BUT, he had provided them with a home and financially supported them in Vietnam while their father was in Australia. Did they owe him some loyalty after all?

All these questions were discussed by Rosalie and me in our post-session debriefing. For us, they represented 'unfinished business'. However, as experienced SST practitioners we were aware we would always have to tolerate and deal with a level of uncertainty. When we reflected on the session with a focus on our original aims:

to engage a resistant and reluctant participant (Bing)

to provide Lok with the opportunity to see his children in a supervised space

and for Lok and Bing to be given the opportunity to discuss options

We felt confident the SST had been helpful. The family had made significant gains and we were satisfied with the contribution we had made. We were a small part of a whole, and now needed to trust in the experience and expertise of the other workers who would continue offering service to the family, and of the family members' "own capacity for self-healing and problem solving" (Hoyt, Rosenbaum & Talmon, 1992). And, as with all SST sessions, we had left an 'open door' for further work if we were needed.

Conclusion

Although I originally focused on SST as a waiting list management tool, the usefulness of SST is much broader, especially in the area of engaging reluctant participants and in cross-cultural counselling, as the above cases demonstrate. I now find all my sessions are informed by SST principles. I value the first session as therapeutic, rather than 'just an intake' and even in longer term counselling, I view each session as a whole, accepting that all we have is 'now', that it may be the only opportunity I have to be helpful to the client, and that every opportunity should be seized, even if it does mean taking therapeutically calculated risks.

References

Boyhan, P. (1996). Clients' perceptions of single session consultations as an option to waiting for family therapy. *Australian and New Zealand Journal of Family Therapy,* 17(2), 85–96.

Hampson, R., O'Hanlon, J., Franklin, A., Pentony, M., Fridgant, L., & Heins, T. (1999). The place of single session family consultations: Five years' experience in Canberra. *Australian and New Zealand Journal of Family Therapy,* 20(4), 195–200.

Hoyt, M.F., Rosenbaum, R., & Talmon, M., (1992). Planned single session psychotherapy. In S.H. Budman, M.F. Hoyt, & S. Friedman (Eds.) *The first session in brief therapy* (pp. 59–86). New York: Guilford Press.

Price, C. (1994). Open days: Making family therapy accessible in working class suburbs. *Australian and New Zealand Journal of Family Therapy,* 15(4), 191–196.

St. Luke's "Strength Cards for Kids." (1996). Cards taken from the 40 card set, card size 14.5 x 21 cms. St. Luke's Innovative Resources, Bendigo (Publisher).

Talmon, M., (1990). *Single session therapy: Maximising the effect of the first (and often only) therapeutic encounter.* San Francisco: Jossey-Bass.

Talmon, M. (2001). *Single session workshop.* Bouverie Family Therapy Session, Melbourne, Victoria, Australia.

Chapter Ten

Walk-In Single Session Therapy at the Eastside Family Centre

*Nancy McElheran, Janet Stewart, Dean Soenen,
Jennifer Newman, and Bruce MacLaurin*

The inception of the Eastside Family Centre's (EFC) Walk-in Single Session Therapy service occurred in response to pressing community need for immediate, readily accessible and affordable mental health services that are at no cost to the client and are based in the community. The Centre was founded in 1990, at a time when funding and other resources for people with mental health problems were diminishing while demand for locally based services was increasing.

The EFC walk-in service is a program of Wood's Homes, a not-for-profit mental health organization that delivers residential and community based mental health services to children, adolescents and their families. Wood's Homes, in Calgary, Alberta, Canada, has been offering services since 1914 and is committed to serving people in their home communities.

The EFC walk-in single session therapy service is the first of its kind in Canada. Now in its 25th year of operation, it is located in a shopping mall in an ethnically diverse, high-density, lower socio-economic area. It serves people from all parts of the city

A version of this chapter was presented as a keynote address at the *Capture the Moment: The Inaugural Symposium on Single-Session Therapies and Walk-In Services* held on Phillip Island, Victoria, Australia, in March 2012 as well as surrounding communities and works in collaboration with community services such as schools, social service agencies, hospitals, mental health services and the justice system. The EFC is also a primary care network for family physicians. Details as to the earlier development of the Centre and the central role of its community advisory committee can be found in Harper-Jaques, McElheran, Slive, & Leahey (2008) and Clements, McElheran, Hackney, & Park (2011).

Description of the EFC Walk-In Service

Utilization data indicates that 35% of EFC clients who access the walk-in service return for additional walk-in sessions as needed at some point following the initial session. Clients may return several times over a few weeks, or might return a few years later based on their positive earlier experience. They sometimes also send their friends and relatives, again based on their own positive experience.

In keeping with the notion that people will seek mental health services when they are ready and not before, the EFC has organized itself so that clients can walk in to the Centre between the hours of 11 a.m.–7 p.m. on weekdays and 11 a.m.–2 p.m. on Saturdays. The walk-in is located on the second floor of an office building and is set up to optimize anonymity for the client by not separating it as a mental health service from the other professional services surrounding it, a request of the original Community Advisory Committee.

Clients arriving at the walk-in are greeted by a friendly receptionist who shows them to comfortable seating and gives them two forms to complete. The first form describes the service and how the session works. This form also elicits basic demographic information and family constellation.

The second form is called the "Green Sheet." Key items ask:

- What is the single most important concern that you wish to share today?
- Emotionally, who is most affected/least affected?
- With regards to your concerns today, what things have you tried?
- Please identify your sources of strength (e.g., humor, stubbornness, courage, creativity, family, friends)

- Have you had previous therapy?/Are you currently in therapy?
- What would you like from today's session?
- For some people a single session with a therapist is sufficient to take action. What will tell you that things are headed in the right direction?
- Name of person completing this form.

Clients then rate their distress level on a scale (Duncan, et al., 2004). In this way, and from the outset, the attempt is to engage the client in what will be a collaborative relationship with the therapist in the session to follow. In completing the forms clients are consenting to treatment that includes a team of multi-disciplinary professionals working with them. Clients also consent to or decline the use of a one-way mirror.

The language on the forms is clear and straightforward, recognizing that clients are most often in significant distress. For clients where English is their second language, the receptionist will assist them with the form and/or they can orally describe, rather than write, their concerns to the therapy team.

Once the forms are completed, clients are asked to wait for a brief period while the therapy team reviews their concerns as reported on the forms. Eastside Family Centre data indicates the wait time from walking in the door to the therapy team receiving the forms is approximately 20 minutes. If there are more clients who walk in than therapy teams to receive them, they will be given the option of staying in the waiting area or engaging in an activity of their choosing. Clients can go shopping in the adjacent mall, go for a coffee or read a magazine in the waiting area. There is a part of this area set aside for children to play. Feedback from clients indicates this is a satisfactory way of managing their wait time.

The Therapy Team

Therapy teams are comprised of mental health professionals from the disciplines of social work, psychology, nursing and family therapy, as well as graduate students from these disciplines. Consulting psychiatrists are on-site weekly. They provide their particular expertise to address high-risk issues such as suicide, a psychotic episode or a psychiatric problem that requires hospitalization and/or referral to a hospital emergency service. Medical practice residents and psychiatry interns join a team during their rotation through the center with their psychiatric consultant.

A therapy team is available for a four-to-six hour shift. Most often there are four team members per shift. Therapists take turns seeing clients based on their interest in and/or expertise with the presenting concern. One member of the team, with advanced knowledge, is called the shift coordinator. This person is responsible for the quality of the service delivered, the management of risk and also serves as a support behind the one-way mirror. The other therapy team members see clients as they walk in the door. Potentially, three or four clients may be seen at any given time. If there happens to be more therapists than clients, then the therapist not seeing a client will also become a support behind the one-way mirror with client consent.

The therapy team has a two-fold responsibility. One is to conduct a single session of therapy with a client and the other is to consult with other team members about their clients and to assist in creating interventions. The process of therapist-client-team interaction and feedback creates a context whereby the client is involved in a consultative process with the team and the team is collaborating with the client around his/her issue.

Current therapy teams are comprised of clinical staff of Wood's Homes, multi-disciplinary contracted consultants, psychiatrists, graduate students and community therapists. Community therapists are professionals who work at other community organizations and who donate their professional time to the walk-in for personal fulfillment reasons (Whitford, 1994).

Most therapy teams are quite diverse, comprised of people from different work backgrounds and graduate level professional education. Their knowledge and interests add to the energy that is created in the conversation as to the need(s) of the client. As teams are created with each shift, there is constantly an eclectic mix of both expertise and experience brought by the team to each walk-in session.

The Session

Each session is 50–60 minutes in length and has a five-part sequential organization consistent with the Milan model (Boscolo, Cecchin, Hoffman & Penn, 1987): (1) pre-session where the forms the client has completed are reviewed by the team, hypotheses are generated as to the possible nature of the issues presented and a plan of action for the session is formed; (2) the session with the client wherein the therapist and client collaborate on addressing the presenting issue; (3) an inter-session consultation where the therapy team reviews the problem construction that has been co-created with the client and therapist and an intervention is formed; (4) delivery of the intervention by the therapist on behalf of the whole team; (5) a post-session debriefing, in the absence of the client, that focuses on whether, from the team's perspective, the session met the client's need and suggestions are made as to future directions, should the client return. The therapist then completes a session note that incorporates the discussion.

At the end of each session clients are informed that should they decide to return they are welcome to do so but will not necessarily see the same therapist. They will, however, receive the same service and their note(s) from the previous session will be available to the next team. Implicit in this procedure is that the client's relationship is with the service, not any particular therapist.

When there are issues of risk, the shift coordinator and the team create a safety plan with the client. The safety plan could include consulting with children's services on behalf of a child at risk, calling a family member to assist the client, connecting the client with other community resources such as a crisis line or supporting them in getting to a hospital emergency room.

When their session finishes, clients are provided with a feedback form that has been adapted from the Duncan and Miller Outcome Rating Scale (Duncan, Miller, & Sparks, 2004). A measure of their post-session distress is requested and the clients are asked to provide feedback as to the goodness-of-fit of the session for them, as well as their alliance with the therapist and team for their session. The few clients who rate their session as unsatisfactory are later contacted by the center manager to explore their dissatisfaction and to be offered another session.

The Clinical Framework and Approach

From the outset, the intent of the EFC walk-in single session therapy service was to provide a whole therapy in one hour. Each session was conceived as having a beginning, middle, and end.

Theoretical influences on this process have included systemic, postmodern, social constructionist, and Ericksonian ideas. Therapeutic models derived from these influences, such as solution-focused and narrative as well as elements of MRI and strategic approaches contribute to the therapy work (Talmon, 1990; Hoyt, 1998; Hubble, et al., 1999; Slive, et al., 2008, 2011). However, and consistent with postmodern thinking, no one theoretical model will fit for every client or therapist. Choosing an approach that is a good fit for clients and their issue, and is pragmatic in perspective, is central to the therapeutic conversation (Amundson, 1996; Slive, et al., 2008). That rapid change is both possible and common in the human experience, and that the greatest opportunity for change comes early in the therapy process (Bloom, 2001), is a basic tenet implicit in the walk-in therapy context.

Therapists who work at the EFC often must make a shift in their beliefs about therapy and change. Most importantly, this involves construing the nature of their relationship with the client as different at a walk-in service where, as noted, the focus is on connecting the client with the service rather than with any particular therapist.

Therapists new to a walk-in single session approach to therapy sometimes find it a challenge to consider the possibility that they can provide effective help to a client they may never see again. Most therapists, however, can embrace the idea that clients are the experts regarding their situation, will seek help at moments of need and have problem-solving capabilities that can be accessed in therapy. This typically occurs in a consultative and collaborative relationship co-created with a therapist and team (Harper–Jaques & Leahey, 2011).

Principles inherent in the model have been well-articulated by Slive, et al. (2008; 2011) but bear repeating as they are central to the walk-in practice at the EFC:

a) Given that a session is only one hour, building a therapeutic alliance quickly is essential.

b) Asking clients to focus on their immediate concern using interventive questions (Tomm, 1987, 1988) such as "If there was one question you could have answered during our time together what would that be?" (Wright, 1989) assist in determining what the client needs.

c) Narrowing the database by keeping a focus on the problem in the present and guiding the conversation to the present and/or future assists the client to address his/her immediate concern.

d) Addressing the common factors as articulated by Duncan, et al. (2004) by building a therapeutic alliance.

e) Determining what is the best fit for the client versus any one model of therapy assists with effectively moving a session forward.

f) Embracing the principle that it is a whole therapy in one hour is essential.

g) The therapist and the client are engaged in a collaborative process.

h) The therapist is creating a context for the client to discover his/her own resources and solutions.

Conducting a Walk-in Session

In practice, the goal of the EFC walk-in single session therapy service is to provide clients with a sense of relief from their problem, some hope their life situation could improve and some sense of a self-defined positive outcome. To assist with this process we have created a session format that asks clients what they want from their session, how it is that the problem is a problem for them now, what they have done in an attempt to resolve their problem and who or what they would cite are resources useful to them. Asking about resources takes into account the systemic notion that family, in whatever form it takes, is relevant to the client's situation.

Some clients see themselves as bereft of internal resources but identify external ones such as family, while others see themselves as quite isolated but having internal strengths that assist them in times of stress. Clients who identify a balance between internal and external resources are also encouraged to think about how they would use their resources to arrive at possible solutions.

The use of solution-focused, strength-based, and resource-based language assists in building a co-operative client-therapist relationship and co-creating solutions that are both achievable and incorporate the client's belief system about change. Questions, such as "What will work for you today? What one question would you like answered today or if there were a question you would like me to ask, but I have not yet, what would that be?" (Wright, 1989), support clients' exploration of their situation with the therapist and at the same time situates their pain in the immediate past so that the present and future have new possibilities.

Interventions are based on what clients bring to the session and what they believe would be useful at that particular moment. Interventions are typically offered throughout the session and are a co-creation of possibilities and alternatives to the dominant problem/story and vary in accordance with what will fit for the client. Interventions are often tentative in nature and may include multiple ideas to leave space for the client to decide if what is offered is a fit. Commendations, which are positive statements about the client and what is noted by the therapist/team, are always offered during and at the end of a session as they tend to highlight strengths. Commendations often positively surprise clients in hearing something about themselves they had not appreciated (McElheran & Harper-Jaques, 1994; Houger-Limacher, 2003).

A taxonomy of presenting concerns has assisted with collecting statistical data as to client issues, levels of risk and acuity. Over time the top five concerns are: mental health problems; parent/adolescent/child conflict; couple/family relationship issues; addictions; developmental/life transitions. Acuity is consistently showing moderate to severe levels of distress.

Case Example #1: Belonging

Tyler, age 15, and his mother Sherri, age 34, came to the EFC following a police visit to the home with a concern that Tyler was damaging community property with his friends, a situation that could result in charges if he did not receive "help." The police recommended the EFC as a place to start as they said the mother and son could walk-in and see a therapist right away. Sherri noted on the Green Sheet, and told the therapist who met with them, that Tyler's behavior came as a surprise to her as he was mainly a respectful and responsible boy. She went on to say that in the past six months she had become quite concerned as Tyler was very disrespectful to her and was refusing to participate in any of the family activities or assume responsibilities.

Sherri presented as a quiet and tired woman who was visibly upset with her son's behavior, as exemplified by Tyler interrupting her and saying he did not have to listen to her and that it was her fault he was in trouble. When this happened, she became tearful and said in response to the therapist's question that her hope for this session was for Tyler to be more respectful and responsible.

At the beginning of the session, and with questions from the therapist that focused on the immediate situation, such as who was directly involved in Tyler's life, it was learned that Sherri had, six months earlier, married Dan who, to date, had not been involved with Tyler; that Tyler's dad was a drug dealer and not present in Tyler's life and that Tyler's maternal grandparents were those that Tyler preferred to be with, although he did not see them regularly.

As the session progressed, the team behind the one-way mirror called into the therapist and suggested she focus on what was working in Sherri and Tyler's relationship and what they liked about each other. It emerged that they had both been very involved with one another until Sherri's marriage to Dan. Since that time Sherri had been more occupied with Dan and their new life than with Tyler. The team behind the mirror "wondered" if this new relationship may have created an opening for fear and resentment to creep into the relationship as Tyler became unsettled at the time his mother was getting more involved with Dan. With the support of the team, the therapist asked Tyler if he might like to get to know Dan now that he was a part of his mother's life. Tyler's response was that he might but that he didn't think Dan liked him.

At the inter-session break the therapist and team discussed the recent changes in Sherri and Tyler's life. The team hypothesized that the transitional challenges that were potentially created with the introduction of Dan into Sherri's life may have resulted in the shift in Tyler's behavior as he may have become uncertain as to where and with whom he belongs.

Following this inter-session discussion, the therapist, on behalf of herself and the team, offered commendations to both Sherri and Tyler as individuals and to them as mother and son for recognizing that their relationship may have drifted into fear and resentment because they were spending less time together. The therapy team wondered if experimenting with replacing fear and resentment with love and confidence could meet Sherri's goal of wanting respect and responsibility in the relationship and Tyler's need to feel like he belongs somewhere.

The therapy team suggested they do an experiment by giving fear and resentment a vacation. At the same time, the team suggested Sherri involve Tyler in her and Dan's activities and that Tyler talk with his mother and Dan about his interests and activities.

They were invited to return as they needed and if they wanted to obtain additional ideas. Sherri was invited to thank her parents for "standing in" for her over the past six months but to reassure them it was no longer necessary since she and Tyler were getting back on track.

As the session was coming to an end, Sherri decided that she would go with Tyler to the police station to find out what they needed to do to assure the police he would not be getting involved in any more illegal activity.

They thanked the team and said they would return as needed, but found that the session gave them good ideas. Their feedback form indicated they were very satisfied with their session and their distress level was significantly reduced.

Case Example #2: Shifting Beliefs

Alice and Mike moved to Calgary six months ago from Saskatchewan, where they had farmed, so that Mike could retire and they could be closer to their children. Mike is an aboriginal man who originally lived on one of the reserves close to the town where Alice grew up. They met at a local dance in their teens and married against their collective parents' wishes. Alice commented that, since his retirement, Mike is at home more, which is new for them. She indicated that she finds it difficult having him in the house as they do not have much to say to each other since typically he was always working the land and she was tending the house and children. In addition, Alice states that Mike likes to spend time with elders from his native community, an activity that excludes her. Alice reports her main reason for coming to the walk-in is because she has always had "nerve" difficulty which was treated successfully with anti-depressants until this past summer. She can't account for the change but states she is much more nervous now. She described her nerves as "jumping" in her skin which leaves her feeling very unsettled, unable to sleep and often wishing she could die.

The therapist that met with Alice for the initial session used a team behind the mirror to assist with the process in this session. The therapy team asked the therapist to query if Alice thought the increase in anxiety could be connected in any way to Mike being around more, or if it could be connected to him spending time with his elder friends instead of with her. She rejected both ideas immedi-

ately, stating she thought something physical was wrong with her that she was not responding to the medication.

Alice went on to say she has tried three new medications and none of them have worked very well. Her doctor suggested she come to the EFC to talk, but Alice stated she just wants to "know when the medications will work" and her "nerves" will stop jumping. Given her strong belief that there was something physically wrong, the team decided, at the inter-session break, to offer an intervention that could address the physical effects of her anxiety and, at the same time, offer some suggestions for activities that would begin to include members of her family and her husband to connect with her emotionally.

At the end of the session, the therapist, on behalf of himself and the team, suggested that Alice experiment with becoming more physically active by walking and going to the gym for exercise to see if this would help reduce the intensity of her experience with her nerves. The therapy team also suggested she spend some time with her family doing fun activities and that she and Mike sit down at the kitchen table and talk about what they might do together now that he is home more. She was invited to return to report on her findings whenever she would like.

Alice returned to the walk-in about a week later. At the beginning of this session the therapist asked her what stood out for her from the last session she had. Alice stated that she found the first session helpful and she wanted some more assistance. She said she found being physically active and being around her family was helpful, although she was still experiencing some "jumpiness", particularly when she and Mike were in the house alone and it was quiet. She said they did not talk as she was too worried about what he might say. Her doctor had changed her medication again, which she thought made a small improvement.

Given that this was a new therapist and team for Alice, the therapist decided to explore her relationships with the people in her life. The story that unfolded was that she was never a very popular child growing up, not particularly cared for by her mother, and always felt like she was in the way. She said that after she and Mike got together and married they did not do much together beyond taking care of the farm and their children and now she was at a loss to know what to say to him. She also said that he is a very quiet man and not very affectionate. She went on to say that while she would like to talk with him more she did not know if he would feel the same way as he is very connected to the elders in his community

and she is an outsider. Alice then said that she used to be quite con-
tent to spend time with her children and grandchildren but finds it
is not sufficient now.

With support from the team behind the mirror, the therapist
pursued talking with Alice about her relationship with Mike. Alice
suddenly volunteered that Mike had squeezed her hand in the wait-
ing room today, which was a first. She also volunteered that she
liked him doing that but could not tell him. The team behind the
mirror phoned in again to ask the therapist to offer a commendation
from them to Alice for recognizing that she wanted some affection
from her husband. The therapist asked her what it would take for
her to tell him. Alice smiled shyly and said that perhaps she could
do it if the therapist helped. She went on to say that she had begun
to wonder if what she needs is for someone to hug her as she missed
that all of her life.

At the inter-session break, the therapist and his team agreed to ask
Alice to invite Mike into the end of session feedback so he could hear
from her what she wanted to say. She agreed. The therapist indicated
to Mike that Alice had some things she needed to say and wanted the
support of the team to tell him. With that Alice told Mike how much
she liked him holding her hand. Mike smiled broadly and said that he
has wanted to do that for some time and would like to do more if she
would permit him. The therapy team commended both of them and
suggested they go on a date to a place of their mutual choosing so
they can talk some more about what they like about each other. Alice
was asked to note what happened with her anxiety when they were
together in this new way. They were invited to come back as a couple
or as individuals if they wished.

Approximately one month later, the couple returned and asked
to be seen together. They stated they really just came to let the
therapist and team know they were doing much better. They were
both smiling and said that while Alice's anxiety was not completely
gone, it was significantly reduced. Alice said that for the first time
in their marriage she and Mike were talking and, as she put it,
"getting to know each other." Alice noted that she now believed that
her anxiety was not just a physical problem but was connected to
her feeling lonely, which was abating now that she and Mike were
talking. She also said she was less upset now when he met with his
elder friends as she knew he would come back to her.

The therapy team offered the couple a reflecting team as the
feedback for this session. A psychiatrist was part of this particular

team. The reflecting team commended the couple for the work they were doing in connecting their mutual need for love and affection with Alice's experience of anxiety and Mike spending more time with his elder friends than he wanted. The psychiatrist made a specific comment that Alice was on track with her medications and should continue to work with her family physician. The couple thanked the team for assisting them in getting to know each other. They also said they enjoyed meeting different therapists and teams as they got different ideas each time. On their feedback form they commented that the team and mirror was a good idea and thanked the team for its help.

Case Example #3: Connecting with Hospital Resources

Steven, a 24-year-old Chinese man, came to the EFC walk-in at the suggestion of a mental health worker who talked with him on a local crisis line. He stated on his Green Sheet that he was afraid he was being followed and was not sure what to do. He also stated he was frightened of some of his thoughts. The team that met with him had a consulting psychiatrist who joined the therapist behind the mirror. The therapist who met with Steven asked specifically what was concerning him most today. Steven's response was that he was becoming frightened of his thoughts as he was getting messages through his iPhone that he should harm his girlfriend and that he thought her father was following him. At the suggestion of the psychiatrist, the therapist asked for details about the messages he was getting and if there was a specific method he would use to harm the girl. It unfolded that Steven kept a gun in his house and said he would use it which was why he left the house today. The therapist then asked if Steven had or was using drugs of any type. He offered that he was taking medication for an undisclosed issue when he was living with his parents but had not taken any medications since moving to Canada and living on his own. He also volunteered that he had previously attempted suicide by diving off a bridge into water in the hopes he might drown as a way of getting rid of the thoughts. When he was asked if he was at risk to himself as well as to his girlfriend today, Steven became tearful stating he was frightened and didn't know what to do. The therapist then asked him about people in his life who he might call for help. Steven seemed puzzled by the question but volunteered that he had come to Canada in the past year and that his family was still in Hong Kong.

He met his girlfriend here but had few other resources. At this point, the therapist decided to meet with her team and consult further with the psychiatrist. The therapy team agreed with the psychiatrist that Steven needed to have a full psychiatric assessment, that he was not sufficiently stable at the moment to get himself to the hospital and an ambulance transport would be arranged. The psychiatrist agreed to call the local hospital emergency and facilitate him seeing one of the psychiatrists for possible admission. She also agreed to meet with Steven and the therapist in the therapy room to talk with Steven about her suggestions. Steven was initially reluctant to consider the request that he go to the hospital but quickly agreed when it was explained that this would be the safest solution for him today.

A few weeks later, Steven returned to the walk-in. He stated at this time that he was admitted to the hospital for a 3-week stay, was prescribed new medication for what was diagnosed as a psychotic disorder and was finding that he was calmer and feeling much more safe within himself now. He asked if he could come to the walk-in with his girlfriend as she was still worried about what had happened. The therapist and team of the day supported his wish to bring her and come for a walk-in session whenever they liked.

Teaching and Training within the Professional Community

From the beginning, a culture of teaching and learning was developed at the EFC that continues today and attracts staff, professional volunteers and students from various backgrounds to the Centre.

Currently, training in the walk-in model is offered to interested and qualified mental health practitioners across the country. Workshops are of varying length, depending on the need of the agency requesting. Workshops typically offer both theory and practice in the EFC walk-in single session approach. Certificates are provided that meet standards for continuing competencies for many professional bodies. Students identify the live supervision using the one-way mirror, low student-staff ratio and experience working with multi-disciplinary teams as central to their learning. EFC staff also offer workshops and consult off-site to other organizations working with the model and/or interested in establishing their own walk-in service.

Community Connections

The EFC walk-in service does not stand alone. From the beginning, the intent was to connect the Centre with the community and the community with the Centre to create a safety net of resources that could be accessed by people coming to the walk-in. As a result, and with the advice of the original community advisory committee that was made up of local professional groups, a counseling service for men who are perpetrators of domestic violence was established on-site alongside Wood's Homes crisis team and a family serving agency. Off-site are connections and partnerships with hospital-based services such as emergency rooms and outpatient services, community organizations that provide multi-professional connections in their centers, and immigrant-serving agencies as well as to local schools and to Wood's Homes street services. Our consulting psychiatrists hold leadership roles in the hospital systems and facilitate both communication and connections between the groups. Connections to local politicians, police and community leaders remain a core part of community development planning.

Developing a Framework for Ongoing Research and Evaluation

There is consensus that individuals and families deserve timely access to effective walk-in clinical services; however it is only recently that there has been an emphasis on understanding the short- and long-term outcomes associated with walk-in interventions (Green, et al., 2011). There is growing demand in all fields to understand which interventions are most useful for which clients, for what presenting concerns, and over what time period (Trocmé, MacLaurin, Fallon, Shlonsky, et al., 2009). The Eastside Family Centre (EFC) walk-in has been the focus of a number of research initiatives over the past two decades, and findings suggest that the program has been successful in providing accessible walk-in services and that clients consistently report satisfaction with services received (Hoffart & Hoffart, 1994; Whitford, 1994; Miller, 1996, 2008; Miller & Slive, 2004;). Hoffart & Hoffart (1994) found that 89% of clients were satisfied with the walk-in services and the level of client satisfaction was higher at 6-month follow-up compared to immediately following the session. Miller (2008) examined client satisfaction questionnaires for 403 individual adults, couples or families who completed questionnaires one week post walk-in session. While more than 81% of respondents indicated overall satisfaction (very satisfied or satisfied) with the walk-in team therapy approach, there were clinically significant differences by presenting concern, including marital and couple conflict (83.4%), depression or withdrawal (86.7%), and child behavior problems (93.1%). These independent research initiatives add greatly to the evidence supporting walk-in single session therapy at EFC, and clearly highlight the benefits of collecting outcome data on an ongoing basis.

In 2012, EFC and the Wood's Research Department completed a review of all clinical and outcome data gathered on clients presenting at EFC. Client-level data were well used to inform the clinical process but were underutilized for measuring session outcomes. An outcomes research framework was developed to aggregate pre-session data (demographics, client resources, pre-session distress, presenting concerns, anxiety and depression symptoms) as well as post-session outcomes (distress, satisfaction with services, and therapeutic interventions). A pilot study was conducted in 2012–2013 to test the feasibility of the data collection, entry, and analysis processes for all clients attending a walk-in single session of therapy at EFC over a one-month time period. This pilot project informed refinements to the data collection process and the final set of outcome measures to be tracked.

Preliminary analyses on an initial sample (n = 600) report promising results. For example, a statistically significant decrease in distress from pre- to post-session was noted, indicating that clients are assisted to manage their perceived distress during a 50-minute walk-in session (Stewart & Newman, 2013). A future publication will report on data following the first year of data collection in December, 2013. Based on the initial pilot data, it is predicted that the EFC will add outcome data on approximately 1,500 to 2,000 clients yearly. The outcomes research framework supports further analyses to differentiate which clients achieve greater success as it relates to pre-existing conditions, demographic characteristics, or co-occurring concern. The development of this framework for ongoing client-based outcome data collection provides a strong foundation for research and evaluation that will inform evidence-based practice at the EFC in the future.

References

Amundson, J. (1996). Why pragmatics is probably enough for now. *Family Process, 35*, 473–486.

Bloom, B.L. (2001). Focused single-session psychotherapy: A review of the clinical and research literature. *Brief Treatment and Crisis Intervention, 1*(1), 75–86.

Boscolo, L., Cecchin, G., Hoffman, L., & Penn, P.(1987). *Milan systemic family therapy.* New York: Basic Books.

Clements, R., McElheran, N., Hackney, L., & Park, H. (2011). The Eastside Family Centre: 20 years of single-session walk-in therapy. In A. Slive & M. Bobele (Eds.), *When one hour is all you have: Effective therapy for walk-in clients* (pp. 109–127). Phoenix, AZ: Zeig, Tucker & Theisen.

Duncan, B.L., Miller, S.D., & Sparks, J.A. (2004). *The heroic client: A revolutionary way to improve effectiveness through client-directed, outcome-informed therapy.* San Francisco, CA: Jossey-Bass.

Green, K. E., Correia, T., Bobele, M., & Slive, A. (2011). The research case for walk-in single sessions. In A. Slive & M. Bobele (Eds.), *When one hour is all you have: Effective therapy for walk-in clients* (pp. 23–36). Phoenix, AZ: Zeig, Tucker & Theisen.

Harper-Jaques, S., & Leahey, M. (2011). From imagination to reality: Mental Health Walk-In at the South Calgary Health Centre. In A. Slive & M. Bobele (Eds.), *When one hour is all you have: Effective therapy for walk-in clients* (pp. 167–183). Phoenix, AZ: Zeig, Tucker & Theisen.

Harper-Jaques, S., McElheran, N., Slive, A., & Leahey, M. (2008). A comparison of two approaches to the delivery of walk-in single session mental health therapy. *Journal of Systemic Therapies, 27*(4), 40–53.

Hoffart, B., & Hoffart, I. (1994). *Program evaluation of Eastside Family Centre.* Calgary: Synergy Research Group.

Houger-Limacher, L. (2003). *Commendations: The healing potential of one family systems nursing intervention.* (Unpublished doctoral thesis). Calgary, AB: University of Calgary.

Hoyt, M.F. (Ed.). (1998). *The handbook of constructive therapies.* San Francisco: Jossey-Bass.

Hubble, M.A., Duncan, B.L., & Miller, S.D. (Eds.). (1999). *The heart and soul of change: What works in therapy.* Washington, DC: American Psychological Association.

McElheran, N., & Harper-Jaques, S. (1994). Commendations: A resource intervention for clinical practice. *Clinical Nurse Specialist, 8*(1), 7–10.

Miller, J. K. (1996). Walk-in single session therapy: A study of client satisfaction. *Dissertations Abstracts International, 58*, 421.

Miller, J. K. (2008). Walk-in single session team therapy: A study of client satisfaction. *Journal of Systemic Therapies, 27*, 78–94.

Miller, J. K., & Slive, A. (2004). Breaking down the barriers to clinical service delivery: Walk-in family therapy. *Journal of Marital and Family Therapy, 30*, 95–105.

Slive, A., & Bobele, M. (2011). Making a difference in fifty minutes: A framework for walk-in counselling. In A. Slive & M. Bobele (Eds.), *When one hour is all you have: Effective therapy for walk-in clients* (pp. 167–183). Phoenix, AZ: Zeig, Tucker & Theisen.

Slive, A., McElheran, N., & Lawson, A. (2008). How brief does it get? Walk-in single session therapy. *Journal of Systemic Therapies, 27,* 5–22.

Stewart, J., & Newman, J. (2013). *Evolution of outcome tracking at Eastside Family Centre.* Presentation at the Wood's Homes 3rd Annual Research Symposium, June 14th, 2013, Calgary, AB, Canada.

Talmon, M. (1990). *Single session therapy: Maximizing the effect of the first (and often only) therapeutic encounter.* San Francisco: Jossey-Bass.

Tomm, K. (1988). Interventive interviewing: Part III. Intending to ask linear, circular, strategic or reflexive questions? *Family Process, 27,* 1–15.

Tomm, K. (1987). Interventive interviewing: Part II. Reflexive questioning as a means to enable self-healing. *Family Process, 26,* 167–183.

Trocmé, N., MacLaurin, B., Fallon, B., Shlonsky, A., Mulcahy, M., & Esposito, T. (2009). *National child welfare outcomes indicator matrix (NOM).* Montreal, QC: McGill University, Centre for Research on Children and Families.

Whitford, D. (1994). *Exploration of contributors to volunteer retention at two community based human service programs: Eastside Family Centre and the Community Resource Team.* Calgary: Wood's Homes.

Wood's Homes Research Department (2013). *Eastside Family Centre Wood's Homes outcome measurements (WHOM) report January–December 2012.* Calgary: Wood's Homes.

Wright, L.M. (1989). When clients ask questions: Enriching the therapeutic conversation. *Family Therapy Networker, 13*(6), 15–16.

Chapter Eleven

Single Session Therapy in China

John K. Miller

"A journey of a thousand miles begins with a single step."
—LAO TZU (CHINESE PHILOSOPHER,
6TH CENTURY B.C.)

My journey into the practice and research of single session therapy (SST) began in 1995 after I started reading about the advent of this new form of clinical service delivery and the pioneering work of Drs. Moshe Talmon, Michael Hoyt, Robert Rosenbaum, and Arnold Slive. I was a brief therapist trained in the tradition of the Mental Research Institute (MRI), doing my best to follow in the footsteps of luminaries such as Don Jackson, John Weakland, Jay Haley, Richard Fisch, and Virginia Satir. Later that year I accepted a post in Canada and moved from Virginia to Calgary to work with Dr. Slive and his colleagues who had created a walk-in single session therapy service at the Eastside Family Therapy Centre (see Chapter 10 this volume). I worked there for one year with Dr. Slive and his

The author would like to acknowledge funding support for this project from the U.S. Department of State, Fulbright Senior Research Scholar Program (Research Award #9126) as well as support from the Chinese Ministry of Education, East Asian Academic Exchange the U.S. Embassy in Beijing, and the U..S Bureau of Educational and Cultural Affairs. A version of this chapter was presented as a keynote address at the *Capture the Moment: The Inaugural International Symposium on Single-Session Therapies and Walk-In Servic*es held on Phillip Island, Victoria, Australia, in March 2012.

colleagues, seeing hundreds of single session cases and conducting research on client satisfaction, help-seeking behavior, and the factors that influenced the change process in the walk-in single session service they had created (see Miller, 1996; Miller & Slive, 1997, 2004; Miller, 2008). I was inspired by the many cases I saw in which significant change was accomplished in these single session interventions. After my time at the Eastside Family Centre, I have spent much of my career looking for various ways to overcome the barriers to therapy services that I have witnessed in the U.S., Canada, and throughout the world. This has included "relationship check-up" services developed at the University of Oregon (Miller, 2000), a "healthy nests" project (also at the University of Oregon; see Linville, Todahl, & Miller, 2008; Todahl, Linville, Miller, & Brown, 2009) wherein we offered short-term consultations to new parents; single session therapy services offered after a catastrophic disaster (e.g., Hurricane Katrina; Miller, 2006, 2011a); Internet-based groups reaching out to people who had suicidal thoughts (Miller & Gergen, 1996) and Internet-addiction problems (Su, Fang, Miller, & Wang, 2011); and single session therapy projects for traumatized people in Mexico City and Cambodia in collaboration with my colleague, Dr. Jason Platt (Miller & Platt, 2013; Miller & Tarragona, 2012; also see Chapter 12 this volume).

Eventually this pursuit led to more international interests, as it seemed to me that a single session focus may have special appeal in countries where the concept of therapy was still developing, and the populace may be more open to SST over more traditional, longer-term, and Western modes of treatment.

In 2005, I began traveling to mainland China to teach and collaborate on research regarding clinical delivery and family therapy in the rapidly developing Chinese context. I have been interested in China since my childhood. My father was a chemistry professor who had many mainland Chinese graduate students come to work with him in the 1970's when it was fairly rare to have students from China come to the United States. In 2008, I was awarded a Fulbright Senior Research Scholar award from the U.S. Department of State to live in China and develop and conduct a single session therapy offering in Beijing in collaboration with the faculty and staff at Beijing Normal University (BNU). Under the leadership of Dr. Xiaoyi Fang, the Institute for Developmental Psychology at BNU had developed one of the flagship graduate programs in psychology in China. The faculty, staff and graduate students welcomed the chance to collaborate on the project. During my year in China we developed a walk-in (and well as by appointment) single session therapy offering. The project was a clinical service, an intercultural collaborative training venture, and a research project about client experiences with the service. The following details our experience developing the service, the types of problems we were brought, and how we tailored our understanding of SST practices to fit the Chinese context.

Psychotherapy in the Contemporary Chinese Context

Of all the various types of available therapy services possible in the developing Chinese context, family/interpersonally-based, short-term, problem-focused, brief, and directive approaches have had the greatest appeal and acceptance among the people. This is likely due to unique aspects of Chinese culture such as "filial piety" (*xiào*), a Confucian virtue that includes a central value of respect for parents and family ancestors. Individualistic models of therapy are less relevant in the Chinese context given the Chinese cultural value of collectivism, a concept that recognizes the interdependence of every human being. Generally speaking, Chinese culture values helping professionals who are directive, expert-based, and oriented to solving the problem quickly and pragmatically (Miller & Fang, 2012; Liu, Zhao & Miller, 2012; Liu, Miller, Zhao, Ma, Wang, & Li, 2012). The single session therapy methods I had been practicing since 1995 seemed to be an ideal fit for the emerging field of therapy in China and the preferences of most people seeking services there.

The Problem of Clinical Service Delivery Internationally

Despite the Chinese government's concerted efforts to expand and promote therapy services in China, most people who would likely benefit from therapy do not attempt to access the services that are available. Recent studies have revealed that while 178 million Chinese people suffer from some mental health issue, the overwhelming majority have received no counseling or professional services even though in most situations counseling would likely help. In China, the importance of maintaining reputation and social standing or "face" (*mianzi*) is likely to prevent some people from seeking help for fear of losing respect. The World Health Organization (WHO) and other similar globally-oriented agencies have reported that the worldwide mental health system is plagued with more barriers to services than any other branch of health services. Three main barriers prevent people from seeking help: (1) stigma, (2) accessibility, and (3) cost. Research has demonstrated that SST has the potential to overcome some of these barriers in that the approach is strengths-based (low stigma), highly accessible, and cost-efficient (usually free for clients—paid for by a university clinic, agency, or the government). Also, there is evidence that, while traditional therapy practices have a harder time getting males to access services, males are more likely to utilize an SST service. Likewise, many people who have used an SST service reported that they would not have typically approached more traditional therapy services, but were attracted by the brief, "hassle-free" consultation-based format of SST. Many of these people reported that this was their first therapy experience and that now that they had some exposure to what therapy was really all about, that they would be much more likely to use other therapy services in the future. Of those that came to the service, the majority said they felt that counseling services were not easy to access in their community and that there is a stigma associated with therapy. The project described here is one effort to overcome apparent barriers to therapy service delivery in China.

Introduction to the Walk-In Single Session Therapy Project in Mainland China

The service we developed in Beijing was a walk-in, single session, family-oriented (systemic), collaborative, and action-oriented therapy. The philosophical approach and accompanying techniques that the service was based upon have been presented in more detail elsewhere (Miller, 1996, 2006, 2008; Miller & Slive, 2004), yet warrant a brief description here for the reader who may have an interest in developing a single session service in an international setting.

Like many of the SST offerings described in this volume, our service was designed to provide as much help as possible in a single meeting. Although the goal of the project was not to solve all the problems that people brought to us in the one meeting, the general aim was that this one meeting might provide a valuable first step in the change process. Our hope was that people who would not normally consider accessing services would approach *this* service because it was immediately available, hassle-free, and offered at no cost. All the therapists and researchers volunteered their time to the project. We predicted that most people who would come to the service would have little or no history with therapy and that this one experience might help demystify the concept of therapy and provide a favorable taste of it so that those who felt they needed more services would be more likely to attempt to access them in the future. The service was offered at the training clinic at the Institute for Developmental Psychology at BNU, which also has a more traditional individual and family therapy clinical service that any returning clients were welcomed to visit. The clinic had several therapy rooms and an observation room where a group of up to 10 therapists/supervisors could observe the session. All sessions were supervised by the author and occurred in Chinese. A translator (Chinese-English) was available for every session. A 5-step team approach was used with all sessions, and this approach often involved the team going into the room to talk with the clients toward the end of the session if the client(s) consented. The five steps of the session included:

- a pre-session, based on the available information, to discuss the case before the client(s) entered the therapy room
- session part 1, where the therapist learned about the problem and what the clients wanted from the meeting
- a session break, where the therapist consulted with the team
- session part 2, where the therapist concluded the session with the clients
- a post-session meeting, where the therapist debriefed the session with the team and received supervisory feedback

After the session clients were also invited to meet in another room with a researcher not involved in the team or therapy, who asked questions about the clients' experiences and views of the session.

Most clients welcomed feedback from the team. I have been conducting this type of therapy in the U.S. and Canada for the past 20 years, and my sense was that the clients in this Chinese project welcomed the team feedback even more so than is typical in North America. This may be due to the Chinese value of seeking expert advice and feedback regarding problems. The team stance was collaborative, and was oriented to providing the clients with a useful outcome at the end of the session based on what the clients were seeking in the consultation. All of the therapists in the project were advanced Chinese graduate students trained at BNU to conduct systemically-based individual and family therapy. Most were bilingual (Chinese and English). All 10 therapists who volunteered to provide services attended an 8-hour training regarding best practices in a single session service. The therapists in the project haled from a variety of therapy traditions, but all were systemically trained with at least two years of experience as a therapist. The 8-hour training included role-playing of simulated cases with feedback from the author and Chinese supervisors throughout the process. All therapists participating in the project had to be approved by the Chinese supervisors before seeing cases in the service.

As is common in most single session offerings, we tried to make the most of every contact with the client, including the first phone call. Clients were solicited through advertising and announcements around the campus community and in local newspapers. The notices gave a brief description of the service, and were designed to be appealing, welcoming, and non-stigmatizing. The response to the service was overwhelming, and while we had only planned to offer the service for two months, we had to extend it to three months to see all the clients that called or walked-in requesting a session. We designed a special set of documents for the project that was tailored to the single session nature of the service. This included phone intake documents, "lobby" intake documents, and custom session note forms, etc. The forms were created with intentionality with regard to the limits of the single session. Questions included:

"What are your thoughts about how we might be helpful today?"

"Is there a specific problem you would like to address today?"

"If you have been to counseling in the past, what do you remember as useful or difficult?"

"What are strengths and resources in yourself or your relationship?"

All forms were translated into Mandarin Chinese (the most common dialect in China).

Themes and Common Problems Brought to Single Session Therapy

During the project, our team conducted over 50 single session therapies. The cases were either walk-in or, if requested, by appointment. (About half of the cases were walk-in; the others requested an appointment.) Our group saw a wide variety of cases and presenting concerns. The following three vignettes highlight several common types of issues that were brought to us. As discussed in the comments following each presentation, each represents a unique aspect of therapy and therapy issues in the Chinese culture.

Case 1: Po Xi Wen Ti—The "Mother/Daughter-In-Law Problem"

A heterosexual couple in their mid-twenties and the husband's mother presented for a single session consultation requesting help with "communication" issues that have arisen between the three of them in the last year. During the first part of the session, the wife did the majority of the talking. She explained that the couple was married 3 years ago after they both graduated from college. They had their first child (a boy) one year ago. As is common in Chinese culture, the couple moved into the home of the husband's parents after they married. Chinese families often have at least three generations living under one roof, sometimes four. The husband's father passed away two years ago, a year after the couple moved in. The wife had only limited experience with her mother-in-law before moving in. It is interesting to note that in Chinese culture each position in the family-of-origin has a specific name. For example, in Mandarin, pópo indicates the husband's mother, and xífù indicates the daughter-in-law. This specificity regarding family position (relative to the terms used in the West) indicates the Chinese emphasis on recognizing each member's unique position in the family. The wife explained that at first the relationship between her and the mother-in-law was polite and friendly, but after the birth of the first child, the wife found that her mother-in-law was becoming more and more critical of her as a mother and a wife. The conflict that can arise between the pópo and xífù is commonly referred to in Chinese culture as the "po xi wen ti" which is roughly translated as "mother-in-law problem" (although some of the team members watching the case commented that from a systemic point of view it could also justifiably be called a "daughter-in-law problem" or a "mother-son-wife problem").

Both the husband and wife worked outside the home, leaving the grandmother to take care of the newborn. In modern China, this arrangement is also very common for many families, where the younger working age members of the family work outside the home, leaving the children to the grandparents to raise. The husband's job takes him away from the home more often than the wife's job, leaving the two women of the house together more, and increasingly in conflict. The therapist's goal in the first part of the session was to clarify the problem statement from each member of the family. After some prompting, the husband indicated that he was not sure why the two women he cared about could not get along with each other. He lamented about how hard he was working and that he felt increased pressure to perform in the family after the death of his father. Yet, he was fearful about getting caught in the middle so he had become less and less involved in the family, which he conceded probably made things worse. The mother-in-law indicated that she felt she was only trying to do what was best for the child and that it was her right to offer advice to the daughter-in-law and that she did not feel appreciated or that her opinion mattered. She felt it was the wife's job to help her take care of the child and accept her influence. The mother-in-law conceded that she felt a little offended and hurt that her daughter-in-law did not appear to value her opinions. The daughter-in-law seemed surprised to hear this and said that she did not mean to give this message and that she did value the mother-in-law's views.

The therapist asked if this type of thing had happened before and had it ever turned out in a more favorable way? They all agreed that it had gone well at first, before the father had passed away. They all agreed that in the past when conflict emerged in the house the father would get involved and that this helped resolve things more quickly. Also, the father was a strong support and his death had left a vacuum in the family. The family discussed the father's death, and how they had not really had a chance to fully recognize the loss. After a break in the session, the therapist returned to the therapy room to ask the family if they would like to hear feedback from the team directly (with the team coming into the therapy room to talk to the clients directly), which interested them all greatly. The team shared how they thought that one thing that they all seemed to share was a concern for the family as a whole, the welfare of the newborn, and deep affection for the recently deceased father. One team member reframed the situation as the family going through several challenges that would normally involve conflict between members. The team discussed how families might struggle to make all the adjustments that must occur when a couple marries, has a child, and grieves the death of the father. Recognizing all these challenges and normalizing the struggles that follow seemed to give relief to each family member. One team member noticed how they had reported that when the father was alive, he would get involved more and that this exception to the way the current situation was occurring may be important to consider. The team member invited the family to think about what the father might say to them all now as advice about how to deal with the current dilemma if he were here in the room. Finally, another team member discussed the importance of grieving, and wondered if the family had enough time to fully grieve given all that was happening. Once the team left the room, the family discussed the feedback from the team with the therapist, paying special note to the idea of thinking about what the father would say if he was here and could give them advice. The therapist pointed to an empty chair in the room and asked each, "What do you think he would say if he was sitting here with us?" Each family member took turns and shared what they thought he would advise. They all cried as they talked. They all agreed that his message would be kind, and would encourage them to work together for the welfare of the newborn. In concluding, the therapist suggested that they could have this same sort of conversation at home in the future, bringing the departed father's voice into the conversation. The family was welcomed to return to the clinic anytime in the future when they thought it might help.

Comment: This brief case description highlights many of the useful elements of SST, as well as some unique characteristics of Chinese family life. The research in SST has demonstrated that what many clients say they appreciate about the single session is the ability to have an open conversation about issues, with an objective professional helping to keep things from getting too activated or stuck. Often these clients report that it was not possible to have the conversation they had in the therapy room on their own at home without it turning into an unproductive fight. They report that the neutral, safe, therapy space allows them to have a new type of conversation with one another, which allows for important new insights, understandings, and behaviors to occur.

This case also highlights one of the most important virtues in Chinese family life, that of "filial piety." Filial piety is considered the first of among 100 virtues that Confucius prescribed as the foundation of social harmony. The concept is one of family honor, where younger members of the family show their respect for the older generation by taking care of them and accepting their influence as they grow older. Yet in modern China, this virtue is being challenged with pressures such as rapid urbanization, the mass migration of the young people from the farm life to urban settings, and the increasing elderly population who must be cared for by their only children. In this family, these pressures were clear with the demands on the daughter-in-law to accept the influence of the mother-in-law while also adjusting to her role as a new mother and as a professional (see Lim & Lim, 2012).

Case 2: The "4-2-1 Dilemma" and Academic Achievement

A mother in her 40's and her 18-year-old daughter presented for a single session consultation. The mother began the session by discussing her concern that the daughter was not doing well in school. The mother seemed very anxious about the daughter's school performance, although it seemed that while the daughter's grades had dropped somewhat she was still doing very well in school. The daughter sat quietly listening for the first part of the session as the mother shared her concerns. After some prompting by the therapist, the daughter shared her feeling of being under too much "pressure" and her general sense of worry and anxiety that had been growing since she came to the university. The daughter discussed how the transition had been difficult, especially her worry that she would not be able to continue to make the good grades she had when she was younger. The daughter also reported her worry about her parent's constant attention to her, including daily phone calls and probing inquiries which she felt had become more intense since she came to school. The daughter reported that her sense of worry and pressure had made her feel more and more depressed and she revealed that she had even thought about the meaningless of life. This was new information for the mother, who was alarmed and became more anxious and inquisitive. The therapist inquired further about this, and the daughter denied any self-harming thoughts or behaviors. The therapist asked the daughter to talk about her experiences of feeling under pressure, where those feelings came from, and what she thought would help.

The daughter told about how when she was younger and attending a school outside the city, she had been the best student in the class. This made her happy, as she was the "only child" of two "only child" parents, and that she felt she her academic success had brought honor to her four grandparents and two parents who all loved to brag about her. The daughter reported that when she was younger it was easy to make the top grades, but with each graduation to a new school she was competing more with those few other students from around China who were making the top grades in their classes. Her hard work had paid off when she took the gaokao, *formally known as the "National Higher Education Entrance Examination" in China. Almost all graduating high school students take the* gaokao *each year, and the score they earn determines what university they will be able to attend. College is relatively inexpensive in China and the determination of what school a student is able to attend is highly influenced by the score the student earns on the* gaokao. *If their score is high enough, they are almost guaranteed a spot at a top school as well as financial support to attend. In essence, most people believe the score on this one exam is the most important factor that determines a student's success in life. The daughter had scored very well on the exam and was able to attend a top university.*

Now, she was at a major university and competing with many other students who, like her, were all the top of their class when they were younger. In this environment, it was impossible for all the students that were once the top of their class to remain in this position. She also talked about the worry she had for her parents now that she had left the home. The mother agreed that she had missed the daughter since she had gone to college and that her absence in the house had made things more tense between her and the father. As their only child, the daughter had been the focus of their relationship since her birth and now that she was away at college there was a big hole in their lives.

The mother and daughter welcomed feedback from the team during the break in the session. The team complimented both the mother and the daughter for their concern for the feelings of the other, and their sense of respect for the larger family. They shared how it seemed to make sense how the mother would be anxious about the daughter's performance given her deep devotion to the daughter, and the entire family's investment in her doing well. The team also appreciated the difficult situation the daughter was in, with all the hopes and dreams of four grandparents and two parents leveled on her shoulders. The team talked about the value and cost of pressure, since it had come up so often during the session. Some team members talked about how some amount of pressure is useful to give someone enough energy and motivation to do a difficult thing. Yet there is also a "principle of diminishing returns." This principle states that for any two variables (like pressure and success) that as you increase one, the other increases as well. More pressure will often increase success, up to a certain point. Yet at some point the positive return from this relationship diminishes. Ironically sometimes the relationship seems to go the other direction, where more pressure actually decreases success. The team wondered if they had discovered this limit in the daughter's current situation. The team wondered if this was true, that it still might be very hard for the family to change given that they had all been working this way for a long time. Yet the team encouraged them to consider this point and experiment with lowering pressure. Finally, the team discussed the definition of "success" for the family, and wondered if they had openly discussed the various ways (beyond grades) that someone might be successful. They encouraged the mother and daughter to share this discussion with the father, and perhaps even the grandparents.

After the team left the therapy room, the mother and daughter both agreed that they felt they had reached the "diminishing returns" of pressure on the daughter's academic success. They discussed with the therapist various ways to lower pressure for the daughter, and the daughter was able to offer her own thoughts about what would help. They both agreed to share their thoughts about the conversation with the father the next time they had a meal together. Also, the mother discussed ways to lower her own anxiety and pressure about what was happening, which may include more involvement with her husband.

Comment: This case also highlights several elements of SST that clients often say they appreciate about the session. The clients seemed to be caught in an "attempted solution as the problem" type of situation. Everyone was applying more pressure to the daughter (including the daughter herself) which previously had made things better, but was now making things worse. Many clients caught in this situation continue the same "attempted solution" because the story that they have to explain what is happening does not allow for other alternative "attempted solutions" and they are worried if they stop that things will get worse. The introduction of an "alternative story" to explain what is happening can be a powerful force in opening up new opportunities for the family to try new possibilities that may alleviate the process that maintains the problem. As in the previous case vignette, the session was useful for the family in that it provided a neutral place with a trained professional that would help everyone express themselves without things getting stuck or becoming too out of control. The team was able to normalize what was happening, and compliment everyone for doing what they thought was best. Finally, the team encouraged the family to activate some of their currently existing resources (the larger family unit) in helping address the problem of "diminishing returns." Many clients report that the SST sessions are helpful in that the session helps activate these currently existing resources.

This case also highlights several aspects of Chinese family life that are relevant for the therapist practicing in the Chinese context. The "4-2-1 dilemma" is getting more attention in Chinese society (see Miller & Fang, 2012; Miller, 2012), with the history of China's "only-child" policy producing the unintended consequence of a whole generation of only children getting married to each other and producing an only child. In an environment of "filial piety" it is easy to see how the pressure from four grandparents and two parents on a single child may produce too much pressure for the young person. It is interesting to note that while in the U.S. the most commonly reported presenting concern for therapy is "depression," in China, the most common complaint I have observed over the past decade is "pressure." The difference is perhaps subtle, yet may lie in the differences between an individualistic society like the U.S. and a collectivist society like China. In one situation, happiness and pain may be thought of as emanating from the inside the individual. In another situation, these may be thought of as phenomena that are pressed in upon the individual from the outside.

Case 3: "Flash Marriage" and "Flash Divorce"

A heterosexual couple in their late 20's presented for a single session with concerns about their marital relationship. The couple had married 2 years ago, and reported that there had been more tension in the relationship in the last year. The therapist inquired about their fighting and what the conflict was about. The couple reported that they had married after a short courtship (4 months) and didn't really get a chance to know one another fully before getting married. They both talked about pressure from their families to get married, but they now felt that their courtship was too fast. They argued often about money, household responsibilities, and their relationship with their parents. Their disagreements had reached a crisis point during the last Spring Festival, when they traveled to the husband's home to visit with his family but were not able to visit her family because there was not enough time and her parents lived in a different region.

The Spring Festival (or Chinese New Year celebration) occurs in late January or early February, and is perhaps the most important family holiday in China. Each year in China, much of the population makes a pilgrimage back home to visit with their families of origin to celebrate the coming of Spring. The Spring Festival is also a time to remember and celebrate the family ancestors. With China's 1.8 billion people, each year the Spring Festival migration sets a new world record for the number of people making a migration. In contemporary China, this migration is increasingly younger people who have moved to the bigger cities for work returning home in the countryside to see their families of origin.

The husband's parents were critical of the wife during the visit, implying that she was not doing her duty in the family and taking care of their son properly. She felt they were pressuring her to be less career focused and stay home and devote herself to starting a family and taking care of her husband. Yet the wife felt that financially there was no chance that they would be able to afford for her to stop working with the high cost of living in the city. They both reported that things had not been very happy between them since the visit home for the Spring Festival and that she felt increasingly unhappy in the relationship and was now considering divorce. The husband said he did not want to divorce, but conceded that it was a very unhappy situation and he did not know what to do. They reported that the therapy session was the first time they had been able to talk about the conflict directly because when they brought it up at home the conversation would immediately escalate into an unproductive fight with each eventually retreating to a separate room.

The couple welcomed feedback from the team who entered the therapy room during the break and talked to the couple about the tremendous pressure on both of them from work and family. One team *member talked about the importance of some amount of disagreement early in the relationship so that certain issues in the relationship can get worked out. The team normalized this tension as a typical process for new couples, and wondered if they had enough time in the relationship to work out these issues given their relatively short courtship. Perhaps before making a decision about divorce, they could spend some time deciding what they needed to know to make a good decision about the future and what they would want to have happen? Since both had reported that the therapy conversation had allowed for a new type of discussion to occur between them, the team recommended that they return to consult with one of the therapists at the clinic so that they could make the best decision for the future. The focus of the team was not to keep the couple together or help them to part, but to help them make a good decision about what to do next since it was such a big decision. The couple agreed to this plan and scheduled another appointment at the clinic for the following week.*

Comment: This session involves several aspects of SST that are often reported by clients as useful. The couple had reached a gridlock in the relationship where they were no longer able to communicate productively about the tensions in the relationship. The single session opened up new conversational space between them where they were able to discuss the relationship issues without escalating into conflict. Many clients report that the therapy session provides a neutral space for them to talk things out more calmly with an objective party (the therapist) to help guide them and regulate conflict. This conversational space can be an important starting place for people to begin to get the relationship issues on the table. For this couple, more sessions seemed warranted given these dynamics. The goal of future sessions would not be to keep them together or break them up, but to help them get the issues out and assist them in making the best decision possible.

The session also highlights a unique aspect of couple therapy in China. The divorce rate in China has rapidly increased over the last few decades, going from 25% in 1999 to 39% in 2006 to even higher today. Many social scientists attribute the rapid increase in divorce to a typical process for a developing country that is rapidly modernizing and enjoying more affluence. In the past in China people needed to get permission from their employer to get a divorce; the laws have now changed to simplify the process of divorce. Personality conflicts are also commonly cited as reasons for marriage dissolution in urban cities with 50% of couples in urban settings divorcing after 7 years of marriage. These changes have led to a new social phenomenon among the younger population in China, "flash marriage" and "flash divorce." These terms were coined in the last decade to denote the large numbers of couples that marry after a relatively short courtship (7 months or less) and often subsequently divorce. The pressure to marry sooner is often fueled by financial pressures and family-of-origin pressures. There is a wide concern in China about the rapid societal changes with regard to marriages and divorce (Miller & Fang, 2012).

Client Feedback Regarding the Single Session and How to Open Up Services

At the conclusion of each session all clients were invited to fill out a survey and participate in a debriefing interview with a separate researcher that asked about their experiences and opinions about the service. The intent of the survey and the interview was to find out if the services had been helpful; clients' views about help-seeking behaviors in China; the usefulness of the single session; what was helpful about the session (if anything); and recommendations to improve the service. Almost all of the clients completed the survey and interview at the conclusion of the session. When asked if the single session had met the client's expectations, 81% indicated that it had met their expectations. No clients indicated that it did not meet their expectations. When asked if the one session was useful to them, 79% of the clients indicated that the session was useful, while 21% were neutral on this question. None of the clients indicated that the session was not useful. When asked if the single session alone was sufficient to address the concern they had brought to therapy, 56% indicated that it was sufficient, while the remainder indicted they would likely need more help. These findings roughly match the findings of similar studies conducted throughout the West.

Respondents were also asked about what they thought would improve access to counseling in China. The majority indicated that counseling services were not easy to access in their community (66%) and that there is a negative stigma regarding counseling in China (93%). When asked their opinions about what would make it more likely that people would seek counseling help in China, many talked about the need to have a better sense of who is qualified to provide services and how and where to find proficient therapists. They also discussed the need for some therapist regulation to ensure that the provider is well trained and able to provide competent help. This issue regarding therapist competence and the concern potential clients have about how to find a competent therapist has also been raised in many studies in the West regarding barriers to service (U.S. Department of Health and Human Service, 1999; Miller, 2005; Miller, Todahl & Platt, 2010; Miller, 2010). When asked what was helpful about the session, many clients discussed the objective, professional suggestions made during the session by the therapist and the team. The responses seemed to support the supposition that many people in the Chinese culture prefer a more expert-based service where direct suggestions are given.

Concluding Thoughts about Western Therapy in the Chinese Context

The Ethics of One-Way Exportation: The Importance of a Two-Way Exchange

Much of the practice of therapy in China today is the result of collaborations between Chinese therapists and Western influences. Like many things, this has the potential to produce both positive and negative consequences. The Chinese culture is one of the oldest continuously existing civilizations on the planet and by virtue of its longevity and contiguity, it would be hard to argue that has not been successful. As Western concepts and methods continue to influence Chinese culture, it will be important to keep in mind the natural healing methods and processes that already exist in the Chinese culture and do everything possible to preserve them. A true give-and-take, mutually influencing and influenced environment, will be more healthy for all involved than a one-way delivery of information (from West to East). Chinese family therapy leaders like Dr. Xiaoyi Fang at Beijing Normal University, Dr. Wai Yung Lee at the University of Hong Kong, Dr. Xudong Zhao and his colleagues and students at Tongji University in Shanghai, and Dr. Joyce Ma and her colleagues at the Chinese University of Hong Kong are a few of the important scholarly groups that strive to utilize Western methods of therapy while also preserving, recognizing and promoting Chinese ways of knowing and healing (see Liu, Zhao & Miller, 2012;

Liu, Miller, Zhao, Ma, Wang & Li, 2012; Ma, 2012; Miller, 2011b, 2012; Su, Fang, Miller, & Wang, 2011; Yuhong, Zhao & Miller, 2010). The world of therapy and the clients we serve globally will greatly benefit from our efforts to promote genuine two-way exchanges of knowledge and healing traditions.

The Danger of the Single Story of China

China is a rich tapestry of cultures, ethnicities, and traditions. Far from being one homogenous group, Chinese culture represents over 56 clearly identifiable ethnic groups speaking 129 different languages, excluding dialects and sub-dialects (Miller & Fang, 2012). Yet it is common for many in the West to perceive China as a single cultural group. This is a serious over simplification of a complex and rich culture and peoples. One of the first things I learned when becoming a therapist was not to treat an individual within a group as if they were the whole group that they belong to, nor treat a whole group of individuals as if they could be represented by a stereotypical single individual. My year living in Beijing, and my near decade of work across China, has taught me this basic principle of therapy is especially true when thinking about the wonderful and complex Chinese peoples and culture. To this point I am inspired by the words of the novelist Chimamanda Adichie in her now famous 2009 TED talk about the *Danger of the Single Story*. During her talk she recognizes that we and the groups we belong to are composed of many interlaced stories and that if we hear only the single story of another individual or group we hazard a critical misunderstanding; and that when we reject the single story of a culture (or individual) we can "regain a kind of paradise." As the title of a brief therapy book (Hoyt, 2000) has it, *"Some Stories are Better than Others,"* and in China and around the world we can often help clients find their "better story" in one session.

References

Adichie, C. (2009). The danger of a single story. *TED Talks*. See http://www. ted.com/talks/chimamanda_adichie_the_danger_of_a_single_story.html

Hoyt, M.F. (2000) *Some stories are better than others: Doing what works in brief therapy and managed care*. Philadelphia: Brunner/Mazel.

Lim, S. & Lim, B. (2012). Po xi wen ti: The "mother-in-law problem": Navigating tradition and modernity in transforming familial relationships in the Chinese family. *Journal of Family Psychotherapy*, 23(3), 202–216. DOI: 10.1080/08975353.2012.705649

Linville, D., Todahl, J., & Miller, J. (2008, October). *Healthy Nests: A Pilot Preventive Intervention for New Parent Couples*. Presentation at American Association for Marriage and Family Therapy National Conference. Memphis, TN.

Liu, L., Miller, J. K., Zhao, X., Ma, X, Wang, J., & Li, W. (2012). Systemic family psychotherapy in China: A qualitative analysis of therapy process. *Psychology and Psychotherapy: Theory, Research, and Practice*. Article first published online: Sept. 20, 2012 doi: 10.1111/j.2044-8341.2012.02075.x

Liu, L., Zhao, X., & Miller, J. K. (2012). Use of metaphors in Chinese family therapy: A qualitative study. *Journal of Family Therapy*. Article first published online Feb, 15 2012. doi: 10.1111/j.1467-6427.2012.00582.x

Ma, J. L. C. (2012). *Anorexia nervosa and family therapy in a Chinese context*. Hong Kong: The Chinese University Press.

Miller, J.K. (1996) *Walk-in single-session therapy: A study of client satisfaction*. Dissertation: Virginia Polytechnic Institute and State University.

Miller, J. K. (2000). *Bringing the mountain to Mohamed: Re-thinking clinical delivery. Relationship check-ups*. Paper presented at the 2000 World Congress of the International Family Therapy Association (IFTA), Oslo, Norway.

Miller, J. K. (2005). The question of competence. *Family Therapy Magazine*, 4 (4), 28–31.

Miller, J. K. (2006). First on the scene after disaster strikes: What to expect as a mental health worker. *Family Therapy Magazine*, 5(2), 6–11.

Miller, J. K. (2008). Walk-in single session team therapy: A study of client satisfaction. *Journal of Systemic Therapies*, 27(3), 78–94.

Miller, J. K. (2010). Competency-based training: Using the objective structured clinical exercises (OSCE) in marriage and family therapy. *Journal of Marital and Family Therapy*, 36 (3), 320–332.

Miller, J. K. (2011a). Single session intervention in the wake of Hurricane Katrina: Strategies for disaster mental health counseling. In A. Slive & Bobele, M. (Eds.), *When one hour is all you have: Effective therapy for walk-in clients* (pp. 185–202). Phoenix, AZ: Zeig, Tucker, & Theisen.

Miller, J. K. (2011) Special section: International issues in clinical practice and training. *Journal of Systemic Therapies*, 30(2), 41–42.

Miller, J. K. (2012). Introduction to the special section on marriage and family therapy in China. *Journal of Family Psychotherapy*, 23, 169–172.

Miller, J. K., & Fang, X. (2012). Marriage and family therapy in the People's Republic of China: Current issues and challenges. *Journal of Family Psychotherapy*, 23, 173–183.

Miller, J. K., & Gergen, K.J. (1996). Life on the line: Therapeutic potentials of computer mediated conversation. *Journal of Marital and Family Therapy*, 24(2), 189–202.

Miller, J. K., & Platt, J. (2013, February). *Therapy Needs and Challenges in Post-Genocide Cambodia*. International Family Therapy Association's 21st World Family Therapy Congress, Lake Buena Vista, FL.

Miller, J.K., & Slive, A. (1997) *Walk-in single-session therapy: A model for the 21st century.* Paper presented at the 1997 Annual Conference of the American Association for Marriage and Family Therapy, Atlanta, GA.

Miller, J. K., & Slive, A. (2004). Breaking down the barriers to clinical service delivery: Walk-in family therapy. *Journal of Marital and Family Therapy,* 30(1), 95–103.

Miller, J. K., & Tarragona, M. (2012). International family therapy. In A. Rambo, C. West, A. Schooley, & T.V. Boyd (Eds.), *Family therapy review: Contrasting contemporary models* (pp. 262–264). New York: Routledge.

Miller, J. K., Todahl, J., & Platt, J. (2010). The core competency movement in marriage and family therapy: Key considerations from other disciplines. *Journal of Marriage and Family Therapy,* 36(1), 59–70.

Su, W., Fang, X., Miller, J. K., & Wang, Y. (2011). Internet-based intervention for the treatment of online addiction for college students in China: A pilot study of the healthy online self-helping center. *Cyberpsychology, Behavior, and Social Networking,* 14(9), 497–503.

Todahl, J., Linville, D., Miller, J., & Brown, T. (2009, October). *Healthy Nests: A Preventative Intervention for New Parent Couples.* Presentation at American Association for Marriage and Family Therapy National Conference. Sacramento, CA.

U.S. Department of Health and Human Services. (1999). *Mental health: A report of the Surgeon General—executive summary.* Rockville, MD: U.S. Department of Health and Human Services, Substance Abuse and Mental Health Services Administration, Center for Mental Health Services, National Institutes of Health, National Institute of Mental Health.

Yuhong, Y, Zhao, X., Miller, J. K. (2010). Comparisons of multi-system interpersonal relationship characteristics between Chinese and American college students. *Shanghai Archives of Psychiatry,* 20, 397–400.

Chapter Twelve

Single Session Walk-In Therapy for Street Robbery Victims in Mexico City

Jason J. Platt and Debora Mondellini

An unfortunate reality of life in all large cities is the occurrence of street crimes, and Mexico City is not an exception. The possibility of experiencing a street robbery in Mexico City is something that touches both our personal and professional worlds and the threat of them occurring has an influence on the day-to-day lives of those who live in our community. Indeed, both of us authors have had the experience of being robbed, as have many of our friends, family, students and clients. We recently spoke about street robberies at a family therapy conference in Acapulco and were somewhat surprised to learn that the vast majority of therapists attending also had been robbed at some point.

On the other hand, we recognize that there is an over-focus in recent years on violence in Mexico and we are troubled by the fact that the media paints an unbalanced picture of life and safety here. The majority of the time people are not being robbed and our lives are not dominated by a singular focus on avoiding theft. We are aware that people outside of Mexico are particularly given an incomplete version of reality, promoted by the media, of a single story of Mexico as dangerous. This simplistic and partial story silences important layers and complexities of reality here and it can also have clinical implications. As a mental health training program, we began to consider how we might use our university mental health center, the California Clinic, to provide assistance and be a resource for those who had experienced being robbed on the street.

The California Clinic is a counseling and dialogue center based in Mexico City, one of the planet's largest metropolises with a population of approximately twenty-three million people. Founded in 2011, the clinic was developed to serve as a training and research center for students enrolled in the Masters in International Counseling Psychology program (MAICP) and immersion education students at Alliant International University's Mexico City Campus. The program emphasizes systems theory, Latin American and liberation psychologies, and draws from a social constructionist perspective. Given that the community of students and faculty come from diverse national origins and are largely serving Mexican communities, the program makes considerable effort to avoid relying solely on standardized Western models of mental health and to be mindful of the powerful influence of the national cultural, historical and contemporary contexts in which we provide services.

As we began efforts to develop an onsite clinic, one of our missions has been to provide services to underserved and often impoverished communities. As a component of the services the clinic provides, walk-in single session therapy was selected because of its ability to address many of the barriers to services faced by poor communities, including economic issues and social stigma. Clinic clients generally pay around 50 pesos (less than $5 US), but if they are not able to pay, we will waive the fee. Services are provided in Spanish, unless a client (e.g., an American expat) requests otherwise. In July of 2011, a Fulbright fellowship brought Dr. Monte Bobele, who participated in the development of Our Lady of the Lake University's walk-in clinic (Slive & Bobele, 2011—also see Chapters 5–6 this volume) to help with the initial development of a walk-in infrastructure and to provide single session training to therapist-supervisees working in the clinic. Later, we brought Dr. John K. Miller, who has also worked in several walk-in clinics and has used a single session interventions in working with people following a natural disaster (Miller, 2011—also see Chapter 11 this volume) to provide training in using this approach with clients dealing with trauma. As university faculty, we work with supervisees in adapting interventions for the unique needs of the economically challenged and to be mindful of how the collective memories of violence within Mexico City may shape individual responses to a personal experience with violence.

In this chapter we will share ideas about using single session interventions with clients who have experienced a street robbery. We will start by explaining the context and nature of street violence in Mexico and some of the common clinical implications this experience has in the lives of individuals, couples and families. We will also describe how single session interventions can be integrated with Latin American originating liberation psychology to better serve clients who also live in poverty.

Street Violence in Mexico

A layered and complicated story of violence exists in Mexico, one that can have an influence on the personal and relational wellbeing of individuals and families. One unfortunate example is the disproportionately high number of street robberies that occur in Mexico City. According to the *Procuraduría General de Justicia* (PGJ), in 2012, 43,329 robberies (of any type) were reported—118.1 robberies a day—in Mexico City. For the period of January–May 2013, 133.3 robberies were reported per day. These figures undeniably underrepresent the number of actual robberies given that few people report such crimes in Mexico for reasons that range from the belief that it "wasn't such a serious thing" to a general mistrust in the system's adequacy in investigating the event.

For the purposes of this writing we shall refer to the phenomena we are discussing as *street robberies*, a term consistent with the dictionary definition of robbery as "(1) to take away something by force: steal from; (2) to take personal property by violence or threat." This coincides with Mexico's Penal Code, which typifies a robbery as the act of seizing someone else's property without having a right to them, and/or without consent. We have struggled with how to refer to street robberies given that there are a number of nuanced terms that exists, both in Spanish and in English, such as *hurto*, mugging, assault, *robo*, etc.

Likewise, we have struggled with referring to clients as "victims." We concluded that if we were to use the term, the definition of *victim* that is closer to our purposes is in the United Nation's Resolution 40/34 (1985) that assumes a systemic perspective by referring to the possible "physical, emotional and material consequences of a criminal act on a person as well as their family." Ultimately, for the purposes of clinical work and training, the dialogue with clients about how they name their own experience is what is meaningful. These personal constructions may also provide a window of opportunity for intervention.

The type of street robberies and degree of violence involved varies, and for some people the experience results, among other things, in a loss of a sense of well-being, relational conflicts, and a serious disruption of their daily activities. A loss of a sense of safety is also a common result. Mexicans' perception of safety was studied by the Center for Research and Development (CIDAC, in Spanish) in 2012. They reported that experiencing a street robbery—with or without violence—was among the top eight types of crime that negatively impact people's perception of safety. They also found that for each non-violent street robbery there are three violent street robberies.

A sense of safety is, to some extent, linked to a belief in justice, i.e., the belief that authorities can be trusted to catch the thieves, return the property, and bring the perpetrators to justice. In Mexico, however, there is little—close to no—confidence in the police, whether it is from personal experience or not. For example, "Karina" (age 27) explained, "If I go and say 'this is the thief,' the thieves will learn that I reported it and it is very probable that they can figure out where I live. That is very dangerous and it would just result in more problems."

Therapists working with street robbery survivors often need to discuss with clients issues of justice and impunity. CIDAC (2012) notes that the Public Ministry, the agency that investigates crime, treats all types of crime in the same manner, whether it is a street robbery or a murder, without prioritizing. They also use the same resources for either. And so it is that out of 100 reported cases, only one is punished, resulting in a message of impunity that contributes to people's sense of insecurity and reluctance to report.

The lack of expectation of being helped by formal structures is grounded in the real experiences of many clients. For example, "Garrett", a 30-year-old gay North American expatriate living in Mexico, was robbed twice. After the first incident, when he attempted to report it, he was asked if he was gay. When he responded that he was, he was told he had to go to a special station for crimes against the gay community. No such station existed and he kept being told to go to a different station. Eventually he gave up and when he was robbed a second time he did not report it.

In these types of cases, when justice is unlikely, resolution will need to take another form. Garrett's experience was complicated by a number of contextual factors that it would be essential for a therapist to consider. Clinical work would need to include an understanding of diversity issues in Mexico such as gender, immigration and language abilities. It has been our experience—in our social circles—that the experience of a street robbery and the personal perception of safety influences acculturation. For many people, leaving Mexico is not a viable option at the moment, which can lead to a frustrating sense of feeling trapped. In working with Garrett, having a space for him to clarify therapeutic goals and weigh different options was valuable. As a gay U.S. male student, Garrett reported considering returning home, but ultimately decided to stay after giving more importance to his positive experiences in Mexico and that he only had one year left to graduate.

The Clinical Implications of Street Robbery

In a city where street crimes are relatively common, how then does a person make meaning of his or her own safety, as well as that of their loved ones? How do they make meaning of the experience of being robbed? How do they perceive their sense of support? We believe it is not useful to automatically pathologize the experience of being robbed. We have encountered many people who believe it is expected of any metropolis and they get on with their lives as usual.

When street robbery becomes a normalized probability, it affects a person's sense of safety and so they engage in certain behaviors to avoid being the victim of a crime; for example, changing the way they dress, using or not using public transport, and avoiding certain areas. Unfortunately, the normalization of crime can also become an obstacle for those who feel the need of support from family and friends and are not receiving it, perhaps because of the belief that it happens to everyone at least once. This could lead to minimizing their felt experience, say sleeplessness or heightened tension, which in some way may be disrupting their daily life and relationships. Not having anyone to talk to or feeling unheard, and consequently being unable to find solace given this social construction, can lead to silent suffering, especially in a culture where going to therapy is viewed as elitist, or reserved for the "really serious stuff" (whatever that may be!).

People typically believe in the right to feel safe and protected, and in the belief that we are not vulnerable to the *whims* of strangers who can simply come up and take that which is ours. Otherwise, we would be constantly evaluating events, people and circumstances in terms of potential danger, at the expense of considerable psychic energy, a sense of loss of autonomy and of control (Kennedy, 1983). As therapists, we then encounter such constructs as "no one is safe anymore," "it wasn't even nighttime," "that street used to be safe," etc. (In fact, living in the same city and from personal experience, we couldn't agree with them more!). Needless to say, these have clinical implications when their daily lives and relationships are disrupted, and when they realize their security measures weren't efficient.

A person may find solace in the fact that "at least they only took material things" and that "it could have been worse." Sellin and Wolfgang (1983) found that people's evaluation of the gravity of a delinquent experience is in direct proportion to personal injuries and the monetary equivalent of the loss, and if they deem it as *not so serious*, they tend to view themselves as having been fortunate, rather than as a victim. We believe that in these cases, people react by taking precautions to ensure their safety without seriously disrupting their lifestyle.

Triventi (2008) reported that people's sense of safety can actually improve after a street robbery, because they will take measures to ensure their safety. However, some of these strategies could lead to isolating oneself from their usual activities, including social ones, leading to feelings of depression and yet a very low percentage will seek therapy (Morral, Marshall, Pattison, Macdonald, 2010).

In fact, when we ask clients' reasons for seeking therapy, they tend to posit responsibility on others for suggesting they come because they believe the client has been *traumatized* by the event, and is behaving *hysterically* or *neurotically* (it is important to distinguish the use of these terms in everyday language from their clinical definitions). And when we ask their opinion about such *diagnoses*, they wonder if they really are *locos* (crazy). The flexibility of strategies and/or interventions inherent to a single session approach is efficient in addressing these constructs and, more importantly, in validating the client's reactions and resources.

Another behavior that may disrupt people's lives and bring them to the consulting room is if they find themselves afraid of being alone and feeling vulnerable to the point that they are constantly asking someone to stay with them or accompany them when going somewhere; loved ones may insist on not leaving them alone either. Constant remorse and guilt can be interfering, too, as expressed in thoughts such as "I should not have dressed this way," "I should have used a smaller bag," or "I should not have taken the metrobus."

There are many cultural aspects to consider in our work in Mexico. The influence of gender, race, sexual orientation, and so forth must be considered by the therapist, along with how these variables intersect with Mexican culture. For example, from Mexican men we often hear comments such as, "there were too many to fight off" or "if they didn't have a gun/knife" then they would not have been a victim of crime, suggesting the possibility that being robbed in the street is an affront to their personal and cultural construction of manhood. Also, in Mexico, a predominantly Catholic country, the experience of a crime might shake the faith of some people. Others, though, may draw on their religious beliefs as a form of support. Bible scripture (e.g., "For we must all appear before the judgment seat of Christ, that each one may receive what is due him for the things done while in the body, whether good or bad"—2 Corinthians 5:10) may comfort some with the idea that justice will eventually be served.

The Single Story of Post-Traumatic Stress Disorder

No client constructs exactly the same meaning or reacts in the same way to their experience of a street crime. This has been important for us to realize in our work. Despite the significantly diverse ways people deal with being robbed on the street, we found that we and our supervisees had, in some ways, been socialized through education and the existing resources to primarily conceptualize the experience from one perspective. As we considered and researched frameworks for addressing the experience of a street robbery, invariably we found references to post-traumatic stress disorder (PTSD). Since its inclusion in the *DSM*, this framework has been one of the most successfully exported theories of trauma throughout the world and is often found in the research on street robbery survivors. It should be remembered though that theories reflect the cultural norms and realities of the nations in which they developed. The dominant theory, globally exported, is that when a person experiences a street robbery, they will develop PTSD. While this framework has contributed a useful perspective on trauma, research on it has primarily been based on people from the United States, a country that makes up less than 5% of the world's population. As Arnett (2008, p. 1) highlights, this results in the fact that "the rest of the world's population, the other 95%, is neglected." In our work, we cannot ignore the contributions that a PTSD framework offers for survivors of violence, but we have also recognized it was not developed for this national context and that it is an incomplete framework.

People who have experienced a street robbery may report characteristic PTSD-type responses, including the avoidance of stimuli associated with the robbery, difficulty sleeping, anger, an exaggerated startle reflex, hypervigilance and difficulty concentrating, but seldom do they meet the full clinical criteria for PTSD.

Based on the story of PTSD, traumatic events are often treated though Critical Incident Stress Debriefing (CISD). This approach was first developed in the 1970s with the goal of assisting clients to reclaim a sense of safety and to address problems that impact a person's productivity and personal functioning (Mitchell & Bray, 1990). There are seven stages involved in CISD: (1) Introduction; (2) Fact phase; (3) Thought phase; (4) Reaction phase; (5) Symptoms phase; (6) Teaching phase; and a (7) Re-entry stage. We have found that a number of these stages occur naturally during the stages of single session therapy and those that do not can be easily incorporated. Campfield and Hills (2001) found that immediate use of CISD with people exposed to a noninjurious robbery resulted in clients having significantly fewer symptoms characteristic of posttraumatic stress.

Liberation Psychology

The larger community context in which any given phenomenon takes place has an isomorphic connection to the microsystem of the family and individual. Poverty and crime are two such realities in Mexico City. In regard to street robberies, the majority of people robbed in Mexico are those who are already facing economic oppression. Most models of therapy do not consider how the city the clients live in is part of the system on which to focus a clinical eye. Liberation psychology, in contrast, offers ideas on shifting the systemic lens from the microcosm of the family toward the macro-system of society. Ignacio Martín-Baró, a psychologist and Jesuit priest who was working with economically impoverished and war-torn communities in El Salvador, critiqued the use of U.S.-born individualistic approaches that largely ignore sociocultural contexts. In response he founded Liberation Psychology (Platt, 2010) and argued that "What is needed is for our most basic assumptions in psychological thought to be revised from the bottom up. But this revision cannot be made from our offices; it has to come from a praxis that is committed to the people" (Martín-Baró, 1994, p. 23). An important component of this revisioning of psychological approaches with a preference toward the poor is to help clients gain consciousness of the ways they are impacted by the social contexts. The goal is to help them recognize how their presenting problems are linked to the larger system and also to empower them to find ways to relate differently to and bring about social change within their communities.

"Maximo" (age 40), who had been robbed multiple times, when asked about his perspective on therapy, responded that, "Therapy is something rich people do. We have to work and we do not have time to go sit on a couch." Many people of lower and middle economic classes echo his sentiments about mental health services. The wealthy elite of Mexico, while also impacted by the experience, has options and resources unavailable to the poor. Additionally, dominant theories and the foundations of mental health also were primarily developed to meet the needs of wealthier clients (Martin-Baró, 1994; Platt, 2013); e.g., where services are located, the length of time needed, and the ongoing economic investment that longer-term therapies require. Clinicians are also rarely trained to serve the poor. Researchers Frankel and Frankel (2006) found that therapists, in general, tend to have ambivalent feelings about and relationships with families who are living in poverty. In many ways it makes sense that those who are poor might not see therapy as a relevant or as a viable resource for themselves. To address this reality, therapy services need to go beyond the dominant methods generally used. A single session therapy approach fits nicely within a liberation psychology framework given that it seeks to address three of the primary barriers to services faced by the poor: (1) social stigma, (2) financial barriers, and (3) accessibility (location).

Stages of a Single Session Following a Street Robbery

We draw on the general format for a walk-in session described in Slive and Bobele (2011). Therapy starts with clients being asked to complete a very brief questionnaire that contains questions aimed at orienting clients toward a single session framework. The therapist then further orients clients by explaining that many people find a single meeting to be sufficient. The therapist also explains that they will meet for about 30 minutes and then the therapist will take a break to consult with a team of other therapists. The session would start with general questions, such as, "What is the concern about your experience of the street robbery that you believe is the most important for us to discuss today?" During the meeting, the therapist would highlight the client's strengths and resources and would assist the client in identifying small concrete goals. After the therapist takes a break, the therapist would return to the session to briefly share observations of strengths and resources observed by the team as well as a smorgasbord of options the client might choose to take. For example, for street-crime victims this might include giving the option of returning for additional sessions, information about reporting the crimes, and information about other local resources and agencies. We might also share a list of things ideas other survivors have shared about what they have found useful to do in responding to the experience of street robbery. In addition to these basic steps, if it does not happen organically, we might ask questions based on the seven stages of Critical Incident Stress Debriefing. Given the lack of justice about crimes and the issue of justice, we also might explore ideas the clients have about how to change the system. Consistent with a single session approach, we might identify small but concrete goals for how the client might contribute to influencing change at the macro-level of the city.

Clinical Vignette

In order to illustrate how single session approaches can be used in cases of street crimes, we are providing a fictional vignette. The case example provided is drawn from a mix of actual cases and interviews with people who have experienced a street robbery and includes common phrases we have heard in how they describe their experience.

"Lorena" (age 50) lives in a low SES (socioeconomic status) neighborhood in Mexico City known for its high crime rate. Lorena had experienced two street assaults and came to the California Clinic on recommendation of her *comadre* (godmother), who was worried about recent changes she had seen in Lorena's behavior and relationships since she had been robbed. Lorena had hesitated to come, believing her outbursts were a passing phase, but after a shouting round with her adult son, she thought she'd give it a try and called the clinic.

First Contact and Introductory Phase

During the initial phone call, we talked with Lorena about our services and we suggested that "Sometimes people who have been robbed find it useful to come and talk with us as a way to make sense of their experience and to make sure it is not causing them any trouble. You may find that a single consultation will be enough for this situation." Lorena arrived for a consultation a few days later. We began our session by describing that our goal was for us to see what we might do today to be helpful to her. We told her that, in our clinic, we work with a team and that part way through the session, we would take a break to consult with our colleagues who would be watching the session. She agreed to this arrangement. We let her know that some clients just come to see us one time, but that we are here and available if she found a desire to come back in the future.

Initial Stage of the Session

THERAPIST: What would you like from our meeting today?

LORENA: I am having problems with my son. We had a big argument and I've never shouted at my son like that, and for no reason. Everyone was trying to calm me down and I just burst out crying. It's true I've been behaving like a hysterical, crazy woman and I don't know why. And I don't know what to do about it. My *comadre* said you could help me and I thought, why not? I have nothing to lose.

THERAPIST: So if you thought you had nothing to lose by coming here, do you think you have something to gain? If so, what might be an example of one small thing that might be different, some small change?

LORENA: Well...I don't know...I've never been to therapy, I don't know how it works, but since you're the experts, I thought you could tell me...

(Comment: It has been our experience when working with people from a low SES that we must invest some time challenging this belief, as well as trying to develop a more collaborative stance when developing a therapeutic alliance. The hierarchical culture in Mexico, as it plays out in therapy, is a constant challenge and a paradox: if we want to proceed with a col-

laborative approach, are we behaving 'anti-collaboratively' by imposing our beliefs when a client apparently needs or expects us to be more hierarchical? This debate of course goes beyond this chapter's objectives; however, we have found that emphasizing the client's experience and strengths gradually demystifies this notion as the client becomes more empowered.)

THERAPIST: Hmm...what experience has taught us is that everyone feels, thinks and reacts differently, so it would be impossible for us to be experts on your experience...maybe we can figure it out together?

LORENA: **As you say...**

THERAPIST: You say you thought *it* was a passing phase, but I'm not too sure I understand what you mean by 'it.' Do you mind telling me about 'it,' please? Also, is there a reason you are deciding to come see us now, as opposed to, maybe awhile ago?

LORENA: Well...now that I think about it, I've been feeling on edge, everything and everyone annoys me...*ni yo me aguanto a mí misma!* ("I can't even stand myself.") I want people to leave me alone...but I also don't want to be alone...I'm not like that, I swear! What if I really am going crazy? I thought I should talk to someone now before it gets worse.

THERAPIST: *Híjole* ("Yikes!"), that sounds unbearable—here's hoping we don't annoy you, too...but if you feel it's getting to that point, will you let us know?

LORENA: (smiles) OK.

THERAPIST: So how long has this been going on?

LORENA: ...Not sure...

THERAPIST: Maybe something happened...?

LORENA: ...Not sure...Well, now that you ask, do you think it could have something to do with the time I was mugged?

THERAPIST: Did you feel this way before it happened?

LORENA: I don't think so...

THERAPIST: Would you like to tell us what happened?

LORENA: I was walking to the bus stop to go to work, at 6 a.m., when a couple of men threatened me with a knife. I gave them everything I had, which granted wasn't a lot, just enough to get to work and for any eventuality, and then one of them shouted something nasty—which I really don't want to repeat in front you—and then put his hand inside my blouse to "fish out" my cell phone from my bra. And then, the next morning it happened again! The neighbor's son walked with me for protection, and the same gang came and robbed us both.

THERAPIST: Did you report it to the police?

LORENA: *Uy señorita!* What for? They surely get their cut from them.

THERAPIST: What did you do?

LORENA: What could I do? I went to work anyway, I had some metro tickets in my shoe just in case it happened again…

THERAPIST: That's good thinking! So you were ready this time…

LORENA: *Me llena de rabia!* ("It fills me with rage!") Where were their parents when they were growing up?! How dare they take what little I have when I work so hard for it? (cries)…I'm sorry…What are you going to think about me?

THERAPIST: That I'd be filled with rage, too, just like you…I'm wondering if there's a connection between what happened with you and your son, and this rage you're telling me about?

LORENA: I hadn't thought of it…

THERAPIST:…Does it make sense to you?

LORENA: I guess it does, because I'm really a calm person and people usually turn to me for advice. Now I scare them away!

THERAPIST: Really? What is it about you that makes people come to you?

LORENA: I don't really know…I mean, I help friends and family when they have a problem, or when they are sick…and I do it gladly…They know there's always a *tazita de café* (little cup of coffee) at my home and we can chat.

THERAPIST: And who did you turn to when you were robbed and need a *tazita de café?*

LORENA: I didn't want to bother anyone…I mean, look what happened. They try to help me and they get robbed, too!

THERAPIST: So you're a calm, friendly person with some great advice and a noble heart, because you wanted to protect them...

LORENA: (shrugs shoulder)

THERAPIST: I want to try something that may sound weird, please bear with me. Let's say you were looking at yourself in the mirror in one of those moments when you felt filled with rage, but your reflection is that of calm Lorena, the one with the good advice and a *tazita de café*...what advice do you think she'd have for you?

LORENA: I don't know...I hadn't thought of it that way...I guess...I guess...I would tell her that she should be grateful nothing worse came of it?

THERAPIST: Do you think that would console her?

LORENA: You know, now that I think of it, I am not going to let them take my things and leave me with rage!

THERAPIST: What do you mean?

LORENA: It's like what I used to say to my boys when they'd get in fights at school—if you let the anger get a hold of you, you lose. It's the same thing now—if I continue getting uncontrollably angry, they win. I'm not going to let them win...maybe I can't get the police to help, but they are not going to make me angry and scared all the time!

THERAPIST: That sounds very wise...but can I detect a bit of anger?

LORENA: Yes! Angry at them...and them only! I'm getting my life back, and I'm going to get my calm back!

THERAPIST: Will there be a *tazita de café* at yours again?

LORENA: (laughs) *Sí!*

Session Break and Feedback to Client

After consulting with the team, we returned and reported on some of the observations the team had about what she had shared:

1. We shared the admiration of the team about the strength she had demonstrated. For example, she had gone to work even though she had experienced a street robbery.

2. We shared how the team also saw her cleverness in hiding metro tickets in her shoe and other examples of her resourcefulness.
3. We discussed different strategies she could put in place to detect if she was starting to feel she was getting "filled with rage," including taking time out to calm down like going to the rooftop for some fresh air. She joked she wouldn't go for a walk…what if they robbed her again?
4. The team offered several suggestions about how she can increase the possibility of safety, such as informing the people she worked for that she'd be arriving later in the morning in order to not be walking alone on the streets at a time when no one else was around.
5. We shared some resources for people who have experienced crime that included legal consultation, government agencies, low-cost medical providers.
6. The team also, in line with liberation psychology, suggested ideas about connecting with a Mexican women's collective that gathers to address issues, such as street violence, that impact the lives of women here in Mexico City.

After providing the feedback from the team, the therapist discussed with Lorena whether she would like a referral to see a therapist more regularly. We also shared the option for her to return to the California Clinic. She stated that she was feeling more confidence and felt that she had ideas on how to avoid being a victim again. She did not schedule another session and she has not returned, but she sent us a message a couple of weeks later with her *comadre* telling us she had not returned since she felt the calm was returning and that she felt she had regained more control over her anger.

Concluding Thoughts

We are still in the early stages of implementing single session approaches with people who have experienced a street robbery, but we recognize the great potential this model offers in addressing the consequences of this overly common problem. In our view, the single session model has an intrinsic flexibility that allows us to work efficiently in a culture such as Mexico's, with both the national and expatriate population. Many people can and should be helped by accessible, no-hassle, non-pathologizing SST.

The biggest challenges in working with those who have experienced a street robbery are two-fold: being where they need us to be and encouraging a culture of seeking therapeutic assistance. While the clinic is located in an accessible area near several metro and *metrobus* lines in a centralized area of the city, visibility to those impacted by street robberies could still be increased. While this is valuable and the clinic provides an option for many clients, in the future we will be taking single session work to the people. We are considering options like placing a consulting booth in *tianguises* (street markets) that have fixed locations and dates.

There is a deep-rooted saying in Mexico, *"la ropa sucia se lava en casa"* ("dirty clothes are washed at home"), meaning that personal problems needn't be discussed outside of the home. This belief has often been mentioned by clients when asked about coming to therapy. We believe that part of our social responsibilities as therapists is to demystify therapy and promote its benefits, and single session therapy—which offers minimalist constructive intervention as a small, affordable, and accessible safe first step—might just be the ideal way to get us on the way.

References

Arnett, J. J. (2008). The neglected 95%: Why American psychology needs to become less American. *American Psychologist, 63*, 602–614.

Campfield, K.M., & Hills, A.M. (2001). Effect of timing of critical incident stress debriefing (CISD) on posttraumatic symptoms. *Journal of Traumatic Stress,* 14(2), 1–16.

CIDAC (2012). 8 Delitos primero. Índice delictivo. Retrieved from http://cidac.org/esp/uploads/1/Indice_Delictivo_CIDAC_2012._8_delitos_primero_1.pdf p. 6, 9,10.

Código Penal Federal. (n.d). *Justía México.com Código Penal Federal.* Retrieved from http://mexico.justia.com/federales/codigos/codigo-penal-federal/libro-segundo/titulo-vigesimo-segundo/capitulo-i/http://mexico.justia.com/federales/codigos/codigo-penal-federal/libro-segundo/titulo-vigesimo-segundo/capitulo-i/ Book 1, art. 367.

Frankel, H., & Frankel, S. (2006). Family therapy, family practice, and child and family poverty: Historical perspectives and recent developments. *Journal of Family Social Work,* 10(4), 43–80.

Kennedy, D.B. (1983). Implications of the victimization syndrome for clinical intervention with crime victims. *Personnel and Guidance Journal,* 62(4), 219–222.

Martín-Baró, I. (1994). *Writings for a liberation psychology.* Cambridge, MA: Harvard University Press.

Merriam-Webster (n.d) "Robbery." In Merriam-Webster's online edition. Retrieved from http://www.merriam-webster.com/dictionary/robbery

Miller, J.K. (2011) Single session intervention in the wake of Hurricane Katrina: Strategies for disaster mental health counseling. In A. Slive & M. Bobele (Eds.), *When one hour is all you have: Effective therapy for walk-in clients* (pp. 185–202). Phoenix, AZ: Zeig, Tucker, & Theisen.

Mitchell, J.T., & Bray, G.P. (1990) *Emergency services stress: Guidelines for preserving the health and careers of emergency service personnel.* Englewood Cliffs, NJ: Prentice-Hall.

Morral, P., Marshall, P., Pattison, S., Macdonald, G. (2010) Crime and health: A preliminary study into the effects of crime on mental health of U.K. university students. *Journal of Psychiatric and Mental Health Nursing,* 17, 821–828.

Platt, J.J. (2010). Direct practice with Latino families. In R. Furman & N. Negi (Eds.), *Social work practice with Latinos* (pp. 184–200). Chicago, IL: Lyceum Books.

Platt, J.J. (2013). Stepping over a baby's head: Thoughts on privilege, humanity and liberation. In M. E. Gallardo (Ed.), *Developing cultural humility: Embracing race, privilege and power* (pp. 199–221). Thousand Oaks, CA: Sage.

Procuraduría General Judicial. (2012) Report of robbery. Retrieved http://www.pgjdf.gob.mx/images/Estadisticas/2012.pdf

Sellin, T., & Wolfgang, M. (1964) *The measurement of delinquency.* New York: John Wiley.

Slive, A., & Bobele, M. (Eds.). (2011). *When one hour is all you have: Effective therapy with walk-in clients.* Phoenix: Zeig, Tucker & Theisen.

Triventi, M. (2008) Vittimizzazione e senso di insicurezza nei confronti del crimine: un'analisi empirica sul caso italiano. *Rivista di Criminologia, Vittimologia e Sicurezza,* 2(2), 137–159.

United Nations. (1985). "Victims." *U.N. Resolution 40/34 Declaration of Basic Principles of Justice for Victims of Crime and Abuse of Power.* Retrieved from http://www.un.org/documents/ga/res/40/a40r034.htm Annex A. Victims of Crime 1 & 2.

Chapter Thirteen

Opening the Heart and Mind with Single Session Psychotherapy and Therapeutic Hypnosis: A Final Meeting with Milton H. Erickson, M.D.—Part 1

Kathryn Rossi and Ernest Rossi

This is Part One of a verbal transcript of a 1980 videotape of Milton H. Erickson, M.D. and his personal physician and colleague Marion Moore, M.D., training Ernest Rossi, Ph.D., in a single session of psychotherapy and therapeutic hypnosis. They are seated very closely together in Erickson's small office to deal with Rossi's request that they use therapeutic hypnosis to *"Open my mind to learning everything I need to know to become a good practitioner of therapeutic hypnosis."* Erickson arranged the situation so that Ernest Rossi is seated between Erickson and Marion Moore. This two-hour session provides a surprisingly transparent view of Erickson's concept of the *General Waking Trance* and his style of psychotherapy. Erickson explained the rational for such long sessions with the simple idea, "That is how long it takes to get something done!" This was Rossi's final training session with Erickson just before he passed on. Rossi's initial commentary on this highly edited session was published 28 years later in 2008 when he had very little conscious memory of this final session, but for the first time recognized the significance it had for his later personality development and professional career.[1] In this 33-year follow-up, written in 2013, Rossi reviews some current neuroscience research that supports Erickson's innovative techniques of therapeutic hypnosis and psychotherapy.

Opening the Heart and Mind with Therapeutic Hypnosis

> MILTON H. ERICKSON (MHE): Now we're going to discuss your request to open your mind with therapeutic hypnosis. (Milton hands Ernie a pencil with its eraser replaced with a tiny doll with purple hair and a red heart sewn on it. These pencil dolls apparently were a popular novelty at one time but Rossi was surprised because he had never seen one.)
> ERNEST ROSSI: What is this? (laughing) It must be a witch doctor of a pencil. I notice the purple hair. Well, I can see it has a heart, too.
> MARION MOORE (MM): Do you know what a closed mind is?
> ERNEST ROSSI (ER): A closed mind? Well, I know what it is about, intellectually anyway.

Opening the Mind: Erickson's Novel & Surprising Hypnotic Induction: Open-Ended Questions to Facilitate Ideodynamic Experiences with Implicit Processing Heuristics (IMPs)

> MM: All right. (Marion takes the pencil from Ernie and makes the hair neat and compact.) Now I will let Milton show you how to open up that closed mind.

---

1. The original version of this single training session and commentary can be found in *The Collected Works of Milton H. Erickson*, Volume 3, *Opening the Mind* (Rossi, Erickson-Klein, & Rossi, 2008–2014). It and accompanying figures are used by agreement.

Figures 1a, 1b, 1c (left), 2a, 2b, 2c (right).
Images of Milton Erickson (left) and Marion Moore (right) demonstrating
the hand levitation technique of inducing therapeutic hypnosis in
Ernest Rossi. Erickson and Moore demonstrate three stages of hand
levitation with their unique ways: a) hovering, b) engaging the hand/
wrist, and c) gently releasing the hand/wrist. See detail later in figure 6.

MHE: (*Takes the pencil doll between the palms of his hands and*
rolls the pencil back and forth vigorously so the dolls purple
hair becomes a mess.)
ER: Shake it up!
MM: Now today you've asked us to open your mind up.
ER: I sure have.

MHE: You like to sunbathe, don't you? [Note how this simple and agreeable question actually functions as an *Implicit Processing Heuristic (IMP): a gentle, permissive and empathic suggestion that encourages people to create self-rewarding inner search experiences as possible gateways to accessing their own therapeutic resources for personal problem solving in their own unique ways illustrated in Figure 3*]

ER: I love to sunbathe. Sure. Who doesn't?

MHE: What do you feel when you sunbathe?

ER: Oh, I feel the warmth of the sun. I feel a deep relaxation of not having to do anything for a while. That's probably the best of all—a *kind of warmth. Ease. Comfort. Above all, comfort.* [Note how Erickson has managed the situation with open-ended questions so that Rossi probably already has an auto-induced ideodynamic (ideo-sensory and/or ideo-motor) experience of *"a kind of warmth. Ease. Comfort. Above all, comfort."* These are all positive experiences consistent with the general waking trance, therapeutic hypnosis and an inner search for mind-body healing and well-being.]

MM: On which side? [Note how Moore continues to focus and hopefully intensify Rossi's ideosensory experi-

Figure 3. Implicit Processing Heuristics (IMPs) are gentle, permissive and empathetic therapeutic suggestions that facilitate the Mind-Gene loop of communication and healing (Rossi, 2007, 2012; Rossi & Rossi, 2013).

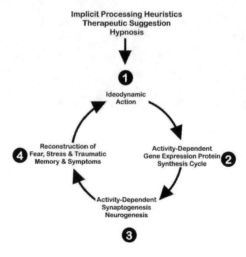

ence with this question. *Rossi, however, cannot really respond to Moore's question without first replaying an inner personal experience to identify, explore, and facilitate his own ideosensory experiences of sunbathing more deeply.* This is another example of an *Implicit Processing Heuristic (IMP): a gentle, permissive and empathic prompt that encourages people to explore self-rewarding inner experiences searching for their own therapeutic resources for personal problem solving via their own unique mind-gene communication loops as illustrated in Figure 3.*]

Recognizing and Facilitating the Natural 4-Stage Creative Process

MHE: *All within yourself!* [Erickson's strong emphasis here *respects and reinforces Rossi's original search within: "Open my mind to learning everything I need to know to become a good practitioner of therapeutic hypnosis." Erickson empathically recognizes Rossi's need for a sense of autonomy and self direction—ultimately to support Rossi's search for own sense of self-control and self-transformation in therapeutically re-framing his own life!* Note how this humanistic approach is in striking contrast to the popular misconceptions of stage hypnosis, which purports to condition people to robot-like obedience of the hypnotist's commands.]

ER: Mm-hum. (*pause*) [Note how Rossi's brief little hum and pause here is a positive but almost non-verbal affirmation of Erickson's injunction "*All within yourself! The pause here probably* indicates that Rossi is beginning to manifest aspects of the general waking trance as Stage 2 (incubation) of the 4-Stage Creative Process when a person is so inwardly focused on their own absorbing and important inner experiencing that they *pause*—they hardly acknowledge and communicate with others as they momentarily focus within.]

MHE: How about that bird that flies between you and the sun? [What bird? Erickson is boldly offering an

Figure 4. The Chronobiological Theory of Rossi's 4-Stage Creative Process (top) from Mind to Gene that takes place naturally about 12 times a day every 90-120 minutes of the Basic-Rest-Activity Cycle (BRAC), (Lloyd & Rossi, 1992, 2008). We hypothesize that this natural BRAC accounts for the therapeutic efficacy of Erickson's long (double) sessions within the natural 24-hour circadian cycle (bottom). Erickson's naturalistic therapy thus utilizes two deep psychobiological rhythms that were selected for their adaptive value by billions of years of evolution (Rossi, 2004, 2007, 2012; Rossi & Rossi, 2013).

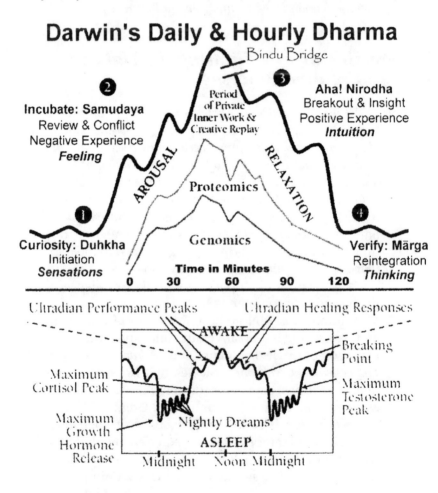

IMP in the form of a question to assess whether Rossi will accept it as a hypnotic suggestion and incorporate it within his inner imagery, which could be even experienced as a visual hallucination! Notice even here, however, Erickson does not make a direct command—Erickson *proffers* an IMP as a question for Rossi to consider. The word *"proffer"* is an interesting fail-safe approach that Erickson often used to describe his subtle verbal assessments of a patient's subjective state during therapeutic hypnosis (See *The Indirect Trance Assessment Scale (ITAS)* in Volume 14 of Erickson's *Collected Works*). *"Proffer"* is derived from the Anglo-French *"por-"*, forth, and *"offrir"*, to offer. *"Proffering" involves making an offer prior to any formal suggestion or negotiation.*]

ER: When I'm sunbathing I probably don't even notice a bird there. [Rossi's negative response implies that he is maintaining his own critical professional perspective at this moment—he is not some gullible dupe of hypnosis.]

MHE: We know that. [Non-directive support.]

MM: We discussed that. [Non-directive support.]

ER: You mean I need to notice the shadow?

MHE: That's right. [Non-leading support of whatever Rossi may be processing inwardly in a private manner. *This is an important distinction between IMPs, which support whatever the person may be exploring, searching or creating versus conventional suggestion in everyday life and directive hypnosis wherein an inappropriate effort is made to insert something into another person's mind. The problem with such conventional suggestions is that many people tend to resent, resist and reject them as foreign intrusions on their personal mental territory.*]

ER: Wow! That would be real sensitivity! How do I develop that kind of sensory sensitivity? [This "Wow!" implies how Rossi may be experiencing positive Stage 3 (*Ah-h!*) of the 4-stage creative process as illustrated in Figure 4. This could be an experience of the Novelty-Numinosum-Neurogenesis Effect (NNNE) wherein activity-dependent gene expression and brain plasticity are being turned on for marshalling creative inner resources for problem solving during an important life turning point as illustrated in Figure 5 (Rossi, 2002).]

Figure 5. The Life Turning Point Cycle when most people seek counseling, psychotherapy and therapeutic hypnosis (Rossi, 1972/1986/2000, 2007, 2012; Rossi & Rossi, 2013). A life turning point gives rise to dreams within the BRACs that usually occur 4 or 5 times during sleep. These dream BRACs also turn on gene expression and brain plasticity (flexibility) to create the transcription/translation cycle of gene expression that underpins brain plasticity for creating new consciousness.

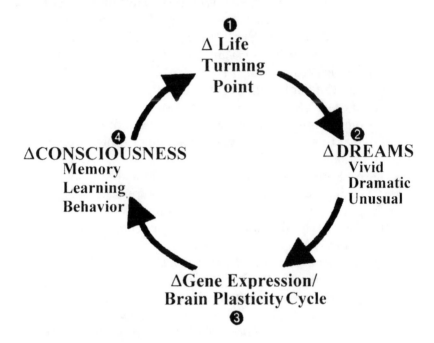

MM: Do you feel the warmth of the sun on both sides of your body when you're facing up...both the same? [Moore is attempting to lead, focus and intensify Rossi's ideosensory experience. We may wish him good luck in taking this risk. But carefully notice how Moore's leading is very different from Erickson's purely open-ended and non-directive IMPs that may facilitate people without the risk of leading them in the wrong direction.]

ER: I usually feel it on one side.

MHE: Where do you feel it best? [Note once again how Erickson's emphasizes the "best" of an inner experience! He is facilitating a possibly self-rewarding ideosensory expe-

*rience that will deepen Rossi's creative inner work. Er-
ickson's IMP is a simple risk-free and fail-safe query that
encourages Rossi to elaborate further on the "best:" Rossi's
own inner search and naturally self-reinforcing path to creating his own consciousness and self* (Rossi, 2012).]

ER: Well, the side that's facing the sun. Maybe on my
stomach I feel it best.

Ideodynamic Inner Search Algorithms to Facilitate Mirror Neurons during the Creative Work of Therapeutic Hypnosis

MHE: [Holds out his left palm and with attention getting
movements by very slowly rotating it with the palm
facing up for a moment and then down for another
moment or two. He is focusing Rossi's attention on
his own ideomotor movements to again facilitate
Rossi's own inner search algorithm (Rossi & Cheek,
1988). Erickson's penchant for using ideodynamic
hand movements to induce therapeutic hypnosis and
facilitate creative inner work was illustrated previously in Figures 1a, 1b and 1c. It is explained here in
detail in Erickson's words and exquisite sensitivity in
Figure 6.

*Figure 6. Thumb and finger placement during a hand
levitation induction of therapeutic hypnosis.*

An Introduction to Milton H. Erickson's Favorite Method of Facilitating Therapeutic Hypnosis and Psychotherapy in a Single Session

We can illustrate Milton H. Erickson's favorite, simplest, and most rapid approach facilitating therapeutic hypnosis and psychotherapy in a single session which he describes as follows:

"You take hold of the wrist very, very gently. What is your purpose? Your purpose is to let the patient feel your hand touching his wrist. That is all. The patient has muscles that will enable him to lift his arm, so why should you do it for him? *The body has learned how to follow minimal cues. You utilize that learning. You give your patient minimal cues. When he starts responding to those minimal cues, he gives more and more attention to any further cues you offer him. As he gives more and more attention to the suggestions you offer, he goes deeper into trance. The art of deepening the trance is not necessarily yelling at him to go deeper and deeper; it is giving minimal suggestion gently, so the patient pays more and more attention to the processes within himself and thus goes deeper and deeper.*

"I think all of you have seen me take hold of a patient's arm and lift it up and move it about in various fashions. I induce a trance in that way. I have tried to teach a number of you how to take hold of a wrist, how to take hold of a hand. You do not grip with all the strength in your hand and squeeze down on the patient's wrist. What you do is take hold of it so as to very, very gently suggest a grip on his wrist, but you don't actually grip it; you just encircle the wrist with your thumb and index finger with light touches. You suggest a movement of the wrist with only the slightest pressure. You suggest a movement of the hand upward. And how do you suggest it upward? You press with your thumb just lightly, while at the same time you move your index finger this way to give a balance (Figure 6). You move your fingers laterally, and while the patient gives attention to that, you have your thumb actually lifting the hand. This is essentially a distraction technique: while the thumb very lightly and consistently directs the hand upward, your other fingers make touches and distracting movements in a variety of other directions that tend to cancel out each other.

"Another approach to guiding the hand upward is to attract the patient's conscious attention with a firm pressure by your fingers on top of his hand and only a gentle guiding pressure by your thumb on the underside of his hand. The only way the firm touch can remain firm is for the patient to keep moving his hand up against your fingers. At the same time the lower touch of your thumb is kept gentle by the patient by constantly moving upward away from it. The therapist needs to practice these movements over and over because they are one of the quickest and easiest ways of distracting the conscious mind and securing the fixation of the unconscious mind.

"You lift the hand in that fashion, letting your fingers linger here and there so that the patient unconsciously gets a sense of the lingering of your hand. You want the patient to have that nice comfortable feeling of the lingering of your hand because you want his attention there in his hand and you want the development of that state of balanced muscle tonicity which is catalepsy. Once that state of balanced muscle tonicity is established to achieve catalepsy, you have enlisted the aid of the unconscious mind throughout the patient's body. Because you can get catalepsy in one hand, there is a good possibility there will be catalepsy in the other hand. If you get catalepsy in the other hand, then you probably have catalepsy in the right foot, in the left foot, and throughout the body, face, and neck. As soon as you get that balanced tonicity of the muscles, then you have a physical state that allows the patient to become unaware of fatigue, unaware of any disturbing sensations. It is normally hard to maintain that balanced muscle tonicity and pay attention to pain. *You want your patient giving all of his attention to that balanced muscle tonicity because that distracts him from pain and other proprioceptive cues so that numbness, analgesia, and anesthesia are frequently experienced in association with catalepsy. If you have balanced muscle tonicity throughout the body, catalepsy throughout the body, you have reduced the sensations that exist within the body to those sensations that go into maintaining that catalepsy. A patient then becomes decidedly responsive to a wealth of other ideas.*"

The introspective comments of subjects who have experienced the induction of catalepsy in this manner tend to support Erickson's view of the dynamics of distraction in the process. Most subjects report that their hand seemed to have a peculiar tendency to move upward and about by itself because they could not distinguish the consistent pressure upward by the therapist's thumb from the distracting touches and movements by his other fingers. The therapist's minimal cues and the patient's responses to them take place at a faster rate than the patient's cognition can follow. Most of the tactile stimuli and responses are mediated automatically by the proprioceptive-cerebellar system so that the patient's ego awareness on cortical levels is bypassed.

ER: [Stares curiously at Erickson's novel and very slow movements then cautiously and slowly imitates Erickson's hand palm turns.]

MHE: What is the difference between the palm and the back of the hand? [Another ideodynamic IMP that can only be answered by Rossi using his own mirror neurons to explore and possibly intuit an inner search algorithm implied by Erickson's movements (Rossi, 2007; Rossi & Rossi, 2006, 2007)]

ER: Ventral, dorsal (*laughs*).

MHE: [Erickson reaches out and touches Ernie's hand.] You can take more pressure here [Erickson touches the palm of Ernie's hand] then you can take here [Erickson touches the back of Ernie's hand.]

ER: Right! There are calluses on the palm.

Opening the Mind by Noticing the New: Exploring Novel Life Options and Feelings

MHE: Now, last night after you looked at the owl. [He is referring to one of the many art pieces in Erickson's personal home collection. They are made of beautifully polished ironwood from Mexico hand-made there by native Indians.]

MHE: What kind of tubular (tunnel) vision did you use?

ER: Well, my tubular (tunnel) vision said that it was an owl?

MHE: No. You did not see the owl.

ER: I did not see the owl?

MHE: Not until it was pointed out to you.

ER: Ah! That's right. I didn't see the owl in the room until you pointed it out to me. Because there were so many other art pieces that I did not pick that one up.

MHE: When you grab hold of something you don't let go. You hang to that one sensation.

ER: I see. The general sensation of the room, I hang on to that rather than seeing all the new things that came into the room since I'd been there last. [*Erickson intimated that Rossi did not notice the new ironwood art piece in Erickson's vast collection around his living room. He is now implying that Rossi needs to notice anything new and novel that appears in familiar settings. Note that "novelty" (the new, surprising, and unexpected) is one of the three major factors neuroscientists now recognize at evoking surprise and facilitating activity-dependent gene expression and brain plasticity. See Chapter 1 of Volume 1 in MHE's Collected Works.]*

MHE: And you like the ironwood don't you?

ER: I love the ironwood! Yes!

MHE: Do you?

ER: Well, I like them. I don't always notice the new ones as they come in.

MHE: How are you sure you like the ironwood?

ER: Well, I look at them. I touch them. The one you gave me as a gift I keep in my office on my desk so I see it every day. I think it's through touch [Ernie nods his head in a "yes" motion]. I sense the fineness of the grain of the wood, the fineness of the workmanship.

MHE: That's one option.

ER: That's one option?

MHE: That's one.

MM: That's one option.

MHE: Ernie, I find when I take people in [to look at his ironwood collection], sometimes there are half a dozen in a group, they just hold a piece of ironwood and feel it—then they go over and feel this, and this, and this.

MM: Right!

ER: They go and feel *all* the pieces of wood sculpture?

MHE: Now, *you* get one feeling, and it's enough.

ER: I tend to stay with one piece. I admire that. I feel that. And then I don't go and touch the others. *You would say that's a self-limitation on my part?* [Notice how Rossi is picking up on MHE's implication for Rossi to expand his awareness of his own feelings and options in life. The therapeutic power of Erickson's implications is facilitated by his IMPs that allow Rossi to create his own interpretation and self prescribed behavioral self-transformations.]

Opening Your Mind: Expanding Sensations and Perceptions in Everyday Life

MM: In the same way with your clothing that you were mentioning last night. Now, I'm going to mention the suit I have on now is over 11 years old. And yet, you would admire the suit that I had on yesterday—the fact that it was still doing so well, and so forth. It is beautiful cloth. How did I know that this cloth would be a good lasting cloth? It is a firm, hard, non-fuzzy weave. So it has lasted—at least wearing it one day a week, every week of the year, virtually since 1969, November.

ER: It looks brand new.

MM: That's what everybody who sees it says. But the quality of things...To a lot of different things...Because we've come close to see it—because we liked the look of things. *But you have to feel it, feel it, feel it!* See what is it going to feel like? See what inward awareness you can obtain from it. And don't do it with one suit, do it with 15 suits!

ER: Yes.

MHE: You start spreading...

ER: *Exploring...*

MM: *Exploring!* Expand that! [Obviously all three participants are now in rapport and using each other's words *("Exploring")* about the central theme of this therapeutic session "to *open my mind to learning everything I need to know to become a good practitioner of therapeutic hypnosis."*]

Opening Your Mind: Art, Beauty, and Truth for Exploring All Possible Routes to a Goal

MHE: When you see a pretty girl, now what does one pretty girl have?

ER: I understand. I should explore many pretty girls. Is that right? *(Laughs)*

MM: No, let's start with what does one pretty girl...?

ER: I would see what characteristic, what features one pretty girl would have?

MHE: All right. Tell me.

ER: Beautiful skin

MM: Any more?

ER: Oh, for another, beautiful eyes, beautiful hair, beautiful disposition. [*Note the role of art, beauty, and truth, etc. in facilitating activity-dependent gene expression and brain plasticity in MHE's* Collected Works.]

MHE: I wonder if I done this with you before? How would you get from this chair to that office?

ER: You told me about exploring all possibilities. I could go directly in. I could go out that door. I could take a taxi to the airport and fly to China and back. I could go around your house and through the back door. You strongly advocate people exploring all routes to a goal.

Opening Your Mind: Non-Verbal Sexual Postures and Cues

MHE: You see a pretty girl. You see her skin. You see the flexibility of features. The curl of her hair—the sensation, the coarseness, the fineness. The way she touches her hair. The way she touches her ear. The way she touches her face. The way she puts her hand on your arm (*Erickson touches Ernie's arm*). How does she cross her legs? You cross your legs because it's comfortable. You did it for comfort, not for feeling.

ER: Not for feeling?

MM: Right. Not for feeling it. Milton, do you want to describe this leg to him? The double wrap leg. (*Marion crosses his legs in a feminine manner.*) The female does that.

MHE: (*Erickson shakes his head in mock disbelief.*)

ER: I can't even do that one!

MM: It is not easy to do. You do one cross over and then stick one leg under like this.

MHE: A man can barely do this. She has a wider pelvis. So when you look at a pretty girl and you see how soft is her skin, the movement of her facial muscles, her hair thick or thin, long or short. The way she tosses her hair. Now when you look at a person, you look at all of their behavior.

ER: The mobility of her facial features, things about her personality, is that—for example?

MHE: Two men sit down on each end of a couch. The girl sits in the middle. You have already looked at her, and then you notice which way she crosses her legs.

MM: And also which way she tends to lean—up to this one or that one. And the leg crossing and the leaning will both be synonymous toward one of the two men.

ER: Toward her preference. And this is nonverbal, without her realizing?

MM: She has no idea. Ninety-nine and four hundredths percent of the time she will have no idea. So this is in a way what I was trying to talk to you about last night and this morning. You were trying to get us to cram into you a whole lifetime of feeling that you want to get in two hours. [Moore is referring to Rossi's request that Erickson use therapeutic hypnosis to open Rossi's mind to learn everything he had to in order to become an effective psychotherapist.]

Opening Your Mind: Early Memory Review of Touch and Family Patterns

MM: I asked Milton about some of your background. Did your parents' use touch a great deal?

ER: Only so-so I would say.

MM: Do you remember sitting in your mother's lap at all?

ER: Oh, yes.

MM: Often? Or was it on special occasions, birthdays, holidays, etc.

ER: I think after the age of four or five it just became on birthdays.

MM: Even a pat on the fanny as he walked by?

ER: Yes, plenty of pats on the fanny.

MM: I don't mean spankings. I'm talking about: "I know you're there, son," as you walk by type of touch.

ER: Not too much.

MM: OK. This is part of the touch that I was telling you about that has been missed in your personal background.

MHE: (*To Rossi*) You've mentioned how much I refer to my father and mother. In their nineties, us kids caught them holding hands and they would blush.

ER: Fantastic. At 90. After 50 years of marriage?

MHE: After 70 years!

Opening Your Mind: Surprising, Non Sequitur Search Algorithms for Exploring New Experiences

MHE: Now how you sit in a chair? How do you sit in the new chair? [Notice this non sequitur question that seems "to come out of the blue." Such questions are slightly jarring and disorienting to the listener. Erickson frequently proffers such surprising, unusual and seemingly random new questions—searching for other areas in which he can encourage new sensations, perceptions, insights, etc. Once again we hypothesize that such questions are novel, attention getting, and focusing via search algorithms, which facilitate activity-dependent gene expression and brain plasticity that tend to open the mind to new experiences.]

ER: With probably more care than an old chair.

MHE: Don't be embarrassed to look at this. Do you ever ride horseback?

ER: Yes.

MHE: Side-saddle?

ER: No, I've never ridden sidesaddle.

MHE: Why not?

ER: I've never been taught. I'm afraid I would fall off. I never got beyond the first stages of horseback riding. I did a little bit of English, but mostly western saddle.

MHE: Did you ride bareback?

ER: I never rode bareback.

MM: You really miss something. I've rode many miles bareback.

ER: I had just taken beginning lessons, really, on the oldest nag in the stable. If I had stayed with it, no doubt, I would have those kinds of experiences.

Open Your Mind: The Searching Game of Can You Top This? Food and Cooking as a Metaphor of Life

MHE: How stereotyped is your diet? [Notice, once again how this slightly surprising, non sequitur question that the pace and supports the agenda of the ongoing searching interaction between all three participants in empathy.]

ER: I love a variety of foods especially when I go out to a restaurant. I like to have all kinds of different foods, different nationalities and different kinds of dishes. At home I do get into a rut of steak, chili, chicken, macaroni, a kind of Italian-American food. That's only because I lack the skill. I've been getting into baking lately, baking my own bread—making up new kinds of breads—new kinds of flavorings. [Notice how Rossi seems to have unwittingly got the point of Erickson's introducing this long series of novel, surprising, open ended, and non sequitur questions here as Rossi now emphasizes all "the different kinds of dishes," etc., that an open mind would be receptive to when cooking. Rossi is, in effect, now answering his own question of *"How to open my mind to all the different things I need to learn to do therapeutic hypnosis?"* It is just like learning all the different things you need to know to cook creatively!]

MHE: You're just starting?

ER: Really, I'm just starting, in the past year or so. Yes.

MHE: And you follow directions? What is the difference of prime rib in one and prime rib in the other?

ER: A lot of things. The thickness in the cut is important. A lot of things: the amount of cooking, the amount of gravy, the tenderness of it.

MHE: Those are the gross things, the weight, the amount.

ER: The textures, the flavors.

MM: Even the aesthetics of the restaurant in which you are eating—from one place to another?

ER: How good the wines are, yes.

MM: They all add to the flavor of the meat, also.

ER: The company you're with. [Notice once again how Rossi seems to be doing his best to join, keep up with, and possibly even outdoing Erickson and Moore in their searching game of, *"Can you top this for novelty and surprising goodness in this creative, wonderful activity we are engaged in together!"]*

MM: The company you're with, plus and the actual seasonings of the meat. The meat can vary widely from one place to the other with prime rib.

Three Would-Be Wise Men Mirror Their Hypnotic Rapport: Participation Mystique and Gentle Loving Care

MHE: The best kind are raw, prime rib of beef comes from the chef who cuts it a certain way.

MM: That's right!

ER: Oh, to cut across the grain?

MHE: No. You're being practical again!

ER: Practical again? *(laughs)*

MHE: *The gentler loving care.*

ER: I see. It's the way they cut the meat.

MHE: *Is there gentle loving care* in cutting the meat, which adds a great deal to the taste?

ER: I didn't know that. Is that of fact? You don't just cut the meat?

MM: No!

MHE: If they just cut you a piece of meat...

ER: *That's all you get.*

MM: That's right. *That's what you get.*

MHE: That's what you get. [Aha...at last, the three would-be wise men now seem to be in perfect empathetic accord! Apparently these three fully-grown gentlemen are sagaciously mirroring each other with the same words and manner about preparing food for cooking, pretty girls, etc. Who is hypnotizing whom here? Is this a modern experience of participation mystique? Is this the essence of the historically famous "hypnotic rapport?" Or are these just 3 guys having fun? Notice how Marion Moore and Milton Erickson are now mirroring Ernest Rossi, supposedly the subject, who first uses the phrase, "That is all you get." Could we speculate that all three participants are illustrating how their mirror neurons are now in focus with each other? (Chapter 1 of Volume 1 of Rossi, Erickson-Klein, & Rossi, 2008–2014; Rossi, 2012).]

MM: And if it's in supposedly an esthetic place you may pay twice the price for what you get, and it's only half as good as what you would get in the other place where it was treated entirely differently. I can vouch for this. Just the other night I had a steak and Milton had told his wife Betty to get me a certain steak, which she did. I brought it out here. Milton said, "You're going to take it out there and ruin it because I like it well done." So I took the steak and *gently* sliced it (*makes hand movements showing* gentle *slow slicing horizontally*) right in half and cooked both sides. I kept turning it over so it would get charred. I got it thoroughly done and it was just as juicy... and I could cut it with a fork. I did not have to take a knife out of the drawer to cut it at all. And that steak was absolutely delicious.

ER: We need to treat our food, our steaks, *gently.*

MHE: I heard from some cousins of mine recently and they brought me a big hunk of Wisconsin cheese. My mouth started watering immediately. They took this cheese out of the wrapping, out of that carry-all. They handled it so delicately and placed it on a table so gently that I knew how good that cheese would taste.

MM: That's right

ER: Because of the *gentle* handling. [Ernest obviously is getting the metaphorical point that one treats patient's *"gently"* with therapeutic hypnosis. This is the second time Rossi mirrors Moore and Erickson's use of the word *"gentle."* He is beginning to get the idea very gradually.]

Summary of Part One

In the first half of Erickson's psychotherapy sessions the client is often in an inquisitive or uncertain state of mind. Rossi, for example, is now beginning to embrace the idea of gentleness, but has not yet integrated this into how to open his mind to become a better therapist. We suggest that at this point Rossi is in Stage 2 of the Creative Process as illustrated in Figure 4—full of questions but not clear on the answers to his questions. In Part 2 Rossi does become clear about what it takes to be an open-minded practitioner of therapeutic hypnosis having experienced the twists and turns of Erickson and Moore helping him to experience for himself the sensitivity of truly looking at and listening to his clients.

References

(All references appear at the end of Part 2.)

Chapter Fourteen

Opening the Heart and Mind with Single Session Psychotherapy: Utilizing the General Waking Trance, Empathy, and Novelty in Life Transitions—Part 2

Ernest Rossi and Kathryn Rossi

This presents Part Two of a highly edited version of a videotape made in 1980 by Marion Moore, M.D., showing Milton H. Erickson and Moore demonstrating novel, activity-dependent approaches to hand-levitation and therapeutic hypnosis on their subject, Ernest Rossi. Erickson's naturalistic and utilization approach is described in his very direct and surprising induction in a trance challenged patient. These novel, and surprising inductions are examples of how Erickson was prescient in developing activity-dependent approaches to therapeutic hypnosis and psychotherapy several generations before modern neuroscience documented the activity-dependent molecular-genomic mechanisms of memory, learning, and behavior change. Erickson describes a case where he utilized what he called, "The General Waking Trance" when he "dared" not use an obvious hypnotic induction. It is proposed that the states of *focused attention, intense mental absorption* and *response attentiveness* are facilitated by the general waking trance are functionally related to the three conditions neuroscientists have identified as *novelty, enrichment, and exercise* (both mental and physical), which can turn on activity-dependent gene expression and activity-dependent brain plasticity. This is the molecular-genomic and neural basis of memory, learning, consciousness, and behavior change. We recommend that the next step in investigating the efficacy of therapeutic hypnosis will be in partnering with neuroscientists to explore the possibilities and limitations of utilizing the activity-dependent approaches to hypnotic induction and the general waking trance in facilitating gene expression and brain plasticity.

A Direct, Surprise Induction of a "Trance Challenged" Woman

Erickson casually begins describing one of his recent cases as follows.

> MHE: She came in and said, "Time to go into a trance! Sixty hours I spent and paid for and I couldn't go into the trance. Now it is a long way from San Francisco here to Phoenix. See if you can try to put me into trance." You should listen to what patients say. She said: "*Try* to put me in trance! I'm really a challenge!" Only she didn't know it. I knew it.
>
> I said, "All right then, go and sit down in that chair there. Relax and lean back. And shut your mouth and shut your eyes and go into a deep trance, *NOW!*" And she did. She came in expecting my kind of treatment. I took her completely by surprise and put her into trance. [Note how this very rapid, direct, abrupt, and somewhat surprising induction is appropriate in this special context where the patient is impatient with having apparently wasted 60 hours with her previous therapist. Note how *Erickson immediately adopts and utilizes her own impatient attitude with this direct and rather abrupt hypnotic induction.* Notice that he takes the patient by surprise, while still giving brief but adequate instructions of how to go into therapeutic hypnosis. This is consistent with current neuroscience research on mirror neurons, empathy, rapport, and behavior

(Buccino, et al., 2004; Carr, et al., 2003; Rizzolatti & Arbib, 1998; Rossi, 2007). Erickson typically adopts and utilizes the patient's own attitudes, behavior, words, and points of view in facilitating therapeutic hypnosis. *This is the essence of Erickson's naturalistic and utilization approach to therapeutic hypnosis and psychotherapy* (Rossi, Erickson-Klein, and Rossi, 2008–2014). This initial matching of the patient's current state by the therapist implies that Erickson is making optimal use of his mirror neurons in synchronizing his own psychobiological state with the patient to facilitate their hypnotic rapport (Rossi & Rossi, 2006.)]

The abrupt and surprising aspect could also function as the type of salient, attention focusing, psychological shock, which we speculate could evoke activity-dependent gene expression and pendent brain plasticity to facilitate creative changes in the patient's consciousness and behavior. This surprise induction is an example of how Erickson was prescient in developing *activity-dependent approaches to therapeutic hypnosis* several generations before modern neuroscience documented the *activity-dependent, molecular-genomic mechanisms of memory, learning, and behavior chan*ge. [See Rossi (1973/2007) for more case examples of how Erickson used psychological shocks to facilitate creative moments in therapeutic hypnosis and psychotherapy.]

MHE: She said, "When I think of 60 hours I wasted in San Francisco. I wish I had come to your first!" I think I would have been much more gentle and unsuccessful if she had.

The First International Erickson Conference in 1980: Communication is Main Problem of Psychotherapy

ER: Jeffery Zeig is organizing the first International Milton H. Erickson Conference in Phoenix this December (1980). We want to learn the main themes about your work that you feel we should present to the audience.

MHE: I think one of the first things to be considered is a fact. *Our main problem in psychotherapy is communication.* We all learn communication without realizing it. We think communication is words. But babies learn by intonations, inflections, and facial expressions. We keep on trying all through childhood to put on certain expressions when we mean something else.

ER: So there is an incongruity between verbal behavior and what is showing on the parents' face?

MHE: We are overdoing our expression. We would like our child to believe medicine tastes good. So the parent puts on the act of tasting it and liking it. But that is not fooling the child a bit!

ER: What's all this got to do with communication in psychotherapy?

MHE: In psychotherapy you are dealing with a lot of problems that are painful to the patient. These are painful to reproduce. They are painful to themselves. Smoking cigarettes! There are painful continuous ways of behavior. Pain has been defined and highly communicated in relationship to this and that.

Novel Activity-Dependent Approaches Therapeutic Hypnosis: Touch and the Psychotherapist

MM: Earlier tonight Ernie and I were discussing the sense of touch and how a child, baby, adult, male or female feels when we touch them. You (MHE) and I have been touching patients for years. Ernie has developed as a no-touch type of professional.

ER: Yes, that's right. You are both physicians with a license to touch. But touching clients is a rather controversial issue for some psychologists.

MM: Yet, this is a very basic form of communication that is very important. It starts with a little bitty baby. They can tell if somebody doesn't like them, or when somebody is uptight holding them, or when somebody is perfectly relaxed in holding the child well. Most cases of colitis and diarrhea in children that I have seen hospitalized usually have a very tense mother. I have worked with mothers to teach them how to be relaxed when they hold their baby and the baby's colic disappears. Problems of this nature start with the very young.

MHE: We very soon learn to have strength. At first it's quite tender. Then we begin to show our strength. We keep developing with pride in our strength. (*Erickson reaches out to touch Rossi's right hand.*) [Note how Erickson continues answering Rossi's inquiry of how to have an open mind with therapeutic hypnosis by again using the hand levitation induction—Erickson's favorite technique.]

We exercise our strength with a *hovering touch.* When I touch somebody's hand like this...[Erickson hand hovers momentarily over Rossi's right arm in Figure 1a (see Part 1 for Images 1a-c and 2a-c). MHE then very gently touches Rossi's forearm. With a slow, slightly sliding motion Erickson shifts his gentle touch toward Rossi's wrist as illustrated in Figure 1b to provide a non-verbal cue for Rossi to lift his arm so that it remains suspended in the air in Figure 1c. Notice how Erickson utilizes a very positive context with empowering words, and phrases such as "We very soon learn to have strength," "quite tender," and "with pride," to support this apparently non-verbal activity-dependent induction of therapeutic hypnosis.]

ER: You are giving me an unconscious cue to lift my hand?

MHE: Now, if I do it this way (*Erickson gently touches the top of Rossi's wrist with a slightly downward motion and Rossi's hand goes down*) I don't get a levitating response [Not illustrated in the figures.]

ER: You cue the hand upward but let the client actually lift his hand. [Likewise patients drop their hand and arm when MHE gives it a gentle downward touch.]

MHE: That's right. [Details of Erickson's activity-dependent approach to hand levitation to inducing therapeutic hypnosis are discussed and illustrated in Volume 11 of the new series of 16+ books on *"The Collected Works of MHE"* (Rossi, Erickson-Klein, & Rossi, 2008–2014).]

Personal, Private, Peripersonal Space: "Very Gently One Goes Into Private Space"

MM: If you do it with such a gentle, expectation touch, as Milton said, it's nothing. (With his thumb, Marion Moore barely touches the underside of Rossi's wrist to give a non-verbal cue for Rossi to lift his hand and arm as illustrated in Figure 2b.)

But if you grab it like this (*Marion firmly grabs Rossi's wrist with a bit of roughness*) they tend to resist you! They want to pull their hand back and put it down rather than let you grab them. Each of us has our little *private space* around us. If someone gets within our private space, inner space, we want to back off. We see this in crowds a great deal. When you see people crowding in you will see this person moving away from that person because they are coming in a little too close to them. It is well known in the schizoids or schizophrenics, but every person alive has their little barrier. [Private, personal, or as the neuroscientists now call it, *"Peripersonal Space"* is a highly flexible, subjective sense of space depending on the context. Peripersonal space generally extends an arm's length around one's body (Blakeslee & Blakeslee, 2007). If any other person or object enters this peripersonal space then special activity-dependent cells are activated throughout the person's brain. Erickson and Moore are obviously entering Rossi's peripersonal space with this "novel and activity-dependent approach" to hypnotic induction and are therefore activating neurons throughout his brain. Research is now needed to explore the possible contributions and limitations of facilitating the efficacy of therapeutic hypnosis and psychotherapy at the cellular, neural, and molecular-genomic level by entering a subject's peripersonal space.]

ER: I wonder if those touch approaches to hypnotic induction entering the private space of the person are getting closer to individual. Closer to places where they...?

MHE: *Great injuries can happen when you go into the private space. Very gently one goes into the private space.* [This reminds us of the still controversial review paper Erickson (1932/2008–2014) published about his earliest experimental and clinical work with hypnosis as follows.

"In the writer's own experience, upon which it unfortunately will be necessary to a large extent to base the elaboration of these various questions, *hypersuggestibility was not noticed*, although the list of individual subjects totals approximately 300 and the number of trances several thousand. Further, a considerable number were hypnotized from 300 to 500 times each over a period of years. Also several of the subjects were immediate relatives with consequent intimate daily contact, and they were trained to respond, in experimentation, quickly and readily to the slightest suggestion. Far from making them hypersuggestible, *it was found necessary to deal very gingerly with them to keep from losing their cooperation*, and it was often felt that they developed a compensatory negativism toward the hypnotist to offset any increased suggestibility. *Subjects trained to go into a deep trance instantly at the snap of a finger would successfully resist when unwilling or more interested in other projects.*" (p. 324, italics added)

There is great consistency over almost 50 years from Erickson's initial 1932 statement of the need to treat hypnotic subjects *"very gingerly...to keep from losing their cooperation"* to his 1980 statement, *"Very gently one goes into the private space."* In this paragraph Erickson is clearly saying, *"hypersuggestibility was not noticed"* and "Subject's trained to go into a deep trance...would successfully resist when unwilling or *more interested in other projects."* Erickson emphasizes the subject's ability to resist the therapist's suggestion in a manner that is consistent with current research on hypnosis and conscious states. Erickson also describes the subject's motivation and state of absorption in being *"more interested in other projects,"* which is consistent with a decade of neuroscience research that describes how experiences of novelty, enrichment, and exercise turn on gene expression and brain plasticity to facilitate memory, learning, and behavior change (Rossi, 2008).]

MM: And do it at the far extremity (of the arm) as I was telling to you (Rossi) earlier. You don't reach up and grab them on the shoulder the first thing. You want to touch them here (*Marion gently places 4 fingers on Rossi's wrist with Marion's thumb supporting and gently cueing levitation on the underside of Rossi's wrist*). When you see they are responding to you (by levitating their arm) then you can go further up (*Marion holds Rossi's forearm near the elbow with both hands*) and they have less resistance (*Marion has one hand on Rossi's shoulder and the other on his elbow*) toward your invading their private space, you see. But it is a behavioral set that the person learns—*if they can trust you*. They learn to trust that you are fine. Then they don't mind that you enter into their private space. A man and woman in love don't mind entering their private spaces at all. They share it—their private space together, so to speak. But when they hate each other—how far do they stay apart?

ER: We are moving in on what we call, "personal or private space." This is an approach to facilitating communication—a more intimate kind of communication.

MHE: *Within the private space.*

ER: Within the private space. This is why you developed this very gentle touch and cuing approach to the hand levitation in the induction of therapeutic hypnosis.

MHE: Yes.

Consummating a Marriage: Letting Her Do It Her Own Way: Choice and Private Space

MHE: A bookkeeper at the hospital fell in love with a girl—they are both very moralistic and idealistic and have a very chaste courtship. The girl's father died either shortly after she was born or just before she was born. The mother never married. The young bookkeeper fell in love with her while attending church. The mother liked him and the girl responded. The mother was agreeable. So they were married in the Greek Orthodox Church.

The upper town priest said: you may now kiss your bride. The groom touched her gently on the shoulder; leaned over and kissed her (*Milton reaches over and touches Rossi's shoulder*). He then goes over to the wedding reception after the marriage ceremony and watches her eyeballs talk. The mother expressed her wishes for grandchildren right away. Everybody is encouraging the birth of children. They went home to the groom's apartment and he started to put his arms around her to kiss her. She developed a hysterical panic.

He could kiss her if he put his hands on her shoulders and leaned forward. But he couldn't hug her or get closer body contact. And yet they had been talking about consummating the marriage all the way home. Now he undressed completely in the nude. She got in bed and he made a movement toward her. She slid out of bed screaming, crying, trembling, shivering, completely hysterical. Days and days this went on. Every time he tried to hug her or touch her in any way, even a blowing kiss—the panic resulted. She didn't like it and he didn't like it. And finally sought me out for therapy.

I gave the girl a Saturday afternoon appointment. She told me the same story he had. You see, she had been keeping that space (*Erickson reaches out to gently touch Rossi's shoulder*). Her mother had taught her all her life to keep her purity and she was a virgin. Yet she picked out a fellow that got her information about sex. So I saw her that afternoon. I listened to her story. And then instead of suggesting any remedy I told her this Saturday afternoon it is entirely possible they could consummate the marriage that night, but I would prefer Friday. Or they might choose Sunday. I prefer Friday. Or they might postpone it until Monday, but I would prefer Friday—or I might decide on Tuesday, but I would prefer Friday. She might decide on Wednesday, but I prefer Friday. Or, she might even decide on Thursday, but I prefer Friday.

ER: Something's brewing here! (*Laughing*) What are you getting at? What are you doing with this?

MHE: I've named all of the days of the year. That's right! *All* of the days of *all* the years yet to come. But Friday is my night. She had been taught to avoid all men and boys. And here was Friday, my night. On Friday morning the husband came in all smiles. He said, "I was asleep at 11:00 last night. *My wife awakened me and raped me!* And we had intercourse several times."

ER: All before Friday, because Friday was your day.

MHE: Yes. *Her* mother had never told her *not* to approach men.

ER: Ah-ha, there is the rub!

MM: Her mother never told her to be aggressive but to avoid those aggressive boys and what they might do to you. So she ate this up. She couldn't go a whole week because Friday would have been his day. And she didn't want to do it to him (*Marion points to Milton*). Friday was his day symbolically to be with him (Milton) and she didn't want to give it to him. She had to go back to her husband and do it but she couldn't let him (her husband) do it. So she just did it to him, which I thought was beautiful.

ER: That's right. She had not received any prohibitions against being the aggressor. Okay, I understand that. But was this psychotherapy or was this hypnotherapy? Was there any hypnotherapy involved?

The General Waking Trance: Intense Mental Absorption and Response Attentiveness

MHE: I didn't *dare* to use anything except my *"General Waking Trance."*

ER: General Waking Trance? What do you mean by that?

MHE: By holding her attention so rigidly that her eyes never left my face.

ER: In other words, your story had such an attention grabbing impact on her—you call that "The General Waking Trance." When a person is looking at you with that intense, what you call, *"Response Attentive-*

ness" you feel they are in a trance even though they are apparently awake?

MHE: Yes. But actually, you realize that when you are looking at a person, the patient, and they are doing that [Intense *Response Attentiveness* indicated by staring back into the therapist's eyes] you know that they are not seeing anything else in the room. They are seeing you. *You see the fixed stare. You will also see the little dilation of the pupils. They will blink their eyes but they will blink more slowly than they would normally blink when you are looking at them.*

MM: That's right. Another person can walk in and take a book out of your bookcase and walk back out and the patient you are talking to will never hear or see them enter and leave. [Patients experience a momentary *dissociation* from anything apart from their intense *absorption* in the focus of their salient response attentiveness on the therapist and what the therapist is saying.]

ER: So this is hypnosis in the sense of *intense focused attention.*

MHE: *Intense focused attention!*

MM: A narrowed area of tubular [tunnel] vision, I call it. I mentioned this to Milton some years ago. I called it, "tubular vision." They also get tubular [tunnel] hearing. They get tubular everything when you really have got their attention. And yet someone else walking in would say they say they are not in a trance because they saw the patient's eyes open, or whatever. The patient's body motility quits and their pupils dilate.

This is why I want you to learn that (*points at Ernie's eyes*). You haven't seen this yet. You would like to see it. Next time I'll fix up my camera set up so that we can put you into trance and we will take pictures both ways and let him (Rossi) see what his pupils are doing both ways (while in and out of intense response attentiveness or therapeutic trance). I think that it is good that he observes this particular thing because sometimes it is so dramatic.

ER: For training of the hypnotherapist it is very important to learn to observe what is actually going on in the patient—to observe minimal eye, facial, and body cues, etc. It is particularly important to recognize the *intense response attentiveness* that indicates when the patient is in a *General Waking Trance*, which is similar to therapeutic hypnosis without a formally recognized hypnotic induction. [The General Waking Trance is equivalent to what has been called "Naturalistic Hypnosis" or "The Common Everyday Trance" (Rossi & Lippincott, 1992; Rossi, 2007). It has been proposed that these states of *intense mental absorption* and *response attentiveness* are functionally related to the three conditions neuroscientists have identified as *novelty, enrichment, and exercise* (both mental and physical) that can turn on *activity-dependent gene expression and activity-dependent brain plasticity, that are the molecular-genomic and neural basis of memory, learning, consciousness, and behavior change* (Rossi, 2007).]

Opening the Mind: The Casual Attention Non Sequitur and Hidden Picture Puzzles

MHE: (*meeting Rossi's gaze*) And by the way, I've been using you as an object to be avoided.

ER: You have been using me as an object to be *avoided?* [Notice Rossi's *immediate intense arousal and response attentiveness* to MHE's casual non sequitur.]

MHE: (*ignoring Rossi's surprised question and shifting his gaze to Marion Moore*) Go over there and get Sandy's picture. [Sandy Sylvester was one of Erickson's students.]

MM: Oh, yes, okay.

ER: I wonder what kind of a scheme you are hatching now (*laughing*)? [It is now obvious MHE has Rossi's humorous and expectant response attentiveness.]

MM: Oh boy! (*Laughing, brings a poster in from the other room.*)

ER: Oh brother. A huge image of a hippopotamus!

MHE: There is a cat there.

ER: (*after a searching pause staring at the poster*) Oh, there *is* a cat's face right there hidden in the image!

MM: Also a walrus with tusks.

ER: A camel.

MHE: An elephant.

ER: Okay, what's the significance of this for learning how to do therapeutic hypnosis?

MHE: When you look at patients look at all of them. Don't miss anything. We have to learn how to read faces— the mood, the expression.

ER: The little wrinkles on the forehead that indicate thought and focus of attention. So this is a classical example, Milton, of why you are always fascinated with puzzles. These puzzles with hidden figures are an aspect of the way you look at the world. You are always looking at the hidden figures. You see the obvious. But what else is there besides what's obvious?

MHE: There is a lot to it. When I was teaching in medical school I taught medical students to see both eyes, both arms, both feet. And now I am teaching Ernie Rossi to see both toes.

Obvious and Minimal Cues in Face Reading: A Lesson Studying Our Own Faces

ER: Yes! I am learning how to do that. For example, with one of my clients this week I noticed that one side of her face is about ½ inch higher than the other side of her face. I don't know why.

MHE: You see that does happen sometimes. So take a look at my face.

MM: His right eyebrow is very bushy and hangs down and you cannot get it back up. The left eyebrow stays perfectly clean and is in line.

ER: The right side seems to have more tonus, or being pulled up more.

MHE: The lips are saggy. They draw a little to the side. Well, you draw down the corners of your mouth, Ernie.

ER: I do?

MM: You drag down the corners of your mouth. Erickson can only do that on one side.

ER: Studying your own physical problems going back to your when you were 17 and having polio for the first time has helped enhance your sensory perceptual sensitivity and this is what you utilize in therapeutic hypnosis.

Erickson's Therapeutic Hypnosis Data Base is Everyday Life: Experience an Open Mind by Observing Minimal Cues

MHE: (Tells an interesting story of how a neighbor recognized the young Erickson because he looked like his mother.)

ER: This is a heart-warming observation I've made about you. You can't talk for more than 5 or 10 minutes without your bringing in your family—your mother, your father, and children.

MM: These are the things he knows about.

ER: That's right. Milton's knowledge of hypnosis is from his real life everyday things—real life observations rather than abstract theoretical conceptions.

MHE: I got my conceptions from people around me.

ER: Yes, that rather than from book. That's part of my despair. I'm a book reader and I'm a writer. I don't observe real life as well as I should and that's a change that I need to make. From a Jungian typology perspective, I am an introverted, thinking, and intuitive type but obviously you are more of an extraverted, sensation type—observing the real world—although also deeply intuitive. A lot of people feel that you must have some kind of ESP—that you must have some kind of extrasensory powers. But there is nothing of this sort. It is just the observing minimal cues—very accurate observation that leads to your skills as a hypnotherapist.

MM: Yes, this is Milton's skill as a hypnotherapist. It can be tremendously helpful to any therapist if he/she can read facial expressions correctly. This is important not only in therapeutic hypnosis but in any therapy. Yes, that is the essence of it.

The General Waking Trance: Unobtrusive Assessment of Hypnotic Amnesias and the General Efficacy of Therapeutic Hypnosis and Psychotherapy

ER: It is important to be able to recognize that patients change their apparent state of consciousness throughout the hour. They can be in that state of *Intense Response Attentiveness* so characteristic of *the General Waking Trance* [with a fixed stare into space, for example, when patients are so absorbed with their own inner preoccupations they don't hear or remember what the therapist is saying. Such patients tend to manifest a spontaneous hypnotic amnesia, which Erickson would frequently carefully assess a few minutes later with a simple unobtrusive query about how the patient understands or feels about what Erickson just said.

In a similar manner Erickson would frequently begin a session with a casual inquiry about what the patient remembered of what was said in the previous session—and whether what was said actually changed the patient's behavior since then. This is often a very valuable way of assessing the patient's responsiveness to therapeutic hypnosis and the general efficacy of any ongoing therapy in facilitating behavior change. A very simple way of making this very important assessment is for the therapist to begin sessions with some variation of the Implicit Processing Heuristic (IMP), "Well, I wonder what we talked about last time that actually changed your life since then?" Patients who are responding well to therapeutic hypnosis and psychotherapy, in general, will become mindful of this assessment technique and soon begin to use it spontaneously on themselves. They will soon open their sessions by reviewing how their behavior changed since the last.]

The Therapist's Tool Kit: Multiple Levels of Communication, Metaphor and Context: Learning to Recognize Minimal Cues in Everyday Life

MHE: That helps patients, you know. How soon did you know that "M" was pregnant?

MM: I knew it the second day. The first day I didn't get to see her at all, to speak of, because I was real busy. They hopped in and already were seated right over here. So I didn't get to see her. Then when she got over here the next day I made mention of the fact of the "state of the union." And they didn't understand that. Then you remember that you brought it out again on Thursday, Milton. They still didn't understand it so I came in and explained it to them and told them that's what we were talking about.

ER: Explain this to me.

MM: Well, the "state of the union" means she is pregnant. They had just gotten married not too many months ago. I saw the flush—the flush that women usually get. The change in the walk from a young girl, or a young girl who has not been pregnant before, etc., to one who is. There is a flush to it and there is a...

MHE: The change in the skin.

MM: The change in the muscle tonus, and the coloring of the skin. There are a number of different things. I teased them on Tuesday and then he brought up the thing about the "state of the union." But nobody gets the "state of the union." We were talking about political guys—the senators and so forth and how they change the state of the union. But in the metaphorical state it is the "state of *their* union!"

ER: *That's communication on two levels!* You were ostensibly talking about politics but you were really talking about pregnancy.

MM: That's right!

MHE: This is a lesson I got from my father. He had one cow that gave 56 quarts of milk a day. I wondered why Betsy could give 56 quarts of milk a day. Now Dolly gave only 28 quarts a day. But father said Dolly was worth twice as much as Betsy. Father said, "Look at that pile of manure behind Betsy. The pile of manure behind Betsy was four times as much as the one behind Dolly. So it cost 4 times as much hay for Betsy's 56 quarts as it did for Dolly's 28 quarts.

ER: So, once again, the successful therapist observes!

MM: (*laughing*) Yes, regardless as to what your observation evolves to.

ER: To be a success in therapeutic hypnosis you have to be an acute observer. I'm convinced! That's the gist of most of your stories: *Observations from everyday life is the best approach to opening your mind to becoming a better psychotherapist.*

How to Anticipate a Kiss: Recognizing Non-Verbal Behavior in Everyday Life

MHE: Yes. Who were the girls that kissed me yesterday? [Notice this provocative non sequitur question that would certainly focus the *response attentiveness* of most listeners.]

MM: Oh, the first one that started it off was the pretty little curly-haired one. She's Betsy and the taller, thinner one was Susan, I believe. And yes, of course, the pretty little blond came over, too.

MHE: Now Betsy, the curly-haired one had been advertising to me all day.

MM: I could see it, but there was no way I could get the camera around with that light. I always get them in the wrong light. I shouldn't say always—last year I got some beautiful shots...I saw her doing it but I couldn't get the camera to the back row.

ER: How do you mean she was *advertising* to you? What was she doing?

MHE: She kept suggesting a kiss.

MM: Her lips moved.

ER: I see your lips moving in a funny puckering sort of way. She was doing that?

MM: Yes, her lips were puckering. I tried to catch her on camera.

ER: Now did she realize what she was doing?

MHE: She did it just today.

ER: In other words, she was making minimal kissing motions with her lips.

MHE: Unknowingly!

ER: Unknowingly. Unconscious. And later when the interview was over she did, in fact, come over and kiss you?

MHE: That's right!

ER: So you were able to read that across the room—her very minimal lip movements, which she was unaware of making, indicating that she was going to give you a kiss. How come I never notice these things?

MHE: And when you see a girl narrow her eyes when she looks at you. (*Milton leans forward to Rossi, gets close to him, narrows his eyes and imitates the behavior just before a kiss.*)

ER: (*laughing*) It is like when a horse's ears go back!

MM: You have to get away from the hind feet! (*laughing*)

MHE: That's right.

ER: There is no school for face reading, posture reading, voice inflection reading—except the school of every-day life. Wow! This is the kind of intelligence I need to develop if I want to become a hypnotherapist? Working out these puzzles?

MHE: *You better be aware of it.*

ER: Better be aware of it? Why? What?

MHE: If you are aware of it, basic facial expressions and so forth, I will help you to understand.

MM: Not only that. If you don't begin to understand after a few sessions, that patient leaves you and you wonder why. What was it that made them leave you without ever saying anything to you? They just don't show up any more. And later you may find they have another therapist.

ER: So we have to learn how to read faces. We have to find out how to understand the inflection of words, mini-mal cues that patients give us about their underlying problem. That's what this is all about!

MHE: Yes.

ER: That's a lot of work! You don't just sit there and talk and empathize.

MHE: Yes!

Overview and Summary

We can now summarize Parts 1 and 2 of Rossi's final training session with Erickson in this overview of the deep psychobiology of psychotherapy. As can be seen, Erickson utilized observ-

Figure 7. Our Psychosocial Genomic Update of the deep psychobiology of Milton H. Erickson's psychotherapy and therapeutic hypnosis.

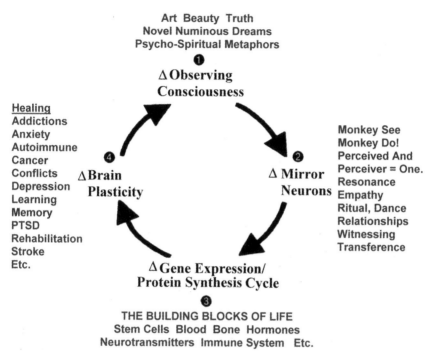

ing consciousness as a meta-level or secondary level of awareness with people found engaging in self-reflective cognitions and feelings about their own cognitions and feelings (illustrated here in Figure 7).

Many types of self-reflection are generally taught as mind-body techniques for facilitating meditation, psychotherapy and psychoneuroimmunology that engage mirror neurons (Iacoboni, 2008; Rizzolatti & Sinigaglia, 2008). Mirror neurons are epigenomic bridges between nature and nurture (Rossi, 2002, 2004, 2007, 2012). We demonstrated in great detail how Erickson's techniques on the cognitive behavioral levels of art, beauty and truth could activate the gene expression/protein synthesis cycle, brain plasticity and their consequent transformations in consciousness, attitudes and plans during important life turning points (Rossi & Rossi, 2013).

References

Blakeslee, S., & Blakeslee, M. (2007). *The body has a mind of its own.* New York: Random House.

Buccino, G., Vogt, S., Ritzl, A., Fink, G., Zilles, K., Freund, H., & Rizzolatti, G. (2004). Neural circuits underlying imitation learning of hand actions; an event-related fMRI study. *Neuron, 42,* 323–334.

Carr, L., Iacoboni, M., Dubeau, M., Mazziotta, J., & Lenzi, G. (2003). Neural mechanisms of empathy in humans: A relay from neural systems for imitation to limbic areas. *Proceedings of the National Academy of Scientists, 100,* 5497–5502.

Erickson, M. (1932/2008–2014). Possible detrimental effects of experimental hypnosis. *The Journal of Abnormal and Social Psychology, 37,* 321–327. Reprinted in E. Rossi, R. Erickson-Klein, & K. Rossi, K. (Eds.) (2008–2014). *The collected works of Milton H. Erickson, M.D.* (Vol. 8). Phoenix, AZ: The Milton H. Erickson Foundation Press.

Iacoboni, M. (2008). *Mirroring people: The new science of how we connect with others.* New York: Farrar, Straus and Giroux.

Lloyd, D., & Rossi, E. (1992). *Ultradian rhythms in life processes: An inquiry into fundamental principles of chronobiology and psychobiology.* London: Springer-Verlag.

Lloyd, D., & Rossi, E. (2008). *Ultradian rhythms from molecules to mind: A new vision of life.* London: Springer.

Rizzolatti, G., & Arbib, M. (1998) Language within our grasp. *Trends in Neurosciences, 21*(5), 188–194.

Rizzolatti, G., & Sinigaglia. C. (2008). *Mirrors in the brain: How our minds share actions and emotions.* New York: Oxford University Press.

Rossi, E., (1972/1986/2000). *Dreams, consciousness and spirit: The quantum experience of self-reflection and co-creation.* (3rd ed. of *Dreams and the growth of personality*). Phoenix, AZ: Zeig, Tucker, Theisen.

Rossi, E. (1973/2007). Psychological shocks and creative moments in psychotherapy. *The American Journal of Clinical Hypnosis, 16,* 9–22. Republished in E. Rossi (2007), *The breakout heuristic: The new neuroscience of mirror neurons, consciousness and creativity in human relationships: Selected papers of Ernest Lawrence Rossi* (Vol. 1). Phoenix, AZ: The Milton H. Erickson Foundation Press.

Rossi, E. (2002). *The psychobiology of gene expression: Neuroscience and neurogenesis in therapeutic hypnosis and the healing arts.* New York: Norton.

Rossi, E. (2004). *A discourse with our genes: The psychosocial and cultural genomics of therapeutic hypnosis and psychotherapy.* Available in English and Italian. (ISBN –89396-01-6) San Lorenzo Maggiore, Italy: Editris s.a.s.

Rossi, E. (2007). *The breakout heuristic: The new neuroscience of mirror neurons, consciousness and creativity in human relationships: Selected papers of Ernest Lawrence Rossi.* Phoenix, AZ: The Milton H. Erickson Foundation Press.

Rossi, E. (2008). The neuroscience of therapeutic hypnosis, psychotherapy, and rehabilitation. In E. Rossi, R. Erickson-Klein, & K. Rossi (Eds.),

2008–2014, *The collected works of Milton H. Erickson, M.D* (Vol.1, Ch. 1). Phoenix, AZ: The Milton H. Erickson Foundation Press.

Rossi, E. (2012). *Creating consciousness: How therapists can facilitate wonder, wisdom, truth and beauty: Vol. 2. Selected papers of Ernest Lawrence Rossi.* Phoenix, AZ: The Milton H. Erickson Foundation Press.

Rossi, E., & Cheek, D. (1988). *Mind-body therapy: Methods of ideodynamic healing in hypnosis.* New York: Norton.

Rossi, E., Erickson-Klein, R. & Rossi, K., (2008–2014). *Experiencing hypnosis: Therapeutic approaches to altered states.* In *The collected works of Milton H. Erickson, M.D.* (Vol. 11). Phoenix, AZ: The Milton H. Erickson Foundation Press.

Rossi, E, & Lippincott, B. (1992). The wave nature of being: Ultradian rhythms and mind-body communication. In D. Lloyd & E. Rossi, (Eds.) *Ultradian rhythms in life processes: A fundamental inquiry into chronobiology and psychobiology* (pp. 371–402). New York: Springer-Verlag.

Rossi, E., & Rossi, K. (2006). The neuroscience of observing consciousness and mirror neurons in therapeutic hypnosis. *American Journal of Clinical Hypnosis, 48*: 283–278.

Rossi, E., & Rossi, K. (2007). What is a suggestion? The neuroscience of implicit processing heuristics in therapeutic hypnosis and psychotherapy. *The American Journal of Clinical Hypnosis. 49,* 267–281.

Rossi, E., & Rossi, K. (2013). *Creating new consciousness in everyday life: The psychosocial genomics of self creation* [a video eBook on Amazon.com]. Los Osos, CA: Palisades Gateway Publishing.

Chapter Fifteen

SST with NLP:
Rapid Transformations Using
Content-Free Instructions

Steve Andreas

Based on their analysis of the patterns underlying the therapeutic mastery of Milton Erickson and Virginia Satir, Neurolinguistic Programming (NLP) was initially developed by Richard Bandler and John Grinder (1975; Bandler, Grinder, & DeLozier, 1976; Bandler, Grinder, & Satir, 1976). Earlier in my career I studied with them (as well as with Abraham Maslow), and for the past 30+ years, my wife Connirae Andreas and I (see Andreas, 1991, 2002a, 2006, 2011, 2012; Andreas & Andreas, 1989; Andreas, et al., 1987) have been investigating the various patterns that create psychological problems and developing change principles and interventions designed to help people resolve them quickly and effectively. We focus on *how* the client constructs his or her subjective world, the ways they create and hold experience, and endeavor to help them modify or alter problematic constructions. Because our interventions are instructions to change the *processes* of representation, rather than their contents, we can often guide people to change and eliminate how they disturb themselves without knowing or "working through" all the specific details of what was bothering

---

Case Example 1 is adapted from Andreas and Andreas (1989); used with permission. Case Example 2 is adapted from an e-book, *Help with Negative Self-Talk* (Andreas, 2010a); used with permission.

them. These second-order changes in perspective can often be accomplished in one session.

When we meet with a client, we establish rapport and alliance, find out what the client would like as a therapeutic goal, and engage them in changing the thought processes that have created and maintained the problem. In what follows, two examples are provided, one involving resolving a specific phobia and the other involving transforming a troublesome internal voice. Both occurred as workshop demonstrations. We believe that for the study of psychotherapy to progress, it is important to see what actually occurs between client and clinician, so we have presented the complete verbatim transcripts of each session (with some orienting commentary and interspersed comments).

Example 1: Resolving Phobias and Intrusive Flashback Memories

There are many different theories about traumatic memories, involving "schemas," "consolidated memories," "core emotional meanings," "symptom-requiring emotional learnings," and often even more metaphoric descriptions, such as "frozen memories," "navigate the maze of trauma," or "trauma burrows deep; it buries itself in the body and lurks behind half-held memories." These poetic descriptions don't tell you anything about what you can actually *do* to "thaw" a frozen memory, or what sort of compass to use to "navigate," or how to locate or look behind "half-held memories," or how to "dig into the body to extract a troublesome memory."

The mechanism of a phobia or a flashback is actually *far* simpler, and much more straightforward. A client experiencing a phobia remembers a horrible and shocking experience as if it were happening again, and the client is *inside* it again, seeing out of their eyes. Since this is a full experiential replication of what happened during the original traumatic event, they again feel all the horrible feelings they experienced in the actual event.

However, there is another way to remember a horrible experience. You can see the memory as a movie in a movie theater, watching it from a distance as an objective observer. From this perspective you may have feelings of compassion for the person on the movie screen going through that horrible experience, but without experiencing the feelings that you had in that event.

You can easily test this in your own experience. Think of an unpleasant memory, and notice if you are looking out of your own eyes, or if you are viewing it as a distant movie on a movie screen…Then whichever way you spontaneously remembered that experience, reverse it. If you were *inside* the memory, step back out of it and view it from the *outside* as an observer; if you were observing that memory from *outside*, step into it as if stepping into a room until you are *inside* it…Go back and forth as many times as you need to, in order to notice how your feelings are different in each of these different ways of remembering.

This ability to take on the viewpoint of a detached observer is a skill that everyone uses in certain contexts, but many people don't realize it and thus don't have the choice to use it in a deliberate way. Resolving a phobia is simply a matter of teaching the client to apply an existing skill that they already have to the traumatic memory.

In the verbatim transcript below (Andreas & Andreas, 1989) taken from the video (Andreas, 1984), I demonstrate the complete process, which took place in a weekend workshop my wife and I taught to a group of mental health professionals. The demonstration subject was a friend of a participant in the workshop, and the friend asked her if she would like to be a demonstration subject. Lori was a completely naïve client who knew nothing about the process, nor anything about the methodology underlying it. The process of eliminating her phobia took 7 minutes. A 25-year follow-up videotaped interview with Lori is also available (Andreas, 2010).

When Lori was eleven years old, she fell into a bee's nest and was stung hundreds of times. Her whole body swelled up so much that her rings had to be cut off. None of her clothes fit, so she had to wear her father's bathrobe for several days. Since then, she had a severe phobia of bees. As she put it, "If a bee is in the house, I'm not!" If a bee got in her car, she had to pull over, stop, open the doors, and wait until the bee left. She also avoided flowerbeds because of the likelihood of bees.

Lori, whom I hadn't met before, had walked into the back of the training room a few minutes before I asked her to join me at the front. In order to emphasize the steps in the process, I did not tell the group the content of Lori's phobia. Below is a complete verbatim transcript of this seven-minute session, with explanatory comments italicized in parentheses. I began with some "small talk" to gain rapport.

STEVE: Lori, I haven't spoken to you at all.
LORI: No.
STEVE: You talked with Michael, I guess.
LORI: Umhmm.
STEVE: I don't know what kind of outrageous promises he's made. *(smiling)*
LORI: *(laughing)* I won't tell you. I won't tell you what he promised.
STEVE: Anyway, you have a phobia, which we won't tell them (the group) about, OK?
LORI: All right.
STEVE: And, it's a very specific thing, right?
LORI: Umhmm.
STEVE: Is it just one thing, or is it kind of a class of things?
LORI: It's one thing.
STEVE: Just one. OK. And what I'd like you to do first— well, think of it right now. If one of these were flying around right now—
LORI: Ohhh! *(She rolls her head around in a counter-clockwise circle, laughing tensely. Now that I have seen Lori's phobic response, later I will be able to recognize when her response is different. Now, however, I need to get her out of this state before proceeding with the process. I do this with specific instructions, distracting, offering my hand, reassuring, and asking her about her friend, Michael.)*
STEVE: This is what we call a "pretest." That's fine; come back. *(Lori is still laughing nervously.)* Look at the people here. Look at me. Hold my hand.
LORI: *(she takes my hand)* Thank you. OK.
STEVE: We're not going to do stuff like that, right? OK.
LORI: OK. Whew!
STEVE: Now look out at the folks here. How is it just being in front of these folks? *(Lori looks out at the group.)* Is that a little nervous-making, too? *(Lori breathes out strongly.)*
LORI: Not bad.
STEVE: Is that OK?
LORI: Yeah, that's fine.
STEVE: OK. You've got a friend [Michael] over there, right?
LORI: Yeah.
STEVE: He's got a nice smile.
LORI: He sure does. He's a great friend.

STEVE: Yeah, good. *(Now Lori is back to a pleasant normal state, so I can begin the method.)* OK. Now what I'd like you to do first, before we do anything—the whole procedure by the way is very simple, and you won't have to feel bad, and stuff like that. But we need to make a few preparations. *("Preparations" implies that we are not yet doing the process, which makes it easier for Lori to just follow my instructions, and not be self-conscious or worry about the process itself.)* What I'd like you to do first is imagine being in a movie theater.

LORI: OK.

STEVE: And this might be easier with your eyes closed...

LORI: All right. *(She closes her eyes.)*

STEVE: And I want you to see a picture up on the screen, of yourself—a black and white snapshot. And it could be of the way you're sitting right now, or something you do at home or at work...Can you see a picture of yourself?

LORI: *(nodding)* Umhm.

STEVE: Is that pretty easy for you?

LORI: Uhuh.

STEVE: Good. Now I want you to leave that black-and-white picture on the screen, and I want you to float out of your body that's sitting here in the chair, up to the projection booth of the movie theater. Can you do that? Take a little while...

LORI: OK.

STEVE: OK, so from now on I want you to stay up in that projection booth. Can you see yourself down in the audience, there? *(Lori smiles slightly and says "Umhm.")* And you can also see the black-and-white picture up on the screen?

LORI: Yeah. OK.

STEVE: Of yourself?

LORI: Yeah.

STEVE: Pretty interesting.

LORI: *(laughing)* It's good.

STEVE: Do you know you could go to a workshop on "Astral Travel" and pay $250 to learn how to do this? *(Lori laughs.)* OK, now I want you to stay up in that projection booth, and see yourself down in the audience, and see that black-and-white picture on the screen of yourself.

LORI: Umhm.

STEVE: Got that?

LORI: Umhm.

STEVE: OK, I want you to stay up in that projection booth, until I tell you to do something else.

LORI: OK.

STEVE: So you can kind of see through the glass, and there are holes in the glass so you can hear the movie—because we're going to show a movie pretty soon. What I want you to do is run a movie of yourself in one of those bad times when you used to respond to that particular thing. And run it from beginning to end, and you stay back in that projection booth. You might even put your fingers on the glass and feel the glass. *(This instruction draws her attention to the feelings in her hands, making it more difficult to notice other feelings, including her phobic response.)* Just run a whole movie, clear to the end. See yourself freaking out over there, in response to one of those situations. That's right. Take all the time you need, and just let me know when you get to the end. *(Seeing a movie in a movie theater has a number of implications, including "This is not real; this is not now; this is only a record of something that happened long ago." I am watching Lori closely for any nonverbal signs that she might be falling back into the phobic response, but she remains resourceful.)* . . .

LORI: It's hard to get to the end.

STEVE: OK. What makes it difficult?

LORI: It just seems to stop. The thing seems to go over and over. *(Gesturing with her right hand in a small circle.)* The particular incident goes over and over and over and doesn't seem to have an end, although I know it ended. *(This kind of short repeating "tape loop" is one of the ways that a client with a phobia or PTSD becomes trapped in their experience. The other main way is to see a still image of the worst moment of the trauma; since it is a still picture, it doesn't change, and seems to go on forever. This is the internal experience that is often described metaphorically as being "frozen in time.")*

STEVE: OK. So it tends to go over and over and over.

LORI: Umhm.

STEVE: OK. Let's speed up the movie. How many times does it have to go over and over before you can get to the end? *(My instruction presupposes that it will exit the loop in a finite number of repetitions, and that it won't take very long.)*

LORI: Um, half a dozen.

STEVE: OK. So let it flip through half a dozen, so it'll let you get to the end,... and when I say "end," I mean after the whole thing happened and you're back normal again. *(This extends her movie far beyond what she previously experienced, giving her a much longer perspective in time than the short tape-loop.)*

LORI: OK.

STEVE: OK. Got to the end?

LORI: Umhmm.

STEVE: *(Although I have not seen any sign of her phobic response, I want to check by asking her.)* Was that fairly comfortable for you, watching that?

LORI: A little uncomfortable, but not bad.

STEVE: "A little uncomfortable, but not bad." Not like the real thing.

LORI: No.

STEVE: OK. Now in a minute I'm going to ask you to do something, and I don't want you to do it until I tell you to go ahead. What I want you to do is to get out of the projection booth, and out of that chair in the audience, and go into the movie at the very end, when everything's OK and comfortable. And then I want you to run the whole movie backwards, including those six times around. Have you ever seen a movie backwards, in high school or something? *(Running the movie backwards while inside it does several things: it reverses the usual cause-effect sequence of her experience— the emotional response occurs before the stimulus—and it also offers her a choice of direction. If she unwittingly falls into the movie at any point, she now has the additional choice to experience it rapidly in reverse, and she will end up before anything bad happened.)*

LORI: Yeah.

STEVE: OK. I'm going to have you run it backwards in color, and I want you to be *inside* it, so it's just like you took a real experience, only you ran it backwards in time, and I want you to do it in about a second and a half. *(Watching the movie in black and white as an observer has reduced its emotional impact; now we add color back in, and speed up the movie, which makes the unpleasantness go by much more quickly.)* So it will go "Bezzzoooouuuuuurrrrrpppp," about like that. *(My sound makes it very clear how long I want her to take doing this.)*

LORI: OK.

STEVE: OK. Go ahead. Do that...*(Lori takes a deep breath, and shudders.)*

LORI: Whooof!

STEVE: OK. Did you come out on the other side all right?

LORI: Yeah. *(laughing)*

STEVE: A little weird in the middle there, eh?

LORI: *(shaking her head and continuing to laugh)* Ooooh.

STEVE: OK. Now I'd like you to do that a couple more times, and do it *faster*. So go into the end, right at the end, jump into it, and then go "Bezourrp," real fast, through the whole thing...*(Most people only need to run the movie backwards once, and usually have no significant response. But because of Lori's brief discomfort, I thought it would be helpful to do it several more times. This time Lori responds much less, sighing a little at the end.)* Now do it a third time, real fast...

LORI: OK.

STEVE: OK. Was it easier the third time?

LORI: Umhm.

STEVE: OK. Now, that's all there is to it. *(Lori opens her eyes, looking very skeptical, grabs the arms of her chair with both hands, shakes her head, and then starts laughing loudly. After about eight seconds of laughter, she says, "I'm glad I didn't pay for this one!" and then continues to laugh for another twelve seconds. Although Lori has been very willing and cooperative throughout the process, her response demonstrates that she certainly has absolutely NO belief that what we did has made any difference—there is no placebo effect. Lori's skepticism is very familiar to us. Even though we have guided literally hundreds of people through this process, we are still amazed that such a simple process can have such a profound impact. My next comments are both to acknowledge her disbelief, and to allow a little time to pass before testing her response to bees again.)*

STEVE: Fine. It's all right. We love to joke. Joking is one of the nicest ways to dissociate. Think about it. When you're joking, when you're having a humorous response to something, there's really no way to do it other than popping out for a while, looking at yourself, and sort of putting a different frame around what's happening, such that it's funny. It's a really valuable way of dissociating. We believe that dissociation is the essence of a lot of humor—not all; there are different kinds of humor, and so on. But we definitely recommend it. Now, Lori, would you imagine now that one of these little critters—came. *(Steve gestures with one finger, like the flight of a bee, toward Lori, in order to test her response. Lori pauses, looks momentarily worried, then thoughtful, but does not go into the tense fear response that she demonstrated at the beginning of the session.)*

STEVE: What's it like?

LORI: Um hay de hay. *(Lori is at a loss for words, and begins laughing.)* Um...

STEVE: Do you still have it [the phobia]?

LORI: *(Looking down, surprised.)* No! She laughs and puts one hand on her chest.

STEVE: *(speaking to workshop audience)* This is a nice response because it looks like, "What?" Consciously she's expecting to have this [old] response. She's had it for—*(speaks to Lori)* How long have you had this?

LORI: Twenty years.

STEVE: *(to audience)* She's had the response very, very dependably for twenty years. It's been a very unpleasant and overwhelming response. There's a very strong conscious expectation. And what you saw here, was this conscious expectation, "Ooooh! It's going to be terrible...*(turns to Lori)* What?

LORI: *(laughing)* It's true.

STEVE: Now let's make it a real bad one, you know. Have one come in and land on your hand or something. *(Lori looks down at her hand.)* Can you imagine that?

LORI: Umhm. *(She shakes her head in disbelief.)* Whew!

STEVE: What's it like?

LORI: Ummm... *(in a neutral tone of voice, shrugging her shoulders)* It's like having one sitting on my hand.

STEVE: That's a typical answer—is what's so funny. "It's like being in an elevator, you know." Isn't that a mind-boggler?

LORI: Yeah, it is! Because I had that happen within the first year after the first incident, I had one land on me, Woof!

STEVE: And it was different, right?

LORI: Yeah! *(looking down at her hand again, still puzzled)*

Lori's nonverbal response to bees in her imagination is clearly very different at the end of the session than it was at the beginning. Several times during the next summer we called her and asked if she had seen any bees, because we wanted to know what her real-world response had been. Each time she said she hadn't seen any bees, which seemed unlikely to us. Finally in December (11 months later) we took a jar with about a dozen honeybees to her house. In a videotaped follow-up interview she comfortably held the jar with bees and examined them closely. When we let several of them out of the jar, she watched them crawling on her living room window without any reaction. A bee was in her house, and this time, so was she. Two years after the session, Lori reported that she still hadn't noticed any bees, though she admitted, "They must have been around me."

It's actually fairly common that people become completely oblivious to what had been the stimulus for their phobia. What used to terrorize them becomes so normal and ordinary it's not worth noticing. When we called one woman a few weeks after eliminating her elevator phobia, she realized she had ridden in several elevators without noticing!

Some people diagnosed with PTSD may have only the kind of immediate phobic response that Lori had. However, frequently they also have other responses that require different specific methods. It is useful to be able to recognize and sort out the different responses, so that you can intervene appropriately. For instance, some people talk about "moral injury," but that doesn't tell you how to heal it. It is simpler to describe this response as being shame or guilt. If the client has shame about how they responded in the traumatic event, or guilt about what they did or didn't do during the traumatic event, then these aspects of their experience need to be treated using additional processes. My wife and I developed a dependable process for shame years ago (Andreas, 1990, 2002b,) and a different process for guilt (Andreas, 2012b)

If the trauma resulted in someone dying or in permanent damage or disability to the client, they may experience grief over these losses, and a method for resolving grief can be used for this (C. Andreas, 1987, S. Andreas & C. Andreas, 2002). Other issues could also be associated with the traumatic experience, and they would require additional specific interventions.

Example 2: Transforming a Troublesome Internal Voice Using Content-Free Process Instructions

Content-free process instructions can be used to enrich and change a client's experience of a troublesome internal voice. A broader and more detailed perspective (the "big picture") spontaneously elicits a much more comfortable and useful response.

The verbatim transcript below was made from the recording of a presentation on working with belief systems at the Milton H. Erickson Foundation Brief Therapy Conference in 2008 (Andreas, 2008). Rather than just talk about how to work with belief systems, I decided to start with a demonstration, and asked for a volunteer:

> STEVE: What I would like to have is someone up here who has a troublesome voice. It could be a critical voice; it could be one that forecasts horrible futures or anything like that, but something that bugs you a bunch of times. And in a sense this *is* a belief, because if you didn't believe in this voice, it wouldn't be a problem, right? I mean, every once in a while have you had someone say to you something really "off the wall" and you just think, "Well, I guess they're schizophrenic or something—it doesn't have anything to do with me."
>
> So if you listen to a troublesome voice and if you're troubled by it, then it means you believe it, right? So there's one little piece, and I'd like to show you *one* way of working with beliefs. There are lots and lots of ways. So who would be interested? (*A woman raises her hand.*) OK, good. And you are—?

LYNNE: Lynne.

STEVE: Lynne. OK, great. You get to hold the "rock star" [hand-held] mic. OK. And I'm going to do this content-free, by the way. And a lot of the forms of reframing [see Andreas, 2011] require that you know some content, but this is a way of doing reframing without any content at all. OK? Is that OK with you?

LYNNE: If you can do it.

STEVE: *(confidently)* Oh, yeah, I can do it. *(laughter)*

LYNNE: OK.

STEVE: OK, so you hear a voice, right?

LYNNE: I do.

STEVE: Can you hear it right now?

LYNNE: Mmhm.

STEVE: Great. Do you know whose voice this is?

LYNNE: Mmhm.

STEVE: Great. Now I want you to listen to the tonality of the voice for starters. It's probably unpleasant, so I won't have you do this too long, but just close your eyes and listen to the tonality, and the details, the hesitations, the emphasis, the verbal emphasis, what part is loud, what part is soft, and so on, as it speaks to you...OK? And you know who it is, right? Can you see their face? *(Lynne sighs.)* You know who it is, so I want you to see their face *as* they say these words to you.

LYNNE: Can I comment?

STEVE: Sure, sure. Anytime. Give me feedback any time, *all* the time.

LYNNE: A little content. This happened a very long time ago.

STEVE: That's fine, but I don't want the content.

LYNNE: No, I wasn't going to tell you, but—so I remember the impact of it better than I remember the actual words.

STEVE: Right, you remember the impact, the emotional impact.

LYNNE: And I'm still carrying the impact.

STEVE: Exactly, and that's what we want to change. Now in order to change that, I need you to do some other things.

LYNNE: OK.

STEVE: OK? So close your eyes and do your best to visualize this person. It doesn't have to be totally clear.

People have freak-out phobias with very, very dull, dim images. You don't have to have a crystal clear positive hallucination or anything.

LYNNE: OK.

STEVE: Can you see the person's face *as* they say this to you?

LYNNE: Yeah.

STEVE: Can you see it now?

LYNNE: Yes.

STEVE: When you see this person's face, does it make any difference in your understanding of the meaning of the words? It may or may not.

LYNNE: Not much.

STEVE: You say "not much"; does that mean it's a *little* different? Or the same? *(Lynne is near tears.)* It's really getting to you, isn't it?

STEVE: OK. We'll change this real fast. So take a little break. And I want you to see the larger context around this interaction. Can you see that? So there is this person speaking to you. *Where* are they speaking to you? And again I don't want to know the answer, but I want you to visualize the larger context...

LYNNE: Mmhm.

STEVE: Now, when you see the larger context, does that change the meaning? Again, it might or it might not.

LYNNE: *(in a more lively voice)* I think it did.

STEVE: OK. And we can explore that later. I just want you to notice. So the larger context made a difference, right?

LYNNE: Yeah.

STEVE: OK. You look like it's more comfortable now.

LYNNE: Yeah.

STEVE: OK. Great. Actually, give me a *little* bit of a report, without revealing content, just how is it different seeing the whole context?

LYNNE: I like the place.

STEVE: You like the place. OK. So the place is comfortable, or pretty, or—you like it in some way.

LYNNE: Mmhm.

STEVE: OK. Great. Now I want you to expand the context in another way. What happened just before this event?

LYNNE: I don't actually know.

STEVE: Well, hallucinate it then. Make it up. What do you think happened just before this, in the few minutes or the half hour before this event?...And also what happened after? Expand your sense of this event in time, both before and after. And let me know when you've done that...

LYNNE: I can't do before.

STEVE: You can't do before. OK. You can't even *imagine* what might have happened before?

LYNNE: Well—

STEVE: What if you just made it up. What do think *might* have happened?

LYNNE: Umhmn.

STEVE: Does that change it at all?

LYNNE: *(taking a deep breath)* Well, in the sense that we shifted away from the event.

STEVE: OK. Good. *(to the audience)* So, can you hear her? Some not and some yes. *(to Lynne)* I know it's a chore *[to hold up the microphone]*. But if you can—say again what you said—something about shifting the attention away from the—

LYNNE: It shifts the attention away from the actual event. It just lightens it.

STEVE: So it lightens it, right. This is called "perspective," seeing something in a larger context, and often it shifts the meaning. At least it makes the emotional impact different, even if it doesn't shift the meaning. OK? Now, you know this person, is that right?

LYNNE: Mmm.

STEVE: Very well?

LYNNE: Mmm.

STEVE: OK. Now I want you to contemplate their strengths, their limitations, who they are as a person, their history, all the background that this comment came out of. They said something to you. And initially we started with just the voice, and then we added in all these other things, and now I'm asking you to add in your knowledge of this person and their limitations and their difficulties, their history, their hopes, their desires—anything you know about this person. *(long pause)*...

LYNNE: Do you want feedback?

STEVE: Yeah, a little bit. Again, not content, but just if it shifts your experience I would be interested in some little report.

LYNNE: *(softly)* I'm feeling sorry for them.

STEVE: Feeling sorry for them. Oh, that's a very different feeling than you had a just little while ago, is that right?

LYNNE: Mmhm.

STEVE: Before it was feeling somehow diminished or terrorized, or something—I don't know what, right? And now you are feeling sorry for them.

LYNNE: Mmhm.

STEVE: Great. That's a very useful change, I think. Now I want you to do one more—well several more things, but the next thing—I'm going to give you a whole bunch of good stuff here. Ask that voice—ask that person—"If you could tell me fully what you meant to say by what you said, including the background—your feelings, the experience that this statement came out of, what would you say?" And just listen for her response, or his response... *(Lynne is showing strong feelings.)* I can tell that's very powerful for you. I don't know the details. Is it useful? Can you tell me?... (Lynne takes a deep breath.) "Are you learning something?" is another way of saying it.

LYNNE: I think so.

STEVE: Yes? Do you want to do that a little more, or do you want to go on?... We can always come back later, of course. *(Lynne laughs.)* It's your brain, and you're stuck with it.

LYNNE: *(laughing)* OK.

STEVE: OK? So it told you—it clarified the message in some way?

LYNNE: More information. *(Lynne begins to have some soft tears.)*

STEVE: More information, yeah—a larger background?

LYNNE: Yes.

STEVE: Does anybody have any Kleenex? In the front row here? Well here *(offering)*, this is a *relatively* clean handkerchief.

LYNNE: *(laughing)* It will probably get makeup all over it.

STEVE: I don't care about that. *(Someone in the front row offers some Kleenex.)* OK, now we're all set.

LYNNE: *(to the person who provided Kleenex)* Thank you.

STEVE: Thank you. OK. So this person told you in greater detail the—Ah, you have more of a basis to understand what this person said, is that right?

LYNNE: Yes.

STEVE: Great. Close your eyes. *(Lynne takes a deep breath.)* And *thank* this person *(Lynne laughs)* for the clarification. It might sound silly.

LYNNE: No it wasn't that. It wasn't that it was silly.

STEVE: OK. All right. *(Lynne takes several deep breaths.)* ...You're getting quite a few changes out of this. *(Lynne laughs.)* And you let me know if there's any time that there is some kind of problem, or...I'm sure this is useful; I've done this a bunch.

LYNNE: Yeah.

STEVE: OK. The next thing I want you to do is ask that person for their positive intent when they spoke to you in that way. What was their positive intent? It could be a very *limited* positive intent coming out of their own frustration—they just needed to yell at somebody at that moment. It could have been that they were worried about you, and they spoke out of their worry, and they were not very good at communicating, so they said it in a crummy way that made you feel bad all these years. And ask them for their positive intent. And then listen to what they say back.

LYNNE: I'm not sure how much information I can give you.

STEVE: That's all right.

LYNNE: They were mostly defending someone else.

STEVE: OK. So they were trying to protect somebody else?

LYNNE: It wasn't about hurting me.

STEVE: What was that?

LYNNE: It wasn't about hurting me.

STEVE: It wasn't about hurting you, yeah. Good. OK, great. And, again, thank them for that—for their communication. *(There is a long pause while Lynne repeatedly breathes deeply.)* ...That's pretty different now, isn't it?

LYNNE: They're sorry...

STEVE: Yeah, they're sorry. Oh, good. Do you have any questions about this?…Would it be OK if people asked you questions, as long as you have total freedom to not answer anything they ask?

LYNNE: *Yes!*

STEVE: OK. There's a mic there if anybody would like to ask her questions. Please sort out your questions between her and me. You know, questions for me about the method, or what I'm doing or what's going on—theory stuff. And her—it's just about her experience if you have any questions for her…

MAN: *(in audience)* Steve, after you do this kind of work—

STEVE: Wait, you're asking me? First, any questions for her, and then we can let her rest.

MAN: OK, the question for you [Lynne] is the same. Now that you've done the work, what's the affective response to the event that occurred to you a long time ago?

LYNNE: I'm sorry. I didn't hear you; can you ask louder?

MAN: You worked through a belief system based on an event. The question is, "What is your emotional, affective—"

STEVE: *(translating)* "How do you feel now?" *(Lynne laughs.)* How's that?

LYNNE: Thank you.

MAN: Thank you.

STEVE: These psychiatrist types can go on *forever!* *(The audience laughs, Lynne laughs, and the man asking the question chuckles.)*

MAN: How do you feel about what happened to you when you were little, right now? What are you feeling now?

LYNNE: Better, better.

MAN: What does "better" mean?

LYNNE: Yeah. A little relieved. A little relieved. It's interesting because I didn't get any information I didn't have before, but there was something different about the way I got it—I'm not sure that answers the question.

(Throughout the process, Lynne's nonverbal behavior—tears, sighing, facial expression, relaxation, smiling, etc.—was eloquent in demonstrating the various changes that she was going through, and how much better she was feeling at the end. I wish that I had said something to point out

at the time that to attach specific words to the changes was not really necessary.)

STEVE: Any other questions for her? Use the mic—Well, go ahead.

WOMAN 1: *(in audience)* Was it hard to thank the person?

STEVE: *(repeating)* Was it hard to thank the person?

LYNNE: *(firmly)* No. No.

STEVE: Very congruent answer, right? One more question for her and then—

WOMAN 2: *(in audience)* I may have missed this in the beginning, but what was your belief, and how has that changed?

STEVE: We don't know, because I wanted to do this without content.

WOMAN 2: Without the content—

STEVE: All I know is there was some kind of voice that terrorized her or made her feel terrible at the beginning.

WOMAN 2: OK. But the belief you had has changed?

STEVE: Ask her.

WOMAN 2: Yeah. *(Lynne takes a deep breath.)...(Again, the question asks for the content of the belief, and a request for a verbal confirmation that she has changed, when her nonverbal behavior was already eloquent.)*

STEVE: Let me ask her—here's a better way to do it. Lynne, can you hear the original voice now?

LYNNE: I don't *feel* the way I felt.

STEVE: Right. You can still *hear* the original voice, but you feel differently.

LYNNE: But I feel differently.

STEVE: Right.

LYNNE: *Yes.*

STEVE: That's a real concrete specific thing. If you talk too much about words and beliefs you can get a little lost, but she feels different and she feels more ah, whole, more settled, more—

LYNNE: Freer.

STEVE: Freer. Yeah. That's really the answer. OK, thanks very much.

LYNNE: Thank you. *(audience applause)*

(The demonstration and commentary above took 19 minutes.)

Now let me just say a couple of words about this. Beliefs are not just words. Beliefs are generalizations that are usually based on concrete, very specific experiences. If you stay with the words, you can get really lost, and you can wander around in the swamp forever. If you have a specific example—this is called a "prototype" in cognitive linguistics—then you work with the prototype. All I did here was repeatedly increase the scope of what she was experiencing, in both space and time, what is often described as "seeing the big picture." Initially she just has a set of words. You get the face, the person, the background of the person, the context. I keep expanding the scope of her experience, and when you do that, the meaning typically changes, sometimes *radically.*

Just one very simple example, and then I'll stop. One woman had two sisters who belittled her all the time, and so she had these voices of her sisters yammering at her all the time. All she did—when she saw the sisters' faces, she realized they were *jealous.* The belittling had nothing to do with her. It had to do with *their* feeling bad, *their* feeling diminished, and the only way they could deal with that was to defensively belittle her. That totally changed the meaning of the whole thing, and her response was completely different. Usually it changes all along, or sometimes one thing doesn't make a difference but another thing does, but here's a whole series of things that you can do.

But basically, you start with the voice, whose voice is it, you add the face, you get the context—the immediate context, the larger context, the time context—what happened before, what's happening after—and then you go for the background—who is this person, what is their positive intent, what lifestyle is this coming out of, what is their stance in life, blah, blah, blah. But it's a concrete, *specific* experience, and that's what makes it work.

Lynne said, "I didn't get any information I didn't have before, but there was something different about the way I got it," and I'd like to say a bit about my understanding of how it was different, and why it got a more useful response:

1. We took a specific, concrete experience and worked with that, rather than with an abstract generalization *about* that experience.
2. Using pure process instructions I asked her to attend to many different aspects of that experience that she had not been attending to, enlarging the context in both space and time.

3. As she enriched her understanding of the voice in many ways, she experienced all this together *simultaneously* (rather than separately, or sequentially).

4. By expanding her experience of the voice she could see "the big picture," and she had a different response to this richer perspective.

Although a conference demonstration is a unique situation, the events in this transcript are typical of the sequence of changes that someone experiences as I offer them a series of instructions that are completely content-free. This is quite different from most therapies, which are usually focused on content, and are often meandering, and don't produce dependable results. After each intervention, I ask her to report any changes. After some of the interventions she experiences little or no change, but major changes with others.

Since I have *no* idea what her internal voice is saying to her, there is no possibility that she could be embarrassed by revealing any sensitive personal information. Working without content also makes it impossible for me to influence her experience with my values or opinions about the content, either verbally or nonverbally.

After each intervention, I ask her to report any change, so that I have instant feedback. I am also carefully monitoring her nonverbal responses to make my own assessment of any changes, comparing what I see and hear in the moment with her initial state, or her state immediately preceding the intervention. This provides me with immediate feedback, so that I can adjust what I do to be sure that I am communicating effectively, and that she is successfully doing what I ask her to. In contrast, feedback at the end of a session—or much later—is always much more global, and doesn't permit the kind of adjustments that I can make in response to responses in the moment.

At the end of this example, Lynne realizes that the words that had troubled her were intended to protect someone else, and were not intended to hurt her. Lynne is sorry for the person whose voice has been making her feel bad for so many years, and the voice is sorry about it, too. The voice is now a cooperative ally, speaking to her as a friend, and they are no longer opponents in conflict.

I recently (2013) got some nice 5-year follow-up from Lynne. She wrote: "I have made major changes in my life, and although I don't credit the work I did with you completely, I do think it was a significant piece. The voice I heard was my mother telling me to protect my sister's feelings by—and of course this was my interpretation—

hiding my own gifts. So I created a very compartmentalized life in which I kept the secret of all the things I can do: people who knew me as a therapist didn't know I was also a singer/songwriter and vice-versa. When I recorded a CD I not only refused to have my picture on it, I forgot to put my name on the CD itself! So those who got the CD without the jacket wouldn't know who it was, and had no way to get in touch with me. Three years ago I agreed to host an Internet radio show (thelynneshow.com)—more public, but still not visible. Then I began writing a one-woman musical piece; I didn't understand until it was almost finished that it was a challenge to this life-long taboo. I produced and performed *Under the Radar* last year, on my 70th birthday. It was the most terrifying thing I'd ever done—until I played the video for my family, including my sister."

References

Andreas, C. (1987) "Resolving Grief" (video). Available at http://www.real-peoplepress.com/resolving-grief-video-download-p-97.html.

Andreas, C., & Andreas, S. (1989) *Heart of the mind: Engaging your inner power to change with NLP*. Boulder, CO: Real People Press.

Andreas, C., Andreas, S., Bennett, M.E., & Wilson, D. (1987) *Change your mind—and keep the change*. Boulder, CO: Real People Press.

Andreas, S. (1984) "The NLP Fast Phobia Cure" (video) Available at http://www.youtube.com/watch?v=mss8dndyakQ.

Andreas, S. (1990) "Resolving Shame" (video) Available at http://www.real-peoplepress.com/resolving-shame-video-download-p-103.html.

Andreas, S. (1991) *Virginia Satir: The patterns of her magic*. Boulder, CO: Real People Press.

Andreas, S. (2002a) *Transforming your self: Becoming who you want to be*. Boulder, CO: Real People Press.

Andreas, S. (2002b) "Resolving Shame" (article) Available at http://www.steveandreas.com/Articles/shame.html.

Andreas, S. (2006) *Six blind elephants: Understanding ourselves and each other* (Vols. 1 & 2). Boulder, CO: Real People Press.

Andreas, S. (2008) "Changing Beliefs." (audio) Milton H. Erickson Foundation Brief Therapy Conference, BT08 Dialogue 5.

Andreas, S. (2010) "The NLP Fast Phobia Cure: 25-Year Follow-Up." (video) Available at http://www.youtube.com/watch?v=TjjCzhrYJDQ.

Andreas, S. (2011) "Using Reframing Patterns Recursively." Available at http://realpeoplepress.com/blog/using-reframing-patterns-recursively-free-vide-clip-of-a-new-nlp-dvd.

Andreas, S. (2012a) *Transforming negative self-talk: Practical, effective exercises*. New York: Norton.

Andreas, S. (2012b) "Resolving Guilt" (article) Available at http://realpeoplepress.com/blog/guilt-and-values-conflicts.

Andreas, S. (2014) *More transforming negative self-talk: Practical, effective exercises.* New York: Norton.

Andreas, S., & Andreas, C. (2002) "Resolving Grief" (article) Available at http://www.steveandreas.com/Articles/grief02.html.

Bandler, R., & Grinder, J. (1975) *Patterns in the hypnotic techniques of Milton H. Erickson, M.D.* (vol. 1). Cupertino, CA: Meta Publications.

Bandler, R., Grinder, J., & DeLozier, J. (1976) *Patterns in the hypnotic techniques of Milton H. Erickson, M.D.* (Vol. 2). Cupertino, CA: Meta Publications.

Bandler, R., Grinder, J., & Satir, V. (1976) *Changing with families.* Palo Alto, CA: Science & Behavior Books.

Chapter Sixteen

Clinical EFT (Emotional Freedom Techniques) as Single Session Therapy: Cases, Research, Indications, and Cautions

Dawson Church

One of the best-known single session case histories in the field of energy psychology was described by psychologist Roger Callahan (2013). A client he calls "Mary" had a longstanding phobia of water. Her parents reported that she had exhibited a marked phobic response to water since infancy. Now in her 40s, she was still frightened every time it rained. She could not take baths in a tub full of water. Though she lived near the ocean, the mere sight of it caused her so much anxiety that she never visited the beach. She had frequent nightmares of being engulfed by water. Callahan worked with Mary using conventional techniques for 18 months but made little progress. He had a swimming pool near his home office, which he used to test her phobic reaction. The best result he had been able to obtain was having her sit on the edge of the pool and dangle her legs in the water, though even this degree of proximity triggered marked anxiety.

Figure 1 (Hand Point) and Figure 2 (Head and Torso Points) ©Dawson Church. Used with permission.

Mary had told Callahan that when she thought of water, she had a sick feeling in the pit of her stomach. Callahan had recently learned about acupuncture points and meridians, and knew that the end point of the stomach meridian was located under the pupil of the eyes. During one session, "not expecting much of anything to happen," Callahan suggested she use her fingertips to tap under her eyes. She did so, and exclaimed that the feeling in her stomach had vanished. She leaped from her chair and ran to the pool. Her fear of water had vanished. The nightmares ceased, and when followed up almost thirty years later, Mary's water phobia had not reappeared.

This experience led Callahan to experiment with a variety of acupressure points for a variety of psychological conditions, and publish his findings (Callahan, 1985). Manual stimulation of acupuncture points is called acupressure, and is used in a variety of therapies such as Shiatsu massage as an alternative to the insertion of acupuncture needles. A randomized controlled trial showed pressure on the points (acupressure) to be as effective as needling (Cherkin, Sherman, & Avins, 2009). Callahan first learned about manual acupoint stimulation from John Diamond, a chiropractor who developed a technique called Applied Kinesiology (Diamond, 1985). Callahan developed an extensive set of diagnostic and treatment techniques which he called Thought Field Therapy (TFT; Callahan, 2000). The acupoints tapped were usually on the endpoints of acupuncture meridians as identified in traditional Oriental medicine (Gallo, 1999).

Oriental medicine identifies 14 of these meridians, which are believed to be conduits along which energy flows in the body. Modern equipment has allowed investigators to detect electromagnetic differences between acupuncture points and the surrounding skin (Syldona & Rein, 1999). Investigators using fluorescent nanoparticles have traced the paths of tiny threadlike structures called Bonghan Ducts running through acupuncture meridian pathways (Johng, et al., 2007). Acupuncture points have an electromagnetic resistance much lower than that of the surrounding skin, and may easily be found by a practitioner using a hand-held galvanometer. TFT has practitioners first diagnose which meridians to treat, then has them tap on a series of points prescribed for that particular condition (Callahan, 2000).

One of Callahan's students, an engineer and performance coach named Gary Craig, then simplified TFT and called his version Emotional Freedom Techniques or EFT (Craig & Fowlie, 1995). He discarded TFTs lengthy diagnostic protocols, reasoning that since there are only 14 meridians, and each one takes only a few seconds to tap, a complete round of acupoint stimulation can be completed in less than a minute. Unlike Callahan, Craig did not believe that the order in which the points were tapped was essential to effective treatment. EFT and TFT also use elements of exposure therapy and cognitive therapy, combining these with acupoint tapping (Feinstein, 2012). Cognitive and exposure therapies were identified as effective treatments for PTSD in a review by the U.S. government's Institute of Medicine (Institute of Medicine, 2007). Acupuncture has also been used successfully to treat PTSD (Zhang, Feng, Xie, Xu, & Chen, 2011). The acupoint tapping component of EFT has been shown to be an active ingredient in treatment, and not merely a placebo (Fox, 2013). There are many methods similar to TFT and EFT, as well as variants of both; Gallo (1999) coined the term "energy psychology" to describe this class of therapies.

A robust research base has emerged to support both EFT and TFT, with Feinstein (2012) identifying 51 clinical trials of the two methods (Research.EFTuniverse.com). Feinstein (2012) compares the research with the standards for "empirically validated treatments" published by Division 12 (Clinical Psychology) of the American Psychological Association (APA), and finds that they meet criteria as an evidence-based practice for anxiety, depression, phobias, and PTSD. One of the seven "essential" APA criteria is that a written manual must document the method so that it can be performed consistently across clinical trials and training programs. *The EFT Manual* (Craig & Fowlie, 1995; Church, 2013a) has provided EFT with such a consistent source since the inception of the method. The EFT method as validated in research performed to APA standards is called "Clinical EFT" (ClinicalEFT.com).

As outcome studies have demonstrated efficacy for energy psychology, investigators have turned their attention to the underlying physiological mechanisms of action involved. A large triple-blind randomized controlled trial investigated the role of the stress hormone cortisol in treatment (Church, Yount, & Brooks, 2012). In this study, one group received a single hour-long EFT session. A second group received an hour of conventional talk therapy in the form of a supportive interview. A third group simply rested. Psychological symptoms were assessed using a valid and reliable instrument called the Symptom Assessment 45 (SA-45; Davison, et al., 1997). The SA-45 has two global scales for the breadth and depth of psychological conditions, as well as nine subscales measuring specific conditions such as anxiety and depression. Clients are asked to respond to the 45 items based on their experience over the prior 7 days.

Analysis revealed that overall symptoms declined by more than twice as much in the EFT group as in the other two groups ($p < .001$), and a significant drop of 24% in cortisol was measured ($p < .03$). EFT thus produced both psychological and physiological change. The degree of psychological change in a single session was significantly correlated with the drop in stress hormones.

Hormones such as cortisol are one part of the body's physiological response to stress. It can also be assessed in the autonomic nervous system and brain using measures like EEG, EMG, heart rate variability, and galvanic skin response. Paralleling the results of the cortisol trial, studies using EEG find reductions in the brain wave frequencies associated with stress after an energy psychology treatment (Swingle, Pulos, & Swingle, 2003; Lambrou, Pratt, & Chevalier, 2005; Swingle, 2010).

EFT can be briefly explained to a client as a stress reduction method that combines acupressure with techniques drawn from conventional psychotherapy. Many practitioners refer to it as "psychological acupuncture." Clinical experience shows that most clients will try EFT after a very brief explanation; once they experience a "felt sense" of it in their bodies, the value of the protocol is self-evident. Clinical experience further suggests that prolonged explanations of the meridians and acupuncture points, the efficacy of acupressure, and reviews of the evidence base can be counterproductive with a new client since the physical experience alone is usually sufficient.

EFT's essential protocol is called the Basic Recipe. It consists of remembering an emotionally triggering event, and giving the intensity a rating on an 11-point Likert scale. Zero represents no intensity, and 10 represents the maximum possible intensity. This scale is drawn from the work of Wolpe (1973) and is called Subjective Units of Distress or SUD. The client then incorporates the traumatic memory into a "Setup Statement." This statement is verbalized three times while tapping seven to 10 times on a meridian on the outer side of the hand with the fingertips of the other hand (see Figure 1). The setup statement combines exposure with cognitive reprocessing in the form of self-acceptance. A typical setup statement might be: "Even though I was in that terrible car crash [*exposure*], I deeply and completely accept myself [*cognitive self-acceptance*]." Then, seven additional points on the face and torso are tapped, repeating the exposure statement "terrible car crash" each time (see Figure 2).

Figure 1: Hand Point

Figure 2: Head and Torso Points

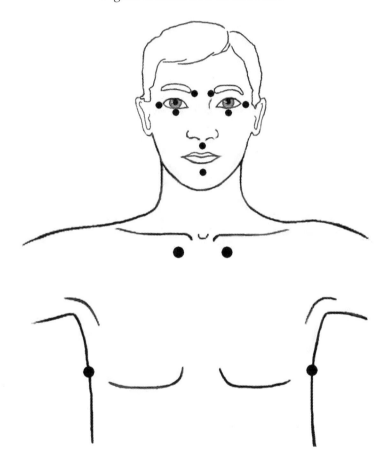

After completing this sequence, called a "round" of EFT, SUD is re-assessed. Typically, distress scores drop substantially. If they do not, additional procedures are used, such as a set of bilateral eye movements drawn from TFT and similar to EMDR (Eye Movement Desensitization and Reprocessing). The Basic Recipe contains the first 9 elements of Clinical EFT (ClinicalEFT.com). There are additional 39 methods in which practitioners are trained. These apply EFT to various clinical dilemmas such as dissociation, emotion, persistent catastrophic cognitions, pain, physical symptoms, and incomplete work at the end of a psychotherapy session.

EFT sessions vary widely in length. Church (2009) found that a 15-minute session improved basketball free throws by 38% in a group of elite athletes. Baker and Siegel (2010) applied EFT to phobias and found that a single 45-minute session was efficacious and that participant results held over time. Traditional Oriental medicine uses a 2-hour clock, with the prescription that there are optimal times of day to insert acupuncture needles for particular conditions, and some clinicians report that EFT sessions ranging in length from 90 to 120 minutes are more effective than the traditional 50-minute psychotherapy hour (Church, 2013b). EFT is often applied situationally, e.g., a public speaker tapping for five minutes before a speech, an acrophobic client tapping just before boarding an airplane, a prisoner tapping when confronted by a gang member (Lubin & Schneider, 2009). SUD can be used by the client to assess the results of EFT when applied briefly in such situations.

Case Histories

Case 1: Grief and Cortisol

I performed a second cortisol test with one of the participants in the cortisol study. The subject, a 58-year-old male psychiatric nurse, was randomized to the supportive interview group. His indicators of psychological distress were as high after the interview as before, unlike other members of the group, who experienced a modest decline.

In the second treatment session, performed outside of the main study, I used EFT. I selected this participant because I was curious whether his scores on the SA-45 would change after EFT as they had not done after talk therapy. The way EFT was administered was typical of the standardized protocol described in *The EFT Manual* (Craig & Fowlie, 1995). This consistent and manualized form of EFT has been used in research, and is termed Clinical EFT (Church, 2013). I scheduled this session as close to the same time of day as the first session as possible, because cortisol rises and falls in a stable diurnal rhythm. For best results, cortisol assays must be administered at chronologically synchronous intervals. The supportive interview began at noon, while the EFT session began at 10 a.m.

A Clinical EFT session usually begins by having the client focus on a particular event with a high degree of emotional charge. For this client, the triggering event occurred when he was 5 years old. He saw a television advertisement in which Gina Lollobrigida was touted as "the most beautiful woman in the world." After watching the advertisement, he went to the bathroom, climbed up onto a stool, and looked at himself in the mirror. He concluded that he was not good looking, and realized he never would be. His somatic experience as he described the memory was a pain in his solar plexus, which he assessed as a 3 out of 10 intensity.

Clinical EFT uses a scale called SUD or Subjective Units of Distress, first popularized by Wolpe (1973). This 11-point Likert scale has clients rate their distress on a continuum from 0 (no distress) to 10 (maximum distress). Clinical EFT practitioners typically ask the client for a SUD score when remembering a traumatic emotional event, and again after treatment. In this way, client progress is self-rated.

The client's second memory was working on the assembly line at Bendix Brake Corporation at the age of 20. He could not assemble the parts fast enough, and he was fired. His SUD around this incident was a 2. He had now provided me with two specific memories, which though he remembered them as highly emotional, he scored at a low level on the SUD scale. This suggested to me that the client might have a pattern of dissociating from troubling emotions. He appeared to be "in his head," approaching troubling incidents by way of mental evaluation rather than actually feeling them.

He then said that every day he thinks about the million unborn babies that will be born into a life of suffering. He felt "deep sadness, anger at myself, depression" accompanying these ideations. His SUD intensity was a 3.

Finally he described a breakup with a girlfriend. He stated that he thinks about this breakup every day. He said that on the final day of their contact, he drove his girlfriend to the airport and put her on an airplane to the opposite coast where she was moving. The fragment that was most emotionally poignant to him was where she looked back as she walked up the jetway "with stunned regret." Yet his SUD intensity remained low, self-reported as a 3.

In an attempt to induce the client to get in touch with his feelings, I probed for additional details of the event, such as his girlfriend's physical appearance, and the last words she said. His SUD then rose to a 6, and he became tearful and red-faced. He described his feelings as a "soggy sponge" with the locus being, again, the solar plexus. Given the intensity of his feelings I assumed that the breakup was recent, but inquiry revealed that it occurred 8 years previously. Yet he could clearly remember the details, and shifted to describing the event in the present tense rather than in the past tense. Ruden (2005) notes that traumatic events are often "frozen in time," with all the sensory channels, sight, sound, smell, taste and touch, encapsulated in that present moment rather than being integrated into the psyche as part of the past.

After tapping on the Gina Lollobrigida incident, we reassessed his intensity around the other incidents as well as that one. The mirror incident had decreased to a 0. The Bendix assembly line remained at a 2. The "million unborn babies" thought diminished to a 1. The breakup incident diminished to a 1, as assessed by the intensity of the feeling in his solar plexus. After the session, I had him fill out a second SA-45, and administered a second cortisol assay.

When presented with the clipboard to which the SA-45 was attached and asked to fill it out, the client said, "This is ridiculous. This is asking me about the last 7 days. How can I have changed in an hour?" He proceeded to write down the exact same scores as he had provided on pretest. He remembered his earlier scores, and duplicated them precisely on the second assessment.

In my experience of administering well over 1,000 SA-45s in numerous studies, this response by a client is highly unusual. Even though the SA-45 instructions tell the client to recall the previous week, scores usually drop after a single EFT session. The events may be the same, but the cognitive frame through which the client views them may be very different, as we will see in subsequent case histories presented here. Objective reality might not have changed, but when subjective reality changes a reduction in psychological symptoms can result.

When the cortisol results arrived back from the lab (SabreLabs. com) a few days later, they showed that the subject's cortisol levels had dropped from 4.61 ng/ml to 2.42 ng/ml, or -48%. This was at the extreme low end of the range of cortisol reductions found in the EFT group as a whole. After his talk therapy session the subject's cortisol had risen from 2.16 ng/ml to 3.02 ng/ml, an increase of 40%.

The lesson for me in this case was that a practitioner receives messages from the client's mind, and messages from the body. They might not be congruent, especially with dissociative clients. This client showed no improvement in psychological scores, but a massive drop in cortisol. Psychological assessment alone would have led me to conclude that the EFT session was unsuccessful, or at best a modest success based on client-rated SUD. Physiological assessment showed that the client had experienced a large reduction in stress at the biological level, despite the interpretation of his mind.

A typical feature of this case is the reduction in SUD for all the client's emotionally troubling events. In EFT this is called the Generalization Effect (Church, 2013). Note that in this session we did not work on any of the adult events, only on the single childhood event. Once the SUD for the childhood event went down, SUD for all the adult events reduced too.

Therapists hypothesize that the reason clients are bothered by adult events is that they resemble childhood events. These associations are usually unconscious, and often surprising, as shown by the following brief case report. Clinical EFT practitioners are trained to look for, and work on, early events. Experience has shown that tapping on adult events often results in temporary improvement, but only finding the roots of patterns of emotional triggering in childhood events results in permanent rehabilitation.

Case 2: Performance Anxiety and Specific Events

Clients typically present with a general issue such as a phobia or performance anxiety. Clinical EFT cautions against working with such global issues, training practitioners instead to identify particular events. The reason for this directive is that global diagnoses usually originate in specific events. When emotional traumas are encoded in our brains, they're engraved in episodic memory in the brain's hippocampus as specific events. So while a client may present with a general issue such as performance anxiety, the issue did not start out as a general problem with performance anxiety. The performance anxiety arises out of an aggregation of specific events, and only after they'd all accumulated can we identify and name a general problem. The following case illustrates this pattern.

"Jeanette," a woman in her early 20s was a participant at a Clinical EFT workshop, and volunteered for a demonstration session in front of the whole group. Her presenting issue was performance anxiety. She said she had no problem during a performance, but felt "horrible anxiety" every day leading up to one. She had an actual performance coming up in 2 weeks, and I asked her for a SUD score as she imagined it. She reported a 10, and the physical location as a burning sensation in her chest.

I guided her into finding several events that had contributed to the problem by asking, "Tell me about one of the first times in your life you remember feeling that exact same sensation in your chest." The first one Jeanette identified was performing solos in Music Tech class at the age of 11. "There was one girl who looked so smug," Jeanette said. "Her name was Melanie, and she knew she was the best singer. She'd look at me while I was performing, and I knew her look meant 'You know I'm the best.'"

"Was it only solos?" I asked. She said "Yes," that when they sang together as a group in choir, no one could hear the individual voices. But when they sang solos in Music Tech, all eyes were upon her. We performed several EFT sequences on the incident.

In another incident, Jeanette had to give a talk about her summer vacation in front of the class in first grade. She prepared for days in advance, and wrote careful notes. When the day arrived, she opened her back pack, only to discover that she'd left her notes at home. She was very nervous, and even though the speech went well, the event left a lasting emotional impression. We tapped on that event too, till she reported a SUD of 0.

Jeanette described another event around the age of 9. She'd been asked to sing in the church choir, and went to rehearsals to practice with the group. She enjoyed the singing and the companionship of the rehearsals, and eventually the great day dawned when they had to sing in front of the congregation. When they assembled in the choir room just before the service, the choir master discovered that most of the sets of music sheets were missing. So each group of three choir members had to share a sheet of music. Jeanette was too far away from the friend holding the sheet to be able to see it properly, and felt under great stress, even though the performance went "fairly well." We tapped on this final event.

When I asked Jeanette to characterize her anxiety now as she imagined her upcoming performance, her SUD score was a 0 out of 10. Note that we had not done EFT on her performance anxiety or the upcoming performance, only on individual childhood events that contributed to the presenting issue. Jeanette's results are consistent with those of a randomized controlled trial of EFT for public speaking anxiety (Jones, Thornton, & Andrews, 2011). These investigators found that a single session of EFT was sufficient to address both behavioral and psychological blocks to public speaking.

A single EFT session can also make a significant different in sports performance. A randomized controlled trial of soccer players found a significant improvement in free kick performance (Llewellyn-Edwards & Llewellyn-Edwards, 2012). A similar trial found that basketball players receiving a 15-minute EFT session scored 38% more free throws (p < .05) than a placebo control group (Church, 2009). A 20-minute EFT session was found to increase confidence and decrease anxiety in an uncontrolled study of female college-aged athletes (Church & Downs, 2012).

Case 3: The Worst or the First, and the Apex Effect

While a client may seek therapeutic intervention for a general problem like performance anxiety, self-esteem, or procrastination, the roots of these problems are usually found in a sequence of specific events. For instance, a client with self-esteem problems might have self-talk such as, "I'm worthless. My needs don't matter. I don't amount to anything in the world." These are global negative cognitions that arose from traumatic events early in childhood. Each event may have been only a few seconds or a few minutes in duration, but collectively they influence the client. The client makes meaning of the event by locating it in a cognitive frame, such as, "My needs don't matter."

Clinical EFT training directs practitioners to search for the earliest events. There are usually many events, leading to the question of how to identify which ones should be the therapeutic target. A useful filter is the concept of finding "the worst or the first" event. One client I worked with in a group had been beaten often by his father when he was a child. I asked him to describe "the worst or the first" beating and he described a particular beating that occurred when he was eight years old. His father hit him so hard that he broke the child's jaw.

This particular client reported a SUD level of 10 when recalling this traumatic event. We worked on many aspects of the event, such as his father's words, the expression on his father's face, his father's tone of voice, the circumstances surrounding the event (a birthday party with the client's childhood friends). Once we had tapped on all the aspects of the event, the client's SUD went down to 0.

Obtaining pre- and post SUD scores, as well as intermediate assessments, is vital to good EFT practice. The reason for this is that clients often forget how high their distress was before treatment. One veteran treated successfully for PTSD told his therapist after receiving six sessions of EFT that he wasn't in bad shape and probably never had PTSD to begin with. She showed him is pre-treatment scores on the PTSD Checklist—Military (PCL-M; Weathers, Huska, & Keane, 1991). He was astonished at how high his scores had been prior to treatment. This therapist was one of a group of about 400 therapists who treat veterans as part of a national organization called the Veterans Stress Project (StressProject.org). Many Veterans Stress Project therapists report similar cases. The phenomenon of clients forgetting the severity of their former problems is noted so frequently in EFT and TFT treatment that Callahan coined a term for it, the "Apex Effect" (Callahan, 2000). The neurological processes that underlie the Apex Effect are beyond the scope of this chapter, but the Apex Effect presents an argument for the importance to both client and practitioner of recording frequent SUD scores.

In the case of the client who had been beaten by his father, the drop in SUD for the specific event was reflected in a drop in SUD for the collective experience of being beaten. At the end of the session the client said, "My father did the best he could. He wasn't very good at it, but he tried. And when he was a kid, his dad beat him far worse than he beat me." This language indicated a cognitive shift in the client, from a position of helpless childhood victim to an adult perspective of reflection and assessment. This type of cognitive shift is typical of successful EFT treatment. Clinical EFT practitioners are trained to watch carefully for cognitive shifts in clients. A shift in the cognitive frame in which a client holds an event may be an indicator of treatment progress. Cognitive shifts are a method of testing the results of treatment that possess more nuance than the rudimentary yardstick of SUD.

The limbic system in the mammalian midbrain, and especially the hippocampus, has been developed in a long evolutionary cycle to make associations. Proximate sensory cues are compared to historical events in order to determine if they present a threat to survival. If the hippocampus finds a match between a new event and an old one, it signals the amygdala to initiate a full-fledged stress response (Phelps & LeDoux, 2005). Therapy sessions that address current problems might provide some relief, but experience with EFT has shown that fast and permanent symptom change is usually accomplished by targeting old events.

When the soothing somatic input of acupressure signals the hippocampus that no objective threat is present, even when the brain's prefrontal cortex is simultaneously presenting the limbic system with a troubling subjective memory, the association between the forebrain signal and the stress response may be broken for all similar memories. Once this conditioned response has been interrupted one time, the link is often permanently broken. The individual may have the same troubling emotional thought again, but it is no longer encoded by the hippocampus as an objective threat to survival. The hippocampus therefore does not signal the amygdala to initiate a systemic stress response even though the mental stimulus is present. Once the association has been broken for the most traumatic childhood memory, the hippocampus may generalize this counterconditioning to embrace all other memories with a similar emotional content. Clinical EFT makes use of this "generalization effect" so that the client does not have to work on every single memory.

The associations made by the hippocampus are often surprising to both practitioner and client, as the following case demonstrates.

Case 4: Acrophobia and Hippocampal Associations

At an EFT workshop I worked with a retired gentleman on acrophobia. He said he hadn't been able to go near a balcony for years, and he avoided going to the city because he'd have to deal with high-rise buildings. He joked about friends saying things like, "Let's go to the Transamerica tower and see the view from the observation deck." I asked him when it was worst ("the worst or the first"), and he identified it as a building with floor-to-ceiling windows. The workshop was being held in a single floor building with no opportunity to test his SUD level *in vivo*, so I asked him to imagine in his mind's eye walking up to a floor-to-ceiling window and tell me how closely he could get without stopping. He said he could get within 6 feet of the window and at which his SUD level was a 9, and the physical sensation was in his throat.

I asked him to identify the first time in his life he had felt the same physical feeling in his body. He said that when he was three years old that his family lived in a house near a mine. It was very noisy, and miners disappeared down a shaft every day. He didn't know why that experience was so emotionally troubling for him, but we tapped on it anyway. He then shifted to another event, when he was two years old, when his father started up his motorcycle in the driveway. It also made a loud and startling noise. As we tapped, the SUD on the motorcycle event went down to a 1, after which I tapped on as many aspects of the mine as he could recall.

At that point I tested our results by asking him to again imagine approaching a floor-to-ceiling window. He was able to walk all the way up to the window and his highest SUD level was a 2. He stated that felt as though he could now handle going to the city with its tall buildings.

Why did the client associate the sound of the mine with a fear of heights? Neither the client nor I could make the link with our conscious minds. Yet the client's hippocampus did associate the two. One of the challenges in Clinical EFT practice is to avoid assumptions. Associations between disparate events may be hidden in surprising niches in the psyche, with physiological correlates in neural pathways in the hippocampus. Only by listening very carefully, and respecting the client's reports, can they be identified and treated. Clinical EFT training emphasizes the importance of the therapist "getting out of the way" in order to allow insight to emerge organically from within the client's own psychological processes and neurological configuration.

Clients and practitioners have been recording case histories in an online database for over a decade, and amassed some 5,000 anecdotal accounts (EFTuniverse.com). Several hundred of these stories describe recovery from phobias. Besides this clinical evidence, EFTs efficacy for phobias has been demonstrated in three randomized controlled trials.

Three randomized clinical trials have examined the effects of EFT on phobias and found that a single session is usually enough to resolve a phobia (Wells, Polglase, Andrews, & Carrington, 2003; Baker & Siegel, 2010; Salas, Brooks, & Rowe, 2011). All three studies included a follow-up period and found that the phobic responses of participants remained significantly lower than before treatment. These studies show that EFT meets the standards of APAs Division 12 Task Force on Empirically Validated Treatments (Chambless & Hollon, 1998) as an effective single session remedy for phobias.

In terms of treatment speed, I conceptualize phobias as one end of the spectrum of anxiety disorders, with PTSD at the other end. While there are very few accounts of a phobia requiring more than one EFT session, PTSD has been described as a "treatment-resistant" condition (Seal, et al., 2010). Only a third of veterans referred to a comprehensive yearlong PTSD program at a Veterans Administration hospital complete the prescribed course of treatment (Seal, et al., 2010).

EFT for PTSD

EFT has been evaluated in several studies of PTSD. Most of these use several treatment sessions, and a detailed discussion of these results is beyond the scope of this paper. However, there is one study of a single session of EFT for PTSD that is of interest, and it is helpful to locate this study within the body of research for this condition.

A hospital in Britain's National Health Service (NHS) conducted a study of EFT for PTSD in its patients (Karatzias, et al, 2011). The NHS study compared EFT to Eye Movement Desensitization and Reprocessing (EMDR: Shapiro, 2001), and found that both remediated clinical PTSD levels in an average of four sessions. A randomized controlled trial of veterans with clinical levels of PTSD symptoms found that they could be successfully treated in six EFT sessions (Church, et al., 2013). Pilot studies that preceded these randomized controlled trials shows similar results (Church, Geronilla, Dinter, & Brooks, 2009; Church, 2010). Outcome studies of traumatized populations such as Haitian earthquake victims (Gurret, Caufour, Palmer-Hoffman, & Church, 2012) and Congolese women (Nemiro, 2013) also demonstrate EFTs effectiveness for PTSD.

The population for the single session study was drawn from a group of male adolescents in a group home (Church, Piña, Reategui, & Brooks, 2012). The boys in the institution had been committed its care by a judge because of physical or emotional abuse at home. This randomized controlled trial compared participants who received EFT to a control group receiving no treatment beyond that routinely offered by the institution. All participants scored in the "clinical" range on the Impact of Events Scale (IES: Horowitz, et al., 1979). Each participant in the EFT group (n = 8) was asked to recall a specific traumatic incident ("the worst"). Thereafter, they received an hour-long comprehensive session from an experienced practitioner. Aspects of the experience, such as the physical appearance of their abuser, the tone of voice, and physical sensations, were addressed. Participants received a posttest 30 days after treatment, and all participant symptoms scored in the "non-clinical" range (p < .001).

The Karatzias, et al. (2011) study found that an average of 4 sessions was required to remediate PTSD in hospital patients, a treatment time frame similar to the 6 sessions used with veterans in Church, et al. (2013). Why did the Church, et al. (2012) study of adolescents find that a single session might be sufficient? The reason may lie in the age differential between the populations. This is suggested by a randomized controlled trial of depression in which clinically depressed teenagers were given EFT group therapy (Church, De Asis, & Brooks, 2012). On follow-up, scores for the EFT group were in the "non-depressed" range of the Beck Depression Inventory (Beck, Steer, & Carbin, 1988). Hebbs' Law is simply expressed as "neurons that fire together, wire together," and studies of PTSD show that it produces durable changes in the brain over time (Vasterling & Brewin, 2005). While neural plasticity is helpful when applied to positive stimulation such as learning new skills, it can work to our disadvantage when our brain repeatedly processes the signals of stress, such as the intrusive thoughts, flashbacks and nightmares typical of PTSD. Over time, parts of the brain responsible for cognitive function, and the conversion of short-term to long-term memories, shrink in volume in PTSD patients (Vasterling & Brewin, 2005).

I also believe that practitioner training plays a part in such a quick outcome. I speak from the perspective of supervising a large group of Clinical EFT trainers, as well as having conducted many practitioner trainings myself. I read over a thousand case histories annually in the course of practitioner evaluation. This has led me to conclude that a thorough knowledge of all 48 Clinical EFT techniques, as well as training in other psychotherapeutic methods, plus a diversity of clinical experience, leads to the best client outcomes. The veterans PTSD study (Church, et al., 2013) used 14 practitioners with a variety of backgrounds and levels of training, while the adolescent male study (Church, et al., 2010) used a single expert practitioner. While EFT is a useful way to reduce the emotional intensity of traumatic memories, much more is required for a client with complex PTSD and co-morbid conditions.

However, even a single session usually produces some results for PTSD patients. Church, et al. (2013) used an intermediate assessment after three sessions, in addition the post-treatment assessment after 6 sessions. The three session evaluation showed that symptoms of PTSD, depression, and anxiety were reduced, along with physical symptoms of insomnia, pain and traumatic brain injury (TBI). Anecdotally, veterans often reported some improvement after the first session. During the second session, several reported to their practitioners that they had experienced their first unin-terrupted night's sleep since they returned from Vietnam. I now present some case histories of clients with PTSD drawn from the Church, et al. (2013) study.

Case 5: Vietnam Nurse and Allergies

Subject's body was so sensitive that she was unable to tolerate EFT tapping on any part of it without getting violently nauseous. Subject reported many incidents of physical abuse starting in early childhood, and was so physically sensitive that she was easily trig-gered by physical stimuli. She couldn't wear socks or shoes, and couldn't tolerate physical touch by others. Her companion, report-ing that their life situation was "unbearable," and that she was "in complete desperation," arranged for coaching.

Subject's intolerance to touch presented a challenge to finding a way to let her apply EFT. She found that she was able to tolerate tapping between her eyebrows, so that was the only point used in the first session, which focused on fear and safety issues.

Halfway through the second session, she noticed that she could now tap on every EFT point, including the collarbone point, which had previously been her most sensitive spot. During this and sub-sequent sessions, the client worked with three specific war memo-ries, and two physical symptoms, among other issues. These five coaching targets are summarized below.

(1) Subject had rescued some Vietnamese village people, elderly and children and was treating them in her field hospital. A U.S. Army sergeant came in and ordered her to discharge them imme-diately because the space was required to treat American service personnel. The subject outranked the sergeant, and refused. At that point, he withdrew his service revolver from its holster and put the barrel to her head. He said he was going to kill the villagers one way or the other, and her only choice was whether or not she was going to die first.

Realizing the rage he was in, she knew she had no choice, and rescuing the villagers was completely out of her control. She knew that the only thing she could do was to allow for them to go in peace and with dignity, with no fear or panic, in the tradition of their culture. To insulate them to the violence of the sergeant, she very gently pulled the IVs out of their arms, allowed the children to gather around the elders for support, and encouraged them to leave the hospital as a group. Once outside, they were shot by the sergeant.

The nurse never recovered emotionally from the experience. She blamed herself for being responsible for the killing. She continued to have nightmares about the incident even decades later.

During the EFT session, subject tapped on the separate scenes of this traumatic event. She began to feel a sense of connection with the villagers, and come to an understanding that they were actually grateful for her. They had witnessed the gun at her head and they knew that there was nothing more she could do. They didn't blame her but appreciated that she did the best she could. After this cognitive shift, the nightmares about the incident did not recur.

(2) The subject lives close to a military base. Helicopters frequently fly overhead, and she would go into involuntary panic at the sound. After several rounds of EFT, subject said that she now simply noticed the sound of the helicopters, without panic or agitation.

(3) One of the subject's most traumatic memories was of an incident in which the hospital she was working in was bombarded by friendly fire and collapsed on her. At the time the bombardment began, she had been walking down a corridor. Two children were present, and she grabbed them and threw herself over them, protecting them with her body while the hospital roof collapsed. She was the only person pulled out alive from the rubble. She spent many months in hospital and rehabilitation following the incident. She had frequent nightmares about the scene. After EFT, the memory no longer held emotional triggers. She was able to recount the incident calmly, without the emotional upheaval that she reported before.

(4) Subject had an allergic reaction whenever she consumed ice cream. She used EFT for the substance itself, and for her symptoms. Subject recounted that, in Vietnam, there were two things that wounded men requested: steak, and ice cream. Both were difficult to obtain, and represented the comforts of home. When subject would eat ice cream, she felt connected with the pain that she had witnessed. After EFT, the allergy subsided.

(5) Subject had a hearing impairment, due to scar tissue from various injuries. She identified shutting off her hearing as a defense mechanism, and repeated application of EFT was required. After EFT, her hearing improved to the point where she could hear the clicking of the keys on her computer keyboard.

Case 6: Vietnam Combat Veteran

Subject had a violent, alcoholic father. He was drafted to serve in Vietnam. He worked on two specific memories, among others:

(1) The first night in Vietnam, he woke up in horror, realizing he was in imminent danger, when an enemy artillery bombardment began at 2:30 a.m. The camp was completely unprepared, with plywood floors and no security, and the draftees had not yet been issued weapons with which to defend themselves. Their anger at the army for not being prepared for them and keeping them safe was enormous. The subject remembered drinking a bottle of scotch whiskey and smoking a pack of cigarettes the first night, while a friend of his, newly married, sobbed helplessly. The recruits slept uneasily under their beds. The artillery fire resumed every night at 2:30 a.m. Before the first EFT session, subject would wake up every morning at this time. After EFT, he was able to sleep through the night.

(2) Some of the workers in the camp were Vietnamese. They pretended to be friendly, but their families were connected to the enemy, and the subject discovered that they were secretly passing information about the base to the Vietcong. So he and the other recruits were never safe. Subject felt a sense of betrayal, and being unsafe, ever since, and was able to reduce his SUD score around these issues with EFT.

Other Combat Memory Examples

The following are examples of specific memories on which EFT reduced SUD scores to 0 during the course of a single session:

(1) An Iraq veteran described an incident in which the Humvee in which his best friend was the driver hit an Improvised Explosive Device (or IED) and was unable to extricate himself. He burned to death. The veteran used EFT for the incident. He then began to spontaneously recall the funerals of other people who had loved him. After reducing his SUD score for each one, he began to relax.

(2) Another Iraq veteran was the driver of a transport truck, and in charge of transporting the men inside safely. At night, he had a very limited field of vision through the vehicle's armor. The lack of peripheral vision made the drive very stressful for him. His passengers yelled at him for his inadequate driving, and he felt overwhelming anger for their resentment while he was so stressed and trying to do a good job. He performed EFT for these memories, as well as for find-

ing forgiveness, and tapped while imagining the other soldiers asking for forgiveness, using phrases like, "Sorry, man, for yelling at you. It wasn't personal," coupled with the EFT self-acceptance statement.

(3) A former Vietnam officer described ongoing threats from his subordinates. He described huge tension between white and black soldiers. He had stood up for a Vietnamese woman who was about to be raped, and prevented the rape by his comrades. As a result, he was harassed by his compatriots for months.

One of his soldiers went into a rage after drinking heavily and pointed his rifle through the tent door at the soldier while he was asleep. The officer handcuffed his opponent outside the bar until he sobered up. From that moment on, the soldier tried to shoot the officer wherever his back was turned. The officer did not have a safe moment until the subordinate was killed in a firefight.

(4) Another veteran shot a 9-year-old girl who was pointing a rifle at him. He said, "I only saw the rifle! I was trained to shoot when somebody point a rifle at me! I found out later that it wasn't loaded. She is always with me, smiling, and she never says a word. I have asked for forgiveness, I have asked my life to be taken for hers, but it hasn't. I have to live with this memory every day, and I always see her. I wish I'd never come back from Vietnam." The little girl was with him as a flashback for 44 years, quietly smiling at him. After EFT, she now disappeared. Most veterans report severe childhood trauma in addition to combat trauma. Issues include sexual abuse, parental alcoholism, physical abuse, poverty, and neglect. Some reported that releasing childhood trauma was more effective than releasing war memories in producing a reduction in emotional distress levels.

Limitations and Cautions in Using EFT

With a research psychologist colleague at the Psychology Department of the University of Arizona, I conducted an outcome study of healthcare workers (Church & Brooks, 2010). Participants were 216 healthcare professionals at 5 professional conferences. After a single day-long EFT workshop, their symptoms of psychological conditions such as anxiety and depression declined by a mean of 45% ($p < .0001$). We found these results striking, since most of their gains were maintained on follow-up.

Before publishing these findings, after receiving the data analysis from my colleague, I interviewed a number of experienced EFT practitioners, seeking to understand the surprising magnitude of the symptom reductions noted. Their consensus was that such improvements were the norm with EFT, but that the results obtained during the first set of EFT sessions was not necessarily an indicator of what might be required for further improvement. The most superficial layer of psychological distress might yield readily to treatment, but the next and more highly conditioned layer might not. Early results can rarely be extrapolated out to the future.

Training in Clinical EFT stresses this limitation, and instructs practitioners against becoming overly enthusiastic after witnessing early results with EFT. Practitioner allegiance to the method can result in pressure on the client to live up to the practitioner's expectancy by reporting lower SUD scores. Practitioner training counters this tendency by emphasizing the importance of validating the client's experience, especially when SUD scores rise. A rise in scores is frequently encountered with dissociative clients, who might get in touch with their emotions for the first time in many years. Paradoxically, in these cases a rise in scores is an indicator of client progress. Practitioner neutrality and client validation is therefore a cornerstone of good EFT practice.

A phrase used in EFT to describe rapid treatment success is "one minute wonders." The EFT case history archive (EFTuniverse.com) contains hundreds of such stories detailing alleviation of psychological distress, as well as physical symptoms such as pain, swelling, headaches, and autoimmune diseases. However, practitioners who experience one minute wonders can then develop the expectancy that every condition, psychological and physical, will respond as quickly. They soon discover that this is not the case. Some problems are multifaceted, complex, and treatment-resistant. Certain conditions, such as tinnitus, rarely respond to EFT treatment. Addictions are also often difficult to treat, with uncertain outcomes (Lake, 2013). While 86% of the veterans in the PTSD study (Church, et al., 2013) were subclinical after six sessions of EFT, 14% experienced no improvement. Like any other therapy, EFT is not a panacea.

EFT targets specific events held in episodic memory in the limbic system. Clients who cannot remember events for whatever reason present a challenge. When asked for an event that underlies their presenting condition, some clients respond with phrases like, "I can't remember a single event" or "I can't feel anything in my body when I think of the event." Clinical EFT has developed a number of techniques for such situations. The most commonly used one is drawn from TFT and is called the 9 Gamut procedure (Church & Marohn, 2013). It uses eye movements reminiscent of EMDR, and clients without memories, or without the ability to anchor emotion in physical sensation, usually report relief after using the 9 Gamut. While it can be self-applied, it is complex, and execution is usually more successful with the help of a practitioner. Clients who cannot remember childhood events can find EFT challenging to use without expert professional support.

A different treatment challenge is presented by clients who experience overwhelming emotion. At one workshop I conducted, I talked to a middle-aged man who appeared very sad. He said, "I have so much grief, it feels like a huge reservoir. I have my finger in the dam. If I take my finger out and allow even a little bit of that grief to come out through the hole, the dam will burst and obliterate me." Three EFT techniques called the Gentle Techniques have been developed to accommodate such situations (Church & Marohn, 2013). They deliberately induce dissociation in order to give the client a sense of distance from the problem. Once the client's SUD level for the distantly held event drops, they may be able to approach the memory directly. Generally, if a practitioner keeps a client tapping even while experiencing overwhelming emotion, the degree of distress diminishes. Several clinicians have emphasized EFT's safety when treating mental health conditions (Flint, Lammers, & Mitnick, 2005; Mollon, 2007).

Conclusions

The evidence base for Clinical EFT as a single session therapy for certain conditions like phobias is robust. EFT practitioners test client progress often during a session using SUD scores and noting cognitive shifts. Spontaneous cognitive reframes by clients are common. Good EFT practice targets specific childhood events rather than generalities, and EFT works best on conditions rooted in episodic memories. Clinical EFT practitioners are also trained in specialized techniques designed to address treatment challenges such as overwhelming emotional intensity and dissociation. Clients typically report significant reductions of their symptoms of anxiety, depression, and PTSD in a single session, though longer courses of treatment are indicated for these diagnoses. Certain treatment-resistant conditions like complex co-morbid PTSD can require prolonged treatment, therapeutic expertise, and support from other therapy techniques. Research indicates that EFT remediates a complex of co-occurring conditions, with

PTSD, depression, and anxiety symptoms dropping simultaneously. In tandem with improvements in mental health, physical symptoms such as pain and autoimmune conditions can improve as the hormonal and brain wave correlates of stress are reduced.

Single sessions of EFT can encourage clients to persist with prescribed treatment by providing them with an experience showing that even psychological problems of long duration can be relieved. This may enhance their compliance with a full treatment program involving many other modalities. For these reasons, EFT is recommended as an efficient and effective frontline primary-care and mental health intervention.

References

Baker, A. H. (2010). A re-examination of Church's (2009) study into the effects of Emotional Freedom Techniques (EFT) on basketball free-throw performance. *Energy Psychology: Theory, Research, & Treatment, 2*(2), 39–44.

Baker, A. H., & Siegel, M. A. (2010). Emotional Freedom Techniques (EFT) reduces intense fears: A partial replication and extension of Wells et al. *Energy Psychology: Theory, Research, and Treatment, 2*(2), 13–30. doi:10.9769. EPJ.2010.2.2.AHB.

Beck, A. T., Steer, R. A., & Carbin, M. G. (1988). Psychometric properties of the Beck Depression Inventory: Twenty-five years of evaluation. *Clinical Psychology Review, 8*(1), 77–100.

Callahan, R. (2000). *Tapping the healer within: Using Thought Field Therapy to instantly conquer your fears, anxieties, and emotional distress.* New York: McGraw-Hill.

Callahan, R. (2013). Thirty years of Thought Field Therapy. Accessed 8/3/13 at http://www.rogercallahan.com/news/30-years-of-thought-field-therapy/case-studies.

Callahan, R. (1985). *Five minute phobia cure: Dr. Callahan's treatment for fears, phobias and self-sabotage.* Blair, NE: Enterprise.

Cherkin, D. C., Sherman, K. J., Avins, A. L., et al. (2009), A randomized trial comparing acupuncture, simulated acupuncture, and usual care for chronic low back pain. *Archives of Internal Medicine, 169*(9), 858–866.

Chambless, D., & Hollon, S. D. (1998). Defining empirically supported therapies. *Journal of Consulting and Clinical Psychology, 66,* 7–18.

Church, D. (2009). The effect of EFT (Emotional Freedom Techniques) on athletic performance: A randomized controlled blind trial. *Open Sports Sciences, 2,* 94–99.

Church, D. (2010a). The treatment of combat trauma in veterans using EFT (Emotional Freedom Techniques): A pilot protocol. *Traumatology, 16*(1), 55–65. http://dx.doi.org/10.1177/1534765609347549.

Church, D. (2013a). *The EFT manual* (3rd ed.). Santa Rosa, CA: Energy Psychology Press.

Church, D. (2013b). Clinical EFT as an evidence-based practice for the treatment of psychological and physiological conditions. *Psychology*, 4(8), 645–654. doi:10.4236/psych.2013.48092.

Church, D., & Brooks, A. J. (2010). The effect of a brief EFT (Emotional Freedom Techniques) self-intervention on anxiety, depression, pain and cravings in healthcare workers. *Integrative Medicine: A Clinician's Journal*, 9(4), 40–44.

Church, D., De Asis, M. A., & Brooks, A. J. (2012). Brief group intervention using EFT (Emotional Freedom Techniques) for depression in college students: A randomized controlled trial. *Depression Research and* Treatment, 1–7. doi:10.1155/2012/257172.

Church, D., & Downs, D. (2012). Sports confidence and critical incident intensity after a brief application of Emotional Freedom Techniques: A pilot study. *Sport Journal*, 15.

Church, D., Geronilla, L., & Dinter, I. (2009). Psychological symptom change in veterans after six sessions of EFT (Emotional Freedom Techniques): An observational study. *International Journal of Healing and Caring*, 9(1).

Church, D., Hawk, C., Brooks, A., Toukolehto, O., Wren, M., Dinter, I., & Stein, P. (2013). Psychological trauma symptom improvement in veterans using EFT (Emotional Freedom Techniques): A randomized controlled trial. *Journal of Nervous and Mental Disease*, 201, 153–160.

Church, D., & Marohn, S. (Eds.) (2013). *The clinical EFT handbook: A definitive resource for practitioners, scholars, clinicians and researchers* . Santa Rosa, CA : Energy Psychology Press.

Church, D., Piña, O., Reategui, C., & Brooks, A. (2012). Single session reduction of the intensity of traumatic memories in abused adolescents after EFT: A randomized controlled pilot study. *Traumatology*, 18(3), 73–79. doi:10.1177/1534765611426788.

Church, D., Yount, G., & Brooks, A. J. (2012). The effect of Emotional Freedom Techniques (EFT) on stress biochemistry: A randomized controlled trial. *Journal of Nervous and Mental Disease*, 200, 891–896. doi:10.1097/NMD.0b013e31826b9fc1.

Craig, G., & Fowlie, A. (1995). *Emotional freedom techniques: The manual*. Sea Ranch, CA: Gary Craig.

Davison, M. L., Bershadsky, B., Bieber, J., Silversmith, D., Maruish, M. E., & Kane, R. L. (1997). Development of a brief, multidimensional, self-report instrument for treatment outcomes assessment in psychiatric settings: Preliminary findings. *Assessment*, 4, 259–275.

Diamond, J. (1985). *Life energy*, New York: Dodd, Mead.

Feinstein, D. (2012). Acupoint stimulation in treating psychological disorders: Evidence of efficacy. *Review of General Psychology*, 16, 364–380. doi:10.1037/a0028602.

Flint, G. A., Lammers, W., & Mitnick, D. G. (2005). Emotional Freedom Techniques: A safe treatment intervention for many trauma-based issues. In

J. Garrick & M. B. Williams (Eds.), *Trauma treatment techniques: Innovative trends* (pp. 125–150). New York: Routledge.

Fox, L. (2013). Improvement in study-related emotions in undergraduates following Emotional Freedom Techniques (EFT): A single blind controlled study. *Energy Psychology: Theory, Research, and Treatment* (in press).

Gallo, F. P. (1999). *Energy psychology*. Boca Raton, FL: CRC Press.

Gurret, J. M., Caufour, C., Palmer-Hoffman, J., & Church, D. (2012). Post-earthquake rehabilitation of clinical PTSD in Haitian seminarians. *Energy Psychology, 4*(2).

Horowitz, M. J., Wilner, N. J., & Alvarez, W. (1979). Impact of events scale: A measure of subjective stress. *Psychosomatic Medicine, 41,* 209–218.

Institute of Medicine, Committee on Treatment of Posttraumatic Stress Disorder. (2007). *Treatment of posttraumatic stress disorder: An assessment of the evidence.* Washington, DC: Institute of Medicine. Retrieved from http://www.nap.edu/catalog/11955.html.

Johng, H. M., Lee, C. H., Yoo, J. S., Yoon, T. J., Shin, H. S., Lee, B. C., & Soh, K. S. (2007, January). Nanoparticles for tracing acupuncture meridians and Bonghan ducts. In *World Congress on Medical Physics and Biomedical Engineering 2006* (pp. 3584–3586). Berlin and Heidelberg : Springer.

Jones, S., Thornton, J., & Andrews, H. (2011). Efficacy of EFT in reducing public speaking anxiety: A randomized controlled trial. *Energy Psychology: Theory, Research, and Treatment, 3*(1), 19–32. doi:10.9769. EPJ.2011.3.1.SJ.

Karatzias, T., Power, K., Brown, K., McGoldrick, T., Begum, M., Young, J.,...Adams, S. (2011). A controlled comparison of the effectiveness and efficiency of two psychological therapies for posttraumatic stress disorder: Eye Movement Desensitization and Reprocessing vs. Emotional Freedom Techniques. *Journal of Nervous and Mental Disease, 199*(6), 372–378. doi:10.1097/NMD.0b013e31821cd262

Lambrou, P.T., Pratt, G.J., & Chevalier, G. (2003) Physiological and psychological effects of a mind/body therapy on claustrophobia. *Subtle Energies and Energy Medicine, 14,* 239–251.

Lake, D. (2013). Strategies for an integrative medicine practice. In D. Church & S. Marohn (Eds.), *The Clinical EFT handbook* (Vol. 1, pp. 347–358). Santa Rosa, CA : Energy Psychology Press.

Llewellyn-Edwards, T., & Llewellyn-Edwards, M. (2012). The effect of Emotional Freedom Techniques (EFT) on soccer performance. *Fidelity: Journal for the National Council of Psychotherapy, 47,* 14–21.

Lubin, H., & Schneider, T. (2009). Change is possible : EFT (Emotional Freedom Techniques) with life-sentence and veteran prisoners at San Quentin State Prison. *Energy Psychology: Theory, Research, and Treatment, 1*(1), 83–33.

Mollon, P. (2007). Thought Field Therapy and its derivatives: Rapid relief of mental health problems through tapping on the body. *Primary Care and Community Psychiatry, 12*(3–4), 123–127.

Nemiro, A. (2013, May). EFT vs. CBT in the treatment of sexual gender based violence in the Democratic Republic of the Congo. Presented at the conference of the Association for Comprehensive Energy Psychology (ACEP), San Diego, CA.

Phelps, E. A., & LeDoux, J. E. (2005). Contributions of the amygdala to emotion processing: From animal models to human behavior. *Neuron, 48,* 175–187.

Ruden, R. A. (2005). A neurological basis for the observed peripheral sensory modulation of emotional responses. *Traumatology,* 11(3), 145–158.

Salas, M. M., Brooks, A. J., & Rowe, J. E. (2011). The immediate effect of a brief energy psychology intervention (Emotional Freedom Techniques) on specific phobias: A pilot study. *Explore: The Journal of Science and Healing,* 7(3), 255–260.

Seal, K. H., Maguen, S., Cohen, B., Gima, K. S., Metzler, T. J., Ren, L., Bertental, D., Marmar, C. R. (2010). VA mental health services utilization in Iraq and Afghanistan veterans in the first year of receiving new mental health diagnoses. *Journal of Traumatic Stress,* 23(1), 5–16.

Shapiro, F. (2001) Eye movement desensitization and reprocessing (EMDR): Basic principles, protocols, and procedures (2nd ed.). New York: Guilford Press.

Swingle, P.G. (2010) EFT in the neurotherapeutic treatment of seizure disorders. *Energy Psychology: Theory, Research, and Treatment,* 2(1), 27–38. Doi : 10.9769.EPJ.2010.2.1.PGS

Swingle, P.G., Pulos, L.,& Swingle, M.K. (2004) Neurophysiological indicators of EFT treatment of posttraumatic stress. *Subtle Energies and Energy Medicine,* 15(1), 75–86.

Syldona, M., & Rein, G. (1999). The use of DC electrodermal potential measurements and healer's felt sense to assess the energetic nature of Qi. *The Journal of Alternative and Complementary Medicine,* 5(4), 329–347.

Vasterling, J. J., & Brewin, C. R. (Eds.). (2005). *Neuropsychology of PTSD: Biological, cognitive, and clinical perspectives.* New York: Guilford Press.

Weathers, F., Huska, J., & Keane, T. (1991). The PTSD checklist military version (PCL-M). Boston, MA: National Center for PTSD.

Wells, S., Polglase, K., Andrews, H. B., Carrington, P., & Baker, A. H. (2003). Evaluation of a meridian-based intervention, Emotional Freedom Techniques (EFT), for reducing specific phobias of small animals. *Journal of Clinical Psychology,* 59, 943–966. doi:10.1002/jclp.10189.

Wolpe, J. (1973). *The practice of behavior therapy* (2nd ed.). New York: Pergamon Press.

Zhang, Y., Feng, B., Xie, J. P., Xu, F. Z., Chen, J. (2011). Clinical study on treatment of the earthquake-caused post-traumatic stress disorder by cognitive-behavior therapy and acupoint stimulation. *Journal of Traditional Chinese Medicine,* 31, 60–63. doi: 10.1016/S0254-6272(11)60014-9.

Chapter Seventeen

Love Is All Around: A Single Session Solution-Focused Therapy

Chris Iveson, Evan George, and Harvey Ratner

Solution-Focused Brief Therapy is a work in progress. Its beginnings are to be found in the work of Steve de Shazer, Insoo Kim Berg and the team at the Brief Family Therapy Center in Milwaukee, Wisconsin (Nunnally, et al., 1986; de Shazer, et al., 1986), although its earlier roots extend through the Mental Research Institute in Palo Alto, California (Weakland, et al., 1974) to Milton Erickson (Haley, 1973). The first "full form" of the Solution-Focused model is to be found in de Shazer's (1988) *Clues: Investigating Solutions in Brief Therapy* and from this early blueprint many variations have evolved. At BRIEF, founded by the authors in 1989, the guiding principle has been Ockham's Razor, the dynamic minimalism propounded by the 14th century philosopher, William of Ockham, and adopted by the Milwaukee team from its earliest days: "What can be achieved with fewer means is done in vain with many." The most dramatic result of this philosophical principle was the Milwaukee team's realization that knowing the problem was not a requirement for effective therapy—at the time a revolutionary idea. BRIEF's continued application of Ockham's Razor has been a rather slower revolution but nevertheless one which has reduced the components of effective therapy even further—as we will discuss in what follows.

Coming across the SFBT approach in 1986 and setting up the following year a solution-focused workshop in a community-based mental health clinic in London, our work—in common with other so-lution-focused practitioners throughout the world at that time—was centered on the therapeutic map sketched out in *Keys to Solution in Brief Therapy* (de Shazer, 1985) and further developed and clarified in *Clues*. By adopting de Shazer's advice to treat each session, including the first, as potentially the last, we quickly discovered that effective, single session therapy was no fluke: in fact it was more common than any other number of sessions. Now, approximately half of our clinic-based therapies are single sessions—which at one time we would have regarded as abject failure. However, our five outcome studies between 1990 and 2010 (Shennan & Iveson, 2011) showed no signifi-cant difference in outcome related to the number of sessions. For very many clients one session appears to be sufficient and, as we have found no way of knowing who these clients are before we begin, we must treat every first session with every client as potentially the last.

During this twenty-year period the average number of session also reduced—from five to 2.5 (though this excludes a very small number of clients for whom the work continues over a number of years—"brief" to us means taking the shortest route we can find and if it turns out to be a long way, so be it). We associate this drop in the average number of sessions with the use we have made of Ock-ham's Razor, the use of which has been monitored by our outcome studies so we have been able to test that the cutting out of a particu-lar technique has not been at the expense of effectiveness. Overall our effectiveness based on client report (80% reporting some lasting improvement) has been consistent apart from one small blip (a 5% reduction) associated with a cut too far. (Shennan & Iveson, 2011)

In our earliest form (George, Iveson and Ratner, 1990) a first ses-sion (which sometimes was also the last) would follow this eight-step pattern:

1. "Problem-free talk" or rapport-building
2. Identify the problem
3. Pose the "miracle question" as "life without the problem"
4. Seek exceptions to the problem pattern
5. Scale progress towards the resolution
6. Identify the next steps
7. Give compliments
8. Finish with a task assignment or directive, the form of which being based on the client's level of motivation (customer, complainant or visitor in solution-focused parlance).

As we worked at that time in a service where most clients were both mandated and reluctant we assumed low levels of motivation. The first outcome study, surprisingly, showed no outcome difference related to the assessed level of motivation. Since then, we have treated all clients as motivated, with part of the therapist's task being to help the client discover what they are motivated for. We have also found that there is no noticeable difference either in the number of sessions or in the effectiveness of the therapy related to the route of referral. Reluctant and mandated clients do just as well (or badly) as the most eager client and with the same number of sessions. Like de Shazer before us, we are discovering that many of the major issues in the therapy literature are socially constructed and have no "objective" basis. Motivation, and its lack, is created more by therapists than by clients.

Our second big shift was to excuse our clients from the need to tell us about their problem. As problem information was not used in the therapeutic conversation except as the starting point for the miracle and exception questions it seemed irrelevant for us to know so we began to ask not "What brings you here?" but "What are your best hopes as a result of coming here?" "Where to?" instead of "Where from?" From this point the model could be entirely based on outcome, leaving it a matter of client choice whether or not we were given information about problems. The miracle question (or more commonly the less dramatic "tomorrow" question ("If you woke up tomorrow to find yourself moving towards these hopes what would be the first sign?") was then used to describe a preferred future followed by scales, compliments and tasks.

Then we began to notice that task-performance did not seem to be related to outcome so we experimented with dropping tasks which led to a major and unexpected shift in our thinking. Solution-focused tasks are not plucked out of the air, they are crafted and the crafting is part of the session. Watch any tape of Steve de Shazer working and about one-third of the way through his questions will begin to have an element of task development within them. To do this the therapist needs to be in two places: (1) with the client, and, (2) in his own head processing the answers for clues about the type of task to go for. When we stopped giving tasks and were thus able to give all our attention to the client, our listening changed and we became more curious about the client's hoped-for future and progress towards this future. In consequence descriptions became richer and more detailed and as the average number of sessions declined we assumed these descriptions were a force for change. Gradually, as this realization of the power of description sank in we started to remove from our questions and, as far as we are able, from our minds, any stakehold in what the client did the next day: we try to make it *not our business*. This is not to say that we don't wish our clients well or ourselves success but in the end these are not our lives and our clients must live them as they choose. We stopped trying to shape their behavior and instead devote ourselves to helping them create elaborate descriptions of their best wishes—even if it means, on some occasions, potential dire consequences like loss of their freedom or children.

This reliance on description and only description (which we try to maintain although often fail) we associate with the most recent reduction in the average number of sessions and increase in single session therapies. As we began writing this chapter a typical first session (and thus, around 50% of last sessions) would take the following three- or four-stage form (Ratner, George & Iveson, 2012):

1. *What are your best hopes from this visit?*
   Often then some dialogue to establish a working outcome
2. *If you woke up tomorrow and found yourself moving towards...?*
   Followed by a description of this preferred future often taking up most of the session
3. *On a zero-to-ten scale...?*
   Used to find out what the client is already doing that might contribute to the hoped-for future and sometimes used to elicit more description of future signs of progress. (Never used to plan steps.)
4. (Sometimes) *A brief summary highlighting the main elements of the client's preferred future and steps already taken towards it.*

As will be seen at the end of this chapter, Solution-Focused Brief Therapy continues to be a work in progress and the addition of an extra stage (or the return of an old stage but in a different position) may well turn out to be a significant factor in single session therapy.

The session with Carrie[1] that follows is clear evidence of the shift since then in our team's conceptualization about the nature of change and a radically altered view of what we are doing with clients during therapy, coaching, or consultation sessions (Iveson,

---

1. Our thanks to "Carrie" and her family, whose details have been altered to protect their anonymity. Thanks also to "James," the social worker who believed enough in his client to offer her this opportunity.

et al., 2012; Ratner, et al., 2012). As described in Shennan and Iveson (2011), we have moved from goals to preferred futures, from exceptions (to the problem) to instances (of the preferred future), from end-of-session tasks to in-session conversation, from compliments to summaries—all in the service of leaving the problem behind. The structure of the conversation is evident. The therapist opens by asking what the client hopes to achieve from the session: *"What are your best hopes from this meeting?"* This question is the most significant driver of the changes in our approach. It at once focuses the client on outcome, what the client is trying to achieve rather than what it might be that is bothering the client and it centralizes the client from the very start of the process.

Having determined the *best hopes* we are interested in inviting the client to describe those *best hopes happening* in as much everyday, lived-life detail as possible. The emerging picture is not intended to commit the client; the picture is always provisional and subject to possible change. It is the engagement of the client in the process of describing that seems to be important and the therapist will have no evaluative interest in the detail of the client's answers. In this way, no answer that the client could give is any more right or wrong than any other although it may be more or less useful in opening up possibilities for change. Following the detailed description of the preferred future a scale question of the degree of progress towards the preferred outcome allows the client to describe what is already present in her life that fits with the preferred future. Asking the question at this point, after the client has both described the preferred future and experienced themselves describing that future, is associated with clients noticing more than they otherwise might of what is already in place. Pre-experiencing a little of the future that is being described and the associated feelings often leads to the client re-viewing the present and recent past from a different perspective, from a place of hopefulness and possibility, and from this place the client literally sees different things and sees things differently. The session is concluded with a summary of what the client has said during the session that fits with the idea that progress in their preferred direction is possible and if a further session is agreed it will be to "review progress."

At the heart of the BRIEF approach is *description* and it is the task of the therapist to facilitate and support the client in this process of description. The therapist is not trying to make sense of, is not attempting to understand the client or her world. The questions asked do not seek information. One could almost say that the therapist has no particular interest in the specifics of the client's answers. True to de Shazer and Berg's (1992; also see Miller, 1997) "post-structural re-vision," the questions are merely invitations to the client to describe in a very particular way. The challenge to the therapist is literally to stay on the surface, working in and with the client's description rather than peering beneath in a search for meaning:

> You've got what you've got and that's all there is. There is no need to look behind or beneath since everything you need is readily available and open to view. Nothing is hidden. (de Shazer & Berg, 1992, p. 75)

and

> The miracle question was not designed to create or prompt miracles. All the miracle question is designed to do is to allow clients to describe what it is they want out of therapy without having to concern themselves with the problem and the traditional assumption that the solution is somehow connected with understanding and eliminating the problem. (de Shazer, *Words Were Originally Magic*, 1994, p. 267)

Transcript and Commentary

This single session took place during an introductory course in Solution Focused Brief Therapy for child protection social workers. The daughter of a particular client of the social work service, Suzie, was causing concern and the trainer, Chris Iveson, offered to see the client, either during or after the course. The client, Carrie, said she could come right away if we didn't mind her bringing Billy, her baby. It is not unusual for us to see clients during trainings but mostly they come to our clinic at BRIEF having made a prior appointment. Though some clients pay most we see without charge since we are able to earn enough from our teaching to not need money from therapy. This means we can see poorer and more troubled clients most of whom come via public agencies often with very serious issues in their lives. As an independent clinic we choose to have no other referral process than a phone call to take the client's name and telephone number and fix a time. Any public agency can refer provided their client is in serious need. We particularly welcome mandated clients and have never turned a referral down. When clients arrive they are asked simply to confirm their contact details and whether or not they will permit the session to be videoed for training purposes. About 30% agree. We have detected no difference between videoed and other sessions.

Carrie arrived for her session half an hour after she'd received the invitation. It lasted fifty minutes (a typical session length). Sitting beside the client was James, the social worker, while the rest of the course participants were a little further away. Billy was held by James, Carrie, and the therapist in turn giving each of them a chance to drink their tea during the session. This is the transcript of the session as it was recorded at the time with changes of name and some details to protect the client's identity.

> THERAPIST: What are your best hopes from this meeting?
> CARRIE: I was intrigued.
> THERAPIST: And if being intrigued turns out to be a good idea what do you hope it might lead to?
> CARRIE: A better future for my kids; a better future for me.
> THERAPIST: Okay.
> CARRIE: No more worries. No more thinking.
> THERAPIST: No more—?
> CARRIE: Thinking—the worst!
> THERAPIST: What would you be thinking instead?
> CARRIE: Well, there are still things there that go through my head—
> THERAPIST: Okay.
> CARRIE:—from the past, so no more of that.
> THERAPIST: So what do you hope would replace those sorts of thoughts?
> CARRIE: Um—good thoughts for the future, instead of thinking about the past.
> THERAPIST: It sounds like the past is messing with your future a bit?
> CARRIE: It does, yes.

Billy wakes up in his buggy, looks around and gives everyone a big smile. Carrie picks him up and he laughs.

> THERAPIST: How have you brought him up to be such a happy and placid baby?

At first Carrie says it's in his nature but then goes on to say that there have been a lot of changes for the better. She looks to the group and says how much they have helped. She explains that she came from London to escape a violent relationship. Her three eldest sons were removed from her care and had been brought up by her mother but she was determined to do better for her younger ones, Aaron and Charlie. They had been very aggressive and in trouble with the law but with help she had brought them under control and the family was very much calmer. Billy remains calm, curious and responsive throughout this five-minute period—and for the rest of the meeting. (See additional note on this part of the session in the conclusions.)

Commentary

Right from the start the therapist works from the assumption that the client has come for a good reason and without preamble demonstrates his trust in her with his first question. As it is a question only the client can answer the therapist is entirely in her hands. From that point on it will be the task of the therapist to ask questions only the client can answer so that she remains in sole charge of the content. It is in those answers which contain words that she has never spoken before which we assume carry the possibilities of change.

> THERAPIST: So let's imagine a little miracle happens tonight and it stops the past messing with your future so you are no longer being held back from where you want to be—
>
> CARRIE: *(interjects with the beginning of a sense of wonderment)* I don't know what I'd do with it!
>
> THERAPIST:—what's the first thing you'd notice when you woke up tomorrow that somehow gave you the first hint that the past was no longer messing with your future?
>
> CARRIE: Oh my god! Not to think about it would be a miracle!
>
> THERAPIST: So what would be the first thing you'd notice tomorrow?
>
> CARRIE: *(beginning to smile)* I think it would be more what I'd do!

THERAPIST: What would you do?

CARRIE: Everything!! Everything I've always wanted to do! I want to learn to drive, I want to go to college—that would be the first thing. Yes. Everything! And for the kids.

THERAPIST: So what time will you wake up tomorrow?

CARRIE: Because of the baby it's usually at about five o'clock in the morning.

THERAPIST: So what might be the very first thing you'd notice at five o'clock if the past was not got rid of but was no longer messing with your future?

CARRIE: Wow! What a question. I don't know what I'd do! (*big smile*) I think I'd have to get used to the idea first!

THERAPIST: So what would be the first hint that the idea was there?

CARRIE: I think me being different—yes.

THERAPIST: So what would Billy notice about you at five o'clock that began to show the first sign of that difference?

CARRIE: What would he notice?

THERAPIST: And I appreciate that it might be just a small difference—

CARRIE: There'd have to be a spark. There'd have to be a small difference somewhere.

THERAPIST: Okay.

CARRIE: I think he'd be a lot more happy in the morning than he usually is.

THERAPIST: So how would you know that he'd seen that spark?

CARRIE: Well with Billy when he's happy like that he hugs me and kisses me and I think it would be a lot more for him. He'd notice a difference in me.

THERAPIST: What would you notice about the way he hugged you back?

CARRIE: I think with a lot more loving.

THERAPIST: Okay.

CARRIE: I don't know if I can explain how I would be—I think I'd just be in shock!

THERAPIST: Would you be able to go back to sleep again?

CARRIE: No, not at all!

THERAPIST: So what—

CARRIE: I'd want to get up straight away and do something—do something about it.

THERAPIST: What would you do?

CARRIE: Oh, what would I do?

THERAPIST: How long does it take to feed him in the morning?

CARRIE: He has his breakfast at about half-past-eight—

THERAPIST: And at five o'clock?

CARRIE: He has his feed and then he goes back to sleep.

THERAPIST: And what will you do then?

CARRIE: I'd get all my housework done—I think I'd be too excited to sit down! And then after I'd seen to Billy that would be the time to start getting my life sorted out.

THERAPIST: And what are your other children called?

CARRIE: There's Aaron who's twelve and Charlie who's ten.

THERAPIST: What time do they get up?

CARRIE: They all get up at seven o'clock.

THERAPIST: Maybe a bit before seven if you're going round hoovering [vacuum cleaning] their bedrooms at five o'clock!

CARRIE: *(laughing)* That's true!

THERAPIST: So what would be the first sign to Aaron that you'd got this spark?

CARRIE: Aaron—well, he always asks me, whatever mood I'm in, "Are you all right, Mum?"

THERAPIST: So where would you first see him?

CARRIE: When he comes down at seven. He'll know there's something wrong if I go hoovering his bedroom at five o'clock in the morning!

THERAPIST: And where would you be when he came down?

CARRIE: In the kitchen ready to make their cups of tea.

THERAPIST: So what's the first thing he'd notice about you that tells him you've got this spark?

CARRIE: I think he'd want to know what was making me feel so happy.

THERAPIST: How would he know you were happy?

CARRIE: Too much energy! The look in my face.

THERAPIST: So he'd see the look in your face and he'd ask you, so what would you say?

CARRIE: I think I'd say, "I don't know what's wrong with me but I feel like something has been lifted."

THERAPIST: Will he be pleased?

CARRIE: Yes.

THERAPIST: What effect will it have on him?

CARRIE: He'll hug me.

THERAPIST: And what would you notice about the way you hug him back?

CARRIE: A lot more love into it! Everything—putting everything into it.

THERAPIST: I guess you love him anyway so what would be different that showed it was a love coming with spark?

CARRIE: I don't think it would be just the love I think it would be the feeling that it's a new day.

THERAPIST: Okay.

CARRIE: Yes—a new day, a new start.

Commentary

This next sequence begins to give a sense of the sort of description that the therapist is inviting the client into. The future that is being pictured is carefully and specifically prescribed. Carrie is not being invited to imagine that the past somehow never occurred, merely that it is no longer interfering with the present. Carrie's response is marked by an almost palpable sense of excitement on her part, a sense of wonder, that we can imagine is very different from the client's response were she to be asked to describe what is bothering her. (Hoyt, 2009, p. 184, describes this as enhancing "*solution sight*.") The sort of description that the therapist appears to be prioritizing through his questioning is rooted in the client's everyday reality; it may be a miracle that she is considering, but this is a miracle that is happening within her daily routine, within her home, with her children present as both witnesses and participants.

THERAPIST: Okay. And Charlie, what would Charlie notice?

CARRIE: Charlie has a lot of energy anyway so he'll probably think I'm just ready for him! No, I think he would notice the difference. Yes, he would, definitely.

THERAPIST: So what would he notice about the way you were making the tea for them that fits with you having this spark back in your life?

CARRIE: I think it's because in the morning with getting up at five o'clock I'm feeling a bit *yucky* but if I had that happen I think it would be the energy. I think that's what they'd notice.

THERAPIST: How would that show as you were making the tea?

CARRIE: *(smiling)* With a smile on my face—definitely!

THERAPIST: And then they go off to school?

SOCIAL WORKER: There's Suzie as well.

THERAPIST: How old is Suzie?

CARRIE: She's nine.

THERAPIST: Okay, what's Suzie going to notice?

CARRIE: I think—with Suzie—I don't think she would notice.

THERAPIST: Of course she would! She's a girl!

CARRIE: Or she'd think, 'What's the matter with Mum to-day?'

THERAPIST: So what would she see that made her have that question?

CARRIE: That I've actually made her a cup of tea because she never drinks her tea. So it would be that I actually made her one.

THERAPIST: Okay.

CARRIE: No. I think she'd want to know what the difference was. She would! She's full of questions and she'd want to know!

THERAPIST: Okay, so she'd want to know?

CARRIE: Yes, she'd want to know everything.

THERAPIST: And what effect would it have on her seeing that spark?

CARRIE: I like to put with Suzie that she's capable of anything. She's joined a basketball team and I say to her whether she wins or loses that she's good. She's good at anything she puts her mind to and there's a lot more that she wants us to do and if I could do all that and fit it in for her she'd see the difference.

THERAPIST: And tomorrow morning, what difference would it make to her seeing you with that spark at that moment?

CARRIE: "Maybe I've got my mum back."

THERAPIST: Oh wow! How will you know she's having that thought?

CARRIE: She'd tell me—she tells me everything.
THERAPIST: Does she?
CARRIE: Yes, she tells me what she thinks.
THERAPIST: And if she told you "I think I've got my Mum back" how would you respond.
CARRIE: I think I'd cry. Yes, I would, I'd cry.
THERAPIST: And then?
CARRIE: I'd give her a hug.
THERAPIST: And what would she notice about the hug?
CARRIE: The fact that I'm giving her a hug—she's not one of those girls that likes hugs. You'd think being a girl she'd be more... she's not a close person, Suzie isn't and I think with the things that she's gone through that's part of it but she's slowly coming back and I think I'd know that she knew if I was getting it back myself.
THERAPIST: Would she like that hug then if it was coming from getting her mum back?
CARRIE: Yes
THERAPIST: How would you know that she liked it? What would you feel when she hugged you back?
CARRIE: I'd love it, I'd love it, no matter how she hugged me. I think it's the fact that she's hugging me.
THERAPIST: And when she's giving you that hug what will you notice that tells you that she realizes she's got her Mum back?
CARRIE: The feeling she puts into it—yes.
THERAPIST: How will you know?
CARRIE: She'd be holding me tight, not pulling away. I think that will make the difference.

Commentary

As the session progresses we begin to notice more. The therapist is persistent, inviting the client into describing multiple layers of difference. The first answer that the client gives becomes the foundation for more questions: if a hug happens in the preferred future, what will be different about that hug and what will the parent notice about herself and what will she notice about the child's response to her response? The almost-forgotten Suzie is scooped into the story with a very moving change of description as the therapist stays with the immediacy of the miracle morning. The picture is rooted in an interactional framework: people do things, others respond and then we respond to those responses. The therapist's detailed tracking of events builds clearly defined sequences of difference, each detail opening new possibilities for action though there is never even a hint of pressure on Carrie to perform her 'miracle'.

> THERAPIST: Okay. And when they are off to school what would Aaron notice about the way you said goodbye to him?
>
> CARRIE: He'd probably look at me funny, actually, and give me a big hug, a big kiss and "See you later!" Yes, he'd give me a look!
>
> THERAPIST: And Charlie?
>
> CARRIE: He'd probably think I'd gone a bit weird! He'd give me a weird look as well!
>
> THERAPIST: And what about Suzie?
>
> CARRIE: Oh, she'd definitely look at me weird!
>
> THERAPIST: Okay! So you'd get three weird looks!
>
> CARRIE: Definitely!
>
> THERAPIST: And then?
>
> CARRIE: Get Billy up, get him sorted, breakfast and then I can't wait to get out of the house—you know how you feel when you don't want to go out...
>
> THERAPIST: So where might you go?
>
> CARRIE: Anywhere. Maybe somewhere I've not been before, where I'd been too nervous to go. Just get on a bus!
>
> THERAPIST: To?
>
> *CARRIE:* Well actually I'm meeting a friend in town tomorrow—we're going to do our shopping together.

For the next ten minutes the conversation explores the differences Carrie and her friend will be noticing during their trip to town and then it returns briefly to the children. We are now 29 minutes into the conversation.

> THERAPIST: What would Aaron notice about you when he got home from school?
>
> CARRIE: I think he'd check to see if I was in the same mood.
>
> THERAPIST: So how would he know that you were?

CARRIE: He'd probably ask me—he'd probably ask if I was on drugs or something!

THERAPIST: And what difference would it start to make to him, and to all the family, when they began to realize this was the real you and you were here to stay?

CARRIE: A big difference! Yes, a big effect! It'll give them more inspiration about what they want to do; it'll change the way they act, the way they are with each other, the way they are with me. It would be the happiest home they'd ever, ever seen. I think that would be the big change for all of them. I don't even know how I'd deal with it—I think I'd just let it go with the flow.

THERAPIST: So what will this bring out in you because I guess this is the real you?

CARRIE: Yes. A lot more confidence. A lot more confidence, in myself—I'm capable of doing things.

THERAPIST: What difference would that make, feeling more confidence?

CARRIE: A big difference. A very, very, very big difference.

THERAPIST: And who outside the family would be the next to notice this difference.

CARRIE: I think my Mum.

THERAPIST: When will you next see her?

CARRIE: I'm going up to see her next month.

THERAPIST: How would your Mum know when you arrive that you've arrived with this spark, this confidence back in your life?

CARRIE: She'd probably say go away, it ain't me!

THERAPIST: What'd be the first thing she'd see?

CARRIE: She'd ask me, she'd ask me what's changed.

THERAPIST: What would she be seeing that tells her this change has happened?

CARRIE: I think something in me, something in the kids, how we act, how we are with each other.

THERAPIST: So what will she be seeing between you and the kids?

CARRIE: Well, she's seen happiness between me and the kids but she hasn't seen much happiness within me. No.

THERAPIST: How would she know you've got your happiness back?

CARRIE: She'd know!

THERAPIST: How?

CARRIE: Me and my Mum are close.

THERAPIST: What will she see?

CARRIE: Everything. It's the excitement, the...I wish I could explain how I'd really feel but I don't think I can. I can feel it! You know, just having the thought of all that!

THERAPIST: So what will your Mum see when you arrive that conveys that you have all this feeling going on in you?

CARRIE: *(a long thoughtful pause)* A shine. How I am. How I am towards everything.

THERAPIST: So what will she see?

CARRIE: The fact that I'm more...the smile...nothing bothers me. I think that's what she'll see more.

THERAPIST: Okay, so do you have a key, do you knock? Where would you first see her?

CARRIE: She's already on the doorstep waiting for me by the time I get there.

THERAPIST: How are you travelling?

CARRIE: By train and then a taxi to hers.

THERAPIST: So she'd be there on the doorstep, the taxi pulls up, she sees you getting out of the taxi; even before you speak to her what will tell her—

CARRIE: She'd ask me who I am!

THERAPIST: And what would she notice about you as you are getting out of the taxi that gave her the first clue?

CARRIE: I'd just run up, hug her and tell her how much I love her.

THERAPIST: Okay! Would she be surprised or is that something you do anyway?

CARRIE: I do anyway but I think it would be the feeling I put into it, the way I say it and the way I act. Then she'll know.

THERAPIST: What will you be noticing about yourself as you're running towards her from the taxi to give her that hug?

CARRIE: *(pause, eyes looking up, small smile)* God! *(longer pause)* I don't know—just...

THERAPIST: In those few steps as you are running towards her?

CARRIE: Just how much I miss her; how different I feel being back there but *good!* Good.

THERAPIST: And what will your Mum feel in that hug that conveys this?

CARRIE: She'll know—when I hold her tight. I do anyway but she'll notice the difference.

THERAPIST: How will you know? What will you notice about her hug back?

CARRIE: I'll tell her I love her. I'm back!

THERAPIST: What will you feel in her hug back?

CARRIE: She'll probably tell me it's nice to have me back.

THERAPIST: And what difference might that make?

CARRIE: More love. I'd feel better about myself, better about the kids—better about life! That's the difference she'll see.

Commentary

As the client is invited into a picturing of a life in which the past no longer messes with the future, she spontaneously expresses her excitement: "It's the excitement, the...I wish I could explain how I'd really feel but I don't think I can. I can feel it! You know, just having the thought of all that!" As she describes that life and especially as she describes the difference in the hugs she gives and receives, the emotions that fit the descriptions come alive for her. And perhaps what is particularly striking is the therapist's refusal to blur the picturing by suggesting at any time that the client should take action, should put into practice any of these different ways of living. He sticks purely at deriving description and nothing else. There is no pressure, no problem-solving, no action-oriented suggestions.

THERAPIST: So...*(pause)* Let's have a scale with ten being your life is like that—how you want it to be—and zero is the worst it's ever been; where would you say you are between having the life with spark and the worst it's ever been?

CARRIE: I think I'm just fi...on a six.

THERAPIST: A six!

CARRIE: For some reason—I don't know—I just feel that I'll wake up one day and it will happen! Actually, I do think so! I really feel good at the moment! I *do*!

THERAPIST: So how have you got from—

CARRIE: Actually, *(laughing)* I'm feeling like I'm there already!

THERAPIST: Okay.

CARRIE: I think talking about it and saying how you feel and how you want to feel, and what you want and what you do, I think—um—it puts a lot in your head. What you want can really happen.

THERAPIST: So how much of it is already happening, now you think about it?

CARRIE: A lot of it! I don't think I've really thought about it before.

THERAPIST: So how much of it is already happening?

CARRIE: A lot of this life is happening. The kids, the kids are happy—they have their moments between each other but they're getting so much better, so much better...*(pause)* Yes. *(pause)* I didn't realize—I didn't realize myself, actually. *(pause)* Actually I feel good right now.

THERAPIST: Okay—So let me bring you down to earth with a bang!

CARRIE: *(laughs)* Yes, you'd better!

THERAPIST: It sounds from what you said earlier that you have come such a long way and sometimes it's like climbing a mountain—when it's such a hard struggle we don't realize we're almost at the top.

CARRIE: Yes.

THERAPIST: And life is always full of troubles! What will you be noticing when you've got your spark back, what will you be noticing about how you deal with life's difficulties?

CARRIE: It's true, some things I do find difficult but I've got the kids and it's not fair for them but talking to them and saying how we're going to handle things, how I'm going to handle things makes it...yes...I think I have handled things quite well, really! From what I expected I've done well. And it's making a difference to the kids—a big difference; their behavior, the violence isn't there anymore. I thought with my daughter it wasn't going to happen but we've had a

really good talk and for the past week she's been handling things very well—no retaliations, no taking it
out on the boys. Slowly she's coming back. So she'll
get there. Yes she will.

THERAPIST: So what might be the next small sign that you
are even closer to getting back that spark, getting on
with your future?

CARRIE: The next step is more me! The kids are doing really well!

THERAPIST: So what will be the first sign of you giving
yourself some of that good attention?

CARRIE: Believing in myself.

THERAPIST: So what will be the next sign?

CARRIE: Believing that I can do things, I'm not useless, not
stupid, not…I know I'm capable of a lot. Of achieving a lot. *(pause)* I can't believe I've just said that. I
never thought I'd ever say that again!

THERAPIST: Okay. *(pause)* I think I've run out of questions.
Is there anything I haven't asked you that I should
have done? Anything you wanted to say that I didn't
give you a chance to say?

CARRIE: *(pause)* I think you've asked me everything.
(pause) It's putting things into my head of what I've
already done and what things can be like.

THERAPIST: Okay. Good.

*The therapist then explains to Carrie that the group had been
asked to look out for all her strengths and achievements and he asks
everyone to give her feedback. This included that she, Carrie, was
a strong woman, had a lovely relationship with her children evidenced by the way she smiled as she spoke of them, her appreciation
of how much she had achieved and the genuine realization that a
better life was possible. Carrie several times commented back: "It's
the questions, just answering the questions makes you realize!"*

Commentary

Being invited to examine her life out of her miracle picture, fresh
from the description and the experiencing, Carrie notices things that
she hasn't noticed until then. The change in the children's behavior

suddenly becomes obvious and she begins to see her life, past, present and future in a quite different light. And she is able to hear herself saying things that she never thought she'd ever say again.

We are unsure of the value of the closing feedback in this session. When working alone we rarely end a session with compliments, mainly because it gives import to the therapist's words when we believe it is the client's words that count. Our outcomes did not appear to be affected by dropping compliments so we assume they are unnecessary. However, when we have a group watching as we often do in our various training programs we do not want them to be an audience of voyeurs; we want the client to know that they are as much engaged in the work as we are. Having them give affirmative feedback, either directly or through the therapist, seems a good way to convey this.

Outcome

Six months later, Chris received the following email from the referring social worker:

> I wanted to feed back to you the impact your session had on her.... Over the next few weeks after having the session with you I saw a dramatic change in her confidence and ability to prioritize and effectively deal with situations. I saw her planning for a future she used to dread and for the first time in the 2 years we had worked with her, she was thinking forwards, planning for her children's needs and was emotionally far more resilient and calm.
>
> The difference in her, her self-esteem and confidence was amazing. She obtained coping strategies which had previously been missing and a new found positivity. Consequently her children became much more settled, communicative and emotionally contained. She had envisaged a visit to her mum's during the session which actually took place two weeks after the session. The visit went pretty much as well as she had hoped, only this time, when she returned she was actually happy to be home and was feeling more independent. On her previous trips to see family she always returned feeling emotionally needy, alone and unable to manage.

I just wanted to let you know how beneficial the impact you had on, not only Carrie's life, but that of her children and our group as a whole.

Case Conclusion

Accounts of sessions such as this session involving Carrie and Chris can at times defy belief. How do we explain what happened here? It may be helpful to recall de Shazer's (1993, pp. 146–147, italics in original) caution:

> Looking at therapy as a conversation can be useful because it helps to keep the therapist and client in the same picture, thus helping us to focus on the interaction. The danger [John] Weakland [1993] points out is that it is altogether too easy to slip from this descriptive mode into an explanatory mode. Once this happens, once the "therapeutic conversation" is seen as *the* curative factor in therapy or an explanation of therapy, then it will at least obscure our picture and blind us to what else is going on that might be worthy of note.

We can describe what the therapist *did*, the invitation to imagine a different way of living, the invitation to do that in some detail and to embed those descriptions in the client's daily living and key relationships. As she describes she seems to tell us that she is experiencing something different but is that a key component of the change or might just as great a transformation (or indeed perhaps a greater one) have occurred without the experiencing? Clearly something occurs that allows the client to notice things about her children that she states she had not previously noticed and is able to say things about herself that she did not expect to hear again. And yet on other occasions the change can be just as dramatic with no such moments of epiphany in the session, just a routine, somewhat mundane, low-key description. So in our attempts to make sense of this, what, provisionally, seems important to us? What helped to make it a one-session success? Probably the centering of the session on the client's best hopes, establishing what the client wants and keeping this central in the talking. Probably the detailed picturing of the preferred future divorced from any pressure of suggestion that the client should take any particular action—leading to the striking consequence that change is more likely when it is not required or expected of the client. Probably a disconnection from any interest in the specifics of the client's answers—just description. And probably the detailed tracking of the client's answers, building questions on each answer, thereby validating the client's answer and inviting the client on, beyond the answer that they have just given. And maybe we should add that feature that is inevitably missing from a transcript, namely the way the therapist interacted with his client: the smiles, the nods, the encouraging gestures that reveal his belief in the possibility of rapid change, as well as his openness to the possibility that this single meeting today might be enough.

Change is Constant—Is it Possible to be Briefer?

In our early work (George, et al., 1990, 1999) we began our sessions with "problem free talk"—a few minutes of talking with the client about anything but the problem in order to bring into focus the competent side of the client. Eventually, we found this ritual unnecessary and so omitted it.

Recently we have been interested in the ground-breaking work with couples undertaken by Elliott Connie (2013) in which he introduces "problem free" (or competency-based) talk immediately after determining the client's best hopes from the session. His argument for this is that he is able to listen differently since he knows the direction the client is wanting to take. The "interlude" near the beginning of the session with Carrie in which she explains why Billy is happy and placid also emphasises Carrie's competence as a parent (something she wants more of as well as something that has been seriously questioned). When Chris eventually asks the miracle question it is clear that it opens a surprise (to Carrie) door to a future she had thought impossible *even before she began to answer the question.*

Between the first drafting of this chapter and its present form Elliott Connie visited BRIEF and saw a client for a single session demonstration interview. This same awakening of hope and possibility occurred when, after a few minutes of competency-talk, he asked the miracle question—the client's eyes lit up and a note of wonderment came into her voice. Two swallows do not make a Summer but in the tradition of the original Milwaukee team we need to be constantly on the alert, looking for what works as well as what might be unnecessary. During the writing of this paper there was the opportunity to further test this idea. A new client was to be seen during the BRIEF International Summer School, watched live by brief therapists from around the world (see www.brief.org.uk). They were asked to look out for any evidence that competency-talk between the "best hopes" and "miracle" questions had any noticeable impact on the client's openness to change. Within a minute of beginning to explore the depressed client's preferred future he began to smile and he spontaneously declared that for some reason he had started to feel happy. Only "three swallows" but if a period of competency-talk ("What do you do for fun?" as Connie will often ask) between asking for the client's hopes and the miracle (or "tomorrow") question might possibly lead to the client becoming more readily open to change, then it is worth investigating and, who knows, it might make single session therapy the norm.

References

Connie, E. (2013) *Solution building couples therapy.* New York: Springer.

de Shazer, S. (1985) *Keys to solution in brief therapy.* New York: Norton.

de Shazer, S. (1988) *Clues: Investigating solutions in brief therapy.* New York: Norton.

de Shazer, S. (1993) Commentary. In S. Gilligan & R. Price (Eds.), *Therapeutic conversations* (pp. 146–147). New York: Norton.

de Shazer, S. (1994) *Words were originally magic.* New York: Norton.

de Shazer, S., & Berg, I.K. (1992) Doing therapy: A post-structural revision. *Journal of Marital and Family Therapy, 18,* 71–81.

George, E., Iveson, C., & Ratner, H. (1990; revised and expanded 1999) *Problem to solution: Brief therapy with individuals and families.* London: BT Press.

Haley, J. (1973) *Uncommon therapy.* New York: Norton

Hoyt, M.F. (2009) Solution-focused couple therapy. In *Brief psychotherapies: Principles and practices* (pp. 139–196). Phoenix, AZ: Zeig, Tucker & Theisen.

Iveson, C., George, E., Ratner, H. (2012) *Brief coaching: A solution focused approach.* London: Routledge

Miller, G. (1997) *Becoming miracle workers: Language and meaning in brief therapy.* Hawthorne, NY: Aldine de Gruyter.

Nunnally, E., de Shazer, S., Lipchik, E., & Berg, I. (1986) A study of change: Therapeutic theory in action. In D.E. Efron (Ed.) *Journeys: Expansion of the strategic-systemic therapies.* New York: Bruner/Mazel

Ratner, H., George, E., Iveson, C. (2012) *Solution focused brief therapy: 100 key points and techniques*. London: Routledge.

Shennan, G., & Iveson, C. (2011) From solution to description: Practice and research in tandem. In C. Franklin, T.S. Tepper, W.J. Gingerich, & E.E. McCollum (Eds.), *Solution-focused brief therapy: A handbook of evidence-based practice* (pp. 281–298). New York: Oxford University Press.

Weakland, J.H. (1993) Conversation—but what kind? In S. Gilligan & R. Price (Eds.), *Therapeutic conversations* (pp. 136–145). New York: Norton.

Chapter Eighteen

Single Session Medical Family Therapy and the Patient-Centered Medical Home

Tziporah Rosenberg and Susan H. McDaniel

Some years ago I (S.H.M.) consulted regarding a 68-year-old woman named Karen who was admitted to the hospital 3 days after a myocardial infarction (MI), or heart attack. Her 10 adult children were enraged with her for delaying seeing a doctor. Their health beliefs matched those of the healthcare providers: "Go to the doctor immediately and accept intervention." Karen, on the other hand, drove the hospital team to distraction as she refused one after another intervention. She was so oppositional that her depression was missed, until her family physician called a family meeting. Fairly intimidated by this woman and her large family, he came to me, his on-site family therapist, and asked for help. "I have no idea how to conduct this family meeting, but I'm sure we need one."

Seated in a large circle in a family conference room, we learned that her husband had died 10 months previously of a heart attack (something that the hospital staff did not know). After raising 10 children and taking care of her diabetic husband for 40 years, Karen felt her role as caretaker was over. In terms of family history, the women in Karen's family lived long lives and many were miserable and wheelchair-bound with severe arthritis; while the men died young of heart attacks. Because of this scripting, Karen first did not believe she was having a heart attack. However, once her symptoms persisted, she decided a shorter life without disability was preferable to a longer one in a wheelchair.

My role in this session was to create space for each party to tell his or her story, and to help them negotiate a common goal. I worked with the physician to support the patient's right to make choices about her life and her treatment, while at the same time challenging some of her depressive beliefs.

After a few attempts by the family physician to convince Karen that she really should call him if she had chest pain, he took the cue from me and backed off. Karen was tough: he told her to call him if she had symptoms that required her to take 3 nitroglycerin tablets. Given this rule, she would only take 2 so as not to have to call him!

During the 40-minute session, we negotiated a mutually agreed-upon treatment plan, a common mission that recognized the value Karen placed on her own independence, as well as her children's desire for her to be as healthy as possible. This plan included more home care and a greater sense of control than is typical for a patient with a recent MI. By us supporting Karen's autonomy, she then accepted my offer of counseling around the loss of her husband. Both the physician and I strongly suspect this one brief session saved the healthcare system a considerable amount of money and frustration, allowed Karen to function according to her values, and potentially saved her family a considerable amount of angst and worry.

Negotiating a common mission can be difficult, especially when patients, family members, and even family therapists, physicians, and other members of the healthcare team accept a difficult diagnosis on different timelines. At any given time we each occupy a space on a continuum of illness acceptance; some may be optimistic, while others occupy what they feel is a more "realistic" view. It often seems almost as if someone needs to deny the illness and advocate for life to go on, while others grapple with the hard realities. Families and friends can get polarized and move into major conflict over this. Our job as medical family therapists in these single meetings is to create a space where defenses can be respected, while also providing patients and families with the information they need and want to have.

Karen denied much of her illness. Of course, the more she did that, the more her children and her healthcare team tried to convince her she was sick. At one point in the session, one of her children said, "Mom, there is such a thing as a 'silent heart attack.'" Karen said, "I know,

I know. They gave me 3 different papers on that when I was in the hospital." Her problem was not one of ignorance in need of education. Rather, it was that her level of acceptance and the meaning she gave the illness differed from others' (including her family and her physician).

The Case for Medical Family Therapy and Integrated Care

Cases like these demand thinking outside the box, but even more they demand working in close coordination/collaboration with other care providers. Two core paradigms (*medical family therapy* and *integrated care*) nicely fit this demand. Medical family therapy has as its foundation the biopsychosocial model (Engel, 1977; Frankel, Quill, & McDaniel, 2003), and joins a whole-person orientation with the critically important social, relational, and community contexts in which we are each situated. In its original conceptualization (see McDaniel, Hepworth, & Doherty, 1992), medical family therapy was developed as a biopsychosocial treatment approach optimized by collaboration among all healthcare providers as well as individual patients and their families. More recently, the element of integrated care has come to the fore, not because it is a novel idea but because many are recognizing that fragmented and siloed care is both inefficient and not patient-centered. Particularly true in primary care settings (like Family Medicine, OB/GYN, and Pediatrics), where such a large proportion of patient families struggle with psychosocial and mental health issues in addition to those stresses brought on by illness, integration of behavioral and biomedical aspects of care is essential (McDaniel, Hepworth, & Doherty, 2014).

From the perspective of patients and families, this approach to care is exactly what is embodied by the concept of the patient-centered medical home (PCMH; PCPCC, 2007). The PCMH is a healthcare delivery paradigm in which care coordination, communication, and collaboration among patients/families, professionals and support staff are paramount (NCQA, 2013). Primary care practices increasingly are moving to this model because it seeks to improve health for a given population while providing (1) a high quality, (2) accessible and reliable patient and family experience, while (3) controlling overall cost. This is called the Triple Aim of primary care (Berwick, 2008) and requires an integration of systems and those who function within them (Institute for Healthcare Improvement,

IHI, 2009). Wagner (2013) adds a fourth dimension: supporting the health and vitality of the healthcare team itself. Collaborative single session interventions such as the one described above represent precisely the vision of efficiency and satisfaction of the PCMH achieving this Quadruple Aim.

Challenges of Coordination

Integration may make good clinical sense, but it is not always easy to achieve. Issues related to time, access, ease of coordination, and funding pose potential stumbling blocks. Professionals from different disciplines have differing cultural perspectives on time; primary-care medicine visits are typically scheduled for 10–15 minutes, for example, while the psychotherapy "hour" may be 45–50 minutes. Medical practices rely on clinicians spending only the time necessary to address the presenting problem in any given meeting; many psychotherapists spend the same amount of time in session independent of the focus for any given day. Bridging these cultures in an asynchronous manner, via the use of phone calls or emails or messages through a shared medical record, can be very helpful in opening or maintaining the communication channels among clinicians and/or between clinicians and the patient and family. However, alone, asynchronous communication can risk missing important information. Around "hotspots" such as challenging moments or times surrounding critical decisions, it may be best to bring everyone together. Joint meetings including patients, family members, and relevant professionals are important opportunities to align agendas, clarify perspectives, and coordinate treatment plans that address what is most important to all who are at the table.

Single Session Medical Family Therapy

Single session interventions are common in collaborative, biopsychosocial health care. Certain clinical scenarios are best suited for these kinds of intervention. These scenarios include interdisciplinary meetings in the hospital as well as in outpatient clinics, around critical moments in clinical care, and as consultations to existing care relationships or teams.

General guidelines

McDaniel, Campbell, Hepworth, and Lorenz (2005) suggest several guidelines for conducting a family meeting, independent of setting. These guidelines include:

1. creating a warm environment welcoming to everyone;
2. affirming the importance of each person's contribution;
3. acknowledging and allowing for emotional expression;
4. emphasizing strengths;
5. helping members to clarify their thoughts; and
6. maintaining a stance of empathy and acceptance.

These family therapy/family physician collaborators also suggest avoiding behaviors that may interfere with the accomplishment of the meeting's stated goals, such as: allowing one person to monopolize the conversation, allowing members to speak for others, offering too-early interpretations, creating coalitions by taking sides, and breaching the patient's confidentiality. Efficient family and interdisciplinary meetings rely on a clear rationale for bringing members together, having an established and mutually agreed upon agenda, setting clear limits on time, and negotiating the desired outcomes of the meeting itself.

Sample Cases

Here are some typical scenarios involving single session medical family therapy:

1. Hospital-based family meetings.
The case scenario presented above highlights the utility of the family meeting during the course of an inpatient hospitalization. The genesis of these hospitalizations can be acute medical illness as well as acute psychiatric illness. Hospital-based meetings that bring together patients and their important others, as well as key members of the care team, provide a forum in which to get everyone on the same page. These meetings are not without challenges. As in the case of Karen and the systems of support around her, including the healthcare team, emotions can run high. Fear or guilt about diagnosis or outcome, or perceived failures in care, for example, can create

obstacles to the openness, creativity, psychological safety, and clarity of purpose upon which a successful family meeting is contingent.

Hospital-based single session family meetings may also be useful opportunities to align care providers and family members around what happens after discharge. Involving family members in the course of hospitalization can help them ready themselves to take on helpful healthcare responsibilities after discharge. Medication changes, new diagnoses, post-surgical recovery regimens and simply trying to get back to "life as usual" is a challenge for any patient and family. If the next steps are complicated, contradictory to pre-hospital routines, or generally unwanted, seeing them through can be that much more difficult. Bringing these key stakeholders together prior to discharge in a single medical family therapy session allows for a review of the hospitalization course, any new diagnoses or treatments, and post-hospital changes to medications or daily routines. It can create opportunity for all to ask important questions and express concerns during a time when those concerns can be addressed and plans modified, based on what the patient and family may be able to handle. Reducing family members' anxiety can help reduce patients' anxiety, too, with the added benefit of promoting adherence to the plan and a quicker recovery (McDaniel, Campbell, Hepworth, & Lorenz, 2005).

2. Outpatient family meetings around new diagnosis, treatment adherence, or bad news.

Jeannette was a 31-year-old mother of two, tough, independent, funny, and seemingly fearless. She had noticed that she was struggling to keep up with her children, carry in the groceries, and get up and down the stairs as easily as she had. She had also noticed pain in her body, diffuse and in most of her joints. Some days it was debilitating. Her primary care clinician performed a physical exam but found no apparent cause for her symptoms. Follow-up bloodwork, however, revealed the presence of antinuclear antibodies and other autoantibodies, confirming a diagnosis of systemic lupus erythematosus (SLE, or lupus). She was devastated to learn of this news. Her father had been diagnosed with lupus when she was in primary school, and she knew all too well the damage it could cause. His condition was characterized by involvement of several major organs, rendering him intermittently completed disabled, and ultimately taking away much of his ability to participate in and enjoy his family. Jeannette didn't know much about whether lupus would do the same to her, but she was certainly fearful of it. And when she recalled images of her father throughout her own growing up, she was even more fearful of telling her family what was happening to her.

Jeanette had a longstanding relationship with her primary care physician and her team. She had entrusted them with the delivery of both of her children, and management of the health of her entire family. She knew she could entrust them once again with her very real fears and confusion about this new diagnosis. Her primary care physician listened attentively to Jeannette and felt strongly that convening her support systems (personal and professional) might help her feel part of a team, less alone, and better equipped to plan for what she might need to do to accommodate the demands of lupus. He invited her to a family meeting. Together with the medical family therapist on the team, they requested that her parents and her best friend join her in a special office visit to learn about her lupus, how it was similar to but different from her father's, and to discuss her concerns about her health and her family. They sat around a table in the conference room, not an exam room, for this single session meeting. Jeannette shared her fears that the same fate would befall her as had her father, that she would lose the ability to play with her children and care for them, that she would become dependent and unable to manage her life with the same level of independence to which she had necessarily grown accustomed. The collaborative primary care team took turns responding to her fears. The physician explained that her lupus appeared to manifest differently than her father's, that she did not appear to have any major organ involvement right now, and that the myalgias seem to be the most prominent symptom for her. The medical family therapist paused to see what she understood of the differences, and to ensure her questions were answered. The physician went on to explain the course of treatment he would recommend, and the likely impact on her daily functioning, which he believed would be minimal. The medical family therapist invited her family to share their concerns as well, and explored how they might support her as she began the treatment, learned how to make room for lupus in her family's life, and built the systems she needed to get back to "life as usual." The best friend offered instrumental support with the children and housework during this initial flare, with the promise to do the same in future flares. Jeannette noted feeling better informed, clear on the next steps, and surrounded by love and community, all of which were exactly what she needed.

These single session interventions, whether around a new diagnosis as was the case with Jeannette, "bad news" or treatment adherence, aim to increase the patient's sense of both agency and communion (Bakan, 1966). Agency refers to the feeling of self-efficacy, empowerment, awareness, engagement, and mastery over one's condition, while communion refers to the ability to bring together important others, to create a sense of warmth and connectedness, and to ensure the support necessary especially during times of medical crisis. Often these meetings maximize the opportunity to address patient and family concerns, directly address their expressed and implicit emotions about the illness, and to plan in specific ways how the network of people around the "patient" can become activated when it is most needed.

3. Consultation by a behavioral health or biomedical provider.

Not infrequently, behavioral health and biomedical providers alike may seek out one another or their colleagues for a consultation relative to a specific patient, diagnosis, prognosis, or treatment decision. This consultant may have a one-time opportunity to evaluate and assess, provide education, or offer a second opinion for a patient/family in a critical healthcare moment. Once the referral information has been provided, and the professionals have coordinated about the rationale for the consult, the consultant may be invited to meet with the patient, whether that meeting is with the preexisting provider or outside of that relationship with close communication before and afterwards. The patients know in advance that it will likely be a one-time meeting.

Couples seeking in vitro fertilization using donor eggs or sperm is a classic application of this model. Psychological evaluation and counseling is the standard of care for couples who seek to use others' gametes as part of reproductive technology interventions. These sessions include an evaluation to affirm decision-making competence about pursuing treatment and psychoeducational counseling about the psychological and interpersonal complexities of choosing to do so. Donors go through a similar process. This typically single session intervention has potential for profound impact, not only for the hopeful recipient couple/individual, but also for those whose generosity gifts another with hope for growing their family.

Linda, 41, and her husband Richard, 48, were referred by the Fertility Clinic for a single session of evaluation and counseling prior to embarking on donor in-vitro fertilization from an anonymous egg donor. Richard had been married briefly before and had an 18-year-old son that lived with his ex-wife in another state. He wanted to have the experience of raising a child, and he knew Linda badly wanted the experience of pregnancy and motherhood. Medical tests revealed no obvious cause for their infertility, other than Linda's relatively advanced age.

In addition to taking a Personality Assessment Inventory (both scored within the normal range on all sub-scales), I (S.H.M.) drew a genogram of both sides of their families. The couple told the story of how they met working at an advertising agency, and some history of their relationship. ("We do everything together. We are best friends. Everyone says we have the 'perfect' relationship, except for never having kids.")

Richard was the oldest of two boys in an Italian-American family. His younger brother was married, with 3 children, no problems conceiving. His father was a recovering alcoholic. His parents were both retired. Neither brother used alcohol or any other mind-altering substances because of awareness of their family risk. He reported no other mental health problems. Linda said she was the middle of 3 children in an Irish-American family, with an older brother and younger sister. The older brother had 2 children, the younger sister divorced without children. Her mother had 2 miscarriages in addition to her successful births. Her father died of a heart attack at age 64, 3 years ago. Linda was deeply saddened that she did not have children before his death. She had one abortion at age 19 ("I was definitely not ready then"), and had not been pregnant since. She reported her maternal grandmother became very depressed after her grandfather died, but seemed to have "snapped out of it" after 3 years. No other reported mental health or substance abuse problems. Both families were Catholic. Linda said her family was so intent on wanting her to have children that they had no concerns about IVF as a method. Richard's parents were very religious; Richard and Linda had not told them for fear of lack of support.

"If the procedure fails..." After taking a history, I led with: "I sincerely hope you will be successful with IVF, but as you know it is not always. How will you feel if it doesn't work?" Richard looked at Linda. She said: "I will be very, very disappointed...but we will move on. We can't afford to do more than one attempt, so we just have to play our odds." Richard said: "I'll be fine. I just worry about her." I asked about previous losses, and how they handled them.

Linda said: "The worst was my father's sudden death. He was the rock of our family. I was devastated, but knew that he'd want me to care for my mother and my siblings. I keep him in my heart." When I asked how long Linda was out of work after her father's death; she said "just one week." Given that both members of the couple seemed to have managed previous losses fairly well, I suggested the couple talk to each other and plan ahead how they might handle an unsuccessful IVF cycle: taking a weekend away, acknowledging the loss, and any other ritual that would help them in this situation.

"If the procedure succeeds..." They then turned to talk about if the IVF succeeded, including issues about the egg donor, and disclosure to the child. First, I asked about their choice of an anonymous versus known donor. They said that Linda's sister was too old to be a donor, and besides they preferred to not know the person. I asked what if the child wanted to know who the donor was, or information about his/her genetic background. Linda and Richard said they had not thought about that. I said that, for now, the records are sealed and that is likely how it would remain. But, given that some adoptees now want to know about their birth parents and pursue information, it is possible that their child would also go after the information. Linda said, "That would be weird, but I guess we could handle it." I went on to ask what they planned to tell the child about his/her birth. They said they didn't think they needed to say anything to the child. When I asked if Linda's family knew about the planned IVF, she nodded. I recommended they be open with the child from the beginning, for a number of reasons. First, given that her family and some friends know, the chances that this secret would not come out are very low. As parents, they should control how it happens and not have it slip out at some unplanned time. Also, given advances in genetic medicine, the chances are high that a future physician will know, or need to know, about the child's genetic make-up. Again, better to be in charge of this from the beginning rather than have it emerge during an illness. Linda and Richard looked surprised. After a moment of silence, Linda said: "I see what you mean. I just never thought about it. I just have focused on wanting a baby. How would we talk to a child about this? At what age?" We talked through a number of ideas. "I understand you've been focused on hoping for a child. There's no reason why you would have thought this through. That's why you're here to see me! I tell all my patients to make a baby book with this information from the beginning, that Mommy's tummy was broken and this *wonderful lady wanted them to have a baby so donated her eggs so Mommy and Daddy could have her. It will be your child's special story, a story of love. Also, you don't want to imply by keeping it secret from the child that there's anything at all shameful about what you're doing. You're trying very hard to have a baby, and it is a wonderful thing. I hope you'll be successful."*

Linda and Richard thanked me, saying they had much more to think about. They were appreciative and promised to let me know the outcome. The time we'd spent together had served its purpose, and they were free to choose their next steps knowing they had thought through some of the most challenging aspects of their family planning decisions.

4. Team-based pre-clinic huddles.

Sometimes the single session intervention can happen outside of the patient-clinician interaction. Growing in popularity in primary care practices, *huddles* (Institute for Healthcare Improvement, 2004) allow all team members and any consultants for the day to convene briefly with the purposes of checking in, planning ahead, and foreseeing challenging encounters. Huddles occurring before patient appointments promote teamwork by including all members of the healthcare team, and draw on the expertise and perspective of each. They enable the team to be prepared for complicated patients, those managing chronic conditions, those who have highly complex psychosocial presentations or who struggle with adherence, and any acute issues that might have arisen since the previous clinic session (Stewart & Johnson, 2007). These brief interactions may occur daily, although each time they occur, they necessarily focus on a specific list of patients coming in to receive care that day. Given that all members of the team participate, including behavioral health practitioners, huddles are also opportunities for brief intervention.

At a recent morning clinic, for example, one of our therapists joined other members of the primary-care team in pre-clinic huddle to plan for their patient's arrival. One of the patients was a 19-year old, impoverished young man with a trauma history. The PCP (primary care physician) had seen him for over a year before she convinced him to enter behavioral health. She addressed his gastrointestinal issues and headaches, likely exacerbated by stress, which did not seem to respond to intervention. The behavioral health therapist had also seen him, addressing his depression and history of abuse, including a string of recent violent episodes with a family member. On that particular morning, the therapist and PCP jointly planned to talk with him and his girlfriend about entering a higher level of care due to worsening depressive symptoms. The pre-clinic huddle allowed for a team-based conversation about how delicately the team would approach this suggestion given the patient's high likelihood of rejecting it and potentially becoming agitated as he had in previous disagreements. The medical secretary and the medical assistant offered a helpful reminder that this patient, even though he could become recalcitrant, often responded well to kindness and warmth. The nurse chose to offer a flu vaccine before the PCP and therapist entered the room. The PCP and therapist planned with the others for how they would like to structure the visit and its potential fallout, should he become frustrated or afraid. The team was well prepared, and the physician and medical family therapist had a chance to rehearse the interaction, all before the patient and his girlfriend even arrived.

The visit went according to plan, with the PCP and therapist sharing leadership of the session; the PCP addressed her concerns and linked his worsening physical symptoms with the heightened psychosocial stressors while the therapist expressed concerns about safety for the patient, his girlfriend, and the family. Both endorsed connection with a day treatment program with the goal of symptoms stabilization. Both leaned on the rapport and history they had established, as well as the judgment and concerns of the other professional. They elicited the patient's and girlfriend's concerns regarding his safety and health overall, who collaboratively decided to accept the referral. The medical secretary warmly greeted the couple at check out and offered to help with setting the appointment as well as transportation to get there.

Critical Elements for All Professionals in Learning these Interventions

Skills to conduct these single session interventions are not always inherent in either primary-care or behavioral health training. Teaching collaborative, interdisciplinary skills may be even less common. The many complexities involved in the examples above highlight the importance of complementary training and bringing clinicians from different disciplines together to learn in the same clinical laboratory. Models include teaching mental health professionals about primary care, coaching primary-care residents to conduct primary-care counseling, and offering guidelines to all participating in, leading, and supporting interdisciplinary meetings with patients and their families. These lessons are best imparted through a balance of promoting strong professional identities and respect (not criticism) of other professionals. Some of our favorite resources for teaching these skills on interprofessional collaboration are *Family-Oriented Primary Care* (McDaniel, Campbell, Hepworth, & Lorenz, 2005), *Models of Collaboration* (Seaburn, Lorenz, Gunn, Gawinski, & Mauksch, 2003), *The Shared Experience of Illness: Stories of Patients, Families, and Their Therapists* (McDaniel, Hepworth, & Doherty, 1997), and *The Collaborative Psychotherapist: Creating Reciprocal Relationships with Medical Professionals* (Ruddy, Borresen, & Gunn, 2008). Finally, Nash, Khatri, Cubic, and Baird (2013) have recently published competency guidelines for psychologists working in patient-centered medical home settings. Each resource offers specific suggestions for all healthcare professionals regarding the fundamental steps to functioning as a true team on behalf of patients, their families, and their communities.

References

Bakan, D. (1966) *The duality of human existence: An essay on psychology and religion.* New York: Rand McNally.

Berwick, DM. (2008) The Triple Aim: Care, health and cost. *Health Affairs*, 27 (3): 759–769.

Engel, G.L. (1977) The need for a new medical model: A challenge for biomedicine. *Science*, 196, 129–136.

Frankel, R.M., Quill, T.E., & McDaniel, S.H. (Eds.) (2003) *The biopsychosocial approach: Past, present, future.* Rochester, NY: University of Rochester Press.

Institute for Healthcare Improvement. (2004). Meeting tools: Huddles. http://www.ihi.org/knowledge/Pages/Tools/Huddles.aspx. Last accessed November 17, 2013.

Institute for Healthcare Improvement. (2009). The Triple Aim: Optimizing health, care, and cost. Reprinted from *Healthcare Executive*, January/February 2009.

McDaniel, S. H., Campbell, T. L., Hepworth, J., & Lorenz, A. (2005). *Family-oriented primary care* . Springer Publishing Co.

McDaniel, S.H., Hepworth, J., & Doherty, W. J. (1992). *Medical family therapy: A biopsychosocial approach to families with health problems.* Basic Books.

McDaniel, S.H., Doherty, W. J., & Hepworth, J. (2014). *Medical family therapy and integrated care (2nd edition).* Washington DC: American Psychological Association.

McDaniel, S.H., Hepworth, J., & Doherty, W.J. (Eds.) (1997) *The shared experience of illness: Stories of patients, families, and their therapists*. New York: Basic Books.

Nash, J.M., Khatri, P., Cubic, B.A., & Baird, M.A. (2013) Essential competencies for psychologists in patient centered medical homes. *Professional Psychology: Research and Practice*, 44(3), 331–342.

National Committee for Quality Assurance. Patient centered medical home. http://www.ncqa.org/tabid/631/default.aspx. Last accessed November 11, 2013.

Patient-Centered Primary Care Collaborative. (2007). "Joint principles of the patient centered medical home." http://www. pcpcc. net/node/14 (last accessed November 11, 2013).

Ruddy, N., Borresen, D., & Gunn, W.B., Jr. (2008) *The collaborative psychotherapist: Creating reciprocal relationships with medical professionals*. Washington, DC: APA Books.

Seaburn, D. B., Lorenz, A. D., Gunn, Jr., W. B., Gawinski, B. A., & Mauksch, L. B. (Eds.). (2003). *Models of collaboration: A guide for mental health professionals working with health care practitioners*. Basic Books.

Stewart, E.E., & Johnson, B.C. (2007). Huddles: Increased efficiency in mere minutes a day. http://www.transformed.com/workingPapers/Huddles.pdf. Last accessed November 15, 2013.

Wagner, E.H. (2013). Primary care and the future of American medical care. Personal communication.

Chapter Nineteen

Collisions of the Social Body and the Individual Body in an Hour's One-Time Consultation

James P. Gustafson

While this is indeed about how single sessions of consultation in a Brief Psychotherapy Clinic can be helpful like those of D.W. Winnicott in his *Therapeutic Consultations in Child Psychiatry* (1971), it is also more deeply about a much larger subject. Yes, I do draw upon Winnicott's method of bringing a case along with the resident until the patient is ready for such a single session of consultation, and I do follow the patient afterward with the resident to work through the core of the consultation.

The context is this. The patient and resident and I meet in our audio-visual room for one hour. The session is recorded on DVD, with the cameraman behind a one-way mirror and the other residents in the Brief Psychotherapy Clinic down the hall watching the session on closed-circuit television. The following week the residents and I will watch the session over again on DVD to study how it works. The patient understands it is a chance for a one-time hour's consultation.

However, I am chiefly concerned in this essay with the greater subject of **the enormous scale of collisions between social body and the individual body** and **their intersection where they explode into each other**. This is about the tragedy of this, not only in tornadoes in the Mississippi River Valley, but on **the world scale** of the **corporate hot engines** colliding with **our cold engine natures**, and needing a **third position transformer** to **bring down the voltage** to **modulate the forces** and **result in a comedy.**

I will give the reader the core of the consultation similarly to how I presented it in *Lecture Twelve, Taking in the Whole Situation from a Third Position* (July 6, 2012), in my series on *Maps for Psychiatry* of thirty-six lectures on my *Jim Gustafson Channel of YouTube* (type in *Jim Gustafson Channel* on *YouTube*, and you will find the channel folder of all thirty-six lectures). I will also give a two-year followup and discussion of what was accomplished by the single session, and what remained to accomplish and still remains unfinished business for the patient. The patient has read the entire manuscript and agrees with the accuracy of the account.

Taking In the Whole Situation from the Third Position

I am going to have to be **fairly telegraphic** in reporting a consultation, leaving out many remarkable aspects of the hour, to **point to the decisive forces.** Let me suffice to say that our patient found herself **bullied** in corporate life to the point of not being able to continue, in continual panic, and in despair. Her huge pair of dreams conducted in **the company warehouse under spotlights** shows the whole situation in two extremes, a week apart.

Let us turn to the first drawing, which I drew and showed to the patient **to see if I imagined rightly what she saw in the dream and she confirmed that I did.**

The first dream finds her in the middle of a circle of chairs of her superiors and co-workers, standing on a chair herself with a noose around her neck. The decision point is that she can **lift off** the noose with her hands, or she can step off the chair and **be strangled.**

As we discuss her predicament, she seems quite ready to free herself. **As** she felt in the dream, the noose seemed like a *security blanket*, a kind of *addiction*, difficult to dispense with. This security blanket/noose goes way back in her history in her family, where material security and prestige are its very honor.

The second dream is in the very same warehouse, under the very same spotlights, but her **positioning** has **totally changed.** Now, she is walking up and down in front of her hated superiors and co-workers who **menaced her, menacing them**, with the

Figure 1. First Pair of Dreams

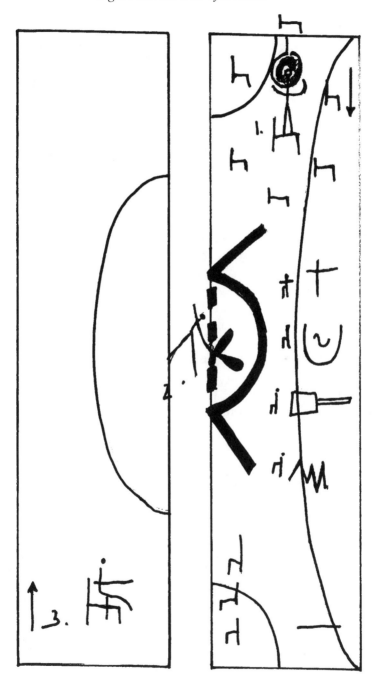

motion of cutting with a pair of **scissors,** so polished that they **flash brilliantly**. Not only that. The first and most hated boss is about to be *killed by crucifixion* on the cross behind him, the second boss by *drowning* in a huge tub, the first co-worker by *lethal injection,* and the second co-worker by a *funeral pyre.*

I ask her feeling, and she says it is a feeling of *power,* of *great satisfaction,* in *getting even.* I ask her how the second dream bears on her predicament of getting out of her pain and doing what she wants. The **shears** seem **decisive** to her and to me, and **come from her home**—they have been an instrument of **creating** things. Now, they are instruments of a kind of **creating of evil,** of **an eye for an eye.** I ask her if she has read Dante's *Inferno,* and she has and she agrees this is the originality like his of inventing **suitable deaths** for those who have tormented her. I ask her how that helps.

She says it helps her to get out of the box of sales in the company, of security with a noose ever tightening around her neck, **strangling** her [quite like the patients of Breuer and Freud (1955, original work published 1893–1895 in German)]. She feels ready to use her powers of creating in a more suitable position in the company. More immediately, the final detail of the dream, of *ordering her assistant to put the first nail in the hand* of the first supervisor *nailing him to the cross,* feels to her like a *suitable menace* to the other three tormentors *not to mess* with her.

My letter (emailed to the patient the day following the consultation) summarizing the consultation ran as follows:

> Your dramatic pair of dreams portrays the two extreme positions.
>
> The **first position** is of being surrounded by the firm with a noose around your neck.
>
> The **second position** is of menacing them, twirling your scissors flashing in the light.
>
> Of course, the **first position is of surrender,** and the **second position assumes a power** it is **impossible to wield.**
>
> So, the **third position** is **implicit** in the **comparison of the first two:** it is possible to have a **certain quiet fierceness** to **look out for** what you want while negotiating with what they are **willing to offer.** I imagine your subsequent dreams will make your third position, which takes in the whole situation, more **explicit.**

It is pleasure to work with you on this.

Two days after the consultation, I met with her and the resident again and I was struck immediately by finding her in a third place. She looked **ten years younger**, and was **full of sharp, comic wit** of the **reduction to absurdity** of her current boss's insecure rigidity. She was much less intimidated by her, and even felt sorry for her. Of course, the working through of her third position in negotiations with the company is just about to begin.

The Study Necessary to Conduct This Consultation

I recall 41 years ago this spring when I graduated from my residency in June of 1971. Like our residents now, I would get keen on one idea and think psychotherapy was all about that — like the idea of confronting resistance. You can imagine for yourself how that would **miscarry** with our patient, who needs to be **in charge herself** of what we talk about, and at what pace, and in what order.

As Michel Serres (1982, original work published in French, 1975) argued, in his thermodynamics, patients **get sick** from being **unable to construct the intersection** of **radically different spaces with radically different energies** in which they find themselves. Their **bodies explode**. More precisely, **one surface explodes into the other surface. The patient's body is the intersection** (p. 44, *Language and Space: From Oedipus to Zola*). One of our residents watching the consultation (Fred Langheim, personal communication, 2012) sent me a note by email of the relevance of the laws of thermodynamics for this consultation, which would neatly allow us to consider **the three kinds of energy** in our patient **from three different positions.**

She begins in the first third of the hour-long consultation **very coolly**, scientifically, explaining her anxiety and depression. In the second third, things are much more **charged up** with her at the decision point standing on the chair with the noose around her neck, and her hands on the noose. In the third, she is **quite unleashed, eyes flashing** with the **satisfaction of revenge**. Here is where **the fiery, pent up body** is on the **verge of explosion.**

Already in the last five minutes, carried over to the next meeting, the **third energy** is **being modulated** to a **sharpness**: she is **twirling her glittering scissors**, with a **sharp wit** that is a **modulation of**

Figure 2. Intersection of Radically Different Energies

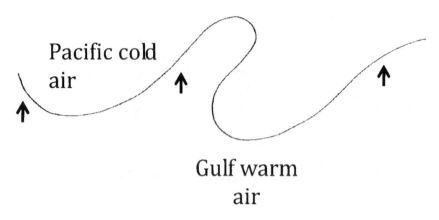

Pacific cold air

Gulf warm air

murder, into a **beautiful capacity** for **the reduction to absurdity of her antagonists.**

Like the influx of warm air from the Gulf of Mexico coming into collision with cold air from the Pacific Ocean in the Mississippi River Valley, **the danger of discharge** from **lightning and tornado** becomes greater and greater as **the gradient of temperatures between the two fronts gets steeper.**

Let us go to the second drawing by myself and compare it to the first drawing.

So this is the kind of **intersection of hot and cold** that sets up **tremendous voltages** in our Mississippi Valley and in our patient on a much smaller scale. Thus, we could place the corporate warehouse as a tiny segment of this enormous front. As I argued in my last book (Gustafson, 2010, *22nd Theorem*) borrowing from Rene Thom's biology (1988, original work published 1972 in French), **everything depends** on **how close you are to the potential explosion.** In other words, **everything depends** on the **distance** of **the body from the social body.** In other words, how do the **body and social body intersect?**

In position one, the corporation would **swallow up our patient.** In position two, our patient **explodes into the corporation.** In position three, she can **negotiate sharply.** Fortunately, I could find in her a kind of **transformer** to bring the **voltages down to an intensity** she could make **sharp use of** vis-à-vis **the corporate world.**

As Wallace Stevens (1997, original work published 1942, p. 665) wrote about **the nobility of poetry: "It is a violence from within** (pause) **that protects us from a violence without."**

Two-Year Follow-Up and My Concluding Discussion

Two-Year Summary of Follow-Up

I would like briefly to comment on what has happened since the hour-long consultation. I followed the patient with the resident about every two weeks (I would be present for a third of each of these hours) for three months until he graduated. In the last nine months, I have seen the patient about monthly for forty-five minutes, each time by myself.

From my perspective, she handled **the profound clash** between the **social body** of the **corporation** and a very similar **corporate social body** of her **family of origin** with that of her own **body**, by deciding to stay home and enjoy mothering her five-year-old daughter and enjoy quite a vigorous athletic training regime and begin to consider an alternative career in some **truly helping profession** in place of being a **traveling saleswoman** for the corporate world. She also began to separate herself from the **corporate regime** of her family of origin, by seeing much less of them, and reducing the **domination** over **her purposes** that the **extended family** loved to **dictate to her.**

This was financially possible for two years because her husband had a successful job and because she had been put on disability for depression by the resident. If there was **a drawback** to the last two years, and there was, she became **less confident** that she could return to the corporate world and keep up its daily schedule and top-down dictation, but she also **felt less confidence** in entering the social world at all, as with friends, other mothers, and other community events.

She tried out a number of alternative careers in her mind, and has been experimenting with teaching by being a teacher's assistant in her daughter's kindergarten. This has felt much more meaningful to her than being a corporate saleswoman. This also helps her to gain confidence in her abilities to work with children and other adults.

In the last several months she has felt quite well and ready to apply to begin applying to the corporate world again, this time in management of distribution of the company's products for a company that she respects and respects her.

Our one-session consultation with the interpretation of her two dreams was a turning point, then supported by the ongoing therapy with the resident and then with myself.

Concluding Discussion

As discussed by Studs Terkel in *Working* (1972) and more recently Karen Ho in *Liquidated: An Ethnography of Wall Street* (2009), there are very few of us in the corporate world who are not **dominated and de-centered** by the corporate hierarchy imposing its **will** by **threat**, both explicit and implicit. Lewis Mumford in *The First Megamachine* (1995) traced it back to the machinery of top-down **orders** descending from the Pharaoh through the priesthood to the slave labor drafted by violence from the poor farmers. At every level of this descending hierarchy, the **obligation** is to carry out orders as precisely as possible and **invent nothing!** The **results of this terror** were extremely precise results in the laying of massive stones down to a tolerance of a few millimeters or centimeters over square miles of pyramid!

Little has changed in such megamachines in three thousand years except that they run at **much faster speeds!**

Thus, it is quite exceptional to belong to a profession as a **truly individual member** who originates and enjoys making meaningful contributions. Rather, the rule is to be a **membership-individual** who **only complies**, or a **singleton** that is **not allowed to belong** (Turquet, 1975).

In Terkel's book, there is but one of several hundred interviewed, *The Stone Mason*, who enjoyed this kind of **being an individual member.** Every day he drove to work in the Ohio River Valley, he could stop and pause over one of his previous constructions, so **the portfolio of his development** as a mason was there for him to taste and smell and see and consider, and take it forward into his current project.

This is what I would call **real working** and it is very difficult **to arrange.** I think our patient would like something more like this than what she has had so far!

References

Alighieri, D. (2006). *The inferno* (R. and J. Hollander, Trans.) New York: Doubleday. (original work published in Italian about 1300)

Breuer, J., &Freud, S. (1955). *Studies on hysteria.* In *The standard edition of the complete psychological works of Sigmund Freud* (Vol. 2, pp. 1–319). London: Hogarth Press. (original work published in German in 1893–1895)

Gustafson, J.P. (2010). *Twenty-four theorems of the topology of captivity and deliverance.* Madison, WI: James P. Gustafson, Publisher. Also available as an electronic book on his web site at http://psychiatry.wisc.edu/gustafson.

Ho, K. (2009). *Liquidated: An ethnography of Wall Street*. Durham and London: Duke University Press.

Mumford, L (1995). The first megamachine. In D.L. Miller (Ed.), *The Lewis Mumford Reader*. Athens, GA: University of Georgia Press.

Serres, M. (1982). *Hermes: Literature, science, philosophy* (J.V. Harari &D.F. Bell, Eds.). Baltimore, MD: Johns Hopkins University Press. (original work published in French 1975).

Stevens, W. (1997). The noble rider and the sound of words. In *Wallace Stevens: Collected poetry and prose*. New York: Library of America. (original work published in 1942).

Terkel, S. (1972). *Working*. New York: Avon Press.

Thom, R. (1988). *Structural stability and morphogenesis* (D.H. Fowler, Trans.). Boulder, CO: Westview Press. (original work published in French in 1972)

Turquet, P.M. (1975). Threats to identity in the large group. In L. Kreeger (Ed.), *The large group, dynamics and therapy* (pp. 87–144). London: Constable.

Winnicott, D.W. (1971). *Therapeutic consultations in child psychiatry*. New York: Basic Books.

Chapter Twenty

One-Session Therapy: Fast New Stance Using the Slo-Mo Three-Minute Trance

Michele Ritterman

"[S]ometimes brief psychotherapy can be remarkably effective...[and] the concept of time distortion lends itself in a remarkable way to clinical therapeutic work."
—MILTON H. ERICKSON (IN COOPER & ERICKSON, 1959, P. 247)

Since the late 1980s, I have taught and written that the world has changed in ways that our therapies must catch up to. The key issues today are in present-time, present-space and synchronicity. Space is about personal space and our reduced sense of freedom, especially within intimate relationships, manifested in the often-heard colloquialism, "I need some space." Synchronicity is about the need for many related things to happen at once in a concurrent and cooperative manner toward the same result for experiential change to occur. Time and the experience of time is perhaps most important in life and healing today. Changing how a person feels inside is not strong enough medicine. If there are no mirrored or corresponding changes in their interactional realities of love/work/etc., the social environment will tend

Based on keynote speech, "The Three-Minute Trance to Adjust Your Stance and Avoid Medications," presented on November 18, 2011, at the annual convention of the Mexican Psychological Association, held in Puebla, Mexico.

to dominate. Therefore, affecting our use of experiential time and producing the proper stance for action in the world becomes paramount.

My primary work experience is in the clinical world, so I will speak to that here. How can we use special skills of our mind to maneuver through the world today? The big secret as I wrote in *The Tao of a Woman* (Ritterman, 2009) comes from a Chilean saying: *Despacito por las piedras.* "If you are in a big hurry, slow down." But we must know **exactly when and how** to slow down while living in a machine-fast world. So let's see how **the speeding up of social time** impacts the **time pressures** upon our **state of mind** and **upon the stances** we take in our life.

I will explain how I learned that **time** sense is as important a variable in therapy as the past and memories, sensations and perceptions in general, and I will explain what **time** has to do with **trance states** or **states of mind** and **what it has to do** with our problems and how we handle them. It pertains especially to the kind of therapy we are called upon to do today. I will discuss and illustrate, in single session interventions and within those sessions, the significance of what I call **the slo-mo state** and the three-minute trance. We'll begin with a beginning, then four explanatory and demonstrative parts, then a conclusion.

To Begin at a Beginning...

It was in the late 1980s that I realized that the human experience of time had changed forever and that psychological methods and most long-term therapies hadn't caught up with that change. This became clear to me in my own home, the first night I was to use a brand new microwave. Until that night, I had cooked a nice three-course dinner for my family of four and we had enjoyed meal time as family time no matter what else we all had done apart each day.

That fateful night, my eight-year-old son was playing Nintendo in the living room and he asked me, "Mom, when will dinner be ready?" and I looked at this new dial on the microwave oven, and instead of saying "half an hour" as I always had, I said, "35 seconds"...and he said, "That's too long!" And I understood, even as I unplugged the bulky microwave and lugged it out into the backyard in protest—complete with the defrosting "healthy choice" meal inside and my son calling upstairs, "Dad, Dad, Mom's flipped!"—that my son was already living in a dimension of time that was different from what I had known and that if this new perception of time was not part of the understandings in my own life and my own field of psychotherapy, then the field of psychology was off the mark (Ritterman, 1995). It was apparent then that crude technological time was destroying the delicate rhythms of home time, leaving families like little orchestras in which each musician plays at a different beat, and all of them are out of sync. I later wrote "A Five-Part Poetic Induction in Favor of Human Decency (Countering the Hate Movements)" in which I concluded that it was easy to hate and harm quickly, but that "Love and healing take time" (Ritterman, 1994, p. 481).

Now, this issue of time is even more evident. Come with me in your mind to one week ago in my therapy office. A couple comes in, and no sooner had they settled into their places on the couch than each of them **simultaneously** pulled out their cell phone from their jackets, as if drawing guns from their holsters. Each one had a saved text to read quickly about what had irritated them about the other the week before. Before they could read their texts to me, the husband hurried to say to his wife: "Listen, I don't like how my mom is treating you on **Facebook**. I want you to know that it is OK with me if you **unfriend** my mother"—a many years long relationship between daughter-in-law and mother-in-law, to be dismantled with the click of a box on a screen!

Today, in this world of nanoseconds, economic pressures and social and political upheaval, our longer slower therapies do not always address the **urgencies** our clients feel in the moment. For all of us **time**, **timing** and our **sense of time** is **now**. This is perhaps the central issue in determining the therapies we need.

> *Perhaps we have learned to swim in the river,*
> *but suddenly we come to a rapids and we have no idea how*
> > *to handle it,*
> *or a sink hole appears,*
> *and we have no idea*
> *how to be in the moment with this new challenge.*
> *And this new time urgency*
> *that began as minds competing with technology,*
> *and leaves us open to quick fixes*
> *like the dream of the magic pill,*
> *rather than what we need*
> *which is new skill*
> *at making quick shifts:*

Quick but holistic shifts internally
and quick but informed interactional shifts.

It is my dream that psychologists and some psychiatrists, even working individual by individual, can help the people of the world to deal with the pressures of time without jumping without just cause to medications, as if there is something defective about our brains. What I call "brain-blame" ought to be our last recourse. First let us create a more human-friendly society, and when we can't, let's help people use their creativity to respond to the madness outside of themselves. This means having tools to help our clients be present in this moment. Every day in my office I watch the beauty of minds, like flowers with time-lapse photography, opening.

Part One: Trance and Stance or the 'Slo-Mo' Three-Minute Trance

I will tell you how I first learned about the idea for this tool and I will demonstrate it with you the reader, and I will show how I used this tool with several clients. I call this tool or technique my Prozac without addiction or side effects (such as shrinking of the brain organ). It is designed to deal with the present fast pace of life, both internally and externally and it is a friend of one-session intervention and therapy to help people get **unstuck fast**.

It was 1975, and I was a 28-year-old Psychology student, starting to conduct my four-year Ph.D. dissertation research, which was one of the first controlled studies comparing a new drug, just out, called Ritalin, with placebo and family therapy for a group of boys now identified with a vaguely defined syndrome that was hypothesized without evidence-based research to make young boys jumpy in their classrooms. I was doing this as a student of Jay Haley, Salvador Minuchin, and Bernice Rosman at Philadelphia Child Guidance Clinic and Children's Hospital of Philadelphia. A young psychiatrist from my clinic came back with a first professionally produced video (Erickson & Lustig, 1975) of the father of hypnotherapy, Dr. Milton Erickson, to show to Dr. Salvador Minuchin, one of the fathers of family systems therapy. Sal, who was my boss and mentor, invited me into this private viewing. And, as they say, the rest is history...

Dr. Erickson's subject in the video was Mondy, a beautiful African-American woman in her twenties. She reported to Dr. Erickson that she became overwhelmed entering social situations, her heart racing, her mind spinning. (If Mondy were seen by most North American psychiatrists today, she would probably be given a ten-minute interview without any blood tests or x-rays, and she would leave the office with a medical diagnosis as if she were part of some diseased cohort and suffered certain biochemical brain deficits needing to be medicated. Mondy's medical records would state that she suffered Social Anxiety Disorder and she would likely be prescribed Paxil or Zoloft or Celexa—which is like assuming fevers are caused by taking too little aspirin.)

Dr. Erickson was a M.D. psychiatrist, but one who was very cautious in the prescription of medications because he preferred to work with the whole mind and body. He was also a psychologist with a pragmatic problem-solving approach to human difficulties. Let's see how he treated this problem with Mondy in one session, in the video I watched with Sal.

He asked her **exactly** what situations made **her** feel anxious. She got nervous when she had to walk into a room with other people in it. She became self-conscious.

He went deeper and deeper into the specifics of this state for her: the unique details of **her** anxiety. In short, he slowed time down with her, in their rapport, in order to be invited to rapidly enter into the world of **this moment before she enters a group, the world of that moment for her.** To do so, he used trance to help her turn to the channels in her mind that could help to explore what exactly went on inside of her mind, in order to connect with her emotionally so that he could establish **a rapid and powerful therapeutic relationship** with Mondy, and to identify what was going on inside of her that was then seemingly automatically producing **an agitated stance** in certain social situations. **This particular anxiety**: He did not look at her complaint as if all people who feel anxiousness suffer the same underlying unitary defect. He pondered: What's **this** anxiety making her feel, think and do that isn't working for her **now? In this moment?** (Just as Walt Whitman called his book of poems *Leaves of Grass* because every leaf of grass is a different color of green.)

He maintained a deep emotional rapport throughout as he gathered the unique details to:

1. **Identify her current trance** and
2. **The resulting** (maladaptive) **stance.**

He used the trance state **to help her bring him inside of her mind**. When she revisited the feeling she got approaching a group, he learned quickly that she was showing herself many disturbing memories like old T.V. shows in her mind. The worst old program was a beating she got with a hairbrush by her mother for doing something naughty when she was a child. Erickson had her relive and memorize that most terrible experience of humiliation and shame that was unconsciously triggered for her when she thought of entering a group. He learned that **just before** entering a group, she imagined the group as big and powerful like her mother was, and herself, small and beaten, as a child. She showed physical changes, such as an altered rate of respiration, she grimaced and winced and her body tightened and contracted during the reliving of the beatings.

Now Erickson **knew** what was triggering **her** social anxiety. Not someone else's anxiety, as if it were just a brain problem with no mental or emotional content. Now, still in **the world of the moment she enters into before going into a group,** he then—only minutes into this single session—had her turn to a **different channel** in her **own** mind where she remembered herself feeling quite the opposite, the brain channel of her happy times. She remembered playing with abandon chasing ducks. She was the big powerful force and she was laughing and dancing and clapping her hands as they were flapping their wings and hopping about to escape her. She was playing with abandon, without self-consciousness.

During the reliving of these memories, she smiled, opening her eyes, still in trance, her face radiant with a child's mischief and delight. When she did, he beamed approvingly at her, giving her a heavy dose of unconditional love to look at and to use to project onto groups. **Still in the moment before she would normally become anxious,** he had her go back and forth from one state to another: From the shameful and humiliated state of Mommy's bad girl taking a painful beating with the brush again and again, to the happy child playing with abandon, chasing ducks. And he taught her to move quickly to the good one.

Then he taught her how to take that beating, the imagined disapproval of others, that everyone was looking at her with disapproval and judgment, like her mother had done and have that trigger her to switch to her happy self and instead project onto the faces of the people in the group a loving look. The kind of look people might give to a happy child playing with abandon. The kind of look he was giving to her. They were playing with her usual trance and stance followed automatically by her new trance and stance. He trained her to open her eyes, feel triggered with upset, close her eyes and literally in the blink of an eye, to add into her old natural sequence a feeling of playing with abandon, a new internal and external trance, a projection of love. He taught her a skill instead of giving her a pill.

I don't have long-term follow-up on Mondy, but after watching this video, at age 28, I decided to work personally and directly with Erickson for the next five plus years, until he died in 1980. (See Ritterman, 2013, for a further account of my time with Erickson.)

I knew I'd witnessed something I was not being taught in graduate school! Erickson's one-session therapy with Mondy was and remains the single best piece of clinical work I've ever witnessed. All of this went into my own unconscious mind, where I would be developing my one-session interventions, and then the tool of the three-minute trance.

Although I finished my four-year research on Ritalin, I had already concluded that jumpy little boys needed to learn how to concentrate. They needed skills not pills.[1] I began to understand that instead of a diagnosis and a hypothesis of underlying brain damage, which was becoming the model of choice for the American Psychiatric Association and was pressuring the field of psychology as well, Erickson gave Mondy the tools to discover **the automatic trance** she was entering unconsciously in social situations, and to switch to the **trance state and stance** needed to spontaneously handle social situations. He offered her a way to be present in the moment and to give this moment a chance to be different from what she'd anticipated it would be.

Part Two: The Value of Training in Trance and Stance: Subjective Time and the Slo-Mo

Even when our clients take yoga classes, study meditation, or learn to use trance states, they do not know how **to bring those pauses precisely into** the challenging sequences of automatic responses and interactions specific to their own fast-paced daily lives. If they cannot **act** or **take the best stance** in the moment, automatically, drawing on these learnings, using their meditations

---

1. For more on the overemphasis of neuropsychiatry and medication at the expense of social and psychological factors with "ADD" clients, see Mate (1999).

and trances at the moment of need, they will be chronically over-whelmed and break down one way or another at their own point of biophysiological fragility.

For the past 36 years, I have developed these methods I first ob-served in Erickson's work with Mondy, and have used them with considerable success with a variety of clients:

- survivors of Hurricane Katrina in New Orleans, and of do-mestic violence;
- a wife depressed after her husband left her;
- a breadwinner denied the life-long pension promised by his job;
- a couple in which the wife's drug addiction is ravaging the whole family;
- a little boy who becomes wild and out of control at school;
- a man who has panic attacks when he goes out dancing with beautiful women.

I also use Slo-Mo in my own life to learn ever more about being present here, now, in this moment we share.

I assume that most of us would like to try simpler possibilities first, before we refer the students we see or our clients or ourselves to the psychiatrist for the magic pill—or even for longer-term thera-pies. Let's say we ourselves would like to live more in the moment and be able to have a wider range of responses available to us than the ones we usually use. So, **how** did Erickson accomplish this im-portant practice for Mondy, something she will need to do again and again and again, until it is automatic, just like tai chi, or sun saluta-tion in yoga, or practicing the piano, or learning to sing a new song in a new way? How did he help Mondy **shift** from a bad trance and an unhelpful stance to a good trance and a helpful stance? But first, I'd like you to experience subjective time for a few minutes of clock time.

Part Three: Experiencing Subjective Time and Slo-Mo

I have talked about entering into the world of this moment. Now I will tell you how to do it. Remember, though, that just as impor-tant as this shift is that people "wake up" and "do something dif-ferent" afterward in their social context.

Erickson only wrote half of one book, *Time Distortion in Hypnosis: An Experimental and Clinical Investigation* (Cooper & Erickson, 1959/2002). The rest were his articles or books others wrote about his work. This one book, however, was about subjective time or experiential time. I see this work as the most important thing Erickson understood. Erickson had his finger on the pulse of how people have control over themselves and how they lose control over themselves. He worked with what I will call **slo-mo**.

Slo-mo comes into play in shock. Many people have experienced **slo-mo** in an upsetting experience, like a car accident. It is a capacity of mind that makes us **really be present** and to remember and observe in an incredibly detailed way.

Let me give three quick examples:

1. When the Loma Prieta Earthquake struck the San Francisco Bay area on October 17, 1989 at 5:04 P.M., I was in my office working with a man remembering in a trance being molested by his mother when he was about age four, just before she committed suicide. My client was a big handsome man and as the first shaking hit, I wanted to jump into his arms and have him save me. This would have been bad for him, especially given his revivifying having had a mother who not only did not mother him, but harmed him! Instead, I wracked my brain for what to do, and recalled that standing under a door jamb was safest. I then calmly asked that he awaken slowly and step with me under the door jamb. And he did, and we rode out the earthquake together. But the important part of this story is that when people asked me what the earthquake was like, I'd said "Not that bad—it only lasted 20 minutes." But, in fact, I later learned, the earthquake which had leveled highways had lasted only 20 seconds, and all the careful thinking and acting I did with my client occurred in a few breaths.

2. The mind can also contract time, so that a long thing positive or negative can be experienced as happening faster than the clock moves. I spent 7 hours with Erickson one day. When he asked me how long we'd been together I guessed four hours.

3. Elizabeth "Betty" Erickson (Erickson & Erickson, 1958; also discussed in Cooper & Erickson, 1959, pp. 191–192) called attention to "the first experimentally and clinically significant instance of hypnotic time condensation," reporting that

during her birth labor with her first child events seemed "remarkably rapid," including the minute hand of her bedside clock and the minute hand on the wall clock in the delivery room "moving with the speed of a second hand." When time condensation occurs, it is as if the hands of the clock spin. This use of perceived time also can be marvelous for long-distance airplane travel. Kay Thompson, a dentist who was a lifelong student of Milton's (see Kane & Olness, 2004), personally helped me with that process.

I call this **slo-mo**. Subjective time. When **experienced time does not match the clock time. This becomes a skill we can use to deal with the rush of time in many ways.** It happens in a heartbeat. **In the blinking of an eye.** In a specific instant. In a moment, time opens up like a huge chasm for a person and there one's whole sense of life can be up for grabs. On the negative, this opening of time can happen when one is sad, and it can feel like "forever." I know of a young woman, a teenager, a friend of a client of mine, who drank too much at her San Francisco condo, and in a moment shifted from happy-party mode to deeply despondent and jumped off her deck to her death!

I also worked with a young woman who, in trance, revealed how she had responded to a post-hypnotic suggestion she had not known she had received and thus saved herself. She had many years earlier taken one self-defense class for women and a wise teacher said: "If you are ever being attacked from behind, when you need this method, you will remember it." Right before she came to see me, a would-be rapist had entered her apartment. He forced her at gunpoint into her bedroom. The rest happened without her awareness, an automatic seeming stance: Looking in a mirror out of the corner of her eye, she saw the assailant behind her, momentarily distracted as he undid his pants. And automatically, in the blink of an eye, she recalled the lesson, scraped his shin with her shoe, elbowed him in the ribs and punched him in the head and escaped!

So let's think how this works. The mind is like cable television. There are many channels and you can turn on one or the other of the channels. Hypnosis depends upon this activation of several different channels within the programming of what the Western world calls the "unconscious mind." In the method I am describing, we want to pinpoint the moments that make a person automatically turn on a certain channel in their mind, a certain state that I am calling a trance state, and from that place that they automatically or unconsciously adopt a certain stance that does not work for them— such as Mondy taking a fearful stance approaching new groups as opposed to a stance of curiosity or playful anticipation.

Before I describe six cases of the three-minute trance or the Slo-Mo Mind in single session therapies, I would like to demonstrate three minutes of clock time versus three minutes of slo-mo time. I want to take 3–6 minutes of egg-timer time[2] to show you experientially how dramatically our minds can change states into a positive state. To have the effect of a positive meditational/hypnotic experience, right within the flow of your life right now, allow our 3–6 minutes, one or two turns of an egg-timer, to help you right here and now to feel a bit of what it means to shift into an alternative state of mind.

Slo-mo is where our brain has the most play to relax and let the mind shift. First we must stop the clock. Please consider these two verses from *The Tao of a Woman* (Ritterman, 2009), designed to help stop the clock and enter into the slo-mo mind, where we can practice shifting stance quickly.

Your Mind[3]

Just as your respiratory system
does the best it can
to take in the air that is useful to you
and let go what is not,
and just as your digestive system
does the best it can
to take in what is digestible from what you eat
and eliminate when is not,
so also your mind has the right
to take in what is helpful to you
and let go what is not,
with each breath.

---

2. Here is another example of how the times they are a'changing! An "egg timer" is an "old-school" analogic hour-glass device a cook uses, turned upside down with sand running through it, to measure how long to boil an egg. Nowadays modern cooks might just set their Smart Phone alarm for 3 minutes! When I teach, I hand out egg-timers to the students to take home as a post-hypnotic cue for themselves after our class has ended.

3. From M. Ritterman (2009). *The Tao of a Woman*. Berkeley, CA: Skipping Stones Editions (p. 139). ©Michele Ritterman 2009. Used with permission.

Is some heavy energy spinning your way?
Observe its course.
Step aside.

Allow yourself now to attain the calm that is helpful (but not essential) in searching your brain for the memories and experiences most useful to you in this moment.

To Attain Calm[4]

Breathe in, and then
exhale slowly
and deeply.
Remind yourself:
"I have done what I can
for the moment
about everything
outside of me.
[Breathe in. Loooong exhale.
That's right.
Now let yourself know:]
I have all the time I need
in the time that I have."
As your body naturally
inhales again,
daydream.
Watch how the clouds change shape.

Here alone with me while you are reading this suggestion, this wish from me to you, as your lengthened exhales continue, you may have a moment when you feel you do not belong, you are not as smart as someone else, or your job is not as good, or you do not feel as special or informed or qualified...From that place, from that precise moment, you may have a series of memories you don't like or recognize a tendency to behave in a way you do not like. These are a default setting in your mind. But your unconscious mind knows the way to shift to another state! I want you to take two minutes of clock time to relive a time you felt unconditionally loved for

---

4. From M. Ritterman (2009), *The Tao of a Woman*. Berkeley, CA: Skipping Stones Editions (p. 135). ©Michele Ritterman 2009. Used with permission.

who you are, more than for your job or your education or your status, loved for your very being. Appreciated. In one moment of your life. Allow yourself to enter into that place in which you felt totally acceptable and worthy just being who you are. Memorize that moment. Were there the smells of food cooking or flowers, the sounds of music or ocean, was some person or favorite dog or cat looking deep into your eyes, was the temperature warm or cool? Feel that moment in which you knew in the core of your being that you were as valuable on this planet as anyone. Your Unconscious Mind can continue this search for you at ease inside your skin, the trillions of cells inside the galaxy of your being shining inside you, and you can memorize these feelings just like you did the letters of the alphabet, learning what gets dotted and what gets crossed, shaping your way into your future. And through the many years and channels of your mind when you brush your teeth tonight or when you wake up tomorrow and brush your teeth, and throughout the rest of your life, so that you will spontaneously feel appreciated. And you can unconsciously shift from feeling less-then to feeling good-enough. Shift from the road that leads you backward to sorrow to the track that leads you forward to well-being and good dreams, and the stance you need for this moment. What is inside of you is most important. And you can then work to actualize your inner state in the outer world, even without conscious intention.

Part Four: Six Single Session Clinical Examples of the Three-Minute Trance

Here are six one-session client vignettes in which I used Slo-Mo Trance and Stance tools.

Case #1

A handsome young Asian-American man in his late thirties came to me in a deep depression. He'd gone to the family psychiatrist who saw him for ten minutes and prescribed anti-depressants and then he heard about me and decided to work with me instead.

My goal was to find out what was making him sad. He reported that he just couldn't seem to do anything. He barely could get out of bed in the morning. He'd always been a happy guy. "What was the immediate cause?" I asked, hoping that he would **stop clock time and begin to let me into his mind**. His beautiful young wife, the love of his life, had just been diagnosed with terminal cancer. He could understand her being paralyzed with sorrow, but why him? He was supposed to take care of her. She was the one with the disease. His sorrow was compounded with shame.

Clearly all of this would be cause enough for depression. But I wanted to know about **his depression**, to go inside of the moment in his mind where he got lost and incompetence became his stance. So we used **stop the clock and go into subjective time**. We can **never know what we may find when we use slo-mo to zoom inside a person**.

In trance, he reported that what was hard for him really was he felt helpless. He felt that once she died he could not take care of himself. He couldn't go on without her. This report was different and deeper, underlying the sorrow and shame. Now we had the problem identified. The so-called depression (the unrelenting streaming of sad shows on that cable channel of his mind) was on top of his deeper fear channel in which he saw programs in which he was unable to take care of himself.

Using the **slo-mo** time trance induction, I asked him to search for a moment in his life when he had felt he could take care of himself. He recalled "**The color blue**." "**Blue**?" What could that mean? I asked that he look closer. "**Blue what**?" (If I asked each reader what does the color blue bring to your mind, we would all have a different answer: sky blue nail polish, my dad's favorite shirt, the color of a sailboat....As therapists we might think: "Oh, blue, that's sad, that's the blues" but don't go there—see what the client thinks of as "blue.")

"Ah, a blue glass pitcher," he said.

"**Where**?" I asked.

In the refrigerator of his childhood home. At first he and I were both surprised. When I asked him to tell me more about the blue glass pitcher, he revealed that he was four years old and the fridge was very big and on a shelf, his mother had left him the blue bottle filled with milk and a box of cereal, because he had said he was a big boy and he could wake up and make breakfast for himself. It is Saturday morning. Everyone is asleep but him. He goes to the fridge and sees the big blue glass milk pitcher and he knows he can make his own breakfast and he feels proud and competent. This memory alone did the job for him. The entire slo-mo experience lasted for about ten minutes. He required one session. No meds, ever. And he got the tool that he needed.

So let's track what happened. He imagines his wife is gone. That is where his anxiety starts. Not in the care-taking. He is afraid he can't go on. He is powerless, helpless without her. He is regressed from the current pain back to before the age of 4. We introduce a rest as in music, a pause, and help him shift to a different mental state based on his own experiences that are on a different "channel" of his mind—his own memory of competence. He comes up with the medicine that is the antidote. And what do you think it is? A blue glass pitcher of milk! This memory allows him to alter his stance toward his situation.

Case #2

A couple in a long-term relationship comes in complaining about a many-years-long problem with their sex life, but they are shy to discuss it. I tell them we can talk about whatever they like. (Other subjects will automatically metaphorically address this underlying issue.) She says she baked him a platter of Christmas cookies and there were many varieties. She'd prepared all day. He walked in the door, saw the platter, raced over with enthusiasm and began downing some of them. After working all afternoon to prepare this treat for him, she felt enraged and wanted "to kill him" when he grabbed the cookies!

Next step in the faster-than-the-speed-of-light reaction sequence that happens with them: He felt absolutely baffled. What did she want him to do? Ignore the gorgeous cookies? Did she not want **him** to be the one to eat them? Was he not **good enough** for the cookies?

Looking at the man and woman, we could see how she might call him self-centered and he might accuse her of offering and then withholding. But what if we just look at the hypnotic sequence? What is making her suggestion to him unclear? We stopped the clock, using the slo-mo, three-minute trance to suggest the wife let the husband know **at just the right moment** what she really wants, which she reveals calmly, is to hear how much she would like him to **admire** her cookies. What if the husband finds within himself the pause button that lets him locate trust that the wife does want him to enjoy the cookies, but that she needs him **to slow down**, **approach more slowly** and **admire the cookies** before he touches them? Different way of thinking and observing—think about it!

This couple went home and made love after the cookie story three-minute trance provided a sequence of delicious interactions.

This couple went home and made love after the cookie story three-minute trance provided a sequence of delicious interactions.

Case #3

I had a single session in front of a large group with a country-and-western singer who had never recovered from over-dosing on the stage. In a three-minute trance, I helped him remember before he had his overdose so vividly that he could wake up and face the audience and feel fully comfortable. Then flip into the post-drug memory, in which with open eyes he stared in panic at the audience, frozen like a statue, and then, close his eyes, opening them again to the comfortable space of singing before his overdose. He learned quickly how to move out of the debilitating state and back into his channel of thousands of moments when he felt confident and connected to both his guitar and the audience.

Case #4

I saw a man who'd married a woman who'd not resolved her sexual conflicts after prolonged incest with her father and hadn't wanted a marriage with sex. After her therapy, she wanted sex. He then came in for a single session. He had no recollections of early childhood affection. No happy physical memories. In the three-minute trance, he recalled floating through the air on giant hands.

I think of the Netter (2006) books of medical drawings of the body. There is an illustration of the representation in the brain of information from the hands and feet alone. They take up much of the brain. I realized that even a single memory or sensation can occupy our brain for better or worse and carry much weight. In the negative, an obsessional thought can rule our lives! In the positive, a single memory can be used to transform a person's experience of him/herself.

From this single memory of being held as a baby by his mother, he recalled that he'd received much maternal affection until he was five and became a "big boy," and that his mother's mother had disapproved of coddling a "big boy." From these memories that came out like scarves from the magician's sleeves, he was able to re-member his body and move rapidly to enjoying his manhood and sexuality.

Case #5

I worked with a mother and daughter. For years the daughter had harbored hatred of the mother for an affair she had over many years with a man in another state. In this one session, I helped them stop the clock, and let the mother reveal her husband's—the girl's father's—lifetime of infidelities, her hidden desire to protect the family and preserve it, by having a supplementary affair of her own, and helped the daughter identify her own longing to be number one for her mother.

They had then identified within themselves all the experiential feelings needed from the various channels of their minds, to create a different stance toward one another. The family continued on a different footing all the way through to the death of the father, who was considerably older than the mother, five years later. They did this without the need for other intervention.

Case #6

In Puebla, Mexico in November, 2011, I worked therapeutically (speaking in Spanish) with a woman who had only a week before experienced a bus hijacking. I was ill at that time, and actually had been resting in bed at the home of a therapist who'd offered to care for me before I left town. So the client and I had under an hour to accomplish anything before I needed to return to sleeping.

My years of experience working with torture and trauma before the diagnosis of PTSD had been created taught me that the closer in time the treatment to the traumatic assault, usually the more effective. She had already talked to many friends about it, but no one had stopped the clock, helped her enter into what I now call Slo-Mo, and found out *what bothered her?*

What bothered her was not that the driver could have been in on it, not that a gun was held to her neck, not that they stole her cell phone. She had digested and eliminated those poisons.

What bothered *her* was that she heard an older woman behind her on the bus cry and she couldn't help her because she had to sit statue-still with her head down. She knew that there were two children up front and she feared that they would cry out and get killed. As soon as the hijackers left the bus with the passengers' money and cell phones, she was the person who took charge of the situation and got everyone calmed down.

The undigested part of the trauma, obtained only by my with-holding the idea that I understood or could guess what bothered *her*, and by *stopping the clock to enter into her meticulous recounting* of the micro-moments of the event, revealed that this woman felt bad that she couldn't be who she is, during the assault. In half an hour of talking with me, she was a bit improved and less depersonalized. As she finally cried with release, she told me, "You came inside. You got it. You helped me get to the real injury underneath the ob-vious." I also read her a poem from *El Tao de Una Mujer* (Ritterman, 2009; translated beautifully into Spanish by Leandro Wolfson):

My Teacher's Last Gift[5]

My teacher received a visit
From a very old Japanese man.
The visitor told my teacher that he saw his life
As he stood on the top of a mountain
Looking down over the climb that he had taken.
The jagged rocks and sharp weeds
That cut him along the ascent
Had become overgrown with moss
And wildflowers.

Conclusion

When I met Erickson in my late twenties, he said that I was too young and too pretty to be taken seriously and that I needed to wait until my hair was as white as his to express my opinions. Well, if it weren't for my hairdresser, Frank, clearly my time has come! At this point in my life, I am old enough to say that my life's work has been about the power of human interactions to heal people mentally and emotionally or to make them sick or even to die, as in voodoo. I have studied human interaction at many levels, from family inter-actions that drive children or members of a couple mad in my book *Using Hypnosis in Family Therapy* (1983/2005); to social forces and torture by the state in my book *Hope Under Siege: Terror and Fam-*

---

5. From M. Ritterman (2009), *The Tao of a Woman*. Berkeley, CA: Skipping Stones Editions (p. 157). ©Michele Ritterman 2009. Used with permission.

ily Support in Chile (1991); to spiritual levels of interaction among people, in *The Tao of a Woman* (2009).

We need to help clients learn to bring their trance states, their **slo-mo**, their rest notes, right into the ongoing interactions in their lives, right into the environments that would otherwise trigger them **faster than thought** to get stressed and overwhelmed. The martial arts teach us that we need to know many stances in life that we can move to quickly to handle any challenge at hand. We as therapists now need to teach our clients how to **utilize** their **slo-mo** states to attain the **proper stance** for any one moment. This is a tall order. But it is as necessary as understanding their early childhood relationships or processing their feelings. If they cannot **act** on these learnings, they will be chronically stressed and overwhelmed and may break down one way or another.

You might want to propose that they become non-violent urban warriors, people who have the skills necessary to stand up to the challenges of this moment—to save their own minds and hearts, and to heal with unconditional love.

So I close saying to you:

> *Occupy your mind.*
> *It is your final and own territory.*
> *Don't let anyone conquer your mind.*

References

Cooper, L.F., & Erickson, M.H. (1959) *Time distortion in hypnosis: An experimental and clinical investigation*. Baltimore, MD: Williams & Watkins. (Reissued 2002 by Crown House Publishing, Williston, VT.)

Erickson, M.H., & Erickson, E.M. (1958) Further considerations of time distortion: Subjective time condensation as distinct from time expansion. *American Journal of Clinical Hypnosis*, 1, 83–88.

Erickson, M.H., & Lustig, H. (1975) *The artistry of Milton H. Erickson*. Phoenix, AZ: Milton H. Erickson Foundation.

Kane, S., & Olness, K. (Eds.) (2004) *The art of therapeutic communication: The collected works of Kay F. Thompson*. Williston, VT: Crown House Publishing.

Mate, G. (1999) *Scattered: How attention deficit disorder originates and what you can do about it*. New York: Dutton.

Netter, F.H. (2006) *Atlas of human anatomy* (4th ed.). Philadelphia: Saunders Elsevier.

Ritterman, M. (1991) *Hope under siege: Terror and family support in Chile* (Foreword by Isabelle Allende). Norwood, NJ: Ablex.

Ritterman, M. (1994) A five-part poetic induction in favor of human decency (countering the hate movements). In J.K. Zeig (Ed.), *Ericksonian methods: The essence of the story* (pp. 465–481). New York: Brunner/Mazel.

Ritterman, M. (1995, January/February) Stopping the clock. *Family Therapy Networker*, 19(1), 44–51.

Ritterman, M. (2005) *Using hypnosis in family therapy* (2nd ed.). Phoenix, AZ: Zeig, Tucker & Theisen. (Work originally published 1983.)

Ritterman, M. (2009) *The tao of a woman: 100 ways to turn.* Berkeley, CA: Skipping Stones Editions. (Available in Spanish as *El tao de una mujer.*)

Ritterman, M. (2013) The tao of a woman. In M.F. Hoyt (Ed.), *Therapist stories of inspiration, passion, and renewal: What's love got to do with it?* (pp. 217–231). New York: Routledge/Taylor & Francis Group.

Chapter Twenty-One

Expectation: The Essence of Very Brief Therapy

Rubin Battino

We can perhaps consider Sigmund Freud, the "father" of psycho-analysis, to be also the "father" of single session therapy (SST). On August 6, 1910, in Leyden, The Netherlands, in a deep state of de-pression, the composer Gustav Mahler met with Freud (see Kuehn, 1965). Apparently, Mahler had put off this meeting several times, and this was the last occasion when he could meet with Freud who was vacationing there with his family. For four hours a psychoana-lytic session occurred while they walked along the canals of the city. Mahler feared that his wife, Alma, would leave him: there was a "psychosexual disorder" and a "mother fixation." This example of SST apparently worked, although the actual details of the four-hour session are not known. What we do know is that Mahler (and Freud) knew there would only be the one meeting.

My own introduction to SST began by attending a presenta-tion by Moshe Talmon, Michael Hoyt, and Robert Rosenbaum at the 1988 Brief Therapy Erickson Congress; and then subsequently reading Talmon's (1990) book, *Single Session Therapy*. Their studies at Kaiser Permanente gave the results summarized below:

- The most frequent length of therapy for every one of the ther-apists in their retrospective study was a single session, with 30% of all patients choosing to come for only one session.

- The therapeutic orientation of the therapists had no impact on the total number of SSTs.
- In their prospective study, 34 of 58 patients elected to have a single session. On follow-up 88% of the SST patients contacted reported either "much improvement" or "improvement" since the session and 65% also reported having other positive changes that might be attributed to the ripple effect.
- There was little correspondence between what the patient (in his/her memory) thought helped them in the session and what the therapist thought was helpful.

Some years ago I also heard Steve de Shazer (see de Shazer, 1982) describe a research project they did at the Brief Family Therapy Center (BFTC) in Milwaukee. At the initial intake clients randomly were told that for their particular concern it typically took therapists either five or ten sessions to help them. The therapists did not know what their clients were told. A follow-up one year later showed that the "five-session clients" started doing "significant" work in the fourth session and that the "ten-session clients" in the eighth or ninth session. The client's *expectation* had a profound effect on how soon they got down to business. (This is an example of what Appelbaum [1975] calls "Parkinson's Law in Psychotherapy"—work expands or contracts to fit the time allotted.) Being a "hard" scientist (I have spent most of my professional life as a professor of chemistry), I immediately graphed these results and came to the conclusion that if I told my clients that I *expected* to be able to help them in one session that *their expectation* would be the same. So, I tell all of my clients at initial contact that I rarely see people more than one or two times, and that I will do everything I can so that it is only one session. Since I work for myself and my "office" is in my home, my sessions are always open-ended and can last several hours (usually 90 minutes or so). Almost all of my sessions with clients for the past few years have been single. On the other hand, I always tell my clients that I will be available to see them again if they feel that would be helpful for them.

In effect, *expectation* is the essence for me of doing SST.

The Nature of Expectation

There is a vast literature on the subjects of expectation, expectancies, and the placebo effect. I just cite three papers by Kirsch

(1985, 1990, 2010) here. His basic conclusion is that psychotherapy is more effective when the client has positive expectations. We can also quote various statements from another paper by Kirsch (1994):

> Of course, psychotherapy is a placebo. [p. 96].... When people expect changes in their own responses and reactions, their expectations can produce those changes.... Because expectations can maintain psychological symptoms, the removal of those symptoms may require that those expectancies be changed. [p. 97].... Not only does expectancy determine when hypnotic responses occur, but it also determines what subjects experience and how they behave in hypnotic situations. [p. 98].... Although patients' initial expectancies play an important role in determining the outcome of therapy, it is equally important to monitor and influence changing expectations throughout the course of therapy. This is facilitated by including therapeutic procedures that are likely to provide clients with feedback indicating that treatment is successfully producing therapeutic changes. [pp. 103–104]

We know from the many double-blind studies that pharmaceutical companies and medical and other researchers have carried out that the placebo effect is effective in producing both physical *and* mental changes in people. Kirsch categorically states above that psychotherapy is a placebo. I agree. The early expectation in psychodynamic approaches was that clients would come for years. Post-World War II, therapists typically expected clients to come for 1–3 years. In recent years managed care has actually prescribed 8–12 sessions for various diagnoses. Very brief therapy proponents (like the authors in this volume) propose the possibility and practicality of SST (or just a few sessions). My expectation for everyone who comes to see me is one session, and my clients are told this directly in the initial contact. In the vernacular this might be expressed as "Let's cut out all of the bullshit and get down to work!" I am sure that there is a place for testing and time spent on getting sufficient information to diagnose (or "DSM") the client. I have never found that to be useful in my practice.

Some SST Approaches I Use

My book on expectation (Battino, 2006) details many on the things that I do. Here I am only going to give some information on the ones I use most frequently. In the last section I will describe "chatting" which is my preferred method of being with clients and being their guide.

1. As-If and the Miracle Question

One of the absolutely remarkable things that human beings are capable of is acting "as-if" something was true about themselves and finding that this acting then becomes real. I had a client not too long ago who told me in our first session that she had decided recently that she was going to be happy, and that she was. She then told me some of her life story and it sounded like a soap opera where almost everything in her life that could have gone wrong did go wrong. What she came to see me about was not about these past difficulties (after all, she was now happy!), however, but about some concerns having to do with her daughter. So that was what we worked on in that session, and in a follow-up session where I spent the time with her daughter. The issue with her daughter was apparently resolved.

The word "apparently" in the previous sentence should have you asking for more information, which I cannot supply in this instance or for most of the people I see just once. They generally do not come back or call or write to me, and it is my assumption that they got what they wanted in that single session. I do occasionally get feedback at long intervals from clients I run into in my small community, or infer a satisfactory outcome via people they refer to me.

You can get a client to act "as-if" what they came to consult with you about has been resolved by directly suggesting to them that they do so. The Mental Research Institute in Palo Alto (Fisch, et al., 1982) pioneered this idea in working with troubled couples. The couple was given directions for one of them to toss a coin every evening for two weeks. If the coin came up heads, then they were to act the following day as if everything in their marriage was working fine. If it came up tails, then they would act "normally" the next day. They kept separate records with the non-tosser recording a judgment of which side of the coin came up the previous night. At the next session two weeks later the therapist was generally told that the patients had stopped the experiment fairly early, and that their lives had taken a positive turn for the better. This is an example of "injecting" a family with a change agent (the coin-tosser) who changed the dynamics of the system.

The Miracle Question, which was initially developed by Insoo Kim Berg of the BFTC (see Miller & Berg, 1995, p. 37; Berg & Dolan, 2001, pp. 5–7), is my favorite as-if approach. At an appropriate time in the session (usually fairly early) the following is said to the client:

> Suppose that tonight, after our session, you go home and fall asleep, and while you are sleeping a miracle occurs. The miracle is that the concerns that brought you here are resolved realistically, and to your satisfaction. But, you don't know that the miracle has occurred since you are asleep. When you wake up in the morning, what is the first thing you will notice that tells you that this miracle has occurred?

Then, for the next twenty to thirty minutes you lead your client through his/her day asking for details about what is different in their day post-miracle. If they were able to step outside of themselves and observe themselves, what would they notice about their posture, their facial expressions, what they say and do? What would their spouse notice, their children? Ask more for observable behaviors than about feelings. What would people who know them well at work notice? Assume they call up a parent that evening—what would that parent notice that is different about the way that they talk, the things that they say? The more information you get about post-miracle behavior, the more the "miraculous" changes become reified. The more they describe their own behavior post-miracle, the more real it becomes. In a way this is an elaborate reframe in which *they tell you* the new way in which they perceive themselves and how they think of themselves. This as-if miraculous new life then takes on a reality of its own.

Steve Andreas (2012) has an exercise for transforming negative self-talk that involves a person saying to herself when she enters her home or walks around her house, "I am sitting in this happy chair. There is this happy table. There are the happy windows with happy curtains." The client is asked to do this every day for 10–15 minutes. Other words like "calm," "peaceful," "relaxed," "active," "smiling," and "creative" can also be used for this exercise.

2. Bill O'Hanlon's Inclusivity

Almost all clients and therapists operate out of an either/or mode with respect to describing what is going on in the client's life. That is, the person is either depressed or happy; passive or active; anxious or calm; tense or peaceful; and compulsive or casual. Bill O'Hanlon (2003) hit on the idea of *both/and* (or *inclusivity*) with a client and expanded this into a useful and delightful (versus ponderous!) book that describes 26 methods of respectful resistance-dissolving therapy involving this idea.

Just imagine your client's response when you say one of the following to her after attentively listening to her troubles. "I wonder what it would be like to be _____."

- happily depressed *or* depressingly happy
- actively inactive *or* inactively active
- anxiously calm *or* calmly anxious
- tensely peaceful *or* peacefully tense
- compulsively unconcerned *or* unconcernedly compulsive
- stupidly intelligent *or* intelligently stupid
- beautifully unattractive *or* unattractively beautiful
- a successive failure *or* a failing success
- humorously sad *or* sadly humorous
- alone in company *or* companionly alone
- assertively withdrawn *or* withdrawing assertively
- lovingly hateful *or* hatefully loving.

The inclusivity approach is essentially oxymoronic in combining apparently opposite emotions and feelings. (Classic oxymorons are the *down escalator* and *jumbo shrimp*.) The implication in both/and is that a person need not be stuck in one or the other of these states. Thinking about being "happily depressed" scrambles the mind of the listener and they are forced into opening up to new possibilities in their lives. Inclusivity has the nature of a second-order change which is outside the system in which they have been stuck. Inclusivity can also be considered to be a reframing, leading the client into thinking about herself and her behavior from a completely different (and even absurd!) perspective. When I have used these oxymorons with my clients they appear to go into a trance state while they work out the puzzle in their minds of who they are and what they do. We therapists are in the business of guiding clients into discovering new ways of taking care of themselves, of thinking outside of the box.

I am certain that your clients will provide you with many opportunities for oxymoronic brain scrambling. I am also certain that you will be able to playfully create serious oxymorons and seriously create playful ones. (A side effect of inclusivity work is that it is fun!)

3. Reframing

Reframing (Watzlawick, Weakland, & Fisch, 1974) is a second-order change process which is external or meta to the main concern of the client. Second-order changes are surprising, paradoxical, strange, and different than first-order changes which are doing more of the same. (If it does not or has not worked, do something different!) Context reframing involves altering the framework or context within which the concern occurs. For example, some marital difficulties have been resolved by simply getting the couple to change their habitual side of the bed! Content reframing has to do with changing the perspective of the concern, i.e., seeing their behavior from a different angle or interpretation. A "standard" reframe at the beginning of a session is to tell the client how brave or strong he is to actually be there and be interested in facing his difficulties. "I know it really takes a lot of strength to be here." The Gestalt Therapy two-chair procedure can be considered to be reframing, as well as any of the as-if methods. Dissociating and observing oneself in various situations works well. Looking at oneself over your spouse's shoulder is another way. A crystal-ball approach (Erickson, 1954) like having a client observe herself from some time in the future when this particular concern has been resolved, and asking the client to tell you what she did that brought about the change, also works.

I have observed many top therapists do demonstrations at venues like the Ericksonian Congresses. When I analyze what they are doing I find that a main ingredient is invariably reframing, getting the volunteer to think differently about their presenting concern. (You may have noticed that I avoid the word "problem" since problems are harder to work with than concerns or troubles or difficulties. This change in language is, of course, itself a reframe into a more useful language—see Battino, 2011.)

4. Narrative Therapy: Externalization and Exorcism

Narrative therapy was developed by Michael White and David Epston (1990). Their approach is quite rich with many aspects; the one I mostly use is the idea of *externalization*. This is based on their principle of "The person is not the problem, the problem is the problem." Somehow there is a controlling entity of some kind within them that causes them to behave the way that they do. I have yet to have a client who has not accepted this idea since it provides them with an "out" for the behavior they would like to change. This can be illustrated by the following case.

Case Example: The Big D

The client (Bill) had been diagnosed as being depressed. Bill was 35 years old, single, and told me that he had low energy, slept a lot, felt "down" most of the time, and had no "get up and go." He had been this way most of his life, but still managed to hold down a job and have a few friends and sporadic relationships. Bill was tired of living like this and was willing to do most anything to be "okay."

I explained that there was probably somebody or something inside of him that caused him to be depressed, that controlled his life. I asked him to give this "thing" a name, and he came up with the "Big D." Then I asked him if there were some times when he was able to defy Big D, to hold up his hand and say "Stop!" or "I am not going to listen to you now." He thought for a minute and said, "Yes, there have been a few times when I have defied him and ignored him and went on to have a good time." I asked, "What was different about those times? How did you manage to do that?" He replied: "I just felt strong and in control at those times." We explored this a bit more.

I then told Bill that, even though I was not a priest, that what was needed was an exorcism, and that I could help him with that. The strange thing that happened at this point was that Bill agreed that this was what was needed. (Although this keeps surprising me, I have yet to have a client who did not accept the idea of an exorcism to rid himself of the Big D, or whatever had been controlling him.) I said, "Do you have a sense or an idea of what external force or being can banish Big D away forever?" Bill said, "The Holy Spirit." I asked: "Would it be okay now if we had a hypnosis session that incorporated the Holy Spirit and maybe other useful powerful helpers?" Bill agreed.

The hypnosis included an initial relaxation, a trip within Bill's mind to a safe and protected place that was uniquely his, a visit (visitation?) by the Holy Spirit and other spiritual entities who exorcized Big D and sent him off into outer space never to return, an affirmation that whenever Bill needed the Holy Spirit it would be with him and protect him and that Bill would remember when he needed it and as he needed it what went on in this session. The session concluded when I thanked Bill for his attention and trust and returned him to the present time and location. *Follow-up*: About two years later I ran into Bill. We chatted for a while, and he told me was happily and actively living his life.

Here are two more SST cases.

Case Example: Quacking and Weight Control

Dianne consulted with me for weight control. She was in her early sixties, and her husband of many years had died just a few years earlier. Since then she had put on some weight and was feeling uncomfortable with the extra poundage. With weight control clients I spend some time talking about the physiology of weight control (calories do count; decreasing caloric intake and increasing exercise are the best way to move permanently to a lower weight). I also point out that almost everyone I have worked with or otherwise know who has made a permanent change in smoking or over-eating has done so via an internal transformation (much like a religious "conversion"). An innocuous kinesthetic anchor of touching her ear was introduced and practiced to remind Dianne that she no longer needed to over-eat, even though she could enjoy the sight and odor of good foods. Dianne felt that she was beginning to "waddle" like a fat person when she walked. She pounced on the idea of hearing quacking in her head every time she was tempted to over-eat (this, of course, was also rehearsed in our meeting). An abbreviated transcript of the hypnosis portion of the session follows to give you a sense of how hypnosis can be used for weight control. There has been no follow-up (frequently the case in SSTs). However, Dianne left looking determined, relieved, and buoyant.

Hypnosis Session

"Well, Dianne, I generally like to start out with asking people to pay attention to their breathing. Please find some way of being comfortable, knowing that you can move and adjust your position... Yes. And, within your mind now you can just drift off to that camping place you loved. It is morning, and you can smell the bacon cooking. And, there is the sound of water flowing in the nearby stream. There may be a gentle breeze, and the smell of the forest around you. A bird sings somewhere... While you are enjoying being there you may be wondering how this is going to help in changing your lifestyle so that you will be lighter and healthier and more able to do things physically with comfort and ease. In this place and this time you feel the Lord's[1] presence. It is simpler and easier with His help, with His love, with His support. And, you can also most sense, can you not, that with His help, His Presence, that somehow, somehow, somewhere inside you a switch has been flipped. A decision has been made. From this time on you will find a lightness of being.... The un-needed and extra weight that has been weighing you down and has been in the way, simply and easily and naturally slips and slides away... permanently...

"At this time you know, you just know deep inside yourself, you will eat just what your body needs, and do so for the rest of your life. That switch has clicked. Old pathways have been eliminated, and new pathways established. In some fashion, some way, your brain has been re-wired, your physiology has altered and changed and accommodated to the new you who is emerging... Touching and being touched, loving and being loved, laughing with, that smile, bird song in the morning, sunsets and sunrises, the moon in the morning, this moment, this breath, this heartbeat... That inner sense that the switch has been made, that inner conviction that from now on... This breath and the next one. And, you should know, Dianne, that your mind is somewhat like a tape recorder so that whatever has happened in this session, today, that is useful and helpful to you, for you, will be with you as you need it and when you need it. I want to thank you, Dianne, for your trust,

---

1. When I do hypnosis or guided imagery work (see South & Battino, 2005; Battino, 2007), I always follow the lead of the client as to what agent or imagery will work for her. For Dianne this was "The Lord."

your confidence, and your attention. And, when you are ready,
you can just take a deep breath or two, blink your eyes, stretch a
bit, and come back to this room here and now. . . . Yes and Yes and
Yes . . . Thank you."

Case Example: Four Issues

Marilyn first came to see me over 15 years ago as part of my volunteer work with people who have life-challenging diseases. She had been diagnosed with cancer and I used guided imagery among other things to help her through all of the treatments and recovery. Marilyn has been cancer-free for many years now. She has come to consult with me about a variety of issues at long intervals. I saw her about two months ago and the previous session was nine months before that. The issues that she raises are all different and are effectively resolved within one session. The session last year was about having an allergy which was significantly affecting her life since it had to do with house mold. I used the NLP "fast-allergy" cure (http://www.shcredo.com/nlp-interventions/fast-allergy-cure) and she has been free of allergic reactions since then. In the particular session to be detailed here we worked on four issues:

Issue 1: Pushing Out Teeth

The solution here was a reframing and appeared to be the sentence, "I'm safer than I feel." Marilyn was to say this to herself before going to sleep (she was doing the pushing out while she slept). It was also suggested that she say to herself that she can use her tongue for what she wants and needs to say (and not push out her teeth!). A light went on in her eyes, and she knew that this was all she needed (and not dental contraptions).

Issue 2: Stepson is Getting Divorced and Has Returned to Live with Them

There was, of course, some disruption in household routines. Also, 35-year-old George is a big and physically powerful person.

He is not aware that his presence and voice can be threatening. George works in an environment with other men that can be dangerous. So, he can be loud and boisterous. It was suggested to Marilyn that she have a calm, quiet, adult-to-adult talk with George. She was to tell him that she loved him, cared for him, and wanted to be closer. Marilyn was also to tell him in this quiet way that he just did not know that some of his reactions and behaviors actually triggered old bad memories in her. This made a lot of sense to Marilyn and she felt that she could do this.

Issue 3: 19 year-old Daughter Elena

There were actually two issues here: (1) Elena's boyfriend was older, out of work, and a "loser"; and (2) Elena has almost finished college and appears to not be interested in getting her degree. I suggested to Marilyn regarding #1 that she paradoxically praise the "loser" boyfriend for various aspects of his lifestyle and his free behavior and independence. Elena is a bright person and the paradox was designed to get her to observe and think on her own (rather than have her mother tell her what a good-for-nothing he was). Marilyn never managed to go to college and get the degree she wanted due to major difficulties in her life. So, with #2 I suggested that Marilyn at suitable occasions talk quietly with Elena with nostalgia about how she never managed to achieve her dreams, and how that still bothers her. Marilyn felt that talking about herself would have more effect than giving parental advice.

Issue 4: Husband Harry Not Setting Limits for His Son

Marilyn was to share quietly with Harry her concerns that he can actually better help his son and daughter (from his first marriage) by, in addition to unconditionally loving them, setting the limits that parents need to set to protect them. This was particularly the case with George who was now living with them.

Here were four new concerns that were resolved to Marilyn's satisfaction (she now knew what to do) in a single session. I am sure that she will have something new in a year or so. In issues 2, 3, and 4 Marilyn was "injected" into her home situation as a *change agent*.

That is, by changing *her* behaviors she will be able to influence and change the behaviors of those around her.

Sequential Single Session Therapy (SSST)

The previous case study (Marilyn) is an example of *sequential single session therapy* (*SSST*), a term to be added to the literature. In my private practice it has not been unusual for clients to come back after a period of years for a "tune-up" or presenting a new and different concern. We meet for one session and I may or may not see them again for several years. The interval is occasionally less than one year and is almost always about something new that has shown up in their life. For some therapists (and clients) these return visits may involve several sessions, and may then be called *sequential multiple session therapy (SMST)*!

Some Concluding Comments about "Chatting"

Although I have written above about some of the most frequent things I do in SST, my style has evolved into something I call "chatting." My clients know that I work in a very brief therapy mode. After listening to them describe what troubles them, we generally "chat" and just have a comfortable discussion. I may tell stories that are relevant, and I may share personal things and stories that are also pertinent. Of course, they know that I am a therapist who is going to use his skills and knowledge to help them resolve the concerns they presented. The emphasis, however, is not on doing interventions and exercises and following various approaches. In that isolated room two people spend time together being with each other, and sharing in the wonder of being human and fallible. We may explore new ideas and ways of thinking about what is going on in their life. These are more in the way of experiments than prescriptions. This person-to-person interaction has overtones of the placebo effect in the sense that it is my expectation that spending quality time together, being with each other, and sharing the commonality of our humanity will allow them to discover new and useful and realistic ways of being. There is something magical, even miraculous, about the kind of intimacy that chatting brings about. Most chatting sessions end with some brief hypnosis to consolidate and extend what has occurred before. I suspect that this way of functioning is not for all therapists—it appears to work for me and my clients.

References

Andreas, S. (2012) *Transforming negative self-talk: Practical effective exercises.* New York: Norton.

Appelbaum, S.A. (1975) Parkinson's Law in psychotherapy. *International Journal of Psychoanalytic Psychotherapy, 4,* 426–436.

Battino, R. (2006). *Expectation: The very brief therapy book.* Bethel, CT: Crown House Publishing.

Battino, R. (2007) *Guided imagery: Psychotherapy and healing through the mind-body connection.* Bethel, CT: Crown House Publishing.

Battino, R. (2011) *Healing language: A guide for physicians, dentists, nurses, psychologists, social workers, and counselors.* www.Lulu.com.

Berg, I.K., & Dolan, Y.D. (2001) *Tales of solutions: A collection of hope-inspiring stories.* New York: Norton.

de Shazer, S. (1982) *Patterns of brief family therapy.* New York: Guilford Press.

Erickson, M.H. (1954) Pseudo-orientation in time as a hypnotic procedure. *Journal of Clinical and Experimental Hypnosis, 6,* 183–207.

Fisch, R., Weakland, J.H., & Segal, L. (1982) *The tactics of change: Doing therapy briefly.* San Francisco: Jossey-Bass.

Kirsch, I. (1985). Response expectancy as a determinant of experience and behavior. *American Psychologist, 40,* 1189–1202.

Kirsch, I. (1990). *How expectancies shape experience.* Washington, DC: APA Books.

Kirsch, I. (1994). Clinical hypnosis as a nondeceptive placebo. *American Journal of Clinical Hypnosis, 37,* 95–106.

Kirsch, I. (2010). *The emperor's new drugs: Exploding the antidepressant myth.* New York: Basic Books.

Kuehn, J.L. (1965) Encounter at Leyden: Gustav Mahler consults Sigmund Freud. *Psychoanalytic Review, 52,* 345–364.

Miller, S.D., & Berg, I.K. (1995) *The miracle method.* New York: Norton.

O'Hanlon, B. (2003). *A guide to inclusive therapy: 26 methods of respectful, resistance-dissolving therapy.* New York: Norton.

South, T.L., & Battino, R. (2005) *Ericksonian approaches: A comprehensive manual* (2nd ed.). Bethel, CT: Crown House Publishing.

Talmon, M. (1990). *Single session therapy: Maximizing the effect of the first (and often only) therapeutic encounter.* San Francisco: Jossey-Bass.

Watzlawick, P., Weakland, J.H., & Fisch, R. (1974) *Change: Principles of problem formation and problem resolution.* New York: Norton.

White, M., & Epston, D. (1990). *Narrative means to therapeutic ends.* New York: Norton.

Chapter Twenty-Two

Quickies:
Single Session Sex Therapy

Douglas Flemons and Shelley Green

As brief therapists, we are committed to working as efficiently as possible (Watzlawick, Weakland, & Fisch, 1974), facilitating change in client conundrums in a way that underscores clients' resources, expertise, and capacity for transformation. Although we don't restrict our practice to single session appointments (we are comfortable with therapy unfolding over multiple visits if it makes sense to us and is experienced by the clients as helpful), we are attuned to the importance of expectancy in potentiating and orienting therapeutic change (Kirsch, 1999). Thus, we approach each session with clients as a singular opportunity for initiating a significant shift in their experience.

We are known for our application of brief therapy ideas and methods to individuals and couples with sexual concerns (Flemons & Green, 2007, 2013), so other clinicians will sometimes send (or more often accompany) their clients to us for one-session sex therapy consultations. This chapter describes one such case. It illustrates how we think about and practice therapy (particularly our single session work), how we make sense of sexual experience, and how we involve ourselves in resolving clients' sexual difficulties.

Therapeutic Principles and Practicalities

We recognize that minds are embodied (Lakoff & Johnson, 1999) and bodies are mindful (Varela, 1979), and, following Bateson (2000,

2002), we consider mind a quintessentially communicational phenomenon that is best understood systemically, in terms of circular patterns of relationship within and between individuals. As therapists, and particularly as sex therapists, we act so as to preserve and protect the integrity and change-ability of minds and bodies, and so we are always taking into consideration and exercising curiosity about the challenges and possibilities inherent in relationships—relationships within and between bodies and minds, between the individuals in a couple or family, between the clients and their complaint, and between the clients and us.

Practically speaking, this means that when clients come to us with a worry or concern about some problematic part of their personal or interpersonal experience, we accord respect to and curiosity about both the person(s) and the problem itself. Clients may think of the problem as an isolable entity, as something that, with our help, could perhaps be better controlled or even eradicated from their experience. But we assume that problems are composed of and contribute to mindful networks of relationship. Such patterns don't obey the same laws as entities. It is possible to toss a problematic thing—a broken lamp, an empty bottle—into the trash or recycling bin and be done with it, but if you try to eradicate a problematic relationship—with a spouse, with a substance to which you're addicted, with a sexual difficulty—you risk rendering the relationship more complex and the problem more entrenched. You can't throw the problem away, but you *can* alter the patterns of relationship that constitute and contextualize it. This realization, and the relational ideas underpinning it, inform and infuse the therapeutic principles that guide our single session work and the therapeutic techniques that characterize it.

Our orientation to change respects the communicational properties and relational integrity of bodies and minds. You can't do sex therapy without having a realistic understanding of how bodies work, how desire and arousal work, how orgasm works. We go in search of our clients' intra- and interpersonal resources, rather than their deficits, and we invite resolutions to problems via connections, rather than negations (Flemons, 1991, 2002; Flemons & Green, 2007). We are always curious to explore how a resourceful pattern in one area of a couple's mind-body experience could be relevant and helpfully transported to a problematic area. Have they already found some success in dealing with the problem? If so, what were they doing at the time? Have they solved analogous problems? How so? What skills, abilities, talents do the clients have? When and how do they access these? What essential element in these resources could be helpful in responding differently to the problem?

We also listen for how our clients' well-intentioned efforts to resolve their problem may have been unintentionally contributing to its maintenance or even exacerbating it (Watzlawick, et al., 1974). This can happen when the focus is on eliminating or controlling the problem, so we keep an ear open for whether this is the case, and we explore possibilities for an alternative orientation.

This search for and grasp of the complexity of clients' struggles helps us to develop our empathic understanding. If we can recognize clients' challenges and opportunities, and if we can communicate this understanding to the clients, they will be better equipped to decide whether they can trust the connection with us enough to be safely vulnerable. You have to feel safe if you're going to divulge intimate sexual concerns to a stranger and risk asking for help in changing them. We suspect that the relative anonymity that accompanies the "one-night-stand" aspect of a single session appointment allows some clients to feel more comfortable speaking frankly about their sexual relationship; however, others are tentative about opening up when they "really don't know us that well." Empathy is particularly important when working with those who are cautious or shy.

Recognizing that meaning is dependent on context and that problems are held in place by assumptions held about them, we invite our clients to make sense of their problem in a way that allows them and us to orient to it differently. We define it as a pattern that is mutable, which helps create an expectancy for some kind of therapeutic movement. Not only do we assume that the problem can shift in some meaningful way, but we are open to discovering that it has already started changing or that it can begin changing now or soon. Such an attitude or expectancy lies at the heart of all reframing—in keeping with a change in how the problem is understood, the couple can find themselves responding to their situation and each other with a shift in thoughts, emotions, and/or behaviors.

When it comes to sex, at least part of any change will be nonvolitional in nature. Desire, arousal, and orgasm can't be consciously controlled and thus don't respond well to willful efforts to change them. We normalize dilemmas and desires and pleasures and anxieties, as this can help clients relax their ineffective efforts to negate or to *other* whatever they hate or fear, and we invite non-volitional shifts in attitude, effort, response, belief, or anticipation.

Although we teach in the same university family therapy program, team up at times on workshop presentations, and co-direct a private practice, we don't regularly get a chance to see clients together. We look forward, then, to requests for one-session joint consultations, particularly sex therapy cases, as they offer us an opportunity to think and improvise together, combining our perspectives to see and offer more than we might, were we working individually.

We don't charge any more for Quickies consultations involving both of us than for therapy sessions with just one of us. If we were solely dependent on our income from private practice, then such an approach probably wouldn't be economically viable, but our private practice is a secondary part of our professional lives, and we enjoy the opportunity to collaborate, so our clients get the benefit of two heads for the cost of one. (In fact, we saw the case discussed here in our university's family therapy training clinic, the Brief Therapy Institute, so we collected no fee.)

Referrals come primarily from other therapists, who often, but not always, accompany their clients to the session. The clients know coming in that we will be meeting with them just once—we are clear that we will not take over the therapy from the referring clinician—and that the time involvement will be 1½ to 2 hours. We like the pun of referring to our one-session sex consultations as a "Quickie," but we generally keep this play on words to ourselves (and to the readers of our work). Before arriving, the clients have been told by their therapists that we have the necessary expertise and experience to perhaps be helpful with their sexual difficulty in the course of a one-shot consultation.

When clients aren't brought in or sent by another clinician for a consultation but, instead, contact us on their own for therapy, they often ask how many sessions they should anticipate attending. We tell them that as brief therapists, we are committed to seeing them for the fewest number of appointments necessary. We offer the possibility that they may not need to come more than once, but add that if they do wish to return, we will welcome them back (should they and we believe that it would be helpful to do so). This way, we orient them to the possibility of attending a single session *and* protect them from being anxiously concerned before and during that first appointment that they might need more time. We aim for them to feel comfortably expectant that significant change is within easy reach.

Case Study

We would like to tell you about a Quickies consultation that was initiated by a therapist, Lauryn, a few months into her working with a couple in their forties, whom we'll call Ed and Michelle. The three of them had been addressing a variety of complaints, and the couple had made significant headway; however, Michelle had recently voiced the concern that the core of their problems had a sexual origin that needed to be addressed if they were to save the marriage. Lauryn responded by telling the couple about us, and with their encouragement, she contacted us for an appointment. The resulting video-recorded session, which was attended by Ed, Michelle, and Lauryn, lasted close to two hours.

Inspired by de Shazer (de Shazer & Dolan, 2007), we typically inquire at the beginning of our consultations about whether the clients have recently initiated or noticed any changes in their relationship or their problem. If they have, we explore the implication that such a head start can expedite our work together. In response to our posing such a question, we learned straight away that Ed and Michelle worked together in a small business they jointly owned; however, after 5 years of marriage (Ed's first, Michelle's second) and much contentious fighting, Ed had recently moved out of their house and stopped drinking. They both asserted their deep love for each other, despite the fighting and Michelle's experiencing Ed as abusive.

> ED: I started AA [Alcoholics Anonymous] four weeks ago, thinking there were some issues there...and I go every day. I come from a family of alcoholics...I never believed I was, but now I've started that path.
>
> DOUGLAS: That's a huge change. What other changes have you made since [starting therapy with Lauryn]?

If you think of a marriage (or any system) as a complex pattern of interactions, then you will assume that a positive alteration in one part of the pattern will possibly be occasioned by an analogous shift somewhere else—ramifying the significance and helpfulness of the change.

> MICHELLE: We communicate now.
>
> ED: Yeah, we talk a lot better now; our communication has opened a lot...

MICHELLE: But it's awful hard, given some of the stuff that's being said, to not let the emotions come in and get hurt.

SHELLEY: Yeah, because you do love him.

Shelley's comment acknowledged that Michelle's pain was heightened by the depth of her feelings for her husband.

DOUGLAS: Who made the decision to live separately?

ED: I did.

MICHELLE: Oh yeah, he did. It got real bad.

DOUGLAS: Is it working?

ED: Yeah, in a sense, it is.

MICHELLE: He says it is; in my eyes it isn't.

We look for resources everywhere, while simultaneously acknowledging the severity of our clients' concerns. If Ed made the decision to live separately, then we could have acknowledged his willingness to take responsibility for creating a context for safety. If Michelle had made the decision, we would have been able to remark on her willingness to take a stand to protect herself. Throughout the session, in interchanges not always included below, we managed on several occasions to do both—to discover instances where Ed was initiating efforts to protect Michelle and where Michelle was "putting her foot down" to protect herself. But first we needed to know the nature of the danger. From what was Michelle needing to protect herself? Safety is a foundation for everything we do.

SHELLEY: You said "it got real bad." Was there physical violence?

MICHELLE: Oh no. He would never do that. But he would yell at me, just scream and holler at me.

Ed's commitment not to hit could be construed as a strength, as could Michelle's firm trust that she was physically safe. With that reassurance, we felt comfortable proceeding to explore other possibilities for trust.

SHELLEY: [Ed] has a mindset right now not to drink, and to be committed to that. Do you have faith in that, and believe him?

MICHELLE: Yes I do.
SHELLEY: He sets his mind to something and that's what
he's going to do. So you have trust in that?
MICHELLE: Oh yes. I see a lot of changes in him.

Shelley highlighted that Michelle trusted Ed's ability to commit to change and to follow through on it. We saw this as a hopeful sign that they would be able to follow through on any changes to their sexual relationship that might arise from our consult.

The couple proceeded to describe painful conversations they'd been having about past betrayals and disappointments. Rather than get caught up in the details of the problems and the distress they had caused, Shelley commented on the couple's ability to forthrightly address the hurts, and she sought to establish whether this was also a recent development.

SHELLEY: You guys have had some brutally honest conversations. Is that new and different?
MICHELLE: We sure have!
ED: Yeah, and that's one of the good things, one of the
good positive changes I see.

As much as we inquire about, attend to, and underscore strengths and positive changes, our relational approach dictates that we never take up residence on only one side of an important distinction (Flemons, 1991). We honor what's been working and what's better and hopeful, *and* we pay close attention to and acknowledge what's been causing pain and distress. During a discussion of the couple's many arguments, Michelle gave additional examples of lingering anger and resentment. Shelley was able to legitimize her concerns without getting caught up in the details:

SHELLEY: Well, it sounds like there is…both hostility and
lack of forgiveness in some cases, *and then* there is some
sort of love and deep caring that brought you guys here.
MICHELLE: Oh, yeah! I mean, if we didn't care, we
wouldn't be trying to do this.
ED: Absolutely.

About 25 minutes into our consultation, we asked the couple what they'd like to get out of their session with us. We don't always wait so long to pose this essential orienting question, but, like Eve Lipchik (1994), we assiduously avoid the *rush* to be brief, lest it slow us down and obscure what could turn out to be vital contextualizing information about the clients and their struggles. Allergic to recipe-focused therapy, we don't impose a rigid structure on our sessions. For us, there's no one place to start and no particular order of queries to pose when letting our curiosity roam. Instead, we're organized by two commitments. First, we want to flesh out a relational understanding of how the problem *makes sense*—how it fits within the complex of intra- and interpersonal relationships of which it is a part and that contribute to its meaning. And second, we want to invite one or more small changes in the fabric of one or more of those relationships. The session ends once we've offered a comprehensive empathic grasp of the complexities the clients are facing, followed by some imagined possibilities that sketch out alternatives to trying to constrain or negate the problem.

> DOUGLAS: How were you thinking that we could be helpful? I don't know [turning to Ed], was it your idea that we would meet with you?
>
> MICHELLE: It was my idea to meet with you! I was done, and she [Lauryn, the therapist] asked me, "Are you going to divorce [me], too?" [laughter] I was just done with the marriage and the therapy. And I said, "No one's getting it." 'Cause we were talking about the kids, we were talking about all the little things.... [but] we haven't been talking about the major thing.
>
> SHELLEY: What is the big thing that we need to talk about?
>
> MICHELLE: The major thing is, well, he drank a lot, and when he drinks, he has this thing about strip clubs.... He's told me, off and on, that he's not sexually attracted to me.
>
> DOUGLAS: So this is the major thing for you that had you thinking it would be good for you to come in to us to talk about?
>
> MICHELLE: Yes. Because a lot of things he does, it's like he *needs* to see strippers, he *needs* to go on porn sites.... We'd be in bed together and be all lovey-dovey, and he told me that "something's wrong, you know, it's just not working" [i.e., he couldn't maintain an erection]. And then I find out later, he gets up and goes

and takes a shower and he's jerking off. Well, I'm sorry, that bothers me. That hurts me, because he can't be with me, he can only be with himself.

If we were traditional sex therapists, and if we had agreed to be organized by Michelle's description of the problem, then we probably would have focused the session on issues of sex addiction and erectile dysfunction. But as brief, relationally focused therapists, we endorse Haley's (1991) advice to define the problem interactively, in a way that leaves open the possibility for change.

> SHELLEY: So is that a betrayal for you?
> MICHELLE: It's just, it was a lie. Because he told me there was something the matter with him and there really wasn't. So I'm sitting there saying, I mean, I have a libido, you know? So I pushed my feelings off to the side, and I love him for who he is, so if we can't do that [have intercourse], I'll accept that...
> SHELLEY: But [now] knowing that physically... [it is possible for him to] be sexual, then you want it to be with you.
> MICHELLE: Yeah, that was a kick in my face.
> DOUGLAS: So, then, if you could be sexual *together*...
> ED: That would be fantastic.
> SHELLEY: [turning to Ed] For you, too?
> ED: Absolutely.

The goal of the session was now defined, for us, for the clients' therapist, and for the clients themselves, as finding the means for the couple to "be sexual together." We pursued that direction by finding out more about what had drawn Ed to strip clubs. He told us that he started visiting them over 20 years earlier, at a time when he was struggling to cope with several devastating losses. Ed puzzled about the fact that he had always found the strip-club environment "soothing." Shelley offered a way of making sense of it.

> SHELLEY: You weren't interacting physically in the strip clubs...right? Just observing?
> ED: No, well, sometimes I would get a lap dance, but mostly...
> SHELLEY: In a strip club, there were no demands on you...It's sort of a passive activity. You can watch,

be aroused, enjoy; there was no one really expecting anything from you. So there was nothing directed at you in terms of your performance.

ED: Right, nothing was expected of me.

SHELLEY: So I can see how that would be soothing and arousing.

DOUGLAS: Talk about stuff put on your lap. You'd been handed the death of [three of the most important people in your life], and you're [just] 18....

Douglas referred back to Ed's getting lap dances as a means of empathically elaborating on the idea that for Ed, arousal and emotional safety went hand in hand.

MICHELLE: See, that was the thing I told him, I mean, I'm not a counselor or anything, but it seems like he was looking for something, and that's what he found.

SHELLEY: That was his comfort....

DOUGLAS: So what triggers your need for comfort?

ED: My need for comfort?

SHELLEY: When do you need to soothe yourself?

ED: Interesting question...Ummmm, actually *after* we have sex. *After* we have sex! Not when we're having sex. And I don't understand it.

SHELLEY: So that's when you would usually go check out a porn site?

ED: Right, afterwards.

We strive to normalize our clients' experiences, to make sense of them in non-pathologizing, non-othering ways. Behaviors are easier to change when you're not consumed with or defending yourself against recriminations from yourself or significant others. When we offer such understandings, we credit the clients themselves with having inspired them, and we offer them tentatively. We don't want to impose our views on clients, as we're committed to the therapy being a collaboration.

Michelle speculated further about the timing and meaning of Ed's attraction to porn and strip clubs, to which Douglas responded.

DOUGLAS: So, if Michelle's got her finger on something, the need for soothing happens after sex with someone you love, and it happens when you're afraid that if you get too close you could lose the whole thing. Is that...[accurate]?

ED: Yeah...

SHELLEY: And I'm thinking, after sex with someone you love, you're probably at your most vulnerable moment...potentially. Maybe not...

ED: Yeah...

Ed was a little hesitant in affirming Shelley's idea, so we continued exploring it. We didn't want to move on without being sure that it fit for him. Douglas mentioned as a possible example the erection problems Michelle had alluded to earlier.

DOUGLAS: [I imagine that] if you're making love and you're finding...that you're not able to perform, that [would have to be] a very vulnerable place to be.

ED: Right...because she would try to stimulate me, and it wasn't working. I was starting to think, and like [Michelle] said, I made her believe there was something physically wrong. I, physically, myself, was starting to think there *was* something wrong...

If, like us, you consider bodies to be mindful, then when you hear that a body part like a penis is reluctant to participate wholeheartedly in an enterprise like sex, then your first thought won't be, "What's wrong with the penis?" Sex and analogous activities—creative brainstorming, improvisational theater or music, playing a team sport—necessitate integrated engagement and interactive communication and cooperation. So, instead of going in search of a deficiency, you'll look for how the body part's reluctance *makes sense*, given the demands it is facing from other parts within the whole. Arousal and pleasure and orgasm are automatic body responses that can't be imposed or dictated by a person's or partner's conscious mind. Bodies are much too systemically wise to permit such attempted interference.

DOUGLAS: It also would make sense to me, if you're with Michelle, and [your erection's] not happening, and you're starting to worry about that, if there's something wrong, [then a] great way to reassure yourself [would be] to jack off in the shower, or go to a strip club, to reassure yourself, "I guess I am OK."

ED: Good, right. Because I was doing that for a while to make sure it was working, because I thought, wait a minute, why is it not happening here? And she got upset about it one night, and said, "What's wrong?" And I'm like, "I don't know what's wrong!"

SHELLEY: But then would that be reassuring to you, when you'd go to porn site or strip club?

ED: Yeah,

SHELLEY: So then it's like, "Whew! At least we know that's working."

ED: Yeah.

This reframe of Ed's attraction to porn and strip clubs cast Ed in a respectful light. Instead of a sex addict in search of alienated stimulation, he became a vulnerable man in anxious need of reassurance about his sexuality. He had been trying unsuccessfully to solve this problem by withdrawing into non-demand opportunities to feel sexually successful. His attempts to resolve his sexual anxiety and thus to "soothe himself" enough to be sexual with Michelle unintentionally alienated her. A therapeutic alternative to turning away from Michelle was to turn toward her, to make intimacy possible. We noted that Ed was attracted to strong, assertive women, but we distinguished between the pseudo strength of a stripper and the real strength of Michelle—a strength that offered both challenges and possibilities.

DOUGLAS: [to Michelle] I was just thinking about the frightening part [for Ed] of your being the strong woman that you can be.... [to Ed] It's very arousing [when] a stripper [is] making eye contact and being overtly sexual towards you. That's a very assertive thing [for her] to do. But when Michelle is being strong, that places demands on you; the difference is the stripper doesn't place demands.

SHELLEY: The stripper doesn't come home with you and need you emotionally.

Both Ed and Michelle felt betrayed by the other, and each talked about wanting to forgive the other in order to move forward. We explored the idea with them, but we tied the desire and effort back to the theme of vulnerability, remarking on the benefits of not letting go of resentment too soon and normalizing the conflict that had plagued their relationship.

> DOUGLAS: Forgiving is…a very vulnerable thing to do. 'Cause as long as you can hold resentment, it's okay to have a wall you can retreat behind.
>
> SHELLEY: And the [person you resent] can't hurt you. [You can feel safe behind] a wall of "maybe she's not the right one for me."
>
> DOUGLAS: Ed, if you were to, I don't know if you have yet, but if you were to fully forgive Michelle, [then] at that point, you're vulnerable again, because you can't retreat behind a wall of resentment. It sure seems to me that you're experimenting with some incredibly important ways to be safe: [You're reaching out] without alcohol to protect you, without resentment to protect you, without other relationships to protect you. It means you're raw.
>
> ED: I am…
>
> SHELLEY: So right now you're in a place of kind of letting all that go, and questioning every bit of it. And you don't know what it's gonna look like on the other side yet.
>
> ED: Right.
>
> SHELLEY: It's kind of a scary place to be, to be willing to put yourself in this place. Scary not to know where you're headed. It's kind of amazing that you're willing to do this.
>
> ED: I'm not completely convinced that we're going to make it through this. I hope we do, but uh, but with my desire for sexuality, we just may not be compatible.

Ed expressed one of many uncertainties that he and Michelle were facing. Shelley bridged from the possibility that they wouldn't make it as a couple to other uncertainties that necessarily followed from Ed's willingness to experiment with making so many changes.

> SHELLEY: But also, you don't really know what your and Michelle's potential is—[you've] never [before]

> put yourself in this place of emotional vulnerability,
> with no anesthesia, no alcohol, all the other ways that
> you...[in the past, went in search of] comfort. You
> don't really know what's gonna be there.

Perhaps one of the primary constraints of offering one-session consultations is that we as therapists don't have the luxury of allowing understandings and shifts in perspective to happen gradually, over the course of multiple appointments. This means for us that when we're seeing people only one time, we tend to be more actively involved in the construction of such changed meanings. One of the primary delights in this highly efficient mode of working is that we are sometimes privileged to witness the therapeutic equivalent of time-lapse photography—a relational transformation in an individual's sexual experience or a couple's sexual relationship that unfurls in the space of one or two hours.

We see it as our responsibility to offer anticipation for change in an open, yet compelling way. Therapeutic opportunities are easier for clients to embrace if expectancy for them to occur is heightened.

> DOUGLAS: It seems to me that you're on the verge of dis-
> covering the strength of vulnerability, of being with
> an assertive woman, and what it means to lose your-
> self in her eyes. You're experimenting with that, in a
> sense for the first time. And that's, that's huge.
> SHELLEY: That's huge, and I think that, we talked a lot
> about the role of pornography, and it sounded to me
> like you were thinking somehow if you were going
> down to a porn site and jacking off, before, during, or
> after sex—or instead of having sex—with Michelle,
> that that said something about whether you guys
> were compatible. And the more I've listened to what
> you've said, the more I think [that your attraction to
> porn and strip clubs] tells us a lot about what's been
> soothing and comforting to you in the past, and that
> makes a lot of sense. But I think right now, you guys
> are really experimenting with...moving way beyond
> stuff that's worked for you in the past. It doesn't tell
> us about what's going on between you now; it seems
> like it just says a lot about what's worked for you in

the past. But what I'm hearing is you don't want the same things anymore.

Douglas reinforced Shelley's prediction by speculating about possible next steps.

DOUGLAS: My guess is that [new ways of relating] are going to start to get invented. I don't know if it will be [to Michelle] you finding ways [to offer soothing to Ed] or you [to Ed] finding ways to ask [Michelle] for soothing, ah, some soothing after sex, so that you don't have to go down the hall to the computer.

MICHELLE: If we could sit there and talk and cuddle, he wouldn't have to go down there. I think it is a bad habit.

SHELLEY: It has been comfortable and familiar, whether it worked or not. And we don't know what's going to work now.

DOUGLAS: Cause everything is unfamiliar now.

MICHELLE: Exactly.

SHELLEY: I'm really curious to talk to Lauryn later to find out what you guys have found that works, and where you have taken this. You have taken some amazing risks already, and that's a huge start.

The consultation ended at this point, with Lauryn feeling comfortable and confident that key points from our session could be used as organizing principles for future sessions with Ed and Michelle. If Lauryn hadn't been able to accompany the clients, we would have provided her with an in-depth letter that outlined our relational sense of what had been going on with the couple, where we saw potentials for change, and how, given this understanding, it might be helpful to focus future appointments. Just as we underscore the integrity of our clients, so too we are deeply respectful of therapists and the work they have been doing. We want to be sure that anyone willing to venture in a new direction, whether client or therapist, isn't, as a result of coming to see us, at risk of losing face. We thus don't propose changes that entail the negation of previous efforts but, rather, a *sense-able* reimagining of possibilities.

The couple continued to see Lauryn, so, with their permission, she was able to provide us with follow-up information. Three months after our seeing them, they reported that they weren't arguing nearly as much as before and were having "lots of sex," which Ed defined as "lovemaking." As he put it, "We made love this week.... [It was] more intimate, [with] no derogatory or kinky language. Just more natural—holding each other and telling each other we love each other." At a follow-up a year after that, they, no longer in therapy, were still together and doing well. Michelle was asserting herself and Ed wasn't having to distance from her as a means of handling her strength.

Our relational approach to single session consultations is grounded in an understanding of how relationships change: A small shift in part of a pattern can ramify throughout the rest of it, thereby altering the whole of it. We bring this sensibility into what we listen for, what we ask about, how we respond, and what we suggest. We begin by tuning into relevant relationships—between mind and body, between the couple and the problem, and between the two individuals—and then we invite small shifts in each or any of them. When our Quickies consultations are successful, they re-orient a couple's efforts to solve their problem and alter the relationship between them, such that their future sexual relationship reflects or even enhances the changes initiated during our single session together.

References

Bateson, G. (2000). *Steps to an ecology of mind.* Chicago, IL: University of Chicago Press.

Bateson, G. (2002). *Mind and nature: A necessary unity.* Cresskill, NJ: Hampton Press.

de Shazer, S., & Dolan, Y. (2007). *More than miracles: The state of the art of solution-focused brief therapy.* Binghamton, NY: Haworth Press.

Flemons, D. (1991). *Completing distinctions.* Boston, MA: Shambhala.

Flemons, D. (2002). *Of one mind: The logic of hypnosis, the practice of therapy.* New York: Norton.

Flemons, D., & Green, S. (2007). Just between us: A relational approach to sex therapy. In S. Green & D. Flemons (Eds.), *Quickies: The handbook of brief sex therapy.* New York: Norton.

Flemons, D., & Green, S. (2013). Brief sex therapy. In A. Rambo, C. West, A. Schooley, & T. V. Boyd (Eds.), *Family therapy review: Contrasting contemporary models* (pp. 234–236). New York: Routledge.

Haley, J. (1991). *Problem-solving therapy* (2nd ed.). New York: Harper & Row.

Kirsch, I. (Ed.). (1999). *How expectancies shape experience*. Washington, DC: American Psychological Association.

Lakoff, G., & Johnson, M. (1999). *Philosophy in the flesh: The embodied mind and its challenge to Western thought*. New York: Basic Books.

Lipchik, E. (1994). The rush to be brief. *Family Therapy Networker*, 35–39.

Varela, F. (1979). *Principles of biological autonomy*. New York: Elsevier North Holland.

Watzlawick, P., Weakland, J., & Fisch, R. (1974). *Change: Principles of problem formulation and problem resolution*. New York: Norton.

Chapter Twenty-Three

Horse Sense: Equine Assisted Single Session Consultations

Shelley Green

A relatively new and often-misunderstood clinical approach, equine assisted therapy invites clinicians to temporarily leave their "talk therapy" techniques at the office and emerge into the realm of nature, engaging with large, powerful, yet typically gentle animals who, for a short time, become co-therapists in a clinically rich and unpredictable therapeutic dance. There are multiple and varied approaches to incorporating horses into clinical work; the range of those approaches will be reviewed briefly here.

The particular work described in this chapter is fundamentally grounded in the relational, systemic assumptions that have informed the brief therapy field (Cade & O'Hanlon, 1993; Flemons & Green, 2007; Flemons, 2002; Green, 2013; Watzlawick, Weakland & Fisch, 1974).

1. Our work is intentionally strength-based, non-normative, and non-pathologizing.
2. We seek out our clients' solutions rather than imposing our own, and we attend carefully to how our clients' behaviors make sense in context, assuming there is systemic wisdom in their current actions that we need to understand and respect.

3. Our effort is always to understand and utilize this wisdom rather than to simply offer conventional ideas about relationship health and satisfaction.

4. We strive to honor and punctuate our clients' strengths, to avoid pathologizing interpretations of their behavior, and to create—through our observations of their encounters with the horses—new meanings and understandings that can enhance their relationships.

These clinical assumptions provide a solid theoretical foundation that offers clinical clarity within an experiential model that relies largely on non-verbal communication, spontaneity, careful observation, and creativity in learning to observe and utilize the immediate and powerful interactions between humans and horses to facilitate therapeutic change.

Our equine assisted approach lends itself particularly well to single session consultations, as the clinical work often fast-forwards client understandings of their current situation. A single session with the horses offers clients an embodied experience of awareness and transformation that they may return to in future therapy sessions and also in their day-to-day interactions with each other. This chapter introduces the broad field of equine assisted therapies, describes in detail the model we developed, and offers a case study that illustrates the potential of a single equine assisted clinical session to transform couple dynamics.

History of Horses and Humans

Humans partnering with horses is not new—for thousands of years we have shared a bond with these beautiful and fascinating creatures, using them to carry warriors into battle, to haul burdens, plow fields, drive cattle across the range, and, in more modern days, to earn millions for their owners on the race track and in the show ring. Within the past 30 years, occupational and physical therapists have embraced the physical benefits of horseback riding to create successful therapeutic riding programs for individuals with physical limitations, as well as for children dealing with the effects of autism and developmental delays (Frewin & Gardner, 2005; Masini, 2010). The sheer range of life-enhancing services provided by horses over the centuries is staggering, particularly given that they are prey animals, and thus, naturally inclined to flee all potential predators. Humans have acted as both predators and partners, and have over the centuries perpetrated much harm as we have bent these beautiful creatures to our will and determined the course of their lives. As Hamilton (2011, p. 7) notes, "Because horses function from the premise of a herd identity, they see relationships as partnerships. They struggle to include us in their concept of a herd—a huge leap considering they are the ultimate prey species and we the uber predators." However, oddly enough, horses still find it within themselves to connect with humans, often becoming willing and trusting partners in a wide range of endeavors.

Development of Equine Assisted Psychotherapy

Within the past 20 years, increasing attention has been devoted to exploring the potential of horses to enhance lives not only through physical activity and riding experiences, but also through their unique way of relating to humans. While the range of animal assisted therapies includes clinical work that partners humans with a wide variety of animals (dogs, dolphins, cats, pigs, rabbits, and even elephants) (Chandler, 2012), the basic assumptions of utilizing horses therapeutically are unique, as the animals themselves offer a singularly different relationship with humans. As prey animals, horses do not automatically assume they are safe in the company of humans. Because their survival for thousands of years has depended entirely on their ability to attune to their immediate surroundings and detect danger in time to flee, they are exquisitely sensitive to context. They attend carefully to minute changes in body language—of humans, other horses, or other predators—and they respond with immediacy and honesty.

It has been said that "horses can't lie." Without anthropomorphizing, it remains clear through observing horse-human interaction that horses have a unique capacity to attune themselves quickly to the non-verbal communication of humans, to determine whether the intentions conveyed by that communication allow for a safe environment for the horse, and to respond accordingly and immediately. They read human behavior quickly, and are intuitive and responsive to that behavior. Horses have no ability, as humans do, to edit, misrepresent, or manipulate through communication; this alone alters the context of therapy considerably.

Assumptions of Equine Assisted Models

Many equine assisted programs have been developed for at-risk adolescents, allowing them the opportunity to groom, care for, interact with, and perhaps ride the horses, with the guiding assumption that all of these activities will, in general, be beneficial in building self-esteem, developing responsibility and accountability, and offering much-needed companionship (Chandler, 2012; Frewin & Gardner, 2005). Other programs have more specific clinical aims, utilizing horses in therapeutic settings run by licensed mental health professionals to treat specific issues such as substance abuse, eating disorders, domestic violence, trauma, PTSD, and physical or sexual abuse (Masini, 2010). A number of organizations have emerged, each informed by a slightly different approach or set of assumptions, to train and in some cases certify equine and mental health professionals to conduct this work. These include the Equine Assisted Growth and Learning Association (EAGALA), and the Professional Association for Therapeutic Horsemanship, International (PATH, Intl), among others. Most of these programs offer an atheoretical approach that assumes each licensed mental health professional will bring his or her own clinical expertise and model to the work, while integrating the therapeutic potential of including horses as partners in the sessions.

Theoretical Framework

A brief, relational approach to therapy provides the foundation for our equine assisted model (Green, 2013). Clients are assumed to be the experts on their own lives, and a non-normative, non-pathologizing stance is maintained; thus, we don't assume that clients' "hidden agendas" or pathologies will reveal themselves through their work with the horses. Rather, we believe the session will provide an opportunity for clients to try something new and to experience success in the moment; this experiential process can then offer new meanings for the behaviors that have been troubling to them. Informed by the work of the Mental Research Institute (MRI), we assume that our clients are often stuck in their own well-meaning attempts to resolve problems, and that those attempts may be exacerbating their difficulties (Watzlawick, et al., 1974). Clients often experience, in one session, a transformation of the premises, meanings, and assumptions that have defined their relationship—

transformations we understand as second-order change (Fraser & Solovey, 2007; Watzlawick, et al., 1974).

The goal of our work, then, is to alter the clients' relationship to their problem, rather than to explore underlying causes. Our focus is consistently on relationships, rather than on individual motivations or characteristics; we seek to enhance relational freedom, so that our clients may change or remain stable in coordination, rather than competition, with each other (Flemons, 2002; Flemons & Green, 2007). We assume that clients are doing the best they can, given their circumstances, and that their solution attempts have made sense in some significant way. Understanding "patterns as habits" (Cade & O'Hanlon, 1993), we hope to offer our clients, through a unique and unpredictable interaction with the horses, a way out of those habits into a less constrained and less troubling relationship. Paramount in all of our sessions is our acknowledgment that clients are taking risks just to be present and engaged with the horses and each other, as well as our deep respect for and desire to understand our clients' expertise and strength. We trust that through our observation of their interactions with each other and the horses, we will be able, within the single session, to observe and highlight those risks and strengths in ways that lead to transformed relationships.

Structure of Session

Each session is organized around simple tasks that can easily be revised or even omitted as the session evolves; the point is never the completion of the task—rather, tasks are simply jumping off points for observing client behaviors and interactions. A team, including a mental health professional and a trained equine specialist, conduct all sessions. The therapist's job is to avoid becoming invested in the clients actually completing the task, and to focus on the experiential process, honing observation skills about "how" the clients attempt the task, noticing clients' investment in finishing, or perhaps their desire to connect, or to try, or to give up, or to ask for help. Clients may be asked to observe and describe horses, catch and lead them, name them, paint them with finger paints, walk them through obstacle courses, or gather them in a herd. The possibilities for tasks are endless, and are guided by the collaboration between the clinician and the equine specialist, balancing safety with risk, and offering opportunities for clients to be challenged personally and relationally.

There is often very little talk throughout the completion of a task; the therapy team observes closely, and considers ways the clients' behaviors are making sense given their context and constraints (i.e., their in-the-moment context with the horses, as well as the larger context of their relationship). Observation of the horses' behavior is paramount, as the horses' response to human behaviors often becomes a pivotal component in the clients' experience. We do not interpret equine behavior for our clients; rather, we ask them what sense the behavior makes to them, and they often share compelling stories that are relevant and close to their own experiences. In this way, the experiential potential of equine assisted work is maximized.

As mentioned earlier, all work is un-mounted; there is no attention to horsemanship or to "teaching" clients how best to work with or engage with the horses (EAGALA, 2009). We seek instead to learn from clients how they typically interact with each other, and with themselves when faced with uncertainty, ambiguity, fear, tension, and unusual expectations. All of these are common factors in any equine session; our ability to observe and comment therapeutically on how our clients manage these concerns provides the heart of our clinical work, as it offers the potential for creating relational freedom rather than constraint. We attempt to both make sense of their challenges and frustrations, and to notice and comment on strengths they may not have observed in terms of their unique efforts to resolve these challenges.

Equine assisted work thus offers an alternative context, apart from a content-based discussion of problem behaviors, which may allow clients to experience change and then apply that change back to their current life situations. The following case study will offer an illustration of this model in practice.

Clinical Illustration

As I have specialized in couples therapy and sexuality concerns for the past 20 years, I have been particularly interested in bridging couples work with an equine assisted approach. Given that couples are often entrenched in long-standing, consistent, and often particularly painful interactional patterns that can be difficult to interrupt or transform, altering the therapeutic context can be a welcome change. Moving outside the therapy room and engaging with horses offers an innovative way for couples to experience, process, and understand their relationship dynamics, typically without a focus on the ongoing, familiar discussion of old hurts and resentments.

The case example presented here reflects the work that I developed and refined in collaboration with Valerie Judd, who serves as the equine specialist in all our couples' sessions. In this role, Valerie not only attends to the safety of the horses and people, but also observes the equine behavior closely, adding a different perspective to the clinical observations. An experienced horsewoman and trained equine specialist, she is able to notice subtle but relevant aspects of the horses' behavior that can become an integral part of our clinical interactions. We collaborate continuously throughout each session, comparing our observations and allowing the flow and direction to evolve in ways that maximize the clinical potential of the interactions between horses and humans.

I originally trained with EAGALA, and Valerie is certified as an equine specialist through PATH International. Our work together, however, has emphasized the specific incorporation of the brief, systemic therapy assumptions described above. We have witnessed first-hand the power of grounding an equine assisted approach in a solid theoretical framework that privileges a non-normative, non-pathologizing stance, punctuates clients' existing strengths, and shines a light on the unique ways they may already have found to connect as a couple.

Our work has been enriched by partnering with an innovative clinical practice here in South Florida, Couples on the Brink (couplesonthebrink.com) that specializes in intensive therapy for couples in crisis. Valerie and I developed a consultation model that maximizes the power of our equine assisted approach and tailors it to working with distressed couples. The therapy team at Couples on the Brink (COTB) contracts with couples for 12 hours of intensive, in-office talk therapy, typically allocated in three 4-hour sessions. They also offer follow-up telephone sessions after the intensive work is completed. As a means of adding an experiential component to their intensive therapy, the clinicians at COTB refer these couples to us for an equine session lasting approximately 90 minutes. Most of the couples are unfamiliar with equine assisted therapy, but they have been intrigued and receptive to trying a new approach. The primary therapists are always welcome to join us to observe the session if their time permits. As illustrated below, we send a follow-up therapeutic letter to the couple (White & Epston, 1990), in care of the therapists, to be shared at their next appointment.

The referring therapists do not share specific information with us about the couple's situation prior to our consultation. Upon meeting the couple, I spend 10–15 minutes going over paperwork, getting a signed release of information to communicate with the referring therapists, and hearing from them a very brief overview about their current situation and their work in intensive therapy. Our focus in this brief interview is to find out about any changes that have occurred since they began their intensive sessions, and to understand what hopes they currently have for their relationship. We discuss only minimal content or background about their situation, and then we "take it to the horses."

Case Study: Aaron and Laura

Aaron and Laura were referred to us by COTB. They had been married for 8 years and had no children; both were in their mid-thirties. They were both independently employed in demanding and creative fields, and had devoted the years of their marriage to collaborating on their professional pursuits, traveling, and embracing life. Both were highly educated, articulate, reflective, and passionate. In addition to a powerful emotional and sexual connection, the couple shared intense synergy and creative collaboration, and supported each other as they built their careers. They had also endured hardship; Laura had suffered both severe injury and chronic, debilitating health issues within the previous 3 years, resulting in her needing a great deal of physical care and attention from Aaron. Only in the past few months had she experienced significant health improvements that allowed her to attempt embracing life again with her characteristic enthusiasm and abandon; even so, her health was an ongoing concern for both of them.

They came to COTB as they were currently experiencing ongoing conflict and were in great distress. They couldn't imagine how they could love each other so deeply and be so committed to their relationship, and simultaneously find themselves in such emotional pain. They described Laura as a steamroller, moving over Aaron and demanding that he comply with her wishes, which he generally did but with much resentment. Laura believed he needed to commit more time and energy to her, so she demanded it. He wanted to be with her, but feared that her demands would overwhelm him. They both hoped that through intensive couple therapy, they could reclaim the passion and move beyond the conflict that currently threatened their relationship. We spoke very little regarding the content of their conflict, but went out and introduced them to the horses. While they had each ridden horses recreationally a few times, they had little other experience with horses, and neither of them had experienced equine assisted therapy before; both were intrigued by the prospect.

Immediately as we approached the arena, Aaron and Laura were engaged, curious, and receptive to exploring what these horses might have to offer. We allowed them to simply observe, finding whatever way worked for them to get to know the horses and see what they could learn about them. We did not direct them in terms of how to approach the two mares they would be working with, whether they could or should touch them, or how the horses might respond, as we wanted to learn from the couple about the different ways they would each attempt to get to know our equine partners. We also did not share any information with them about the horses, such as names, histories, or typical behaviors/personality characteristics.

Aaron initially approached a grey mare (who he later decided to call "Sanchez") and noted that the other horse, an Appaloosa mare, seemed to hold back at first and make sure she wanted to engage (she later was christened "Dolittle" by both Aaron and Laura). Laura described being amazed by the horses' "gentle quiet presence," noting that while they are so big they emanate such presence and sense of calm. As we entered the ring, Laura observed the horses but did not approach them; the horses both went immediately to Aaron and stood quite near him, seeming to desire his presence. Dolittle began to nuzzle Aaron and nudge him repeatedly, moving her large head up and down his body, rubbing particularly forcefully against his crotch. Sanchez was more calm and passive in her demands, but nevertheless, stood patiently near Aaron, maintaining a constant gaze upon him and making clear she wanted to be in his presence. Neither horse approached Laura nor indicated that they noticed her.

We made no comment about the horse's intentions or behaviors, but asked Laura simply what she noticed about what was occurring. She said immediately that Dolittle asked for Aaron's attention the way she herself usually does (and which she said that Aaron hates); she said that Sanchez was asking for attention in the way that would work for Aaron—calmly and quietly. She stated that when she requests attention and caring from Aaron in the way that Dolittle was attempting, he gets angry and doesn't want to be with her. However, Aaron quickly corrected her and noted that while he is at times angry at her attempts, he still wants very much to connect with her. This desire for connection came as a surprise to Laura.

We then asked them to catch a horse, take it for a walk, and bring it to a place they wanted it to be. We did not provide any specifics about how they were to do this—we didn't suggest that they do it together or individually, nor did we indicate what they were to use to catch the horse(s), nor what tools or approach might work best. Our goal was to leave as much ambiguity as possible and then attend to how each of them attempted to accomplish the task. As they began, we paid careful attention to their actions, their interactions with each other and the horses, and the horses' behavior throughout.

Laura and Aaron initiated this task independently, in very different ways, with Laura offering Sanchez a beach ball and playfully inviting her to interact as she repeatedly said, "Come on, this will be fun—you will love it!" This invitation to play continued even as Aaron laughingly commented that horses don't play with balls. As her efforts to engage Sanchez continued to be ineffective, she rather abruptly pushed Sanchez, and then apologized, saying, rather emphatically, "I don't want to hurt you but we have a task to accomplish!" Sanchez turned her head and walked away.

During this interaction with Laura and Sanchez, Aaron was calmly retrieving halters from the center of the ring and trying to put them on the horses, while acknowledging repeatedly that he had no idea how to do so. This didn't stop him, and he commented that he was always eager to try new things and figure them out. After 5–10 minutes of trying unsuccessfully to gain cooperation from the horses, he asked Laura several times to come and help him figure out the halter. While she initially resisted, she ultimately complied and they spent much time attempting to put on the halters, always making sure the horses were safe and comfortable and that the halters weren't going to harm them in any way. The horses were calm and compliant throughout this process, never wandering away or disengaging. Following this patient and careful process, they then each separately took a horse for a walk, commenting throughout to each other on how they were able to do so and what that was like for them.

After we observed them walking for a few moments, we stopped them and commented very briefly on a couple things we had noticed; Valerie mentioned Laura's comment to Sanchez about "having a task to accomplish." Laura immediately noted that this is what she does to Aaron—inviting/demanding that the tasks she needs his help with will be fun. We then mentioned her unsuccessful attempts to entice Sanchez with the ball, and she elaborated further, noting that with Aaron, she pushes and cajoles, demanding that he will have fun "working on our household budget." Aaron quietly observed this discussion.

We then commented on their careful attention to keeping the horses safe and comfortable, and their sensitivity to the horses' experience. We also mentioned Aaron's desire to figure things out and his repeated invitations to Laura to help him do so. Laura noted how painful it is for her that his invitations only come when he wants/needs her intellect—not when he wants to "share his heart" with her. He heard this, and he agreed that they can connect intellectually and professionally, but they are missing the heart connection that they both value deeply.

At this point in a typical session, we would most likely have asked the couple to do a bit more elaborate task with the horses; however, this couple had already made significant connections between their interactions with the horses and their typical behaviors with each other. We seemed to have quite a good sense of their frustration, their pain, and their desire for connection. So instead, we then asked them to remove the halters from the horses and to arrange themselves and the horses in a way that would represent where they would like to be as a couple right now. Within 15–20 seconds, Aaron and Laura were standing between the two horses, with their hands outstretched, fingertips lightly touching each horse. Initially, Laura's back was to Aaron, although she was very close to him—almost spooning. However, she almost immediately turned around and faced him, with their noses almost touching and their eyes meeting, while remaining in contact with both horses, which stood quietly, nose to tail. The horses' cooperative response to their efforts to array them was immediate and compelling.

The couple shared a very powerful moment while standing in the midst of the two horses, tears streaming down their faces. After some time of allowing them to experience this connection, we asked them simply what was happening. They said that in that brief moment, they were able to connect in a way that "filled them up" rather than drained them in any way. Aaron described his fear that if he were responsive to Laura's demands to connect with her, that it would take too much time and limit his ability to accomplish his work. What surprised him was how much he in fact felt filled up—not just that he was filling her up—and that the moment was powerful and brief, and would allow him to connect with her and with his life in a significant and positive way. We asked them if they could give a name to the configuration they created, and they said that it represented the "cradle" that they hoped they would be able to return to.

They were both deeply touched by the power of this moment; I took a picture of them in their "cradle" with the horses, and texted it to them while still in the session. They said they would frame it and have it displayed in their home, to bring them back to what they learned about how to embrace their heart connection. They shared that with all they have experienced in life, this had been one of the most meaningful and powerful experiences of all, and that it would stay with them forever.

As mentioned earlier, because we only have a brief time with these couples prior to their return to their intensive therapy sessions, we follow up our equine assisted therapy session with a letter that is sent to the primary therapy team at COTB and read together in the couple's next session. In each of these letters, we describe what we believe to be the pivotal moments from the session, and we offer our observations regarding how their interactions with the horses may be relevant within their relationship. The intent of each letter is to offer a strengths-based, non-pathologizing and, ideally, generative description of the couples' encounter with the horses. The single session, along with the therapeutic letter, often punctuates themes that may have already been developing within the couples' intensive therapy sessions. The single session with the horses allows the couple to move away from talking about their struggles and to experience them in a powerful, embodied way. One of the liberations for me, as an experienced "talk-therapy" professional, is that I can watch our clients "see" and experience, in one session, changes that I might otherwise have discussed with clients for weeks, with little result. Below are excerpts from the therapeutic letter that we sent to Laura and Aaron:

Dear Laura and Aaron,

It was our honor and pleasure to meet with you last week, and to witness the powerful work that you were able to do with the horses. Both of you demonstrated a commitment to consider your actions and your responses to each other within the context of your history, your love, and your challenges, and to find your path to a new way of being together.

We were captivated as the session began and you both began to notice the horses' ways of being and to make sense of their behaviors. Laura, you quickly began to notice parallels between how the horses were inviting Aaron's presence and the ways that you find to ask Aaron to be with you. Your ability to examine your own behavior, and to watch Aaron's reactions to Sanchez and Dolittle's different sorts of invitations, seemed to provide a foundation for the rest of the session. With no defensiveness or emotional protection, you both immersed yourselves in the possibilities for learning and growing in this moment. Laura, we also were struck at that moment by your impression that when you invite Aaron's presence in the way that Dolittle was asking, he tends to become angry and not want to connect. What we heard from him, clearly, was that even in anger or frustration, he still wants very much to connect with you—anger and connection can coexist. We wonder how this understanding will inform you as you find new ways to connect with each other.

As we asked you to catch a horse and take her for a walk, we noticed your unique ways of reaching out. Laura, you offered an invitation to play and a promise of enjoyment and fun, and seemed to become frustrated when that invitation was not accepted. As Valerie observed, you then moved Sanchez while apologizing to her, and reminding her of your shared task. It sounds as though the tasks that you invite Aaron to "love" are not always the activities he wants to "love" with you. Aaron, you enthusiastically embraced the challenge of trying something you had no idea how to do, and then invited Laura to help you several times. We noticed that it was very important to you to know the "right way" to put the halter on; we wonder how your desire to respond to Laura in the "right way" has at times kept you from responding at all. As you and Laura worked together to find a way to halter the horses, we were so touched by your careful attention to the horses' safety and comfort. You wanted to make sure, above all, that you were attuned to their needs. Your tenderness and sensitivity were so apparent to us even as you were in the midst of struggling with invitations that were not received as you had hoped.

Aaron, when you invited Laura to help you figure out this new challenge, we saw that this invitation to her intellect, but not to her heart, has perhaps been standing in the way of the heart-filled connection that you both have been missing. The poetry with which you both turned away from these frustrated invitations and towards each other, turning the horses into a cradle that connected your hearts, astounded us in its brevity and its elegance. Without a doubt, the two of you know exactly how to find a heart-to-heart connection, to grasp it fully and immediately, and to fill each other up in the moment. We trust that you will find many ways to claim that connection and to be filled by it. Thank you both for sharing a piece of your story with us. We would always love to hear from you.

We were fortunate to be able to follow up with the couple's intensive therapy team, and to learn that a year after treatment, they were doing well. While they had had some ongoing and significant challenges with Laura's health concerns—challenges that threatened the peace and connection they had developed—they were able to find ways again to connect and support each other, and to renew the intimacy they had created. A month after a follow-up session with their intensive therapy team, they reported that they were stronger than ever.

Conclusions and Implications

This case represents our commitment to embracing and amplifying the strengths and wisdom our clients bring, and to finding experiential ways to interrupt the "habits" that have prevented them from enjoying the relational freedom they desire. Our clinical assumptions help us focus on the creation of new meaning and interactions, without attention to pathology, causes, or negative intent. Always, we maintain a non-expert stance; we don't impose our views, and we choose to frame, rather than interpret, client interactions. Similarly, we have no desire to educate our clients on how to have a "healthy" relationship—we believe they have their own ideas about this that simply need to be accessed and privileged. This fits well within an equine-assisted model that is not informed by a need to educate clients about how best to interact with horses; in the clients' efforts to find their own way with the horses, they demonstrate for us their relational strengths.

We have found this to be a transformative experiential process, with little discussion of "how things are" but a significant focus on observation and meaning. Interestingly, while the referring therapists do not provide us with specific details about the couples' relationship prior to our session, our impressions of the clients' struggles are always strikingly similar to those of the intensive therapy team, as we learn upon conferring with them after the session. We hope to enhance the overall therapeutic process—but we don't take the place of it; our therapeutic letters offer a way to connect the equine work back with the ongoing intensive therapy, and provide a new perspective. We offer consultations as a way of dealing with stuck cases as well, for other therapists in the community.

Not all of our equine-assisted sessions are single session; we also do ongoing clinical work that includes horses, and we work with a wide range of clients (children and adolescents, couples, families, and groups), struggling with issues such as eating disorders, substance abuse, domestic violence, anxiety, school problems, conflict, and crisis. In all cases, we hold on to our foundational clinical assumptions, while letting go of our desire to "talk about" the context of the struggle and instead, watch it unfold. Sometimes, a single session is all that's needed, and in those cases, we celebrate the ability of our equine co-therapists to invite clients into new ways of interacting and making sense of their struggles.

Making the decision to partner with horses in my clinical work has been exhilarating, challenging, frustrating, and inspiring. I have questioned my sanity many times as I have dealt with the complexities of adding a herd of large, hungry, curious, opinionated, and feisty co-therapists to my practice. Valerie and I have learned to manage safety concerns, calm our own anxieties, pay attention to the horses' behavior, watch, learn, and trust the process. I have learned to let go of my need to "talk" in session and simply observe; Valerie has learned that our human clients don't have to put a halter on the "right" way, and that the horses won't mind, as long as they are treated with respect and kindness. We have both learned how much the horses can show us about how our clients engage, develop relationship, push too hard (and thus encounter a fleeing horse), create trust, initiate cooperation, face and overcome fears, and find new ways to connect with each other in loving and yet complex relationships. Each session is unique, unpredictable, and demanding in its requirement that we observe and utilize what's happening in the moment, rather than hold onto any commitment about what "should" be happening. The horses are often our greatest clinical asset, as they communicate very clearly with the clients about how their behavior is being received. When clients change their attempts in the moment, their equine partners respond with immediacy and grace.

While certainly not every therapist may have access to the unique setting necessary—or the desire—to include horses in their work, we encourage readers to seek out opportunities to collaborate with professionals who do conduct relational, strength-based equine assisted models. In one session, it will add horse sense to your practice, and innovation to your ongoing clinical work.

References

Cade, B., & O'Hanlon, W. (1993). *A brief guide to brief therapy*. New York: Norton.

Chandler, C. (2012). *Animal assisted therapy in counseling* (2nd ed.). New York: Routledge.

Couples on the Brink (2013). www.couplesonthebrink.com

EAGALA. (2009). Fundamentals of EAGALA model practice: Equine assisted psychotherapy certification program. Equine Assisted Growth and Learning Association (www.eagala.org).

Flemons, D. (2002). *Of one mind: The logic of hypnosis, the practice of therapy*. New York: Norton.

Flemons, D., & Green, S. (2007). *Quickies: The handbook of brief sex therapy*. New York: Norton.

Fraser, J. S., & Solovey, A. D. (2007). *Second-order change in psychotherapy: The golden thread that unifies effective treatments*. Washington, DC: APA Books.

Frewin, K., & Gardiner, B. (2005). New age or old sage? A review of equine assisted psychotherapy. *The Australian Journal of Counselling Psychology*, 6, 13–17.

Green, S. (2013). Horses and families: Bringing equine assisted approaches to family therapy. In A. Rambo, T. Boyd, A. Schooley & C. West (Eds.). *Family therapy review: Contrasting contemporary models* (pp. 256–258). New York: Routledge.

Hamilton, A. (2011). *Zen mind, Zen horse: The science and spirituality of working with horses*. N. Adams, MA: Storey Publishing.

Masini, A. (2010). Equine assisted therapy in clinical practice. *Journal of Psychosocial Nursing*, 48(10), pp. 30–3).

PATH Intl. (2013). Professional Association of Therapeutic Horsemanship, International. (www.pathintl.org).

Watzlawick, P., Weakland, J. & Fisch, R. (1974). *Change: Principles of problem formation and problem resolution*. New York: Norton.

White, M., & Epston, D. (1990). *Narrative means to therapeutic ends*. New York: Norton.

Chapter Twenty-Four

Deconstructing Therapy: Case Study of a Single Session Crisis Intervention

Hillary Keeney and Bradford Keeney

We present a case study that exemplifies how single session therapy can be guided by the overarching structure of a three-act dramatic play (Keeney, 2009; Keeney & Keeney, 2013). The beginning act with its communications concerning problems and crisis is bridged to a middle act that enables more choices of understanding and action that, in turn, enables further movement toward a resource-focused final act. Here "act" not only demarcates the interactional plot line of a session, it is a metaphor for the contextual frames constructed through therapeutic interaction, indicating how particular distinctions that arise—any communicated metaphors, actions, reports of behavior or experiences—ought to be regarded and handled (Keeney & Keeney, 2013; Keeney, Keeney, & Chenail, 2013). For example, a family's report of their adolescent son's behavior may be regarded by a therapist as evidence of a mental health disorder and given an ADHD or bipolar diagnosis. Alternatively, that same behavior can be more resourcefully framed as signs that a young man is full of an extraordinary amount of joy and creative life force that he doesn't yet know how to handle. Whereas a mental health diagnosis serves constructing a reality in which a family must learn to treat and medicate their problem son, the latter invites exploration of how a family can together experiment with ways to better foster and support a son's special gift.

We refer to this as the construction of a more "resourceful" frame (Keeney & Ray, 1996), a metaphor for a therapeutic context that highlights and brings forth more of clients' strengths, choices for positive action, and avenues for growth. A shift from "problems" and "solutions" (note that each implies the other, whether intended or not) to a "resource" has the advantage of helping lessen a problematic emphasis, provides a solution to the way solution talk implies "something that is solved," and is more expansive and inclusive than either a problem or solution focus. Once a resourceful frame is built, it initiates the turning of a virtuous circle, the momentum of which is maintained by a continued focus on whatever resourceful metaphors, actions, or communications have uniquely arisen in the session. We find ourselves entering the final act when the session starts to feel alive and more effortlessly sustained inside this more enriching context. To get there, however, every session must move through a middle act that serves as a kind of fulcrum that teeters back and forth between problem maintenance and movement toward change. Change in therapy cannot happen without movement through a transitional middle, the passage or bridge that carries us from a limiting, impoverished beginning to a more resourceful, transformed ending. This doesn't necessarily mark the end of therapy (nor does it necessarily have anything to do with reaching a "solution"). It simply means we experience a session as complete or well-formed, the way we experience the finale of a live performance (Keeney & Keeney, 2013).

As the anatomy of a therapy session is deconstructed to reveal the handling of its primary distinctions and frames, the constructivist nature of therapeutic interaction is revealed. In every session a therapeutic reality is created that either feeds a continued focus on pathology (including the vicious cycle of problem-solution interaction) or delivers more choice, creative possibility, and change (Keeney & Keeney, 2012). The structure of a three-act dramatic play provides a tool for practitioners to discern whether a session has moved in a resourceful direction, recycled the same order of discourse, or further hardened an already impoverished context.

This orientation provides a "single session mindset" which can be applied to any session, independent of whether the therapeutic offering is reified as single session therapy, long-term therapy, multiple single session therapy, or indeterminate-duration therapy. We apply a single session mindset to every session we conduct, whether we are contracted to provide a consultation for a social service agency or clinic (as in the case that follows) or in our private practice. We have no purposeful intention that defines our therapy as requiring completion in a single session, nor are we attached to any idea that more sessions are ever needed. Our sessions may last between 30 and 45 minutes (and we tell our clients that if they ask), though we are unattached to whether they last 10 minutes or 70. A single session mindset is an intervention for the practitioner, intended to help bring forth their best performance. We consider any determinations regarding length or number of sessions made prior to a session as presumptuous. When organized by systemic interaction and participation, it is not possible for a therapist to know anything about how a session or a course of therapy will or ought to unfold until that session begins. Furthermore, any determinations made inside the interaction must be subject to change as clients and practitioners change.

We simply see each session as a whole therapy. Unless the therapy is done, we invite clients to come back for another session. If we see the client again, we approach him as if we are seeing him for the first time with no importance given to whether he will continue, while utilizing any relevant distinctions or momentum from the previous session. If clients ask how many sessions our work requires, which they seldom do, we are more likely to absurdly tease them in order to imply that duration is an unimportant organizing principle. We might say, "It might require either a single session or a lifetime. It depends on how difficult it is to get you ready for your next lifetime." With this way of working we find that most of our clinical work, whether involving individuals, couples, or families in any kind of crisis or complex situation, typically do not last more than 1–3 sessions, even though we give no value to having a low number of sessions. What matters is the single session mindset. Single session therapists in crisis-intervention settings have the advantage of a certain urgency to maximize their efforts in every session to bring forth change. We regard this as a resource rather than a limitation. In fact, we encourage all practitioners to become single session therapists, regardless of their preferred orientation. Whether a therapist intends to conduct one session with a client or many, a single session approach guided by the structure of a three-act performance itself delivers a more resourceful context for the practice of therapy. By attending only to the dramatic plot line of a session and the deconstruction/construction of contextual frames that serve change, practitioners are released from the constraints of any model that dictates how therapeutic interaction can and should unfold. This includes presumptions about how long a session should last or how many sessions will be required for a client to change. With an emphasis on live therapeutic performance, therapists discover their capacity in every session to creatively and improvisationally act in order to bring forth a unique, life-changing session with each and every client they encounter. This immersion into interactivity rather than narrativity, something advocated by the experientially-oriented work of Carl Whitaker (1976), invites liberation from the hindrance of interpretive theory, something that unnecessarily extends the duration of therapeutic performance (see Keeney & Keeney, 2013, for further discussion).

Case Study: The Family Overflowing with Life

This session took place at a university clinic in Louisiana in a systemic family therapy program. The therapist involved was a doctoral student being supervised by Bradford Keeney, who was watching the session behind a one-way mirror. The family had been to the clinic briefly for a handful of sessions a few months prior for help with their son, Jacob, who is 13 years old. This evening the family—father, mother, and teenage older sister—arrived to the clinic without Jacob, explaining that a few days prior they had checked Jacob into Oakville, a local psychiatric facility. The family explained that Jacob had staged a break-in and robbery of their home in an attempt to implicate one of the neighbor kids who had been bullying him. At the recommendation of law enforcement, the parents decided to send Jacob to a psychiatric facility rather than juvenile detention. The family also reported that recently Jacob had been "having a lot of problems," including several times pretending to be sick so that his parents would pull him out of school.

Mapping the progression of the session through the structure of a three-act play, we analyze the minimization of problem discourse and the highlighting of resourceful themes. A more detailed analysis of this session would likely show its movement through several transitional acts. For the sake of brevity, we widen the scope to illustrate that no matter how many acts comprise a single session, a well-formed case will reveal a clear beginning, middle, and end. The session below is shown moving from an impoverished context in which the family is struggling with how to handle the psychiatric treatment of their son, to one that provides more choice for positive action that includes participation of the whole family. Therapy itself becomes rendered a less resourceful contextual frame in favor of the family shifting to their needing something different that mobilizes the parents to take more responsibility for their leadership.

Act One: Psychiatric Treatment

After exchanging greetings, the session begins with both parents explaining to the therapist the events that led to Jacob's hospitalization.

FATHER: It wasn't their [the police's] decision. We are the ones who called Oakville and took him there. They didn't force us, but we didn't know what else to do. And we wanted him to get help. We have been thinking that he probably needs to go back and get reevaluated, to throw all the medicine out and get reevaluated, to see if this time we can get a more accurate diagnosis.

MOTHER: But he was having problems at school. He was showing a lot of anxiety, a lot of paranoia. But now since he's been at Oakville they have cleared him of all of his medicines except for two. Jacob has been diagnosed as bipolar disorder type 1 severe, ADHD, impulse control disorder, and severe anxiety disorder. They said that in group therapy the other day he was fine until some boys sat behind him. They said then his paranoia came back and he kept looking over his shoulder.

FATHER: We've been told a few times by the psychiatrist that he needed individual counseling, and now the counselors at Oakville are reinforcing that. We had come here to this clinic before as a family, but they want Jacob to have individual counseling.

MOTHER: One on one. They say he needs one-on-one counseling. Just specifically for him. And according to the therapist at Oakville, they said that in his case Jacob is not only exhibiting high levels of anxiety and paranoia, but they say Jacob also has a way of manipulating everything to his advantage. She said "for kids that are manipulative" they do something—what's she call it?—a role play or something.

FATHER: Because you can't manipulate that. I don't know. That was over my head. I didn't understand exactly

what she was talking about. I guess I'm not familiar
with what she was talking about. [To the therapist]
Maybe you know what they are talking about since
you're in the biz. Anyway, that's where we are.

MOTHER: There's a lot we don't understand right now.

In terms of the plot line of this session, Act One begins with a report from the parents on the crisis of Jacob's hospitalization, his recent problems, psychiatric diagnoses, and history of treatment and
medication. On the one hand, the family accepts the advice offered by
the psychiatrists that Jacob has multiple mental health disorders that
require medication and individual counseling. On the other hand,
they are uncertain about their chosen course of action, express a lack
of understanding of the psychiatrists' recommendations, and have
come to the clinic seeking additional professional guidance—much
like a second opinion. Though the family may not be formally aware
of the theoretical differences between psychiatry and systemic family
therapy, their previous experience at this clinic included an expressed
emphasis by the therapist on working with all family members at
once and the absence of mental health diagnosis and medication.

As a systemically-oriented clinic, we never offer mental health
diagnoses, prescribe medication, or recommend individual therapy.
It's important to note, however, that we regard the specific nature of
any problem diagnosis as less relevant than discerning how it keeps
a family caught inside the same vicious cycle of problems and attempted solutions. It matters less whether a problem is understood
to be caused by bad brain chemistry, cultural oppression, a hoodoo
spell, or past trauma, than how a therapist acts in order to interrupt the vicious cycle of problem discourse that keeps a session and
a family stuck (Keeney & Keeney, 2013). In other words, whether
or not a client "really has" a psychiatric disorder—including ADD,
bipolar and anxiety disorder—is less relevant to change-oriented
therapy than the way communication about pathological nomen-
clature organizes social interaction. Similarly, if a diagnostic manual
for happiness and wellbeing were created as a counter-manual to today's pathological taxonomy, the possible diagnoses of ASO (attention sufficient order), unipolar, and cool-as-a-cucumber syndrome,
would be less a concern in working with clients than the way they
use these metaphors to participate in everyday interaction.

In addition, therapists often assume that more time spent gather-
ing information, history, and commentary on the presenting crisis

or problem means more is being accomplished, as if it is critically important to "know what is *really* happening," versus discerning how such talk plays a part—if it does—in the everyday performance of clients' lives. When analyzed through the structure of a three-act performance it is more readily revealed how this kind of investigation can keep a session from moving past the beginning act. From a constructivist perspective, there is no such thing as "discovery" in therapy, only continuous invention and reinvention through live interaction (Keeney & Keeney, 2012). In this particular session, the family is already operating inside the impoverished frame of psychiatric diagnosis and treatment. More time spent feeding this same order of discourse simply keeps the session and the family from moving anywhere different. For a further discussion of how to avoid the trap of pathological frames, see Keeney and Keeney (2013).

At this point, the therapist asks Catie, the sister, if she has anything she'd like to say. Catie states: "If God ever gave me a choice for Jacob to keep his problem or for me take it, I would totally take his problem so he could be more normal and wouldn't have to worry about any of this." Sister introduces the metaphor "normal," in reference to her brother, which is quickly picked up on and repeated by Father and Mother.

> FATHER: You know what, Catie? Jacob probably has the same problems. He probably wants worse than any of us to be normal. He just doesn't know what it's like because he never was normal. He just can't get there.
>
> SISTER: I just want so badly for him to be able to experience being normal for a day. I don't tell him I want him to be normal because then I worry that he's going to feel like, "Oh, so you don't like me for the way I am?" I love him. But it's hard to watch him have to go what he goes through.
>
> MOTHER: That's why we're trying everything we know how to do, Catie, to make him as normal as possible. I don't know how to make him normal. We're trying, you know. They [the psychiatrists] tell me I need to desensitize him. I don't have a clue what desensitizing means. I know what they told me to do, but is that really going to work? You know?
>
> FATHER: This kind of messes me up, too. I come home expecting a fight every day at 5 o'clock. When I come

home now and open the door and there's nothing—
no fight, no argument, no screaming, no yelling, nothing broken—it's strange. I know. But you know what
that tells me? We've got a messed up sense of normal,
really. Our normal is not like everybody else's.

MOTHER: Normal is so overrated.

The family has on their own moved from a focus on Jacob alone
to a more systemic inclusion of the whole family, and the conversation has now shifted to address not only Jacob's but the whole family's relationship to being "normal." Mother responds to Father's
comment "our normal is not like everybody else's" by saying, "normal is so overrated." In particular, this last comment delivers the
opening to move the conversation toward a context where being
"not normal" may actually be indicative of something unique and
special about the whole family, rather than something problematic.
Learning to identify a potential resource requires practice, especially for therapists indoctrinated in seeing clients through a pathological or problem/solution lens (see Keeney & Keeney, 2013, for
practical exercises that help develop resource focused perception).
Brad Keeney, who has been watching behind the one-way mirror,
recognizes this opening and enters the room.

BK: Well, let's start with the good news.

FATHER: What's that? Jacob is getting out?

BK: The good news is that you all care about your son and
your brother. The good news is you want what's best
for him and what's best for your family. Let's own
that and celebrate that to start with. Now for the surprising news. The surprising news is the last thing
you all want is to be normal. [Mother, Father, and Sister laugh]

By acknowledging and celebrating that the family wants what is
best for Jacob, it creates a context in which the family's uncertainty
about their recent choice of action can be addressed without judgment. Brad quickly returns to theme of "normal is overrated," but
makes it even stronger by saying "the last thing you all want is
to be normal." Calling this "surprising news" echoes the family's
previous communication that their sense of normal—and therefore
their family life—is unique and not like everybody else's.

FATHER: You're probably right.

BK: Because none of you are normal.

MOTHER: You didn't hear what I said a minute ago, did you?

BK: I did hear what you said. You said, "Normal is over-rated." That's when I jumped in here. I'm just here to underline that. Because being normal is like being boring and trying to figure out how to be alive. And when that happens then you do all kinds of stupid things, and live a miserable life.

Brad continues to reinforce the theme that "normal is overrated." (As editor Michael Hoyt has suggested [personal communication, 2013], "the three mental illnesses are psychosis, neurosis, and normosis.") Whereas previously being "not normal" was a metaphor for Jacob's problems, now it is indicative of something positive about both Jacob and the whole family: they are not boring and know how to be alive. Utilizing the opening created by Mother's comment to highlight a family strength helps advance the session past the opening context of a family struggling to navigate the treatment of a problem son. Now that the goal of trying to be normal (treating a psychiatric disorder) has been released, the stage is set for a more resourceful direction that allows more possibilities to be explored for how to relate to what makes Jacob and the family unique.

BK: Okay, now for the confusing news. You've heard about different opinions. As you know, there are times when you are sick, and you go to the doctor and he says you need to have your appendix taken out or you need to have your inner ear worked on. And when that happens sometimes you go get a second opinion.

FATHER: Right.

BK: Well, when it's something related to your organs it's easier, because all doctors go to the same medical school or they're all going to use the same x-rays and blood tests. But when it comes to the challenges of living life, you're going to get a hundred different opinions about what's going on. And that's the confusing news. So, if you go seek the opinion of a retired marine sergeant, he would just say your son needs boot camp. He would probably say, without a doubt, that all this psychiatric stuff is a bunch of bullshit. He'd say Jacob just needs boot camp, because that's the way a marine sergeant sees the world.

MOTHER: It's all a sergeant knows.

BK: Right. Likewise, let's say we could put you in a time machine and take you back to a hundred years ago in Mississippi—even Louisiana—certainly Kentucky, where the church was so alive that they had revivals that lasted ten hours a day for ten days. If you asked for their opinion, they would say he just needs to go through a good revival and get some religion. Are you following me? But if you go to the psychiatrist, they're going to say he needs at least ten—if not thirty—years of individual therapy and five hundred different pills and this and that, so he can keep all those people employed. And if you come here and you ask me, if you ask the people who work at this clinic, "Does he need individual therapy?" We would say sure, if he lived in a universe where he was the only person in it.

FATHER: Yeah, I'm following you now.

BK: But he lives with other people. So you've got to work with him in relationship with other people.

FATHER: Right.

Rather than set up an either/or choice between following the professional advice of either psychiatry or family therapy, Brad expands the possibilities for helping Jacob to include those that fall outside the boundaries of the mental health professions. This makes the point that any diagnosis and prescription for treatment, whether it's boot camp, pills, or religion, reflects the particular worldview of the person offering the advice, rather than any absolute truth. Interactionally speaking, Brad has created a context inside which he can share his opinion freely as one of many possible views, while acknowledging the leadership of the parents as the ones who must ultimately navigate all the different professional advice they receive.

BK: If you were to ask me, I'd say in my professional opinion, what Jacob is learning and what he's looking for, is how to handle an abundance of overflowing life. That kid was not born with a 75% shot of life, or life force. He's not even 100%. He is overflowing with life. He bubbles so much with life that he sits there looking like a rocket. [Brad had observed Jacob with the family a few months prior to this session.] You can just see the countdown. All right—five, four, three—he's going to launch! And you know, the thing about that launch, when I see him, it's actually joy. It's like, I have so much happiness and joy to share, I can't wait to share it, and then he's so frustrated when it can't launch all the time. Now, I don't believe in labels like hyperactive and bipolar. I'll tell you why: because they're all made up. They weren't around a long time ago, and they have no scientific proof. But, you can go ahead and choose to believe it. You can also choose to believe a marine sergeant. You can choose to believe anything. The confusing news is that you have to choose what world you're going to live in and what world you want your son to live in. If you want him to live in a world where he doesn't relate to any other person, then get him one-on-one counseling. Now don't get me going on that because clearly I don't buy that. So the question to you all is: what world do you want to live in? My diagnosis is that you have a young man overflowing with life and joy and he doesn't know how to control the faucet. It's just on full blast.

Act Two: A Son Overflowing with Life—To Channel It or Turn It Off?

Here we mark the transition to the middle act, set in motion when Brad offers his professional "diagnosis" that Jacob is a boy who was born with an extra amount of joy and life force which he doesn't yet know how to handle. This new frame, "overflowing with life," includes both the presenting problem of a family seeking help for their son, as well as the introduction of a more benign way of relating to Jacob's behavior that is absent of pathological diagnoses. Suggesting that Jacob "doesn't know how to control the faucet" acknowledges there is room for change, while transforming what was previously regarded as a psychiatric disorder into a question of Jacob struggling to handle his gift.

Mapping the progression of the session thus far, we see the first resourceful theme, "normal is overrated," helped advance the session past the beginning context of a family dealing with the psychiatric treatment of a son with multiple diagnoses. Once it was established that not being normal is actually a family strength and that the parents have more choice when it comes to helping Jacob, the momentum was created to further move the session in a more resourceful direction. With the introduction of the frame, "overflowing with life," a virtuous circle of interaction is sparked and fed by more communication on the part of both Brad and the parents about Jacob's strengths and talents.

> MOTHER: He's smart, as smart as smart can be. I would just love to figure out what area he's the smartest in. You know what I'm saying? Because he is smart. He can figure things out. He can do things. I know he is smart. I just never found his niche.
>
> BK: He's overflowing with life force. He can make it go in any direction.
>
> FATHER: We really need to figure out how to help him have his faucet on without—
>
> MOTHER: Exploding? [laughs]
>
> FATHER: Without keeping just the hot water on all the time. [Mother nods]
>
> BK: Remember what else we saw in our session before. We saw Jacob move from "rocket launch" to somebody who was very still and calm and loving to you when we turned the light off and asked both of you [Mom and Dad] to tell your kids some words of wisdom, as if it were the last time you'd be able to talk to them. We saw that Jacob has that switch inside him. Do you remember that moment when the light came on? Here he was sitting right next to you and he was peaceful and calm. So he's got that switch in him.
>
> MOTHER: We've just got to figure how to control it.
>
> FATHER: That's right. I remember that. We turned the lights out to say that prayer and Jacob leaned over and put his head on my shoulder.
>
> SISTER: [to her father] He was loving on you.
>
> FATHER: He completely laid over on me that day.

In the previous session some months earlier, we turned off the lights and asked the parents to offer their kids some words of important wisdom. This was a way of re-establishing the parents to-gether as the leaders and wise elders in the family by enacting it in the session. It was a very tender and loving moment, during which Jacob fell silent and cuddled up next to his father. Brad's recalling of this experience brings what was positive and transformative about that interaction, including the parents' leadership and Jacob's abil-ity to be calm, into the context of the current session.

Now that the interaction is fully inside the resourceful frame of relating to Jacob's overflowing amount of joy and life, it elic-its a flood of additional communication from the family concern-ing other positive things about Jacob, including Mother saying she hears from her friends how Jacob is "such a sweet boy" and "a per-fect gentleman." Sister and Mother start sharing about all the times they have fun at home with Jacob being silly and laughing wildly together, including dancing in the house.

When a virtuous circle begins to turn, it naturally elicits more of whatever communication further feeds movement toward positive change. The same is true, however, for the vicious circles of interaction that feed and harden impoverished frames. In the beginning of the session, all communication from Mother and Father concerning Jacob arose from inside the frame of psychiatric treatment. Once a frame is built, it brings forth the necessary distinctions to fit the reality that has been constructed, organizing the participation of all concerned including clients, families, and professionals, however well intended they may be. When a session begins drowning in the kind of prob-lem-saturated discourse that feeds vicious circles, it must be inter-rupted so that another more virtuous, enriching circularity can be set in motion (Keeney & Keeney, 2013). Change in therapy is principally about choosing which kind of circularity you will help feed—one that brings forth more of the same or one that delivers more imagination, creativity, joy, choice, hope, dreaming, and life force. When we feed resourceful communication in a session, the interaction itself becomes a virtuous circle that brings forth more of the kind of distinctions and metaphors that maintain presence inside whatever more enriching context has been constructed. When this happens, we experience the fulcrum of the middle act tilt forward, and this momentum can be utilized to help carry the session toward the final act.

Note that while a solution focus may appear to be a step removed from a problem emphasis, it is not far enough removed and may easily slip back into addressing something (the named or unnamed problem) that is presumed to require solving. In other words, neither problems nor solutions exist *in vitro*. The work of Watzlawick, Weakland, and Fisch (1974) clearly demonstrated that problems and solutions are an interactional pattern, something that is arguably misunderstood by solution-focused therapists. Solution-focused work, like most therapies, does not necessarily dissolve a problem focus any more than a daytime focus dissolves the night, as day and night are a complementary gestalt. A focus on resources is further removed from both the problems and solutions of problem-solution interaction. We invite therapists to move from problems to solutions, and then move past both, advancing toward resourceful experience which can include either a problem or solution, or neither.

> BK: I've got a hypothesis.
>
> MOTHER: What's that?
>
> BK: Not only is Jacob full of life, not only is he overflowing with joy, not only is his curiosity meter going wild. Not only is he interested in every subject in the world, not only does he want everything for you, he wants you to have 125% of everything like him. And when he sees you aren't as happy as he is, he wants you to have it. He thinks you all need the joy he has. Without even knowing it, maybe deep in his unconscious, I think it's possible he's looking at you all and saying...
>
> MOTHER: We're boring and...
>
> FATHER: We need some help.
>
> BK: Right. That you need help. He may be thinking that you need as much happiness as he has. He's trying to fix you all because he loves you so much.
>
> FATHER: He does lead us all the time.

The cost of individual therapy and diagnosis is that it ignores how behaviors are held inside the complexities of relational dynamics. The suggestion that Jacob is actually trying to help or "fix" his family, rather than the other way around, places Jacob's behavior inside the context of relationship where it can be addressed as a family interactional dynamic rather than an individual psychological disorder. This sets the stage for a strategic prescription for action (below). Here it is the other family members who are asked to change and become more like Jacob, amplifying their expression of joy and excitement.

BK: It's just really amazing. It will be really amazing if this kid can just figure out how to have a relationship to his gifts and all the things you have given to him. Jacob reminds me of those old comic books about superheroes with super powers. When super heroes were kids, it was really awkward for them because if they played baseball and hit the ball it was ripped to shreds and went—

FATHER: To the moon.

BK: Exactly. You're living with someone who's almost like a superhero, and what he wants to give you, if he could, would be of superhero proportions. And I think—this sounds really out there—but when I close my eyes, in my imagination I can just see, if you suddenly were as excited about life as he is, all of a sudden he would just start to chill.

MOTHER: He'd be surprised, like, "Wow."

FATHER: Yeah, we'd be at the same speed he is.

BK: But it would bring him down a bit. Because I think in some kind of crazy way, without even knowing it, he thinks unless you're feeling as much joy as he is, he's got to rev you up. So you have a choice. It's not going to be easy. None of these choices are easy. Boot camp isn't easy, psychiatry isn't easy, and it's not easy trying to find a way to show your son that you're actually happy and he doesn't have to worry about trying to fix you, without saying it. Because he doesn't know why he's doing it. It's just an automatic thing deep inside him that's happening. Just think if he had the talent of being a singer and had put that energy on stage.

FATHER: That's what I was telling his grandfather the other day. If he could ever go in a positive direction with something there is no telling how far he could go. Because he's so talented. It's just not being channeled.

BK: That's one of your choices. It's your choice: do you channel that and go for helping it deliver the success that you all want to see, or do you try to turn it off?

Brad's question delivers the climax for the middle act, highlighting the primary choice the parents face when it comes to helping their son. Jacob is no longer a psychiatric patient, but a superhero. Whether they decide to help channel his special power or turn it off, the choice remains inside the resourceful context of helping a son utilize his gift to live a successful life.

> FATHER: No, you don't turn it off. You know, suddenly right now I feel so commercialized. Like somebody has tried to sell me on some idea. I've been told he needs to talk to these people and he needs to take this pill and he probably needs to take this pill and he needs to go to this therapist and he needs to do this activity and on and on. You know.
>
> BK: You know the pill he needs? I'll tell you the pill he needs.
>
> FATHER: Life.
>
> BK: Right. Life, he needs life.

As we show below, Brad was going to say the "pill" Jacob needs is a bowl of Rice Krispies. Before he could continue, however, Father answered, and did so with such a tone of love and authority in his voice that those of us watching behind the one-way mirror looked at each other and gasped. We could see and hear him change from a parent confused and unclear about what to do, into a father ready to embrace a different way of helping his gifted son.

Act 3: Life Coaching

Now that the decision has been made to help Jacob learn to channel his gift rather than turn it off, the session transitions to Act Three with the following prescription for action.

> BK: I'll tell you what else he could use. I'll write a prescription for it. I'll take a piece of paper and write it out. Three times a day you need to feed him a bowl of Rice Krispies. Pour the milk on it, and for as long as it's making a sound, have him listen to it without talking. And then he can eat it. He needs to learn to listen to snap—
>
> MOTHER: Crackle and pop. That's right. [nodding]
>
> BK: Yes. And you all need to show him some snap, crackle, and pop.
>
> FATHER: Since you said that and it started coming together, I have this vision of standing on the beach with the waves and Jacob just running in a pair of shorts and

nothing else, just mad crazy down the beach, splashing in the water, kicking in the sand, somewhere where he could just let it go.

BK: Well, if somebody saw that in India, they'd make him a saint. They'd say he has found true happiness.

FATHER: You know what I mean?

BK: Yes. And you know what? A hundred people would say, "Show us how we can be that happy."

Now that Jacob's overflowing joy and life is regarded as a gift, a vision of Jacob running "mad crazy" down the beach comes forth as an inspiring fantasy rather than a sign of mental illness. Brad underscores this as evidence of Jacob's joy and happiness, and again suggests that this comes as a teaching to those around him.

FATHER: He does have to control it to some extent, doesn't he?

BK: It's the challenge of how not to turn it off but—

FATHER: Just to control the volume.

BK: Yes, learning how to use his abundance of life force as a resource and not as something that gets him into trouble. He thinks you all need some snap, crackle, and pop.

Brad shifts the focus back to the participation of the whole family, reemphasizing that helping Jacob "control the volume" is as much about the family *showing* Jacob more "snap, crackle, and pop" as it is about Jacob learning to *listen* to the sound of a bowl of Rice Krispies.

MOTHER: Well hell, he ain't the one that needs the damn therapy, we are!

BK: Actually, in all honesty, I don't think any of you need therapy. You know what you need? You all are not normal, which is why I like you so much. What you need is coaching in how not to be normal and enjoy it. You need a coach.

Since the context of the session has shifted entirely away from the beginning act—navigating psychiatric treatment—to a "not normal" family learning how to work together to better support a son with overflowing joy and life energy, the opening is created to abandon therapy altogether. Therapy treats problems, whereas life coaching offers a more resourceful context for seeking help, one that is more about strategies for maximizing already present talents and potential. While generally speaking we regard the difference between therapy and coaching to be irrelevant, at this moment in the interaction it helps draw an important distinction that marks the change that has occurred in the session. If we had declared the end of therapy and a shift to coaching in the beginning act, it would have had little transformative currency, especially if the focus had remained on treating a son with mental and behavioral disorders. Now "coaching" ushers in a new contextual frame that affirms all of the family's strengths and resources.

> FATHER: Yeah, I was just thinking that. When you said "You all don't need therapy," the first thing that came into my mind is that what we need is more like a life coach.
>
> BK: That's exactly what you need. Let's end therapy right now. Let's give this family some coaching on how to handle all that which is not normal and beautiful in this family and all the life force that bubbles outside of you and through you. Can we end therapy right now?
>
> THERAPIST: We can.
>
> BK: Can we move to coaching?
>
> FATHER: Yes, yes.
>
> BK: Awesome. That's a big step. [Brad leans forward and shakes the father's hand]
>
> SISTER: That was a good conversation.
>
> MOTHER: Wonderful. [Shaking Brad's hand]
>
> FATHER: Yes.
>
> BK: I mean really. You all can decide which reality you want. This was real. We shook hands. No more therapy. Let's get coaching, and let's tell Jacob about the button he has, which he can push and calm himself down. He has a button he can push. And you're going to have to show him and not tell him anything about it, because the teaching is for his unconscious mind, the deepest part of him, the parts that are deeply sensitive inside his heart in the realm of mystery; things no mind can understand. Jacob is trying to give you snap, crackle, and pop. I mean it when I say he needs a Rice Krispies prescription. In fact, the whole family should sit with a bowl of Rice Krispies and see who can listen the most.

This is a family overflowing with life. You've got to find a way of communicating to this boy that you guys have as much snap, crackle, and pop in you as he does, because you do, and he's going to learn how to hear the snap, crackle, and pop when you give it. And that's why that cereal, as weird as it, is a very powerful prescription. You have to be quiet. All of you have to be quiet. If he can have three bowls of Rice Krispies a day, when he is quiet and listens to the snap, crackle, and pop, that's all the medicine he's going to need because in that time he's learning to turn the switch off to listen.

MOTHER: Wow. Let's do it.

BK: Okay? Okay [speaking to the family and the therapist], you guys can wrap things up. I know I'm going to think about you because there's something about you all that really is special, and you know that. [pointing to the parents] You guys have everything you need. It's just time for you to not listen to other people and start being the teachers. [Brad exits the room]

After Brad left the room the family and the therapist continued to celebrate that she was now going to be their life coach instead of their therapist. They discussed all the ways the family could show Jacob more of their "snap, crackle, and pop." The next day, the family called the therapist to tell her that they pulled Jacob out of the psychiatric facility and brought him home. A few weeks later, the whole family returned to the clinic to let the therapist know they were doing well, and were continuing to experiment with how to share more joy and abundant life energy with one another. They concluded their therapy, but said they would come back whenever they felt they needed some more coaching.

In summary, the plot line of the session can be mapped as follows:

Figure 1. Summary of the Session in 3 Acts

Act 1	→	Act 2	→	Act 3
Psychiatric Treatment		A Son Overflowing with Life: To Channel It or Turn It Off?		Life Coaching

In the beginning, a family came seeking help because their son, who had a history of psychiatric diagnosis and treatment, had been committed to a psychiatric facility. Confused and uncertain about their choices and best course of action, they came seeking additional guidance. Utilizing every communication on the part of the family that delivered any possible exit from pathological discourse, Brad highlighted what was unique and special not only about Jacob, but about the whole family. Utilizing Mother's wisdom that "normal is overrated" and Jacob's visible abundant expression of joy, the session moved from treating a son with psychiatric disorders (trying to "make him normal") to a question of how best to help Jacob learn to handle his gift—an overflowing amount of life. When faced with the choice of whether to channel it or turn it off, both parents affirmed that they wanted to see Jacob channel it in a positive direction. Two prescriptions for action were then created, one that asked the family to show Jacob they were as excited about life as he was, and another that asked Jacob to tune into the sound of a bowl of Rice Krispies as a way of helping him get in touch with his inner "button" or "switch." Both parents accepted these new strategies that involved the whole family. As they step into their new role of teaching their son to "control the faucet" or the "volume," Brad again reminds them that not being normal is a gift to celebrate rather a disorder to medicate. Therapy itself is now rendered irrelevant, as the family has shifted toward needing life coaching—literally coaching in how to handle and foster an overflowing amount of life.

Like this family, therapists need to be reminded that there is always more choice and possibility for how to relate to your clients and your therapy that invite more creativity, more joy, and more life force. When you find yourself feeding the vicious circle of diagnosing and fixing problems (whether you do so through the constructs of psychiatry, systemic therapy, psychoanalysis, solution-focused therapy or some other model) remember that, when it comes to both life and therapy, normal is overrated. If you're lucky, you'll be reminded of that by a client like Jacob, someone overflowing with joy and life, ready to shake you up and teach you how to have more snap, crackle, and pop in your sessions. When he and his family arrive, however, you'll have to know what to listen for. Therapists, like families, easily become lost in all the noise generated by diagnostic categories, therapy jargon, and intervention models. Instead, tune in to the snap, crackle, and pop that are waiting to be discovered and amplified in every interaction. Let the sound of life, rather than the patter of therapy mind, speak more in your sessions. Dare to fully express your joy and awaken more life force in the room. Rather than be a therapist who tries to fix problems, become a single session life coach, or even better, a three-act theatre host who helps clients live as fully as they can.

References

Keeney, B. P. (2009). *The creative therapist: The art of awakening a session*. New York: Routledge.

Keeney, H., & Keeney, B. (2012). *Circular therapeutics: Giving therapy a healing heart*. Phoenix, AZ: Zeig, Tucker, & Theisen.

Keeney, H., & Keeney, B. (2013). *Creative therapeutic technique: Skills for the art of bringing forth change*. Phoenix, AZ: Zeig, Tucker, & Theisen.

Keeney, H., Keeney, B., & Chenail, R. (2013). Recursive frame analysis: A practitioner's tool for mapping therapeutic conversation. In H. Keeney & B. Keeney, *Creative therapeutic technique: Skills for the art of bringing forth change* (Appendix, pp. 191–211). Phoenix, AZ: Zeig, Tucker, & Theisen.

Keeney, B. P., & Ray, W. (1996). Resource-focused therapy. In M.F. Hoyt (Ed.), *Constructive therapies* (Vol. 2, pp. 334–346). New York: Guilford Press.

Watzlawick, P., Weakland, J., and Fisch, R. (1974). *Change: Principles of problem formation and problem resolution*. New York: Norton.

Whitaker, C. (1976). The hindrance of theory in clinical work. In P. Guerin (Ed.), *Family therapy: Theory and practice* (pp. 154–164). New York: Gardner Press.

Chapter Twenty-Five

Moments Are Forever: SST and Walk-In Services Now and In The Future

Moshe Talmon and Michael F. Hoyt

As we joyfully conclude the long process of editing this book we feel lucky and blessed. Scientific findings in general and psychotherapy studies in particular often first report what appear to be significant results that later are disputed and refuted (Lehrer, 2010). Nearly 30 years ago we conducted a modest exploratory study on SST (Talmon, 1990). Our sample was small, the follow-up was short, and the setting was very specific. The three therapists who conducted 58 attempts at planned single sessions had little to no knowledge of how to conduct therapy that starts and ends in one session. Reviewing the extensive research data (see Appendix A) on single session encounters, we are delighted to find that our data and initial findings were replicated and validated many times over by dozens of other studies.

Most important, it expands them and enriches them in many more ways than we could ever imagine:

- The research and clinical data presented in this book are based on a much larger and more diverse sample than we had in our original study. For example, the contact behavior of more than 100,000 cases was studied in the State of Victoria, Australia (see Chapter 7), with more than 40% electing to complete their therapy in one visit even when more visits were available. Many more thousands of one-session cases were conducted all over the world, reports coming from China, Mexico, England, Ireland, Turkey, Sweden, Chile, Israel, Australia, New Zealand, and Canada as well as from across the United States;

- In our original research project we were able to follow-up with our clients anywhere from three months in most cases to two years in fewer cases. In this book, studies and cases are presented with follow-ups ranging from two years to 25 years, thus validating SST as a model for brief intervention with lasting results;

- We originally thought SST might work mostly with non-psychologically-minded "first-timers" who could be considered to be the "worried well" or at most diagnosed as having "adjustment disorders." When we thought about a possible candidate for SST we thought about patients who come to therapy for a well-defined and focused reason with the right timing and proper state of readiness to work for easily reachable change. This book, however, presents detailed accounts of effective SST conducted with serious, longstanding, and diverse conditions ranging across PTSD, suicide threats, addictions, family violence, anxiety and depression, ADHD, bipolar affective disorder, and life-challenging medical illnesses; as well as clients who present multiple problems and could be easily assessed in *DSM* terms as meeting criteria for having dual or even multiple psychiatric diagnoses. The available data now strongly refute the idea that SST can help only "light" problems of highly resourceful clients.

Most of this book's contributors agree that it would be unwise to try to pre-determine what conditions will fit SST (and how much time will be needed). Thus, Hillary and Brad Keeney (Chapter 24) write: "We consider any determinations regarding length or number of sessions made prior to a session as presumptuous. When organized by systemic interaction and participation, it is not possible for a therapist to know anything about how a session or a course of therapy will or ought to unfold until that session begins. Furthermore, any determinations made inside the interaction must be subject to change as clients and practitioners change." In our editors' introduction (Chapter 1) we noted that "Because we were open to the *possibility* of one session being enough but did not insist on a single session, cases that required more than one visit were not thought of as 'failures in SST' but rather simply as cases needing more time. The basic idea was 'making the most of each session,' no more than needed." Or, as Arnie Slive and Monte Bobele (Chapter 5) nicely put it, "We are pleased when a client returns for another session. We think this means we have done a good job. We want our clients to be satisfied enough that they will come back as needed."

SST: Useful in a Variety of Settings

Some of the work described in this volume is conducted in settings where SST is a natural and very sensible fit for the common reality of everyday life, such as public clinics with high demands, limited staff, and long waiting lists; walk-in services in low-income neighborhoods or with populations that are very reluctant to use psychotherapy services; as well as other places where "no appointment necessary" is very common in many other services. Nancy McElheran and her colleagues at the Eastside Family Centre (Chapter 10) in Calgary, Slive and Bobele (Chapters 5–6) in Texas, Jeff Young and his colleagues (Chapters 7–9) in Australia, John Miller (Chapter 11) in China, and Jason Platt and Debora Mondellini (Chapter 12) in Mexico City all describe such applications. Health maintenance organizations (HMOs) that contract to provide "prepaid" services and thus operate with a "Get 'em in and get 'em out as quick as possible" mentality might welcome single sessions, but we caution that they need to be very careful that patients are receiving what is needed—not just what is less expensive to provide (see Hoyt, 2000, pp. 77–108). The wider appropriate use of SSTs may help conserve needed resources for other clients who need more, but SST is not a panacea: more resources and better care are needed.

Other obvious settings for SSTs may include:

- Community mental health services
- Alcohol and drug treatment services
- Problem gambling services
- University and school counseling services
- Primary care and medical services (see Chandler & Mason, 1995; McNeilly, 1994; Greenberg, et al., 2001; also see Chapter 18 this volume)
- Emergency rooms and on-call centers.

In the Australian project, it was found that single sessions were often employed by professionals who do not identify themselves necessarily as "therapists," e.g., primary-care physicians, intake and case managers, maternal and child-health workers, hospital social workers, and youth workers. They found using the term *single session work* (*SSW*) a useful framework because their clients often do not attend regular, multiple, or scheduled appointments; or because the workers were acting as *occasional counselors* in between providing other services such as case management or practical support.

Utilizing SSTs/SSWs as a common or preferred mode of therapy sometimes can be a very challenging option for the provider. In the first few years after the publication of *Single Session Therapy* (Talmon, 1990), we were mostly invited to present our work to the "early adopters," namely therapists who are interested in brief, systemic, resource-based, strength-based, solution-focused therapy. In later years, one of us (M.T.) experienced a major shift when he was invited to teach and consult more and more by organizations and professionals who work with cancer patients, sexually and physically abused women in shelters, patients in psychiatric wards and in various inpatient medical hospital departments. When Moshe questioned how much his limited experience with such psychotherapy patients would be relevant to their work, they all insisted that they had so many single session cases that they must devote some time to learn how to use SST to the advantage of the patient as well as to help their own morale working under such pressure in very challenging situations. In this book we learn many more ways to effectively use single session encounters with difficult and complex cases. There is a lot here that could be used in a first session, in an only session, or in any session.

Another important challenge involves money. Most independent private practitioners make their living on a fee-for-time basis.[1] Where more is economically better for the provider, it pays to hold on to your clients for as frequent and as many visits as possible. In such situations, one is more inclined to adopt "more is better" and "longer is better" notions. Meeting a client for the first time who has

---

1. Jay Haley (1990, pp. 14–15): "When we look at the history of therapy, the most important decision ever made was to charge for therapy by the hour. Historians will someday reveal who thought of this idea. The ideology and practice of therapy was largely determined when therapists chose to sit with a client and be paid for durations of time rather than by results." Or, as Hoyt (2009, p.

a very painful, complex, and longstanding difficulty in life, it can be very tempting to join them for as long a journey as possible and to adopt pessimistic views about the nature of people and life such as "Most people resist change and if and when they do change, it will take a very long time." There are also undoubted emotional rewards to spending many months or years with a client, sharing their pain and rejoicing in their happiness as they go through life in an ever-deepening relationship. However, beliefs that a client's "presenting problem" is only a symptom of much larger and deeper underlying and unconscious conflicts ("the tip of the iceberg"), which must be addressed and "resolved" thoroughly for therapy to be effective and useful (see Haley, 1963, especially pp. 179–201, on "therapeutic paradoxes," one-up/one-down relationships, and the illusion of "deeper"; as well as de Shazer [in Hoyt, 1994, p. 14; and Hoyt, 1996a, pp. 70–80] on Wittgenstein, language games, and "You've got what you've got, and that's all there is"), may lead some clinicians to resist or ignore all the clients that elect to come only once or a few times.

In addition to issues of money and the psychoanalytic notion of "deeper is better," there is also the strong image from Judeo-Christian tradition of the powerful bond between the great sufferer-victim and his/her savior-rescuer, which is quite present in our culture. When a therapist with a strong need to be needed meets with a client who is strongly attached to his or her experience of being a victim, both parties may try to hold on to one another for dear life.

Quite a few of the contributors to this volume have no financial incentives to conduct SSTs, especially when they operate in a fee-for-service solo or small group private practice setting. They work fee-for-service but elect to continue doing SSTs. What is our incentive in working "briefly" when it is clearly working against our own financial interests? What could be the incentive for therapists—including both the editors, who were originally trained in psychoanalytically and psychodynamically oriented models—to embrace the possibility of single session encounters? Looking across the chapters comprising this volume, despite the differences in theories and techniques, three synergistically interrelated themes may be suggested.

---

8) has expressed it: "[T]here are essentially three factors that tend to determine the length of treatment: 1. The theoretical orientation of the therapist[....]2. Money—how much and for how long the patient can afford to pay, 3. The patient's problems, situation, personality, psychopathology, expectations, and capacities."

Three Key Themes

Mindset

Embracing and implementing single session therapy is largely a result of a creative mindset much more than a response to a specific psychodiagnostic cluster or the employment of a particular method or school of psychotherapy. Each session is approached as a singular event. Monte Bobele and Arnie Slive (Chapter 6, emphasis in original) articulate their SST mindset:

> [O]ur belief [is] that any session could be the last session. We don't conduct any session as if there will be another session. In other words, we do *one session at a time....* Of course another session may have occurred before the current one, and other sessions may follow, but the current session is complete and stands on its own.... We have come to believe that this single session mindset is essential to be effective as a walk-in therapist.... Therefore, a crucial element for conducting successful single session therapy is the therapists' own beliefs about the effectiveness of brief therapy. Therapists' expectations are communicated overtly and covertly to their clients about how rapid and how much change can be expected.... We have also developed a motto that we repeat like a mantra to our trainees: *Every case has the potential to be a single session case!*

Expectation is a central part of the SST mindset. Thus, Rubin Battino (Chapter 21, emphasis in original) writes:

> The client's expectation had a profound effect on how soon they got down to business. (This is an example of what Appelbaum [1975] calls "Parkinsons' Law in Psychotherapy"—work expands or contracts to fit the time allotted.).... I immediately graphed these results and came to the conclusion that if I told my clients that I *expected* to be able to help them in one session that *their expectation* would be the same. So, I tell all of my clients at initial contact that I rarely see people more than one or two times, and that I will do everything I can so that it is only one session.... Very brief therapy proponents (like the authors in this volume)

propose the possibility and practicality of SST (or just a few sessions). My expectation for everyone who comes to see me is one session, and my clients are told this directly in the initial contact. In the vernacular this might be expressed as "Let's cut out all of the bullshit and get down to work!"

Hillary and Brad Keeney (Chapter 24) similarly approach each session as a whole unto itself:

> This orientation provides a "single session mindset" which can be applied to any session, independent of whether the therapeutic offering is reified as single session therapy, long-term therapy, multiple single session therapy[2], or indeterminate-duration therapy. We apply a single session mindset to every session we conduct....A single session mindset is an intervention for the practitioner, intended to help bring forth their best performance. We regard this as a resource rather than a limitation. In fact, we encourage all practitioners to become single session therapists, regardless of their preferred orientation. Therapists discover their capacity in every session to creatively and improvisationally act in order to bring forth a unique, life-changing session with each and every client they encounter...Therapists need to be reminded that there is always more choice and possibility for how to relate to your clients and your therapy that invite more creativity, more joy, and more life force.

Time

Single session therapy is predicated on the belief and expectation that change can occur *in the moment*. Thus, Bobele and Slive (Chapter 6) remind us of the capaciousness of the moment: "When you

---

2. Adding to our list of SST terminology (see Chapter 1, pp. 11–15), Battino (Chapter 21) offers the term *Sequential Single-Session Therapy* (and its acronym, *SSST*); many patients who have a SST will return another time to have another SST (or ongoing therapy). Young et al. (Chapter 7) also introduce the term *Single Session Family Consultation* (*SSFC*) to refer to SST/SSW (Single Session Therapy/Single Session Work) involving more than one person (families, partners, social networks, etc.).

have a WHOLE hour." Michele Ritterman (Chapter 20) describes "Slo-Mo" techniques to expand and go inside the moment with her clients. Hoyt (1990) advises that we're "on time in brief therapy" and reminds us (in Chapter 4) that "Verily: life is a single session. Capture the moment and count your blessings." Bob Rosenbaum (in Hoyt, et al., 1992, p. 81) says "My desire is not to see everyone for one session; my desire is to see everyone for one full moment, as long as that takes" and explains (in Chapter 3) that there really is only the present and that each moment, while ungraspable, is "The Time of Your Life."

Indeed, there is no time but the present. This was recognized by St. Augustine in his 4th century *Confessions* (quoted in Boscolo & Bertrando, 1993, p. 34): "What is by now evident and clear is that neither future nor past exists, and it is inexact language to speak of three times—past, present, and future. Perhaps it would be exact to say: 'there are three times, a present of things past, a present of things present, a present of things to come. In the soul there are these three aspects of time, and I do not see them anywhere else. The present considering the past is the memory, the present considering the future is expectation'."

Yapko (1989, 1990) notes that three factors determine whether a patient will benefit from brief therapy interventions: (1) the person's primary temporal orientation (toward past, present, or future); (2) the general value given to "change," whether he or she is more invested in maintaining tradition or seeking change; and (3) the patient's belief system about what constitutes a complete therapeutic experience. Different cultures may structure time differently. In addition to the chapters cited above that explicitly address issues of time, Chapter 11 about SST in China (by John Miller) and Chapter 12 about SST in Mexico City (by Jason Platt and Debora Mondellini) give some glimpses of how time orientation may influence therapeutic process in non-North American/European contexts.

Change (or stasis) always happens NOW (Gilbert, 2005; Goulding & Goulding, 1979; Hoyt, 1990; Stern, 2004; Tolle, 1999). Herman Hesse (1943/1969) tells us that "In all beginnings dwells a magic force." E.E. Cummings (1972, p. 743) celebrates "we who have wandered down from fragrant mountains of eternal now." Nikos Kazantzakis (1961/1965) says "This was another divinely beautiful day. Each morning the world rediscovers its virginity; it seems to have issued fresh from God's hands at that very instant....It experiences the present moment as an eternity. No other moment exists;

before and behind this moment is Nothing." Maya Angelou (1993) tells us "the horizon leans forward."

"Moments are forever," so rather than saying "Capture the moment" perhaps it would be easier to simply say, "And now?" Whatever their particular theory or technique, the various authors in this volume all approach the session with the assumption that something good can happen NOW (and that what happens can have enduring benefits).

Patient Empowerment

The fundamental assumption of all forms of deliberate brief therapy, including SST, is an attitude and expectation—supported by various theories, methodologies, and findings—that *clients/patients have the capacity to alter their thoughts, emotions, and behaviors in order to bring about significant and beneficial changes.* Furthermore, they share a general faith that once a person has made a change, this can be magnified and reinforced by subsequent life experiences so that there is a positive cascade of "ripple effects." Thus, Haley (1982, p. 23) writes: "The small change invariably led to the larger one. As Erickson put it, if you want a large change you should ask for a small one."

People can make a difference. Again, regardless of specific theory or technique, all of the authors approach meeting their patient/ client with the belief that with skillful facilitation, *the patient/client has the potential to make a change in the moment.*

SST as a "talking cure" is based on the minimal and very inexpensive tool of a conversation that opens up the opportunity that when two (or more) people meet, anything can happen and that the main goal at any point in this process is to help patients help themselves and be helped primarily by their natural internal and external support systems. The therapists all "believe in" their clients—the role of encouragement (see Watts & Pietrzak, 2000) is important in patient empowerment. The therapists meet their patient wherever he or she is at—and then confidently guide them forward. Getting a description of the person's desired goal or change is very useful. It helps to organize the conversation, providing purpose and direction. (See Appendix B). As Hoyt (2000, p. 6) wrote, using a metaphor from the sport of golf: "It's a long day on the course if you don't know where the hole is." Hope is stirred and client involvement amplified by the therapists' optimistic support and by their asking about the client's goals—what will be different when change occurs? Finishing sessions with some discussion of next steps is also often helpful.

We like to help people use their resources and strengths to get better as soon as possible.

As described in Chapter 4 (p. 67), a "Context of Competence" is created wherein the therapeutic alliance is used to help goals and resources converge. The patient is aided to bring forward his or her strengths, and the single session of therapy helps to set into motion multi-faceted intrapsychic and interpersonal processes. The work is not superficial or simply technique-oriented; it is precise and beneficial, often yielding enduring long-term benefits as well as more immediate gains. Depending on the client's goals, the intention may be improved morale and "less of the same" better coping (no mean feat!) and/or a second-order change that shifts the rules that govern the system's organization and undesired patterns of interaction. With the therapist's guidance, in one session (or more, if needed), the client is encouraged to make a move to break out of his/her/their painful, reiterating cyclical behavioral trap (Gustafson, 2005) by truly "doing one thing different" (O'Hanlon, 1999). This can be understood in a variety of ways, including: the disruption of the attempted solution that actually maintains the problem *a la* MRI's (Fisch, et al, 1982; Fraser & Solovey, 2007) strategic-interactional perspective; the recognition and amplification of an *exception* to the problem (not just "more of the same") *a la* solution-focused therapy (de Shazer, 1988) or a *sparkling moment a la* narrative therapy (White & Epston, 1990); the therapeutic counterinduction of a family's hypnotic symptom trance (Ritterman, 2005); the encouragement of "opposite action" (Linehan, 1993); or the juxtaposition of contradictory cognitive schemas (Ecker, et al., 2012; Padesky, 2012). How you look influences what you see, and what you see influences what you do (Hoyt, 2000, 2009)—multiple theoretical perspectives allow for multiple intervention strategies.

Mere explanation by itself does not usually produce change; rather, clients are better served when facilitated, in different ways, to have a new and powerful *experience*. They come away seeing themselves and their situation differently. Being "taken seriously" (see de Shazer & Weakland, in Hoyt, 1994a), listened to and treated with deep respect, helps to make a "forever moment" lasting impression that goes beyond mere intellectual explanation.

Many Different Ways to Have a Successful SST

Some of the contributors in this volume mostly guide and support the patient's own nascent voice (and choices), as in the solution-focused approaches described by Slive and Bobele (Chapters 5–6), Young, et al. (Chapters 7–9) and Iveson, et al. (Chapter 17); others do it by creating a hypnotic experience that stimulates the patient's unconscious problem-solving, as described by Hoyt (Chapter 4), Rossi and Rossi (Chapters 13–14),[3] Ritterman (Chapter 20), and Battino (Chapter 21); others help alter the patient's problem-governing rules, as described by Flemons and Green (Chapter 22), Green (Chapter 23), and Keeney and Keeney (Chapter 24); and others do it by guiding patients through an experience that alters their energy and the information-processing/construction of their reality, as described by Andreas using NLP (Chapter 15) and Church using EFT (Chapter 16).

While most of the therapist-authors employ more traditional "talking cure" therapies, others also use alternative and nonverbal methods involving acupoint tapping (Church, Chapter 16) and interacting with horses (Green, Chapter 23). Rosenberg and McDaniel (Chapter 18) draw from a biopsychosocial model, combining medical family therapy and integrated healthcare. Some of the therapists mostly "lead by following," whereas others are quite active and persuasive. Brad Keeney (Chapter 24) deconstructs therapy (for therapeutic purposes) in his resource-based therapy, Steve Andreas (Chapter 15) gives specific NLP-based instructions for how his clients should picture their problems: whereas Chris Iveson (Chapter 17) uses a minimalist, solution-focused approach. Their word-by-word accounts help to illustrate their respective practices. Although Keeney, Andreas, and Iveson all are supportive and encouraging, technically they could hardly be more different than one another—yet all are able to mobilize their clients to a whole new place within a one-hour session. They have different styles but reach the same goal: making each therapy session as effective as possible, seeing

---

3. The influence of Milton H. Erickson is visible in a number of cases, both those directly involving hypnosis as well as others that draw from other strategic methods that were derived from Erickson's work. Interestingly, in the two reports that involve the respective author as a SST *client/patient*; the therapist's name was "Erickson"—for Rossi (Chapters 13–14), Dr. Erickson himself; and for Hoyt (Chapter 4), Carol Erickson (Milton's oldest daughter).

each session potentially as the last one, being devoted to clients' strengths and resources and aiming to keep all treatments as brief as possible with a strong preference toward relational-systemic-family approaches to therapy. All the cases are successful.

In this volume we also have included one case (Chapter 19, Jim Gustafson) that draws from psychoanalytic thinking. Although not a "true" SST or single session consultation (SSC) in the sense of being a stand-alone, one-off meeting (the patient was being seen by a psychiatry resident, and after the consultation with Gustafson continued to be seen by the resident and Gustafson for two years), the consultation illustrates a significant one-session turning point in which the contents of one of the patient's violent dreams were interpreted to her as a source of power to help her overcome her feelings of powerlessness. This might be thought of as a watershed moment, a "pivot chord" (Rosenbaum, et al., 1990) or "critical intervention" (Omer, 1994). As Gustafson has written elsewhere (1986, p. 279): "The opening is concerned with where to take hold. The middle is for getting different illuminations of this focus. The end provides a concluding punctuation. Condense, widen, and condense again. Exposition, development and recapitulation." Rosenbaum (2008, p. 8) amplifies: "Psychotherapy depends instead on 'good moments' where something profound shifts for a client. All the rest is preparation and consolidation." Sometimes this can all be accomplished in one session and the patient can carry on by herself—other times, more support may be needed to consolidate the change.

Many people view Sigmund Freud's psychoanalysis as the foundation of modern psychotherapy and the basis for the assumption that psychotherapy should be a very long process lasting years. We note that, in fact, it was also Freud who was the first to record single session therapies. In his successful SSTs with Katarina and with Gustav Mahler (see A. Freud, 1960; Gay, 1988; Kuehn, 1965), Freud broke most of the rules of his newly developed method of psychoanalysis. They were conducted without lying on the analyst's couch. A long walk along the canals in Leyden, Holland was the setting for Mahler's case and a single meeting at a ski resort in the Alps, where Freud was on vacation and young Katarina was the daughter of the owners, was the setting for the other. The SST sessions lasted longer than the "holy" 50-minute hour—in Mahler's case, it lasted four hours. Katarina's case involved sexual abuse; Mahler's involved impotence and depression. The outcomes of these two SSTs were much more positive than most of Freud's reported longer-term, much better known cases. We don't know the full accounts of the sessions, but we do know that Mahler, Katarina, and Freud knew that there would only be that one meeting. Although Katarina's and Mahler's problems were real and severe, the good doctor recognized both the external conditions (availability) and respected the patients' preferences, broke his own rules, and the patients benefitted greatly. Parkinson's Law in Psychotherapy (Appelbaum, 1975) holds true here. Necessity may be the mother (or father) of effective intervention as well as invention!

Reading about these cases and other early "one session" reports helped to inspire us to "think outside the box" and try something new. "Ever run the short way," wrote Marcus Aurelius (c. 167 A.D./1964) in his *Meditations*, "and the short way is the way of nature, with perfect soundness in each word and deed as the goal." We had to shift our thinking:

> How could it be called therapy if therapy implies deep and long-term changes in personality? I was trained to see therapy as a relatively long process, and my own therapy terminated only after several years. Originally, the very idea of therapy lasting for only one session struck me as incredible. It took hundreds of single session cases and two years of research for me to fully appreciate the therapeutic potential of the first and only session." (Talmon, 1990, p. xv)

Still, we were (pleasantly) surprised when clinical experience and systematic data began to accumulate that unequivocally answered in the affirmative the question with which we began our introduction in Chapter 1: "Could one therapy session be enough for some people?"

It is now very well established and many times proven (see Appendix A) that single sessions are the most common length of therapy and that the so-called "ultra-brief therapies" (up to six sessions) cover the vast majority of all treated cases—and that many patients want and benefit from these meetings. SST is both a mindset (making the most of each session, maybe only needing one) and a clinical phenomenon (given that many clients elect to only come once, what we actually do during the meeting), the basic purpose being not a reduction in services but actually better services that "capture the moment" by aligning with many clients' natural preferences while freeing time and resources for other clients needing different lengths of therapy.

In our original study we found that when both therapists and clients initially agreed to make the most of the first session, about one-half the cases successfully finished with the one session. Our colleagues who have established walk-in services have found that single sessions can work out well with up to 80% of clients. All the walk-in services welcome return clients and continuously help them within the one-at-a-time framework.

The general walk-in model described in this book and employed in Canada, the U.S., Australia, China, and Mexico is in more than one way a much more "pure" version of SST and the constructive minimalistic approach than what we originally presented. It is understood in advance that there will be only one face-to-face meeting. It usually lasts for one hour. It has no pre-session phone call and no follow-up phone conversation. Most of the time, there is no routine psychodiagnostic ("*DSM*") assessment. All that is needed is a group of therapists who believe in the concept and are trained to carry it out as often and as well as possible. They make their accessible, ethical, and effective counseling service available to thousands of people who are not very likely to attend a more formal therapy with traditional pre-scheduled appointments. They make their services available in friendly and easily approachable places like shopping malls and on street corners with "Walk-Ins Welcome" and "No Appointment Needed" signs, a simple and very useful application to modern urban life.

One of the unique contributions of this book is that it is not limited to presenting strong research data and many clinical examples and guidelines for how to conduct effective SSTs. Our Australian, Canadian, and American colleagues also present information on the much longer processes of providing implementation and ongoing training. Slive and Bobele (Chapters 5–6) and McElheran (Chapter 10) have played important leadership roles in this area. Since 1996, the Bouverie Centre (see Chapters 7–8; also Young, et al., 2012) has trained thousands of individual practitioners in SST and has helped hundreds of organizations implement SST into their services. It has been found that the stronger the link between practitioner values and the philosophy of the organization, the easier implementation will be. For example, the Australians have had greater success implementing SST in services which embrace a social model of health and celebrate client empowerment and less success with services which primarily value the expertise of the professional staff to determine the direction of client care. Clearly, when the expertise is in individual work it will be much harder to implement family work, when the expertise is in a medical model it will be much harder to employ non-medical or non-pathology language, and so on. In the same way, extensive history taking and problem-saturated talk makes "solution sight" (Hoyt, 2008, p. 282) much less likely to take place.

Being that therapy is a collaborative effort, the mindset and attitude of the therapist can be of great help to clients to help themselves—as well as helping both the therapist and client to experience a more enjoyable and co-creative process. As Steve de Shazer said (in Hoyt, 1994a, p. 13):

> [E]very session is somehow a unique event, and the main thing that the therapist has to do is listen and keep it simple. And if you do it, I think, the clients will tell you what to do...[E]ven people who have been in the field for a long time and have lots of "experience" get married to their theories, as we all do. But they won't pay attention to what works. Even stuff they do. So I think that's what's really difficult, to me, with the older, more experienced practitioners, usually, is that they know all this stuff about what works but they don't know they know it. And they get hung up on looking at what doesn't work. It's good to know what doesn't work, but it's really helpful to know what does.

Many of the chapter contributors have found it most useful to integrate methods from various schools of therapy—including the MRI model, solution-focused, narrative, Haley's problem-solving, and Ericksonian hypnotherapy—that have been collectively subsumed under the umbrella of *constructive therapies* (Hoyt, 1994b, 1996b, 1998). Shifting toward approaches that focus on client strengths and resources (rather than on putative pathology) entails a rethinking of our roles. Again using golf as a metaphor, Hoyt (2000b, p. 8, emphasis in original) thus advised: "Collaborative, competency-based therapists may like the thought: 'I'm the caddy, not the player—my job is often to hand them one of *their* clubs, offer encouragement, and maybe give some advice about traps and strange winds.'"

With the growing pressure for industrialization and cost-effectiveness of psychotherapy services we have witnessed a growing number of evidence-based unified protocols offered for specific diagnostic groups. Although we gladly provide in this book several general guidelines for SST processes (e.g., see Appendix B), we strongly believe that any attempts for "one-size-fits-all" detailed manuals are most likely to hinder both the effectiveness as well as the creative and surprising elements of each first session and each first encounter.

We are pleased to acknowledge the many different models, techniques, and theoretical backgrounds reported in this book. We have noticed, however, that "theoretical orientation" rarely matters to the client. Our theoretical stand is important for our professional identity. The evidence (see Duncan & Miller, 2000; Duncan, Miller, Wampold, & Hubble, 2010) says that it is the contribution of the client—not the therapist—that really makes the difference. Preferably, let your next client's worldview and theory of change (Duncan, Hubble, Miller, & Coleman, 1998) lead the way in your next session.

On the Past, Present, and Future of Our Time

As our esteemed colleague and partner in the original SST research project, Bob Rosenbaum, elegantly notes in Chapter 3: "This is the time of our life and we are the time of our life." By the traditional chronological clock, the editors of this volume are, by now, elders who were young when we first attempted to study planned and unplanned SSTs during the 1980s.

We both can still experience right now the same enthusiasm, devotion, and excitement we felt as young therapists who were "the new kids on the block" during the 1980s. We also now, at the very same moment, have the perspective (and, we hope, the wisdom) of elders who between us have conducted psychotherapy for more than 65 years and have seen thousands of individuals, couples, and families for an SST—as well as others for an intermittent and sometimes ongoing, open-ended therapy (some of which have lasted, in much fewer instances, for many years). We can experience ourselves as both very young as well as old and can take advantage of both the enthusiasm of a "beginner's mind" combined with the perspective and wisdom of elders.

All the contributors in this book are also well experienced. Each of us has seen plenty of single session cases in various ways. Most of us continue to see patients regularly and still find it a meaningful and rewarding work of passion and love. As noted by most of the contributors to this volume, SST is about expanding and enriching mental health services and making them more accessible and more respectful of clients' choices, resources, and strengths. Doing therapy is an adventure. It is forever evolving, changing, and always presenting new and surprising information that constantly challenges us with every beginning of a first session.

The overwhelming data about the high frequency and strong efficacy of SST is by now a well-established fact all around the world. Many clients know and appreciate it. Managers who are concerned about cost-effectiveness gladly welcome and embrace SSTs and wish to implement them into their services. The on-going challenge was and still is with the providers. Given the accumulated evidence of SST effectiveness coupled with the great need to provide services to many more people, why has SST not yet been more widely embraced by clinicians? We think there are several issues—and constructive answers:

- Many clinicians are busy in their practices and not yet aware of the mounting evidence. As the information contained in this volume becomes more widely known, some providers will be more open to trying briefer (including single session) interventions. Long ago, impressed by their experiences with short-term therapies, psychoanalysts Lewis Wolberg (1965), David Malan (1976), and Michael Franz Basch (1995) all recommended trying briefer approaches first before assuming the need for and moving on to longer approaches. Their example can now be extended: *for lots of patients, try "very brief or ultra-brief" (i.e., maybe one session) first, then "brief," and only if that doesn't work, then "longer."* Recognizing that many patients *de facto* are only going to appear once—including those who self-select by walking into clinics expecting single session therapy as well as those seen in other settings where therapy could have gone on longer but they decide to stop after one or a few meetings—it also makes sense to develop ways to enhance the likelihood that these brief encounters will be useful and satisfying for all involved. For some, this will require adjusting mindsets, both those of the clinician and the client.
- Some therapists may also be concerned that if they begin practicing more shorter-term therapies with some clients, that "the system" (read: insurance, HMOs) will somehow use that to claim that *all* therapy should be one-session or at least very brief and may curtail treatment and not provide longer-term care for those who need it. As Cummings (2000, p. 77) has advised, "Indeed, sometimes there are single ses-

sion treatments that can be the right thing for some patients, but this should not be interpreted too broadly. It is for those who choose a single session that the benefits can be significant." It will be important for clients, therapists, patient advocates, healthcare coverage purchasers, insurance companies, and unions to assure that short-term models are not applied inappropriately. Again, we want to make explicit that we strongly favor larger budgets and better care being allocated for those in need, including the underprivileged.

· For some providers, however, there are still the beliefs that "more is almost always better," "deeper is better," and that "real therapy takes a long time" and that other approaches are simply "superficial" or palliative "quick-fixes" without effecting any meaningful, "significant" improvement—despite lots of evidence to the contrary (see Appendix A). Slive and Bobele (2011; also see Chapter 5) note how single session (and brief) therapy is sometimes dismissed as a "Band-Aid"—even though Band-Aids have been shown to be very helpful in allowing the body's natural healing processes to occur! Hoyt (1995) and Duval, et al. (2012) have also adumbrated lists of therapist resistances, including the need to be needed and difficulties saying goodbye; Hoyt and Budman (1996) describe being vilified for suggesting a short-term approach as the treatment of choice for some patients. We have more than once encountered the "status game" wherein an earnest, well-meaning colleague in private practice learns of our interest in brief, time-sensitive therapy and looks down his or her nose, proudly saying "Oh, I used to do that—but now I see my patients for as long as I can." (There is sometimes also the underlying belief that "It took me, a highly-educated mental health professional, three years with Dr. X to get my stuff together—so how can this poor devil hope to get anything in just a visit or two?") Some therapists feel a strong need to be the "hero" or "central figure" rather than seeing their expertise as primarily assisting the client/patient. They want to "be there" as the client makes changes, rather than accepting a more momentary role of some contact, support, and direction…and then having to live with not knowing what happened. (Budman and Gurman, 1988, p. 11, nicely contrast the dominant values of the long-term and short-term therapist.) Graduate school professors and workshop presenters sometimes reinforce this "need to be needed" by demonstrating their own brilliance rather than focusing on helping identify the client's "brilliance" or "resourcefulness." In single session and walk-in services, clients come when they want, most report that they got what they came for, and they know that they can return when they want to. We hope that readers will be attracted to the elegance of doing more with less. In 1656 the French philosopher Blaise Pascal (quoted in Benham, 1914, p. 718) finished a letter to a friend by writing: "I have only made this letter rather long because I have not had time to make it shorter." (*"Je n'ai fait celle-ci plus longue que parceque ju n'ai pas eu le loisir de la faire plus courte."*) Indeed, it takes time and skill both to write concisely and to practice therapy concisely, especially in a single session!

- In addition to intellectual, theoretical, technical, and cultural considerations (including the archetype or meme of the wise savior rescuing the afflicted)…*follow the money!* Especially with a tight economy and managed care already restricting services, it is hard to let a full-fee patient go. Sometimes helping someone quickly will result in developing a reputation for results and will generate other referrals, but in the short run "longer" tends to be more predictable (not needing as often to fill empty appointment slots with new patients) and more lucrative. We don't think that there are many venal clinicians who deliberately extend treatment simply to make more money, but we have certainly noticed—in ourselves as well as others—that it is easier to justify extending treatment (e.g., "working through," "consolidating gains," "relapse prevention," "exploring issues," "promoting deeper healing," "following the patient") when the patient is attractive and financially able. Briefer forms of therapy will probably continue to be the mainstay of clinics and training centers and, as we have noted several times, single session (and other brief) therapy is not always enough, but the need to make money needs to be balanced against the awareness that we are ultimately in a service profession, and that our prime directive should be serving the needs of our clients rather than our pocketbooks.

Perhaps the greatest challenge in being an SST therapist in the current climate is grappling with the ever-present message our society sends that "more is better." In fact, when we first presented our research at the American Psychological Association's 1989 annual convention, the theme of the convention that year, displayed on a large banner in the conference hall, was "More is Better." As therapists we are not immune to this message: we can be tempted by more prestige by being "The Expert" in therapy sessions; we can be tempted by feeling more needed by clients seen as more needy; and we can be tempted by more income from more sessions. We would do well to remember the warning voiced 2500 years ago in the *Tao Te Ching* (Rosenbaum, 2013):

> *No curse is worse than grasping at more.*
> *The contentment that comes from knowing enough is enough*
> *Is abiding contentment in truth.*

We hope that this volume will help therapists from all orientations, settings, and habits of practice. As Michele Ritterman notes in Chapter 20: "*Time* and the *experience of time* is perhaps the most important element in life and healing today. For all of us **time, timing** and **our sense of time** is **now**. This is perhaps the central issue in determining the therapies we need."

As many clients and therapists have discovered, SST can be as up-to-date as tomorrow's sunrise.

References

Angelou, M. (1993) *On the pulse of morning*. New York: Random House.

Appelbaum, S.A. (1975) Parkinson's Law in psychotherapy. *International Journal of Psychoanalytic Psychotherapy*, 4, 426–436.

Aurelius, M. (1964) *Meditations*. (M. Staniforth, Trans.) London, England: Penguin Books. (original work written in Greek around A.D. 167)

Basch, M.F. (1995) *Doing therapy briefly*. New York: Basic Books.

Benham, W.G. (1914) *Cassell's book of quotations* (rev. ed.). London: Cassell & Company.

Boscolo, L., & Bertrando, P. (1993) *The times of time*. New York: Norton.

Budman, S.H., & Gurman, A.S. (1988) *Theory and practice of brief therapy*. New York: Guilford Press.

Chandler, M., & Mason, W. (1995) Solution-focused therapy: An alternative approach to addictions nursing. *Perspectives on Psychiatric Care*, 31(1), 8–13.

Cummings, E.E. (1972) "stand with your lover on the ending earth." In *Complete poems 1913–1962* (p. 743). Orlando, FL: Harcourt Brace Jovanovich. (work originally published 1958)

Cummings, N.A. (2000) The single session misunderstanding. In *The collected papers of Nicholas A. Cummings. Vol. 1: The value of psychological treatment* (p. 77). Phoenix, AZ: Zeig, Tucker, & Theisen.

de Shazer, S. (1988) *Clues: Investigating solutions in brief therapy*. New York: Norton.

Duncan, B.L., Hubble, M.A., Miller, S.D., & Coleman, S.T. (1998) Escaping from the lost worlds of impossibility: Honoring clients' language, motivation, and theories of change. In M.F. Hoyt (Ed.), *The handbook of constructive therapies* (pp. 293–313). San Francisco: Jossey-Bass.

Duncan, B.L., & Miller, S.D. (2000) *The heroic client: Doing client-directed, outcome-oriented therapy*. San Francisco: Jossey-Bass.

Duncan, B.L., Miller, S.D., Wampold, B.E., & Hubble, M.A. (Eds.) (2010) *The heart and soul of change: Delivering what works in therapy*. Washington, DC: APA Books.

Duval, J., Young, K., & Kays-Burden, A. (2012, November) *No more, no less: Brief mental health services for children and youth*. Policy paper, Ontario Centre of Excellence for Child and Youth Mental Health. Available from www.excellenceforchildrenandyouth.ca.

Ecker, B., Ticic, R., & Hulley, L. (2012) *Unlocking the emotional brain: Eliminating symptoms at their roots using memory reconsolidation*. New York: Routledge.

Fisch, R., Weakland, J.H., & Segal, L. (1982) *The tactics of change: Doing therapy briefly*. San Francisco: Jossey-Bass.

Fraser, J.S., & Solovey, A.D. (2007) *Second-order change in psychotherapy: The golden thread that unifies effective treatments*. Washington, DC: APA Books.

Freud, A. (Ed.) (1960) *Letters of Sigmund Freud*. New York: Basic Books.

Gay, P. (1988) *Freud: A life for our times*. New York: Norton.

Gilbert, D. (2005) *Stumbling on happiness*. New York: Knopf.

Goulding, M.M., & Goulding, R.L. (1979) *Changing lives through redecision therapy*. New York: Grove Press.

Greenberg, G., Ganshorn, K., & Danilkewich, A. (2001) Solution-focused therapy: Counseling model for busy family physicians. *Canadian Family Physician, 47*, 2289–2295.

Gustafson, J.P. (1986) *The complex secret of brief psychotherapy*. New York: Norton.

Gustafson, J.P. (2005) *Very brief psychotherapy*. New York: Routledge.

Haley, J. (1963) *Strategies of psychotherapy*. New York: Grune & Stratton.

Haley, J. (1982) The contribution to therapy of Milton H. Erickson, M.D. In J.K. Zeig (Ed.), *Ericksonian approaches to hypnosis and psychotherapy* (pp. 5–25). New York: Brunner/Mazel.

Haley, J. (1990) Why not long-term therapy? In J.K. Zeig & S.G. Gilligan (Eds.), *Brief therapy: Myths, methods, and metaphors* (pp. 3–17). New York: Brunner/Mazel.

Hesse, H. (1969) *The glass bead game* (R. Winston & C. Winston, Trans.). Troy, MO: Holt, Rinehart, & Winston. (work originally published in German 1943)

Hoyt, M.F. (1990) On time in brief therapy. In R.A. Wells & V.J. Giannetti (Eds.), *Handbook of the brief psychotherapies* (pp. 115–143). New York: Plenum.

Hoyt, M.F. (1994a) On the importance of keeping it simple and taking the patient seriously: A conversation with Steve de Shazer and John Weakland. In M.F. Hoyt (Ed.), *Constructive therapies* (pp. 11–40). New York: Guilford Press.

Hoyt, M.F. (Ed.) (1994b) *Constructive therapies*. New York: Guilford Press.

Hoyt, M.F. (1995) Therapist resistances to short-term dynamic psychotherapy. In *Brief therapy and managed care: Readings for contemporary practice* (pp. 219–235). San Francisco: Jossey-Bass.

Hoyt, M.F. (1996a) Solution building and language games: A conversation with Steve de Shazer (and some after words with Insoo Kim Berg). In M.F. Hoyt (Ed.), *Constructive therapies* (Vol. 2, pp. 69–85). New York: Guilford Press.

Hoyt, M.F. (Ed.) (1996b) *Constructive therapies* (Vol. 2). New York: Guilford Press.

Hoyt, M.F. (Ed.) (1998) *The handbook of constructive therapies*. San Francisco: Jossey-Bass.

Hoyt, M.F. (2000) *Some stories are better than others: Doing what works in brief therapy and managed care*. Philadelphia: Brunner/Mazel.

Hoyt, M.F. (2008) Solution-focused couple therapy. In A.S. Gurman (Ed.), *Clinical handbook of couple therapy* (4th ed., pp. 259–295). New York: Guilford Press.

Hoyt, M.F. (2009) *Brief psychotherapies: Principles and practices*. Phoenix, AZ: Zeig, Tucker, & Theisen.

Hoyt, M.F., & Budman, S.H. (1996) Fear and loathing on the managed-care trail: A response to Pipal (1995). *Psychotherapy, 33*, 121–123.

Hoyt, M.F., Rosenbaum, R., & Talmon, M. (1992) Planned single session psychotherapy. In S.H. Budman, M.F. Hoyt, & S. Friedman (Eds.), *The first session in brief therapy* (pp. 59–86). New York: Guilford Press.

Kazantzakis, N. (1965) *Report to Greco*. New York: Bantam Books. (work originally published in Greek 1961)

Kuehn, J.L. (1965) Encounter at Leyden: Gustav Mahler consults Sigmund Freud. *Psychoanalytic Review, 52*, 345–364.

Lehrer, J. (2010, December 10) The truth wears off. *The New Yorker*, 52–57.

Linehan, M.M. (1993) *Cognitive-behavioral treatment of borderline personality disorder*. New York: Guilford Press.

Malan, D.H. (1976) *The frontier of brief psychotherapy*. New York: Plenum.

McNeilly, R. (1994) Solution-oriented counseling: A 20-minute format for medical practice. *Australian Family Physician, 23*, 228–230.

O'Hanlon, W.H. (1999) *Do one thing different: And other uncommonly sensible solutions to life's persistent problems*. New York: William Morrow.

Omer, H. (1994) *Critical interventions in psychotherapy: From impasse to turning point*. New York: Norton.

Padesky, C.A. (2012) *Simplifying personality disorder treatment: A new paradigm for CBT*. Workshop, Santa Rosa, CA, April 27–28.

Ritterman, M. (2005) *Using hypnosis in family therapy* (rev. ed.). Phoenix, AZ: Zeig, Tucker, & Theisen.

Rosenbaum, R. (2013) *Walking the way: 81 Zen encounters with the Tao Te Ching.* Boston, MA: Wisdom Publications.

Rosenbaum, R., Hoyt, M.F., & Talmon, M. (1990) The challenge of single session therapies: Creating pivotal moments. In R.A. Wells & V.J. Giannetti (Eds.), *Handbook of the brief psychotherapies* (pp. 165–189). New York: Plenum.

Slive, A., & Bobele, M. (Eds.) (2011) *When one hour is all you have: Effective therapy for walk-in clients.* Phoenix, AZ: Zeig, Tucker, & Theisen.

Stern, D.N. (2004) *The present moment in psychotherapy and everyday life.* New York: Norton.

Talmon, M. (1990) *Single session therapy: Maximizing the effect of the first (and often only) therapeutic encounter.* San Francisco: Jossey-Bass.

Tolle, E. (1999) *The power of now: A guide to spiritual enlightenment.* Novato, CA: New World Library.

Watts, R.E., & Pietrzak, D. (2000) Adlerian "encouragement" and the therapeutic process of solution-focused brief therapy. *Journal of Counseling and Development, 78,* 442–447.

White, M., & Epston, D. (1990) *Narrative means to therapeutic ends.* New York: Norton.

Wolberg, L.R. (Ed.) (1965) *Short-term psychotherapy.* New York: Grune & Stratton.

Yapko, M.D. (1989) Disturbances of temporal orientation as a feature of depression. In M.D. Yapko (Ed.), *Brief therapy approaches to treating anxiety and depression* (pp. 106–118). New York: Brunner/Mazel.

Yapko, M.D. (1990) Brief therapy tactics in longer-term psychotherapies. In J.K. Zeig & S.G. Gilligan (Eds.), *Brief therapy: Myths, methods, and metaphors* (pp. 185–195). New York: Brunner/Mazel.

Young, J., Weir, S., & Rycroft, P. (2012) Implementing single session therapy. *Australian and New Zealand Journal of Family Therapy, 33*(1), 84–97.

Appendix A

What the Literature Says: An Annotated Bibliography

Michael F. Hoyt and Moshe Talmon

In addition to the preceding chapters and the citations therein, the number of SST case reports continues to mount, including those from practitioners whose theoretical models do not necessarily intend to be one session. For some examples drawn from various approaches, see:

Adlerian/Individual Therapy

Carlson, J. (2005) *Adlerian therapy*. Washington, DC: APA Books (APA Psychotherapy Video Series).
Powers, R.L., & Griffith, J. (1989) Single-session psychotherapy involving two therapists. *Individual Psychology*, 45 (1–2), 99–125.

Bereavement Counseling

Shakian, B.J., & Charlesworth, G. (1994) Masked bereavement presenting as agoraphobia. *Behavioural and Cognitive Psychotherapy*, 22(2), 177–180.

Cognitive Analytic Therapy

Cowmeadow, P. (1995) Very brief psychotherapeutic interventions with deliberate self-harmers. In A. Ryle (Ed.), *Cognitive analytic therapy: Developments in theory and practice* (pp. 55–66). New York: Wiley.

Coherence Therapy

Ecker, B., & Hulley, L. (2008) Coherence therapy: Swift change at the core of symptom production. In J.D. Raskin & S.K. Bridges (Eds.), *Studies in meaning 3* (pp. 57–83). New York: Pace University Press.

Ericksonian Therapy

Erickson, M.H. (2008) Burden of responsibility in effective psychotherapy. In *Collected works of Milton H. Erickson* (Vol. 3, pp. 67–71; E. Rossi, R. Erickson-Klein, & K. Rossi, Eds.). Phoenix, AZ: Milton H. Erickson Foundation Press. (work originally published 1964)

Flemons, D., & Gralnik, L.M. (2013). *Relational suicide assessment: Risks, resources, and possibilities for safety* (pp. 50–51). New York: Norton

Hoyt, M.F. (1995) *Brief therapy and managed care: Readings for contemporary practice* (pp. 163–176). San Francisco: Jossey-Bass.

Hoyt, M.F. (2000) What can we learn from Milton Erickson's therapeutic failures? In *Some stories are better than others* (pp. 189–194).

> *This book chapter discusses how Erickson struggled to find explanations for why some of his single session cases did not succeed. Being a strategic therapist, he looked to himself to make something happen (or assumed responsibility if it did not); but, recognizing the cardinal importance of the patient's contribution (on which rests the principle of utilization), he also included the client's motivations and effort in his search.*

Hoyt, M.F., & Ritterman, M. (2012) Brief therapy in a taxi. *The Milton H. Erickson Foundation Newsletter, 32*(2), 7.

Lankton, S.R., & Erickson, K.K. (Eds.) (1994) The essence of a single session success. *Ericksonian Monographs, 9*, vii–164.

Marcus, J.D. (1999) An Ericksonian approach to crack cocaine addiction: A single-session intervention. *Contemporary Hypnosis, 16*, 95–102.

O'Hanlon, W.H., & Hexum, A.L. (1990) *An uncommon casebook: The complete clinical work of Milton H. Erickson, M.D.* New York: Norton.

> *This work reviews all of the then-known reports of Erickson's "complete clinical cases, that is, cases in which there was a clear presenting problem and/or request for treatment and a conclusion, whether success, failure, or dismissal" (p. x). At the time of their writing, the authors were able to identify and summarize 316 cases. Of these, 67 involved a single session treatment for a wide variety of problems, including smoking cessation, pain control, bedwetting, marital and sexual problems, debilitating test anxiety, sleep difficulties, and even a block/ resistance in psychoanalysis. A potpourri of strategies and techniques were employed, and success was reported in 62 of the cases, failure in 5.*

Ritterman, M. (2005) *Using hypnosis in family therapy* (2nd ed.). Phoenix, AZ: Zeig, Tucker & Theisen. (work originally published 1983)

Ritterman, M. (2013) The tao of a woman. In M.F. Hoyt (Ed.), *Therapist stories of inspiration, passion and renewal: What's love got to do with it?* (pp.

214–231). New York: Routledge. Short, D. (2013) Finding humanity in darkness. In M.F. Hoyt (Ed.), *Therapist stories of inspiration, passion and renewal: What's love got to do with it?* (pp. 251–262). New York: Routledge.

Yapko, M. (1990) The case of Vicki: Hypnosis for coping with cancer. In *Trancework* (2nd ed.; pp. 347–404). New York: Brunner/Mazel.

Zeig, J.K. (2006) *Confluence: The selected papers of Jeffrey K. Zeig* (Vol. 1). Phoenix, AZ: Zeig, Tucker, & Theisen.

Experiential Therapy

Mahrer, A.R., & Robege, M. (1993) Single-session experiential therapy with any person whatsoever. In R.A. Wells & V.J. Giannetti (Eds.), *Casebook of the brief psychotherapies* (pp. 179–196). New York: Plenum.

Kottler, J., & Carlson, J. (2008) *Their finest hour: Master therapists share their greatest success stories* (pp. 219–228, "The Gardener Who Dug Very Deep: A Case from Alvin Mahrer"). Bethel, CT: Crown House Publishing.

Exposure Therapy

Tolchard, B., Thomas, L., & Battersby, M. (2006) Case reports and single session exposure therapy for problem gambling: A single-case experimental design. *Behavior Change*, 23(2), 148–155.

Eye Movement Desensitization and Reprocessing (EMDR)

Jarero, I., & Uribe, S. (2011) The EMDR protocol for recent critical incidents: Brief report of an application in a human massacre situation. *Journal of EMDR Practice and Research*, 5(4), 156–165.

Kutz, I., Resnik, V., & Dekel, R. (2008) The effect of single-session modified EMDR on acute stress syndromes. *Journal of EMDR Practice and Research*, 2(3), 190–200.

McCann, D.L. (1992) Post-traumatic stress disorder due to devastating burns overcome by a single session of eye movement desensitization. *Journal of Behavior Therapy and Experimental Psychiatry*, 23(4), 319–323.

Newgent, R., Paladino, D., & Reynolds, C. (2006) Single session treatment of nontraumatic fear of flying with eye movement desensitization reprocessing: Pre- and post-September 11. *Clinical Case Studies*, 5(1), 25–36.

Focused Acceptance and Commitment Therapy (FACT)

Strosahl, K., Gustavvson, T., & Robinson, P. (2012) *Brief interventions for radical behavior change: Principles and practice of focused acceptance and commitment therapy.* Oakland, CA: New Harbinger Publications.

Gestalt Therapy

Harman, R. (1995) Gestalt therapy as brief therapy. *Gestalt Journal*, 18, 77–85.

Hypnosis

Singh, R. (1992) Single-session hypnotic treatment of insomnia in religious context. *Australian Journal of Clinical and Experimental Hypnosis*, 20(2), 111–116.

Narrative Therapy

Phillips, P. (2002) Shoulder to shoulder: A single session success story. *Journal of College Student Psychotherapy*, 16(3/4), 225–237.

Young, K. (2011a) When all the time you have is NOW: Re-visiting practices and narrative therapy in a walk-in clinic. In J. Duvall & L. Beres (Eds.), *Innovations in narrative therapy: Connecting practice, training, and research* (pp. 147–166). New York: Norton.

Young, K. (2011b) Narrative practices at a walk-in therapy clinic. In A. Slive & M. Bobele (Eds.), *When one session is all you have: Effective therapy for walk-in clients* (pp. 149–166). Phoenix, AZ: Zeig, Tucker, & Theisen.

Neurolinguistic Programming (NLP)

Austin, A.T. (2007) *The rainbow machine: Tales from a neurolinguist's journal.* Boulder, CO: Real People Press.

Psychoanalytic/Psychodynamic Therapy

Davanloo, H. (1978) Short-term dynamic psychotherapy of one or two sessions' duration. In H. Davanloo (Ed.), *Basic principles and techniques in short-term dynamic* psychotherapy (pp. 307–326). New York: Spectrum Publications.

Kuehn, J.L. (1965) Encounter at Leyden: Gustav Mahler consults Sigmund Freud. *Psychoanalytic Review*, 52, 345–364.

Oremland, J.D. (1976) A curious resolution of a hysterical symptom. *International Review of Psychoanalysis*, 3, 473–477.

Springmann, R.R. (1978) Single session psychotherapy in secondary male impotence. *Mental Health and Society*, 5, 86–93.

Springmann, R.R. (1982) Some remarks on psychotherapy by a single interpretation. *Journal of Psychiatric Treatment and Education*, 4, 327–332.

Stadter, M. (1996) *Object relations brief therapy: The therapeutic relationship in short-term work* (pp. 226–232). Northvale, NJ: Jason Aronson.

Rational Emotive Behavior Therapy

Ellis, A. (1989) Using rational-emotive therapy (RET) as crisis intervention: A single session with a suicidal client. *Individual Psychology*, 45, 75–81.

Ellis, A. (1996) *Better, deeper and more enduring brief therapy*. New York: Routledge/Mazel.

Kottler, J. (2013) Love is a four-letter word in therapy. In M.F. Hoyt (Ed.), *Therapist stories of inspiration, passion, and renewal: What's love got to do with it?* (pp. 175–180). New York: Routledge.

Redecision Therapy

Hoyt, M.F. (1995) *Brief therapy and managed care: Readings for contemporary practice* (pp. 99–101). San Francisco: Jossey-Bass.

Sex Therapy

Green, S.K., & Flemons, D. (Eds.) (2004) *Quickies: The handbook of brief sex therapy*. New York: Norton.

Solution-Focused Anxiety Management

Quick, E.K. (2013) *Solution-focused anxiety management: A treatment and training manual* (pp. 147–148). San Diego, CA: Academic Press.

Strategic Therapy

Blymer, D., (1991) The rapid resolution of auditory hallucinations. *Journal of Strategic and Systemic Therapies*, 10(2), 1–5.

Boscolo, L., & Bertrando, P. (1993) *The times of time*. New York: Norton.

Wetchler, J.L. (1994) Brief strategic treatment of a male with HIV hypochondria. *Journal of Family Psychotherapy*, 5, 1–9.

Multi-Subject Studies

A number of SST reviews, involving various cohorts of patients, also have been published:

Bloom, B.L. (1981) Focused single-session therapy: Initial development and evaluation. In S.H. Budman (Ed.), *Forms of brief therapy* (pp. 167–216). New York: Guilford Press.

Bloom, B.L. (1992) Bloom's focused single-session therapy. In *Planned short-term psychotherapy: A clinical handbook* (2nd ed.; pp. 97–121). Boston: Allyn & Bacon.

Bloom, B.L. (2001) Focused single-session psychotherapy: A review of the clinical and research literature. *Brief Treatment and Crisis Intervention*, 1, 75–86.

Boyhan, P.A. (1996) Clients' perceptions of single session consultations as an option to waiting for family therapy. *Australian and New Zealand Journal of Family Therapy*, 17(2), 85–96.

Cameron, C. (2007) Single session and walk-in psychotherapy: A descriptive account of the literature. *Counselling and Psychotherapy Research*, 7(4), 245–249.

Campbell, A. (1999) Single session interventions: An example of clinical research in practice. *Australian and New Zealand Journal of Family Therapy*, 20(4), 183–194.

Campbell, A. (2012) Single session approaches to therapy: A time to review. *Australian and New Zealand Journal of Family Therapy*, 33(1), 15–26.

Duval, J., Young, K., & Kays-Burden, A. (2012, November) *No more, No less: Brief mental health services for children and youth*. Policy paper, Ontario Centre of Excellence for Child and Youth Mental Health. Available from www.excellenceforchildandyouth.ca.

Hoyt, M.F. (1994) Single session solutions. In M.F. Hoyt (Ed.), *Constructive therapies* (pp. 140–159). New York: Guilford Press.

Hoyt, M.F. (2009) *Brief psychotherapies: Principles and practices*. Phoenix, AZ: Zeig, Tucker & Theisen

Hoyt, M.F., Rosenbaum, R., & Talmon, M. (1992) Planned single-session psychotherapy. In S.H. Budman, M.F. Hoyt, & S. Friedman (Eds.), *The first session in brief therapy* (pp. 59–86). New York: Guilford Press.

Hurn, R. (2005) Single-session therapy: Planned success or unplanned failure? *CounsellingPsychology Review*, 20(4), 33–40.

Hymmen, P., Stalker, C., & Cait, C.-A. (2012). The case for single-session therapy: Does the empirical evidence support the increased prevalence of this service delivery model? *Journal of Mental Health*, Early Online, 1–12.

Littlepage, G.E., Kosloski, K.D., Schnelle, J.F., McNees, M.P., & Gendrich, J.C. (1976) The problem of early outpatient terminations from community mental health centers: A problem for whom? *Journal of Community Psychology*, 4, 164–167.

Paul, K.E., & van Ommeren, M. (2013) A primer on single session therapy and its potential application in humanitarian situations. *Intervention*, 11(1), 8–23.

Rockwell, W.J.K., & Pinkerton, R.S. (1982) Single-session psychotherapy. *American Journal of Psychotherapy*, 36, 32–40.

Rosenbaum, R., Hoyt, M.F., & Talmon, M. (1990) The challenge of single-session therapies: Creating pivotal moments. In R.A. Wells & V.J. Giannetti (Eds.), *Handbook of the brief psychotherapies* (pp. 165–189). New York: Plenum Press.

Silverman, W.H., & Beech, R.P. (1979) Are dropouts, dropouts? *Journal of Community Psychology*, 7, 236–242.

Slive, A., & Bobele, M. (Eds.) (2011) *When one hour is all you have: Effective therapy for walk-in clients*. Phoenix, AZ: Zeig, Tucker & Theisen.

Spoerl, O.H. (1975) Single-session psychotherapy. *Diseases of the Nervous System*, 36, 283–285.

Talmon, M. (1990) *Single session therapy: Maximizing the effect of the first (and often only) therapeutic encounter*. San Francisco: Jossey-Bass.

Talmon, M. (1993) *Single session solutions: A guide to practical, effective, and affordable therapy*. Reading, MA: Addison-Wesley.

Here is a sampling of what the research (some cited in the reviews above, some not) says:

The most common (modal) length of therapy is one visit, with 20%–58% of general psychiatric/psychotherapy patients not returning—for better or worse—after their initial visit.

Baekeland, F., & Lundwall, L. (1975) Dropping out of treatment: A critical review. *Psychological Bulletin*, 82, 738–783.

Bloom, B.L. (2001) Focused single-session psychotherapy: A review of the clinical and research literature. *Brief Treatment and Crisis Intervention*, 1(1), 75–86.

Brandt, L.W. (1965) Studies of "dropout" patients in psychotherapy: A review of findings. *Psychotherapy: Theory, Research, and Practice*, 2, 2–13.

Kaffman, M. (1995) Brief therapy in the Israeli kibbutz. *Contemporary Family Therapy*, 17, 449–468.

Pekarik, G. (1992a) Relationship of clients' reasons for dropping out of treatment to outcome and satisfaction. *Journal of Clinical Psychology*, 48, 91–98.

Pekarik, G. (1992b) Posttreatment adjustment of clients who drop out early vs. late in treatment. *Journal of Clinical Psychology*, 48, 379–387.

Scamardo, M., Bobele, M., & Biever, J.L. (2004) A new perspective on client dropouts. *Journal of Systemic Therapies*, 23(2), 27–38.

Simon, G.E., Imel, Z.E., Ludman, E.J., & Steinfeld, B.J. (2012) Is dropout after a first psychotherapy visit always a bad outcome? *Psychiatric Services*, 63(7), 705.

Talmon, M. (1990) *Single session therapy: Maximizing the effect of the first (and often only) therapeutic encounter*. San Francisco: Jossey-Bass.

From clients' point of view, a single session is often what is needed.

Carey, T. A., Tai, S. J., & Stiles, W. B. (2013). Effective and efficient: Using patient-led appointment scheduling in routine mental health practice in remote Australia. *Professional Psychology: Research and Practice*, 44(6), 405–414.

> *Data from Alice Springs, Australia supports the "effective and efficient" practice of allowing patients to call for appointments when wanted, rather than having regularly scheduled visits; they also report that 25 of 92 studied patients chose to attend for a single session (even though more were available).*

Hoyt, M. F., Rosenbaum, R., & Talmon, M. (1992). Planned single-session psychotherapy. In S.H. Budman, M.F. Hoyt, & S. Friedman (Eds.), *The first session in brief therapy* (pp. 59–86). New York: Guilford Press.
> *See Talmon (1990) in this section for more information.*

Hymmen, P., Stalker, C., & Cait, C. A. (2012). The case for single-session therapy: Does the empirical evidence support the increased prevalence of this service delivery model? *Journal of Mental Health*, Early Online, 1–12.
> *This article reviewed seven studies of walk-in single-session therapy and found "that the SST has been sufficient from the clients' perspective approximately 60.9% of the time, which is remarkably similar to the 58.6% that Hoyt, et al. (1992) reported 20 year ago."*

Talmon, M. (1990). *Single session therapy: Maximizing the effect of the first (and often only) therapeutic encounter.* San Francisco, CA: Jossey-Bass.
> *Patients elected to complete their treatment with a single visit in 58.6% (34 of 58) of potential SSTs in a study (see Chapters 1–2this volume) conducted at Kaiser Permanente by Talmon, Rosenbaum, and Hoyt.*

Weir, S., Wills, M., Young, J., & Perlesz, A. (2008). *The implementation of single-session work in community health.* Brunswick, Victoria, Australia: The Bouverie Centre, La Trobe University.
> *This three-year review (see Chapters 7–9 this volume) at community health counseling services in Victoria, Australia, involved more than 100,000 patients and found that 42% of those seen chose to have only a single session even when more sessions were offered.*

Therapist versus client preferences for how long therapy should last—clients usually expect a shorter course than do their therapists.

Barrett, M.S., Chua, W.-J., Crits-Christoph, P., Gibbons, M.B., & Thompson, D. (2008) Early withdrawal from mental health treatment: Implications for psychotherapy practice. *Psychotherapy: Theory, Research, Practice, Training*, 45(2), 247–267.

Hatchett, G.T., & Park, H.L. (2003) Comparison of four operational definitions of premature termination. *Psychotherapy: Theory, Research, Practice, Training*, 40, 226–231.

Hunsley, J., Aubry, T.D., Verstervelt, C.M., & Vito, D. (1999) Comparing therapist and client perspectives on reasons for psychotherapy termination. *Psychotherapy*, 36(4), 380–388. Lowry, J.L., & Ross, M.J. (1997) Expectations of psychotherapy duration: How long should psychotherapy last? *Psychotherapy*, 34, 272–277.

Pekarik, G. (1991) Relationship of expected and actual treatment duration for adult and child clients. *Journal of Clinical Child Psychology*, 20(2), 121–125.

Pekarik, G. (1992a Relationship of clients' reasons for dropping out of treatment to outcome and satisfaction. *Journal of Clinical Psychology*, 48, 91–98.
Pekarik, G. (1992b) Posttreatment adjustment of clients who drop out early vs. late in treatment. *Journal of Clinical Psychology*, 48, 379–387.
Scarmardo, M., Bobele, M., & Biever, J.L. (2004) A new perspective on client dropouts. *Journal of Systemic Therapies*, 23(2), 27–38.

Studies have reported significant reduction of distress and problem severity, as well as improvements in client satisfaction, after a single session.

Green, K, Correia, T., Bobele, M., & Slive, A. (2011) The research case for walk-in single sessions. In A. Slive & M. Bobele (Eds.), *When one hour is all you have: Effective therapy for walk-in clients* (pp.23–36). Phoenix, AZ: Zeig, Tucker & Theisen.
Miller, J.K. (2008) Walk-in single-session team therapy: A study of client satisfaction. *Journal of Systemic Therapies*, 27(3), 78–94.
Silverman, W.H., & Beech, R.P. (1984) Length of intervention and client assessed outcome. *Journal of Clinical Psychology*, 40, 475–480.
Talmon, M. (1990) *Single session therapy: Maximizing the effect of the first (and often only) therapeutic encounter.* San Francisco: Jossey-Bass.

Patients have benefitted by being allowed to simply walk-in or "drop-in" for a single session without a scheduled appointment when they wanted to meet with a therapist.

Bobele, M., Lopez, S.S.G., Scamardo, M., & Solórzano, B. (2008) Single-session walk-in therapy with Mexican-American clients. *Journal of Systemic Therapies*, 27(4), 75–89.
   This article reports single session success with patients who were able to simply walk-in to see a counselor at a store-front clinic in San Antonio, Texas.
Bobele, M., Slive, A., Solórzano, B., & Correia, T. (2008) *Practice, Training, and Outcomes in Walk-In, Single-Session Therapy.* Symposium held at annual convention of the American Psychological Association. Boston, August 17.
   This work reports single session success with patients who were able to simply walk-in to see a counselor at a store-front clinic in San Antonio, Texas.
Brown, L.M. (1984) A single-consultation assessment clinic. *British Journal of Psychiatry*, 145, 558.
   This assessment provides an account from Kent, England.
Campbell, A. (1999) Single session interventions: An example of clinical research in practice. *Australian and New Zealand Journal of Family Therapy*, 20(4), 183–194.
   This work demonstrates successful programs with families based in Australia.

Clements, R.E., McElheran, N., Hackney, L., & Park, H. (2011) The Eastside Family Centre: 20 years of single-session walk-in therapy. In A. Slive & M. Bobele (Eds.), *When one session is all you have: Effective therapy for walk-in clients* (pp. 109–127), Phoenix, AZ: Zeig, Theisen & Tucker.
   This report offers accounts of successful one-session therapies at the walk-in clinic at the Eastside Family Centre in Calgary, Canada.
Clouthier, K., Fennema, D., Johnston, J., Veenendaal, K., & Viksne, U. (1996) Expanding the influence of a single-session consultation program. *Journal of Systemic Therapies, 15,* 1–11.
   The authors describe the expanding of a single-session consultation program in London, Ontario, Canada.
Horton, S., Stalker, C.A., Cait, C.A., & Josling, L. (2012) Sustaining walk-in counseling services: An economic assessment from a pilot study. *Healthcare Quarterly, 15*(3), 44–49.
   A pilot study of the favorable clinical, social, and economic impact of walk-in services in Kitchener-Waterloo, Ontario, Canada.
Hymmen, P., Stalker, C., & Cait, C.-A. (2012) The case for single-session therapy: Does the empirical evidence support the increased prevalence of this service delivery model? *Journal of Mental Health,* Early OnLine, 1012.
   Common themes of what walk-in SST clients consider most helpful include: receiving helpful advice about the problem, therapist characteristics, having the opportunity to talk about the problem and feel supported, being referred to other resources, immediate accessibility of the walk-in service.
Manthei, J. (2006) Clients talk about their experiences of seeking counseling. *British Journal of Guidance and Counselling, 34*(4), 519–538.
   Research documenting single-session drop-in success from Christchurch, New Zealand.
McGarry, J., McNicholas, F., Buckley, H., Kelly, B., Atkin, L., & Ross, N. (2008) The clinical effectiveness of a brief consultation and advisory approach compared to treatment as usual in child and adolescent mental health services. *Clinical Child Psychology and Psychiatry, 13*(3), 365–376.
   A report on the use of a very brief consultation approach in child and adolescent mental health services in Ireland.
Miller, J.K. (2008) Walk-in single-session team therapy: A study of client satisfaction. *Journal of Systemic Therapies, 27*(3), 78–94.
   A study on successful one-session therapies at the walk-in clinic at the Eastside Family Centre in Calgary, Canada.
Miller, J.K. (2011) Single-session intervention in the wake of Hurricane Katrina: Strategies for disaster mental health counseling. In A. Slive & M. Bobele (Eds.), *When one hour is all you have: Effective therapy for walk-in clients* (pp. 185–202). Phoenix, AZ: Zeig, Tucker & Theisen.
   A documentation of valuable one-session therapies in the aftermath of Hurricane Katrina.
Miller, J.K., & Slive, A. (2004) Breaking down the barriers to clinical service delivery: Walk-in family therapy. *Journal of Marital and Family Therapy, 30,* 95–105.

An article on successful one-session therapies at the walk-in clinic at the Eastside Family Centre in Calgary, Canada.

Paul, K.E., & van Ommeren, M. (2013) A primer on single session therapy and its potential application in humanitarian situations. *Intervention,* 11(1), 8–23.

This work provides an excellent primer on the potential application of SST in humanitarian-emergency situations.

Perkins, R. (2006) The effectiveness of one session of therapy using a single-session therapy approach for children and adolescents with mental health problems. *Psychology and Psychotherapy: Theory, Research and Practice,* 79, 215–227.

This article documents another successful Australian study, including assessment at 18-month follow-up, with children and adolescents seen at a mental health clinic.

Perkins, R., & Scarlett, G. (2008) The effectiveness of single session therapy in child and adolescent mental health. Part 2: An 18-month follow-up study. *Psychology and Psychotherapy: Theory, Research and Practice,* 81, 143–156.

Part II of the report on another successful Australian study, including assessment at 18-month follow-up, with children and adolescents seen at a mental health clinic.

Price, C. (1994) Open days: Making family therapy accessible in working class suburbs. *Australian and New Zealand Journal of Family Therapy,* 15(4), 191–196.

A description of successful programs with families based in Australia.

Slive, A., MacLaurin, B., Oakander, M., & Amundson, J. (1995) Walk-in single sessions: A new paradigm in clinical service delivery. *Journal of Systemic Therapies,* 14, 3–11.

A report on successful one-session therapies at the walk-in clinic at the Eastside Family Centre in Calgary, Canada.

Slive, A., McElheran, N., & Lawson, A. (2009) How brief does it get? Walk-in single session therapy. *Journal of Systemic Therapies,* 27, 5–22.

This work reports successful one-session therapies at the walk-in clinic at the Eastside Family Centre in Calgary, Canada.

Stalker, C.A., Horton, S., & Cait, C.A. (2012) Single-session therapy in a walk-in counseling clinic: A pilot study. *Journal of Systemic Therapies,* 31(1), 38–52.

In this study, the authors report a pilot study of the favorable clinical, social, and economic impact of walk-in services in Kitchener-Waterloo, Ontario, Canada.

Young, Y. (2011a) When all the time you have is NOW: Re-visiting practices and narrative therapy in a walk-in clinic. In J. Duvall & L. Beres (Eds.), *Innovations in narrative therapy: Connecting practice, training, and research* (pp. 147–166). New York: Norton.

This work describes effective single-session walk-ins from Toronto, Canada.

Young, K. (2011b) Narrative practices at a walk-in therapy clinic. In A. Slive & M. Bobele (Eds.), *When one session is all you have: Effective therapy for walk-in clients* (pp. 149–166). Phoenix, AZ: Zeig, Tucker, & Theisen.

This chapter provides examples of effective single session walk-ins from Toronto, Canada.

Young, K., & Cooper, S. (2008) Toward co-composing an evidence base: The narrative therapy re-visiting project. *Journal of Systemic Therapies*, 27, 67–83.
This article describes cases of effective single-session walk-ins from Toronto, Canada.

Young, K., Dick, M., Herring, K., & Lee, J. (2008) From waiting lists to walk-in: Stories from a walk-in therapy clinic. *Journal of Systemic Therapies*, 27, 23–39.
This article describes effective single-session walk-ins from Toronto, Canada.

Studies demonstrate the effectiveness of a single session with problems of anxiety.

Barkham, M., Shapiro, D.A., Hardy, G.E., & Rees, A. (1999) Psychotherapy in two-plus-one sessions: Outcomes of a randomized controlled trial of cognitive-behavioral and psychodynamic-interpersonal therapy. *Journal of Consulting and Clinical Psychology*, 67, 201–211.
A study on how clients with mild depression benefitted from what the authors termed "2 + 1 ultra-brief therapy" (two treatment sessions of cognitive-behavioral and psychodynamic-interpersonal therapy, plus a follow-up session).

Basoglu, M., Salcioglu, E., & Livanou, M. (2007) A randomized controlled study of single session behavioral treatment of earthquake-related post-traumatic stress disorder using an earthquake simulator. *Psychological Medicine*, 37(2), 203–213.
An experimental design that studied the use of exposure therapy for PTSD with 31 survivors of the 1999 Turkish earthquakes found large effect sizes for all measures. The study notes that the positive results were essentially the same for one-session as multi-session interventions.

Breitholtz, E., & Ost, L.G. (1997) Therapist behavior during one-session exposure treatment of spider phobia: Individual vs. group setting. *Scandinavian Journal of Behaviour Therapy*, 26(4), 171–180.
A randomized clinical trial in which one-session exposure was found to yield superior results.

Denner, S., & Reeves, S. (1997) Single session assessment and therapy for new referrals to CMHTS. *Journal of Mental Health*, 6(3), 275–279.
A study of 13 subjects having a single session of assessment and therapy at a U.K. community mental health center. It reported significant decreases in anxiety and depression at 6-week follow-up.

Hauner, K.K., Mineka, S., Voss, J.L., & Paller, K.A. (2012) Exposure therapy triggers lasting reorganization of neural fear processing. *Proceeding of the National Academy of Sciences*, Published online before print May 23, 2012, doi: 10.1073/pnas.1205242109.
The authors used brain-imaging techniques to study the neural mechanisms underlying successful single-session exposure therapy.

Kashdan, T.B., Adams, L., Read, J., & Hawk, Jr., L. (2012) Can a one-hour session of exposure treatment modulate startle response and reduce spider fears? *Psychiatry Research*, 196, 79–82.
    A randomized clinical trial in which one-session exposure was found to yield superior results.
Kozak, A.T., Spates, C.R., McChargue, D.E., Bailey, K.C., Schneider, K.L., & Liepman, M.R. (2007) Naltrexone renders one-session exposure therapy less effective: A controlled pilot study. *Journal of Anxiety Disorders*, 21, 142–152.
    A study of 15 anxious subjects which notes that the effects of one-session exposure therapy are lessened if the opioid antagonist naltrexone is administered prior to exposure.
Nuthall, A., & Townend, M. (2007) CBT-based early intervention to prevent panic disorder: A pilot study. *Behavioral and Cognitive Psychotherapy*, 35(1), 15–30.
    A report about one-session CBT-based early intervention to prevent panic disorder.
Ollendick, T.H., Oest, L.G., Reuterskiold, L., Costa, N., Cederlund, R., Sirbu, C., & Davis, T.E. (2009) One-session treatment of specific phobias in youth: A randomized clinical trial in the United States and Sweden. *Journal of Consulting and Clinical Psychology*, 77(3), 504–516.
    The authors conducted a randomized clinical trial using a one-session exposure treatment, an educational support treatment, or a wait-list control for 196 American and Swedish young people diagnosed with a specific (spider) phobia. One-session exposure was found to yield superior results, with outcomes maintained at six-month follow-up.
Ost, L.G. (1989) One-session treatment for specific phobias. *Behavior Research and Therapy*, 7, 1–7.
    A randomized clinical trial in which one-session exposure was found to yield superior results.

Two effective single session treatments for chronic recurring nightmares have been described with supporting data.

Kellner, R., Neidhardt, J., Krakow, B., & Pathak, D. (1992) Changes in chronic nightmares after one session of desensitization or rehearsal instruction. *American Journal of Psychiatry*, 149, 659–663.
    A study conducted at the University of New Mexico-Albuquerque that successfully treated 23 patients with chronic nightmares with one session of desensitization or rehearsal training. In both conditions, patients were taught progressive relaxation. Half the patients were then instructed to work their way up an exposure hierarchy, practicing imagining the nightmare while relaxed; while the other half were instructed to write a modified, "happy ending" version and then practice rehearsing the changed version in imagery while in a relaxed state. In both conditions, patients were seen once and were to practice at home.

After two weeks, most patients in both conditions reported the nightmares were significantly reduced (in four patients, the nightmares ceased), whereas subjects in a waiting list control condition did not report improvement.

Medical utilization is often reduced after SST.

Brooks, M. (2013, June 5) Single-session group CBT effective for insomnia. *Medscape Medical News* from SLEEP 2013: Associated Professional Sleep Societies 27th Annual Meeting, Baltimore, MD.
  Studies done independently in the United Kingdom and by researchers at Kaiser Permanente in Fontana, California that have documented single-session group CBT effective for insomnia.
Coverly, C.T., Garralda, M.E., & Bowman, F. (1995) Psychiatric intervention in primary care for mothers whose schoolchildren have psychiatric disorder. *British Journal of General Practice, 45,* 235–237.
  A study conducted in Manchester, England which found that a single one-hour meeting with mothers whose schoolchildren have psychiatric disorder was helpful in improving the majority of the children's behavior, emotional and health problems, as well as the mothers' confidence in dealing with them.
Cummings, N.A., & Follette, W.T. (1976) Brief therapy and medical utilization. In H. Dorken et al., (Eds.), *The professional psychologist today* (pp. 76–197). San Francisco: Jossey-Bass.
  Reports the benefits of SST still in effect after 8 years and concludes that decreased medical utilization was due to a reduction in physical symptoms related to emotional stress.
De Jongh, A., Mucis, P., ter Horst, G., & van Zuuren, F. (1995) One-session cognitive treatment of dental phobia: Preparing dental phobics for treatment by restructuring negative cognitions. *Behavior Research and Therapy, 33,* 947–954.
  A report of successful one-session cognitive treatment of patients with dental phobia.
Flowers, J.V., Miller, T.E., Smith, N., & Booraem, C.D. (1994) The repeatability of a single-session group to promote safe sex behavior in a male at-risk population. *Research on Social Work Practices, 4(2),* 240–247.
  The authors conducted studies with young men and found single-session small-group interventions effective in reducing unsafe sexual practices.
Follette, W.T., & Cummings, N.A. (1967) Psychiatric services and medical utilization in a prepaid health care setting. *Medical Care, 5,* 25–35.
  The study finds a 60% reduction over 5-year follow-up after a single session of psychotherapy in another study done at the Kaiser Permanente Health Plan (the largest health maintenance organization in the U.S.)
Kunik, M.E., Braun, U., Stanley, M.A., Wristers, K., Molinari, V., Stoebner, D., et al. (2001) One session cognitive behavioral therapy for elderly patients with chronic obstructive pulmonary disease. *Psychological Medicine: A Journal of Research in Psychiatry and the Allied Sciences, 31(4),* 717–723.

Study of one-session cognitive-behavioral therapy benefits for elderly patients with chronic obstructive pulmonary disease.

Loskshin, B., Lindgren, S., Weinberger, J., & Koviach, J. (1991) Outcome of habit cough in children treated with a brief session of suggestion therapy. *Annals of Allergy, 67,* 579–582.

Effective single-session therapy for children with habit cough.

Mumford, E., Schlesinger, H., Glass, G.V., Patrick, C., & Cuerdon, B.A. (1984) A new look at evidence about reduced cost of medical utilization following mental health treatment. *American Journal of Psychiatry, 141,* 1145–1158.

Reviews multiple replications of medical offset utilization phenomena after one or a few visits.

Paniak, C., Toller-Lobe, G., Durand, A., & Nagy, J. (1998) A randomized trial of two treatments for mild traumatic brain injury. *Brain Injury, 12,* 1011–1023.

This work found that single-session educationally-oriented interventions soon after mild brain injuries appeared to be adequate for most subjects.

Patterson, T.L., Shaw, W.S., & Semple, S.J. (2003) Reducing the sexual risk behavior of HIV+ individuals: Outcome of a randomized controlled trial. *Annals of Behavioral Medicine, 25,* 137–145.

The authors conducted studies with young men and found single-session small-group interventions effective in reducing unsafe sexual practices.

Schade, N., Torres, P., & Beyerbach, M. (2011) Cost-efficiency of a brief family intervention for somatoform patients in primary care. *Families, Systems & Health, 29*(3), 197–205.

The authors report a study from Santiago, Chile, in which a brief family intervention (a one-hour session with two shorter follow-up meetings) significantly reduced the medical costs for somatoform patients seen in primary care settings.

Tudiver, F., Myers, T., Kurtz, R.G., Orr, K., Rowe, C., Jackson, E., & Bullock, S.L. (1992) The talking sex project: Results of a randomized controlled trial of small-group AIDS education for 612 gay and bisexual men. *Evaluation and the Health Professions, 15*(1), 26–42.

The authors conducted studies with young men and found single-session small-group interventions effective in reducing unsafe sexual practices.

Families having a planned single session consultation also report significant benefits.

Campbell, A. (1999) Single session interventions: An example of clinical research in practice. *Australian and New Zealand Journal of Family Therapy, 20*(4), 183–194.

Curtis, A., Whittaker, A., Stevens, S., & Lennon, A. (2002) Single session family intervention in a local authority family centre setting. *Journal of Social Work Practice, 16,* 37–41.

Goodman, D., & Happell, B. (2006) The efficacy of family intervention in adolescent health. *International Journal of Psychiatric Nursing Research*, 12, 1364–1377.

Hampson, R., O'Hanlon, J., Franklin, A., Pentony, M., Fridgant, L., & Heins, T. (1999) The place of single session family consultations: Five years' experience in Canberra. *Australian and New Zealand Journal of Family Therapy*, 20(4), 195–200.

Jordan, K., & Quinn, W.H. (1994) Session two outcome of the formula first session task in problem- and solution-focused approaches. *American Journal of Family Therapy*, 22(1), 3–16.

Sommers-Flanagan, J. (2007) Single-session consultations for parents: A preliminary investigation. *The Family Journal: Counseling and Therapy for Couples and Families*, 15, 24–29.

Stacey, K. Allison, S., Dadds, V., Roeger, L., Wood, A., & Martin, G. (2001) Maintaining the gains: What worked in the year after brief family therapy. *Australian and New Zealand Journal of Family Therapy*, 22(4), 181–188.

Turnbull, J.E., Galinsky, M.J., Wilner, M.E., & Meglin, D.E. (1994) Designing research to meet service needs: An evaluation of single session groups for families of psychiatric inpatients. *Research on Social Work Practice*, 4(2), 192–207.

Successful SSTs with adolescents and college students also have been reported in several studies.

Cooper, S., & Archer, J. (1999) Brief therapy in college counseling and mental health. *Journal of American College Health*, 48, 21–28.

Gavazzi, S.M. (1995) The Growing Up FAST: Families and adolescents surviving and thriving-super program. *Journal of Adolescence*, 18(1), 31–47.

Gawrysiak, M., Nicholas, C., & Hopko, D.R. (2009) Behavioral activation for moderately depressed university students: Randomized controlled trial. *Journal of Counseling Psychology*, 56(3), 468–475.

Jerry, P.A. (1994) Winnicott's therapeutic consultation and the adolescent client. *Crisis Intervention and Time-Limited Treatment*, 1, 61–72

Jones, M.P., Kadlubek, R.M., & Marks, W.J. (2006) Single-session treatment: A counseling paradigm for school psychology. *The School Psychologist*, 60, 112–115.

King, L.A. (1992) Early termination from therapy at a university counseling center. *Dissertation Abstracts International*, 43 (12-b), P. 4150.

Littrell, J.M., Malia, J.A., & Vanderwood (1992) Single-session brief counseling in a high school. *Journal of Counseling and Development*, 73 (March/April), 451–458.

Phillips, P. (2002) Shoulder to shoulder: A single session success story. *Journal of College Student Psychotherapy*, 16(3/4), 225–237.

Slaff, B. (1995) Thoughts on short-term and single-session therapy. In R.C. Marohn & S.C. Feinstein (Eds.), *Adolescent psychiatry: Developmental and clinical studies* (Vol. 20, pp. 299–306). Hillsdale, NJ: Analytic Press.

Sundstrom, S.M. (1993) Single session psychotherapy for depression: Is it better to be problem-focused or solution-focused? *Dissertation Abstracts International*, 54 (7-B), p. 3867.

The efficacy of SSTs is not restricted only to "easy" cases but can have more far-reaching effects in many areas, including treatment of alcohol and substance abuse as well as self-harming behavior.

Askevold, F. (1983) What are the helpful factors in psychotherapy for anorexia nervosa? *International Journal of Eating Disorders*, 2, 193–197.
  A study on 42 randomly assigned women with anorexia nervosa to either a single treatment interview, brief psychotherapy, or ongoing psychotherapy; 4–14 years later the group who had received regular psychotherapy was slightly but insignificantly worse off than members of the other two groups.
Baer, J.S., Marlatt, G.A., Kivlahan, D.R., Fromme, K., Larimer, M.E., & Williams, E. (1992) An experimental test of three methods of alcohol risk reductions with young adults. *Journal of Consulting and Clinical Psychology*, 60, 974–979.
  A study done in Great Britain in which one-session intervention was very helpful in getting young adults to reduce problem drinking.
Berman, A.H., Forsberg, L., Durbeej, N., Kallman, H., & Hermansson, U. (2010) Single-session motivational interviewing for drug detoxification inpatients: Effects on self-efficacy, stages of change and substance use. *Substance Use and Misuse*, 2010, 45(3), 384–402.
  In this study of 35 inpatients at a Stockholm drug-user detoxification unit, a single-session of motivational interviewing was found to be more effective than treatment as usual.
Carroll, K.M., Libby, B., Sheehan, J., & Hyland, N. (2001) Motivational interviewing to enhance treatment initiation in substance abusers: An effectiveness study. *American Journal on Addictions*, 10, 335–339.
  A single-session of motivational interviewing was found to be more effective than treatment as usual.
Copeland, J. Swift, W., Roffman, R., & Stephens, R. (2001) A randomized controlled trial of brief cognitive-behavioral interventions for cannabis use disorder. *Journal of Substance Abuse Treatment*, 21, 55–64.
  This study compares 1- and 6-session cognitive-behavioral programs intended to impart cannabis cessation skills and finds benefits for both relative to controls, although only the 6-session group reported significantly reduced levels of cannabis consumption.
Daley, D.C., & Zuckoff, A. (1998) Improving compliance with the initial outpatient session among discharged inpatient dual diagnosis clients. *Social Work*, 43, 470–473.
  This article found that a single session of empathic, motivational interviewing improved subsequent outpatient treatment compliance.

Humfress, H., Igel, V., Lamont, A., Tanner, M., Morgan, J., & Schmidt, U. (2002) The effect of a brief motivational intervention on community psychiatric patients' attitudes to their care, motivation to change, compliance and outcome: A case control study. *Journal of Mental Health, 11*, 155–166.

A single-session of motivational interviewing was found to be more effective than treatment as usual.

Johnson, J.A., & Seale, J.P. (2013, April 25–28) *Screening alone garners long-term reduction in alcohol use.* Poster paper presented at American Society of Addiction Medicine (ASAM) 44th Annual Medical-Scientific Conference, Chicago.

The authors reported long-term reductions in drinking frequency as well as binge drinking after a single "screening" interview.

Lamprecht, H., Laydon, C., McQuillan, C., Wiseman, S., Williams, L., Gash, A., & Reilly, J. (2007) Single-session solution-focused brief therapy and self-harm: A pilot study. *Journal of Psychiatric and Mental Health Nursing, 2007, 14*, 601–602.

A study conducted at Sheffield University in England, of 32 first-time self-harming (overdoses and cutting) patients found that a single (90 minute) session of solution-focused brief therapy reduced subsequent episodes of self-harm over one year.

McCambridge, J., & Strang, J. (2004) The efficacy of single-session motivational interviewing in reducing drug consumption and perceptions of drug-related risk and harm among young people: Results from a multi-site cluster randomized trial. *Addiction, 99*(1), 39–52.

The authors studied 200 substance-abusing young people in a multi-site London-based randomized trial using either a one-hour single-session face-to-face motivational interview or a non-intervention education-as-usual control condition; motivational interviewing was found to be much more effective in reducing self-reported cigarette, alcohol, cannabis and other drug use.

Miller, W.R. (2000) Rediscovering fire: Small interventions, large effects. *Psychology of Addictive Behaviors, 14*, 6–18.

This article found a single session of empathic, motivational interviewing improved subsequent outpatient treatment compliance.

Single sessions of therapy can be associated with generalized life improvements over and above symptom relief.

Significant psychosocial improvements were noted in the Talmon, Rosenbaum, and Hoyt study at Kaiser (Talmon, 1990); 65% of single session clients also reported other positive "ripple" effects, figures that were slightly (and statistically insignificantly) higher than those of the 24 patients seen more than once.

Jacobson, G. (1968) The briefest psychiatric encounter: Acute effects of evaluation. *Archives of General Psychiatry, 18*, 718–724.

Kellner, R., & Sheffield, B.F. (1971) The relief of distress following attendance at a clinic. *British Journal of Psychiatry*, 118, 195–198.

Malan, D.H., Bacal, H.A., Heath, E.S., & Balfour, F.H.G. (1968) A study of psychodynamic changes in untreated neurotic patients: Improvements that are questionable on dynamic criteria. *British Journal of Psychiatry*, 114, 525–551.

A study conducted at the Tavistock Clinic in London found that 51% of "untreated" neurotic patients who had only an intake interview showed less symptomatology.

Malan, D.H., Heath, E., Bascal, H., & Balfour, F.H.G. (1975) Psychodynamic changes in untreated neurotic patients, II. Apparently genuine improvements. *Archives of General Psychiatry*, 32, 110–126.

A study conducted at the Tavistock Clinic in London found that of the 51% of "untreated" neurotic patients who had only an intake interview and showed less symptomatology, half of those patients were also judged to showed increased insight and sense of personal responsibility and to have made important and enduring psychodynamic modifications.

Schwebel, R., Schwebel, A., & Schwebel, M. (1985) The psychological/mediation intervention model. *Professional Psychology: Research and Practice*, 16, 86–97.

The authors describe successful single sessions of psychological mediation in working with a variety of situations involving interpersonal conflict.

Changing viewing changes doing: Two social psychological single-session interventions with clear implications for clinical practice.

Hoyt, M.F., & Janis, I.L. (1975) Increasing adherence to a stressful decision via a motivational balance-sheet procedure: A field experiment on attendance at an exercise class. *Journal of Personality and Social Psychology*, 31, 833–839.

This experiment helped women adhere to a stressful decision via a one-session motivational balance-sheet procedure in which subjects were guided to articulate the pros and cons of continuing to attend an early-morning exercise class.

Miller, W.R., & Rose, G.S. (in press) Motivational interviewing and decisional balance: Contrasting responses to client ambivalence. *Behavioural and Cognitive Psychotherapy*, forthcoming.

This research suggests that a balance-sheet procedure would be more useful after clients have resolved their primary ambivalence lest they be encouraged to voice the "cons" as well as the "pros" for changing a behavior.

Walton, G.M., & Cohen, G.L. (2011) A brief social-belonging intervention improves academic and health outcomes of minority students. *Science*, 331, 1447–1451.

This study improved the long-term academic and health outcomes of African-American college students by having them read and deliver a narrative that framed social adversity in school as shared and short-lived, promoting the stress-inoculation buffering belief that such difficulties were common and transient aspects of the college-adjustment process rather than an indication of some personal deficit or race-specific lack of social belonging. As the authors wrote (pp. 1450–1451): "Changing subjective construal is a fruitful avenue for intervention because many events are ambiguous and amenable to multiple interpretations. Moreover, a change in construal can become self-reinforcing. Students who feel confident in their belonging may experience the social world in a way that reinforced this feeling. They may initiate more relationships and thus obtain more opportunities for belonging and growth. Brief interventions that shore up belonging can thus promote performance and well-being even long after their delivery."

Single session contacts are a common practice in hospital social work.

Block, L.R. (1985) On the potentiality and limits of time: The single-session group and the cancer patient. *Social Work in Groups*, 8(2), 81–99.
  Discusses the benefits of one-session group therapy for patients with cancer.
Gibbons, J., & Plath, D. (2009) Single contacts with hospital social workers: the clients' experiences. *Social Work in Health Care*, 48(8), 721–735.
  The article summarizes three research studies regarding the incidence and nature of single sessions in hospital social work practice in New South Wales, Australia. By surveying the experience of social workers and their clients, the authors conclude that single session work is such a common experience that it needs to become a more recognized part of social work education, practice, and training.
Gibbons, J., & Plath, D. (2012) Single session social work in hospitals. *Australian and New Zealand Journal of Family Therapy*, 33(1), 39–53.
  Further evidence that single session work is such a common experience that it needs to become a more recognized part of social work education, practice, and training.

SST also has been shown to be effective in disability and career counseling.

Barrett, R., Lapsley, H., & Agee, M. (2012) "But they only came once!" The single session in career counselling. *New Zealand Journal of Counselling*, 32(2), 71–82.
  This study, done in New Zealand, followed up with 27 clients who had received one session of career counseling and found that all but one reported that the session had been helpful and that most had made short- or long-term changes as a result.
Jevne, R., Zingle, H., Ryan, D., McDougall, C., & Moretmore, E. (1995) Single-session therapy for teachers with a health disabling condition. *Employee Counselling Today*, 7(1), 5–11.
  This study provided SST to 35 teachers in Edmonton, Canada on long-term disability and reported positive results.

Possible Factors

Severity of complaint and level of distress do not appear to be strong predictors of single session success.

In our original Kaiser study (Talmon, 1990; Hoyt, et al., 1992), we did not find any connection between *DSM* diagnoses and whether patients elected to complete their therapy in one session or continue for more meetings; nor did we find any connection between diagnoses and outcome ratings of improvement. Some patients with longstanding "serious" problems found significant benefit in one visit, while others who seemed to be "only" mildly and recently afflicted did not. Some SST researchers have excluded patients with psychosis, active suicidality, brain injuries, and domestic violence and child abuse—although others see such patients in SST (especially when they "walk in") and make referrals to other resources for continuing care when appropriate. As Slive and Bobele (Chapter 5 this volume) write, "However, walk-in clients choose us, we don't choose them.…Clients are never only their 'diagnosis.' They have many 'normal' issues that can be addressed and helped via a single session of a walk-in therapy."

Campbell, A. (1999) Single session interventions: An example of clinical research in practice. *Australian and New Zealand Journal of Family Therapy*, 20(4), 183–194. Did find stronger family morale to be associated with better outcomes.

Hampson, R., O'Hanlon, J., Franklin, A., Pentony, M., Fridgant, L., & Heins, T. (1999) The place of single session family consultations: Five years' experience in Canberra. *Australian and New Zealand Journal of Family Therapy*, 20(4), 195–200. Did find less severe child behavior problems to be associated with better outcomes.

Hurn, R. (2005) Single-session therapy: Planned success or unplanned failure? *Counselling Psychology Review*, 20(4), 33–40. Cautions against assuming that SST is a panacea, especially in complex, high-risk cases.

Hymmen, P., Stalker, C., & Cait, C.-A. (2012) The case for single-session therapy: Does the empirical evidence support the increased prevalence of this service delivery model? *Journal of Mental Health*, Early OnLine, 1–12. Thorough review notes that "In fact, we have found no advocates of SST who claim this model is sufficient or even appropriate for all clients." We concur.

Patient demographics (age, race, socioeconomic and educational level, etc.) are also not clearly related to SST success (or failure).

Children, adolescents, couples, families, adults and the elderly, as well as persons of varying ethnicities and nationalities, have all reported positive SST experiences. While walk-in single session and other brief interventions may seem to be an obvious fit for persons with limited financial resources and time, there are many reports of college-educated individuals (including two

Ph.D. authors in the present volume—see Chapters 4 and 13–14!) benefitting from a single session of therapy.

The role of client motivation and stage of readiness is also not clear.

An argument (Hoyt, 2011) for walk-in SSTs has been to take advantage of client readiness, although, as Iveson, et al. (Chapter 17 this volume) note, "[Our] first outcome study, surprisingly, showed no outcome difference related to the assessed level of motivation. Since then we have treated all clients as motivated with part of the therapist's task being to help the client discover what they are motivated for."

Hoyt, M.F. (2011) Foreword. In A. Slive & M. Bobele (Eds.), *When one hour is all you have: Effective therapy for walk-in clients* (pp. ix–xv). Phoenix, AZ: Zeig, Tucker, & Theisen.
    Advocates for walk-in SSTs in order to "strike while the iron is hot" (p. xi) as well as for greater accessibility.
Hoyt, M.F., & Miller, S.D. (2000) Stage-appropriate change-oriented brief therapy strategies. In M.F. Hoyt, *Some stories are better than others* (pp. 207–235). Philadelphia: Brunner/Mazel.
    Strategies involve combining Transtheoretical Model of Change with solution-focused and other brief therapy methods.
Norcross, J.C., Krebs, P.M., & Prochaska, J.O. (2011) Stages of change. *Journal of Clinical Psychology: In Session, 67*(2), 143–154.
Description of Transtheoretical Model of Change (wherein patients are assessed to be in the precontemplation, contemplation, preparation/planning, action, *or* maintainance *stage of change).*
Stalker, C.A., Horton, S., & Cait, C.-A. (2012) Single-session therapy in a walk-in counseling clinic: A pilot study. *Journal of Systemic Therapies, 31*(1), 38–52.
    Found only "limited support" for Transtheoretical Model of Change and suggested that "More research is necessary to examine whether it is useful to alter the therapeutic stance according to the client's stage of change in SST, and also whether particular stages of change are more responsive to the therapeutic stances that are integral to narrative, solution-focused, and cognitive-behavioral SST."

Studies of the so-called "dose-effect" (see Howard, et al., 1986; Kopta, et al., 1994) or "dose-response" (Feaster, et al., 2003; Hansen, et al., 2002; Harnett, et al., 2010) relationship in psychotherapy also raise questions.

Feaster, D.J., Newman, F.L., & Rice, C. (2003) Longitudinal analysis when the experimenter does not determine when treatment ends: What is dose-response? *Clinical Psychology and Psychotherapy, 10*(6), 352–360.

Haley, J. (2010) The brief, brief therapy of Milton H. Erickson. In M. Richeport-Haley & J. Carlson (Eds.), *Jay Haley revisited* (pp. 284–306). New York: Routledge.

Haley contends (p. 297) that "the briefer the therapy the more people forget it," which may confound research.

Hansen, N.B., & Lambert, M.J. (2003) An evaluation of the dose-response relationship in naturalistic treatment settings using survival analysis. *Mental Health Services Research,* 5(1), 1–12.

Describes a negatively accelerating pattern in which most change in therapy occurs relatively soon with diminishing yields as time goes on.

Hansen, N.B., Lambert, M.J., & Forman, E.M. (2002) The psychotherapy dose-response effect and its implications for treatment delivery services. *Clinical Psychology: Science and Practice,* 9, 329–343.

Harnett, P., O'Donovan, A., & Lambert, M.J. (2010) The dose-response relationship in psychotherapy: Implications for social policy. *Clinical Psychologist,* 14, 39–44.

The authors seem to suggest that for some patients longer-term therapies may yield greater satisfaction.

Howard, K.I., Kopta, S.M., Kraus, M.S., & Orlinsky, D.E. (1986) The dose-effect relationship in psychotherapy. *American Psychologist,* 41, 159–164.

Hoyt, M.F. (1995) *Brief therapy and managed care: Readings for contemporary practice.* San Francisco: Jossey-Bass.

Argues that even if some patients like and perhaps do benefit from longer therapies, the evidence is clear that many therapies do yield positive results in one or a few sessions. "More is not better; better is better."

Hoyt, M.F., & Austad, C.S. (1992) Psychotherapy in a staff-model HMO: Providing and assuring quality care in the future. *Psychotherapy,* 29, 119–129.

Notes that many dose-effect research studies were based on long-term or open-ended therapies, rather than therapies that were specifically intended to be brief or time-limited and conducted with therapists appropriately oriented and trained.

Kopta, S.M., Howard, K.I., Lowry, J.L., & Beutler, L.E. (1994) Patterns of symptomatic recovery in psychotherapy. *Journal of Consulting and Clinical Psychology,* 62(5), 1009–1016.

Lambert, M., & Foreman, E. (2002) The psychotherapy dose-response effect and its implications for treatment delivery services. *Clinical Psychology: Science and Practice,* 9, 330.

Indicates a negatively accelerating pattern in which most change in therapy occurs relatively soon with diminishing yields as time goes on.

Seligman, M.E.P. (1995) The effectiveness of psychotherapy: The *Consumer Reports* study. *American Psychologist,* 50(12), 965–974.

Evidence suggesting that for some patients longer-term therapies may yield greater satisfaction.

Stacey, K., Allison, S., Dadds, V., Roeger, L., Wood, A., & Martin, G. (2001) Maintaining the gains: What worked in the year after brief family therapy. *Australian and New Zealand Journal of Family Therapy,* 22(4), 181–188.

Patients' self-selection to participate and reliance on patients' self-reports being subject to the confounding of measures of "satisfaction" with "improvement."

Wolgast, B.M., Lambert, M.J., & Puschner, B. (2003) The dose-response relationship at a college counseling center: Implications for setting session limits. *Journal of College Student Psychotherapy*, 18(2), 15–29.

Study that indicates a negatively accelerating pattern in which most change in therapy occurs relatively soon with diminishing yields as time goes on.

But what is "better" (and who really should be the judge)?

Aderka, I.M., Nickerson, A., Boe, H.J., & Hofmann, S.G. (2012) Sudden gains during psychological treatments of anxiety and depression: A meta-analysis. *Journal of Consulting* and Clinical Psychology, 80(1), 93–101.

In their meta-analysis of quantitative studies of sudden gains ["sudden reductions in symptoms that occur between consecutive sessions"] during psychological treatments of anxiety and depression, also found five studies in which significant improvements were reported after the first session of ongoing [not single session] therapies—although these "first session" gains were found to be less stable and more likely to be eroded compared with sudden gains that occurred later in treatments.

Baldwin, S.A., Berkeljon, A., Atkins, D.C., Olsen, J.A., & Nielsen, S.L. (2009) Rates of change in naturalistic psychotherapy: Contrasting dose-effect and good-enough level models of change. *Journal of Consulting and Clinical Psychology*, 77, 203–211.

Provides support for believing that clients who don't return experience "good enough" levels of change.

Barkham, M., Connell, J., Stiles, W.B., Miles, J.N.V., Margison, F., Evans, C., & Mellor-Clark, J. (2006) Dose-effect relations and responsive regulation of treatment duration: The good enough level. *Journal of Consulting and Clinical Psychology*, 74, 160–167.

Provides support for believing that clients who don't return experience "good enough" levels of change.

Barrett, M.S., Chua, W.-J., Crits-Christoph, P., Gibbons, M.B., & Thompson, D. (2008) Early withdrawal from mental health treatment: Implications for psychotherapy practice. *Psychotherapy: Theory, Research, Practice, Training*, 45(2), 247–267.

Although they seem to appreciate that clients often achieve what they came for in a relatively brief period of time, the authors frame much of their review in terms of "early withdrawal" and "attrition" and recommend both investigating "whether various types of clients benefit more or less from such ["brief, ultra-brief, or single-session"] treatments" (p. 261) as well as researching various strategies (e.g., altering the physical appearance of the clinic, incorporating brief models of motivational interviewing or pretherapy role induction procedures) that may help enhance client engagement and retention in therapy.

Cahill, J., Barkham, M., Hardy, G., Rees, A., Shapiro, D.A., Stiles, W.B., & Macaskill, N. (2003) Outcomes of patients completing and not completing cognitive therapy for depression. *British Journal of Clinical Psychology*, 42, 133–143.
> *This work notes that clients may "drop out" after one or a few sessions if their treatment goals of acquiring information, enhancing coping skills, and increasing hopefulness are achieved.*

Fennell, M.J., & Teasdale, J.D. (1987) Cognitive therapy for depression: Individual differences and the process of change. *Cognitive Therapy and Research*, 11, 253–271.
> *The study finds that early positive psychotherapy responders were more likely to maintain gains.*

Gilboa-Schectman, E., & Foa, E.B. (2001) Patterns of recovery after trauma: Individual differences and trauma characteristics. *Journal of Abnormal Psychology*, 110, 392–400.
> *The article found that early positive psychotherapy responders were more likely to maintain gains.*

Gilboa-Schechtman, E., & Shahar, G. (2006) The sooner, the better: Temporal patterns in brief treatment of depression and their role in long-term outcome. *Psychotherapy Research*, 16(3), 374–384.
> *The article found that early positive psychotherapy responders were more likely to maintain gains, and hypothesized that findings of "the sooner, the better" were due to "remoralization" and a "successful integration of new cognitive, interpersonal, and behavioral habits into one's daily routine" (p. 380).*

Given, D.R. (2002) Are we getting better? Psychotherapy dose-response effect: A clinician's comments. *Clinical Psychology: Science and Practice*, 9, 344–347.
> *Notes that clients may "drop out" after one or a few sessions if their treatment goals are achieved.*

Howard, K.I., Lueger, R.J., Maling, M.S., & Martinovich, Z. (1993) A phase model of psychotherapy: Causal mediation of outcome. *Journal of Consulting and Clinical Psychology*, 61, 678–685.
> *The authors proposed a sequential (epigenetic) three-phase model of improvement, clients needing to pass through each stage as a precondition for improvement in the next: (1)remoralization—enhanced feelings of hope and well-being; (2)remediation—symptomatic relief; and (3)rehabilitation—better functioning vis-a-vis life's difficulties. They provide support for the idea that more extensive improvements may require more sessions of conventional psychotherapy.*

Hynan, D.J. (1990) Client reasons and experiences in treatment that influence termination of psychotherapy. *Journal of Clinical Psychology*, 46, 891–895.
> *The authors note that clients may "drop out" after one or a few sessions if their treatment goals are achieved.*

Kopta, S.M., Howard, K.I., Lowry, J.L., & Beutler, L.E. (1994) Patterns of symptomatic recovery in psychotherapy. *Journal of Consulting and Clinical Psychology*, 62(5), 1009–1016.

They divided symptoms into acute distress, chronic distress, and character-ological, and provide support for the idea that more extensive improvements may require more sessions of conventional psychotherapy.

Santor, D.A., & Segal, Z.V. (2001) Predicting symptom return from rate of symptom reduction in cognitive-behavior therapy for depression. *Cognitive Therapy and Research*, 25, 117–135.

The authors found that early positive psychotherapy responders were more likely to maintain gains.

Shapiro, D.A., Barkham, M., Stiles, W.B., Hardy, G.E., Rees, A., Reynolds, S., & Startup, M. (2003) Time is of the essence: A selective review of the fall and rise of brief therapy research. *Psychology and Psychotherapy: Theory, Research and Practice*, 76, 211–235.

Notes that randomized trials are most commonly cognitive-behavioral interventions, whilst naturalistic data have been drawn from predominately psychodynamic and related therapies and concluded: (1)"This indicates the need for systematic evaluation of dose-effect relations in contrasting treatment modalities" (p. 219), and (2)that "current research does not begin....to warrant any rigid prescription of a universal time limit for psychological treatment" (p. 231).

Todd, D.M., Deane, F.P., & Bragdon, R.A. (2003) Client and therapist reasons for termination: A conceptualization and preliminary validation. *Journal of Clinical Psychology*, 59, 133–147.

The article notes that clients may "drop out" after one or a few sessions if their treatment goals are achieved.

The Right Paradigm?

Studies of SST have thus far tended to fall into one of three categories: (1)investigations of walk-in SSTs, modeled on the work of Talmon (1990) and derived from various competence-based approaches, which repeatedly demonstrate the effectiveness (positive outcomes and client satisfaction) of intentional one-session consultations; (2)CBT-based one-session health psychology and anti-anxiety interventions and procedures, and (3)other studies of cases that could have gone for longer treatment durations but which finished after one session. Studies of the so-called "dose-effect" relationship generally have not utilized competence-based, resource-focused therapeutic approaches—such as solution-focused and solution-oriented therapy, narrative therapy, Ericksonian therapy, and strategic-interactional therapy, as well as other methods described in this volume such as systemic family therapy, neurolinguistic programming (NLP), or emotional freedom techniques (EFT)—that have been demonstrated to often yield positive results in a relatively short period of time.

This highlights an additional and overarching conceptual problem: *"dose" is often the wrong metaphor*. Borrowed from the medication-for-medical-illness pharmaceutical research realm ("How many milligrams how many times a day for how many days are needed to eliminate the infection?"), to date the dose-effect research literature has been based largely on some admixture of cognitive-behavioral and psychodynamic interventions (with some motivational interviewing for substance abusers) conducted by therapists more-or-less lacking specific training in deliberately resource-focused, time-sensitive therapy. Therapies which aim to be as efficient as possible and not just an abbreviation of longer therapies operate from different premises, use different processes, and seek different potentials. Most planned brief therapies, including single session, do not attempt to wear down or eradicate "pathogens." It is not about "dosing" patients. Rather, single session (and other brief) therapists endeavor to help clients access and activate overlooked resources, reframe situations, shift meanings and narratives, modify interactional patterns, and spark imagination and inspire creative problem-solving. Interventions are directed toward client empowerment and the constructive reassertion of the client's own preferred voice. The idea is to "get" the client, to connect and appreciate their worldview and to help them amplify something good.

Keeney and Keeney (2013) similarly comment:

> The art of therapy is found in the full complexity of its interactional choreography and cannot be reduced to an isolated action, expression, or prescription for behaving in a session....So-called "evidence-based" therapy research assumes the opposite. In the effort to produce standardized, "best practice" models, therapy is reduced to particular, isolated actions and sequences of actions to be replicated across multiple clinical situations. It follows that clients' problems must also be reduced to a set of isolated variables and lineal causal explanations in order to be "treated" by the established model. The result is assembly line therapy that deemphasizes creating skilled therapists who are able to work with the complexity of each unique client. (p. 29)

Keeney, H., & Keeney, B. (2013) *Creative therapeutic technique: Skills for the art of bringing forth change.* Phoenix, AZ: Zeig, Tucker & Theisen.

The Call for More Research

Asking "Does the empirical evidence support the increased prevalence of this service delivery model?" Hymmen, et al. (2012) conducted a thorough review of relevant databases and observed:

> The findings suggest that the majority of clients attending either previously scheduled or walk-in SST find it sufficient and helpful. The studies imply that this model of service delivery leads to perceived improvement in presenting problems in general, and on specific measures of variables such as depression, anxiety, distress level and confidence in parenting skills. (p.1)

They also noted various methodological issues, however, and concluded:

> Neither SST in practice or research is new....However, what is new is an increase in the number of organizations adopting this approach in the form of walk-in counseling clinics despite the lack of strong empirical evidence in support of its effectiveness. This development provides a significant opportunity to begin a new chapter of SST research. Specifically, future research should involve: more rigorous studies with larger sample sizes, standardized measurement tools, randomization to control or comparison groups and longer-term follow-up; more diverse participants so that its effectiveness with specific client populations and presenting problems can be adequately understood; and in-depth interviews with clients to explore the active therapeutic ingredients involved within a single session intervention. While SST will likely continue to be adopted by resource-stretched community counselling and mental health programs, it remains vital that the field has evidence of the appropriateness and effectiveness of this approach. (Hymmen, et al., 2012, p. 11)

There are many questions to be investigated, and we can imagine a wide variety of research initiatives including:

- Further investigation of the incidence of SSTs with different populations in different settings.
- Meta analyses of all the quantitative and qualitative research presented here.
- Study of therapists' initial mindsets as compared to clients' mindsets and the eventual impact on therapy lengths and results; e.g., the experimental manipulation of both therapist and client expectations about probably length of treatment (such as "People usually get better in one or two visits" versus "People usually take several months to get better") prior to the session.
- Randomized assignment to planned one-session ("one-off") versus multiple-session vs. open-ended/ongoing treatments, including the use of no-treatment control groups.
- Comparison of the use of SST-trained versus untrained clinicians.
- Comparison of client characteristics, presenting problems, and therapy process in "walk-in" versus "by appointment" SSTs.
- Comparison of "SST protocol" (e.g., the Bouverie Centre model) versus "no protocol" SST treatments.
- Comparison of "no diagnosis" versus "full DSM assessment" on therapy process and outcome for SST clients.
- Qualitative studies of "the difference that makes a difference" for clients participating in various kinds of SST.

When research programs are affiliated with a university and are part of graduate and post-graduate studies and training, they can help both to support the clinical service as well as to extend the number of therapists. Although we agree with de Shazer's (1985, p. 18) description of the practice of a team observing and consulting from behind a one-way mirror as a "stimulating but not necessary" arrangement, we as well as other contributors to this volume have often found the input from and discussion with team members to be valuable for the client, for the therapist, and for the further development of the team members. Research and training programs can operate synergistically, as seen at the Eastside Family Centre (Chapter 10), Our Lady of the Lake University (Chapters 5 and 6), and the Bouverie Centre (Chapters 7–8).

We recommend—consistent with the remarks of Keeney and Keeney (2013) quoted above—that we avoid replicating the "best practices" debate and instead focus on identifying what Rycroft and Young (Chapter 8) referred to as "just good practice." It is good to know in general what works best for whom, but even if studied scientifically, the practice of therapy is a craft and an art—one cannot replace imagination with precision and creativity with control.

de Shazer, S. (1985) *Keys to solution in brief therapy*. New York: Norton.
Hymmen, P., Stalker, C., & Cait, C.-A. (2012) The case for single-session therapy: Does the empirical evidence support the increased prevalence of this service delivery model? *Journal of Mental Health*, Early OnLine, 1–12.
Keeney, H., & Keeney, B. (2013) *Creative therapeutic technique: Skills for the art of bringing forth change*. Phoenix, AZ: Zeig, Tucker, & Theisen.

Summary

Numerous case reports and systematic studies—as reported in the preceding chapters as well as summarized here—suggest that when given the choice and the right clinical methodology, a single session of therapy can yield significant and enduring positive effects. Many patients elect to have one-session therapies, whether the session is understood in advance to be a one-time meeting or if more sessions are available but the patient chooses to stop after one; and many patients, with a wide variety of presenting problems and diagnoses, benefit from such one-session experiences—especially if client and clinician are open to the possibility. As Duval, et al. (2012, p. 5) wrote:

Rather than viewing brief services as "the best we can do" in light of fiscal pressures and wait lists, the research indicates that brief modalities show promise for strong clinical outcomes in ways that are economically sound. Innovative research is currently underway, and evaluations of specific interventions indicate that brief services can positively impact wait times, clinical outcomes, and client satisfaction in an efficient and convenient manner. Research shows that for most people, therapy is typically brief.

While more research may help to further explicate which processes will produce the best outcomes for which client/patients, the preponderance of evidence is that sometimes less can be more. As Lazarus and Fay (1990, p. 39) have put it, "[E]ffective treatment depends far less on the hours you put in, than on what you put into those hours."

Duval, J., Young, K., & Kays-Burden, A. (2012, November) *No more, no less: Brief mental health services for children and youth*. Policy paper, Ontario Centre for Excellence for Child and Youth Mental Health. Available from www.excellenceforchildandyouth.ca.

Lazarus, A.A., & Fay, A. (1990) Brief psychotherapy: Tautology or oxymoron? In J.K. Zeig & S.G. Gilligan (Eds.), *Brief therapy: Myths, methods, and metaphors* (pp. 36–51). New York: Brunner/Mazel.

Appendix B

The Temporal Structure of Brief Therapy: Some Questions Often Associated with Different Phases of Sessions and Treatment

Michael F. Hoyt and Moshe Talmon

Here is a basic structure or model to help organize thinking and therapeutic responses when needing to figure out where the client and therapist are and what they may need to do. Of course, this is only a general schema or guideline, one that needs constant adaptation and versatility in its application to particular situations, which is the art and craft of doing therapy. We offer the following as a loose organizational framework that may be of some orienting utility but also recognize that with real clients sessions do not unfold in such a neat order. Moreover, there are also many other aspects to what occurs in a session or therapy (including empathy, encouragement, education, humor, persuasion, role-playing, imagery, reframing, and utilization of various techniques).

With these important provisos in mind, the course of each therapy session can be conceptualized as having five phases or stages: pretreatment, early, middle, late, and follow-through. They tend to be pyramidal or epigenetic—that is, they tend to occur in sequence and each flows from the preceding so that successful work in one preconditions the next. The client elects therapy before forming an alliance; the therapeutic alliance establishes the ground for defining goals; goal setting leads to focusing on specific change strategies; goal attainment leads to discussion about homework, relapse prevention, and leave-taking; and points toward continued growth and possible return to treatment.

Following Gustafson (1986, p. 279: "Just as the entire course of a brief therapy may be seen as having its opening, middle and end game, any particular session may be seen as a microcosm of such thinking"), there is often a microcosm-macrocosm parallelism in which the structure of each therapy session tends to mirror (or parallel) the overall course of treatment. Issues typically involved in the first portion of treatment are similar to those involved in the first portion of each session; the middle of treatment resembles the middle of each session; the issues that characterize the later portions of therapy tend also to characterize the later portions of each session. As biologists might say, "Ontogeny recapitulates phylogeny—the development of the individual mirrors the development of the species"; crystallographers and chaos theorists may prefer to think about how a fragment replicates the whole; poets may conceptualize the parallel as a kind of "synecdoche" in which a part is put forward to represent the whole. Recognizing the respective phases of treatment and their requisite tasks and useful questions, both in each session and in the overall course of treatment, can help to make therapy more effective and efficient.

All of this comes together, of course, when a single session is the entire therapy. Especially when one embarks with a one-session-at-a-time mindset, it can be helpful to think about what would be useful at the beginning, in the middle, and at the conclusion of the meeting to help the client make the most of the session.

Here are some often useful questions (also see DeJong & Berg, 1997; de Shazer, 1988; Haley, 1977; Hoyt, 1990, 2009; Hoyt & Miller, 2000; Slive & Bobele, 2011; Talmon, 1990; Weber, et al., 1985)—drawn from a variety of theoretical perspectives—organized around the dimension of time. Again, this is by no means a complete manual, just some guidelines, and we would advise listening carefully to clients in order to know which questions may be useful at a given moment.

Pretreatment

Change begins even before first contact with the client. He or she or they have decided that there is a problem and would like assistance to resolve the difficulty. Some questions to ask—by therapist or triage screener, on the telephone or by questionnaire—while making an initial appointment:

- What's the problem—why now have you called now (rather than earlier or later)?
- How do you see or understand the situation?
- What do you think will help?
- How have you tried to solve the problem so far—how did that work?
- When the problem isn't present (or isn't so bad), what is going on differently?
- Please notice between now and when we meet, so that you can describe it to me, when the problem isn't so bad [when you and your spouse are getting along, when you're not feeling depressed, when you don't drink too much, and so on], what are you doing differently then?
- This may give us some clues regarding what you need to do more of—identifying exceptions to the problem that led you to call will focus on solutions that may be useful to you. OK?

Early in Treatment and Early in Each Session

As we begin a session and a therapy, we should attend carefully to forming a good alliance, inquiring about possible changes since our last contact, and establishing goals for the session and the therapy. Some useful questions might include:

- Since we last spoke, what have you noticed that may be a bit better or different? How did that happen? What did you do?
- When is the problem not a problem?
- What do you call the problem? What name do you have for it?
- When (and how) does [the problem] influence you; and when (and how) do you influence it?

- What's your idea or theory about what will bring about change? How would your life be better with these changes?
- How can I be most useful to you?
- If we were only going to meet once or a few times, what problem would you want to focus on solving at this point in time?
- What needs to happen here today so that when you leave you can feel this visit was worthwhile?
- What are you willing to change today?
- Given all that you have been through, how have you managed to cope as well as you have?
- If we work hard together, what will be the first small indications that we're going in the right direction?
- If/when you weren't/aren't having this problem, what would/will you be doing with the time? What would/will you be doing differently?
- On a scale of 1 to 10, where is the problem now? Where would it need to be for you to decide that you didn't need to continue coming here?
- Suppose tonight, while you're sleeping, a miracle happens, and the problem that led you here is resolved. When you awaken tomorrow, how will you first notice the miracle has happened? What will be the first sign that things are better? And the next? And the next?
- What are your best hopes for today's meeting?

In the Middle of Treatment and the Middle of Each Session

We need to keep track of the clients' goals and whether we have a good working alliance and are going in the right direction or if some course "corrections" need to be made. Possible refocusing is directed by the client's responses to questions such as these:

- How did that work? What did you do to help it happen?
- Is this being helpful to you? What would make it more so?
- Do you have any questions you'd like to ask me?
- Are we working on what you want to work on?
- I might have missed something you wish to say—what might it be?
- What can I do to be more helpful to you now?

Late in Treatment and Late in Each Session

Termination—extracting the therapist from the successful equation—becomes central. There are a number of issues to be addressed, as the following guideline questions suggest:

Goal Attainment/Homework/Post-Session Tasks

- Has this been helpful to you? How so?
- Which of the helpful things you've been doing do you think you should continue to do? How can you do this?
- Between now and the next time we meet [or, to keep things going in the right direction], would you be willing to do _____?
- Before we stop in a couple of minutes, when I'll walk you back to the waiting room, let's discuss what's next...
- When you leave in a few minutes, what are you most likely to do with today's session?
- Who can be helpful to you in doing _____? What might interfere, and how can you prepare to deal with those challenges?

Goal Maintenance and Relapse Prevention

- You know that problems often come and go. What would be a signal that the problems you were having might be returning? How can you respond if you see that developing?
- You know we all have the capacity to be our best friends as well as our worse enemies.
- Suppose you wanted to go back to all of the problems you were having when you first came in—what would you need to do to make this happen, if you wanted to sabotage yourself?
- How might [the problem] try to trick you into letting it take over again? What can you do to resist that?
- What will you need to do to increase the odds that things will work out OK even if you were not to come in for a while?
- Who will be glad to hear about your progress? Who in your present or past [family, friends, colleagues] would support your efforts?

Leavetaking

- Would you like to make another appointment now, or wait and see how things go and call me as needed?
- Would you like to make our next appointment for 1, 3, or 6 weeks, or would you prefer to wait a bit longer?
- What is the longest you can imagine handling things on your own?

References

DeJong, P., & Berg, I.K. (1997) *Interviewing for solutions.* Pacific Grove, CA: Brook/Cole.

de Shazer, S. (1988) *Clues: Investigating solutions in brief therapy.* New York: Norton.

Gustafson, J.P. (1986) *The complex secret of brief psychotherapy.* New York: Norton.

Haley, J. (1977) *Problem-solving therapy.* San Francisco: Jossey-Bass.

Hoyt, M.F. (1990) On time in brief therapy. In *Brief therapy and managed care* (pp. 69–104). San Francisco: Jossey-Bass.

Hoyt, M.F. (2009) *Brief psychotherapies: Principles and practices.* Phoenix, AZ: Zeig, Tucker & Theisen.

Hoyt, M.F., & Miller, S.D. (2000) Stage-appropriate change-oriented brief therapy strategies. In M.F. Hoyt, *Some stories are better than others: Doing what works in brief therapy and managed care* (pp. 207–235). Philadelphia: Brunner-Mazel.

Slive, A., & Bobele, M. (Eds.) (2011) *When one hour is all you have: Effective therapy for walk-in clients.* Phoenix, AZ: Zeig, Tucker, & Theisen.

Talmon, M. (1990) *Single session therapy: Making the most of the first (and often only) therapeutic encounter.* San Francisco: Jossey-Bass.

Weber, T., McDaniel, S.H., & McKiever, J. (1985) A beginner's guide to the problem-oriented first family interview. *Family Process, 24*(3), 356–364.